RESEARCH GUIDE TO AMERICAN HISTORICAL BIOGRAPHY

Volume IV
Appendices I, II
Cumulative Index

Suzanne Niemeyer
Editor

Beacham Publishing

RESEARCH GUIDE TO AMERICAN HISTORICAL BIOGRAPHY

Editor
Suzanne Niemeyer

Staff Editors
Jessica A. Dorman
David W. Lowe
Katharine D. McLucas
Charles J. Moseley

Library of Congress
Cataloging-in-Publication Data

Research Guide to American Historical Biography: Volume 4 / edited by
Suzanne Niemeyer—Washington, D.C.: Beacham Publishing, Inc.

Bibliography
Cumulative index

1. United States—Biography—Handbooks, manuals, etc. 2. United
States—Bio-bibliography. I. Niemeyer, Suzanne, 1964.

CT214.R47   1990   920'.073—dc19   88-19316

Description and evaluation of the most important secondary and
primary sources for 371 American historical figures in all four volumes.

Library of Congress Card Number: 88-19316
ISBN: 0-933833-21-0

Printed in the United States of America
First printing, November 1990

PREFACE

Volume IV of the *Research Guide to American Historical Biography* contains bibliographical and other reference aids that allow the reader to explore more fully the lives of ninety-three prominent men and women who have helped to shape the contours of United States history. In response to requests from librarians, professors, and students, this volume of the *Research Guide* focuses on women, Native Americans, and minorities. A fifth volume covering explorers, entertainers, colonial and Civil War figures, and additional minorities who could not be included here will follow.

The *Research Guide* is designed to facilitate the research process for college and secondary school term papers, to assist graduate students and professors in areas outside their fields of expertise, and to provide librarians with an acquisitions tool, information to expedite interlibrary loans, and a ready reference. Our contributors, most of whom are affiliated with universities or special collections, have sifted through the available sources to direct the reader to those that are most useful.

Each entry is divided into several sections for quick reference: the *Chronology* provides a synopsis of major events in the subject's life; *Activities of Historical Significance* interprets the subject's accomplishments and places them in context; *Overview of Biographical Sources* notes any difficulties that the subject's biographers have encountered and comments on changes in scholarly opinion that have occurred over the years; *Evaluation of Principal Biographical Sources* is an annotated bibliography that evaluates the most important secondary sources for content, readability, and accuracy; *Evaluation of Biographies for Young People* a separate listing of biographies written for a young audience, which appears in articles whose subjects have inspired at least three works in this genre; *Overview and Evaluation of Primary Sources* cites autobiographical works by the subject, memoirs by the subject's family and acquaintances, pertinent government documents, and manuscript collections that contain an abundance of unpublished material; *Fiction and Adaptations* describes novels, films, plays, or other creative interpretations of the subject's activities; *Museums, Historical Landmarks, Societies* provides the name, location, and a brief description of relevant organizations or points of interest; and *Other Sources* is a bibliography of journal and encyclopedia articles, monographs, and works on the subject's era that put his or her role in historical context. The works cited in *Evaluation of Principal Biographical Sources* and in *Overview and Evaluation of Primary Sources* have A, G, or Y designations appended to the bibliographical information to indicate whether the work is most appropriate for an academic, general, or young audience. A work's audience designation is based on a combination of readability, subject matter, and availability.

As a further aid to students not well versed in all areas of American history, we have designed an appendix that groups the contents by the era in which each subject made his or her greatest contributions. Also included is an appendix that groups by state the most popular sites described in the *Museums, Historical Landmarks, Societies* section of the articles. If the figure to whom the site pertains is not self-evident, his or her name follows in parentheses.

Because this reference work is a basic research tool, the contents are largely a reflection of the availability of biographical and primary sources that are appropriate for our intended audience rather than a reflection of an editorial judgment about a given individual's historical significance. We have endeavored to include here or in forthcoming volume 5 every woman or minority figure who is the subject of at least two book-length biographical or autobiographical works. Numerous important individuals have been excluded simply because of the paucity of published sources. Literary figures are generally excluded because they are covered in Beacham Publishing's *Research Guide to Biography and Criticism*, though a few representative writers are covered here as well.

The *Research Guide to American Historical Biography* owes its existence to the labor of many individuals who have given generously of their time and talent, and I wish to acknowledge my gratitude to all our contributors. I also wish to thank Robert Muccigrosso, the editor of the original three volumes of the *Research Guide*. Although Professor Muccigrosso was not involved in the publication of this volume, the supplement incorporates the format and the editorial standards that he helped to establish.

Beacham Publishing is continually interested in producing books devoted to improving the research capabilities of students, and welcomes any suggestions for revising this title or ideas for other types of books. Write to: Beacham Publishing, Inc., 2100 "S" Street, NW, Washington, D.C. 20008.

Suzanne Niemeyer

CONTRIBUTORS

Steven Agoratus

Jim Baird
University of North Texas

Jean V. Berlin
Correspondence of William T.
Sherman, Arizona State University

Larry G. Bowman
University of North Texas

John Braeman
University of Nebraska
Lincoln

Mary Jo Bratton
East Carolina University

Patricia Brauch
Brooklyn College Library
Citu University of New York

Lester S. Brooks
Illinois State University

Allan Carlson
The Rockford Institute

Lewis H. Carlson
Western Michigan University

Betty Boyd Caroli
Kingsborough Community College
City University of New York

Paolo Coletta
U.S. Naval Academy (Ret.)

Lynda Lasswell Crist
The Papers of Jefferson Davis
Rice University

Mary B. Davis
Museum of the American Indian
Huntington Free Library

Frank Day
Clemson University

Julian J. DelGaudio
USAF Space Systems Division
History Office
Los Angeles Air Force Base

Richard C. Dickey
University of North Texas

Justus D. Doenecke
New College of the University of
South Florida

Jacob H. Dorn
Wright State University

Maurice G. Fortin
University of North Texas

Jan Furman
University of Michigan, Flint

William M. Gargan
Brooklyn College
City University of New York

Dennis Goldsberry
College of Charleston

Paul R. Griffin
Wright State University

Lynn Haney

Maryhelen C. Harmon
University of South Florida

Donald E. Heidenreich, Jr.
Kemper College

Diane Long Hoeveler
Marquette University

Gerald Horne
University of California
Santa Barbara

Charles F. Howlett

William E. Hull
Illinois State University

Evelyn E. Hunt
Cleveland State University

Mary Anne Hutchinson
Utica College of Syracuse University

Veda Jones

William M. Leary
University of Georgia

Cynthia L. Marshall
Community College of Beaver County

Joseph M. McCarthy
Suffolk University

Joan E. Organ
Case Western Reserve University

Beverly Wilson Palmer
Pomona College

Jack Patrick
Youngstown State University

Donald K. Pickens
University of North Texas

Keith Ian Polakoff
California State University
Long Beach

Paul M. Pruitt, Jr.
University of Alabama
School of Law Library

Sharon M. Rambo
Michigan State University

Daniel Dean Roland

Susan Shaw

Jack Shreve
Allegany Community College

John Y. Simon
Ulysses S. Grant Association
Southern Illinois University

Brooks Donohue Simpson
Arizona State University

Sheldon Spear
Luzerne County Community College

Jacob L. Susskind
Pennsylvania State University

Gretchen R. Sutherland
Cornell College

Warren C. Swindell
Center for Afro-American Studies
Indiana State University

William T. Walker
Philadelphia College of
Pharmacy and Science

Peter Wallenstein
Virginia Polytechnic Institute and
State University

Carol Wilson
West Virgina University

Charles E. Wynes
University of Georgia

Angela Howard Zophy
University of Houston, Clear Lake

CONTENTS

RESEARCH GUIDE
TO AMERICAN
HISTORICAL BIOGRAPHY

RICHARD ALLEN
1760-1831

Chronology

Born Richard Allen on February 14, 1760, a slave of Benjamin Chew of Philadelphia, Pennsylvania, the youngest son of three children of slave parents; *1767* he and his family are sold to a slaveholder, Mr. Stokely of Dover, Delaware; *1767-1776* works on the Stokely plantation for nine years; *1777* converted after hearing the preaching of a white Methodist clergyman; attends Methodist class meetings and receives a "call" to preach; he and his older brother purchase their freedom from Stokely for two thousand dollars; *1778-1783* works as a wood cutter, a laborer in a brickyard, and a driver of a salt wagon; begins preaching to small groups of slaves and free blacks; *1784* becomes assistant to Bishop Francis Asbury—the first American Methodist bishop—following the famous Christmas Conference that gave rise to American Methodism; *1785-1787* travels with Bishop Asbury, preaching to slaves and free blacks in Philadelphia and Dover; *1787* joins with Absalom Jones to found the Free African Society; *November 1787* leads a "walkout" of twenty-three blacks from St. George's Methodist Church in Philadelphia because of a segregated seating policy; *1788* expelled from Free African Society because of his efforts to transform it into a church; responds by purchasing a lot on the corner of Sixth and Lombard Streets in anticipation of building and organizing his own church; *1789-1793* becomes one of the more successful black businessmen of Philadelphia, operating a shoemaking trade and a chimney-sweep service; continues preaching to slaves and free blacks; works as a shoemaker; *1794* forms a group of nine blacks to convert a former blacksmith shop into a church; dedicates church as "Mother Bethel" African Church; *1796* forms a Board of Trustees for Bethel Church, petitions the Supreme Court of Pennsylvania for Articles of Association, formally names his church the African Methodist Episcopal Church of Philadelphia; *1799* ordained as itinerant deacon by Bishop Asbury, thus becoming the first black to receive ordination status from the white Methodist Episcopal Church; *1807* engages in what would become a nine-year legal battle with white Methodists over the use of their denominational name; *1814-1815* forms alliances with African Methodist Societies which had formed over the past two decades in Baltimore, Maryland; Wilmington, Delaware; Attleborough, Pennsylvania; and Salem, New Jersey; *1816* arranges a conference between the various African Methodist Societies to incorporate them into a single body as the African Methodist Episcopal Church of the United States; *April 11, 1816* following the unexplained resignation of Bishop Daniel Coker, becomes the first bishop of the newly independent African Methodist Episcopal Church of America; adopts without alterations the Discipline used by the white Methodist Church as the official Discipline of his own denomination; *1817* holds the denomination's first annual conferences in the cities of Philadelphia and Baltimore; *1820* holds first General Conference of the African Methodist Episcopal Church in Philadelphia; unsuccessfully attempts to unify the African Methodist Episcopal Zion Church with his denomination; *1820-1831* directs the expansion of the African Methodist Episcopal Church into West Virginia, Ohio, Indiana, and Missouri; *1830* helps organize the first national Negro Convention which meets at his Bethel Church; *1831* dies on March 26 at the age of seventy-one in Philadelphia.

Activities of Historical Significance

Allen was one of the most influential black leaders in America from the 1780s until his death in 1831. His role in founding the Free African Society; his leadership against segregation in St. George's Methodist Church, Philadelphia, in 1787; and his founding of the African Methodist Episcopal Church (A.M.E.) in 1816 are considered pivotal moments in the history of the Afro-American struggle for equality in American society. Over the past two centuries, Afro-Americans often have referred to Allen's activities as inspiration in their continuing struggle for justice and equality.

Although his driving ambition was to organize a church where free Afro-Americans could worship without racial oppression and where slaves could find some measure of peace and dignity in the midst of their enslavement, Allen was also concerned with elevating the aspirations and social position of his race. To this end he organized Sabbath schools to teach literacy skills to Afro-American children and helped organize the national Negro Convention and similar organizations to define and institute political strategies for ending segregation and slavery. Allen's activities are remarkable considering that, as a slave for seventeen years, he had no formal education.

Overview of Biographical Sources

Brief references to Allen are found in almost every study of Afro-American religious history, and numerous eulogies have appeared in denominational publications since his death. Two of the best are Daniel A. Payne, *A History of the African Methodist Episcopal Church 1816-1856* (1891), and Richard R. Wright, Jr., *Encyclopedia of African Methodism, 1816-1916* (1916).

Three comprehensive studies of his life and activities have been written: Charles H. Wesley, *Richard Allen: Apostle of Freedom* (1935); Marcia M. Mathews, *Richard Allen* (1963); and Carol V. George, *Segregated Sabbaths: Richard Allen and the Emergence of Independent Black Churches, 1760-1840*

(1973). Allen's inability to write—he dictated his thoughts to others—and a paucity of other firsthand accounts have left few biographical materials.

Evaluation of Principal Biographical Sources

George, Carol V. *Segregated Sabbaths: Richard Allen and the Emergence of Independent Black Churches, 1760-1840.* London: Oxford University Press, 1973. (**A, G**) This work presents excellent biographical information about Allen and his struggles to build his own African Methodist Church. It places Allen's efforts to build a denomination within the socio-political context of the late eighteenth and early nineteenth centuries.

Mathews, Marcia M. *Richard Allen.* Baltimore, MD: Helicon Press, 1963. (**G**) Though a fictionalized biographical account, Matthew's book provides some useful general information about Allen. Her sources are not documented.

Wesley, Charles H. *Richard Allen: Apostle of Freedom.* Washington, DC: Associated Publishers, 1935. (**A, G**) This excellent study provides extensive biographical information and thorough analysis of Allen's religious and political activities. The author portrays Allen sympathetically while examining his weaknesses. Wesley fails to adequately explain Allen's theology.

Overview and Evaluation of Primary Sources

Primary information on Allen exists only in one major source, *The Life Experiences and Gospel Labors of the Rt. Rev. Richard Allen* (1830. Reprint. Nashville, TN: Abingdon, 1960), which are his reflections on slavery and his work with the church, as dictated to his secretary. Appended are several public addresses and short sermons that offer insight into his religious thought.

Newspapers of his day such as the *Philadelphia Gazette* and other contemporary publications such as *The Freemen's Journal,* Vol. I, 34 (November 2, 1827), also are useful sources of information about his activities.

Museums, Historical Landmarks, Societies

Allen is buried in the crypt of "Mother Bethel" A.M.E. Church in Philadelphia, Pennsylvania. Numerous churches throughout the United States and Africa are named after him as is The Richard Allen Christian Endeavor Fellowship—a society within the African Methodist Episcopal Denomination that provides guidance and services for youth.

Other Sources
Simmons, William J. *Men of Mark: Eminent, Progressive and Rising.* Cleveland: George Rewell, 1887. Devotes a short chapter to Allen's life and the founding of the African Methodist Episcopal Church.

Wilmore, Gayraud. *Black Religion, Black Radicalism.* New York: Orbis Books, 1983. Wilmore provides a brief but interesting discussion of Allen's theological beliefs and the socio-political rationale behind the Free African Society and the African Methodist Episcopal Church.

Paul R. Griffin
Wright State University

MARIAN ANDERSON
b. 1902

Chronology

Born Marian Anderson on February 17, 1902, in Philadelphia, Pennsylvania, the eldest of three daughters of John Anderson, a loader at the Reading Terminal Market, and Anna Anderson, a former schoolteacher; *1908* joins the junior choir at the Union Baptist Church at age six; performs a duet with her friend Viola Johnson in her first public performance; *1912* her father dies; *1915-1924* sings in the junior and adult church choirs and begins accepting payment for recitals in nearby communities; attracts attention of internationally known tenor Roland Hayes, who takes a personal interest in the development of her career; takes voice lessons from Mary Saunders Patterson, who accepts no money for her services; begins taking voice lessons from Giuseppe Boghetti with "Marian Anderson's Future" funds raised by family, friends, and fellow church members; *April 23, 1924* is heartbroken when her recital at Town Hall in New York City is poorly attended; nearly abandons her singing career; *August 1925* enters the Lewisohn Stadium Concert Contest where she places first among 300 entrants; *1926* tours the eastern and southern United States with accompanist Billy King, developing her talent and repertoire; managed by Arthur Judson Agency, who help broaden her audience; *1930* performs at Carnegie Hall on March 2; granted a Julius Rosenwald Fund Fellowship and travels to Europe; has official world debut at the Bachsaal in Berlin; teams up with accompanist Kosti Vehanen; *1930-1935* performs a series of concerts abroad, furthering her musical reputation; *1935* despite a broken ankle, embarks on tour of U.S. arranged by new manager Sol Hurok; *December 1935* performs a successful recital in Town Hall, New York City; *1936* appears in Carnegie Hall and the Philadelphia Forum; *1939* banned from Constitution Hall in Washington, D.C., by the Daughters of the American Revolution because of her race, but invited by Secretary of the Interior Harold L. Ickes to sing at the Lincoln Memorial on Easter Sunday, a landmark moment for civil rights in the U.S.; receives the Spingarn Award from the NAACP; *1940* presented with the prestigious Finnish decoration, the Probenignitate Humana; *1941* becomes one of the highest paid concert performers in the U.S.; *1943* marries longtime friend Orpheus H. Fisher (known as "King" or "Razzle"); invited to return and performs at Constitution Hall; *1955* becomes first black to sing a major role at the Metropolitan Opera in New York; *1957* tours India and the Far East as a goodwill ambassador for the U.S. State Department; is the first foreigner invited to speak at the Mahatma Gandhi memorial statue in India; *1958* appointed by President Eisenhower as a delegate to the United Nations; *1963* awarded American Freedom Medal by

President Johnson; *April 19, 1965* gives her final performance at Carnegie Hall as part of a farewell tour; *1977* Congress passes a joint resolution to create a gold medal in honor of her 75th birthday; *1986* presented with National Medal of Arts by President Reagan; *November 1989* saluted in honor of the fiftieth anniversary of the Lincoln Memorial concert; *1990* resides in Danbury, Connecticut, after outliving her husband.

Activities of Historical Significance

From the beginning, family and church have played an important role in Marian Anderson's life. Friends, associates, and family members recognized early on that she possessed a unique contralto voice that enthralled audiences. Over the years, Anderson performed to great acclaim in many countries, becoming known as the "box office avalanche" in South America. Anderson has been honored with numerous awards and has entertained royalty, presidents, and dignitaries across the globe. She has been described as a citizen of the world and ranked as a woman of the century.

In 1939 Howard University invited Anderson to sing in Washington, D.C., and Anderson's manager selected Constitution Hall as the most appropriate venue. The Daughters of the American Revolution (DAR) barred her from the hall on grounds of race, but Secretary of the Interior Harold L. Ickes invited her to sing at the Lincoln Memorial, instead. Seventy-five thousand people attended this concert on April 9.

In response to the DAR's action, Eleanor Roosevelt resigned her membership from the organization, and many artists who were scheduled to perform in Constitution Hall immediately cancelled their engagements. The DAR eventually recanted its position, and in January 1943 Anderson performed in Constitution Hall. Anderson's brush with the DAR catapulted her into the national spotlight as a victim of racial discrimination. In a more positive light, her Lincoln Memorial concert secured her place as a triumphant struggle for black equality and civil rights. In July 1939 the NAACP awarded Anderson the Spingarn Medal in recognition of "noblest achievement by the American Negro," and Eleanor Roosevelt personally presented the citation. To commemorate the historic Lincoln Memorial concert, a nationwide contest was conducted to create a mural depicting the Easter Sunday event, with the winning artwork placed on permanent display in the Interior Building in March 1942.

Anderson's Lincoln Memorial performance was an event of such significance that its impact transcended the bounds of the musical world. Considered within the context of her entire career, however, it may be seen as just one of many highlights.

On August 27, 1925, Anderson performed "O Mio Fernando" from Donizetti's 'La Favorita" with the New York Philharmonic Orchestra as the winner—selected from a field of three hundred contestants—of the Lewisohn Stadium Concert Contest. Her singing abilities consistently garnered her high praise from music greats. When she performed in Salzberg in 1935, conductor Arturo Toscanini stated that she possessed a voice "that comes along only once in a hundred years." Finnish composer Jean Sibelius was so impressed with her voice that he dedicated his "Solitude" to her.

In 1930 Anderson became the first black female to sing in Carnegie Hall. Some twenty-five years later, she became the first black artist to perform a major role at the New York Metropolitan Opera, playing "Ulrica" in Verdi's "Uno Ballo in Maschera" on January 7, 1955. Anderson's performance of Schubert's "Ave Maria" is considered by many to be one of the finest interpretations of the work in the past century.

Anderson has been the recipient of numerous prestigious awards, including the Probenignitate Humana (1940) and the American Freedom Medal (1963). She used the $10,000 prize from one such honor—the city of Philadelphia's 1941 Bok Award for "outstanding citizenship and meritorious achievement" —to establish the Marian Anderson Scholarship Fund for "gifted young singers in the furtherance of their careers." Now boasting a much-expanded endowment, this scholarship program is still active today.

In July 1958 President Eisenhower appointed Anderson as United Nations ambassador to the Thirteenth General Assembly. On March 8, 1977, Congress created a gold medal in honor of Anderson's seventy-fifth birthday to recognize her "highly distinguished and impressive career . . . her untiring and unselfish devotion to the promotion of the arts . . . her strong and imaginative support to humanitarian causes . . . and her contributions to the cause of world peace."

Overview of Biographical Sources

Two relatively good biographies of Anderson are available. *Marian Anderson: Lady from Philadelphia* (1966) by Shirlee P. Newman is generally informative but aimed more for the general reader than the researcher. A second biography, by Anderson's former European accompanist Kosti Vehanen, *Marian Anderson: A Portrait* (1941), provides a more intimate portrait of the singer and accentuates moments in her lifelong struggle against prejudice.

An excellent book-length bibliography, Janet L. Sims, *Marian Anderson: An Annotated Bibliography and Discography* (1981), will immediately guide the reader to any number of specialized avenues for research. Several books devote chapters to Anderson. Included below are those that are most informative. For journal and newspaper articles, Sims provides an excellent list of sources.

Evaluation of Principal Biographical Sources

Newman, Shirlee P. *Marian Anderson: Lady from Philadelphia*. Philadelphia: Westminster Press, 1966. (G, Y) A personable biography, simplistic in style, this volume is basically a condensed version of Anderson's autobiography. Contains a helpful bibliography.

Sims, Janet L., ed. *Marian Anderson: An Annotated Bibliography and Discography*. Westport, CT: Greenwood Press, 1981. (A) Divided into categories of personal data, interviews and recollections, career activities, and awards and honors. This is the definitive book of sources up to 1980. Appendix includes a list of manuscript holdings and locations, along with a discography, all of which is essential for the serious researcher.

Vehanen, Kosti. *Marian Anderson: A Portrait*. 1941. Reprint. Westport, CT: Greenwood, 1970. (G) A personal view of Anderson's achievements and fight against prejudice by her friend and European accompanist. Centered on her travels abroad and written before the autobiography.

Evaluation of Biographies for Young People

Brown, Vashti, and Jack Brown. "World in Her Hands." In *Proudly We Hail*. Boston: Houghton Mifflin, 1968. Young adult story which describes Anderson's constant struggle with bigotry and how she achieved recognition in Europe before she was accepted by the American public.

Forsee, Aylesa. "Marian Anderson: Grace Before Greatness." In *American Women Who Scored Firsts*. Philadelphia: Macrae Smith, 1958. This biography emphasizes Anderson's strong religious belief that if one has faith in oneself then anything can be achieved. Her success is explained as the result of her high standards for herself as a performer and as an individual.

Tobias, Tobi. *Marian Anderson*. New York: Crowell, 1972. Young adult interpretation of Anderson's life as a contralto.

Overview and Evaluation of Primary Sources

Marian Anderson's autobiography, *My Lord, What a Morning* (New York: Viking Press, 1956) is a commendable, if now somewhat dated, documentation of her life. In keeping with her character, these recollections are unusually humble for such a worldwide achiever.

For a more intensive study, Anderson's personal papers are collected at the University of Pennsylvania's Van Pelt Library. This collection contains diaries, letters, manuscripts, photographs, promotional pamphlets, music scores, recordings, and other correspondence. These materials provide a well-rounded picture of Anderson's career. A complete catalog is available: Neda M. Westlake and Otto E. Albrecht, eds., *Marian Anderson: a Catalog of the Collection at the University of Pennsylvania Library* (Philadelphia: University of Pennsylvania, 1981).

There are also smaller yet useful collections at Atlanta University's Trevor Arnett Library; the Julius Rosenwald Fund Records in the Amistad Research Center at Tulane University, New Orleans; the Schomburg Collection at the New York Public Library; and the Moorland-Spingarn Research Center at Howard University, Washington, D.C.

Since Anderson has been called this century's most unique contralto, a researcher should experience her recordings to understand the full range of moods and expressions created by her magnificent voice. All music libraries and public libraries with music collections will likely have many of Anderson's most famous works. Her recordings are currently available in all formats, including CD. For a list of original recordings, consult Sims or David Hall and Abner Levin, eds., *The Disc Book* (New York: Long Player, 1955).

Fiction and Adaptations

Lenore Spivey's book *Singing Heart: A Story Based on the Life of Marian Anderson* (1966) is a fictionalized account of Anderson's career.

Museums, Historical Landmarks, Societies

Arts Hall of Fame (Birmingham, AL). Anderson was inducted in 1972.

Marian Anderson Scholarship (Philadelphia, PA). Foundation to help gifted young artists in the furtherance of their careers; sponsors an annual contest.

Mural (Washington, DC). Depicts the 1939 Easter Sunday concert at the Lincoln Memorial. Located in the U.S. Interior Building.

Women's Hall of Fame (Seneca Falls, NY). Anderson was inducted in 1973.

Other Sources

Embree, Edwin R. "Marian Anderson: Deep River of Song." In *Thirteen Against the Odds*. 1944. Reprint. New York: Kennikat Press, 1968. The entry on Anderson discusses major highlights in her career and mentions her humbleness and graciousness as a human being.

Hurok, Solomon and Ruth Goode. *Impresario*. New York: Random House, 1946. A book about the many accomplishments of Sol Hurok, Anderson's manager for many years. Hurok devotes a section to Anderson which provides "behind-the-scenes" information about the Constitution Hall controversy.

Richardson, Ben. "Marian Anderson." In *Great Black Americans*. New York: Crowell, 1976. Summarizes Anderson's entire career in a brief entry.

Rodgers, J. A. "Marian Anderson: The Voice of the Century." In *World's Great Men of Color*. 1947. Reprint. New York: Macmillan, 1972. Very short entry, but contains a good bibliography.

Roosevelt, Felicia Warburg. *Doers and Dowagers*. New York: Doubleday, 1975. Chapter in the "Achievers" section emphasizes Anderson's ability to keep a busy and rigorous schedule.

Richard C. Dickey
University of North Texas

LOUIS ARMSTRONG
1901-1971

Chronology

Born Louis Armstrong around August 4, 1901 in New Orleans, Louisiana, son of William Armstrong, a laborer, and Mary Albert, a teenager who had come to the city from the nearby sugar cane fields of Bourre, Louisiana; (for most of his life Armstrong's date of birth was listed as July 4, 1900, but recent research suggests the August 1901 date); *1901-1915* grows up in the poorest black neighborhood in New Orleans; reared largely in a single parent, female-headed household; sent to the Jones Home (Waifs Home), for delinquent and neglected children where he begins the study of instrumental music; *1915-1917* sporadic performance jobs; forms a short-lived six-piece band; *1918* marries Daisy Parker; joins Edward "Kid" Ory's band as a replacement for "King" Oliver; *1922-1924* joins King Oliver's band in Chicago; marries Lil Hardin, the band's pianist; joins Fletcher Henderson's swing band in New York; *1925-1928* returns to Chicago; records with the Hot Five and Hot Seven bands; *1929-1947* returns to New York where he begins to concentrate on popular music as a soloist with large swing bands; marries Alpha Smith, then Lucille Wilson, who was to remain his wife until his death; has his own national radio program in late 1940s; *1947-1971* returns to the music of his youth and performs with a modified dixieland group laced with popular vocal stylings; performs throughout the world, often under the sponsorship of the United States State Department; health declines after a heart attack in 1959; dies in New York City on July 6, 1971.

Activities of Historical Significance

During his formative years in New Orleans, Louis Armstrong was exposed to a wide variety of music—blues, ragtime, the new "hot" jazz called dixieland, marching bands, folk music, African-American church music, and concert bands. His own music, one of the most important single contributions in the history of jazz, was a unique fusion of aspects of African and European music. He improvised over European harmonic structures and based his trumpet tone on European and American models, while his use of slides, growls, and shouts are some of the Africanisms he incorporated into his style.

Armstrong's mother and father dissolved their common-law relationship shortly after his birth, and he grew up in the households of his paternal grandmother, Josephine, and his mother. During his boyhood he paid close attention to the various kinds of music that saturated his environment.

Armstrong learned many survival skills from the pimps, prostitutes, gamblers, hustlers, and others who lived by their wits in his neighborhood. Later, after becoming a musician, he was protected from the pervasive violence of the area by the bouncers and toughs who frequented the neighborhood nightspots. He was proud of the lessons learned through his "street education" and held his "teachers" in highest esteem throughout his life, always alluding to them in his writings and interviews.

The new racial policies of white supremacy, which became law just before Armstong's birth, had a profound affect on shaping his personality and influencing his behavior throughout his career. African Americans had to find ways of surviving and adjusting to their inferior social satus. This often meant conforming to stereotypes, accommodating to the system of segregation, and looking to powerful whites as benefactors. Armstrong conformed to the stereotypes and later was to use his manager, Joe Glaser, as a means of access to the white entertainment establishment.

The speed with which Armstrong learned to play his instrument implies that he was essentially a self-taught musician. This lack of formal training caused problems which affected his entire career. His *embouchure,* or "lip placement" on the cornet mouthpiece was formed incorrectly, and limited his ability to play high notes. Only his determination to succeed enabled Armstrong to produce a fine tone despite this handicap. As a result, his lips were permanently disfigured.

Many of the older musicians in New Orleans noticed the musical talent in young Armstrong and encouraged him. Joseph "King" Oliver gave him a used cornet, taught him informally, and found him performance opportunities. Other black musicians who functioned as role models were William "Bunk" Johnson, Charles "Buddy" Bolden, and Freddie Keppard. He also listened to white musicians such as Emmanuel Perez, Alphonse Picou, and Papa Laine, who influenced his concept of tone.

Armstrong assimilated much of what he heard and gradually developed a new and unique form of expression. By the age of seventeen he had become a professional musician, even forming a short-lived six-piece band. Thereafter, he performed with various groups until the summer of 1918, when he replaced his mentor, King Oliver, in Edward "Kid" Ory's band, one of the premier jazz groups in New Orleans. He soon became aquainted with the characters who frequented the bars and bordellos where he played, including the ladies of the night. One of them, Daisy Parker, became his wife in 1918.

Their marriage was marked by discord and domestic violence. After one particular night of fighting with Daisy, Armstrong awakened the next morning to find her holding a knife above his throat. At that point he decided that nothing or nobody, including his wife, would interfere with his goal of achieving musical distinction. Musical expression became his foremost reason for living. All other activities and relationships would be secondary. Shortly thereafter he ended his relationship with Daisy.

Between 1918 and 1922 Armstrong's genius began to manifest itself. While continuing to perform with Kid Ory's band, he broadened his style by performing with other bands in clubs, dance halls, and the riverboats which traveled up and down the Mississippi River each summer.

The large influx of African Americans into Northern cities after World War I increased the demand for musicians and entertainers. In 1922 King Oliver, who had made a successful move to Chicago, invited Armstrong to travel north to join his band. Almost immediately, Armstrong's playing brought increased popularity to Oliver's band.

Oliver taught Armstrong to swing a lead and play a melody, and he was soon recognized as the master of the new music, which was becoming known as "jazz." From 1923 until the 1930s, an entire generation of jazz musicians came under Armstong's influence. They studied his creativity, improvisational ideas, technique, and style. Many even memorized certain passages from his recorded solos and "quoted" or used them in their own improvisations.

Armstrong's musical growth during this period was phenomenal. Undoubtedly, much of his progress was due to his relationship with the pianist in the band, Lillian Hardin, whom he married in 1924. Hardin was of middle-class origin and an outstanding musician. She had studied music at Fisk University and lead her own groups before joining Oliver. Her formal knowledge of music theory, particularly chord progressions, was invaluable to Armstrong.

Perhaps concluding that Armstrong had reached a creative ceiling with Oliver's band, Hardin urged him to join the Fletcher Henderson band in New York City. Henderson, too, was a college graduate and had initially gone to New York to do graduate work in chemistry at Columbia University. Henderson's musicians were more sophisticated and progressive than those in the Oliver group.

While with Henderson, Armstrong grew musically, became a fully developed soloist, traveled extensively, and earned a national reputation. But his relationship with Henderson was for the most part strained. He complained that he was given the demeaning third cornet part and that the length of his solos was shortened. Controlling the length of improvisations, however, had begun earlier by Jelly Roll Morton. After 1924 more concise improvisations were becoming the rule and eventually became an integral part of the formal structure of the new swing arrangements that superseded dixieland jazz. Armstrong, cast into the throes of rapid change, concluded that Henderson did not care for him.

In addition to musical change, a social revolution was occurring among African Americans in New York City when Armstrong arrived there in 1924. As larger numbers of blacks began to move into the cities during the 1920s, they brought a new response to the institution of white supremacy. Growing more confident, segments of the African-American community began to rebel against the racial accommodationism of the past.

Given his impoverished background and exposure to the violence of racism, Armstrong became confused, disoriented, and ambivalent about this new social revolution. For several decades, he was considered as a turncoat by many African-American musicians and intellectuals. This alienation from many of his people caused him guilt, pain, and inner conflicts, which surfaced years later when he publicly criticized President Eisenhower on the issue of civil rights. During interviews he acknowledged that his people had been mistreated over the years. But white people had been good to him, personally, he asserted. Therefore, he held no grudges. His true feelings, however, probably emerged when he recorded "Black and Blue."

The problems of performing with Henderson coupled with the social climate in New York City were disturbing to Armstrong. In 1925 his wife persuaded him to return to Chicago, and during this era he reached his creative zenith. From 1925 to 1926, he performed with his wife's band, "Lil Hardin Armstrong's Dreamland Syncopators." He subsequently worked with Erskine Tate (1926), Carroll Dickerson (1926-1927), and Clarence Jones (1927-1928). During parts of 1927 and 1929 he also led his own bands.

Armstrong's Hot Five and Hot Seven recordings were made during this period. These recordings constitute one of the most important developments in the history of jazz. They reveal Armstrong's rapid growth to artistic maturity, showcasing his technical mastery of the trumpet and the development of an economical and expressive improvisational style.

During this time, he switched from cornet to trumpet and cut his first recording as a scat singer ("Heebie Jeebies"). In the Hot Five and Hot Seven recordings, Armstrong elevated solo improvisation to a place of pre-eminence in jazz. He influenced the direction of jazz to such a powerful degree that virtually every later jazz musician was in some way indebted to him. His genius influenced Fletcher Henderson, Don Redman, Benny Carter, Sy Oliver, John Nesbit, and even Benny Goodman.

Armstrong created a form of jazz which was powerfully expressive of human feeling and experience. Audiences invariably exclaimed that he made everyone feel good through the sheer force of his exuberant emotion, geniality, humor, simplicity, and musical eloquence.

His geniality had been manifested early in his life; during his childhood it had inspired nicknames based on his wide grin. He was called "Gate" or "Gatemouth," and "Dippermouth" or "Dipper." Later on, he acquired additional names characterizing his easy smile, such as "Satchelmouth", "Satch", "Satchmo"(acquired in 1932 when he toured Europe), "Ambassador Satch," or simply "Pops."

When Armstrong's marriage to Hardin began to deteriorate, his creativity waned. Their relationship started to decline around 1929 when his record director, Tommy Rockwell, took him to New York to appear in Andy Razaf's and Fats Waller's Broadway show *Hot Chocolates*. His singing of "Ain't Misbehavin'" was so well received that he began to concentrate on popular entertainment, devoting less of his time to jazz. This change of emphasis was encouraged by Rockwell and later by Joe Glaser, Armstrong's manager from 1935 until his death. Through the astute management of Armstrong's career, Glaser made both himself and Armstrong millionaires.

As a consequence of his concentration on popular music, by the late 1930s Armstrong had been eclipsed as a jazz trumpeter by Roy Eldridge and Dizzy Gillespie. While they and other jazz musicians were assimilating, coalescing, and expanding Armstrong's contributions into new, more complex, and intricate styles, Armstrong traveled an independent path toward more popular and more commercially rewarding music.

When large swing bands were in vogue, Armstrong worked as featured artist with a widely popular band led by Luis Russell. As the big swing band era began to wane, Glaser organized the "Louis Armstrong All-Stars," a smaller group consisting of jazz greats Earl Hines, piano; Jack Teagarden, trombone; Sid Catlet, drums; and Barney Bigard, clarinet. Eventually, as Glaser realized that Armstrong's reputation was the attraction of the group, he replaced some original members with lesser known musicians. In 1949, Armstrong had become so popular that his picture appeared on the cover of *Time*.

By the 1950s Louis Armstrong had become one of the most revered entertainers in the world. For his own enjoyment he occasionally recorded with other renowned musicians, such as Oscar Peterson, Ella Fitzgerald, and Edward "Duke" Ellington. After a heart attack in 1959 his career declined but he continued to record hit records until his last days. Armstrong died on July 6, 1971 in New York City.

Overview of Biographical Sources

As a popular entertainer who was constantly in the limelight, Armstrong was the subject of numerous articles and interviews. All of the long list of books on the history of jazz stress his contribution to the form. Several biographies written after his death attempt to correct inaccurate information contained in earlier accounts. Chief among these are articles written by James Lincoln Collier as well as his impressive biography, *Louis Armstrong: An American Genius* (1983). A more recent work by Gary Giddens, *Satchmo* (1988) challenges a few of the conclusions reached by Collier.

Since Armstrong was a prolific performer who made hundreds of recordings, discographies are vital to understanding his musical contribution. Films and recorded interviews are other essential sources of information. The major biographies contain information on his films, interviews, recordings.

Chapters in Gunther Schuller's *The History of Jazz: Early Jazz, Vol 1.* (1988) and *The Swing Era: The Development of Jazz 1930-1945* (1989) are essential for understanding Armstrong's place as a twentieth-century musician.

Armstrong did not try to slough off those character traits which were reminiscent of his folk origins. But his desire to conform to numerous expectations and a near obsession to become accepted, often caused him personal ambivalence and inner conflicts. Some of his interviews and writings are, therefore, contradictory. It is important to consult the most recent works on this remarkable musician rather than relying on earlier studies.

Some of Armstrong's personal habits such as smoking marijuana and his association with underworld figures were considered unsavory, and, as a result, his early biographies and interviews were heavily edited. Prior to his death, however, he promised to set the record straight in a book which was to be published posthumously. Thus far, the manuscript has not been found.

Evaluation of Principal Biographical Sources

Collier, James Lincoln. *Louis Armstrong: An American Genius*. New York: Oxford University Press, 1983. (**A, G**) This definitive biography of Armstrong corrects most earlier accounts. Contains information on turn-of-the-century New Orleans, including social, economic, racial, and sexual issues. Well documented and scholarly, it contains numerous photographs, a bibliography, a discography, and an index.

Giddens, Gary. *Satchmo*. New York: Doubleday, 1988 (**A, G, Y**) Giddens's recent scholarly biography critiques earlier biographical material, and uses primary documents such as Armstrong's Certificate of Baptism and the Census of 1910 to arrive at a new birth date. Covers the life of Armstrong and reveals new biographical information unearthed since the work of Collier and others.

Goffin, Robert. *Horn of Plenty: The Story of Louis Armstrong*. Translated by James F. Bezou. 1947. Reprint. Westport, CT: Greenwood, 1978. (**A, G**) Armstrong's first biographer, a Belgian who had close access to the musician, infuses the narrative with too much of his own imagination. The result is an interesting, flattering, but unreliable account of Armstrong's life. While adding another dimension to Armstrong's complex career, it must be used with great caution.

Jones, Max, and John Chilton. *Louis: The Louis Armstrong Story, 1900-1971*. London: Studio Vista, 1971 (**A, G**) Jones and Chilton were among the last writers to have access to Armstrong before his death. They interviewed him about his earlier autobiography, about his relationship with his family, and about the development of his musicianship. Contains well-documented research based on newspaper and journal articles, books, and personal interviews with Armstrong and his family. The annotated discography and filmography are worthy of note.

Panassie, Hughes. *Louis Armstrong*. 1971. Reprint. New York: Da Capo Press, 1979. (**A, G**) Contains fewer details but illuminates topics only briefly mentioned in other studies. Of particular interest to readers seeking a broad, synthesized account of Armstrong's life and career. Easy to read and uncluttered with minor information, it includes a significant discography.

Evaluation of Biographies for Young People

Collier, James Lincoln. *Louis Armstrong: An American Success Story*. New York: Macmillan, 1985. Designed to capture the interest of younger readers, the text focuses on Armstrong's career up to the early 1940s. Major events toward the end of his career are covered in less detail.

Eaton, Jeannette. *Trumpeter's Tale: The Story of Young Louis Armstrong*. New York: William Morrow, 1955. Treats Armstrong's early childhood, his struggle to survive, and his early musical experiences. Eaton attempts to capture the essence of African-American culture by interspersing dialect throughout the text. A fine source of information for younger students, it takes the reader through Armstrong's career with King Oliver and Fletcher Henderson.

Millender, Dharathula H. *Louis Armstrong: Young Music Maker*. Indianapolis: Bobbs-Merrill, 1972. A fanciful and fictionalized version of Armstrong's early childhood. The last third of the text treats Armstrong's career and his marriages to Daisy and Lil Hardin.

Sanders, Ruby Wilson. *Jazz Ambassador*. Chicago: Children's Press, 1973. Presented in a storytelling style, this book covers Armstrong's childhood experiences in New Orleans, his close relationship with his mother, his feelings about racism, and the joy he experienced living in the world of music. This is a sensitive treatment about a remarkable musician.

Overview and Evaluation of Primary Sources

Armstrong's autobiographical output is relatively brief. *Satchmo: My Life in New Orleans* (New York: Signet Books, 1955; **A, G**) was written when he was able to recall many of the details of his youth and the unfolding of his early career. It is considered accurate, but reportedly was heavily edited. Although it contains a few errors and misspellings, the book nevertheless offers readers an intriguing first-hand account.

For a list of articles written by Armstrong, Joann Skowronski's *Black Music in America: A Bibliography.* (Metuchen, NJ: The Scarecrow Press, 1981; **A, G, Y**) is a vital source. A listing of primary sources, especially interviews, is included in Collier's biography of Armstrong. An important source of information about early jazz in New Orleans is the Tulane University Archives. CBS Records Archives (New York City) contains information on Armstrong's career and his association with CBS.

Films and Performances

Armstrong appeared in at least sixty films, television programs, and documentaries. On film he appeared with Bing Crosby in *Pennies From Heaven* (1936); with Cosby and Frank Sinatra in *High Society* (1956); with Billie Holliday in *New Orleans* (1947); with James Stewart in *The Glenn Miller Story* (1953); and with Gene Kelly and Barbara Streisand in *Hello Dolly* (1969).

Among his most cherished performances are: "Ain't Misbehavin" from *Hot Chocolates,* composed by Fats Waller; "Hello Dolly," "When it's Sleepy-Time Down South," "Dippermouth Blues," "West End Blues," "On the Sunnyside of the Street," "When the Saints Go Marching In," and "Mack the Knife."

Among his important recordings are the more than sixty made during the Hot Five and Hot Seven era, and over two hundred made with large swing bands. Also notable are early efforts such as: "Chimes Blues" (1923) with King Oliver, his first recorded solo; "Froggie Moore"; "Go 'long Mule" and "Copenhagen" (1924) with Fletcher Henderson; "St. Louis Blues" (1925) with Bessie Smith; "Cake Walkin' Babies" (1924) featuring Sidney Bechet; and "Texas Moaner Blues" (1924) a classic example of Storyville-style blues.

Museums, Historical Landmarks, Societies

CBS Records Archives (New York, NY). Information on Armstrong's career and involvement with CBS.

Queens College (Flushing, NY). Houses Armstrong's archival material.

Tulane University Archives (New Orleans, LA). Important source of information about early jazz in New Orleans, and includes substantial materials on Armstrong.

Other Sources

Collier, James Lincoln. "Armstrong, Louis." In *The New Grove Dictionary of Jazz*. Vol. 1. Edited by Barry Kernfeld. London: Macmillan, 1988. Provides an excellent synopsis of Armstrong's life and his contributions to jazz. Analyzes the major periods of his career, giving careful consideration to the Hot Five and Hot Seven recordings. Includes a bibliography, discography, filmography, and selected musical transcriptions.

Feather, Leonard. *From Satchmo to Miles*. New York: Stein and Day, 1972. Chapter one is devoted to Armstrong. Includes letters from Armstrong to Feather, an important jazz promoter and author.

Floyd, Samuel A., Jr. and Marsha J. Reisser. *Black Music Biography*. White Plains, NY: Kraus International Publications, 1987. Floyd and Reisser offer substantial annotations of biographical works on Armstrong. The annotations are candid and very useful. Book reviews and supplementary information regarding indexes, discographies, filmographies, photographs, and bibliographies are included for each work listed.

Schuller, Gunther. *The History of Jazz: Early Jazz*, vol. 1. New York: Oxford University Press, 1968. The chapter "The First Great Soloist" focuses on Armstrong and his contributions to early jazz. This is one of the most important treatments of Armstrong's musical contributions. Schuller provides a thorough musicological analysis. He examines Armstrong's harmonic and rhythmic syntax, formal (structural) organization, textures, and sonorities. Through a technical comparison of Armstrong's musicianship with that of other performers, Schuller arrives at a basis for judging his importance to twentieth-century music. He lists four notable features of Armstrong's music: his choice of notes; his tone quality; his rhythmic sense (epitomized as "swing," which includes his phrasing and varied rhythmic attacks); and the unique expressive devices such as vibratos and shakes with which Armstrong colors individual notes.

―――――. *The Swing Era: The Development of Jazz 1930-1945*. New York: Oxford University Press, 1989. Schuller brings uncanny insight to his analysis of Armstrong's career during the swing era of the 1930s and 1940s. He includes several transcriptions of Armstrong's trumpet improvisations along with analyses of their musical significance. Schuller contends that without Armstrong's unique contributions, there might not have been a "swing era," or at the least, the music would have been far different.

Skowronski, JoAnn. *Black Music in America: A Bibliography*. Metuchen, NJ: Scarecrow Press, 1981. Skowronski's bibliography includes almost nine hundred books and articles about Armstrong. Some of the foreign sources may be relatively inaccessible, but many of the articles are from major journals found in most libraries. This book is an important source for students writing research papers on Armstrong.

Southern, Eileen. *Biographical Dictionary of Afro-American and African Musicians.* Westport, CT: Greenwood Press, 1982. A few items such as Armstrong's proper name and date of birth have been corrected since Southern's dictionary was published. This is a concise overview of Armstrong's life and career.

Warren C. Swindell
Center for Afro-American Studies
Indiana State University

CRISPUS ATTUCKS
c. 1723-1770

Chronology

Crispus Attucks is born a slave owned by Deacon William Browne in Framingham, Massachusetts, about 1723; *November 1750* escapes and serves as a sailor on a whaling vessel operated by a Captain Folger; *March 5, 1770* killed leading a public protest in what came to be called the Boston Massacre.

Activities of Historical Significance

Crispus Attucks was physically described as being six feet two inches tall and knock-kneed. Historians disagree as to whether he was a mulatto, a member of the Natick Indian tribe, or of mixed black and Native American blood. Although little is known of his personal life other than his birth into slavery, his subsequent escape, and his work as a sailor, he played a significant role in American history. On March 5, 1770, he led a group of sailors and other citizens in a confrontation with the British in Boston, triggering what came to be known as the "Boston Massacre." Protesting the implementation of the Townsend Acts by which Parliment imposed new taxes on the colonies and quartered troops in private homes, Attucks and an angry crowd surrounded a detachment of British soldiers under Captain Preston outside the Customs House on King Street. After an exchange of insults and snowballs, the nervous soldiers fired into the mob, killing Attucks and four others.

The coroner, Benjamin Church, stated in his report that Attucks was felled by two gunshot wounds that entered his chest and exited his body on the left of his spine. This physical evidence, along with testimony by James Bailey at the trial, indicated that Attucks was in the forefront of the protesters. In the trial that followed, Captain Preston was cleared of murder charges, but because of public outrage, most of the Townsend Acts were repealed. Nevertheless, tension worsened between the colonies and Britain.

As a leader of the protesters and the first to fall, Attucks's name was indelibly linked with the massacre and was invoked as a rallying cry at the Boston Tea Party in 1773. After the war for American independence erupted at Lexington and Concord in 1775, Attucks was widely remembered in revolutionary lore as the first "martyr" to die for the cause of freedom.

Overview of Biographical Sources

Very little has been written about Crispus Attucks for the simple reason that little is known. He seems almost to have appeared from nowhere to assume his role in history on the night of March 5, 1770. With his death, he passed from the scene as abruptly as he arrived. Much of what is written dates to the late 1800s, when there was a revival in interest in the origins of the American Revolution. Brief articles by Benjamin Quarles in *American History Illustrated* (1970) and in *The Dictionary of Negro Biography* (1982) summarize and assess these older sources.

Evaluation of Principal Biographical Sources

Fisher, J. B. "Who Was Crispus Attucks?" *American Historical Record* 1 (1872): 531-533. (A, G) A brief and dated biographical article of Attucks; because other information is scarce, however, this is a necessary source.

Fiske, John. "Unpublished Orations . . ." Boston: 1888. (A, G) This essay was delivered in Boston in 1888 at the dedication of the memorial to Crispus Attucks. It is typically laudatory, and describes the events of March 5, 1770, in good versus evil fashion. Attucks is described as a former slave who escaped from his master and began the movement for American independence.

Quarles, Benjamin. "Crispus Attucks." *American History Illustrated* 5 (November 1970): 38-42. (A, G, Y) This is a brief, well-written article. The illustrations are appropriate, and the article discusses the influence of Attucks as a symbol throughout American history.

————. "Crispus Attucks." In *The Dictionary of Negro Biography*, edited by Rayford W. Logan and Michael R. Winston. New York: W. W. Norton, 1982. (A, G) The best brief biography that is available.

Overview and Evaluation of Primary Sources

A narrative of the trial of the British soldiers accused of shooting unarmed Bostonians was published as William Wemms, *The Trial of British Soldiers of the 29th Regiment of Foot for the Murder of Crispus Attucks, Samuel Gray, Samuel Maverick, James Caldwell, and Patrick Carr, on Monday Evening, March 5, 1770, Before the Honorable Benjamin Lynde, John Cushing, Peter Oliver, and Edmund Trowbridge, Esquires, Justices of the Superior Court of Judicature, Court of Assize, and General Gaol Delivery, Held at Boston, by Adjournment, November 27, 1770* (Boston: William Emmons, 1824; A). Unfortunately, this account, which was originally printed in 1770, contains both editorial and factual inaccuracies. No official transcript or record of the trial of Captain Preston survives.

Volume three of the *Legal Papers of John Adams*, edited by L. Kinvin Wroth and Hiller B. Zobel (Cambridge, Massachusetts: 1965; A) does offer a superb account of the trials of Preston and the soldiers. It also contains the full edition of the aforementioned *Trial of British Soldiers* . . ., with an important appendix of the civilian trial not found in any but the 1770 printing, which is very rare. Many of the errors and disordered parts of that work are rectified in the *Adams Papers*.

Fiction and Adaptation

Edmund Curley's *Crispus Attucks—The First to Die* (1973) stresses the fact that the first person to shed blood in America for liberty was a black man. Though well-researched, this work is highly fictionalized and therefore belongs to literature rather than history.

Museums, Historical Landmarks, Societies

Crispus Attucks Monument (Boston, MA). Dedicated in 1888, this monument, located on Lafayette Mall on Boston Common, commemorates the Boston Massacre and the role of Crispus Attucks. Made of granite, it is twenty-five feet high and over ten feet wide at the base. A bas-relief on the monument's base depicts Attucks standing boldly in the foreground before the State House.

Other Sources

Alden, Edmund Kimball. "Crispus Attucks." In the *Dictionary of American Biography*, edited by Allen Johnson and Dumas Malone, vol. 1. New York: Charles Scribner's Sons, 1928-1936. This article on Attucks is dated but contains some useful information.

A Memorial of Crispus Attucks . . . Miami: Mnemosyne, 1969. This pamphlet contains a full description of the monument on Boston Common, a narrative of the unveiling ceremony, and a description of a following meeting at Faneuil Hall. A letter from Frederick Douglass, commenting on Attucks, is included.

Daniel Dean Roland

JOSEPHINE BAKER
1906-1975

Chronology

Born Josephine Freda on June 3, 1906, in St. Louis, Missouri, the illegitimate daughter of Carrie McDonald, a domestic, the descendant of Negro
and Apalachee Indian slaves, and Eddie Carson, an itinerant street drummer;
grows up in humiliating poverty; scavenges for food in the Chestnut Valley,
St. Louis's infamous tenderloin district and the cradle of ragtime; *1917*
embroiled in the East St. Louis race riot on July 2, one of the worst that
America has ever witnessed; marries Willie Wells, a local foundry worker, but
soon leaves him to tour the country on black vaudeville circuit with the
Theater Owners' Booking Association (T.O.B.A.); *1921* while playing Philadelphia, marries Willie Baker, a pullman porter; *1923* separates from husband
when she lands a job as a comedy chorus girl in *Shuffle Along; 1925* moves
to Paris and electrifies Parisians with her exotic dancing in *La Revue Negre*;
stars at the Casino de Paris and the Folies-Bergère; *1926* appears at the
Folies-Bergère in her most famous costume, a girdle of rhinestone-studded
bananas; *1927-1936* remains an international celebrity, tours the world, acts in
movies, and takes a range of lovers that include gigolo Pepito de Abatino,
mystery writer George Simeon, and architect Le Corbusier; *1937* marries
French sugar broker Jean Lion on November 30, but separates from him fourteen months later; *1939-1945* serves as an undercover agent for the French
Resistance; awarded the Légion d'Honneur, Croix de Guerre, and the Rosette
de la Résistance for her bravery; *1947* marries her fourth husband, band
leader Jo Bouillon, on her forty-first birthday; *1951* becomes an outspoken
critic of American racial policies during a triumphal tour of the U.S.; refuses
to appear in cities where she is offerred second-class accommodations, or to
perform in theaters that do not hire black stagehands; *1954-1965* creates her
"rainbow tribe," adopting twelve children of different races and nationalities
to prove to the world that it's possible for people to live together in harmony;
1975 dies in Paris on April 14, in the course of another spectacular comeback
and just five days after celebrating her fiftieth anniversary in French show
business.

Activities of Historical Significance

Josephine Baker is mainly remembered not so much as a great singer—un-
fairly because she possessed a truly remarkable voice, light and sweet like a
bird—but as a supreme visual performer in the great tradition of the Parisian
music hall. She was one of the thrilling stage presences of the twentieth

century, displaying powers of endurance that are granted to few. She was also an affecting actress, although she never found a framework for this ability.

More than a performer, however, she embodied the glamor, pain, and poignancy of the Jazz Age and Paris in the 1920s. As the first black superstar, she became a symbol of new opportunities for her race. The color that caused her so much pain and suffering in her childhood helped catapult her to international fame. Janet Flanner, on assignment for *The New Yorker,* wrote in 1925: "Her magnificent dark body, a new model to the French, proved for the first time that black was beautiful."

She was deeply respected for her courageous and self-sacrificing work for France during World War II with the Resistance, for her championship of civil rights causes during the bleak McCarthy era of the 1950s, and her outspokenness against bigotry of every kind. She traveled anonymously through the American South to see what life under Jim Crow was like for the average African American, marched on Washington, and tried to sue the Stork Club for racism. But she was unlettered and woefully ignorant: she supported Benito Mussolini's invasion of Ethiopia, lavished attention on dictator Juan Peron, who wanted to make her his next Evita, praised Fidel Castro, and extolled race relations in France, ignoring their colonial history.

Overview of Biographical Sources

Lynn Haney's *Naked at the Feast—a Biography of Josephine Baker* (1981) offers the first comprehensive biography of Baker in English. Rose's elegantly written *Jazz Cleopatra—Josephine Baker in her Time* (1989) is a delight to read but often plays loose with sources and attributions. Researchers should consult Hammand and O'Connor's *Josephine Baker* (1988) to understand why she had such a powerful visual impact on audiences.

The critically acclaimed film biography by Christopher Rallings, *Chasing a Rainbow*, is frequently aired on cable television. In a lively documentary format, Rallings visually captures Baker's metamorphosis from sexy dingbat to fiery humanitarian.

Evaluation of Principal Biographical Sources

Abtey, Jacques. *La Guerre Secrète de Joséphine Baker*. Paris: Éditions Sibboney, 1948. (A, G) Although extremely laudatory, the book is the best account of Baker's wartime activities. It includes a prefatory letter by Charles de Gaulle.

Hammond, Bryan, and Patrick O'Connor. *Josephine Baker*. London: Jonathan Cape, 1988. (G) A cornucopia of photographs and postcards, books, magazines and newspaper clippings, posters and theater programs, songsheets and recordings, autographs and correspondence. The visual representations of Baker help to explain her phenomenal appeal in a way that no text possibly could.

Haney, Lynn. *Naked at the Feast—a Biography of Josephine Baker.* London: Robeson Books, 1981. The first well-researched and definitive biography of Baker, it reveals a wealth of facts that had never appeared before anywhere.

Rose, Phyllis. *Jazz Cleopatra—Josephine Baker in her Time.* Garden City, NY: Doubleday, 1989. (A, G) The strength of this book is not in the material—much of which had already been printed—but in the elegant writing style and its ability to capture the cultural and historical circumstances that both shaped and mirrored Baker's life.

Overview and Evaluation of Primary Sources

Baker co-authored five memoirs. The first—*Les Mémoires de Joséphine Baker*, with Marcel Sauvage (Paris: Kra, 1930; A)—is by far the best. Highly whimsical, with only a tenuous connection to fact, it nonetheless captures her febrile essence, uncontrived and unadorned, before she began to think of herself as a legend. Other volumes, written with Marcel Sauvage, include *Voyages et Adventures de Joséphine Baker* (Paris: Kra, 1931; A) and *Les Memoires de Joséphine Baker* (Paris: Kra, 1947; A). With André Rivollet she penned *Une Vie de Toutes les Couleurs* (Grenoble, France: B. Arthaud, 1935; A), and with Jo Bouillon and Jacqueline Cartier, she compiled *Josephine* (Paris: Robert Laffont, 1976; Trans. New York: Harper & Row, 1977; A).

Baker recorded over a hundred songs during her career. Most of her output first appeared on four labels in France: Odéon, Columbia, Pacific, and RCA, though later she occasionally made records for other companies. Her voice combined three disparate qualities, which made it so unique: the tone and innocence of a child's voice, confidence, and wildness.

Baker's film career always seemed to be at the edge of getting off the ground. In 1927 she appeared in *La Sirène de Tropiques*, a silly bit of frippery about a dim-witted girl from the Antilles named Papitou, who abandons her equatorial island to try her luck in Paris. The script was written by Maurice Dekobra, author of the best-selling postwar potboiler, *La Madone des Sleepings*. In 1934 she starred in *Zouzou*, a playful musical about a laundress who becomes a Parisian music hall "vedette." The film co-starred the great French actor Jean Gabin. *Princesse Tam-Tam* (1935), directed by Edmond Gréville and co-starring Albert Préjean and Viviane Romance, was the story of an African beauty foisted on Parisian society as a princess, with Baker, of course, in the lead role.

Libraries housing collections of Baker's letters, programs, and magazine articles include the Performing Arts Research Center of New York Public Library at Lincoln Center; Schomburg Center, New York Public Library; Bibliothèque de l'Arsenal, Paris; La Bibliothèque Municipal in Perigueux; Sterling Library at Yale University; and the Missouri Historical Society. The Center for Jazz Studies at Rutgers University has taped interviews with Baker.

Fiction and Adaptations

Written by Baker's lover Pepito Abatino, *Mon Sang dans tes Veines* (1931) is an amateurish and melodramatic novel that, nevertheless, affords a rare glimpse of Baker's psychological complexity. The heroine sacrifices her life in the manner of Christ suffering on the cross for the sins of man. A novelized account of Baker's wartime activities, *Épisodes de la Vie d'un agent du S. R. et du contre-espionnage Française* (1961), appeared under the pseudonym of J.A. Rémy, a writer who specialized in secret service activities.

Lynn Haney

EMILY GREENE BALCH
1867-1961

Chronology

Born Emily Greene Balch on January 8, 1867, in Jamaica Plain, Massachusetts, the third child of Francis Balch, a lawyer and former secretary to U.S. Senator Charles Sumner, and Ellen Maria Noyes, a former schoolteacher from Illinois; *1885-1889* attends and receives bachelor's degree at Bryn Mawr College, a member of its first graduating class; *1889-1890* studies with noted sociologist Franklin H. Giddings; *1890-1891* receives a Bryn Mawr European Fellowship to study the French system of poverty relief at the Sorbonne; *1891* returns to Boston and becomes involved in social work, gathering information on laws and agencies relating to juvenile delinquency; *1892* establishes Denison House, a social settlement; *1893* publishes *Public Assistance of the Poor in France* and joins the Federal Labor Union, part of the American Federation of Labor; *1895* publishes *Manual for Use in Cases of Juvenile Offenders and Other Minors*; attends graduate school at Harvard University Annex (later Radcliffe) and the University of Chicago; *1895-1896* studies at the University of Berlin; *1896-1914* teaches economics at Wellesley College; *1903* helps establish the Women's Trade Union League; *1905-1906* visits Austria-Hungary to examine emigration patterns and tours Slavic communities in the United States; *1908-1909* serves on the Massachusetts State Commission on Industrial Education; *1910* publishes a popular book on the history of immigration, *Our Slavic Fellow Citizens*; *1913-1914* serves on the Massachusetts State Commission on Immigration; *1915* accompanies Jane Addams and forty-two other American women to the International Congress of Women at The Hague, and co-authors *Women at the Hague*; *1916* participates in Henry Ford's unofficial Neutral Conference for Continuous Mediation, the American Committee Against Militarism, and the Emergency Peace Federation; *1918* Wellesley College trustees refuse to reappoint her professor of economics because of her pacifist views; publishes *Approaches to the Great Settlement*; *1918-1919* works on the editorial staff of the *Nation*; *1919-1922* converts to Quakerism and becomes secretary-treasurer of the Women's International League for Peace and Freedom (WILPF); *1927* publishes anti-imperialist tract, *Occupied Haiti*; *1931* assumes presidency of the American branch of the WILPF; *1931-1934* works with League of Nations on drug control, international aviation, and disarmament; *1934-1935* resumes position, without pay, as international secretary of the WILPF; *1939-1945* reluctantly supports the war in protest against Fascist aggression; helps European refugees settle in America; writes a book of poems, *The Miracle of Living* (1941); works to secure the release of Japanese-Americans in relocation camps; *1946* receives, along with international YMCA leader John R. Mott, the Nobel Peace Prize; *1952-1959* remains active in the WILPF's affairs, and co-chairs the celebration of the hundredth anniversary of the birth of former league president Jane Addams; *1961* dies in a nursing home on January 9 in Cambridge, Massachusetts.

Activities of Historical Significance

Emily Greene Balch's activities on behalf of international peace entitle her to a place in history alongside such other prominent feminist peace workers as Jane Addams, Lucia Ames Mead, Tracy Mygatt, and Dorothy Detzer. She remains one of the twentieth century's most important American pacifists. Already an acknowledged leader within the peace movement, she achieved worldwide recognition when awarded the 1946 Nobel Prize. Balch never married. At the conclusion of World War I, which marked the breakup of the American women's peace movement, Balch helped found and guide the Women's International League for Peace and Freedom (WILPF).

Initially, Balch was interested in settlement work, aid to the urban poor, juvenile delinquency, immigration relief, and the economic status of women. After her graduation from Bryn Mawr, Balch traveled extensively in search of answers to society's economic ills. Influenced by Progressive Era policies, Balch combined an academic career as a professor of economics at Wellesley College with active involvement in numerous social causes. Of particular interest to her were poverty, child labor and education, and immigration.

Before World War I, Balch worked on drafting a Massachusetts minimum wage bill that failed to pass in the legislature. She helped organize the first State Conference of Charities and during 1897-1898 served on the Municipal Board of Trustees, overseeing services for Boston's delinquent and neglected children. In 1912 Balch assisted the Progressive party's committee on immigration. Her interest in the immigration problem dated back to 1904, when she studied emigration in Austria-Hungary and afterwards visited Slavic communities in the United States. Her 1910 publication, *Our Slavic Fellow Citizens*, remains a frequently cited work on histories of immigration. Working with state regulatory commissions was also an important aspect of Balch's activities before she dedicated her energies to pacifism. During the Progressive period she was a member of the Massachusetts State Commission on Industrial Education, the Massachusetts State Commission on Immigration, and the Boston City Planning Board.

Although Balch professed opposition to war and imperialism after the Spanish-American War (1898), she was not fully associated with the peace movement until the outbreak of world war in 1914. The next year she attended the International Congress of Women at The Hague with Jane

Addams and over forty other American delegates. Seeking peace through mediation, the congress sent delegates to neutral countries. Balch visited scandinavia and Russia. She also met with Sir Edward Grey of Britain and U.S. President Woodrow Wilson. She recounts her role as a delegate in *Women at The Hague* (1915), coauthored with Addams and Alice Hamilton. In 1916 Balch was a member of Henry Ford's Stockholm Neutral Conference for Continuous Mediation. Although Ford's Peace Ship Mission was marked by controversy, Balch conducted two studies for constructive peace: proposing a postwar rehabilitation fund, and an international administration of colonies. On leave from Wellesley in 1916, she participated in peace and antiwar groups such as the American Union Against Militarism, the Women's Peace Party, and the Emergency Peace Federation, which she established.

When Congress declared war in April 1917, Balch supported the left-wing People's Council of America. Dismayed by her anti-war activities, the Wellesley trustees refused to renew her contract as professor of economics. Responding to the college president, Balch wrote that she was unable to "reconcile war with the truths of Jesus' teaching."

In 1919 Balch played a leading role with the International Congress of Women in Zurich, Switzerland. Because of factionalism among female peace groups at home, Balch strengthened her international ties. The congress, founded at The Hague, changed its name to the Women's International League for Peace and Freedom and established a permanent headquarters in Geneva. With Jane Addams, Balch believed that there could be no peace without social and economic justice. Other proponents of broad social reform among the league's founders led the WILPF to incorporate the goal of peace and justice into its platform. As the league's first international secretary-treasurer, Balch administered the Geneva headquarters and established organizational guidelines and policy for the league's attack on the causes of war. In 1931 she was elected president of the league's American branch and in 1934 again served as international secretary. Balch's administrative and leadership skills were crucial to the league's success: the league established summer schools on peace education and created new branches in some fifty nations.

Although Balch condemned coercive aspects of its covenant, the WILPF assisted the League of Nations in its scientific, economic, and cultural efforts until World War II. Balch personally worked on drug control, international aviation, refugee protection, disarmament, and the question of Albania's admission.

Balch was also active on other fronts. In 1926 she, University of Chicago economist (and later U.S. senator) Paul Douglas, and four others investigated the occupation of Haiti, under U.S. control since 1915. The peace team criticized the occupation, and Balch published a lengthy report, *Occupied Haiti* (1927), calling for an end to American intervention. Balch supported disarmament agreements, praised the 1928 Kellogg-Briand Pact outlawing war, called for the international administration of Manchuria after Japan invaded the country in 1931, recommended the installation of a moderate Republican government to end the Spanish Civil War, and worked unceasingly to admit European victims of Fascist aggression to the U.S.

World War II tested Balch's pacifist convictions, because she found it difficult not to support an Allied victory. Without criticizing the war effort, Balch remained an active witness for peace, however, working for the release of Japanese-Americans interned in relocation camps, opposing the unconditional surrender policy, and supporting the rights of conscientious objectors. In 1946 she shared the Nobel Peace Prize with international YMCA leader and ecumenical churchman John R. Mott.

During the cold war, Balch supported specialized agencies of the United Nations, but remained skeptical of a world government, which she felt would operate no differently than any nation-state. Balch believed that the hope for peace rested in the international administration of agriculture, aviation, atomic energy, waterways, polar regions, and underdeveloped countries. With the world on the verge of nuclear obliteration, Balch promoted the WILPF as "a body. . .to push the international idea of a world of friendly, cooperative people." She asserted that the peace movement must include working women, as well as leisure-class women, and the young, who could "make the league one of personal friendship among women of different nationalities."

A product of the Progressive Era, Balch based her administrative mechanisms on expert planning, and remained a gradualist, evaluating the relative merits of each strategy. Her leadership, as an extension of a commitment to social reform, made her the guiding light of the WILPF.

Overview of Biographical Sources

Balch and Jane Addams remain the only American women awarded the Nobel Peace Prize. Balch's roles as academic, social reform theorist, and internationalist have, to some degree, been systematically evaluated and analyzed, but her life and writings remain relatively unexplored.

Improper Bostonian: Emily Greene Balch (1964), by Mercedes M. Randall, represents the only full-length biography of the international leader. Randall, a co-worker in the American women's peace movement, presents an insider's account of Balch's contributions that objectively assesses the Women's International League for Peace and Freedom.

Two short biographical sketches detailing Balch's peace work are Olga S. Opfell's chapter "Holy Fire Within: Emily Greene Balch" in *The Lady Laureates: Women Who Have Won the Nobel Prize* (1978), and Barbara Solomon Miller's "Emily Greene Balch" in *Notable American Women* (1980). Opfell's sketch offers an intimate tribute, while Miller analyzes Balch's roles as peace advocate, social reformer, and economist. Both Opfell and Miller stress the contributions of feminists to internationalism and reform.

John Herman Randall, Jr., Columbia University philosopher and historian, and husband of Mercedes, wrote a short pamphlet, *Emily Greene Balch of New England: Citizen of the World* (1946), to emphasize Balch's peace activities. Historian Justus D. Doenecke assesses Balch's effectiveness as a peace leader in "Emily Greene Balch" in *Biographical Dictionary of Modern Peace Leaders* (1985).

Evaluation of Principal Biographical Sources

Doenecke, Justus D. "Emily Greene Balch." In *Biographical Dictionary of Modern Peace Leaders*, edited by Harold Josephson. Westport, CT: Greenwood Press, 1985. (A, G) Assesses the contributions of Balch's peace activism with particular emphasis on her role as a leader in the WILPF. Contains a useful bibliography.

Miller, Barbara Solomon. "Emily Greene Balch." In *Notable American Women*, edited by Barbara Sicherman and Carol Hurd Greene, vol. 4. Cambridge: Harvard University Press, 1980. (A, G) Intended for both a scholarly and general audience, this biographical reference constitutes a thorough sketch of Balch. Emphasizing the feminist perspective, the author brings to light Balch as peace advocate, social reformer, and academic economist. Contains an excellent bibliography.

Opfell, Olga S. *The Lady Laureates: Women Who Have Won the Nobel Prize*. Metuchen, NJ: Scarecrow Press, 1977. (A, G) A chapter devoted to Balch provides an intimate tribute to the feminist peace advocate and recounts Balch's early childhood education and family background. Though short on details of Balch's role in the WILPF, the author covers her peace activities through reminiscences and autobiographical commentary.

Randall, John Herman, Jr. *Emily Greene Balch of New England: Citizen of the World*. Washington, DC: Women's International League for Peace and Freedom, 1946. (A, G) This pamphlet is a tribute to Balch, focusing on her work with the WILPF.

Randall, Mercedes M. *Improper Bostonian: Emily Greene Balch*. New York: Twayne, 1964. (A, G) A full-length biography depicting Balch the pacifist and social reformer. The author relies on Balch's writings, personal papers, and her own firsthand experiences as a co-worker in the interwar women's peace movement. The author knew Balch personally in the context of the peace movement. Balch's leading role in the Women's International

League for Peace and Freedom is also recounted in this scholarly, yet sympathetic, biography.

Overview and Evaluation of Primary Sources

Although Balch did not write an autobiography, her writings have been conveniently compiled and edited by Mercedes Randall in *Beyond Nationalism: The Social Thought of Emily Greene Balch* (New York: Twayne, 1972; A, G). This contains a complete listing of Balch's writings with an introduction to her career. Randall includes Balch's essay honoring Jane Addams and a moving piece entitled "The Earth Is My Home." Balch's scholarly articles and popular views, mainly on world peace, provide excellent insight into her thought and character.

The quiet, unassuming personality revealed in Balch's writings stands in contrast to her enormous influence. A member of a highbrow New England family, she was exceptionally intelligent. Her writings reflect her concern for world cooperation and personal freedom. One poem "To a Bedbug," concludes: "To help my brothers in all lands/ To make wide the doors of comradeship/ Let me lie locked close and alone/ Despised and punished/ By those I seek to serve."

Balch's earliest writings demonstrate a scholarly interest in social and economic change. Her first publication, *Public Assistance of the Poor in France* (Baltimore: American Economic Association, 1893; A), is a historical study of the care for the poor as well as an organizational study of the bureaucratic administration of poor relief. One of the earliest sociological examinations of care for the poor, it includes statistical and demographic information. Balch's technical manuscript on wayward children, *Manual for Use in Cases of Juvenile Offenders and Other Minors in Massachusetts* (Boston: Conference of Child-Helping Societies, 1895, 1908; A) is primarily of interest to social historians. Her most significant academic work is *Our Slavic Fellow Citizens* (1910. Reprint. New York: Arno Press, 1968; A, G), the first major sociological work on the immigration of Slavic groups in Europe and the United States. Richly documented with appendices containing many statistical tables, the book is one of the most frequently cited studies on the histories of immigration. *The Miracle of Living* (New York: Island Press, 1941; G), Balch's only venture away from formal, abstract writing, is a short book of verse providing insight into her care for humankind.

Balch's principal writings on world peace are found in three books. In 1915, Balch, Jane Addams, and Alice Hamilton were members of the American delegation to the International Congress of Women at The Hague. Their joint publication, *Women at The Hague: The International Congress of Women and Its Results* (1915. Reprint. New York: Garland Publishing, 1972; A, G), contains the records of women pacifists and their attempt to bring an end to

World War I. The delegates urged the adoption of continuous mediation, and the publication of this work brought the meeting to worldwide attention. Balch edited *Approaches to the Great Settlement* (New York: B. W. Hubesch, 1918; A, G), a compilation of documents sponsored by the American Union Against Militarism. It includes socialist and labor documents, peace programs, and proposals to end war written by figures such as David Starr Jordan of Stanford University and William Eliot of Harvard University. British pacifist Norman Angell wrote the introduction. In *Occupied Haiti* (1927. Reprint. New York: Garland Publishing, 1973; A, G), Balch compiled a 1926 report on conditions in Haiti. One of six American peace seekers, Balch visited the island and criticized the American military occupation that dated back to 1915. As the report's principal author, Balch called for the restoration of independence to the Negro Republic.

Two important WILPF pamphlets, *A Venture in Internationalism* (1938; G) and *Refugees as Assets* (1940; G), present a history of the WILPF from 1919 to 1938 and Balch's unrelenting conviction that World War II refugees—European Jews—could be culturally and economically advantageous to the United States. In addition to her principal works and pamphlets, two articles written during World War I solidify Balch's antiwar convictions. In "The Effects of War and Militarism on the Status of Women," *Publications of the American Sociological Society* (1915; A) Balch argues that war disrupts societal harmony and places women in a subservient role. "Who's Who Among Pacifists: The Position of the Emergency Peace Federation" (March 20, 1917) Emily Greene Balch Papers, microfilm, Swarthmore College Peace Collection, represents the initial stages of Balch's organizational peace work that would culminate in her leadership role in the WILPF.

In terms of Balch material on world peace, the Swarthmore College Peace Collection contains a wealth of information. The Balch Papers include diaries and calendars (1876-1955), correspondence (1875-1957), autobiographical notes, poetry, manuscripts for articles and speeches, printed articles, subject files, and clippings. Assorted records of the WILPF, including correspondence, minutes, pamphlets, and other printed materials, constitute a large part of the Balch collection. There is also correspondence addressed to Mercedes Randall, Balch's major biographer. Martha P. Shane has edited a 35-mm microfilm version of these materials, *The Papers of Emily Greene Balch, 1875-1961* (Wilmington, DE: Scholarly Resources, 1988; A).

In addition, the Wellesley College Archives contains material on Balch's career as a professor of economics. The Oswald Garrison Villard Papers, Houghton Library, Harvard University, have information pertaining to Balch as a staff member of the *Nation* and her correspondence with the noted editor Villard. The Office of the President, Wellesley College, holds the board of trustees minutes, especially those dealing with the refusal to reappoint Balch to her former position as professor.

Museums, Historical Landmarks, Societies
Swarthmore College Peace Collection (Swarthmore, PA). In addition to holding the core of the Emily Greene Balch Papers, the collection contains photographs of Balch, the Nobel Peace prize scroll, a writing case and portfolio, and numerous miniature sketches. Sometimes there is a small exhibit on Balch and the WILPF in the Peace Collection reading room.

Other Sources
Alonzo, Harriet Hyman. "Suffragists for Peace During the Interwar Years, 1919-1941." *Peace and Change* 14 (July 1989): 243-262. A sound historical account of the creation of four women's peace groups, including the WILPF, in the aftermath of the Great War.

Bussey, Gertrude, and Margaret Tims. *Pioneers for Peace: Women's International League for Peace and Freedom, 1915-1965*. 1965. Reprint. Oxford: Alden Press, 1980. An excellent history of the peace organization and Balch's influential role.

Chatfield, Charles. *For Peace and Justice: Pacifism in America, 1914-1941*. Knoxville: University of Tennessee Press, 1971. The definitive scholarly study of the interwar American peace movement. Balch and the WILPF are given extensive coverage.

Davis, Allen F. *Spearheads for Reform: The Social Settlements and the Progressive Movement, 1890-1914*. New York: Oxford University Press, 1967. Provides a full history of the settlement movement's development, influence, and impact. Balch and Denison House are covered.

DeBenedetti, Charles. *Origins of the Modern American Peace Movement, 1915-1929*. Millwood, NY: KTO Press, 1978. A solid account of a fourteen-year period in which a new breed of peace reformers began organizing into three different types of coalitions: internationalists, conservative and liberal legalists, and feminist and religious peace workers.

————. *The Peace Reform in American History*. Bloomington: Indiana University Press, 1980. A useful survey of the American peace movement as a reform endeavor.

Deegan, Mary Jo. "Emily Greene Balch." In *American Women Writers: A Critical Reference Guide from Colonial Times to the Present*, vol. 1. New York: Frederick Ungar, 1979. Provides a helpful sketch and brief analyses of Balch's principal writings.

Degen, Marie L. *The History of the Woman's Peace Party*. Baltimore: Johns Hopkins University Press, 1939. A comprehensive, in-depth, and scholarly study of the first years of the Women's International League for Peace and Freedom.

Foster, Catherine. *Women for all Seasons: The Story of the Women's International League for Peace and Freedom*. Athens: University of Georgia Press, 1989. Provides more information on the peace organization, focusing on its recent activities. Balch and the historical roots of the peace groups are mentioned.

Marchand, C. Roland. *The American Peace Movement and Social Reform, 1898-1918*. Princeton: Princeton University Press, 1972. Excellent scholarly analysis of the basis of radical peace activism during the Progressive/World War I period.

Pois, Ann Marie. "The U.S. Women's International League for Peace and Freedom and American Neutrality, 1935-1939." *Peace and Change* 14 (July 1989): 263-284. Offers a scholarly assessment of Balch's criticisms of neutrality laws and her call for nonmilitary, international sanctions against Fascist aggression.

Steinson, Barbara J. *American Women's Activism in World War I*. New York: Garland Publishing, 1982. Covers a wide range of feminist activities, including the numerous peace organizations women participated in during the Great War.

Trolander, Judith Ann. "Emily Greene Balch." In *Dictionary of American Biography*, edited by John A. Garraty, supp. 7. New York: Charles Scribner's Sons, 1981. A brief scholarly study of Balch's progressive views, early social reform career, and commitment to world peace. Constitutes a viable and important reference.

Wittner, Lawrence S. *Rebels Against War: The American Peace Movement, 1933-1983*. 1969. Rev. ed. Philadelphia: Temple University Press, 1984. An important scholarly study of the American peace movement that relies on a wide range of pacifist and antiwar literature.

Charles F. Howlett

ETHEL BARRYMORE
1879-1959

Chronology

Born Ethel Barrymore on August 15, 1879, in Philadelphia, daughter of the noted English actor Maurice Barrymore and stage actress Georgiana Drew Barrymore, and sister of Lionel and John Barrymore; *1879-1893* travels with parents on tour; enters convent school, Academy of Notre Dame in Philadelphia; accompanies her tubercular mother to California for treatment; *1893-1901* after her mother dies, lives with maternal grandmother and hardly knows her father; returns to convent school; understudies and acts in London, and becomes part of a social circle that includes Gerald du Maurier, Henry James, Ellen Terry, Mrs. Patrick Campbell, and Winston Churchill; stars in *Captain Jinks of the Horse Marines* in New York, becomes an established actress during the long run of the play; *1901-1928* becomes the leading lady of the American theater, starring in Shakespearean drama and modern plays, such as *A Doll's House* (1901), *Trelawney of Wells* (1911), *Declasse* (1919), *Clair de Lune* (1921), *The Second Mrs. Tanqueray* (1924), *The Constant Wife* (1926), and *Kingdom of God* (1928); stars often in one-act vaudeville play, "The Old Lady Shows her Medals"; marries Russell G. Colt in 1908, has three children, divorces him in 1923; *1933* makes the movie *Rasputin and the Empress* with her brothers; *1940* stars in drama, *The Corn is Green*; *1944* retires from the stage because of health, moves to California, becomes a character actress in the movies; wins Oscar for the best supporting actress in the film, *None but the Lonely Heart*; *1945* appears in *The Paradine Case*, directed by Alfred Hitchcock; *1949* wins critical acclaim for role in *Pinky*; *1953* hosts the television show, *The Ethel Barrymore Theatre*; *1955* writes her autobiography; *1956* appears in her last film *Johnny Trouble*; *1959* dies on June 18 in her sleep in Los Angeles.

Activities of Historical Significance

Barrymore's reign of over forty years as the leading actress of the American theater is unparalleled in American theatrical history. The appearances of Ethel and her brothers, Lionel and John, on the stage, on radio, and in films, made the Barrymore name synonymous with acting for most Americans of the time. After her retirement from the theater, she distinguished herself as a character actress on the screen and worked with such directors as Alfred Hitchcock and Elia Kazan.

Barrymore was among the first to establish a natural style of acting that contrasted with the more florid approach of the late-nineteenth century. She viewed acting, whether on stage or in films, as a natural extension of the performer's personality and thought that an actor or actress should portray a character as a believable person with understandable motivations. Such later famous film stars as Spencer Tracy patterned their performances after Ethel Barrymore's example.

The source of Ethel Barrymore's greatness was her work as a stage actress. She was not fond of the film medium and made it clear that she worked in movies merely to support herself. These film performances, however, reveal some sense of the power and range of her voice and acting style. Barrymore made twenty-two films, but received top-billing only for *Rasputin and the Empress* (1933). She was awarded an Oscar in 1944 as best supporting actress for her role in *None but the Lonely Heart*. She also attracted critical acclaim for her role in *Pinky* in 1949, a ground-breaking racial drama about a black girl passing for white, who returns to her southern home. Her supporting role in *The Paradine Case*, directed by Alfred Hitchcock and starring Gregory Peck, is considered one of her notable film performances.

Overview of Biographical Sources

A standard biography of Ethel Barrymore has not yet been written. However, two biographies aimed at the juvenile audience are available: Mary Fox, *Ethel Barrymore* (1970), and Shirlee Petkin Newman, *Ethel Barrymore, Girl Actress* (1966). Serious researchers should consult the several biographies written about the Barrymore family.

The Barrymores (1964) by Hollis Alpert details the lives and careers of the three Barrymores, and is the best single source for understanding Ethel's career in the context of her family. *The Barrymores: The Royal Family in Hollywood* (1981) by John Kotsilbas-Davis chronicles the activities of the Barrymore children and provides some specific information about Ethel's Hollywood experiences. Kotsilbas-Davis also wrote a biography of Ethel's father, Maurice, *Great Times, Good Times: The Odyssey of Maurice Barrymore* (1977). Both works are profusely illustrated. Much biographical material on Ethel Barrymore can be found in the biography of her brother John, *Good Night, Sweet Prince* (1944), by Gene Fowler.

Ethel Barrymore's career was minutely covered by popular magazines of the day, and *The Reader's Guide to Periodical Literature* is helpful for tracing her key theatrical achievements.

Evaluation of Principal Biographical Sources

Alpert, Hollis. *The Barrymores*. New York: Dial Press, 1964. (G) Alpert relies heavily on Ethel Barrymore's autobiography but provides insight into several private events about which the actress was reticent.

Fowler, Gene. *Good Night, Sweet Prince.* New York: Viking, 1944. (G) This biography details the close relationship between John Barrymore and his sister Ethel, and explores the influence of their parents, who were renowned performers in their own time.

Fox, Mary. *Ethel Barrymore.* Chicago: Reilly and Lee, 1970. (Y) A complete and inspiring biography for a younger audience.

Kotsilbas-Davis, John. *Great Times, Good Times: The Odyssey of Maurice Barrymore.* New York: Crown, 1977. (G) This biography of Ethel Barrymore's father provides a useful context in which to view her expectations and accomplishments.

————. *The Barrymores: The Royal Family in Hollywood.* Garden City, NJ: Doubleday, 1981. (G) An in-depth look at the famous Barrymore family, in which Ethel figures prominently, if somewhat in the shadow of Maurice, John, and Lionel.

Newman, Shirlee Petkin. *Ethel Barrymore, Girl Actress.* Indianapolis, IN: Bobbs-Merrill, 1966 (Y) This biography is part of the Childhood of Famous Americans Series and focuses on Barrymore's relationship with her sick mother, her sensitivity, and her early instincts for acting.

Overview and Evaluation of Primary Sources

Ethel Barrymore's autobiography *Memories* (New York: Harper & Brothers, 1955; A, G) is the major primary source. In a conversational tone, Barrymore describes her career up to her retirement from the theater in 1944. She then briefly refers to her movie career which followed, primarily dismissing films as "factory work." Barrymore highlights her mother's death when she was fourteen and describes her lack of communication with her father. Her account evokes a unique era of British society in the years before her marriage.

Both brothers authored books: Lionel Barrymore, *We Barrymores (As Told to Cameroon Shipp)* (New York: Appleton, Century, Crofts, 1951; G), and John Barrymore, *We Three.* (New York: Saalfield, 1935; G). These personal memoirs provide insight into the brothers' relationships with their sister.

Fiction and Adaptations

In 1927 Edna Ferber and George Kaufman wrote and produced, *The Royal Family*, a drama about a theatrical family named the Cavendishes. While the story is clearly fictional, the three Barrymores were the not-so-hidden inspiration for the characters. Ethel Barrymore makes no reference to the play in her autobiography, but mentions that she met and liked Edna Ferber when she was preparing to perform in *Our Mrs. McChesney,* a play based on a series of Ferber's stories. Hollis Alpert suggests that Barrymore did not like how "she" was portrayed in the play and always bore a grudge against the authors.

Almost all of Barrymore's twenty-two films are frequently shown on television, and many are currently available on videotape for home viewing.

Museums, Historical Landmarks, Societies

Ethel Barrymore Theater (New York, NY). This theater on West Forty-seventh Street opened December 20, 1928 with Barrymore playing in *The Kingdom of God,* followed by leading roles in *The Love Dual, Scarlet Sister Mary,* and *The School for Scandal.* All the Barrymore's played in Cole Porter's *The Gay Divorceé* in 1932. The theater remains active, although there is no evidence of the Barrymore's presence. Nearby, however, is Barrymore's Restaurant at 267 W. 45 Street, which contains hundreds of photos that trace the acting careers of the Barrymores and many other performers.

Other Sources

Robinson, Alice, et al., eds. *Notable Women in the American Theatre.* Westport, CT: Greenwood Press, 1989.

Dennis Goldsberry
College of Charleston

CATHARINE E. BEECHER
1800-1878

Chronology

Born Catharine Esther Beecher on September 6, 1800, in East Hampton, Long Island, New York, the first child of Rev. Lyman Beecher, a Congregational minister, and Roxana Foote Beecher; siblings include Henry Ward Beecher, Edward Beecher, and Harriet Beecher Stowe; *1810* moves with her family to Litchfield, Connecticut; *1816* assumes domestic duties in the family on the death of her mother; *1822* betrothed to Yale mathematician Alexander Metcalf Fisher, who dies at sea in April; *1823* moves to Hartford, Connecticut, and founds the Hartford Female Seminary; *1829* publishes *Suggestions Respecting Improvements in Education,* which advocates enhanced status for teachers and mothers; *1831* publishes *The Elements of Mental and Moral Philosophy,* challenging the Calvinist position on original sin; *1832* moves to Cincinnati and opens a female seminary; *1835* publishes *An Essay on the Education of Female Teachers,* outlining the importance of woman's role as educator of children; *1837* publishes *An Essay on Slavery and Abolitionism,* in which she denounces abolitionism as unchristian and an inappropriate activity for women; *1841* publishes *A Treatise on Domestic Economy,* reissued in fifteen editions through 1856, offering a comprehensive guide to household management and describing woman's special role in American society; *1845* publishes *The Duty of American Women to Their Country;* *1847* helps found the *Central Committee for Promoting National Education,* to send teachers to the newly settled West; *1850* publishes *Truth Stranger than Fiction,* a lengthy attack on Yale University and the male clergy; *1851* authors *The True Remedy for the Wrongs of Women,* which defends domestic science as the practical training for women, and as necessary for shaping children's characters; founds the Milwaukee Normal Institute and High School (later Milwaukee-Downer College); *1856* publishes *Physiology and Calisthenics,* a treatise on family health and exercise; *1857* publishes *Common Sense Applied to Religion,* advocating departures from orthodox Calvinism; *1860* publishes *An Appeal to the People on Behalf of Their Rights as Authorized Interpreters of the Bible,* another subtle assault on clerical authority; *1863* converts to Episcopalianism; *1869* publishes, with sister Harriet Beecher Stowe, *The American Woman's Home,* a powerful argument for the home as combination church, school, and residence, and for woman as a domestic priest; *1872* publishes *Woman's Profession as Mother and Educator, With Views in Opposition to Women's Suffrage,* arguing against giving women the vote; *1874* publishes *Educational Reminiscences and Suggestions,* summarizing her work in women's education; *1878* dies on May 12 of a stroke in Elmira, New York.

Activities of Historical Significance

The eldest daughter of one of nineteenth-century America's most influential families, Catharine Beecher had a strong impact both as an educator and a popular moral philosopher. In education, she served as an advocate for the creation of special women's schools that featured a curriculum combining languages, the humanities, and the sciences with special training in the domestic subjects of motherhood, teaching, and nursing. Beecher founded female seminaries toward these purposes in Hartford, Cincinnati, and Milwaukee. She also was the active force behind the creation of the Central Committee for Promoting National Education and of related groups sending teachers to "civilize" the West.

As a writer on religious subjects, Beecher played a role in challenging the theological basis of the early nineteenth-century evangelical revival known as the Second Great Awakening. Her treatises on original sin and salvation, as well as her subtle assaults on clerical privilege, helped undermine the residual authority of the Puritan ethos.

Beecher's major significance lay in the crafting of a world view for American women, with consequences lasting well into the twentieth century. She called American women to the task of the moral education of children and society. Women were to be nurturers, with special aptitude for the care and training of children, formal teaching, and nursing. She said that women should accept the subservient role given to them by Scripture, yet use their indirect influence on men and institutions to elevate society. In her many books, Beecher focused on strengthening the home as a separate women's sphere. At times, she even reduced men's involvement in the home to a kind of necessary nuisance. The autonomous American home, blending school, chapel, and residence, would be the moral training ground for character and Republican virtue, guided by women in the role of domestic priests.

Her political views were complicated and diverged from those held by other members of her family. Disturbed by what she saw as the excesses of democracy, she criticized both abolitionism and the woman's suffrage movement. Beecher saw the United States as a fragile nation, whose divisions might be healed only by women's nonpolitical nurturing influence.

Overview of Biographical Sources

Before 1970, biographical attention to Catharine Beecher focused primarily on her work in education, emphasizing her "pioneer" status in advancing women's schooling. The feminist revival focused attention on Beecher as a shaper of gender role expectations and as a popular philosopher. In this regard, Kathryn Kish Sklar's *Catharine Beecher* (1973) stands as the definitive work.

Evaluation of Principal Biographical Sources

Bacon, Martha. *Puritan Promenade: An Amused Portrait of Some Ladies Out of Step with Their Time.* Boston: Houghton Mifflin, 1964. (**G, Y**) This volume features an entertaining chapter entitled "Miss Beecher in Hell," which focuses on Catharine Beecher's confrontation with the more dour doctrines of Calvinism. It first appeared in *American Heritage* magazine (1961).

Boydston, Jeanne, Mary Kelley, and Anne Margolis. *The Limits of Sisterhood: The Beecher Sisters on Women's Rights and Woman's Sphere.* Chapel Hill: University of North Carolina Press, 1988. (**A**) Three chapters of this book, supplemented by selected readings from primary documents, focus on Catharine Beecher. The authors emphasize her role in crafting "a gender ideology," and stress (sometimes to an exaggerated degree) the more radical themes hidden beneath the surface of her work. The book features endnotes, research in the primary documents, and an index.

Caskey, Marie. *Chariot of Fire: Religion and the Beecher Family.* New Haven: Yale University Press, 1978. (**A**) This well-researched volume has a chapter on the development of Beecher's religious views. The author emphasizes the growing tension between father and daughter, and Catharine's rejection of Calvinism, eventual embrace of theological Unitarianism, and conversion to the Episcopal Church. Caskey also suggests that, as popular philosopher, Beecher elevated the home in order to counter the influence of the male clergy on children. The volume includes endnotes, a solid bibliography, and an index.

Harveson, Mae Elizabeth. *Catharine Esther Beecher: Pioneer Educator.* 1932. Reprint. New York: Arno Press and the New York Times, 1969. (**A, G**) This one-dimensional treatment gives primary attention to Catharine Beecher's work as an educator and as a founder of schools. It includes a detailed bibliography.

Sklar, Kathryn Kish. *Catharine Beecher: A Study in American Domesticity.* New Haven: Yale University Press, 1973. (**A**) This is, and probably will remain, the definitive work on its subject. The volume features extensive use of manuscript collections, comprehensive endnotes, and a thorough bibliography and index. Sklar's writing is clean and crisp and, while maintaining a feminist perspective, offers nuanced and persuasive interpretations of Beecher as a popular philosopher of home, family, and gender.

Stowe, Lyman Beecher. *Saints, Sinners and Beechers.* Indianapolis: Bobbs-Merrill, 1934. (**G**) The author, a descendant of the family, describes his ancestors as "amusing, lovable and outrageous" and central in American history to "the transition from heaven and theology to this world and service." Chapters on Catharine Beecher focus on the tragic loss of her fiancé, religious quarrels with her father and brothers, and her attempt to use schools to "save the nation." The volume includes a brief bibliography and an index.

Thorp, Margaret Farrand. *Female Persuasion: Six Strong-Minded Women.* New Haven: Yale University Press, 1949. (G) The chapter on Catharine Beecher offers a useful, though conventional, introduction to her life and work. Notes, index, and bibliography are absent.

Overview and Evaluation of Primary Sources

Catharine Beecher's writings include over two dozen books, numerous tracts and magazine articles, and a voluminous correspondence, much of it to be found in scattered libraries and archives.

Her autobiographical work, *Educational Reminiscences and Suggestions* (New York: J. B. Ford, 1874; **A**), focuses on her early years and educational work. Published four years before her death, it also offers a useful summary of her philosophical tenets. An abridged version appears as "Hartford Female Seminary and its Founder," in *The American Journal of Education,* vol. 28 (1878).

Her father's memoirs, *The Autobiography of Lyman Beecher,* edited by Barbara Cross (1863. Reprint. 2 vols. Cambridge: Harvard University Press, Belknap Press, 1961; **A, G**), provide information about the family life of young Catharine and her restless siblings, and insight into the theological tensions within the family.

Catharine Beecher's important books on religion and philosophy included *The Elements of Mental and Moral Philosophy, Founded Upon Experience, Reason, and the Bible* (Hartford: privately printed, 1831; **A**), *Letters on the Difficulties of Religion* (Hartford: Belknap & Hammersley, 1836; **A**), and *Common Sense Applied to Religion, or the Bible and the People* (New York: Harper & Brothers, 1857; **A**).

Beecher's perspective on the appropriate schooling and curricula for young women may be found in *Suggestions Respecting Improvements in Education, Presented to the Trustees* (Hartford: Packard & Butler, 1829; **A**) and *An Essay on the Education of Female Teachers* (New York: Van Nostrand & Dwight, 1835; **A**). Beecher's views on the role of women in American society were worked out in *A Treatise on Domestic Economy for the Use of Young Ladies at Home and at School* (Boston: T. H. Welsh & Co., 1841; **A**), *The Duty of American Women to Their Country* (New York: Harper & Brothers, 1845; **A**), *The Evils Suffered by American Women and American Children: The Causes and the Remedy* (New York: Harper & Brothers, 1846; **A**), *The American*

Woman's Home, or Principles of Domestic Science, written with Harriet Beecher Stowe (New York: J. B. Ford, 1869; **A**), and *Miss Beecher's Housekeeper and Healthkeeper* (New York: Harper & Brothers, 1873; **A**).

Her views on national issues were elaborated in *An Essay on Slavery and Abolitionism with Reference to the Duty of American Females* (Philadelphia: Henry Perkins, 1837; **A**) and *Woman's Profession as Mother and Educator with Views in Opposition to Woman Suffrage* (Philadelphia: Geary Maclean, 1872; **A**).

Other books included a volume on family health and exercise, *Physiology and Calisthenics for Schools and Families* (New York: Harper and Brother, 1856; **A**), and her lengthy, bizarre exposé of a romantic scandal at Yale, *Truth Stranger than Fiction* (New York: privately printed, 1850; **A**), veiling a serious critique of clerical power.

Among articles of special interest are "An Essay on Cause and Effect in Connection with the Difference of Fatalism and Free Will," *American Biblical Repository* 2 (October 1839; **A**), offering a concise summary of her theological views, and "A Christian Neighborhood," *Harper's New Monthly Magazine* 34 (1867; **A**), which describes an ideal suburb.

Important manuscript and letter collections with materials by or about Catharine Beecher include the Beecher-Stowe Collection of the Arthur and Elizabeth Schlesinger Library on the History of Women in America, Radcliffe College, Cambridge, Massachusetts; the Alexander Metcalf Fisher Collection and Mary Dutton-Beecher Letters, in the Beinecke Rare Book and Manuscript Library, Yale University, New Haven, Connecticut; the Beecher Family papers, in the Sterling Memorial Library, Yale University; the Beecher-Perkins Letters of the Cincinnati Historical Society; the Milwaukee-Downer College Papers held by the University of Wisconsin-Milwaukee Library; the Beecher Family Papers, in the Williston Memorial Library, Mt. Holyoke College, South Hadley, Massachusetts; and collections held by the Stowe-Day Foundation, Hartford, Connecticut.

Museums, Historical Landmarks, Societies

Beecher House (Litchfield, CT). Catharine's home from 1810 to 1823 has survived, although it has been moved several hundred yards from its original site. Currently used as a dormitory for the Forman School, it is not open to the public. A plaque marks the home's original site.

Stowe-Day Foundation (Hartford, CT). This organization maintains the Harriet Beecher Stowe House and a research library, which include materials about Catharine Beecher.

Other Sources

Andrews, Benjamin R. "Miss Catharine E. Beecher, the Pioneer in Home Economics." *Journal of Home Economics* 4 (1912): 211-222. An early historical account of Beecher's role in giving systematic meaning to domestic labor.

Kellogg, Louise Phelps. "The Origins of Milwaukee College." *Wisconsin Magazine of History* (June 1926): 386-408. Catharine Beecher's role receives significant attention.

Allan Carlson
The Rockford Institute

RUTH BENEDICT
1887-1948

Chronology

Born Ruth Fulton on June 5, 1887, in New York City, the older of two daughters of Frederick Samuel Fulton, a surgeon and pioneer cancer researcher, and Bertrice Joanna Shattuck Fulton; *1887-1905* at the age of two suffers the traumatic blow of her father's death; lives on a farm near Norwich, New York, and then in St. Joseph, Missouri, and Owatonna, Minnesota, before moving to Buffalo, New York, with her mother, a schoolteacher turned librarian; *1905-1909* attends and graduates from Vassar College; *1909-1914* spends a year traveling in Europe, another year doing charity work in Buffalo, and three years teaching in girls' schools in California before marrying biochemist Stanley R. Benedict and becoming a housewife in the suburbs of New York City; *1914-1923* dabbles at writing, social work, and modern dance before undertaking graduate work in anthropology under Franz Boas at Columbia University; does a study of Native American religion for her dissertation and receives her doctorate; *1923-1931* holds a series of one-year appointments as lecturer in anthropology at Columbia; conducts anthropological fieldwork among the Zuñi, Cochiti, and Pima Native Americans of the Southwest; assumes editorship of the *Journal of American Folklore*; serves as president of the American Ethnological Association; *1931-1943* separates from husband; obtains regular appointment at Columbia as assistant professor; publishes her most important work, *Patterns of Culture* (1934); is promoted to associate professor, and serves as departmental "executive officer"; *1943-1948* serves as head of Basic Analysis Section, Bureau of Overseas Intelligence, Office of War Information; publishes her influential study of Japanese culture and values, *The Chrysanthemum and the Sword* (1946); returns to Columbia, where she organizes and directs project for Research in Contemporary Cultures; is finally promoted to full professor; wins the Achievement Award of the American Association of University Women; is elected vice president of the American Psychopathological Association and president of the American Anthropological Association; *1948* dies on September 17 in New York City from a coronary thrombosis.

Activities of Historical Significance

In contrast to most leading anthropologists of her generation, Benedict did not owe her reputation to her fieldwork. Her doctoral dissertation on Native American religion was based upon library research. And when she later did fieldwork among the tribes of the Southwest she was hampered by her partial

1825

deafness. She used interpreters to collect the large body of folktales and myths published as *Tales of the Cochiti Indians* (1931) and *Zuñi Mythology* (2 vols., 1935).

Benedict accepted her mentor Franz Boas's rejection of racial determinism and his emphasis on cultural explanations of differences among peoples. Throughout her life she remained a champion of cultural relativism and would speak out against racism and intolerance in magazine articles and her book *Race: Science and Politics* (1940).

Benedict's major anthropological work lay in her exploration of the psychological dynamics of cultural conditioning. Her first contribution in this area came in a 1927 paper that analyzed the differences between the Pima and Zuñi Native Americans in terms of two opposing "psychological types," which she termed the Dionysian and the Apollonian. That approach was more fully developed in her most influential work, *Patterns of Culture* (1934). Contrasting the Apollonian Zuñi with the "paranoid" Dobu and the "megalomaniac" Kwakiutl, Benedict pictured cultures as "personality writ large." Each culture selected and elaborated "a certain segment of the great arc of potential human purposes and motivations." Accordingly, psychological normality was culturally defined—the "misfit" was one "whose disposition is not capitalized by his culture."

While with the Office of War Information during World War II, Benedict pioneered the application of anthropological methods and concepts to advanced societies to produce a series of "national character" studies. The most important was her *Chrysanthemum and the Sword* (1946)—an explication of the complicated system of *on* (obligation) and the resulting Japanese "ethic of alternatives" that is still regarded, even by the Japanese, as a perceptive analysis of Japanese culture.

Although many anthropologists have criticized Benedict's tendency to ignore the extent of psychological variations within a culture, her work laid the foundation for the culture and personality movement in anthropology.

Overview of Biographical Sources

The starting point for any student of Benedict's life and thought is the two volumes by Margaret Mead, Benedict's first student and long-time friend and associate (as well as a major figure in her own right in the history of anthropology). Mead knew Benedict intimately and had access to her surviving correspondence, diaries, journals, and unpublished manuscripts. The first volume, *An Anthropologist at Work: Writings of Ruth Benedict* (1959), is a topically organized collection of primary source materials with Mead contributing brief introductions to each section. The second, *Ruth Benedict* (1974), presents a more sustained and chronologically organized biographical sketch with an accompanying selection of her published writings.

Since the Mead volumes, two attempts at full-scale biographies have appeared—Judith Schachter Modell, *Ruth Benedict: Patterns of a Life* (1983), and Margaret M. Caffrey, *Ruth Benedict: Stranger in This Land* (1989). Although both authors recognize the critical role her own psychological tensions played in Benedict's career, their approaches differ—Modell tending more to a psychobiography, while Caffrey's is a more standard intellectual biography.

The more important of the briefer evaluations and appraisals are those by Victor Barnouw, Virginia Wolf Briscoe, Sidney W. Mintz, Takao Sofue, George W. Stocking, Jr., and the contributors to *Ruth Fulton Benedict: A Memorial* (1949).

Evaluation of Principal Biographical Sources

Barnouw, Victor. "Ruth Benedict: Apollonian and Dionysian." *University of Toronto Quarterly* 18 (April 1949): 241-253. (A, G) Barnouw's perceptive analysis of Benedict's work is the finest succinct appraisal available.

Briscoe, Virginia Wolf. "Ruth Benedict: Anthropological Folklorist." *Journal of American Folklore* 92 (October-December 1979): 445-476. (A) An analysis of Benedict's contribution to folklore studies.

Caffrey, Margaret M. *Ruth Benedict: Stranger in This Land.* Austin: University of Texas Press, 1989. (A, G) The most thoroughly researched of the works on Ruth Benedict. Caffrey sees Benedict's importance as extending far beyond the bounds of anthropology. She even argues that Benedict's influence within anthropology was short-lived because she "reintroduced a subjectivity that threatened anthropology's identity as a science." Accordingly, Caffrey emphasizes Benedict's role in promoting the larger cultural transformation that occurred in the twentieth-century United States—the triumph of the modern framework of thought "based on a relative intellectual system rather than an absolute one." She portrays as the driving force in Benedict's life and thought a "cultural feminism. . .focused on changing the values and beliefs that make up the framework of a culture."

Mead, Margaret. *An Anthropologist at Work: Writings of Ruth Benedict.* Boston: Houghton Mifflin, 1959. (A, G) The basic source for students of Benedict's life and work, this volume is topically organized around five major themes: "Search: 1920-1930"; "Anne Singleton: 1889-1934" (Anne Singleton was the pseudonym under which Benedict published her poems and thereby gave expression to her innermost personal feelings); "Patterns of Culture: 1922-1934"; "The Years as Boas' Left Hand"; and "The Postwar Years: The Gathered Threads." Mead contributed brief introductions to each section, providing biographical data and context, but the bulk of the volume consists of primary source materials—including, most importantly, extracts from Benedict's correspondence, diaries, journals, poems, and unpublished papers.

————. *Ruth Benedict*. New York and London: Columbia University Press, 1974. (A, G) A volume in the Columbia University Press Leaders of Modern Anthropology Series under the general editorship of Charles Wagley. Mead presents here a more sustained and chronologically organized biographical sketch than in *An Anthropologist at Work*; this volume's most noteworthy feature is its extensive quotations from Benedict's correspondence and journals. The stronger emphasis than in the earlier volume upon Benedict's struggle as a woman to attain an identity of her own reflects the intellectual climate at the time of its publication. There is an accompanying selection of Benedict's published writings.

Mintz, Sidney W. "Ruth Benedict." In *Totems and Teachers: Perspectives on the History of Anthropology*, edited by Sydel Silverman. New York: Columbia University Press, 1981. (A, G) An admiring brief appraisal that stresses Benedict's fight against racial prejudice.

Modell, Judith Schachter. *Ruth Benedict: Patterns of a Life*. Philadelphia: University of Pennsylvania Press, 1983. (A, G) Modell has done extensive research in the primary sources. But she goes beyond most biographers in the intensity of the personal identification she feels with her subject. Thus, Modell frankly views developments through Benedict's eyes. Methodologically, her goal is to "unravel the threads connecting Ruth Benedict's extraordinary professional achievements to her private struggles and personal dilemmas." Although she eschews a "psychoanalytical approach" that concentrates upon "unconscious and hidden impulses," her focus is upon what she terms "the interaction between unconscious motives and surface manifestations."

Stocking, George W., Jr. "Benedict, Ruth Fulton." In *Dictionary of American Biography, Supp. 4, 1946-1950*, edited by John A. Garraty and Edward T. James. New York: Charles Scribner's Sons, 1974. (A, G) An excellent biographical sketch that succinctly surveys Benedict's career and appraises her work.

Wenner-Gren Foundation for Anthropological Research. *Ruth Fulton Benedict: A Memorial*. New York: Viking Fund, 1949. (A, G) This collection of appreciations and testimonials upon Benedict's death includes contributions from such friends and fellow social scientists as Alfred L. Kroeber, Cora duBois, Erik Erikson, Clyde Kluckhohn, Robert Lynd, and Margaret Mead, with an accompanying bibliography of Benedict's published writings.

Overview and Evaluation of Primary Sources
The basic collection of primary source materials is the Ruth Fulton Benedict Papers, Special Collections, Vassar College Library, Poughkeepsie, New York, ten open and two closed file boxes that contain the bulk of her surviving correspondence, notebooks, diaries, journals, and unpublished papers. But Margaret Mead's *An Anthropologist at Work* remains an indispensable supplement, because it contains materials (e.g., the original copy of Benedict's "Story of My Life," the 1923 diary, some journal segments, and the letters from anthropologist Edward Sapir, who was one of the most important influences upon Benedict's thinking) that are missing from the Vassar College Library collection (although some may be in the still closed portion). Benedict's relationship with Margaret Mead can be traced in the Margaret Mead Papers, Manuscript Division, Library of Congress, Washington, D.C., and in the recollections of Mead's daughter, Mary Catherine Bateson, *With a Daughter's Eye: A Memoir of Margaret Mead and Gregory Bateson* (New York: William Morrow, 1984; **A, G**). Two other important archival collections containing Benedict materials are at the American Philosophical Society, Philadelphia: the Franz Boas Papers and the Elsie Clews Parsons Papers (which has a draft version of *An Anthropologist at Work* that includes extracts from unavailable Benedict letters not in the published version). Abraham Maslow and John Honigmann, eds., "Synergy: Some Notes of Ruth Benedict," *American Anthropologist* 72 (April 1970): 320-333 (**A**), consists of extracts from notes on Benedict's 1941 Ann Howard Shaw Memorial Lectures at Bryn Mawr College concerning the correlation between social structure and character structure, especially aggressiveness.

Other Sources
Harris, Marvin. *The Rise of Anthropological Theory: A History of Theories of Culture*. New York: Thomas Y. Crowell, 1968. The fullest survey of the history of the discipline. Harris is highly critical of "the dubious factual foundation upon which Benedict reared her psychologistic portraits."

Stocking, George W., Jr. "Ideas and Institutions in American Anthropology: Thoughts Toward a History of the Interwar Years." In *Selected Papers from the "American Anthropologist," 1921-1945,* edited by Stocking. Washington, DC: American Anthropological Association, 1976. An excellent brief survey of developments in American anthropology that is invaluable for placing Benedict's work in context.

John Braeman
University of Nebraska-Lincoln

BLACK HAWK
1767-1838

Chronology

Born Black Hawk, or Makataimeshekiakiak in the language of his people, in 1767 in Saukenauk, a Sauk village on Rock Island, Illinois, the son of Pyesa, a war chief of the Sauk; *1767-82* educated by his family and members of his band to be a hunter and a warrior; *1782* kills a man in a raid against the Osage, traditional enemies of the Sauk, permitting him to join in a scalp dance for the first time; *1783* leads a large victorious war party against the Osage, and is soon acknowledged as a war chief of the Sauk; *c. 1784* his father dies in a battle with the Cherokee; *c. 1784-1789* mourns his father and does not engage in raids or battles; *1801-1802* leads victorious campaign against Chippewas, Kaskaskias, and Osages; *1804* learns about treaty between the U.S. government and the Sauk and Fox nations, ceding the Sauk homeland to the U.S.; *1812* joins the British in the War of 1812; *1813* Keokuk, later his rival, becomes a war chief of the Sauk village; *1814* with British artillery, defeats American forces trying to reinforce garrison at Prairie du Chien; *1816* signs treaty that assents to Treaty of 1804 and establishes Sauk and Fox peace with U.S.; *1827* disagrees with Keokuk and other village leaders about proper response to increasing U.S. pressures for land but is convinced to remain peaceful; *1829* returns to village to find home occupied by illegal white squatters and protests their occupancy to no avail; *1831* leaves village for western side of the Mississippi River when threatened with attack by a large group of undisciplined Illinois militia, and agrees not to return to his village; *1832* recrosses the Mississippi with supporters and their families and is defeated in the resulting Black Hawk War; *1832-1833* is a prisoner of war and tours the East, meeting President Jackson; *1833* dictates autobiography, which is subsequently published; *1837* serves as member of Sauk and Fox delegation to Washington; *1838* dies at his home in Davis County, Iowa, on October 3, leaving his wife and three children.

Activities of Historical Significance

The daring but ill-advised resistance of Black Hawk's band of warriors and their families to the numerous forces of the U.S. Army and the volunteer Illinois militia captured public imagination in 1832. Black Hawk's firm conviction that his people had a moral and legal right to remain in their traditional homeland, coupled with incompetent leadership of the Illinois volunteer militia called in to remove the Native Americans, led to the violent confrontation known as the Black Hawk War. The encounter, which resulted in the death or capture of almost all of Black Hawk's band, remains a vivid symbol both of the losses suffered by Native American nations during the nineteenth century and of the ultimate futility of resisting the westward expansion supported by the newly formed United States government. Native American leaders such as Black Hawk, who resisted white encroachment against overwhelming odds, are revered by many modern observers for the morality of their opposition.

Black Hawk's *Autobiography* has also won him a place in literary history. His control over the narrative makes it of particular interest to scholars studying Native American oral traditions.

Overview of Biographical Sources

Given the enormous interest in Black Hawk that followed his 1832 defeat, it is surprising that a full-scale biography has not emerged. A possible exception is Cyrenus Cole's *I Am a Man: the Indian Black Hawk* (1938). Written one hundred years after Black Hawk's death, it is a chronological, relatively uncritical treatment of the warrior's life. All the other book-length sources are primarily concerned with Black Hawk's role in the 1832 Black Hawk War. The nineteenth-century chroniclers were strongly divided in their opinions about Black Hawk and the necessity of the 1832 conflict. Benjamin Drake's *The Life and Adventures of Black Hawk* (1838) was by far the most popular account. Drake was the first to present a pro-Native American view, a perspective that was not seen again until Perry A. Armstrong's *The Sauks and the Black Hawk War* (1887). Armstrong got much of his material from participants in the war and was unfailing in his admiration for Black Hawk. John A. Wakefield's very rare *History of the War Between the United States and the Sac and Fox Nations* (1834; reprinted as *Wakefield's History of the Black Hawk War*, 1908) presents a vehemently anti-Native American viewpoint. This sentiment is echoed in John Reynolds' *My Own Times* (1855). Reynolds, governor of Illinois at the time of the conflict, was responsible for mustering the volunteer militia to fight Black Hawk both in 1831 and 1832. He was vigorous in asserting that Black Hawk understood the language of the Treaty of 1804, and simply defied its terms for his own selfish interests. A rational, scholarly perspective does not enter the literature until Reuben Thwaites's *The Story of the Black Hawk War* (1892), which utilized the growing body of information about the war and its white and Native American participants. William T. Hagan is responsible for a remarkable effort to place the tribal history of the Sauk and Fox nations into the context of nineteenth-century American expansionism. His book, *The Sac and Fox Indians* (1958), also contains the most useful bibliography compiled on the Black Hawk War to date. Anthony F. C. Wallace, in his *Prelude to Disaster: The Course of Indian-White Relations Which Led to the Black Hawk War of 1832* (1970), gives an excellent account of the events leading up to the war. Cecil Eby and Reginald Horseman expand upon the theme of inevitable conflict in *That Disgraceful Affair: the Black Hawk War* (1973), but lack the objectivity toward both white and Native American participants found in Hagan's account.

Evaluation of Principal Biographical Sources

Armstrong, Perry A. *The Sauks and the Black Hawk War, With Biographical Sketches, etc.* Springfield, IL: H. W. Rokker, 1887. (**A, G**) The author, a child in Illinois at the time of the Black Hawk War, gives a valuable account of the war, the times, and Black Hawk himself, of whom he is unabashed in his admiration. His account also provides a great deal of information about Sauk life.

Cole, Cyrenus. *I Am a Man: The Indian Black Hawk; A Book by Cyrenus Cole, Marking the One-Hundredth Anniversary of the Passing of Ma-ka-tai-me-she-kia-kiak.* (**A, G**) Iowa City: The State Historical Society of Iowa, 1938. One of the only works on Black Hawk to focus on the warrior rather than the war, Cole's biography is uncritical in its analysis of materials.

Cunningham, Maggi. *Black Hawk.* Minneapolis: Dillon Press, 1979. (**Y**) A simplistic, sometimes inaccurate treatment written for elementary school children.

Drake, Benjamin. *The Life and Adventures of Black Hawk with Sketches of Keokuk, the Sac and Fox Indians, and the Late Black Hawk War.* Cincinnati: G. Conclin, 1838. (**A, G**) The most popular nineteenth-century account; it is the first strongly pro-Native American book about the war. Illustrated with woodcuts, it still provides information and points of view not found elsewhere.

Eby, Cecil, and Reginald Horseman. *That Disgraceful Affair: The Black Hawk War.* New York: Norton, 1973. (**A, G**) While the primary focus of this book is on the war rather than on Black Hawk, Eby's efforts to put the events into historical perspective make this book valuable for comprehending the inevitability of conflict between Black Hawk and white intruders.

Hagan, William T. *The Sac and Fox Indians.* Norman: University of Oklahoma Press, 1958. (**A, G**) Widely acclaimed, Hagan's treatment of Black Hawk and the war places the conflict in the broader context of nineteenth-century American expansionism and tribal history.

Oppenheim, Joanne. *Black Hawk: Frontier Warrior*. Mahwah, NJ: Troll Associates, 1979. (Y) This is a good account for young readers of the Sauk warrior's early life and his attempt to uphold the rights of his community against encroaching white settlement.

Reynolds, John. *My Own Times: Embracing Also the History of My Life*. Chicago: 1855. (A, G) Reynolds was governor of Illinois at the time of the Black Hawk Wars of 1831 and 1832 and mustered the Illinois volunteers for both encounters. His account embodies the view of those who saw Black Hawk as an evil leader.

Stevens, Frank Everett. *The Black Hawk War, Including a Review of Black Hawk's Life; Illustrated with Upward of Three Hundred Rare and Interesting Portraits and Views*. Chicago: F. E. Stevens, 1903. (A, G) Stevens's account reflects the views of Black Hawk's most adamant detractors. It is one of the most complete sources, however, for Black Hawk's speeches.

Thwaites, Reuben G. *The Story of the Black Hawk War*. Wisconsin Historical Collections 12 (1892). Reprinted in Twaites's *How George Rogers Clark Won the Northwest & Other Essays* (Salem, NH: Ayer, n.d.; facsimile edition). (A, G) This is the first scholarly, unbiased treatment of the war. Thwaites gleaned much of his information from the Draper Collection at the State Historical Society of Wisconsin.

Wallace, Anthony F. C. *Prelude to Disaster: the Course of Indian-White Relations Which Led to the Black Hawk War of 1832*. Springfield: Illinois State Historical Society, 1970. Reprinted from *Black Hawk War, 1831-1832*, edited by Ellen M. Whitney (Springfield: Illinois State Historical Society, 1970-78). (A, G) An excellent account of the events leading to the Black Hawk War, it was written as the introduction to Whitney's monumental compilation of primary source documents.

Overview and Evaluation of Primary Sources

The most important source for studying Black Hawk as an individual is the autobiography he dictated to interpreter Antoine LeClair in 1833. Published later that year, *Life of Ma-Ka-Tai-Me-She-Kia-Kiak, or Black Hawk* (A, G) was edited by John B. Patterson, an Illinois newspaperman. While the authenticity of the work has been questioned, most scholars today believe the certifications by the editor and translator at the beginning of Black Hawk's account attesting to its veracity. The most current of its several editions is *Black Hawk, An Autobiography*, edited by Donald Jackson (Urbana: University of Illinois Press, 1964; A, G), which compensates for inconsistencies found in earlier editions with an excellent introduction and detailed notes to Black Hawk's text. According to interpreter LeClair, Black Hawk narrated his autobiography so that "the people of the United States. . .might know the causes that had impelled him to act as he has done, and the principles by which he was governed." Although Black Hawk was not known for his oratory, the speeches he made during and after the Black Hawk War are another valuable source for his opinions. They have been reprinted in many of the biographical sources noted above.

There is a plethora of primary sources relating to the Black Hawk War. *Black Hawk War, 1831-1832*, edited by Ellen M. Whitney (Springfield: Illinois State Historical Library, 1970-78; A), is by far the most ambitious compilation of primary source material. This four-part publication is meticulously annotated and contains virtually every official document relating to the event. Other institutions also hold collections of primary source materials that are integral to the study of Black Hawk and the 1832 war. For example, the papers of Thomas Forsyth, Sauk agent from 1817 to 1830, comprise most of the Draper Manuscript Collection at the State Historical Society of Wisconsin, in Madison, Wisconsin. The society also has a large number of other collections pertaining directly to the Black Hawk War. The National Archives, in Washington, D.C., the Kansas Historical Society, in Topeka, Kansas, the Missouri Historical Society, in St. Louis, Missouri, and the Oklahoma Historical Society, in Oklahoma City, Oklahoma hold pertinent documents. Newspapers across the country carried accounts of the Black Hawk War and of Black Hawk's subsequent visits to the East. These articles are indispensable for gleaning information given the public during this time.

Fiction and Adaptations

Black Hawk's defeat and subsequent trip through the East attracted a great deal of public attention. Artists were among those seeking to see the group of six Sauk and Fox prisoners. George Catlin may have been the first to paint Black Hawk, visiting the prisoners at Fort Jefferson, near St. Louis, during the winter of 1832-1833. His oil painting of Black Hawk is now in private hands, while other paintings he made of the warrior and his party are in the National Gallery of Art, in Washington, D.C. J. O. Lewis painted Black Hawk in 1833 in Detroit. A lithograph of that work appears in Lewis's *Aboriginal Portfolio* (1835). Charles Bird King, the famous portraitist of American Indians, did two oil paintings of Black Hawk. The first, painted in 1833 during Black Hawk's sojourn in Washington, is now in the Warner Collection of the Gulf State Paper Corporation, in Tuscaloosa, Alabama. The other, commissioned as part of the War Department's Indian Gallery during Black Hawk's 1837 visit to Washington, was later destroyed in the War Department's fire. It was published, however, as a lithograph in McKenney and Hall's *History of the Indian Tribes of North America* (1844-1848).

James Westhall Ford visited the prisoners in 1833 during their short stay in Richmond, Virginia. Two of his portraits remain: one of Black Hawk, his eldest son Nasheaskuh, and Wabokieshiek, commonly referred to as "the Prophet," is now at the Virginia State Library, in Richmond, and the Valentine Museum, also in Richmond, holds a portrait of Black Hawk and the Prophet. John Wesley Jarvis visited Black Hawk while the prisoners were at Fort Monroe, Virginia, painting Black Hawk and Nasheaskuh. This portrait is now at the Thomas L. Gilcrease Institute of American History and Art in Tulsa, Oklahoma. Another visitor to Fort Monroe in 1833 was artist Robert Matthew Sully, whose portrait of Black Hawk is now at the Virginia Historical Society in Richmond. Sully later painted a similar portrait which is now in the State Historical Society of Wisconsin in Madison.

Black Hawk's *Autobiography* drew the attention of novelists and poets, among others. Black Hawk's life was first romanticized in poetry by Elbert H. Smith in *Ma-Ka-Tai-Me-She-Kia-Kiak; or Black Hawk and Scenes in the West, A National Poem* (1848), and again by James H. Craighead in *Black Hawk: A Romance of the Black Hawk War; Told in Spenserian Verse* (1930). Novelists also wrote about Black Hawk. Iona Fuller in *The Shining Trail* (1943) portrays Black Hawk sympathetically, while Cornelia Meigs's Black Hawk is motivated by his irrational hatred of whites in *As the Crow Flies* (1927). In *Thunder on the River* (1949) by Charlton Laird, Black Hawk is a tragic figure, clearly recognizing the destiny of his people.

Museums, Historical Landmarks, Societies

Black Hawk Trail (IA, IL, WI). Numerous plaques mark the trail that Black Hawk, his warriors, and their families followed during the famous encounter of 1832. The trail starts in Iowa on the western bank of the Mississippi, crosses into Illinois, follows the Rock River into Wisconsin to Madison, and ends where the Bad Axe River meets the Mississippi.

Black Hawk State Park (Rock Island, IL). The park is located on the site of Black Hawk's village, Saukenuk. The "Watch Tower," a high observation point referred to by Black Hawk in his *Autobiography* as a place of contemplation, is located in the park, and a statue of Black Hawk by David Richards graces the park's Indian Garden.

Statue (Oregon, IL). Sculpted by Lorado Taft, this statue overlooks the Rock River.

Statue (Lake View, IA). This statue was sculpted by Harry Stinson.

Other Sources

Hallwas, John E. "Black Hawk: A Reassessment." *Annals of Iowa* 45 (Spring 1981): 599-619. The author asserts that the autobiography of Black Hawk, which has never been the subject of intensive analysis, presents a detailed and sincere self-portrait that merits further study.

Josephy, Alvin M. "The Rivalry of Black Hawk and Keokuk." In *The Patriot Chiefs: A Chronicle of American Indian Leadership*. New York: Viking, 1961. A sympathetic view of Black Hawk and his responses to the conflicting forces which surrounded him. Josephy portrays as heroes those tribal leaders who fought against the U.S. government in its push to drive Native American groups from their traditional lands.

Treadway, Sandra. "Triumph in Defeat: Black Hawk's 1833 Visit to Virginia." *Virginia Cavalcade* 35 (1985): 4-17. An illustrated account of Black Hawk's visit to Washington and Virginia that recounts the public's positive reaction to this famous visitor.

Mary B. Davis
Museum of the American Indian
Huntington Free Library

WILLIAM WELLS BROWN
1814-1884

Chronology

Born a slave in Lexington, Kentucky, probably in 1814; his mother was a slave, his father said to be George Higgins, a slaveowner; *1814-1834* works a variety of jobs, including field hand, hotel servant, and slave trader's assistant; *1833* attempts unsuccessful escape with mother; *1834-1835* escapes in Cincinnati, Ohio, with help from the Quaker, Wells Brown, whose name he adds to his given name of William; goes to Cleveland, works on steamer, educates himself, marries Elizabeth Schooner, and begins a family; *1836* moves to Buffalo, New York, where he works on the Underground Railroad helping runaway slaves reach Canada; organizes a black temperance society; *1840* travels to Cuba and Haiti; *1843* begins lecturing for the abolition movement; *1847-1849* moves to Boston; lectures throughout New England as agent of Massachusetts Anti-Slavery Society; *1847* publishes first book, an autobiography; *1849* travels to Paris as delegate to the International Peace Congress; *1849-1854* tours Great Britain, speaking for abolition and temperance; *1851* wife dies; *1853* publishes his first novel, *Clotel*; *1854* British friends purchase his freedom; returns to U.S.; resumes touring for the abolitionist cause; *1860* marries Annie Elizabeth Gray; *1863* recruits black soldiers for the Union Army; *1864* attends National Negro Convention at Syracuse; begins practicing medicine; *1865* narrowly escapes lynching while promoting temperance in Kentucky; lectures in favor of the black franchise; *November 6, 1884* dies at his home in Boston.

Activities of Historical Significance

A self-educated man, Brown authored some ten books, including the most popular, *Narrative of William Wells Brown, A Fugitive Slave* (1847), an account of his escape from slavery. Brown is generally acknowledged as the first American black to publish a novel; *Clotel* appeared to favorable reviews in 1853. His lesser known play, *The Escape* (1858), is considered to be the first play published by an American black. In addition, Brown is sometimes credited with being the first black author of a travelogue, *Three Years in Europe* (1852). Despite good reception during his lifetime, Brown's books are not currently regarded as major literary works and are valued mainly for their historical content.

Brown's reputation as a reformer has held up better. An active abolitionist, Brown worked for years helping runaway slaves escape to Canada on the Underground Railroad. He was a forceful orator who spoke out against slavery in public lectures in the United States and Europe. His speeches and articles, along with biographical data and information on his activities, were often printed in such abolitionist newspapers as William Lloyd Garrison's *Liberator* and the *National Anti-Slavery Standard.*

Also involved in the peace, women's rights, temperance, and prison reform movements, Brown was often held up as a model of the potential of the black race, should the chains of slavery be removed.

Overview of Biographical Sources

William Edward Farrison has made the study of Brown his life's work; the results are numerous articles and the best biography of Brown to date, *William Wells Brown: Author and Reformer* (1969). Brown's life and writings have been the focus of a number of articles in scholarly journals, as well as newspaper pieces written by his contemporaries. Information about him can also be found in introductions to the many editions of Brown's works. Because of his diversified career, Brown is mentioned frequently in general works on slavery, black literature, abolition, and other reform movements.

Evaluation of Principal Biographical Sources

Coleman, Edward M. "William Wells Brown As An Historian." *Journal of Negro History* 31 (January 1946): 47-59. (A) One of the few examinations of Brown's historical writing. Judging him by current standards, Coleman finds Brown lacking as a historian—he rarely documented sources and did not even attempt objectivity. Yet, Coleman notes, few authors of Brown's time would satisfy today's scholarly requirements, especially those subjected to slavery and denied a formal education.

Ellison, Curtis W., and E. W. Metcalf, Jr., eds. *William Wells Brown and Martin R. Delany: A Reference Guide.* Boston: G. K. Hall, 1978. (A) An exhaustive survey of writings on Brown, including scholarly books and articles, contemporary accounts, and mentions of Brown in numerous works on other topics. While Brown's own works are discussed in the introduction, the bibliography includes only works written about him, not by him. Works are organized chronologically.

Farrison, William Edward. *William Wells Brown: Author and Reformer.* Chicago: University of Chicago Press, 1969. (A, G) Commended for its use of primary sources and objectivity, this detailed work traces Brown's life from birth to death. Farrison places Brown's accomplishments as a writer and reformer into historical context and, despite his obvious admiration for Brown, does not forego objectivity. Excellent bibliography.

Heermance, J. Noel. *William Wells Brown and "Clotelle": A Portrait of the Artist in the First Negro Novel.* Hamden, CT: Shoe String Press, 1969. (A) The author focuses on Brown's use of his own experiences (as described in his narrative) in his novel *Clotel.* Included is a reprint of the 1864 edition in which Brown changed the spelling of the title to *Clotelle.* Contains some information on Brown's life, as well as a general discussion of slave narratives. Called full of errors and "worthless" by Farrison in a review.

Yellin, Jean Fagan. *The Intricate Knot: Black Figures in American Literature, 1776-1863.* New York: New York University Press, 1972. (A) Chapter eight examines Brown's experiences and writings, with emphasis on *Clotel,* and compares them with those of other fugitive slave and abolitionist authors, particularly Frederick Douglass and William and Ellen Craft. Yellin finds Brown's inclusion of personal experiences in his novels especially noteworthy. A positive, although not uncritical, assessment of Brown's work.

Overview and Evaluation of Primary Sources
Extremely popular in their own time, Brown's writings fell into obscurity after his death, remaining unnoticed until the efforts of William Edward Farrison helped to re-establish Brown as a major nineteenth-century author. Farrison's writings sparked the interest of other scholars in Brown's work, particularly during the late 1960s and the 1970s, when his views were strongly criticized by black nationalists. Brown has also been faulted for his style, his reworking of material (*Clotel* and several other works were republished with minor changes), and his choice of controversial subject material (Clotel as the "tragic mulatto").

Today's critics are less willing to dismiss Brown as an author, taking into account the number of stumbling blocks he faced—among them a lack of formal education and the pervasive racism of his time. However, he is probably recognized more for his work as an abolitionist than as a literary figure. In addition to his book-length writings, Brown's articles and speeches appeared frequently in the American abolitionist press and in London newspapers throughout the 1840s and 1850s.

The most popular of Brown's works, reprinted in numerous editions and included in several collections of slave narratives, is the *Narrative of William Wells Brown, A Fugitive Slave* (Boston, 1847; A, G). This work is notable among fugitive slave narratives for its use of humor. Brown compiled a collection of the words (but not music) to forty-eight abolitionist songs as *The Anti-Slavery Harp: A Collection of Songs for Anti-Slavery Meetings* (Boston, 1848; A, G).

In *Three Years in Europe: or Places I Have Seen and People I Have Met* (London, 1852; A, G) Brown describes his travels in France and the British

Isles, mainly the latter, where he spent five years lecturing on abolition. Several years later, Brown published an expanded version of this work as *The American Fugitive in Europe; Sketches of People and Places Abroad* .(Boston, 1855; A, G).

Considered the first novel published by a black, *Clotel; or the President's Daughter: A Narrative of Slave Life in the United States* (London: 1853; A, G) is based on the story of Thomas Jefferson's illegitimate daughter by his slave mistress Sally Hemings. The book centers on Clotel's tortured existence in limbo between the white and black worlds. When grown, she goes to Europe, marries a black man, then returns and reconciles with her father, who eventually accepts her husband and works toward overcoming his own racism.

Considered the first play written by a black, *The Escape: or A Leap for Freedom* (Boston, 1858; A, G), was read by Brown before an audience, but it is not known to have been staged. In this play, two slaves, Glen and Melinda, run away to Canada when their master threatens to sell Melinda for refusing his advances. This work is based on the author's experiences as a slave.

The Black Man, His Antecedents, His Genius, and His Achievements (Boston, 1863; A, G) contains more than fifty short biographies of noteworthy blacks. Brown's purpose in writing this work was to reduce white racism by showing black accomplishments. As such, it is more a defense of the black past, rather than a true history. Immediately successful, it sold out its first edition soon after publication, and went into ten printings over the next three years. In *The Negro in the American Rebellion; His Heroism and His Fidelity* (Boston, 1867; A, G), Brown attempts to show the role played by blacks in the Civil War; in *The Rising Son; or the Antecedents and the Advancement of the Colored Race* (Boston, 1873; A, G), Brown traces the history of blacks through Africa, Latin America, and the U.S., and includes more than sixty brief and flattering biographies of notable blacks.

My Southern Home; or The South and Its People (Boston, 1880; A, G) is part narrative, based on Brown's and others' experiences in slavery, and part travelogue, based on his trips in the South in 1879 and 1880. This work is more pessimistic than Brown's earlier books. Having devoted his life to ridding the world of prejudice, and believing the Civil War to be the revolution that would accomplish this, by 1880 Brown realized that whites remained violent and hostile toward blacks. Brown's final admonition was "Black man, emigrate."

Papers relating to Brown are held in the Henry B. Slaughter Collection, The American University library, Washington, D.C.; the Leon Gardiner Collection on Negro History, Harrisburg, Pennsylvania; the Sophie Smith Collection, Smith College library, Northampton, Massachusetts; and the Gerritt Smith Miller Collection, Syracuse University, Syracuse, New York.

For a complete bibliography of Brown's own writings, including the numerous editions and reprints of his works, Farrison (above) is the best source.

Other Sources

Curti, Merle Eugene. *The American Peace Crusade, 1815-1860.* Durham, NC: Duke University Press, 1929. Includes information about Brown's role in the peace movement.

Quarles, Benjamin. *The Negro in the Civil War.* Boston: Little, Brown, 1953. Brown's accomplishments as a writer and abolitionist are discussed.

Carol Wilson
West Virginia University

MARY CASSATT
1844-1926

Chronology

Born Mary Stevenson Cassatt on May 23, 1844 in Allegheny City, Pennsylvania (now part of Pittsburgh), one of seven children of Robert Cassatt, a banker, entrepreneur, and town mayor, and Katherine Kelso Johnston Cassatt; *1846* the family moves to Europe where she is educated at private schools in Paris, Heidelberg, and Darmstadt; becomes fluent in French and German; *1851* the family returns to Philadelphia; *1861* attends the Pennsylvania Academy of Fine Arts completing the course work in 1865; *1866* continues her artistic training in Europe; *1874* studies in Seville, Spain; *1874* begins friendship with Edgar Degas that continues throughout most of their lives; *1877* her parents and her sister Lydia join her in Paris, where she keeps a separate studio but remains very close to the family; *1879* first exhibits work in the Impressionists' Group Art Show; *1880-1886* accepted as an important contributer to several impressionist exhibitions, including the last Salon in 1886; becomes art advisor and purchasing agent for wealthy American collectors, including the Henry Havemeyers and the Andrew Mellons; *1888* debilitated in a riding accident; her father dies; *1890* attends an exhibition of Japanese woodblock prints that deeply affects her style during what is known as her brilliant years; *1891* reveals Japanese influence in paintings such as "The Birth," "The Letter," and "The Fitting"; *1895* her work is exhibited in New York; her mother dies; visits U.S. with intent to stay but returns to Paris within the year; *1901* continues to paint and to buy art for wealthy American art aficionados and philanthropists; *1903* develops a mild interest in spiritualism; *1904* receives the Legion of Honor from the French government; *1910* journeys to Egypt with her brother Gardner and his family; *1911* her brother dies suddenly, and she suffers from depression; in Paris she is diagnosed as suffering from cataracts and diabetes; receives inhalations of radium as a treatment and, possibly as a result, nearly goes blind; *1908* meets Gertrude Stein but never embraces the modernist's ideals; sells portrait of herself painted by Degas as if to signal an end to their relationship; *1914-1917* lives on the French Riviera during World War I; *1921* almost totally blind, she considers her creative years behind her; *1926* dies on June 14 at Chateau de Beaufresne at Oise near Paris.

Activities of Historical Significance

Mary Stevenson Cassatt was the only female impressionist painter to be accepted as an equal into the French Impressionists' Group and was one of the few American woman impressionists to receive international accolades while alive. Although she lived most of her adult life in Paris, Cassatt kept close ties with her native country and maintained a legal residence in Philadelphia. She thought of herself simply as an American living abroad and did not disclaim her heritage, as did many American expatriate artists living in Paris. Although Cassatt was considered aristocratic by many of the Parisian artists, she mingled socially within the impressionists' circle, counting Degas, Manet, Morisot, Renoir, and the poet Mallarme among her friends.

Cassatt worked in a variety of mediums, producing in her lifetime over 225 prints, 300 oils, 400 pastels, and assorted watercolors and drawings. She was a small woman, yet she mastered the physically demanding process of lithography and produced many of her finest works as hand prints.

Cassatt exalted the feminine spirit in her art. Her most popular and beloved paintings treated domestic subjects, in particular the classic symbol of the mother and child. Her intimate images of caring women holding or admiring children, women bathing, and children in repose are recognized among the major artistic accomplishments of late nineteenth-century impressionism. After 1890 Cassatt was significantly influenced by Japanese woodblock printers and by the works of Japanese artists Kitagawa Utamaro and Toyokuni. Adapting a more oriental approach and shifting her emphasis to line and away from form, she brought her printmaking technique to perfection in a series of etchings that included "Woman Bathing" and "The Coiffure."

In addition to her own creative output, Cassatt served as one of the chief promoters of impressionistic art, selecting and purchasing art for wealthy American patrons, such as the Havemeyers and the Mellons. She personally brokered some of the finest paintings by Degas, Manet, Cezanne, and Gauguin, and is largely responsible for the exquisite H. O. Havemeyer Collection in the Metropolitan Museum of Art in New York City.

When reviewing Cassatt's life, one is struck by her artistic ability, her individualistic spirit, and her philosophy of hard work. She sacrificed marriage and family for her career in an age when these were considered essential pursuits of women of her class and standing. She exalted the ideals of femininity in an arena largely dominated by male artists, and made a major contribution to American aesthetic sensibilities.

Overview of Biographical Sources

There are a number of well-written biographies of Cassatt, each seemingly with its own strengths and weaknesses. Nancy Hale's biography, *Mary Cassatt* (1975), is easy to read but offers limited insight into Cassatt's inner life. Much of this may be due to Cassatt's refusal to reveal her private life, but it seems that too many of Hale's sources remembered Cassatt simply as a sharp, old woman. Frederick Sweet, *Miss Mary Cassatt, Impressionist from Pennsylvania* (1966), uses her correspondence from the Havemeyer Collection at the National Gallery to present a more intimate portrayal; but, confusingly, Sweet's dates in many cases do not agree with Hale's. As well, Sweet adopts some views of women that may be considered outdated, thus detracting from an understanding of Cassatt's contributions to feminist ideals in the late nineteenth century. Julia Carson's *Mary Cassatt* (1966) is meticulously researched but lacks the depth of either Hale or Sweet.

Biographies should not be considered the only sources for researching Cassatt's life. The researcher should pursue books that illustrate her works and the paintings of the Impressionists' Group and should also visit galleries that exhibit these works. To gain a fuller perspective of the life and works of Cassatt, the researcher should also examine the life and works of Edgar Degas and the works of Japanese artists who influenced Cassatt in the 1890s. Kitagawa Utamaro's "Woman at Her Toilet Reflected in Hand Mirrors" (1795) is displayed at the Metropolitan Museum of Art, New York City. Two of Degas's most famous pieces are "The Rehearsal on the Stage" (1878) at the Metropolitan Museum of Art, and "Woman Washing Herself in Tub" (1886) at the Musée du Louvre, Paris.

Evaluation of Principal Biographical Sources

Breeskin, Adelyn. *The Graphic Art of Mary Cassatt.* New York: Chanticleer Press/Museum of Graphic Art/Smithsonian Institute, 1967. (G) This text illustrates in black and white the developmental stages of Cassatt's printmaking. Breeskin includes an excellent biography of Cassatt and explains her artistic methods and techniques.

Carson, Julia. *Mary Cassatt.* New York: David McKay, 1966. (G) This readable book has been carefully researched but is overshadowed by the Hale and Sweet biographies.

Dillon, Millicent. *After Egypt.* New York: William Abrahams, 1990. (G) This book compares the personalities of Cassatt and Isadora Duncan, by examining their respective Egyptian visits. Dillon derives common threads from their lives although their experiences in Egypt were years apart and made under different circumstances. Includes fine photographs of Cassatt.

Hale, Nancy. *Mary Cassatt.* New York: Doubleday, 1975. (A) Hale's research is extensive and accurate, but she reveals no strong empathy with Cassatt. The material is presented somewhat blandly. All illustrations of artwork and photographs are in black and white. Includes an extensive bibliography of references.

Sweet, Frederick. *Miss Mary Cassatt, Impressionist from Pennsylvania.* Norman: University of Oklahoma Press, 1966. (A) Sweet, a museum curator, gives a thorough account of Cassatt's life, including a genealogical base for the Cassatt line. Most illustrations are in black and white; some in color.

Williams, William James. *A Heritage of American Paintings.* New York: Rutledge, 1981. (A) A beautifully written book with color illustrations of many American painters' works, including those of Cassatt. There is a lengthy biography of Cassatt that describes her as "rich, intelligent, and sociable." This book is highly recommended for its illustrations of Cassatt's art work.

Wilson, Ellen. *American Painter in Paris, A Life of Mary Cassatt.* New York: Farrar, Strauss, and Giroux, 1971. (G, Y) This brief biography is an excellent source for the beginning researcher or young student who needs a biographical chronology and an overview of Cassatt's works.

Overview and Evaluation of Primary Sources
In the absence of an autobiography, Mary Cassatt's art work should be considered a major primary source for understanding her life. The second most significant source is Cassatt's personal letters collected in "The Havemeyer Collection of Mary Cassatt Letters," at the National Gallery in Washington, D.C.

Louisine Havemeyer, a personal friend of Mary Cassatt, wrote *Sixteen to Sixty* (New York: Metropolitan Museum of Art, 1930; G), a memoir of her husband's and her collecting days. Havemeyer and Cassatt corresponded frequently, and these letters are included with the text.

The following is a partial but representative list of Cassatt's works and where they can be viewed: "Cup of Tea" (1880), Boston Museum of Fine Arts; "The Bath" (1891), Art Institute of Chicago; "The Coiffure" (1891), "The Letter" (1891), and "The Fitting" (1891), Metropolitan Museum of Art, New York City; "Emmie and her Child" (1889), Wichita Art Museum, KS; "Little Girl in a Blue Armchair" (1878) and "Mother and Child" (1905), National Gallery of Art, Washington, DC; "Lydia in a Loge" (1879), Philadelphia Museum of Art; and "Young Woman in Black" (1893), Baltimore Museum of Art.

Other Sources
Dunlop, Ian. *Degas.* New York: Harper and Row, 1979. This oversized book includes bibliographic information on the Cassatt-Degas relationship. Dunlop recognizes that Cassatt had as much influence on Degas's work as he had on hers. The index is extensive, and a bibliography is included.

Leymaric, Jean. *Impressionism*, translated by James Emmons. Munich: Editions d'Art, 1959. A general overview of the impressionist period, this volume provides a chronology of events significant to the painters as a group. Color plates, representative of the works of each artist, are included.

Pool, Phoebe. *Manet*. New York: Harry Abrams, 1967. This critical history of Manet's work offers an extensive list of his paintings and where these can be viewed. Descriptive information on Cassatt and other impressionists is included.

Cynthia L. Marshall
Community College of Beaver County

CARRIE CHAPMAN CATT
1859-1947

Chronology

Born Carrie Clinton Lane on January 9, 1859, in Ripon, Wisconsin, the daughter of Lucius Lane, a farmer, and Maria Clinton Lane; *1866* moves to Charles City, Iowa; *1866-1877* attends local schools, secures teaching certificate, and teaches for a year; *1877-1880* attends and graduates from Iowa State College, Ames; *1880-1881* works in law office; *1881-1885* serves as principal, then superintendent of schools, Mason City, Iowa; *1885* marries newspaper editor Leo Chapman; becomes assistant editor of the *Mason City Republican*; *1886* Leo Chapman dies; *1887* begins lifetime activity in women's suffrage; *1890* marries civil engineer George C. Catt (d. 1905); *1890-1892* lectures and organizes the Iowa Women's Suffrage struggle; *1895* chairs organization committee of the National American Woman Suffrage Association (NAWSA); *1900-1904* serves as president of the NAWSA; *1902-1923* founds and presides over International Women's Suffrage Alliance; *1913-1914* chairs Empire State Campaign for woman suffrage, New York State; *1915* helps found Women's Peace Party; *1915-1947* serves as president of the NAWSA; *1917* member, committee of ten, Women's Committee of the Council of National Defense; *1919* founds League of Women Voters, which becomes independent of the NAWSA in 1920; *1925-1932* chairs Conference on the Cause and Cure of War; *1947* dies on March 9, from a heart attack at her home in New Rochelle, New York.

Activities of Historical Significance

During the first decade of the twentieth century, Catt's name was practically synonymous with the cause of women's suffrage. More than any other individual, Catt was responsible for the passage of the Nineteenth Amendment. She first came to public attention in 1893 through her successful leadership of the Colorado suffrage campaign. From 1900 to 1904, she was successor to Susan B. Anthony as president of the National American Woman Suffrage Association (NAWSA). Though the illness of her husband forced her to turn over the office to Anna Howard Shaw, she resumed the presidency in 1915. As leader of the NAWSA, she devised the "Winning Plan" of 1916, which concentrated on securing a constitutional amendment. It combined pressures on Congress with increasing the number of "suffrage states." She was active internationally as the moving force behind the International Woman Suffrage

Alliance (later the International Alliance of Women). In this capacity, she presided over international congresses, toured much of the world, and established a network of female leaders that encircled the globe.

Catt was also a prominent leader in the peace movement. In 1915, she aided Jane Addams in founding the Women's Peace Party, a body that focused on an immediate end to World War I, long-range plans for an international political order, and woman suffrage. On February 14, 1917, in the wake of the severance of U.S. diplomatic relations with Germany, Catt committed the most criticized act of her career: she pledged that the NAWSA would back the government in case of war. In 1920 she launched the League of Women Voters (LWV) which, she insisted, would remain a strictly nonpartisan organization devoted to political education. Disillusioned by the Senate's rejection of the League of Nations, she secured the backing of nine leading women's organizations to form the Committee on the Cause and Cure of War. Though the committee served mostly as a forum, it endorsed American membership in the World Court and was prominent in the ratification of the Kellogg-Briand Pact.

With a magnetic personality and a commanding platform presence, Catt was an organizational genius. She stressed imaginative publicity techniques and effective fund-raising. A "single issue" reformer, she insisted on keeping the suffrage issue separate from prohibition and feminism. Yet her career exhibited certain paradoxes. Though she lacked respect for politicians, she modelled NAWSA after the dominant political parties. Though she formed the League of Women Voters as the largest non-partisan organization in America, in her own orbit she was a thoroughgoing machine politician. Striving tirelessly for peace and disarmament, she rebuked Jeanette Rankin for voting against U.S entry into World War I. While a dedicated wife to two husbands, she always remained infuriated by the condition of women.

Overview of Biographical Sources

Serious writing on Catt begins with Mary G. Peck, *Carrie Chapman Catt: A Biography* (1944), an admiring account written by an intimate friend. Helen Hill Miller, *Carrie Chapman Catt: The Power of an Idea* (1958), is typical of the brief eulogies bestowed upon her. Political expediency of top NAWSA leadership is claimed in Aileen S. Kraditor, *The Ideas of the Woman Suffrage Movement, 1890-1920* (1965) and William L. O'Neill, *Everyone Was Brave: The Rise and Fall of Feminism in America* (1969), Robert Booth Fowler, *Carrie Catt: Feminist Politician* (1986), and Jacqueline Van Voris, *Carrie Chapman Catt: A Public Life* (1987), are strong additions to the biographical sources.

Evaluation of Principal Biographical Sources

Fowler, Robert Booth. *Carrie Catt: Feminist Politician.* Boston: Northeastern University Press, 1986. (**A, G**) While not a conventional biography, Fowler's account of Catt's life is succinct and perceptive. Fowler's real strength, however, is his ability to place "Progressivism's dutiful daughter" squarely within the early twentieth-century reform movement. In accounting for her opposition to blacks, Hispanics, American Indians, and recent immigration, Fowler stresses that Catt saw such groups manipulated by a ruthless anti-female power structure.

Peck, Mary Gray. *Carrie Chapman Catt: A Biography.* New York: H. W. Wilson, 1944. (**A, G**) Written by a close personal friend, this work was for many years the only full-length biography. It offers rich detail on her suffrage and peace activities, but avoids her private life and contains little analysis.

Van Voris, Jacqueline. *Carrie Chapman Catt: A Public Life.* New York: Feminist Press of the City University of New York, 1987. (**A, G**) In a meticulously researched biography, Van Voris relies on a host of manuscript collections and contemporary journals to trace Catt's suffrage efforts at home and abroad. The biography is particularly strong on Catt's international suffrage and peace work.

Overview and Evaluation of Primary Sources

Although she never wrote an autobiography, Catt gives her own account of the suffrage movement in *Woman Suffrage and Politics: The Inner Story of the Suffrage Movement,* written with Nettie Rogers Schuler (1928. Reprint. Seattle: University of Washington Press, 1969; **A, G**). Schuler, a Buffalo resident, had been corresponding secretary of the NAWSA since 1916 and one of the directors of field work. In some ways, the work is a synopsis and update of the classic six-volume *History of Woman Suffrage* (1881-1886. Reprint. New York: Arno Press and New York Times, 1969; **A**), a collection of documents edited by Elizabeth Cady Stanton, Susan B. Anthony, Ida Husted Harper, and Matilda Joslyn Gage. *Woman Suffrage and Politics* covers the victories and defeats of the suffragists in impassioned detail from the Seneca Falls convention to the passage of the Nineteenth Amendment. As progressives, Catt and Schuler assail the liquor and brewery trade as "the invisible enemy." Moreover, they express strong resentment at being denied the suffrage when "newly emancipated, untrained" blacks and "mainly uneducated" foreign-born males are permitted to vote. Catt collaborated with other suffrage leaders in NAWSA, *Victory: How Women Won It; A Centennial Symposium, 1840-1940* (New York: H. W. Wilson, 1940; **A, G**), a project she supervised.

The Catt papers are scattered. The Library of Congress houses much of Catt's correspondence, particularly that of her later years. These holdings are conveniently listed in *The Blackwell Family, Carrie Chapman Catt, and the National American Woman's Suffrage Association* (Washington DC: Library of Congress, 1975; A, G). Of particular importance is the correspondence with Mary Gray Peck. Catt undoubtedly destroyed most papers dealing with her personal life, for there are no letters to or from her to either husband. The Library of Congress also houses a vast collection of NAWSA and LMV papers, the latter including special folders of Catt correspondence. The New York Public Library has a number of Catt's speeches and letters evaluating the effect of woman's suffrage. For more of Catt's evaluations of the suffrage movement plus her peace work, see the Schlesinger Library, Radcliffe College, where the Maud Wood Paul and Anna Howard Shaw papers are also located. Many Catt materials are in the "Suffrage: U.S." collection at the Sophia Smith Library, Smith College. Catt wrote frequently for *Women Voter, Woman's Journal,* and *Woman Citizen.*

Other Sources

Flexner, Eleanor. "Carrie Chapman Catt." In *Notable American Women,* edited by Edward T. James. Cambridge, MA: Belknap Press of Harvard University Press, 1971. A good, brief account of Catt's life and achievements.

—————. *Century of Struggle: The Woman's Rights Movement in the United States.* 1959. Reprint. New York: Atheneum, 1970. Reprint includes a new preface by the author. A generally sympathetic account of Catt that places her within the broader suffrage movement.

Gleeson-Lindenfelder, Ann. "Carrie Chapman Catt." In *Biographical Dictionary of Modern Peace Leaders,* edited by Harold Josephson. Westport, CT: Greenwood Press, 1985. A good brief account of Catt's peace activities.

Kraditor, Aileen S. *The Ideas of the Woman Suffrage Movement, 1890-1920.* New York: Columbia University Press, 1981. While finding Catt very much part of a suffrage leadership that acted expediently on matters of race, Kraditor stresses Catt's organizational skill: "She transformed the huge, disorganized, and aimless group of women into a purposeful organization, each part of which carried out its assigned task in its leader's grand strategy for victory."

Lemons, J. Stanley. *The Woman Citizen: Social Feminism in the 1920s.* Urbana: University of Illinois Press, 1973. Puts Catt in the context of the continuation of progressivism during the 1920s. Despite harassment from hard-core feminists, discouraging judicial decisions, legislative conservatism, and continued attacks from rightists, the "social feminists" helped developed the issues from which the New Deal would emerge. Lemons shows that Catt saw the LWV as a temporary vehicle by which women would catch up with the present inequities embodied in legislation enacted from the male perspective.

Matthews, Jean. "Adam's Rib." *Canadian Review of American Studies* 2 (Fall 1971): 115-125. Includes critique of Catt and Schuler, *Woman Suffrage and Politics* (1923).

Morgan, David. *Suffragists and Democrats: The Politics of Woman's Suffrage in America.* East Lansing: Michigan State University Press, 1972. Study of woman's suffrage in the Progressive era, when it became a national political issue. In comparing the women's suffrage movement with the black civil rights movements, Morgan finds that Elizabeth Cady Stanton adopted the tactics of a W. E. B. Du Bois whereas Catt used the techniques of a Booker T. Washington or a Roy Wilkins.

O'Neill, William L. *Everyone was Brave: The Rise and Fall of Feminism in America.* Chicago: University of Chicago Press, 1969. O'Neill finds Catt "a magnificent individual," but notes that her position on race and war show that she often could not distinguish between "sensible compromise and mere expediency." By simply behaving as any other suffrage group, O'Neill contends, such suffragists depleted their moral capital.

Young, Louise M. "Carrie Clinton Lane Catt." In *Dictionary of American Biography: Supplement IV, 1946-1950,* edited by John A. Garraty and Edward T. James. New York: Scribner's, 1974. Concise interpretive essay.

Justus D. Doenecke
New College of the
University of South Florida

MARY BOYKIN CHESNUT
1823-1886

Chronology

Born Mary Boykin Miller, March 31, 1823, at Mount Pleasant, the plantation home of her mother's parents, near Statesburg, South Carolina; she is the eldest daughter of Stephen Decatur Miller, later governor of the state, and Mary Boykin Miller; *1823-1835* grows up seven miles from Camden at Plane Hill, her father's plantation, where she attends school; *1836-1838* attends Madam Talvande's French School for Young Ladies in Charleston; *1838-1840* travels to her father's cotton plantation in Mississippi and returns to Plane Hill; *1840* marries James Chesnut, Jr., son and heir of James and Mary Coxe Chesnut of Mulberry plantation near Camden, one of the state's largest up-country plantations; *1840-1848* resides with her husband and in-laws at Mulberry; *1848-1858* resides with her husband in Camden at Frogvale and later Kamchatka; *1858-1860* lives in Washington, D.C., while her husband serves as U.S. Senator; *1861-1865* during the Civil War, lives in Alabama, South Carolina, and Richmond, Virginia, depending on the duties of her husband, who is a member of Confederate Congress, brigadier general in charge of South Carolina conscription, and aide to President Jefferson Davis of the Confederacy; keeps a detailed diary of events and observations; *1865-1873* resides at Mulberry with her husband; writes several unfinished novels and translates volumes from French and German; *1873-1886* resides at Sarsfield, where she expands and revises (at least twice) her original Civil War diaries; *1886* dies at Sarsfield on November 22 from chronic heart disease.

Activities of Historical Significance

Mary Boykin Chesnut wrote one of the most famous firsthand accounts of the Confederacy. Intelligent and cultured, Chesnut moved within the highest circles of Confederate politics and society. She was a celebrated conversationalist, highly opinionated and frequently controversial, whose companionship was much sought after by men and women alike. Wherever she resided —and she moved often following her husband's career—she became a central personality of the social elite. As a sophisticated student of human nature, she kept a detailed account of her experiences and observations of the short-lived Confederacy. In her diary, she included portrayals of Southern society, rural and urban culture, race relations, sex roles, and political issues. For the remainder of her life, she worked at revising and expanding her original diaries into a more complete chronicle of the Civil War years, while retaining the diary format. She died at age sixty-four, relatively obscure and impoverished, her manuscript unpublished.

A heavily edited version of her manuscript was first published in 1905 as *Diary from Dixie* and was a popular success, particularly in the South. Only in 1984 was the manuscript finally published in its entirety without disruptive and unnecessary editorial meddling. The manuscript stands on its own as a distinctive literary accomplishment.

Overview of Biographical Sources

Elisabeth Muhlenfeld's biography, *Mary Boykin Chesnut: A Biography* (1981) is the only full-length treatment of Chesnut's life. C. Vann Woodward includes a biographical sketch in his introduction to *Mary Chesnut's Civil War* (1984), considered the definitive edition of her Civil War chronicle. Although the biographical materials are based largely on Muhlenfeld's work, Woodward adds valuable insight into the cultural and historical factors that influenced Chesnut's writing, and analyzes her views on slavery and the role of women in Southern society. A brief biographical essay is included in Woodward and Muhlenfeld's *The Private Mary Chesnut: The Unpublished Civil War Diaries*, which reproduces in full the original wartime diaries. In *Patriotic Gore* (1962), Edmund Wilson evaluates Civil War literature and considers Chesnut's diary an extraordinary document.

Evaluation of Principal Biographical Sources

Lynn, Kenneth S. "The Masterpiece That Became a Hoax." In *The Airline to Seattle: Studies in Literature and Historical Writing about America*. Chicago: University of Chicago Press, 1983. (**A, G**) Lynn's article questions the authenticity of Chesnut's Civil War diaries, because of her extensive revision and expansion of the original 1861-1865 manuscripts.

Muhlenfeld, Elisabeth. *Mary Boykin Chesnut: A Biography*. Baton Rouge: Louisiana State University Press, 1981. (**A, G**) The only book-length biography of Chesnut traces her life from birth to death in the context of her family and Southern heritage. Based on extensive archival sources, including manuscripts, letters, diaries, and family papers, this work is particularly focused on Chesnut's transformation of her Civil War diaries into an extended chronicle of the Confederacy.

Wilson, Edmund. *Patriotic Gore: Studies in the Literature of the American Civil War*. New York: Oxford University Press, 1962. (**A, G**) Wilson considers Chesnut's diary a literary masterpiece.

Woodward, C. Vann. "Mary Chesnut in Search of Her Genre." *Yale Review* 73, 2 (Winter 1984): 199-209. (A) A laudatory review that refutes Lynn's criticism and traces Chesnut's literary embellishment of her wartime diaries.

Overview and Evaluation of Primary Sources

Mary Boykin Chesnut's Civil War writings consist of her unedited wartime diaries and a much revised and extended manuscript based on the diaries. The original diaries have only recently been published as *The Private Mary Chesnut: The Unpublished Civil War Diaries,* edited by C. Vann Woodward and Elisabeth Muhlenfeld (New York: Oxford University Press, 1984; A, G). The revised manuscript has appeared in at least three editions with varying degrees of editorial tampering.

At the time of her death, Chesnut entrusted the unfinished manuscript to Isabella D. Martin, who was asked to prepare the work for publication. This she did in 1905 with the aid of Myrta Lockett Avary, editor of a volume of Civil War memoirs published by Appleton. The Martin/Avary edition, under the imposing title *A Diary From Dixie, as Written by Mary Boykin Chesnut, Wife of James Chesnut, Jr., United States Senator from South Carolina, 1859-1861, and afterward an Aide to Jefferson Davis and a Brigadier-General in the Confederate Army* (New York: D. Appleton, 1905; A), omitted approximately two-thirds of Chesnut's revised manuscript. The editors deleted much that was inconsistent with current Confederate mythology and any material they considered too personal or controversial.

In 1949 the novelist Ben Ames Williams brought out a second edition of the manuscript, *A Diary From Dixie* (Boston: Houghton Mifflin, 1949; A, G), twice as long as the Martin/Avary edition. This version is more representative of Chesnut's manuscript, although it still omits one-third of the text. More disturbing, however, Williams extracted passages from the original diaries without crediting the source, and went on to invent several passages he thought Chesnut should have written.

Finally, in 1981, C. Vann Woodward published Chesnut's complete manuscript text as *Mary Chesnut's Civil War* (New Haven: Yale University Press, 1981; A, G). With extensive annotations that identify people, places, events, quotations, and literary references, Woodward's volume is considered the definitive edition of Chesnut's Civil War chronicle.

Other Chesnut writings (unfinished semi-autobiographical novels, essays, etc.) are available in Elisabeth Showalter Muhlenfeld, "Mary Boykin Chesnut: The Writer and her Work," a Ph.D. dissertation completed for the University of South Carolina in 1978. For Chestnut's letters, see Alice Patricia Wall, "The Letters of Mary Boykin Chesnut" (M.A. thesis, University of South Carolina, 1977).

The original Chesnut manuscripts are housed in the South Carolina Library, University of South Carolina, Columbia.

Other Sources

Aaron, Daniel. *The Unwritten War: American Writers and the Civil War.* New York, 1973. Suggests that Chesnut was a literary artist who had the "eye and ear of a novelist."

Childs, Margaretta P. "Chesnut, Mary Boykin Miller." In *Notable American Women: 1607-1950*, edited by Edward T. Jones. Cambridge: Harvard University Press, 1971. Excellent brief sketch of Chesnut, containing basic biographical information.

Wiley, Bell Irvin. "Mary Boykin Chesnut: Southern Intellectual." In *Confederate Women.* Contributions in American History, no. 38. Westport, CT: Greenwood, 1975. Gracefully written sketch of Chesnut and her contributions to Confederate lore. Based on the Martin/Avary and Williams editions of *A Diary From Dixie.* Contains little biographical information before or beyond the years 1861-1865.

Mary Jo Bratton
East Carolina University

JOHN COLLIER
1884-1968

Chronology

Born John Collier on May 4, 1884, in Atlanta, Georgia, the fourth of seven children, three boys and four girls, of Charles Allen Collier, a lawyer and banker who would be elected the city's mayor, and Susie Rawson Collier; *1884-1902* grows up in Atlanta; his mother dies when he is thirteen and his father dies three years later; attends private Roman Catholic schools; briefly converts from his family's Methodism to Catholicism before abandoning formal religion under the influence of evolutionary theory; graduates from Atlanta High School; *1902-1907* goes to New York City, where he takes noncredit courses in literature and French drama at Columbia University and studies philosophy, sociology, political theory, and natural sciences with private tutor; becomes secretary of the Associated Charities of Atlanta but resigns because of dispute with board of directors over his plans to emphasize job creation rather than relief; goes to Paris to study abnormal psychology at the College de Paris; marries Lucy Wood on October 20, 1906; *1908-1919* is named civic secretary of the People's Institute in New York City; works with immigrants on the Lower East Side; becomes involved with Greenwich Village radical and bohemian circles; founds the Home School as experiment in the educational philosophy of John Dewey; helps to establish and serves as secretary of the National Community Center Conference; *1919-1922* moves to California and becomes director of Americanization for the California State Housing and Immigration Commission; joins artists' and writers' colony at Taos, New Mexico; becomes fascinated with Native American culture; *1922-1933* begins his crusade to reform federal government Indian policy as research agent for the Indian Welfare Committee of the General Federation of Women's Clubs; helps to defeat Bursum Bill because of its threat to the land and water rights of the Pueblo Indians; founds and serves as executive secretary of the American Indian Defense Association (AIDA); *1933-1945* appointed commissioner of Indian Affairs; provides moving force behind passage of Indian Reorganization Act of 1934; launches broad program of reform popularly known as the Indian New Deal; helps found the Inter-American Institute of the Indian in Mexico City to encourage contact and the exchange of information among tribes throughout the Western Hemisphere; divorces wife and marries Laura Thompson on August 25, 1943; *1945-1954* resigns as Indian commissioner; organizes and serves as president of the Institute of Ethnic Affairs in Washington, D.C.; defends right of self-government for island peoples under U.S. rule in Guam, Samoa, and Micronesia; teaches anthropology and sociology at City College of New York; *1955-1968* divorces second wife; is visiting professor of anthropology at Knox College, Galesburg, Illinois; moves back to Taos; marries Grace Volk on January 26, 1957; writes column for local newspaper and his memoirs; *1968* dies on May 8 in Taos.

Activities of Historical Significance

Until about 1920, John Collier was a familiar type: the financially comfortable, sensitive young man who, repelled by the materialism of the business world, was trying to find a suitable niche as uplifter of the poor and immigrant; he was a neighborhood do-gooder and community activist, and a fellow traveler of radical and bohemian artists and writers. But he differed from the type in three regards: first, he had a knack for organization; second, he formulated a fully developed and articulated philosophy of cultural pluralism; third, he had a distinctive vision of turning the public schools into neighborhood community centers that would integrate art, drama, and spiritual values to combat the disruptive social forces accompanying industrialization and urbanization.

Collier came to what would become his life's work only when he was in his late thirties. There is no question that his campaign to preserve Native American tribal culture against the assimilative pressures of federal government Indian policy was motivated by a romanticized image of tribal life, which he saw as embodying the harmonious communal values that he wished to promote as an alternative to the individualist and competitive ethos of contemporary American society. But he shrewdly propagandized his efforts as protecting Native American rights against heavy-handed bureaucrats and grasping special interests. The major goal of the American Indian Defense Association (AIDA)—which Collier founded in 1923 and directed as its executive secretary—reversed federal government policies that promoted Native American assimilation by terminating tribal governments, and ending tribal land ownership by dividing the land among individual tribe members.

After President Franklin D. Roosevelt appointed him commissioner of Indian Affairs in 1933, Collier implemented his alternative program. He was the principal architect of the Indian Reorganization Act of 1934, which ended land allotment, authorized funds for the purchase of new tribal lands, increased federal assistance for reservation economic development, and encouraged tribal self-government. Collier also pushed to extend New Deal relief programs to Native Americans, protect Native American religious freedom, improve the school curriculum and establish bilingual instruction in Native American schools, establish the Indian Arts and Crafts Board in the Department of the Interior, and to codify federal Indian law by legal scholar Felix S. Cohen. Collier's administration of Indian Affairs from 1933 to 1945 was a matter of much controversy at the time and continues to be debated by historians. Even his admirers acknowledge that his Indian New Deal did not fully attain its objectives, but they blame an obstructive bureaucracy, a penny-pinching Congress, and the resistance of assimilation-minded Native American leaders. Collier's critics see his program as unrealistic and misconceived from the start.

Overview of Biographical Sources

Lawrence C. Kelly has published the first part of a projected two-volume biography. *The Assault on Assimilation: John Collier and the Origins of Indian Policy Reform* (1983) carries Collier's story from boyhood through his successful battle to pass the Indian Oil Act of 1927, a landmark piece of legislation guaranteeing Native Americans royalty payments from subsoil minerals on executive-order reservations. More narrowly focused upon Collier as an Indian policy reformer is Kenneth R. Philp, *John Collier's Crusade for Indian Reform, 1920-1954* (1977). Approximately forty percent of the text covers Collier's activities as executive secretary of the American Indian Defense Association; the rest deals with his service as commissioner of Indian Affairs. Philp strives to present a balanced evaluation. A more negative appraisal of Collier's Indian New Deal is given by Graham D. Taylor, *The New Deal and American Indian Tribalism: The Administration of the Indian Reorganization Act, 1934-45* (1980).

A perceptive brief account of Collier's values is presented in Stephen Kunitz, "The Social Philosophy of John Collier" (1971). Book-length case studies of the implementation of his program are Donald L. Parman (*re* the Navajos), Laurence M. Hauptman (*re* the Iroquois), Harry A. Kersey, Jr. (*re* the Seminoles), and Robert Fay Schrader (*re* the Indian Arts and Crafts Board). Briefer appraisals appear in William H. Kelly, ed., *Indian Affairs and the Indian Reorganization Act* (1954), and Kenneth R. Philp, ed., *Indian Self-Rule* (1985).

Evaluation of Principal Biographical Sources

Hauptman, Laurence M. *The Iroquois and the New Deal.* Syracuse, NY: Syracuse University Press, 1981. (A) A case study that gives a highly negative assessment of the application of Collier's program to the Iroquois. Collier, Hauptman bluntly concludes, "largely did not understand the Iroquois. . . . . Wanting to do good, he was, nevertheless, handicapped by his inability, based upon his background and temperament, to understand them . . . . Romantic notions and good intentions were insufficient to win the day in New York."

Kelly, Lawrence C. *The Assault on Assimilation: John Collier and the Origins of Indian Policy Reform.* Albuquerque: University of New Mexico

Press, 1983. (A, G) The first volume of a projected two-volume biography that is based upon research in an impressive body of archival and government records and will probably stand as the definitive life. The first four chapters deal with Collier's growing up, his involvement with the People's Institute and the community center movement, and his "discovery" of the Native American. The rest of the volume consists of a chapter outlining the development of federal Indian policy up to 1922, followed by a detailed account of Collier's campaign to reform that policy up to the successful passage of the Indian Oil Act of 1927.

Kelly, William H., ed. *Indian Affairs and the Indian Reorganization Act: The Twenty-Year Record.* Tucson: University of Arizona Press, 1954. (A, G) A symposium featuring recollections and commentary by Collier and his leading associates in the Indian New Deal.

Kersey, Harry A., Jr. *The Florida Seminoles and the New Deal, 1933-1942.* Boca Raton: Florida Atlantic University Press, 1989. (A) Finds the Seminoles only slightly affected, for good or ill, by the Indian New Deal because "they were so small a tribe, and so far removed from the mainstream of American Indian affairs, that scant attention was paid to them by the Indian Office bureaucracy or the harried Commissioner Collier."

Kunitz, Stephen. "The Social Philosophy of John Collier." *Ethnohistory* 18 (Summer 1971): 213-229. (A, G) A perceptive analysis of Collier's romanticization of Native American society in his reaction against the individualist and competitive ethos of business America.

Parman, Donald L. *The Navajo and the New Deal.* New Haven: Yale University Press, 1976. (A) Because they were the most numerous of the surviving Native American tribes and occupied the largest reservation, the Navajos were looked upon as the test case for evaluating the Indian New Deal. The tribe became one of the strongholds of resistance to Collier's plans. While acknowledging faults on both sides, Parman places major blame for the conflict between Collier and the Navajos upon Collier's lack of understanding of Navajo psychology.

Philp, Kenneth R. *John Collier's Crusade for Indian Reform, 1920-1954.* Tucson: University of Arizona Press, 1977. (A, G) Approximately forty percent of the text is devoted to relating Collier's resistance to the assimilative thrust of existing Indian policy under Herbert Hoover's presidential administration; the rest of the book treats the implementation, while commissioner of Indian Affairs, of his program of preserving tribal culture and sovereignty. Basing his work upon extensive research in the Collier Papers, the National

Archives, and published government documents, Philp strives to strike a balanced evaluation of Collier. Thus, he praises Collier's "many impressive achievements" while simultaneously acknowledging how his romanticization of Native American communal life, coupled with his authoritarian, even dictatorial, personality, "often led to coercion rather than promotion of social justice or spontaneous community endeavors."

————, ed. *Indian Self-Rule: First-Hand Accounts of Indian-White Relations from Roosevelt to Reagan.* Salt Lake City, UT: Howe Brothers, 1985. (**A, G**) Includes Rupert Costo, "Federal Indian Policy, 1933-1945"; Floyd A. O'Neil, "The Indian New Deal: An Overview"; and Alfonso Ortiz, "Indian Policy, 1933-1945."

Schrader, Robert Fay. *The Indian Arts & Crafts Board: An Aspect of New Deal Indian Policy.* Albuquerque: University of New Mexico Press, 1983. (**A**) A detailed, favorable account of the contribution made by one of Collier's pet initiatives in preserving and promoting Native American arts and crafts.

Taylor, Graham D. *The New Deal and American Indian Tribalism: The Administration of the Indian Reorganization Act, 1934-45.* Lincoln: University of Nebraska Press, 1980. (**A**) Although this detailed investigation of Collier's management of Indian Affairs rests upon much the same sources as Philp's account, Taylor's assessment is more negative. He admits that the limited success of Collier's economic development program can be ascribed in large part to "a niggardly and hostile Congress." But he finds Collier largely to blame for the failure to achieve "genuine Indian self-determination."

Overview and Evaluation of Primary Sources
Through his writings Collier was an active propagandist for his ideas. The most important of these are "The Red Atlantis," *Survey* 49 (October 1922): 15-20+ (**A, G**); "The Indian Bureau's Record," *Nation* 135 (October 5, 1932): 303-305 (**A, G**); "The United States Indian Administration as a Laboratory of Ethnic Relations," *Social Research* 12 (September 1945): 265-303 (**A, G**); *The Indians of the Americas* (New York: W. W. Norton, 1947; **A, G**); and *Patterns and Ceremonials of the Indians of the Southwest* (New York: Dutton, 1949; **A, G**. Reprinted as *On the Gleaming Way: Navajos, Eastern Pueblos, Zunis, Hopis, Apaches, and Their Land, and Their Meaning to the World* [Denver: Sage Books, 1962]). The autobiography that Collier wrote in his last years, *From Every Zenith: A Memoir and Some Essays on Life and Thought* (Denver: Sage Books, 1963; **A, G**), is informative on his early years but is not always factually reliable. Recollections John Collier, Jr., appear as the "Foreword" to Kelly, *The Assault on Assimilation.*

Collier's papers, which are mostly from the post-1922 years, are in the Western Americana Collection, Yale University Library, New Haven, Connecticut. This large body of materials, filling over ninety boxes, includes personal correspondence, unpublished manuscripts, copies of organizational records and publications, and newspaper clippings. The collection has been microfilmed and is available commercially; there is an extensive index. The major source for Collier's pre-Indian reform phase is the two collections of the People's Institute Papers—one in the Cooper-Hewitt Collection of Manuscripts and Archives, Cooper Union Library, New York City, and the other, the larger and more important of the two, in the Manuscript and Archives Division, New York Public Library.

Collier appears prominently in Mabel Dodge Luhan's memoirs, especially *Intimate Memories: Background* (New York: Harcourt, Brace, 1933; **A, G**); *European Experiences: Volume Two of Intimate Memories* (New York: Harcourt, Brace, 1935; **A, G**); and *Movers and Shakers: Volume Three of Intimate Memories* (New York: Harcourt, Brace, 1936; **A, G**). The correspondence between the two in the Mabel Dodge Luhan Papers, Collection of American Literature, Beinecke Rare Book and Manuscript Library, Yale University, is valuable for reconstructing his life and ideas between 1907 and 1920.

The most important source for Collier's activities in the 1920s are the papers of the California League of American Indians (actually the files of the northern California branch of the American Indian Defense Association) at the Bancroft Library, University of California, Berkeley. Indispensable for his service as commissioner of Indian Affairs are the voluminous materials in Record Group 75, records of the Office of Indian Affairs, National Archives, Washington, D.C.; the National Archives has prepared a two-volume guide to Record Group 75.

Other Sources

Berkhofer, Robert F., Jr. *The White Man's Indian: Images of the American Indian from Columbus to the Present.* New York: Alfred A. Knopf, 1978. Invaluable for placing Collier's views in the context of the history of white attitudes toward the Native American.

Downes, Randolph C. "A Crusade for Indian Reform, 1922-1934." *Mississippi Valley Historical Review* 32 (December 1945): 331-354. While downplaying Collier's personal role, Downes documents the growing attack upon the policy of assimilation that emerged in the 1920s.

Philp, Kenneth R. "John Collier and the Controversy over the Wheeler-Howard Bill." In *Indian-White Relations: A Persistent Paradox,* edited by

Jane F. Smith and Robert F. Kvasnicka. Washington, DC: Howard University Press, 1976. A detailed examination of the crosspressures determining the final shape of the Indian Reorganization Act of 1934.

Prucha, Francis Paul. *The Great Father: The United States Government and the American Indians.* 2 vols. Lincoln: University of Nebraska Press, 1984. A comprehensive survey by the dean of historians of federal government Indian policy.

Szasz, Margaret. *Education and the American Indian: The Road to Self-Determination, 1928-1973.* Albuquerque: University of New Mexico Press, 1974. Informative on Collier's efforts to improve Native American education.

Wright, Peter M. "John Collier and the Oklahoma Indian Welfare Act of 1936." *Chronicles of Oklahoma* 50 (Autumn 1972): 347-371. Shows the modifications Collier had to accept in his plans to meet the needs and opposition of the Oklahoma Native Americans who had received individual land allotments.

John Braeman
University of Nebraska-Lincoln

JOHN COLTRANE
1926-1967

Chronology

Born John William Coltrane on September 23, 1926, in Hamlet, North Carolina, son of John R. Coltrane, a minister and owner of a tailor shop, and Alice Coltrane; *1926-1944* grows up in High Point, North Carolina, where he plays tenor saxophone in the high school band; moves to Philadelphia in 1944 where he studies tenor saxophone at Granoff Studios and The Ornstein School of Music; makes debut as professional musician in cocktail lounge band in Philadelphia; *1945* is drafted into the Navy and plays clarinet in a Navy band; *1946* is discharged from Navy and devotes the year to practicing the saxophone; *1947-1949* plays tenor saxophone with Joe Webb, King Kolax, and Eddie Vinson; *1949* joins Dizzy Gillespie's band; *1950* makes his recording debut with Gillespie; *1950-1955* plays alto saxophone with Earl Bostic, Johnny Hodges, Jimmy Smith, and Bud Powell; *1955* marries Naima Gibbs; *1955-1957* plays in Miles Davis's group; *1957* leaves Davis's group to play with Thelonious Monk at the Five Spot Cafe in New York City; *1958-1960* plays in Miles Davis's group intermittantly, and records several solo albums; *1960* leaves Davis's group to form his own quartet; plays the soprano saxophone for the first time; *1961* wins top tenor saxophone, top miscellaneous instrument and top new star awards in *Down Beat* magazine's critics' poll; begins experimenting with African and Indian rhythms and improvisational techniques; *1962-1964* records several albums in different musical styles; *1965* records *A Love Supreme*, his most influential and successful album; sweeps the *Down Beat* readers' poll as Jazzman and tenor saxophone player of the year; *1966* divorces Naima and marries Alice McLeod; tours Japan to rave reviews; *1967* dies on July 17 of liver cancer in Huntington, Long Island.

Activities of Historical Significance

According to his fellow musicians, Coltrane was one of the most dedicated and restlessly experimental of all jazz musicians. Even as a boy he would spend hours practicing, first the clarinet and then the saxophone. After he was discharged from the army, Coltrane heard the saxophone playing of Charlie Parker and decided to spend a year practicing the saxophone. Even in the early years of his career, other musicians were impressed by Coltrane's dedication and the constant improvement in his skill and repertoire. During the years that followed, Coltrane continued to practice relentlessly and to listen to new and different types of music.

Coltrane's incorporation of African and Indian rhythms and scales into jazz later broadened the music's spectrum and opened the ears of younger jazz musicians who were eager to break out of traditional jazz idioms.

His 1960 recording *Giant Steps* was a revolutionary presentation of the saxophone as an instrument of great versatility. Also, the album was one of the few jazz recordings by young artists to avoid standard jazz songs; it contained only Coltrane's original compositions. This bold move angered some critics and jazz enthusiasts, but it spurred many jazz musicians to write and record more of their own music.

In the years following *Giant Steps*, Coltrane continued to push his music in new directions. He recorded in a variety of settings with diverse musicians, and his openness to experimentation led him to record jazz versions of traditional Spanish, African, and Indian music. At the same time, Coltrane breathed new life into jazz standards such as "Body and Soul" and Broadway show tunes such as "My Favorite Things." In the process of recording such diverse material, Coltrane both broadened the boundaries of jazz and, by using recognizable melodies, gaining a wider audience. *My Favorite Things* and *A Love Supreme* were among the biggest selling jazz recordings of the 1960s. Coltrane's dedication to his instrument and to his music has served as inspiration to musicians as diverse as guitarist Carlos Santana and pianist Chick Corea.

Overview of Biographical Sources

Although he was not thought of highly by most critics or fellow musicians during the early years of his career, Coltrane became one of the most respected and influential jazz musicians of the late 1950s and 1960s. His approach to the tenor saxophone, to jazz, and to music in general have continued to influence jazz, rock, and jazz-rock fusion musicians around the world.

As a result, Coltrane has been the subject of several biographies; the most notable are Cuthbert Simpkins's *Coltrane: A Biography* (1975) and Bill Cole's *John Coltrane* (1976). Both combine a discussion of Coltrane's life with personal reminiscences by musicians and by the authors. Each also discusses the mechanics of Coltrane's technique and music.

Another useful work is Brian Priestley's *John Coltrane* (1987), in which Priestley discusses the influence of Coltrane and his music during his lifetime and since his death.

Evaluation of Principal Biographical Sources

Cole, Bill. *John Coltrane*. New York: Schirmer Books, 1976. (A, G) An account of Coltrane's life and career intertwined with the personal reminiscences of Cole and others who knew Coltrane. Cole emphasizes the influence of

African, Middle Eastern, and Latin music on the development of Coltrane's playing techniques. Includes a lengthy bibliography and an appendix containing several sheets of music written by Coltrane.

Priestley, Brian. *John Coltrane*. London: Apollo Press, 1987. (**A, G**) Offers an overview of Coltrane's life and career, with a final chapter devoted to a critique of his most important recordings. Interspersed throughout are reminiscences by fellow musicians. Priestley also discusses important criticism about Coltrane's music and offers his own evaluations. Contains a selected discography.

Simpkins, Cuthbert Ormond. *Coltrane: A Biography*. New York: Herndon House Publishers, 1975. (**A, G**) A biography as well as an exploration of the importance of religion and non-Western forms of music upon Coltrane's style and music. Contains several appendixes with copies of music written in Coltrane's own hand, as well as reprints of interviews with Coltrane, and reviews of some of his recordings.

Overview and Evaluation of Primary Sources

Coltrane's technique continued to change throughout his career, and his successive recordings each reveal a slightly different sound and document his constant experimentation in technique and form.

Though historically significant, Coltrane's first recordings with Dizzy Gilespie's Orchestra do not contain any solos by Coltrane, and his saxophone is often buried in the arrangements. However, Coltrane's 1951 recordings with Gilespie's Sextet, especially "Night in Tunisia" (Oberon 5100), "Birk's Works" (Dee Gee 3601) and "Jumpin' With Symphony Sid" (Oberon 5100) give brief glimpses of the beginnings of Coltrane's style.

The first recordings that displayed Coltrane's solo style were with the Miles Davis Quintet from 1955 to 1957. Among the best of these recordings are *The New Miles Davis Quintet* (Prestige), and *Steamin'* (Prestige). His later work with Davis is best represented on *'Round About Midnight* (Columbia), *Kind of Blue* (Columbia), and *Milestones* (Columbia).

Coltrane's recordings as a band leader are represented on *Blue Trane* (Blue Note, 1957), *Giant Steps* (Atlantic, 1960), *My Favorite Things* (Atlantic, 1961) and *A Love Supreme* (MCA/Impulse, 1965).

A complete listing of Coltrane's recordings as a band member, featured soloist, and band leader is available in David Wild's *Recordings of John Coltrane: A Discography* (2d ed. Ann Arbor, MI: Wildmusic, 1979). Wild also lists recording dates, session members, instruments, song titles, and, in most cases, studio master numbers for each session.

Other Sources
    Clark, Donald, ed. "Coltrane, John." In *The Penguin Encyclopedia of Popular Music.* New York: Viking Penguin, 1989. The writer of this entry encapsulates Coltrane's life and career in two pages, critically evaluates Coltrane's place in jazz history, and recommends selected albums. This is an excellent entry from which to begin a study of Coltrane's life and music.

    Crohn, Burrill, prod. and dir. *John Coltrane: The Coltrane Legacy.* New York, NY: Video Artists International, 1988. This collection of television appearances by Coltrane shows him at what many consider the height of his career, 1961 to 1964. Among the performances are "Afro Blue," "Alabama," "Impressions," and "My Favorite Things." Interspersed among the performances are interviews with drummers Elvin Jones and Jimmy Cobb and bassist Reggie Workman, in which they give their opinions of Coltrane and his music.

    James, Michael. "Coltrane, John (William)." In *The New Grove Dictionary of Music and Musicians,* edited by Stanley Sadie, vol. 2. Washington, DC: Macmillan, 1980. Offers a concise biographical sketch with emphasis on Coltrane's changing style. Also, James includes a short bibliography of useful material about Coltrane.

    Lemieux, Raymond. "John W. Coltrane." In *Dictionary of American Negro Biography,* edited by Rayford W. Logan and Michael R. Winston. New York: Norton, 1982. A biographical sketch that includes a variety of quotes by Coltrane's contemporaries as well as a short discussion of his importance to jazz music.

    Lenz, Gunther H. "Black Poetry and Black Music: History and Tradition: Michael Harper and John Coltrane." In *History and Tradition in Afro-American Culture,* edited by Gunther Lenz. Frankfurt: Campus, 1984. This provocative chapter explores the connections between Coltrane's music and his incorporation of African rhythms and scales into jazz, and the development of an American black aesthetic. Lenz also discusses the connections between Coltrane's music and the poetry of African-Americans.

William E. Hull
Illinois State University

CAPTAIN PAUL CUFFE
1759-1817

Chronology

Born Paul Slocum on January 17, 1759 on the island of Cuttyhunk, near Westport, Massachusetts, the seventh of ten children of Cuffe Slocum, a former slave, and Ruth Moses, a Native American; *1759-1780* grows up on his father's farm with little formal education, but masters the subject of navigation through self-study; secures employment as a seaman; on the initiative of Paul, in 1778, all of Cuffe Slocum's children except the youngest, drop the slave name Slocum and replace it with their father's given name, Cuffe (sometimes spelled Cuffee); *1780* with brother John petitions the Massachusetts General Court and the Court of General Sessions for tax relief claiming that because, as blacks, they lack the rights of citizenship they should not be required to pay taxes; the petition is dismissed, but in 1783 the state grants citizenship rights to free blacks; *1780-1810* maritime activities prosper; his ships, built on a dock on his Westport property, are commanded by black captains and manned by black crews; on February 25, 1783 he marries Alice Pequit, a Native American, with whom he has two sons and six daughters; purchases a farm on the Westport River and shortly thereafter builds and opens a free school on his property; affiliates with the Quakers, attracted by their anti-slavery stance; *1810-1812* Cuffe's interest in Africa is stimulated by information about the West African colony of Sierra Leone, founded by British anti-slavery organizations; sails for Sierra Leone on January 1, 1811, arrives February 24; spends six weeks there before departing for Liverpool to visit British anti-slavery factions; remains in Britain from July 12 to September 20, 1811, then returns to Sierra Leone for a second visit of three months duration; *1812-1815* War of 1812 prevents progress on colonization plans; *1815-1817* sails for Sierra Leone on December 2, 1815 with thirty-eight American blacks as prospective colonists; contributes $4,000 to support their expenses; returns to the U.S. in July 1816; *1817* dies September 9 in Westport, Massachusetts after an illness of several months; leaves an estate valued at $20,000.

Activities of Historical Significance

The 1780 suit of Paul and John Cuffe against the state of Massachusetts— to free them from taxation in the absence of citizenship rights—was an important part of the struggle of blacks to obtain rights in the aftermath of the American Revolution. Although their suit was rejected and they spent a short time in prison, Massachusetts soon granted the gist of what they had demanded: full citizenship for free blacks.

Paul Cuffe's successful career as a shipowner and sea captain is in itself an example of black accomplishment in the face of the prevailing and often vicious racism of the day. In this regard Captain Cuffe belongs in the company of individuals such as Benjamin Banneker, James Forten, and Phillis Wheatley.

Through his activities to establish the colony of Sierra Leone, Cuffe contributed significantly to the African colonization movement that was beginning to gain momentum in the U.S. He believed that blacks would be better off out of America, away from white prejudice, and that their removal would eliminate white dread of a large free black population, a major obstacle to emancipation. Moreover, he wanted industrious, Christian black colonists to serve as a civilizing force among native Africans who, in his view, sullied themselves by selling their racial brothers into slavery. The economic growth bound to accompany colonization would promote the same object by providing alternative trade possibilities. Cuffe's settlement of thirty-eight colonists in Sierra Leone encouraged the leaders of the American Colonization Society in their ambitious colonization schemes, although the great majority of American blacks would soon express their intense hostility to the idea of colonization in Africa.

Overview of Biographical Sources

Many brief biographical sketches of Cuffe appear in journals or in larger works dealing mainly with Afro-American history; some of these date from the nineteenth century. Only one published work comes close to being a full-length biography: Henry N. Sherwood's "Paul Cuffe," in the April 1923 issue of the *Journal of Negro History.*

Evaluation of Principal Biographical Sources

Adams, Russell L. *Great Negroes, Past and Present.* Chicago: Afro-American Publishing, 1969. (**G, Y**) This brief, readable account of Cuffe's life contains a copy of the only known likeness of the captain, an 1812 silhouette.

Cromwell, John W. *The Negro in American History. Men and Women Eminent in the Evolution of the American of African Descent.* Washington, DC: American Negro Academy, 1914. (**A, G**) The chapter on Cuffe is a standard account of his life, with a somewhat erroneous interpretation of the 1780 tax petition.

Franklin, John Hope. *From Slavery to Freedom. A History of Negro Americans.* 3d ed. New York: Alfred A. Knopf, 1967. (A, G) An excellent general history that discusses several aspects of Cuffe's career and provides the political and social context.

Hill, Adelaide Cromwell, and Martin Kilson, eds. *Apropos of Africa. Sentiments of Negro American Leaders on Africa from the 1800s to the 1950s.* New York: Frank Cass, 1969. (A, G) The chapter on Cuffe includes a number of documents, such as a diary entry recounting his first voyage to Sierra Leone and a description of the conditions that he found there.

Howard, Horatio P. *A Self-Made Man. Captain Paul Cuffee.* New Bedford, MA: Frances Press, 1913. (G) A pamphlet-sized work by Cuffe's great grandson, this standard treatment is perhaps most valuable for its discussion of the 1913 dedication of a monument to the captain and its clear reproduction of the 1812 silhouette.

Reid, Inez Smith. "Black Americans and Africa." *The Black American Reference Book,* edited by Mabel M. Smythe. Englewood Cliffs, NJ: Prentice-Hall, 1976. (G) This article dealing with the connection between black Americans and Africa correctly stresses Cuffe's religious convictions as an important factor in his desire to improve the behavior of his "African brethren."

Ricketson, Daniel. *The History of New Bedford.* New Bedford, MA: Anthony & Sons, 1858. (A, G) An old account notable for its discussion of Cuffe within the context of New Bedford's status as a haven for blacks in the antebellum period.

Sherwood, Henry N. "Paul Cuffe." *Journal of Negro History* 8 (April 1923): 153-232. (A) Sherwood's lengthy article is the definitive study of the life of Paul Cuffe. Its thoroughness derives from the fact that it is based almost entirely on the Cuffe Papers in the Free Public Library in New Bedford.

―――――. "Paul Cuffe and His Contribution to the American Colonization Society." *Mississippi Valley Historical Association Proceedings* 6 (1913): 370-402. (A) An examination of the communication between the founders of the American Colonization Society, especially Samuel J. Mills and Robert Finley, and Captain Cuffe, who used Cuffe's experiences in Sierra Leone to strengthen their own resolve to proceed with a colonization scheme.

Overview and Evaluation of Primary Sources

The Cuffe Collection in the Free Public Library in New Bedford, Massachusetts contains Captain Cuffe's letter book, letters to him, a journal, his published pamphlets, as well as deeds, bills of sale, surveyors' plans, and various other papers. It is accessible to scholars on microfilm through interlibrary loan. Another useful source is the *Life of William Allen with Selections from His Correspondence* (2 vols. Philadelphia: n.p., 1847). Allen was a British anti-slavery figure closely associated with Cuffe in his Sierra Leone activities. Also valuable are the following: *Memoir of Captain Paul Cuffe* (York, England: n.p., 1812), Peter Williams *Discourse on the Death of Paul Cuffe, Delivered before the New York African Institution, Oct. 21, 1817*; and *Records of the Court of General Sessions, Taunton, Mass.* (for the 1780 suit).

Museums, Historical Landmarks, Societies

Monument (Westport, MA). In 1913 Horatio P. Howard erected a granite monument to the memory of his great grandfather, Paul Cuffe. It stands five feet high on the elevation in the front part of the Quaker Meeting House in Westport, Massachusetts and bears the following inscription: "In memory of Captain Cuffe, Patriot, Navigator, Educator, Philanthropist, Friend."

Other Sources

Brawley, Benjamin. "Cuffe, Paul." In *Dictionary of American Biography*, edited by Allen Johnson and Dumas Malone. New York: Scribner's, 1964. A succinct account of Cuffe's life.

Cadbury, Henry J. "Negro Membership in the Society of Friends." *Journal of Negro History* 21, 2 (April 1936): 151-213. Contains a brief discussion of Cuffe's Quaker involvement.

Harris, Sheldon H. "Paul Cuffe's White Apprentice." *The American Neptune* (July 1963): 192-196. A very brief article on apprenticeship, focusing on the contract signed by the Swede Abraham Rodin who worked under Cuffe from 1807 until at least 1811.

Sheldon Spear
Luzerne County Community College

ANGELA DAVIS
b. 1944

Chronology

Born Angela Yvonne Davis on January 26, 1944, in Birmingham, Alabama, to B. Frank Davis, a businessman and teacher, and Sally E. Davis, a school teacher; the eldest of four children, she has two brothers, Benjamin and Reginald, and one sister, Fania Davis Jordan; *1950s* her social activism begins when she and her mother demonstrate for civil rights in Birmingham; *1959-1961* attends Elizabeth Irwin High School in New York City on a scholarship; *1965* graduates from Brandeis University; *1965-1967* attends the Johann Wolfgang von Goethe University in Frankfurt, West Germany; *1968* receives a master's degree in philosophy from New York University; becomes a civil rights activist, setting up a Black Student Council, joining the Communist Party, and founding the Soledad Brothers Defense Committee to champion the cause of George Jackson and W. L. Nolen; *1969* begins teaching, then fired from the University of California by the Board of Regents and Governor Ronald Reagan; *1970* implicated in the Marin County (California) Courthouse shootout when guns, purchased by Davis, are used by Jonathan Jackson; the dead include Judge Haley and Jonathan Jackson; warrants are issued for her arrest; *1971* listed by the FBI as one of the ten most-wanted fugitives in the United States. *1972* acquitted of kidnaping, conspiracy, and murder; *1974, 1978, 1984* is the Communist Party's nominee for vice president of the United States; *1979* awarded the Lenin Peace Prize. *1980* marries Hilton Braithwaite, a photographer; currently serves as a professor of philosophy at San Francisco State University and San Francisco Art Institute, specializing in women's studies and the historical contributions of African American women.

Activities of Historical Significance

The Marin County Courthouse Revolt on August 9, 1970, and Davis's subsequent trial and acquittal on charges of conspiracy, kidnaping, and murder, exemplified the strong racial and political divisions within the American cultural fabric. Her intelligence and her ability to articulate and defend her beliefs made it impossible for the American political establishment and media to ignore African-American political activism. On cultural matters, Davis has been a strong proponent of a natural style in hair and clothing for African American women. Politically she is a champion of cultural and political diversity and of civil rights for Americans of all races. She is the founder and co-chair of the National Alliance Against Racist and Political Repression.

Davis is a scholar and the author of four books. Herbert Marcuse once called her "the best student [he] had in more than thirty years of teaching." A popular lecturer, her classes at San Francisco State University are always filled. Her contributions to American society include her 1972 trial, which was a symbol for the need for equal justice for all races; her sympathetic and vocal support for African American prisoners; and her courage in standing up for her intense political beliefs. Recently, Davis has defined her goal as the forging of "a new socialist order—an order which will reestablish socioeconomic priorities so that the quest for monetary profit will never be permitted to take precedence over the real interests of human beings."

Overview of Biographical Sources

Davis's celebrated arrest for conspiracy, kidnapping, and murder made her an instant media celebrity. With the Marin County Courthouse Revolt now more than twenty years in the past, writings about her have become less polemic and more objective. Davis has always been one of the primary sources for her own biographical data and political beliefs. To date, her autobiography, *Angela Davis, An Autobiography* (1974), is the best descriptive source for the activist period of her life, 1967-1973. Two notable books of this period are George Jackson's *Soledad Brothers* (1971), which consists of prison letters written by Jackson to his supporters, including Davis; and *If They Come in the Morning* (New York: Third Press, 1971), a compilation of essays which include writings by Davis. In all books that discuss Davis, the primary themes are civil liberties, freedoms of speech and press, and the rights of African Americans.

Evaluation of Principal Biographical Sources

Major, Reginald. *Justice in the Round*. New York: The Third Press, 1973. (G) This study of Davis's trial includes a day-by-day chronology.

Nadelson, Regina. *Who Is Angela Davis?* New York: Wyden, 1973. (G) Nadelson was a high school friend of Davis. Her book is a sympathetic account of Davis's youth in Birmingham, Alabama. She discusses civil rights violations in Birmingham and Davis's Communist Party involvement.

Parker, J. A. *Angela Davis: the Making of a Revolutionary*. New Rochelle, NY: Arlington House, 1973. (A) Discusses the rise of black militancy through the eyes of a political conservative, who stresses the non-viability of a socialist approach.

Overview and Evaluation of Primary Sources

Davis's writings spell out her Marxist social theory, which proposes change within the American political system. Her writings explore the subjects of sexism, racism, American politics, and the biases of establishment history. Davis is a staunch supporter of prisoners' rights, working class rights, women's rights, and the rights of people of color. Her writing is candid and polemical. A fine speaker, she is a popular lecturer on American college campuses. Her preface to *Angela Davis, An Autobiography* (New York: Random House, 1974; **G**), states that her book is "especially for those who are going to struggle until racism and class injustice are forever banished from our history." The book describes the Marin County Courthouse Revolt and her relationship with George Jackson, as well as her capture by the FBI and her trial. Her 1982 book *Women, Race, and Class* (New York: Random House, 1982; **A**), consists of thirteen essays in which Davis traces historical social injustices such as slavery and lynching and the contemporary problems of rape and reproductive rights.

Her most recent writings are collected in *Women, Culture, and Politics* (New York: Random House, 1989; **A**); they discuss sexism, racism, and class bias in American society, and call for further historical study to unearth the historical contributions of African Americans and women.

Other Sources

Jackson, George. *Blood in My Eye*. New York: Random House, 1972. For those unaware of the anger, frustration, and rage felt by African Americans in prison, this book may be unsettling. In angry terms Jackson describes his hatred for the system in "Amerika."

—————. *Soledad Brothers*. New York: Coward-McCann, 1971. Although criticized by mainstream critics for his non-grammatical writing, Jackson is one of the best sources of information on Davis's life from 1971 to 1974. While a prisoner in Soledad, he compiled a selection of his letters, including those to Davis. These are tough letters. The introduction is by Jean Genet.

Cynthia L. Marshall
Community College of Beaver County

VARINA HOWELL DAVIS
1826-1906

Chronology

Born Varina Banks Howell on May 7, 1826, at Marengo plantation, Concordia Parish, Louisiana, second child and first daughter of Margaret Graham Kempe Howell, Virginia-born daughter of an Irish expatriate, and William Burr Howell, War of 1812 veteran and son of Governor Richard B. Howell of New Jersey; *1826-1840* grows up at The Briars, Natchez, Mississippi, attends school in Philadelphia, is tutored at home, and graduates from Elizabeth Female Academy, Washington, Mississippi; *1845* marries Jefferson Davis (1808-1889), widower-planter of Warren County, Mississippi; *1845-1846* lives in Washington as wife of congressman; *1846-1848* lives at home, Brierfield plantation, near Vicksburg; *1848-1851* lives in Washington as wife of Senator Davis; *1851-1853* at Brierfield; *1852* gives birth to first son; *1853-1861* returns to Washington as wife of secretary of war and senator; *1855, 1857, 1859* gives birth to daughter and two sons; *1861-1865* serves as first lady of the Confederate States of America, Montgomery, Alabama, and Richmond, Virginia; *1861, 1864* gives birth to son and daughter; *1865-1867* lives in Georgia and at Fort Monroe, Virginia, where husband is imprisoned; *1867-1869* lives in Montreal, Canada; *1869-1878* travels abroad and lives in Memphis; *1878-1892* lives at Beauvoir, Biloxi, Mississippi; *1890* publishes *Jefferson Davis: A Memoir*; *1892-1906* lives in New York City and writes occasionally for newspapers; *1906* dies on October 6 of pneumonia in New York and is interred at Richmond.

Activities of Historical Significance

As the wife of Jefferson Davis, Varina Davis was at the center of the most turbulent decades of the nineteenth century. She shared his life in Washington, where he was an important political force before the Civil War, and was first lady of the Confederacy. A well-educated woman, exceptionally intelligent, strong-willed, opinionated, and a keen observer of people and events, she left an invaluable literary legacy in her correspondence and in a biography of her husband, which contains much autobiographical material not found elsewhere.

The friend and confidante of some of the most influential men and women of her day, Varina Davis was also her husband's strongest supporter, particularly in the difficult years after the war when he was imprisoned, then released virtually penniless and in search of a means of livelihood. After his death Varina undertook her own writing career, producing the *Memoir* and various short pieces, and vigorously defended Jefferson Davis against all critics. She helped rear some of her siblings and her own five children in the midst of war, outliving all but one daughter and one sister; all four sons died before 1879—one died at the Confederate White House—and her youngest child, Varina Anne, "Daughter of the Confederacy," died in 1898.

Overview of Biographical Sources

The first serious biography, by Mississippian Eron O. Rowland, was not written until two decades after Varina Davis's death. The standard biography was written in 1958 by a journalist, Ishbel Ross. Naturally, many aspects of Varina Davis's life and personality have been treated in the myriad biographies of her famous husband, and she has received parallel critical or sympathetic appraisals. She has been the subject of many magazine articles written for the general public (mostly of the "moonlight and magnolias" variety) and has appeared on the fringes of countless studies of the Confederacy. At least two modern biographies are in preparation.

Evaluation of Principal Biographical Sources

Bradford, Gamaliel. *Wives.* New York: Harper & Brothers, 1925. (G) This book by a New Englander emphasizes Varina Davis's intellectual and social talents, her influence on Jefferson Davis, and her unflagging support of his career.

Randall, Ruth Painter. *I, Varina: A Biography of the Girl Who Married Jefferson Davis and Became the First Lady of the South.* Boston: Little, Brown, 1962. (G, Y) One of a series of biographies of prominent women by a skilled researcher and writer; the story is lively, factual, and insightful.

Ross, Ishbel. *First Lady of the South: The Life of Mrs. Jefferson Davis.* New York: Harper & Brothers, 1958. (A, G) The standard full-length biography was written by a prize-winning journalist; it is a straightforward, honest appraisal, well-written and utilizing a wide variety of primary sources.

Rowland, Eron O. (Moore). *Varina Howell, Wife of Jefferson Davis.* 2 vols. New York: Macmillan, 1927. (G) Overlong and sentimentally sympathetic to its subject and to Deep South lore, this account is useful because the author interviewed women who had known Varina Davis.

Van der Heuvel, Gerry. *Crowns of Thorns and Glory: Mary Todd Lincoln and Varina Howell Davis—The Two First Ladies of the Civil War.* New York:

Dutton, 1988. (**A, G**) The most recent biography focuses on two women who simultaneously became public figures and analyzes their actions fairly and compassionately.

Wiley, Bell Irwin. *Confederate Women.* Westport, CT: Greenwood Press, 1975. (**A, G**) Written by a renowned Civil War scholar, this study presents Varina Davis as her husband's helpmate and finds her outgoing personality and youthful enthusiasm a vital balance for his life and career.

Overview and Evaluation of Primary Sources

The most important primary source is Varina Davis's *Jefferson Davis: A Memoir by His Wife* (2 vols. New York: Belford, 1890; **A, G**), which is based on recollections of her life with Jefferson Davis and is also a key source for his own reminiscences. Her observations and opinions add considerable color to his writings, which are usually careful and noncommittal. Although her letters have not been collected in a separate edition, many are contained in Hudson Strode, ed., *Jefferson Davis: Private Letters, 1823-1889* (New York: Harcourt, Brace & World, 1966; **A, G**); in a ten-volume set edited by Mississippi archivist Dunbar Rowland, *Jefferson Davis, Constitutionalist* (Jackson: Department of Archives and History, 1923; **A**); and in *The Papers of Jefferson Davis*, an ongoing edition in preparation at Rice University (6 vols. to date. Baton Rouge: Louisiana State University Press, 1971-; **A**).

Like her husband's, Varina Davis's correspondence is scattered among various repositories and in private hands. The most important manuscript collections of her papers are at the Mississippi Department of Archives and History (chiefly personal and including many Howell family documents), the University of Alabama (including items used by Hudson Strode in the preparation of his Davis biography), and especially for the postwar period, Transylvania University, the Library of Congress, and the Museum of the Confederacy.

Fiction and Adaptations

Two historical novels focus on Jefferson Davis's courtship of Varina Howell: Harnett T. Kane's *Bride of Fortune* (1948) is by a master of the craft who tells Varina's story from the day she first met her husband until his release from prison in 1867; Shirley Seifert's *The Proud Way* (1948) encompasses only 1843-1845 but is based on extensive research and is helpful for understanding family relationships.

Museums, Historical Landmarks, Societies

Beauvoir (Biloxi, MS). An 1848 Gulf Coast plantation house was Varina and Jefferson Davis's last home together. She willed it, complete with many personal items and furniture, to the Sons of Confederate Veterans, who have preserved and maintained the house and gardens.

The Briars (Natchez, MS). The house where Varina Davis spent her childhood and where she was married has been restored and is open to the public.

Confederate Memorial Hall (New Orleans, LA). Varina Davis donated some of the Civil War militaria and most of the Davis family items in this small museum.

First White House of the Confederacy (Montgomery, AL). Now located near the Alabama capitol, the house is furnished in the style of the 1860s with many Davis artifacts, clothing, and the furniture used by Varina Davis at the time of her death.

Hollywood Cemetery (Richmond, VA). Burial site of Varina and Jefferson Davis and all their children; beautiful statuary chosen by Varina Davis.

Museum of the Confederacy (Richmond, VA). The Confederate White House, a National Historic Landmark, has been perfectly restored to the period of the Davises' residence and includes some family pieces; the adjacent museum and library hold one of the most significant collections of Confederate memorabilia.

Old Court House Museum (Vicksburg, MS). Also a National Historic Landmark, the courthouse has one room devoted to the Davises, with several personal items and a scale model of Brierfield (no longer extant).

Smithsonian Institution (Washington, DC). Location of many contemporary likenesses of Varina and Jefferson Davis, as well several pieces of her jewelry, including her engagement ring and wedding jewelry.

Other Sources

Dolensky, Suzanne T. "The Daughters of Jefferson Davis: A Study of Contrast." *Journal of Mississippi History* 51 (November 1989): 313-340. Provides interesting insights into Davis family dynamics.

————. "Varina Howell Davis, 1889 to 1906: The Years Alone." *Journal of Mississippi History* 47 (May 1985): 90-109. The only monograph to adequately describe Varina Davis's role as guardian of the images of Jefferson Davis and the Lost Cause.

Evans, Eli N. *Judah P. Benjamin, the Jewish Confederate*. New York: Free Press, 1988. Concerned mainly with the war years, this work is very useful for its close attention to Varina Davis and the Davises' relationships with others.

Strode, Hudson. *Jefferson Davis*. 3 vols. New York: Harcourt, Brace & World, 1955-1964. A colorful and readable but overly sympathetic chronicle that was written with the assistance of Davis family members.

Woodward, C. Vann, ed. *Mary Chesnut's Civil War*. New Haven: Yale University Press, 1981. Like Evans's work, this is valuable for its coverage of the Confederate period.

Lynda Lasswell Crist
The Papers of Jefferson Davis, Rice University

MARTIN DELANY
1812-1885

Chronology

Born Martin Robison Delany on May 6, 1812, in Charleston, Virginia (now West Virginia) to Samuel Delany, a slave, and Pati Peace, a free black; *1822* moves with his mother to Chambersburg, Pennsylvania, after she is threatened with arrest for teaching her children to read; father buys his freedom and joins the family; *1831* moves to Pittsburgh, where he studies medicine; *1843* marries Catherine Richards, with whom he has eleven children; becomes editor of *The Mystery*; *1848* serves with Frederick Douglass as co-editor of *The North Star*; *1850-1851* attends Harvard Medical School; *1852* publishes *The Condition. . .of the Colored People of the United States, Politically Considered*, which advocates emigration as a response to racial inequality; *1854* publishes *The Political Condition of the Colored Race*; *1856* moves to Chatham, Ontario, Canada; *1859* publishes *Blake: Or, The Huts of America*, a novel calling for insurrection; travels to Africa to explore possible sites for a black colony along the Niger River Valley; *1860* visits London and Liverpool to gain support for an African settlement; publishes report of expedition's findings; *1862* upon returning to the U.S., becomes a recruiter for black regiments; *February 1865* is commissioned a major in the United States Army after meeting with Lincoln; upon war's end becomes a sub-assistant commissioner for the Freedman's Bureau in South Carolina; *1869* seeks and fails to obtain appointment as minster to Liberia from President Grant; *1874* runs for lieutenant governor on Independent Republican ticket; *1876* supports Democrat Wade Hampton's successful gubernatorial bid, overlooking anti-black violence perpetrated by Democrats; *1879* revives interest in emigration by becoming involved in a Liberia colonization scheme and publishes a study of ethnology; *1885* dies January 24 in Xenia, Ohio.

Activities of Historical Significance

Martin Delany's pride in his blackness was evident throughout his life. Best known as an advocate of black emigration, his commitment wavered during the Civil War when he saw hope for blacks in the future of the United States. After establishing himself as a doctor and journalist, Delany began to push for separatism in the wake of the Compromise of 1850 and the passage of the Fugitive Slave Law, which marked the nadir of black rights prior to the end of the Civil War. By 1859 he had moved beyond advocacy and commenced searching for a location for a black colony, traveling to Africa's

Niger Valley. At the same time his novel *Blake,* appearing in serial form, suggested insurrection as another solution to the problem of black oppression.

The outbreak of the Civil War presented Delany with an alternative. Perhaps the eradication of slavery and the movement to accord blacks civil and political equality would remove barriers to black citizenship once deemed insurmountable. Delany helped raise black regiments, obtained a commission in 1865, and served three years in the Freedmen's Bureau in South Carolina. Upon his retirement from military service in 1868, he entered South Carolina politics as a Republican. In the 1870s Delany abandoned the Republican party, asserting that blacks' interests were being ignored and their votes taken for granted by the white leadership. He minimized the intimidation and violent suppression of the black electorate by the Democratic party and in 1876 supported the successful gubernatorial candidacy of Wade Hampton. Only when it became obvious that Hampton's promises to recognize black equality were not going to be honored did he turn once more to emigration as the best solution facing black Americans.

Interest in Delany was revived during the 1960s, when advocates of black nationalism and black power looked for historical role models. However, his life and career were not examined on their own merits at first; only with the appearance in the 1970s of studies about Delany's interest in emigration did more objective, discriminating observations emerge.

Overview of Biographical Sources

With the exception of an 1868 biography by Frances Whipper, *Life and Public Services of Martin Delany,* written with Delany's assistance in order to promote his career, Delany was neglected by most scholars until the advent of the black power movement in the late 1960s. Dorothy Sterling, *The Making of an Afro-American: Martin Robison Delany, 1812-1885* (1971) and Victor Ullman, *Martin R. Delany: The Beginnings of Black Nationalism* (1971) reflect the times in which they were written. While both are the product of diligent research, they are manifestoes of black pride; Ullman comes close to calling for a black uprising in his concluding passages. More critical and detached studies appeared in the 1870s, concentrating on Delany's plans for a black colony in Africa. Only Nell Painter's "Martin R. Delany: Elitism and Black Nationalism" (1988) comes close to offering an interpretation of his entire life, emphasizing Delany's elitism and tendency to confuse the prospect for blacks with his own prospects. There is still a need for a scholarly biography of Delany, one which would incorporate the findings of black history over the past twenty years.

Evaluation of Principal Biographical Sources

Blackett, Richard. "Martin R. Delany and Robert Campbell: Black Americans in Search of an African Colony." *Journal of Negro History* 62 (January 1977): 1-25. **(A)** Explores the background of the Niger Valley Exploring Party, Delany's vehicle for finding a site for a black colony.

—————. "In Search of International Support for African Colonization: Martin R. Delany's Visit to England, 1860." *Canadian Journal of History* 10 (December 1975): 307-24. **(A)** Describes Delany's visit to England to gain financing for his planned African colony, claiming that Delany's visit reminded Englishmen of southern support for slavery and the need to press for abolition, thus contributing to England's decision not to support the Confederacy.

Ellison, Curtis W., and E. W. Metcalf. *William Wells Brown and Martin R. Delany: A Reference Guide*. Boston: G. K. Hall, 1978. **(A)** Essential as a guide to the literature on Delany through 1975.

Griffith, Cyril E. *The African Dream: Martin R. Delany and the Emergence of Pan-African Thought*. University Park: Penn State University Press, 1975. **(A)** Perhaps the best single volume on Delany's desire to establish a colony for American blacks in Africa.

Kahn, Robert M. "The Political Ideology of Martin Delany." *Journal of Black Studies* 14 (June 1984): 415-40. **(A)** Argues that Delany's advocacy first of emigration and then of participation in American politics reflected different facets of a consistent ideology of black advancement.

Morrison, Derrick. "Martin R. Delany and the Beginnings of Black Nationalism." *International Socialist Review* 33 (April 1972): 10-13, 38-41. **(G)** A short overview of Delany's career and thought.

Painter, Nell. "Martin R. Delany: Elitism and Black Nationalism." *Black Leaders of the Nineteenth Century*, edited by Leon Litwack and August Meier. Urbana: University of Illinois Press, 1988: 149-72. **(A, G)** Questions celebratory accounts of Delany as father of black nationalism, pointing out that Delany lost interest in emigration when his personal outlook improved. Stresses Delany's elitist perspective relative to the problems facing American blacks after emancipation.

Sterling, Dorothy. *The Making of an Afro-American: Martin Robinson Delany, 1812-1885*. Garden City, NY: Doubleday, 1971 **(G, Y)** Although intended for readers in junior high schools, Sterling's book includes a great deal of helpful information about Delany's life.

Ullman, Victor. *Martin R. Delany: The Beginnings of Black Nationalism.* Boston: Beacon Press, 1971. (A, G) Reflecting the time in which it was written, Ullman's positive portrayal of Delany embraces a violent solution to America's race problem. In so doing, Ullman abandons biography in favor of advocacy. Notwithstanding this fatal flaw, the book contains a great deal of information about Delany and could well serve as a point of departure for a new study.

Whipper, Francis R. [pseud. Frank A. Rollin]. *Life and Public Services of Martin R. Delany.* 1868. Reprint. New York: Kraus Reprint, 1968. (A) Written under Delany's supervision and with his assistance, this celebratory account minimizes Delany's interest in emigration while stressing his military service during the Civil War and with the Freedmen's Bureau in South Carolina.

Zengner, John. "A Note on Martin Delany's *Blake,* and Black Militancy." *Phylon* 32 (Spring 1971): 98-105. (A) Emphasizes Delany's advocacy of violence as a possible solution to racial oppression.

Overview and Evaluation of Primary Sources

There is no single collection of Delany's papers. Scattered collections can be found in the American Colonization Society Papers in the Library of Congress, the files of the Treasury, State, and War Departments in the National Archives, and in the Governors' Papers in the South Carolina State Archives in Columbia, South Carolina.

Some of Delany's writings were made available in new editions in the late 1960s and 1970s. Perhaps his definitive statement of black destiny, *The Condition, Elevation, Emigration and Destiny of the Colored People of the United States,* which appeared in 1852, was reprinted by New York's Arno Press in 1968. "The Political Destiny of the Colored Race," which marked his conversion to emigration in 1854, is reproduced in Sterling Stuckey, ed., *The Ideological Origins of Black Nationalism* (Boston: Beacon Press, 1972; A). Howard H. Bell, ed., *Search for a Place: Black Separatism and Africa, 1860* (Ann Arbor: University of Michigan Press, 1969; A) contains the report of the Niger Valley Exploring Party. Finally, *Blake: or The Huts of America,* edited by Floyd J. Miller (Boston: Beacon Press, 1970; A, G), was published for the first time as a single volume.

Other Sources

Draper, Theodore. *The Rediscovery of Black Nationalism.* New York: Viking, 1969. A searing attack on black nationalism, claiming that it conceals a desire for black domination through violence. Cites Delany as a founding father of the movement.

Glatthaar, Joseph T. *Forged in Battle: The Civil War Alliance of Black Soldiers and White Officers.* New York: The Free Press, 1990. Demonstrates that Delany was neither the only nor the first black officer in the Union Army during the Civil War.

Litwack, Leon F. *North of Slavery: The Negro in the Free States, 1790-1860.* Chicago: University of Chicago Press, 1961. Discusses the growing frustration of blacks in the aftermath of the Compromise of 1850, an environment which promoted the emigrationist alternative.

Miller, Floyd J. *The Search for Black Identity: Black Emigration and Colonization, 1787-1863.* Urbana: University of Illinois Press, 1975. Compares Delany's plans for emigration with other separatist movements.

Moses, Wilson J. *The Golden Age of Black Nationalism, 1850-1925.* Hamden, CT: Archon, 1978. An informative overview of the context of Delany's proposals. Reminds readers that Delany sought white support for his emigration plans.

Pease, Jane H., and William H. Pease. *They Who Would be Free: Blacks' Search for Freedom, 1830-1861.* New York: Atheneum, 1974. The study of northern blacks includes a chapter on the separatism and emigration movement which features Delany.

Quarles, Benjamin. *Black Abolitionists.* New York: Oxford University Press, 1969. A comprehensive overview of black abolitionists, including Delany.

Sweet, Leonard I. *Black Images of America, 1784-1870.* New York: W. W. Norton, 1976. Contains a discussion of Delany's decision to advocate emigration in the 1850s as part of the debate over the destiny of the black race in America.

Brooks Donohue Simpson
Arizona State University

AGNES DeMILLE
b. 1909

Chronology
Born Agnes George DeMille 1909, daughter of William DeMille, brother of famous Hollywood director, Cecil B. DeMille; her mother was the daughter of the famous American economist, Henry George; raised in an upper middle-class environment, full of educational opportunities and stimulation; *1916* appears in *Ragamuffin*, a film produced by her father; graduates in English from the University of California; begins her career as a ballet dancer, studying under Koslov and Karasavina in London; masters the forms of classical ballet, but her *tour de force* would always be her ability to choreograph; *1927* debuts as a concert dancer in "Jenny Loved a Sailor"; *1929* debuts her choreography with "The Black Crook"; *1930s* stages dances for film, as in *Romeo and Juliet,* and on Broadway, *Hooray for What, Hamlet,* and *Midsummer Night's Dream*; her reputation as a choreographer grows; *1941* her choreography for *Black Ritual* is praised for its originality and primitive style; *1943* marries Walter F. Prude; they have one son, Jonathan; *1947* wins Tony Award for *Brigadoon* choreography; *1949* stages *Rodeo* and *The Courting of Burnt Ranch,* her most significant contributions to dance, incorporating the American spirit and its symbols into the choreography; *1951* publishes first volume of her autobiography, *Dance to the Piper*; *1962* wins Tony Award for *Kwamina* choreography; *1965* choreographs two ballets, *The Wind in the Mountains* and *The Four Marys,* and the musical *Carousel* on Broadway; *1971* chroeographs *Come Summer* on Broadway; *1976* honored with Handel Award by the Mayor of New York City; *1979* choreographs *Oklahoma* on Broadway; *1981* publishes latest installment of critically acclaimed autobiography, *Reprieve*; *1990* honored by the American Ballet Theatre as one of the five great twentieth-century choreographers.

Activities of Historical Significance
Agnes DeMille created a classic American dance style, melding classical ballet with American folk dance. An expert in dance form, she choreographed ballets, musicals, and literary formulas to produce uniquely American motifs and forms. Although an accomplished dancer, she says, "I was constructed for endurance . . . . I was built like a mustang, stocky, mettlesome, and sturdy . . . . But the long, cool, serene, classic line was forever denied me." Her contributions to choreography, using what she calls her "taproot" of square dances, round dances, roping, and twirling motions of the American West, are where her genius lies. In her choreography of *Rodeo,* she uses riding, roping,

tap dancing, and comedy to represent the raucous spirited freedom of the individual spirit. DeMille states, "The cowgirl was me. I wanted to compete with men, in a man's way—through my achievements, not through playing coy or flirting."

Fall River Legend, a dark and haunting classic was also based upon the American tale of gothic imagery and perversity, the Lizzie Borden hatchet murder. Part of DeMille's essence is her ability to communicate through words and gestures complex thoughts and symbols. Her choreographs for *Oklahoma*, the film and the play, *Carousel*, and the macabre classic, *Fall River Legend*, are considered American classics. *Rodeo* and *Fall River Legend* were revived in 1990 as part of the American Ballet Theatre's fiftieth season.

In addition to her incomparable choreography, she is also an accomplished writer, who has chronicled her life and the emergence of America's dance theatre so that others can study the role of the choreographer in twentieth-century theatre and film. She has written texts for beginning dancers describing how one prepares for the stage. DeMille's genius was her ability to combine pathos, candor, relevance, and wit in both her uniquely American choreography and in her autobiographies.

Overview of Biographical Sources

Although numerous periodical articles address DeMille's individual accomplishments or offer critiques of her choreography, there has been no standard biography. This may be a direct result of DeMille's control over her own creations. She has chronicled her own life to such an extent that other biographers have not attempted the task.

Evaluation of Principal Biographical Sources

Stratyner, Barbara Cohen, ed. *The Biographical Dictionary of Dance*. New York: Schirmer Books, 1982. (G) Provides a brief overview of DeMille's life and accomplishments.

Atkinson, Brooks. "Review of *Brigadoon*." *New York Times* April 13, 1947. (G) This is one example of many insightful reviews of DeMille's choreography written by *Times* reviewer, Brooks Atkinson. Atkinson remarks that DeMille transformed "the development of ballet into an integral part of a musical fable."

Overview and Evaluation of Primary Sources

In the 1950s with the publication of *Dance to the Piper* (Boston: Little, Brown, 1951; G), DeMille began a series of autobiographical accounts which compiled diaries, journals, reminiscences, and opinions to recount her experiences within the world of dance. In *Promenade Home* (Boston: Little, Brown, 1956; **G**), DeMille discusses her loves during World War II, and her choreography of *Oklahoma* and *Carousel*. *Speak to Me, Dance With Me* (Boston: Little, Brown, 1973; **G**) describes her life in London during the 1930s when she studied under such great dance instructors as Marie Rambert. Her childhood memories are described in *Where the Wings Grow* (New York: Doubleday, 1978; **G**). In 1981 DeMille published *Reprieve* (New York: Doubleday, 1981; **G**), a portrait of her grueling recovery from a stroke, and perhaps her most poignant and heroic work. In it, she describes her feelings of helplessness, the impotence of immobility after an active life, and the psychic damage caused by her stroke.

Most of the criticisms of this autobiographical series stem from the belief that DeMille was a pampered "little rich girl," who likes to be perceived as a struggling middle-class American. These criticisms appear unfounded when one reviews DeMille's life as a whole. Her struggles and triumphs are those which many would shy away from sharing, and yet, DeMille does not flinch from revealing facets of her life which were less than fulfilling or less than promising.

Other noteworthy sources which give insight into DeMille's personal feelings and opinions of the theatre include her *Book of Dance* (New York: Golden Press, 1963; **Y**), and *American Dance* (New York: Macmillan, 1980, **Y**).

Museums, Historical Landmarks, Societies

Agnes DeMille Theatre (Winston-Salem, NC). This performance space at the School of Arts was named in her honor in 1975.

Theatre Hall of Fame (Winnipeg, Manitoba). DeMille has been inducted into the Theatre Hall of Fame.

Other Sources

Bordman, Gerald, ed. *Oxford Companion to American Theater*. New York: Oxford University Press. 1984.

Nadell, Deborah. "Agnes DeMille." In *Notable Women in the American Theater*, edited by Alice M. Robinson, et al. Westport, CT: Greenwood Press, 1989.

Cynthia L. Marshall
Community College of Beaver County

CHARLES RICHARD DREW
1904-1950

Chronology

Born Charles Richard Drew on June 3, 1904, in Washington, D.C., the first of five children of Richard Drew, a carpet-layer, and Nora Rosella Drew; his parents are of mixed ancestry, so that their son is part African, part English, part Scot, and part Native American; *1922* an indifferent student but a superb all-around athlete, he graduates from Washington's famed, though segregated, (Paul Laurence) Dunbar High School; awarded an athletic scholarship to Amherst College; *1926* graduates from Amherst, still an indifferent student; *1926-1928* serves as director of athletics and instructor in biology and chemistry at Morgan College, Baltimore; *1928* accepted as a student by the medical school of McGill University, Montreal, Canada, after first being rejected by Howard University in his hometown because of an "English deficiency"; *1933* earns M.D. degree with distinction; *1933-1935* interns and completes residency in medicine in Montreal hospitals; *1935* returns to Washington, D.C., as instructor in pathology in the medical school of Howard University; *1936-1937* works as an assistant in surgery, Howard University, and resident in surgery at Howard's teaching facility, Freedmen's Hospital; *1937-1938* becomes instructor in surgery, Howard University, and assistant surgeon, Freedmen's Hospital; *1938-1939* takes leave from Howard University as a General Education Board (Rockefeller Foundation) Fellow at Columbia University, New York City; *1939* marries Lenore Robbins on September 23; *1939-1940* resident in surgery at Columbia-Presbyterian Hospital; *1940* still on leave, completes doctoral dissertation, "Banked Blood: A Study in Blood Preservation," and becomes the first black student ever to be awarded the degree doctor of science in medicine; returns briefly to Howard University as assistant professor of surgery and as surgeon at Freedmen's Hospital, before returning to New York on a leave of absence as medical director of the "Blood for Britain" program; *February 1941* moves up to the post of medical director in charge of collection of blood for the U.S. armed forces through the American Red Cross; *April 1941* returns to Howard University following certification by the American Board of Surgery; *October 1941* appointed an examiner for the American Board of Surgery, as its first black member, and promoted to professor of surgery, Howard University, and chief surgeon, Freedmen's Hospital; *1941-1950* at Howard University trains more than half of all the black surgeons certified by the American Board of Surgery during the decade; receives numerous honors and appointments, including the E. S. Jones Award for Research in Medical Science, chief-of-staff at Freedmen's Hospital, the Spingarn Medal for his work collecting blood, chairman of the surgical section of the National Medical Association, vice president of the American-Soviet Medical Society, Fellow of the International College of Surgeons, and consultant to the surgeon general of the United States; *1950* dies on April 4 in the emergency room of the Alamance General Hospital, Burlington, North Carolina, of injuries sustained in an automobile accident.

Activities of Historical Significance

Drew used to say that there were two things that he spent much of his life trying to live down—his athletic record and his work in blood preservation. He was described as one of the best all-around athletes of the first third of the twentieth century, and as a scientist and physician he made contributions to the collection of blood and the processing of blood plasma that were invaluable to the Allied effort in World War II, directly or indirectly saving of tens, if not hundreds, of thousands of lives. He did not lack pride in these accomplishments, but he regarded his chief work in life as that of a trainer of other black surgeons, whose skills, like his own, would be equal to surgeons trained anywhere. Drew was both an inspiring example for his students and a superb teacher who revolutionized the training of black surgeons by black surgeons.

Overview of Biographical Sources

A man of legend surrounded by myth, Drew has, almost exclusively, attracted writers who are content to repeat the myths and to engender the legend. A romantic figure of great personal charm, literally the "super Negro" at a time when there were few such role models, Drew has inspired most biographers to write about him in the fashion in which Parson Weems wrote about George Washington: Drew is presented as a larger than life figure, possessed of no faults or weaknesses, who in the end was killed, it is said, by bigoted white people who refused to give him medical treatment and left him to bleed to death in the street. The only scholarly biography that has appeared thus far is Charles E. Wynes, *Charles Richard Drew: The Man and the Myth* (1988). To date, then, those who would learn about Drew, the athlete, the scientist, the surgeon, the teacher of other surgeons, and the man of letters, are severely limited in published sources.

Evaluation of Principal Biographical Sources

Bims, Hamilton. "Charles Drew's 'Other' Medical Revolution," *Ebony* 30 (February 1974): 88-96. (G) Bims's article is especially useful on Drew's role as a trainer of black surgeons.

Cobb, W. Montague. "Charles Richard Drew, M.D., 1904-1950." *Journal of the National Medical Association* 42 (July 1950): 238-246. **(A, G)** Cobb and Drew grew up together in Washington, they attended Amherst together, and it was Cobb, already on the faculty of the medical school at Howard, who encouraged Drew to go there. This article neither discredits nor repeats the myths surrounding Drew.

Hepburn, David. "The Life of Charles R. Drew." *Our World* (July 1950): 23-29. **(G)** Hepburn provides a brief overview of Drew's life.

Wynes, Charles E. *Charles Richard Drew: The Man and the Myth.* Urbana and Chicago: University of Illinois Press, 1988. **(A, G)** This biography is brief, yet comprehensive, particularly in disproving the myths that surround Drew. The result is the emergence of a more believable, though by no means lesser, figure.

Yancey, Asa G. "The Life of Charles R. Drew, M.D., M.D.Sc.: Perspectives of a Former Resident in General Surgery." In *A Century of Black Surgeons: The U.S.A. Experience*, edited by Claude H. Organ and Margaret M. Kosiba, vol. 1. Norman, OK: Transcript Press, 1987. **(A, G)** Yancey's forty-page essay is similar in content and equal in merit to Cobb's article.

Overview and Evaluation of Primary Sources

The only body of primary sources on the life of Charles Richard Drew is his personal papers, located in the Moorland-Spingarn Research Center, Founders Library, Howard University, Washington, D.C. These papers, by and large, cover only an eleven-year period of Drew's life: from 1939, when he went to New York to study for the doctor of science degree, to 1950, the year of his death. The bulk of the papers consists of letters to his wife, Lenore, that are extremely revealing. The collection contains other scattered correspondence to friends and to the American Medical Association, objecting to the black exclusionary policy of some local AMA chapters, including that of Washington, D.C. Drew was never accepted as a member of the AMA. Also among Drew's papers is a brief and revealing handwritten soliloquy addressed to the New Year, 1930. There are the usual clippings, posters, programs, invitations, and tributes, and for the artifact lover there are Drew's eyeglasses, laboratory coats, football jersey, graduation robe and hoods, a few medical instruments, and prescription pads. Finally, a superb collection of photographs covers Drew's life from infancy to just a few days before his death. In sum, this collection of personal papers and memorabilia is of great value in getting to know the inner man; it is less revealing about the events of Drew's brief life.

For those seeking personal glimpses of Drew, impressionistic articles by those who knew him are also useful: D. O. ("Tuss") McLaughry, "The Best Player I Ever Coached," *Saturday Evening Post* 225 (December 6, 1952): 184 (G); Paul B. Cornely, "Charles R. Drew (1904-1950): An Appreciation," *Phylon* 11 (Second Quarter 1950): 176-177 (G); and Lenore Robbins Drew, "Unforgettable Charlie Drew," *Reader's Digest* (March 1978): 135-140 (G).

Finally, for the persistent but diplomatic student, oral history opportunities abound in the persons of Drew's colleagues, former students and residents, family members, and friends, many of whom are mentioned in Wynes's, *Charles Richard Drew.*

Fiction and Adaptations

Not surprisingly, the 1960s, a time that emphasized the "black pride" concept and the search for black role models, gave rise to two fictionalized biographies of Drew written for juveniles: Richard Hardwick, *Charles Richard Drew: Pioneer in Blood Research* (1967), and Robert Lichello, *Pioneer in Blood Plasma: Charles Richard Drew* (1968). Both books are replete with invented dialogue and the "thoughts" of Drew. Drew also has inspired an original screenplay by Lanette Lind entitled "Dream High: The Story of Dr. Charles R. Drew." It was presented by the Raleigh Ensemble Players, in Raleigh, North Carolina, in March 1989.

Museums, Historical Landmarks, Societies

Charles R. Drew Blood Center (Washington, DC). This facility named in Drew's honor is located in the Red Cross National Headquarters Building.

Charles R. Drew Postgraduate Medical School (Los Angeles, CA). Named in Drew's honor, this school is a part of the California state system.

Drew's Boyhood Home (Arlington, VA). Drew's brother Joseph and Joseph's wife still live in this house located at 2505 First Street, South. The house bears a plaque indicating that it is on the National Register of Historic Places.

Granite Monument (near Haw River, NC). Erected on April 5, 1986, near the site of Drew's fatal accident, this monument is roughly six feet tall and bears a metal plaque that describes his main accomplishments. It also bears a quotation from Drew: "There must always be the continuing struggle to make the increasing knowledge of the world bear some fruit in increased understanding and in the production of human happiness."

Portrait (Washington, DC). A large portrait of Drew, painted by Alfred C. Loang, hangs in the Clinical Center of the National Institutes of Health.

Other Sources

Cobb, W. Montague, "Numa P. G. Adams, M.D., 1885-1940." In *Journal of the National Medical Association* 43 (January 1951): 43-52. A personal tribute that provides an objective assessment of Drew's accomplishments at the Freedmen's hospital.

Holt, Thomas, Casandra Smith-Parker, and Rosalyn Terborg-Penn. *A Special Mission: The Story of Freedmen's Hospital, 1862-1962.* Washington, DC: Academic Affairs Division, Howard University, 1975. A history of the hospital where Drew's students as well as his surgical residents got their training.

Logan, Rayford W. *Howard University: The First Hundred Years, 1867-1967.* New York: New York University Press, 1969. Logan, a well-known and respected historian, was a contemporary of Drew at Howard. This work places Drew in the context of his work at the university.

————, and Michael R. Winston, eds. *Dictionary of American Negro Biography.* New York: W. W. Norton, 1982. This work contains a concise and accurate biographical sketch of Drew written by Logan.

Charles E. Wynes
University of Georgia

ISADORA DUNCAN
1877-1927

Chronology

Born Angela Duncan on May 26, 1877, in San Francisco, California, to the poet Joseph Charles Duncan and Dora Gray, a musician; *1877-1894* grows up in San Francisco, parents divorce; along with sister Elizabeth formulates the "New School" of dance; *1894-1898* travels with mother to Chicago and then to New York where she joins the dance company directed by Augustin Daly; *1898-1904* travels with family to London; acquires support of the actress Mrs. Patrick Campbell; joins the Loie Fuller dance company; travels to Athens; *1904* with assistance from sister Elizabeth opens dance school in Grunewald, a suburb of Berlin, *1905* gives birth to a daughter, Deirdre, fathered by Edward Gordon Craig; gives performance in Russia and is acclaimed by critic Sergey Diaghilev; *1906* meets and falls in love with Paris Singer, heir to a sewing machine fortune and a patron of the arts; *1908* gives birth to a son, Patrick, fathered by Paris Singer; *1913* two children and nurse killed in automobile accident in Paris; does relief work with brother Raymond in Albania; travels to Viareggio, Italy; has a still-born child, believed to have been fathered by an Italian sculptor; *1915* returns to the U.S.; *1916-1917* has unsuccessful performing tours of South America and the U.S.; *1918-1920* holds dance tours of France and Germany; *1920* invited to organize school of dance in Athens, but fall of Greek government negates offer; accepts an invitation to organize a dance school in Moscow; meets the poet Sergey Aleksandrovich Esenin; *1922* marries Esenin on May 2 and travels to the U.S. during the "Red Scare"; *1923* travels to Paris and Moscow; *1924* returns to France; *1925* Esenin commits suicide in Russia; *1927* publishes autobiography *My Life*; dies of broken neck when her scarf is caught in an automobile wheel spoke in Nice on September 14, 1927; buried in Pere la Chaise in Paris.

Activities of Historical Significance

Isadora Duncan made substantial contributions to the development of modern dance. Although contemporary public opinion was more interested in her liberal lifestyle, which included numerous sexual relationships and a general repudiation of conventional morality, artists and critics recognized Duncan's work as innovative and important. Her "New System" of improvisational dance, which was influenced by her study of Greek art, was an interpretation of nature as expressed through poetry, music, and other forms.

Duncan produced an emotive level of dance described by some as "religious." She disseminated her concepts on dance and art through schools in

Germany, Russia, and France. While none of them have survived, Duncan's denouncement of artificiality in dance had considerable impact on dancers and choreographers such as Mary Wigman and Martha Graham.

Overview of Biographical Sources

From the year of her death Isadora Duncan has attracted biographers. Early efforts by students and admirers, such as Irma Duncan and Allan Ross Macdougall's *Isadora Duncan's Russian Days and Her Last Years in France* (1929) and Mary Desti's *The Untold Story: The Life of Isadora Duncan, 1921-1927* (1929), were biased though valuable accounts that did not approach Duncan's life in a scholarly manner. Over the last two decades several important biographies have appeared; they include Walter Terry's *Isadora Duncan: Her Life, Her Art, Her Legacy* (1964), Victor I. Seroff's *The Real Isadora* (1971), and Fredrika Blair's *Isadora: Portrait of the Artist As A Woman* (1986). Blair's book must be considered the most significant and scholarly of the three because of its scope, intellectual rigor, and the author's effective use of sources.

Evaluation of Principal Biographical Sources

Alder, Norma. "Reconstructing the Dances of Isadora Duncan in the United States." *The Drama Review* 28 (Fall 1984): 59-66. (A, G) This significant, scholarly article examines attempts to recreate Duncan's naturalistic dances in the U.S. It provides valuable information on Duncan's approach to dance.

Blair, Fredrika. *Isadora: Portrait of the Artist As A Woman.* New York: McGraw-Hill, 1986. (A, G) This formidable treatment of Duncan from a feminist perspective provides new insights into the historical forces that confronted Duncan. Perhaps the finest Duncan biography in print, it includes an excellent bibliography and an introduction that reviews the availability of primary sources.

Geselbracht, Raymond H. "Transcendental Renaissance in the Arts: 1890-1920." *The New England Quarterly* (December 1975): 463-486. (A) A highly interpretative and provocative approach to the early twentieth-century intellectual synthesis in which Duncan played a major part.

Jones, R. E. "The Gloves of Isadora." *Theatre Arts Magazine* 31 (1947): 17-42. (A, G, Y) An excellent profile of Duncan's life and work.

Kozoday, Ruth. *Isadora Duncan*. New York: Chelsea House, 1988. (A, G) An adequate and sympathetic biography of Duncan with ample documentation.

Macdougall, A. R. *Isadora: A Revolutionary in Art and Love*. New York: Thomas Nelson and Sons, 1960. (A, G, Y) In this sympathetic treatment, Macdougall includes details (especially regarding Duncan in Europe) not found elsewhere.

Magriel, Paul, ed. *Isadora Duncan*. New York: Henry Holt, 1947. (A, G) This extremely valuable work contains the following essays: "Isadora Duncan and Basic Dance" by John Martin; "Duncan Concerts in New York" and "The New Isadora" by Carl Van Vechten; "Isadora Duncan and the Artists" by Allan Ross Macdougall; and "Isadora Duncan: Studies for Six Dance Movements" by Edward Gordon Craig.

McVay, Gordon. *Isadora and Esenin*. Ann Arbor, MI: Ardis, 1980. (A, G) A scholarly examination of the relationship between Duncan and the Russian artist Esenin. McVay thoroughly discusses Esenin's mental collapse and its impact on Duncan.

Schneider, Ilia Ilich. *Isadora Duncan: The Russian Years*. Translated by David Magarshack. New York: Harcourt, Brace, World, 1969. (A, G) A translation of an earlier work by a Russian artist familiar with Duncan.

Seroff, Victor I. *The Real Isadora*. New York: Dial Press, 1971. (A, G) A reliable and not uncritical biography of Duncan by a friend of hers from the mid-1920s.

Steegmuller, Francis, ed. *"Your Isadora": The Love Story of Isadora Duncan and Gordon Craig*. New York: Random House, 1961. (A, G) The definitive study of what may have been the most serious love affair of Duncan's life.

Stokes, Sewell. *Isadora Duncan, An Intimate Portrait*. London: Brentano's, 1923. (G) An uncritical biography that appeared within a year of her death.

Terry, Walter. *Isadora Duncan, An Intimate Portrait*. New York: Dodd, Mead, 1964. (A, G, Y) An adequate introduction to Duncan's life and contribution to dance.

Overview and Evaluation of Primary Sources

The primary sources for studying the life of Isadora Duncan are voluminous and, in most instances, readily available. The most significant archival collections are the Craig-Duncan, Irma Duncan Rogers, and Dance Collections at the Library for the Performing Arts at Lincoln Center (a New York Public Library), the Isadora Duncan file at the Bibliotèque of Conservatoure de Musique in Paris, the Gordon Craig Collection at the Bibliotèque Nationale in Paris, and the Archive Internationale de la Danse at the Bibliotèque de l'Opera in Paris (A). Duncan's autobiography *My Life* (New York: Horace Liveright, 1927; A, G) provides valuable insights into her reflective state of mind during the year prior to her death and defends her innovations in dance. Many of Duncan's students and contemporaries have provided valuable memoirs about Duncan's influence on them and the importance of her achievements in the history of dance and feminism. Among the most notable are Irma Duncan Rogers's *Isadora Duncan: Pioneer in the Art of the Dance* (New York: New York Public Library, 1958; A, G), *Duncan Dancer: An Autobiography* (Middletown, CT: Wesleyan University Press, 1966; A, G), and *The Technique of Isadora Duncan* (Brooklyn, NY: Dance Horizons, 1970; A, G). Irma Duncan and Allan Ross Macdougall collaborated to produce *Isadora Duncan's Russian Days and Her Last Years in France* (New York: Covici-Friede, 1929: A, G). Other generally sympathetic memoirs have been produced by Mary Desti (*The Untold Story: The Life of Isadora Duncan 1921-1927*. New York: Horace Liveright, 1929; A, G), Loie Fuller (*Fifteen Years of A Dancer's Life*. London: H. Jenkins, 1963; A, G), and Constantin Stanislawsky (*My Life in Art*. Translated by J. J. Robbins. Moscow: n.p., 1926; A, G).

Fiction and Adaptations

The volatile life of Isadora Duncan has commanded the interest of several playwrights and film producers. Several films have been produced by such sources as the Public Broadcasting System and the British Broadcasting Corporation. The best known film of Duncan's life is the 1969 British release *The Loves of Isadora*, directed by Karel Reisz and starring Vanessa Redgrave, James Fox, and Jason Robards. At nearly three hours, the film was considered too long by many and a shorter version, running just over two hours and titled simply *Isadora*, was later released.

The poet Richard Howard has written a work entitled "Poem Beginning with a Line by Isadora Duncan"; this poem, which appeared in the *Partisan Review*, opens with the following line: "The third time I resisted D'Annunzio was years after the War."

Other Sources
   McVay, Gordon. "Sergey Esenin in America." *Oxford Slavonic Papers* 6 (1973): 82-91. An important article that focuses on the experiences of Duncan and Esenin in the U.S.

   Walkowitz, Abraham. *Isadora Duncan in Her Dances.* Girard, Kansas: Haldeman-Julius, 1950. This work consists of a limited commentary along with Walkowitz's photographs of Duncan dancing.

William T. Walker
Philadelphia College of Pharmacy and Science

DUKE ELLINGTON
1899-1974

Chronology

Born Edward Kennedy Ellington on April 29, 1899, in Washington, D.C., the older of two children of James Edward Ellington, butler to the family of a socially prominent physician and later a blueprint maker to the Department of the Navy, and Daisy Kennedy Ellington, daughter of a Washington police captain; *1899-1917* grows up in a supportive environment heavily imbued with the values of Washington's aspiring African-American middle class; wins an art scholarship to attend New York's Pratt Institute, but fails to graduate on time from Armstrong Technical High School; *1914-1918* becomes interested in popular music, principally ragtime, although he refuses his mother's offer of formal training, preferring instead to expand his knowledge of piano technique by hanging around Washington poolrooms and cabarets and mixing with other musicians; *1918* marries Edna Thompson, a neighbor and former schoolmate; *1918-1926* gains experience playing in Washington dance clubs, while also managing several bands and painting signs; moves to New York's Harlem as a member of the Washingtonians, a group that begins to attract attention with a long engagement at the Kentucky Club in midtown; *1927-1935* the Washingtonians become known as Duke Ellington and His Orchestra, gain national recognition with nightly radio broadcasts from the Cotton Club, develop their own distinctive "jungle" style, and introduce major hits like "Creole Love Call" and "Mood Indigo"; *1935-1945* as swing becomes the dominant musical style, reaches his creative peak as a composer and his orchestra reigns as one of the most popular big bands in the country; *1945-1955* popularity declines as some of his best side men depart and bebop and a new emphasis on vocalists replace the big bands of the swing era; *1956-1974* Ellington partially reconstructs his swing-era orchestra, achieves a sensational success at the Newport Jazz Festival, and enjoys a new surge in popularity, especially in a series of foreign tours, playing a mixture of music from the earlier era and the extended concert pieces he continued to write; *1974* dies on May 24 from lung cancer in New York City.

Activities of Historical Significance

Ellington was one of the major figures in the development of jazz as a musical form. Although self-taught (like most of his side men), and limited in his ability to read music, he developed a unique style for what was essentially a dance band and insisted on writing most of his own music, rather than only playing the popular tunes of the day. His music first became distinctive when he assembled a group of brass players adept at the use of plunger mutes and other special effects and used them as a contrast to the smoother sounds of the saxophones and clarinets. He also employed dissonant harmonies, unexpected key changes, and unusual instruments like the violin and baritone and soprano saxophones, achieving a broader tonal palette than any other contemporary band.

In his early years Ellington relied heavily on the ability of his side men to improvise around a simple melody. As he became more confident, however, he increasingly experimented with unusual combinations of sounds, unconventional forms, and new devices to showcase the talents of his musicians while imposing a characteristic unity on each piece of music. Ellington drew freely on the ideas of each of his players, yet the end product was always recognizably his own. His output of jazz classics was extraordinary: "Caravan," "Perdido," "Take the A Train," "Satin Doll," "Don't Get Around Much Any More," "I Got It Bad (and That Ain't Good)," "I'm Beginning to See the Light," "Sophisticated Lady," and dozens more.

In 1943 his orchestra performed a suite called *Black, Brown, and Beige* at Carnegie Hall. Although unenthusiastically received by both jazz and classical critics, it established that Ellington was not merely a band leader and songwriter, but a composer. The Ellington Orchestra continued to present annual concerts at Carnegie Hall for a decade, while Ellington himself concentrated on writing extended pieces, drawn mostly from African and African American experience. In his last years he also wrote three "sacred concerts," the third of which was premiered in Westminster Abbey in 1973. Showered with countless awards and honorary degrees after 1956, Duke Ellington was recognized in his own lifetime as one of the most important composers the U.S. has yet produced.

Overview of Biographical Sources

Ellington became an interesting subject for biographers in his own lifetime and has remained so since his death. He attracted attention partly because he was one of the few African American musicians to attract a large white audience long before the civil rights movement and partly because of his orchestra's extraordinary longevity, which extended over nearly half a century. Jazz critic Barry Ulanov's *Duke Ellington* (1946) was the first biography, but it portrayed the orchestra's side men more sharply than it did Ellington himself. In this respect, Ulanov established a pattern that was hard to break. Ellington was extremely protective of his family's privacy and even of his role as leader of his orchestra. More recent biographies have benefited from the collections of oral history interviews with many of Ellington's musicians and business associates. The best are by English jazz writer Derek Jewell, *A*

Portrait of Duke Ellington (1977), and by American jazz historian James L. Collier, *Duke Ellington* (1987).

Evaluation of Principal Biographical Sources

Barclay, Pamela. *Duke Ellington: Ambassador of Music.* Mankato, MN: Creative Education, 1974. (Y) This slim volume provides a brief summary of Ellington's life and achievements, enhanced by some very good color drawings, for use with primary-grade children.

Collier, James Lincoln. *Duke Ellington.* New York: Oxford University Press, 1987. (A, G) The best and most recent biography of Ellington devotes particular attention to his formative years and tries to define and evaluate his creative methods. Collier presents the views of other writers as well as his own, thereby encouraging the reader to draw his or her own conclusions. This book is carefully researched and well-written.

Gammond, Peter, ed. *Duke Ellington: His Life and Music.* London: Phoenix House, 1958. (A, G) This collection of highly complimentary essays by English critics is especially interesting in that the conclusions of the authors are still shared by jazz historians today.

George, Don. *Sweet Man: The Real Life of Duke Ellington.* New York: G. P. Putnam's Sons, 1982. (A, G) George, who worked occasionally as a lyricist for the orchestra, emphasizes the private life of Ellington and his associates. His book is entirely anecdotal, and there are some obvious errors of fact in matters that can be easily verified. It is doubtful that George knew as much about Ellington as he claimed.

Gutman, Bill. *Duke: The Musical Life of Duke Ellington.* New York: Random House, 1977. (Y) Geared toward adolescent readers, this book emphasizes Ellington's racial pride, overlooks his unstable family life, and judiciously and accurately explains what made his music so good.

Jewell, Derek. *Duke: A Portrait of Duke Ellington.* New York: W. W. Norton, 1977. (A, G) Jewell presents an English perspective on Ellington's role in jazz history. Less scholarly than Collier's later book, it is nevertheless a reliable account of Ellington's life and work. Jewell devotes particular attention to the post-World War II period.

Lambert, G. E. *Duke Ellington.* New York: A. S. Barnes, 1961. (G) This extended essay, largely based on previously published secondary sources, constituted one volume in a now outdated series called "Kings of Jazz."

McCarthy, Albert. *Big Band Jazz.* New York: G. P. Putnam's Sons, 1974. (G) A large, well-illustrated volume on the early roots, evolution, triumph, and ultimate decline of big-band music. McCarthy considers Ellington's role at appropriate points throughout his narrative, then devotes a chapter entirely to the Orchestra, fittingly calling it "The Apex of the Big Band Tradition."

Montgomery, Elizabeth Rider. *Duke Ellington: King of Jazz.* Champaign, Illinois: Garrard, 1972. (Y) This book was designed for use with primary-school children. Montgomery offers Ellington as a role model (he was that rarity in the world of jazz who never tried drugs), devoting most of her attention to his childhood years and the drive that led to success in the world of jazz.

Simon, George T. *The Big Bands.* New York: Macmillan, 1967. (G) This general historical account contains a brief but perceptive chapter on Ellington, complete with a few well-chosen photographs.

Townsend, Irving. "Ellington in Private." *Atlantic Monthly* 235 (May 1975): 78-83. (A, G) Townsend, an executive with Columbia Records, structured this brief memoir around the recording session for *A Drum Is a Woman,* one of Ellington's later extended pieces.

Ulanov, Barry. *Duke Ellington.* New York: Creative Age Press, 1946. (A, G) Writing as the orchestra's most popular and creative period was drawing to a close, Ulanov emphasized the struggles Ellington and his players endured to gain acceptance from white audiences in the Jim Crow era. The book offers excellent portraits of individual musicians but is frustratingly hazy about Ellington's role as leader and how he created a consistently distinctive sound. Contains some factual errors and is marred by invented dialogue.

Overview and Evaluation of Primary Sources

The most important source for the study of Ellington and his music is the vast library of recordings by his orchestra and various small groups composed of players from the orchestra. Jerry Valburn, *The Directory of Duke Ellington's Recordings* (Hicksville, New York: Marlor Productions, 1986; A, G), and W. E. Timner, *Ellingtonia: The Recorded Music of Duke Ellington and His Sidemen* (3rd. ed. Metuchen, New Jersey: Institute for Jazz Studies and Scarecrow Press, 1988; A, G), are comprehensive guides to the original issues. Valburn's compendium includes recordings issued on more than eight hundred labels in thirty-five countries. Timner's huge volume is even more thorough, providing dates, locations, personnel, and even matrix numbers where they are known, not only for the full orchestra, but for the small groups of the late 1930s as well. Neither can be used as a guide to subsequent reissues or to what is currently in print. Fortunately, many classic Ellington LP's and LP collections are now reappearing on compact discs, although it is uncertain how long they will be available. For current issues one must consult the latest edition of *Phonolog Reports.*

Although Juan Tizol, Billy Strayhorn, and others prepared working arrangements for the Ellington Orchestra, these were generally little more than reminders to the players of the keys they were to play in or notations of the basic melodic lines. Even these fragmentary arrangements were never systematically maintained and most have been lost. As a result, the only Ellington scores that exist are those prepared by scholars from the recordings.

Similarly, there are virtually no original Ellington manuscripts. He was simply too protective of his personal privacy to preserve anything. Besides, he never really had a permanent home address, living most of his life out of a succession of hotel rooms. Two universities have tried to fill this gap by collecting oral history interviews of Ellington's side men, business associates, and personal friends. These collections may be found in the Duke Ellington Oral History Project at Yale University and the Institute for Jazz Studies at Rutgers University.

English jazz writer Stanley Dance is substantially responsible for three published volumes that provide some insight into the workings of the Ellington Orchestra in its later years. First, he wrote *The World of Duke Ellington* (New York: Charles Scribner's Sons, 1970; **A, G**), based on a series of interviews he conducted with Ellington and most of the side men who were still around. Dance was a close friend who often provided liner notes for Ellington's LP recordings. Much of this book is very interesting, but as Ellington himself noted in the foreword, "I am sure he has not revealed more than he ought!"

Dance next pulled together Ellington's recollections of his career and notes about his players, mostly written on odd scraps of paper, into an autobiography of sorts: Edward Kennedy Ellington, *Music Is My Mistress* (Garden City, NY: Doubleday, 1973; **A, G, Y**). Anyone seriously interested in Ellington must consult this work, yet it is not very revealing. Like Dance's own book, it is best on the 1960s.

Dance then collaborated with Mercer Ellington, Duke's Juilliard-trained son who helped with arrangements and rehearsals for many years and took over the orchestra after Duke's death: Mercer Ellington and Stanley Dance, *Duke Ellington in Person: An Intimate Memoir* (Boston: Houghton Mifflin, 1978; **A, G**). This work is valuable for its insights into Ellington's personal life and values, the more so since its subject was so secretive.

One other memoir of interest is Barney Bigard, *With Louis and the Duke: The Autobiography of a Jazz Clarinetist* (New York: Oxford University Press, 1986; **A**). Transcribed from taped interviews conducted by Barry Martyn and apparently not edited at all, this oral history document of one of Ellington's best side men offers a candid evaluation of his music and of life on the road in the Big Band Era.

Fiction and Adaptations

Memories of the Duke. Produced by Gary Keys for Time-Life Films and released on videocassette in Tokyo by Nikkatsu Video Films (in English, with Japanese subtitles) in 1980. Filmed in the late 1960s, this eighty-one minute work combines footage of the premier of Ellington's *Mexican Suite* (1968), concerts featuring jazz standards such as "Take the A Train," "Satin Doll," "Creole Love Call," and "Mood Indigo," and interviews with clarinetist Russell Procope and trumpeter Cootie Williams, one of the early masters of the plunger mute.

Museums, Historical Landmarks, Societies

Duke Ellington Memorial Bridge (Washington, DC). Located on Calvert Street at Connecticut Avenue, this bridge is currently being refurbished to provide piped-in Ellington music for pedestrians. A plaque offers tribute to Ellington "the statesman."

Duke Ellington Home (Washington, DC). This privately owned home at 1212 T Street, N.W. is where Ellington lived before moving to New York City.

Other Sources

Hoder, André, and Gunther Schuller. "Edward Kennedy (Duke) Ellington." In *The New Grove Dictionary of American Music*, edited by H. Wiley Hitchcock and Stanley Sadie, 4 vols. London: Macmillan, 1986. Schuller's expansion and revision of Hoder's original article for the *New Grove Dictionary of Music and Musicians* (1980) is a useful and reliable reference source. The same jointly authored article appears, with different musical illustrations and an updated bibliography, in Barry Kernfeld, ed., *The New Grove Dictionary of Jazz* (2 vols. London: Macmillan, 1988).

Keith Ian Polakoff
California State University, Long Beach

ZELDA FITZGERALD
1900-1948

Chronology

Born Zelda Sayre on July 24, 1900, in Montgomery, Alabama, daughter of Anthony Dickinson Sayre, an Alabama state supreme court judge, and Minnie B. Machen Sayre; *1900-1918* grows up in Montgomery, Alabama; *1918* graduates from Sidney Lanier High School in Montgomery; meets F. Scott Fitzgerald; *April 3, 1920* marries F. Scott Fitzgerald in New York; *1921-1929* works with F. Scott Fitzgerald and accompanies him on travels to England, France, Italy, and the Holy Land; moves frequently with her husband in the U.S., living in New York, Connecticut, Minnesota, Delaware, Maryland, and California; publishes commentary articles and fiction in the *Saturday Evening Post*, *Metropolitan*, and *Scribner's Magazine*; *1930* suffers serious mental breakdown; *1932* writes *Save Me the Waltz*; *1933* writes play "Scandalabra"; *1934-1948* institutionalized for mental problems; *March 10, 1948* dies in a fire at Highland Hospital in Asheville, North Carolina; buried in Rockville, Maryland.

Activities of Historical Significance

Many students of early twentieth-century American cultural history have viewed Fitzgerald as the flamboyant, disturbed, and not very gifted wife of F. Scott Fitzgerald. Her efforts at serious writing were more generously received than her ballet performances, although she was most appreciated during her lifetime for her artwork. Critics acclaimed her paintings when they were exhibited at Cary Ross's studio in New York City and in Paris.

More recently, Fitzgerald has been recognized as one of several prominent feminists of the 1920s. Her diary and letters were used by her husband as resources for *This Side of Paradise* (1920) and *The Beautiful and Damned* (1922). Scott and Zelda Fitzgerald collaborated on a number of pieces for *The Saturday Evening Post* ("The Millionaire's Girl") and *Esquire* ("Show Mr. and Mrs. F to Number —"). Her novel *Save Me the Waltz* (1932) was dominated by a feminist theme of liberation and the need for equal opportunity; although it has been criticized for problems of organization and style, *Save Me the Waltz* remains a significant contribution to American cultural history. Another novel, *Caesar's Things*, was never completed. Her play "Scandalabra" was produced unsuccessfully in Baltimore in 1933 and has not been revived.

Fitzgerald was confined to various mental institutions for the last fifteen years of her life, this period broken only by occasional visits with her husband or trips to her family's home in Montgomery, Alabama. She died tragically in 1948 when a fire swept through the hospital where she was confined in Asheville, North Carolina.

Overview of Biographical Sources

Not until Nancy Milford published the exhaustive biography *Zelda* in 1971 did Fitzgerald's life become the focus of a major work. Milford's *Zelda*, reissued in 1983, stands as the premier biography. In it Fitzgerald emerges as a dynamic and talented individual whose insecurities were aggravated by a misplaced and unwarranted sense of greatness.

Previously, and many times since, Fitzgerald's life has been approached only in the context of the life and works of her husband. Sara Mayfield's *Exiles from Paradise: Zelda and Scott Fitzgerald* (1971) and James R. Mellow's *Invented Lives: F. Scott and Zelda Fitzgerald* (1984) focus on the marital relationship. The most reliable source on the life of F. Scott Fitzgerald is Matthew J. Bruccoli, *Some Sort of Epic Grandeur: The Life of F. Scott Fitzgerald* (1981).

Evaluation of Principal Biographical Sources

Bruccoli, Matthew J. *Some Sort of Epic Grandeur: The Life of F. Scott Fitzgerald.* New York: Harcourt Brace Jovanovich, 1981. (**A, G**) Although focused on Scott Fitzgerald, this definitive biography by America's preeminent Fitzgerald scholar provides valuable commentary on Zelda Fitzgerald's personality, her influence on her husband, and the significance of her work.

Clemens, Anna Valine. "Zelda Fitzgerald: An Unromantic Revision." *Dalhousie Review* 62, 2 (1982): 196-211. (**A**) An important essay in which the author examines the literature on Zelda Fitzgerald and suggests new approaches for studying this complex and frustrated individual.

Epstein, William H. "Milford's *Zelda* and the Poetics of the New Feminist Biography." *Georgia Review* 36, 2 (1982): 335-350. (**A, G**) A substantive essay that examines Nancy Milford's *Zelda* from the perspective of the feminist tradition and movement.

Going, William T. "Two Alabama Writers: Zelda Sayre Fitzgerald and Sara Haardt Mencken." *The Alabama Review* 23, 1 (1970): 3-29. (**A, G**) A well-written, sympathetic, and provocative comparative essay on the tragic lives of two Alabama women writers who married dominant contributors to American letters during the first half of the twentieth century—F. Scott Fitzgerald and H. L. Mencken.

Halliday, E. M. "Scott and Zelda." *American Heritage* 5, 2 (1974); 3-18. (G, Y) An article that provides an introduction to the relationship and careers of Scott and Zelda Fitzgerald. Numerous photographs accompany the text.

Heath, Mary. "Marriages: Zelda and Scott, Eleanor and Franklin." *The Massachusetts Review* 13, 1-2 (1972): 281-288. (A, G) This comparative essay, written from a feminist perspective, examines the impact of dominant males on the lives of their creative and intelligent wives.

Mayfield, Sara. *Exiles from Paradise: Zelda and Scott Fitzgerald.* New York: Delacorte Press, 1971. (A, G) An important biographical study of Zelda and Scott Fitzgerald that provides valuable insights into the psychological forces underlying their relationship and public lives.

Mellow, James R. *Invented Lives: F. Scott and Zelda Fitzgerald.* Boston: Houghton Mifflin, 1984. (A, G) Mellow presents Zelda Fitzgerald as a victim of a complex and unstable mentality that drifted between reality and fantasy. The nature of her lifestyle and marriage aggravated her condition.

Milford, Nancy. *Zelda.* New York: Harper and Row, 1971. (A, G, Y) Milford's *Zelda* is the most comprehensive and reliable biography of Fitzgerald written to date. Although weak in certain areas—such as commentary on textual issues—this book provides the most comprehensive study of her life.

Smith, Scottie Fitzgerald. "The Maryland Ancestors of Zelda Sayre Fitzgerald." *Maryland Historical Magazine* 78, 3 (Fall 1983): 217-228. (A, G, Y) Written by the Fitzgeralds' daughter, this is a scholarly account of Zelda's ancestry that provides insights into the conditions into which she was born.

Overview and Evaluation of Primary Sources
Zelda Fitzgerald has provided an extensive written legacy, including a novel, a play, numerous short stories, and articles, many of which have been reprinted or collected. *Save Me the Waltz* (New York: Scribner's, 1932; A, G) was Zelda Fitzgerald's major literary effort. While this work is dated, it offers insights into her personality, her relationship with Scott, and her impact on feminist history. "Scandalabra" (Bloomfield Hills, MI: Bruccoli Clark, 1980; A, G) is Fitzgerald's unsuccessful play. *Bits of Paradise* (London: Bodley Head, 1973; A, G, Y), edited by Fitzgerald scholar Matthew Bruccoli, collects all ten of Zelda Fitzgerald pieces of short fiction. These include "Our Own Movie Queen," "The Original Follies Girl," "The Southern Girl," "The Girl the Prince Liked," "The Girl with Talent," "A Millionaire Girl," "Poor Working Girl," "Miss Ella," "The Continental Angle," and "A Couple of

Nuts." A wide range of articles by Fitzgerald appeared in *Metropolitan Magazine, McCall's, Harper's Bazaar, College Humor,* and *Esquire.*

Additional primary materials are available in *The Romantic Egotists: Scott and Zelda Fitzgerald* (New York: Scribner's, 1974; A, G), edited by Matthew Bruccoli, Scottie Fitzgerald Smith, and Joan P. Kerr. This volume provides valuable reprints of notes, correspondence, and memoirs. John Kuehl and Jackson R. Bryer have edited *Dear Scott/Dear Max* (New York; Scribner's, 1971; A, G), which collects the correspondence between editor Maxwell Perkins of Scribner's and F. Scott Fitzgerald; comments on Zelda's writing and health emerge in this correspondence.

Perceptive comments on Zelda Fitzgerald are recorded in Edmund Wilson's notebooks and diaries, *The Twenties,* edited by Leon Edel (New York: Farrar, Straus and Giroux, 1975; A, G) and *The Thirties,* edited by Leon Edel (New York: Farrar, Straus and Giroux, 1980; A, G). Wilson, the dominant literary critic for five decades in American culture, attended Princeton with F. Scott Fitzgerald and maintained contact with Scott and Zelda during the 1920s and 1930s.

Other Sources

A range of articles on the Fitzgeralds, some scholarly and some simply eccentric, may be found in the *Fitzgerald Newsletter,* published from 1958 to 1968 (Washington: NCR Microcard Books, 1969); and the *Fitzgerald/Hemingway Annual* (Washington: NCR Microcard Books, 1969-1973; Englewood, Colorado: Information Handling Services, 1974, 1976; Gale Research, 1977-1979).

William T. Walker
Philadelphia College of Pharmacy and Science

DIAN FOSSEY
1932-1985

Chronology

Born Dian Fossey on January 16, 1932 in San Francisco to George Fossey, an insurance salesman, and Kitty Fossey; *1938* her parents divorce; *1939* her mother remarries Richard Price, a building contractor, who adopts Dian; *1950* enrolls at the University of California at Davis as a pre-veterinary student but fails her second year and transfers to San Jose State; *1954* graduates from San Jose State with a degree in occupational therapy; *1955* accepts a position with the Korsair Children's Hospital in Louisville, Kentucky; *1963* leaves for Africa on safari on September 23, where she meets Louis Leakey and sees the mountain gorillas for the first time; *1966* Louis Leakey comes to Louisville in March and asks her to embark on a long-term study of the mountain gorillas in the Congo, and she leaves for Africa on December 15; *1967* forced to abandon her first camp in the Congo owing to the political situation; imprisoned by Congolese soldiers for several weeks before setting up a new camp at "Karisoke" in the Parc des Volcans in Rwanda on September 24; *1970* a gorilla named "Peanuts" touches her in the course of a routine observation on January 4, marking the first voluntary contact between a human and a mountain gorilla; *1976* receives her Ph.D. from Darwin College, Cambridge University, in May and attends a symposium with Leakey's other "Ape Ladies"; *1977* poachers kill Dian's favorite gorilla, Digit, on December 31, and another favorite, Uncle Bert, in July 1978; *1980-1983* spends several years in the U.S, teaching at Cornell and writing *Gorillas in the Mist*; *1981* helps to lead a joint symposium with the "Ape Ladies"; *1983* *Gorillas in the Mist* is published in the U.S; *June 1985* attends the Morris Animal Foundation annual meeting to accept an award and appears on the Johnny Carson Show to publicize the gorillas' plight; *October 1985* someone tries to poison her pet pigeons and she finds a wooden puff adder, a voodoo token, on her steps on October 24; *December 3, 1985* the secretary-general of immigration renews her passport for two years instead of the normal two months; *December 27, 1985* Fossey is found murdered in her cabin and is buried three days later in the gorilla graveyard at Karisoke.

Activities of Historical Significance

Dian Fossey was one of Louis Leakey's "Ape Ladies," the three women whom he encouraged to research the behavior of chimpanzees, gorillas, and orangutans in order to learn about man's early origins from the social structures and behavior of these advanced primates. For the first few years of her study, Fossey was known to Americans for her first two articles in the *National Geographic* and the documentary film shot by Bob Campbell that captured the moment that the young male gorilla Peanuts reached out to touch her hand. With the killings of two of her favorite gorillas in 1977 and 1978 Fossey turned her back on field research and concentrated on saving the few remaining mountain gorillas from poachers. It was then that she became increasingly suspicious of people and clashed numerous times with visiting students and scientists, Rwandan officials, poachers, and her native workers. Her intransigent stand that the gorillas should be left alone, unmolested by humans, and that their range should be extended, not diminished by Rwandan farmers anxious for land, overlooked the reality that Rwanda was a desperately poor country with little or no available land, and that either the Parc des Volcans should encourage the influx of foreign tourists and their dollars into the economy or else the land would be seized by the desperately hungry people. Park officials viewed Fossey as an officious troublemaker with little sensitivity to the problems of the people, and Fossey did indeed prefer the company of the gorillas to that of most humans. When the news spread that she had received a visa to extend her stay in Rwanda for two additional years, with a further promise that she could stay as long as she wanted, many Africans and western conservationists foresaw a long and troublesome conflict with her. In hindsight, the timing of her murder three and a half weeks later is no surprise.

Fossey accomplished a great deal in her early fieldwork on the social structures and behavior of gorillas. She was undeniably successful in bringing the world's attention to their endangered status and in raising funds for patrols to cut down poachers' traps. Her book *Gorillas in the Mist* was a popular success and brought her and her beloved beasts to the attention of a much wider audience. Ironically, the publicity surrounding her murder has probably ensured the survival of the gorillas for some time to come; far more tourists than ever before want to come and see where Dian Fossey lived and worked and see the animals she loved. The release of the critically acclaimed and popular movie of the same title as her book three years after her death has ensured her place in American popular culture.

Overview of Biographical Sources
   There are only two biographies of Dian Fossey and both have merit. The earliest, by well-known nature writer Farley Mowat, is the richer and more satisfying. Mowat understood and sympathized with Fossey, but at the same time understood that much of what she said and did was unacceptable to many people and that she placed a higher premium on the welfare of the gorillas than on that of humans. He also had extensive access to her diaries and correspondence, and he quotes from them to good effect. Harold Hayes's

book is more recent but undoubtedly suffered from his premature death before the manuscript was finished. He talked to more people than Mowat and was able to assemble a slightly different picture of Fossey, but his understanding of her was not as complete and textured.

Evaluation of Principal Biographical Sources

Hayes, Harold T. P. *The Dark Romance of Dian Fossey*. New York: Simon and Schuster, 1990. **(G)** This is the more recent of the two biographies and benefits from extensive interviews with Fossey friends, enemies, and associates, but suffers from a lack of interviews with Africans and does not create a clear picture of the whole woman.

Mowat, Farley. *Woman in the Mists*. New York: Warner Books, 1987. **(G)** Mowat's work is a joy to read, and his extensive use of Fossey's own letters and journals, as well as interviews with others, give a complete and rounded picture of this troubled woman.

Overview and Evaluation of Primary Sources

Mowat's biography of Fossey gives some hint as to the riches that await scholars in her personal collection of papers; literally thousands of pages of notes and observations of the gorillas are there along with her more personal manuscripts. At last word, the papers were boxed and placed in storage in Ithaca, New York; scholars hope that Fossey's mother and stepfather will donate them to Cornell or some other university.

Her own book, *Gorillas in the Mist* (Boston: Houghton Mifflin, 1983; **G**) and three articles for *National Geographic* magazine reflect her preference for gorilla over human companionship. Her book in particular reveals her scorn for most other researchers in the field, as well as Africans in general, and her preoccupation with keeping the gorillas isolated from all human contact except her own. The articles published in *National Geographic* are: "Making Friends with Mountain Gorillas," *National Geographic* 137 (January 1970): 48-67, her first article on her work with the gorillas; "More Years with the Mountain Gorillas," *National Geographic* 140 (October 1971): 574-585, which describes her early fieldwork; and "The Imperiled Mountain Gorillas," *National Geographic* 159 (April 1981): 501-523, revealing Fossey's rage after the killings of Digit and Uncle Bert. These writings are essential for those who wish to understand Fossey.

Fiction and Adaptations

Sigourney Weaver was an inspired choice to play Fossey in the movie adaptation of her book, *Gorillas in the Mist,* which also relied heavily on Mowat's biography. Released in 1988, the film starred Australian actor Bryan Brown as the respected wildlife photographer Bob Campbell, who captured much of Fossey's early interaction with the gorillas on film. The movie was filmed on location in Africa, and the fine performances of the actors make it a film worth watching, although its depiction of Fossey and her relationship with Campbell is romanticized.

Museums, Historical Landmarks, Societies

Karisoke Centre for Mountain Gorilla Research (Parc National des Volcans, Rwanda). This portion of the Virunga chain of volcanic mountains in central Africa lies very near the country's borders with Zaire and Uganda. It was here that Fossey accomplished all her research and was murdered. Her camp still exists at "Karisoke," the high mountain meadow in the saddle between two mountains, and international scholars and students still gather there for research.

Other Sources

Kevles, Bettyann. *Watching the Wild Apes: The Primate Studies of Goodall, Fossey, and Galdikas.* New York: E. P. Dutton, 1976. A good basic introduction to what Fossey was trying to do and the activities of Leakey's other "Ape Ladies."

Shoumatoff, Alex. "The Woman Who Loved Gorillas." In *African Madness.* New York: Random House, 1989. This essay first appeared in *Vanity Fair* and is an interesting meditation on Fossey and her relationship with humans.

Jean V. Berlin
Correspondence of William T. Sherman

JESSIE BENTON FRÉMONT
1824-1902

Chronology

Born Jessie Anne Benton on May 31, 1824 at "Cherry Grove," the vast plantation of her maternal grandparents in the Blue Ridge Mountains, near Lexington, Virginia; daughter of Thomas Hart Benton and Elizabeth McDowell Benton; *1838-1841* attends Miss English's Select Academy in Washington, D.C.; *1841* marries John Charles Frémont, a lieutenant in the Topographical Corps on October 19 in a Catholic ceremony in Washington, D.C.; *1842* her husband returns from his important expedition to the West and her first child Elizabeth is born in Washington, D.C.; *1842-1843* works daily on the report of her husband's journey to Oregon and Northern California; *1843* suppresses official correspondence that endangers her husband's second expedition, and then, after the expedition is safely underway, writes to the colonel who had sent the order, explaining what she had done; *1844-1845* husband and wife collaborate on the report of Frémont's second expedition; *1848* Frémont is court-martialled for action taken in California and Jessie appeals in person to President Polk; Polk is evasive and Frémont resigns from the army; *1850* Jessie watches from the gallery of the Capitol as Frémont takes his seat as California's first senator; *1851* her home in San Francisco burns to the ground; *1852-1853* tours England and France with her husband; *1855-1856* encourages her husband to take a firm stand against slavery and to accept the nascent Republican party's nomination for the presidency; *1857* refuses her father's invitation to visit a resort in Virginia because she fears hostility for her anti-slavery views; instead sails for France while Frémont travels to California to look after his vast gold-rich Mariposas estate; *1858* while she is in transit to join her husband in California, Thomas Hart Benton dies; *1861* Frémont, given command of the Department of the West at St. Louis, proclaims the emancipation of all slaves owned by Missouri rebels, whereupon President Lincoln relieves him of his command; in September, she travels by train from St. Louis to Washington, D.C. to protest her husband's removal, but her interview with President Lincoln is unsatisfactory; *1863* publication of her book, *The Story of the Guard: A Chronicle of the War*, about the heroic charge made at Springfield, Missouri by her husband's Zagonyi Guard, which had been criticized as un-American for its Hungarian membership; *1865* refuses to sign a petition for women's rights given to her by Elizabeth Cady Stanton; the Frémonts purchase a gray stone mansion overlooking the Hudson River near Tarrytown, New York and call their estate "Pocaho"; *1868* attends the unveiling of a statue of her father Thomas Hart Benton in St. Louis; *1878* her husband is appointed governor of the Arizona Territory in the midst of a mining boom; teaches informal history classes at the public high school in Prescott, Arizona; *1879* returns to New York to manage her husband's financial interests; *1881* her husband resigns as governor and returns to New York; *1884* the couple travel to Washington, D.C. to lobby in favor of a bill that would give Frémont a military pension for his services as an explorer and Civil War general, but without success; falls ill of rheumatism and nervous prostration; *1887* her husband's autobiography is published, containing a biographical sketch she had written about her father; publishes *Souvenirs of My Time,* a collection of magazine pieces; *1888-1889* acclimates herself to the balmy climate of southern California, where she will spend the rest of her life; her husband shuttles between California and New York; *1890* her husband dies on July 13 in New York City; his recently awarded pension ceases, leaving her in financial straits; Congress passes a bill granting her a widow's pension of $2,000 per year; *1891* moves into a spacious new home in Los Angeles built with money raised by a charitable committee of women; *1902* dies on December 27; her ashes are sent back to New York where they are interred with the remains of her husband.

Activities of Historical Significance

Jessie Benton Frémont was in her time one of America's great popular heroines. Daughter of one of the West's most famous statesmen and wife of its most romanticized explorer, she possessed qualities of loyalty, tenacity, altruism and optimism that made her notable in her own right. As a speaker of French and Spanish, she was an ambassadress of good will in French-speaking St. Louis of the 1840s and in Hispanic San Francisco of the 1840s and 1850s. In California, her shining example as a Southern woman who abhorred slavery was claimed to have been a source of inspiration to state legislators in their decision not to endorse the "peculiar institution." During the Civil War she served on the Sanitary Commission (forerunner of the Red Cross) and afterwards helped to raise funds for the defeated South. Stoically she endured the alienation from her Southern relatives as they realized the strength of her political convictions; and although she detested Abraham Lincoln, her recommendation that her husband not split the Republican ticket of 1864 assured Lincoln's reelection.

It is difficult to assess Jessie's specific contributions because they were so often made through the medium of her husband. The flourish she added to his reports, for example, made them more attractive to the public than if he had written them alone; the first report is a classic in the genre of exploration literature and influenced countless Americans to move west. More than any other work of its kind, it made the West come alive and a generation of Americans were made to feel its allure.

Without Jessie's ambition, Frémont's abilities might never have become known to his admirers. So great was public awareness of her presence in the campaign of 1856 that the Republican ticket was perceived by many as more a matter of "Frémont and Jessie" than "Frémont and Dayton." American women were just beginning to emerge from the shell of conventional propriety, and Jessie embodied all that was best in the new womanhood, exemplifying personal dynamism and political savvy that nonetheless did not as yet conflict with devotion to home and family. The mother of five children, Jessie was also associated with the earliest official movements for child welfare and public education.

In addition to catalyzing the career of John C. Frémont, her natural exuberance also encouraged other young talents. In San Francisco she maintained a kind of literary salon frequented by Bret Harte, then a struggling, unknown writer. Even as she prepared to leave California in 1861, she found the time to secure from friends an office job for Harte so he could support himself while doing his writing. Many years later, also in California, she encouraged the youthful Gutzon Borglum, future sculptor of Mt. Rushmore. After inspecting his equestrian casts and drawings at his studio in 1889, Jessie predicted, "Here is one sculptor who will ride to fame on horseback!" When Borglum went east to work, Jessie furnished him with introductions to influential members of New York society, including Theodore Roosevelt, then police commissioner, who became Borglum's lifelong friend. For an exhibit of his work in Omaha, Jessie lent him his painting of her husband with these words, "He is well known enough to draw a crowd, even if, as yet, you are not."

Overview of Biographical Sources

Catherine Coffin Phillips's *Jessie Benton Frémont* (1935), privately but magnificently printed by John Henry Nash of San Francisco, was for many years the only book-length biography. It is still an invaluable source because Phillips was personally acquainted with her during the last six years of her life and has included copious anecdotes. Pamela Herr's *Jessie Benton Frémont* (1987) supersedes Phillips's uncritical biography in the modernity of its idiom and interpretation and the inclusion of new source material that has come to light in the last half century.

Several historians have undertaken dual biographies of the Frémonts. Allan Nevins wrote *Frémont, The West's Greatest Adventurer, Being a Biography From Certain Hitherto Unpublished Sources of General John C. Frémont Together with his Wife Jessie Benton Frémont and Some Account of the Period of Expansion which Found a Brilliant Leader in the Pathfinder* (1928), but his final critical revision of the work a quarter of a century later dropped the goal of duality from the title and became *Frémont: Pathmarker of the West* (1955).

Another dual biography, *The Famous Frémonts and Their America* (1948; rev. 1961) by Alice Eyre was written for the 1949 California Centennial year and naturally emphasizes the California experiences of the famous couple.

Evaluation of Principal Biographical Sources

Herr, Pamela. *Jessie Benton Frémont*. New York: Franklin Watts, 1987. (G) Making use of valuable new material that takes Jessie out from the shadows of her famous father and husband, this biography nonetheless leaves unresolved some of the contradictions of her life and behavior. Lamentably the book contains no supporting photographs, and its index is inadequate to its aspirations of definitive biography.

Morrison, Dorothy Nafus. *Under a Strong Wind: The Adventures of Jessie Benton Frémont*. New York: Atheneum, 1983. (Y) Written for young adults, this book is lavishly illustrated with prints and photographs, some of which are reproduced from the Phillips biography. Contains a thorough bibliography.

Phillips, Catherine Coffin. *Jesse Benton Frémont: A Woman Who Made History*. San Francisco: John Henry Nash, 1935. (G) Although this biography is now dated, it remains unsurpassed for the minute detail of its bibliography of Jessie Frémont's magazine articles and for its abundant photographic reproductions.

Randall, Ruth Painter. *I Jessie*. Boston: Little, Brown, 1963. (Y) One of a series by the author providing a close-up view for young adults of Civil War-era heroines.

Wagoner, Jean Brown. *Jessie Frémont: Girl of Capitol Hill*. Indianapolis: Bobbs, Merrill, 1956; 1960. (Y) Written for very young children, this book stresses Jessie's migratory childhood in St. Louis, Washington, D.C., and her grandparents' plantation in Virginia, and ends in 1850 when her husband is sworn in as senator from the new state of California.

Overview and Evaluation of Primary Sources

By 1883 Jessie was busy writing "fireside" sketches of various dignitaries she had known (such as General Grant and Dolly Madison) for the popular children's magazine *Wide Awake*. These were later assembled into book form as *Souvenirs of My Time* (Boston: D. Lothrop, 1887; G, Y). She characterized these sketches as "nursery pudding without hurtful ingredients of complete facts." In addition to sketches, she wrote juvenile fiction, often about animals, and fairy tales. A series of articles for *Wide Awake* about her experiences at

Bear Valley, California were published as *Far West Sketches* (Boston: D. Lothrop, 1890; **G, Y**).

In addition, she wrote "A Year of American Travel" (vols. 55-56, *Harper's Magazine*, 1878), reprinted with an introduction by Patrice Manahan (San Francisco: Book Club of California, 1960; **G**) and a reminiscence of the California gold-rush experience that was not published in book form until 1970 as *Mother Lode Narrative*, edited and annotated by Shirley Sargent (Ashland, OR: Lewis Osborne, 1970; **G**).

Her unpublished memoirs, written with some assistance from her son Frank and intended to be the sequel to her husband's *Memoirs of My Life, A Retrospect of Fifty Years* (Chicago: Belford, Clark, 1887; **G**), are located in manuscript form at the University of California at Berkeley, as is a notebook kept by her daughter Elizabeth Benton Frémont and her own scrapbook of clippings. As Allan Nevins observed, it is regrettable that these memoirs are not more complete and that the first volume of the published *Memoirs* did not meet with a sufficient sale to merit publication of the second.

The more than one hundred letters from Jessie to Elizabeth Blair Lee are housed at Princeton University, and some of her letters to her protégé Nellie Haskell Browne are found among the Frémont papers at the Bancroft Library at Berkeley. Jessie's sensitive biographical sketch of her father serves as a prologue to John C. Frémont's above cited *Memoirs of My Life*. Her daughter's book *Recollections of Elizabeth Benton Frémont*, compiled by I. A. Martin (New York: F. H. Hitchcock, 1912; **G**) offers many colorful insights into her mother's life and is especially revealing about the years spent in California and Arizona.

Fiction and Adaptations

In 1944 Irving Stone wrote a bio-historical novel, *Immortal Wife: The Biographical Novel of Jessie Benton Frémont*, which no less a critic than Frémont biographer Allan Nevins called a fine blend of biography and fiction. It was immensely popular and its sales broke the selling record for Doubleday. Stone appended a meticulous four-page bibliography to his novel, which concludes with the death of John C. Frémont in 1890. In 1984 David Nevin wrote a popular novel about the Frémonts, *Dream West*, published by G. P. Putnam's Sons. The novel was adapted rather unsuccessfully to the screen by CBS two years later as a seven-hour mini-series. Alice Krige played Jessie and Richard Chamberlain starred as John C. Frémont.

Museums, Historical Landmarks, Societies

Frémont House (Prescott, AZ). The Frémonts lived in this house, now part of the Sharlott Hall Museum, during his first year as territorial governor.

Frémont Tomb (Piermont-on-the-Hudson, NY). Near the brink of a bluff looking out over the broad Tappan Zee and their old home, "Pocaho," is the tomb of John and Jessie Frémont. The monument, erected by the state of New York, is granite with a bronze sword and medallion of John C. Frémont.

Southwest Museum (Los Angeles, CA). Has the oil portrait of Jessie Benton Frémont by Thomas Buchanan Read.

Other Sources
Dobson, Eleanor Robinette. "Jessie Benton Frémont." In *The Dictionary of American Biography*, edited by Allen Johnson. 1927. Reprint. New York: Scribner's, 1964. A noteworthy encyclopedia treatment.

Eyre, Alice. *The Famous Frémonts and Their America.* 2d ed. Boston: Christopher Publishing House, 1961. A dual biography that relates their lives primarily to the history of California.

Nevins, Allan. *Frémont, the West's Greatest Adventurer, Being a Biography From Certain Hitherto Unpublished Sources of General John C. Frémont Together with his Wife Jessie Benton Frémont and Some Account of the Period of Expansion Which Found a Brilliant Leader in the Pathfinder.* New York: Harper & Brothers, 1928. Although his final critical revision (1955) dropped Jessie from the title, this work by the premier Frémont scholar is invaluable to the understanding of Jessie's life.

Spence, Mary Lee. "Frémont, Jessie (Anne) Benton." In *The Reader's Encyclopedia of the American West*, edited by Howard R. Lamar. New York: Thomas Y. Crowell, 1977. A noteworthy encyclopedia treatment by the co-editor of the critical edition of *The Expeditions of John Charles Frémont*, 3 vols. (Urbana: University of Illinois Press, 1970-1984).

Jack Shreve
Allegany Community College

ISABELLA STEWART GARDNER
1840-1924

Chronology

Born Isabella ("Belle") Stewart on April 14, 1840, in New York City, the first of five children of David Stewart, a wealthy industrialist and importer, and Adelia Smith Stewart; her father is a second-generation American and a descendant of the twelfth-century Scottish house of Robert Bruce and Mary Stuart, and her mother is a descendant of Richard Smith, an English Puritan who settled in Boston in 1650; *1840-1856* grows up in New York City, spending summers on Long Island; educated in private schools for girls; learns French and takes dancing and drawing lessons; a brother and sister die in childhood; *1856* taken to Europe by parents; attends French finishing school in Paris; *1857* visits Italy, returns to New York City; *1860* marries John Lowell Gardner III, or "Jackie"; will become universally known as "Mrs. Jack"; *1865* following death of son, suffers from illness and depression; *1867* regains health and spirit in Europe, experiencing first keen interest in architectural design; *1868* returns to Boston and begins purchasing artwork to be included later in her museum; *1874* returns to Europe and becomes patron of young writers and musicians; begins famous jewel collection; *1875* returns to Boston and assumes care of three orphaned nephews; *1878* attends art history lectures at Harvard; *1879-1882* enlarges home to contain growing art collection; *1883-1884* travels around the world, returning via Venice and staying in a palazzo on the Grand Canal that will be her home for many succeeding summer visits; *1885* sponsors musicians who will form Boston Symphony Orchestra; *1887* sponsors European tour of young Bernard Berenson, an art historian who will become her chief advisor; *1888-1890* continues to purchase European and Oriental art; *1891* receives inheritance at father's death and accelerates purchases of fine art; *1893* attends World's Columbian Exposition in Chicago; *1894-1895* continues art purchases; *1896* begins plans for a museum to house collection; *1898* her husband dies, leaving her in complete control of a large fortune; *1899-1901* plans and builds "Fenway Court," the museum now known as the Isabella Stewart Gardner Museum; *1903* Fenway Court completed and opened to public, the top floor her home until her death; *1904-1906* continues to acquire art on European trips; *1908* suffers financial difficulties with United States Customs and Treasury Department on her importations of European art; *1912* becomes passionate baseball fan of Boston Red Sox, who win World Series; *1919* suffers paralytic stroke; *1924* dies on July 17 of heart attack, her will providing maintenance for the Museum "for the education and enjoyment of the public forever" provided that her arrangement of its holdings is left unchanged.

Activities of Historical Significance

America's post-Civil War economic development is reflected in the personal art collections of Isabella Steward Gardner and others who accumulated great wealth as a result of the Industrial Revolution. Many critics argue that the era of great American collections began with Gardner's acquisitive passion, and that her taste in art influenced American museums as well as other collectors. These late nineteenth- and early twentieth-century collectors often shunned American art for European, especially favoring the work of the Old Masters. The westward flow of great art, following the flow of wealth, alarmed Europeans of the time—a situation that recalls the concern today accompanying the flow of western art to the Orient.

Gardner's eclectic art collection is an extremely personal one, still displayed in the exact dramatic settings she arranged. It remains quintessentially her collection, a time capsule infused with her spirit in a house she built. So strong was Gardner's conviction that perfection had been attained at Fenway Court that she stated in her will that the entire collection was to be broken up and auctioned off if it was altered in any way. Although judged by some to be an eccentric egotist—ruthless in her pursuits, domineering, insatiably vain, and stubborn—Gardner posssessed curiosity, intelligence, taste, and a genius for friendship that softened the edges of her colorful personality.

Gardner's generous patronage is legendary; artists of all sorts benefited from her monetary and spiritual wealth. In turn these artists enriched countless others, who enjoyed—whether as collaborators or audience—the talents that Gardner helped to develop. Gardner's museum, filled with priceless treasures, is still accessible to the public, supported by the funds she earmarked for its permanent maintenance. Most visitors to Fenway Court initially are stunned by the visual and emotional experience of this small palace, its Italianate design strongly influenced by its owner's many visits to Venice.

Most critics and visitors to Fenway Court agree that the Gardner collection is far more than a museum; the building and its contents together form a masterpiece unique in the western world. Adding to its importance is the fact that many of the great collections that once rivalled Gardner's have since been incorporated into the collections of giant art museums, or broken up—leaving the Gardner collection one of the few still maintaining its autonomy.

Gardner's importance as a biographical subject ultimately lies in the legends that she herself created, as well as in her fame both as a patron of the arts and as one of the foremost art collectors of the late nineteenth and early twentieth centuries.

Overview of Biographical Sources

A fascinating, controversial, and multifaceted personality such as Gardner attracted her share of media attention, some of it quite mean-spirited. Her flamboyant zest for life made her "good copy," and during her lifetime she courted publicity—even notoriety—by flouting conventional Boston behavioral expectations, speaking plainly, and making provocative public appearances. Journalists and photographers chronicled every adventure; gossip magazines, especially *Town Topics* (founded in 1874 as *Andrews' Bazaar*) are the source of much lively comment concerning her life.

Further biographical data can be found in works about the great American art collections, formed when the vast wealth of the so-called "robber-barons" of industry and commerce brought European and Oriental art to America by the shipload. Additional material on Gardner can also be found in various publications of the Board of Trustees of the Gardner Museum.

The first biography of Gardner was written by Morris Carter (1926), the initial director of her collection and her "companion-in-chief."

Evaluation of Principal Biographical Sources

Carter, Morris. *Isabella Stewart Gardner and Fenway Court.* 3d ed. Boston: Houghton Mifflin, 1973. (A, G) The first director of the Gardner Museum, Carter worked with Gardner in cataloguing her collection. Access to her art and to her personal and professional archives provided him with authentic data. Succeeding biographies owe a debt to Carter's basic work.

Saarinen, Aline B. *The Proud Possessors.* New York: Random House, 1958. (A, G, Y) One chapter in this survey of the lives, times, and tastes of American art collectors captures the zest for living that friends always recognized in Mrs. Gardner. A concise appraisal of her collection is included, and its unique status is recognized.

Tharp, Louise Hall. *Mrs. Jack.* Boston: Little, Brown, 1965. (A, G, Y) A chatty, gossipy, and readable biography, this highly detailed work is well-documented and illustrated with many photographs. Tharp sorts out the facts about Gardner from the legends, and recaptures the atmosphere of Boston during her lifetime.

Thorndike, Joseph J., Jr. *The Magnificent Builders and Their Dream Houses.* New York: American Heritage, 1978. (A, G) This beautifully illustrated work includes the fascinating story of Gardner and Fenway Court as part of a chronology of dreamers and builders from antiquity to the present.

Overview and Evaluation of Primary Sources

Gardner never published any of her writings, but insightful evidence can be gleaned from the extensive private correspondence between her and the famous and would-be famous people who filled her life. Especially interesting is her correspondence with the writer Henry James and the eminent historian Henry Adams. Collected primary material relating to her, including her journal, is catalogued in the archives of the Isabella Stewart Gardner Museum in Boston.

Museums, Historical Landmarks, Societies

Isabella Stewart Gardner Museum (2 Palace Road, Boston, MA). Gardner's final home contains her collection, spanning thirty centuries, of approximately 290 paintings, 280 pieces of sculpture, 200 drawings and prints, 460 pieces of furniture, 250 textiles, and over 600 art objects, as well as thousands of pages of manuscripts and rare books. There are also innumerable architectural elements incorporated in the three-story building. A large central courtyard is always filled with seasonal flowers, and music rooms feature concerts on a regular schedule. On March 18, 1990, thieves stole a number of the most valuable works in her collection, none of which to date have been recovered.

Other Sources

Brooks, Van Wyck. *New England: Indian Summer 1865-1915.* New York: E. P. Dutton, 1940. Contains a discussion of Gardner as a natural product of the culture-hungry leisure class enjoying the wealth of the post-Civil War Industrial Revolution, and also as a pathetic "barbarian" living in her meretricious Venetian palace in Boston.

Coborn, Frederick W. "Isabella Stewart Gardner." In *The Dictionary of American Biography,* edited by Allen Johnson and Dumas Malone. New York: Scribner's, 1960. Concise biographical sketch of "a daughter of the Renaissance."

Van Holst, Niels. *Creators, Collectors, and Connoisseurs.* New York: Putnam, 1967. Recognizes Gardner's position in the art world.

Maryhelen C. Harmon
University of South Florida

HENRY HIGHLAND GARNET
1815-1882

Chronology

Born a slave on December 23, 1815, on the plantation of Colonel William Spencer at New Market in Kent County, Maryland, the son of slave parents, George and Henrietta Garnet; is the grandson of a former prince in the Mandingo empire in West Africa; *1824-1825* escapes slavery with his parents, sister and eight other relatives and settles in New Hope, Bucks County, Pennsylvania; the family moves to New York City where his father renames his son Henry, his wife Elizabeth, and his daughter Elisa; *1826-1828* enrolls at the New York Free African School where he studies under Charles C. Andrews; his classmates include Charles L. Reason, who would become a leading educator; Ira Aldridge, who would become a Shakespearian actor; and Alexander Crummell, who would be ordained as an Episcopalian priest and become a fiery antislavery orator; *1828* leaves the Free African School and is employed as a cabin worker on a ship; *1829-1830* returns to New York City to discover that fugitive slave hunters have forcibly returned his parents to Maryland; returns to the Free African School until his mentor Charles Andrews is dismissed because of his antislavery sentiments; *1831-1834* studies classical languages at a high school for black youths in New York City; is befriended by Reverend Theodore S. Wright, a black clergyman at the First Presbyterian Church; converts to Presbyterianism; *1835* enrolls with Alexander Crummell at Noyes Academy in Canaan, New Hampshire, a school founded by abolitionists to educate promising black youths; the Academy is disrupted by a group of racists, who threaten the lives of the students; *1836* moves to Whitesboro, New York, to study at the Oneida Institute, a Presbyterian-affiliated school that actively recruits black students; *1838-1839* delivers an address commemorating the emancipation of blacks in the West Indies; organizes a student committee to protest the Episcopal Church's failure to support Crummell's admission to its General Theological Seminary; *1840-1841* graduates from Oneida Institute; moves to Troy, New York, where he teaches at a local black school and studies for the ministry under the guidance of Reverend Wright and Reverend Amos Beman, a highly regarded black Presbyterian minister; serves as the general agent for *Colored American*, the first black newspaper in America; undergoes amputation of his leg which he first injured in 1829; *February 18, 1841* delivers an address on civil rights before the judiciary committee of the New York state legislature on proposed legislation to grant blacks suffrage and equal citizenship; *1842* licensed to preach in the Presbyterian Church; marries Julia Williams, whom he met at the Noyes Academy; publishes the *National Watchman* in collaboration with

William Allen, a black educator; leaves the *Watchman* to publish his own newspaper called the *Clarion*; serves as a delegate to the white liberal Liberty Party convention in Massachusetts where he endorses the party's opposition to slavery; *1843* ordained a church elder and appointed pastor of Liberty Street Presbyterian Church in Troy, New York; delivers a radical address before the National Convention of Colored Citizens at Buffalo, New York, entitled "An Address To The Slaves Of The United States Of America," in which he encourages slaves to use whatever means necessary to overthrow slavery; contends with more moderate members of the Convention led by Frederick Douglass, the famous abolitionist; *1844-1847* delivers addresses before the National Negro Convention and the New York state legislature; *1848* delivers his famous address entitled "The Past And The Present Condition And The Destiny Of The Colored Race" before a Troy benevolent society; severely beaten by a railroad conductor for refusing to give up his seat in a section reserved for whites; *1849* attempts to organize a Christian convention to develop strategies for black advancement; defends a proposal to send Bibles to slaves over Frederick Douglass's opposition; advocates voluntary emigration to Africa as the only solution to the black struggle for freedom; *1850* travels to England where he lectures against slavery; is active in the Free Produce Movement, founded in 1838 by American abolitionist Gerrit Smith to promote free labor and boycott goods made by slaves; *1851* lectures against slavery in Germany and Scotland; helps establish a Free Produce group at Frankfurt-am-Main, Germany; *1852* is commissioned by the United Presbyterian Church of Scotland to serve as a missionary in Jamaica; *1853* sends letter to newspapers in the U.S., recruiting seventy blacks to work on a Jamaican estate; letter provokes conflict with Frederick Douglass, who interprets it as a part of Garnet's emigration plan; *1856* returns to America and accepts the pulpit at Shiloh Presbyterian Church in New York City upon the death of his friend and mentor Reverend Wright; *1858* helps found and is elected the first president of the African Civilization Society whose purpose is to wreck the slave trade by establishing political and economic ties with Africa; *1859* addresses the New England Colored Citizens Convention where he denounces moderate black leaders for misrepresenting the motives of his African Civilization Society; *1860-1863* increasingly rejected by moderate black leaders because of his emigration plan; remains pastor of Shiloh Church and president of the African Civilization Society; *1864* accepts call to pastor the Fifteenth Street Presbyterian Church, Washington, D.C.; *February 14, 1865* delivers "A Memorial Discourse In The House Of Representatives, Washington, D.C." before Congress at the invitation of President Abraham Lincoln; following Lincoln's assassination, organizes the National Monument Association in the District of Columbia; unsuccessfully attempts to fund a National Lincoln Memorial Institute to educate black people; *July 1865* leaves the pastorate of the Fifteenth Street Church; travels as an exploring agent among freedmen in the South for the American Home Missionary Society; also works as an editor of *The Anglo-African* magazine; *1869-1870* serves as president of Avery College, a Presbyterian school in Allegheny, Pennsylvania; *1870-1880* appeals to federal and state governments to enact legislation to help elevate his race; *1881* appointed U.S. minister-in-residence and consul general to Liberia; *1882* travels to Monrovia, Liberia, where he contracts yellow fever and dies on February 12.

Activities of Historical Significance

Although considered radical by most of his more moderate black colleagues, Garnet contributed mightily to the struggle to overcome slavery and racism during the mid-nineteenth century. His 1843 address to slaves in which he encouraged violent rebellion drew national attention and inspired abolitionists to intensify their efforts to end the slave system. This address is one of the most widely read documents in Afro-American writings.

During an era when many black leaders were careful not to arouse white hostility, Garnet boldly proposed radical and immediate reforms. He did not shy away from demanding that Afro-Americans use whatever means were necessary to attain freedom and equality. Although Frederick Douglass became Garnet's most outspoken critic, he subsequently embraced several of Garnet's methods. Douglass was particularly influenced by Garnet's successful efforts to convince the Liberty Party to make black suffrage a part of their platform in 1843. Douglass later adopted Garnet's strategy of pleading the antislavery cause to elected state and federal officials.

Increasingly convinced in the late 1840s that freedom and justice were unattainable in this country, Garnet articulated a black nationalist ideology that asserted voluntary emigration to Africa or Haiti as the best solution for the plight of Afro-Americans. This ideology strongly influenced other well-known nineteenth-century black leaders, including Martin R. Delany and Henry McNeal Turner, and contributed to a tradition of ideas about racial elevation in America that finds echoes in the thoughts and activities of modern Afro-American leaders. Many of Garnet's ideas were invoked during the civil rights struggles of the 1960s and 1970s, revealing the importance of his legacy to Afro-American life and history.

Overview of Biographical Sources

Brief references to Garnet appear in numerous monographs and articles on Afro-American history but few offer comprehensive analyses of his life or activities. Among the earliest short biographical works was James McCune Smith's "Sketch of the Life and Labors of Rev. Henry Highland Garnet," which appeared as an introductory note in Henry Highland Garnet, *A Memorial Discourse Delivered in the Hall of the House of Representatives* (1865). Another early biography was William J. Simmons, *Men of Mark: Eminent, Progressive And Rising* (1887).

Two book-length studies of Garnet exist: Earl Ofari, *"Let Your Motto Be Resistance": The Life and Thought of Henry Highland Garnet* (1972); and Joel Schor, *Henry Highland Garnet: A Voice of Black Radicalism in the Nineteenth Century* (1977).

Evaluation of Principal Biographical Sources

McMaster, Richard K. "Henry Highland Garnet and the African Civilization Society." In *Black Apostles at Home and Abroad: Afro-Americans and the Christian Mission from the Revolution to Reconstruction.* Boston: G. K. Hall, 1982. (A, G) This article provides a concise and exciting examination of one of several organizations Garnet founded during his life—the African Civilization Society—and offers elementary biographical details for Garnet.

Ofari, Earl. *"Let Your Motto Be Resistance": The Life and Thought of Henry Highland Garnet.* Boston: Beacon, 1972. (A, G) The first comprehensive study to place Garnet within the context of the Afro-American experience. This work traces the roots of radical liberation and nationalist sentiments back to Garnet's religious and socio-political views. Drawing on a wide range of primary sources, the study provides excellent biographical details and a lively comparison of Garnet with his more moderate contemporaries, particularly Frederick Douglass.

Schor, Joel. *Henry Highland Garnet: A Voice of Black Radicalism in the Nineteenth Century.* Westport, CT: Greenwood Press, 1977. (A) Schor demonstrates that nineteenth-century Afro-American leaders of widely divergent views often drew on Garnet as a catalyst for their own activities. Schor also seeks to dispel the popular opinion that Afro-American abolitionists were either "optimistic" integrationists or "pessimistic" emigrationists, with little common ground. The study provides a detailed biography of Garnet and analyzes significant moments in his life.

Overview and Evaluation of Primary Sources

Garnet never wrote an autobiography and a number of his writings have been lost, but a significant body of extant addresses, speeches, and letters, some unpublished, remain to enable a critical interpretation of his ideas and work. One common theme flows through all of his writings—the liberation of Afro-Americans.

Foremost among published sources are: "An Address to the Slaves of the United States" in Henry Highland Garnet, *David Walker's Appeal* (Troy, NY: J. H. Tobitt, 1848; **A, G**); *The Past and The Present Condition, and the Destiny of the Colored Race: A Discourse Delivered at the Fifteenth Anniversary of the Female Benevolent Society of Troy, New York* (Troy, NY: J. C. Kneeland, 1848; **A, G**); and *A Memorial Discourse Delivered in the Hall of the House of Representatives, Washington, D.C. on the Sabbath, February 12, 1865* (Philadelphia: J. M. Wilson, 1865; **A, G**). Each of these addresses argues against slavery, asserts the equal humanity of all races, and proclaims the divine right of Afro-Americans to freedom and equality in America.

Several of Garnet's shorter writings are included in Ofari's biography, *"Let Your Motto Be Resistance"*: "Speech Delivered At The Seventh Anniversary Of The American Anti-Slavery Society, 1840;" "Report On The Best Means For The Promotion Of The Enfranchisement Of Our People, 1844;" and "Speech Delivered At The Liberty Party Convention, Massachusetts, 1842."

Museums, Historical Landmarks, Societies

Garnet's Grave (Monrovia, Liberia). A memorial to Garnet in Palm Grove Cemetery marks his grave.

Other Sources

Bracey, John H., August Meier, and Elliott Rudwick, eds. *Black Nationalism in America*. Indianapolis: Bobbs-Merrill, 1970. Contains portions of Garnet's two major writings: "Address to the Slaves" and *The Past and The Present Condition and the Destiny of the Colored Race* and sets them within the context of other nineteenth- and twentieth-century black nationalist literature.

Cromwell, John. *The Negro In American History: Men And Women Eminent In The Evolution Of The American Of African Descent*. Washington, DC: American Negro Academy, 1914. Cromwell, an early pioneer in the study of Afro-American history, devotes a brief but useful chapter to Garnet's rise to prominence as an antislavery crusader and race leader.

Mays, Benjamin E. *The Negro's God*. 1938. New York: Atheneum, 1973. Gives brief biographical information about Garnet and places his views within the context of other nineteenth- and early twentieth-century Afro-American religious writings.

Paul R. Griffin
Wright State University

GERONIMO
1829-1909

Chronology

Born a member of the Warm Springs Apache tribe in No-doyohn Canyon, Arizona in 1829, and given the name Goyakla (also written Goyathlay, Go khlä yeh, Gokliya, or Goyahkla), which means "one who yawns"; *1846* accepted as a warrior by his tribe; marries his first wife, Alope, with whom he has three children; *1858* mother, wife, and children are killed by a Mexican raiding party; develops an undying hatred of Mexicans; *1859* Mexicans give him the name Geronimo, a nickname derived from the Spanish variant of Jerome; *1859-1877* serves his tribe as war chief and becomes famous for his skill and ruthlessness in leading raiding parties in the American and Mexican southwest; *1877* captured by Indian agent John Clum, who forces Geronimo and his band to live on the San Carlos Indian Reservation in Arizona; *1881-1884* flees reservation with hereditary chiefs Nachez (also written Natchez, Nachite, and Naiche) and Juh (also written Ju, Woo, and Whoa) and resumes raiding while hiding out in the mountains of Arizona and Mexico; *1884* surrenders and returns to San Carlos Reservation; *1885* leaves reservation and resumes raiding; *March 1886* surrenders in Mexico to American General George Crook, but on the way back to Arizona escapes again to his mountain stronghold; *September 1886* surrenders to the cavalry under General Nelson A. Miles and is incarcerated at Fort Pickens, Florida; *1887* transferred to Mount Vernon Barracks, Alabama; *1894* transferred to Fort Sill, Oklahoma; *1898* attends Trans-Mississippi Exposition in Omaha where he confronts his old opponent, General Miles; *1901* attends exposition in Buffalo, New York; *1904* appears at St. Louis World's Fair where he sells handmade bows and autographs pictures; *1905* appears in Washington, D.C., in inaugural parade of President Theodore Roosevelt; *February 1909* falls from his horse while intoxicated and spends the night in the open air; dies of pneumonia on February 17 and is buried in the Apache Cemetery at Fort Sill.

Activities of Historical Significance

For centuries, the Apaches inhabited the region of what is now southwestern New Mexico, southeastern Arizona, and the northern parts of the Mexican states of Sonora and Chihuahua. Consisting of several sub-tribes and clans, the Apaches were hunter-gatherers and fierce warriors who often raided the villages of neighboring tribes, such as the Pimas and Papagos, and later those of Anglo and Mexican settlers. The Apaches were experts at guerrilla warfare in the rugged mountains and barren deserts of their homeland, swooping down on unsuspecting enemies and then disappearing into the land-scape. Their favorite tactic was the ambush, and at mountain fighting they were unequalled. Their tactics have been studied and copied by many rebels, such as Cuba's Che Guevara, faced with an enemy possessing logistical or technological superiority. One name above all others is exalted as the most skilled Apache warrior ever to have lived—Geronimo.

As American "civilization" pushed into the Southwest in the last half of the nineteenth century, a collision with the Apaches seems to have been inevitable. The nomadic way of life of the Apaches did not fit the reservation policy established by the Department of the Interior, which demanded that the tribes take up farming even though the arid land was unsuitable for crops. Some limited agriculture could be practiced only on the Warm Springs Reservation in southwestern New Mexico. Of course, the Warm Springs land was coveted by settlers and miners. In 1863 a great Apache chief, Mangas Coloradas (Red Sleeves), was deceitfully captured and killed by whites, a deed that Geronimo described as "the greatest wrong ever done to the Indians."

Settlers to the region saw the Apaches only as a menace. Apache men commonly beat their wives or cut off the nose of an unfaithful spouse, customs that civilized whites viewed with horror. These same settlers, however, were not averse to exploiting the Apaches' low tolerance for alcohol by supplying them with copious amounts of whiskey. To further complicate matters, a group of citizens, called the "Tucson Ring," continually stirred up conflict with the Apaches because they profited from selling supplies to the army. Vigilante bands or cavalry detachments in search of Apache raiding parties sometimes attacked peaceful villages, killing women, children, and the elderly. In one such raid by Mexicans in 1858, Geronimo's own family was murdered.

The Chiricahua branch of the Apache tribe, under their chief Cochise, made peace with the American government and was granted a reservation in their home mountains in southeastern Arizona, but Apache raiders began using this reservation for incursions into Mexico. In 1872 the U.S. government responded to the raiding by establishing a new reservation, the San Carlos, near the confluence of the Gila and Salt Rivers. The Interior Department, backed by the army, attempted to relocate 4,000 members of the various Apache bands onto this reservation. But the land of the San Carlos reservation was so inhospitable that the Apaches there were forced to depend on rations supplied by the government.

Several hundred Apaches refused to tolerate these conditions and left the reservation under the leadership of Geronimo, the most skilled, feared, and respected war chief of the Warm Springs tribe. Geronimo usually rode with Nachez, Cochise's son and nominal head of the Chiricahua tribe, but Geronimo was the real leader of the band. Geronimo led his warriors in bloody reprisals, plunging the region into turmoil.

Geronimo's warriors could travel scores of miles a day on foot through inhospitable terrain, surviving only on a handful of grain and sugar. They used their horses to travel over level terrain but did not hesitate to abandon the animals or slaughter them for food if the need arose, knowing that they could steal more horses later. For many years, the U.S. army was forbidden to cross the Rio Grande into Mexico, so Geronimo and his band would duck back and forth across the border to avoid pursuit. Ultimately, permission was granted for the cavalry to cross the border.

For ten months in 1885-1886 Geronimo eluded the efforts of the army under General George F. Crook to capture and pacify him in what came to be known as the "Geronimo Campaign." In March 1886, using diplomacy and negotiation, Crook personally got Geronimo to surrender, but he slipped back into the hills when a bootlegger started the rumor that the Apaches were going to be murdered. Because of the controversy over this incident, Crook was relieved of his command and replaced by General Nelson A. Miles, a glory-seeker who thought that Geronimo should be brought to bay by military force.

Miles sent an expedition into Mexico, which after nearly six months tracked Geronimo to his camp in the Sonora Mountains. Miles then arranged a negotiated surrender through Lt. Charles Gatewood, one of Crook's men and the only officer the Native Americans would trust. Geronimo asked what Gatewood thought he should do, and Gatewood simply told him to surrender and trust General Miles. Thus, although Crook had been personally disgraced, his strategy of diplomacy prevailed. Miles insisted that his military tactics forced the final surrender, and the battle to claim credit for Geronimo's capture continued in the press long after all parties were dead.

When Geronimo surrendered to Miles, he was told that he would be reunited with his family, and that his group would be held only for a short time in Florida before being allowed to return to Arizona. None of these promises were kept. Instead, he was shipped to Fort Pickens in Florida and then put to work on a labor gang. Even the peaceful Apaches, some of whom helped track down Geronimo, were sent there, solving the Apache "problem" once and for all to the satisfaction of the settlers. Many Apaches suffered from illness and died in the humid Florida climate. Geronimo was transferred to Mount Vernon Barracks, Alabama, and then to Fort Sill, Oklahoma. He remained in captivity until after 1894 and never saw Arizona again.

Undeniably a crafty warrior, Geronimo could be duplicitous and cruel, as well. Once Geronimo taunted a Mexican captive, making him remove and hand over his shirt. Then Geronimo killed the unarmed prisoner, explaining that he hadn't wanted to get blood on such a nice shirt. Geronimo often returned to the reservation when winter began to close in, pledging peace and drawing government rations, only to leave again when spring and good hunting returned. He would lie to fellow Apache leaders for personal gain. Once he lied to Nachez and Chihuahua, getting them to leave the reservation by telling them of a non-existent plot against their lives. In spite of several half-hearted attempts later in life, Geronimo never adapted to the demands of American civilization, as did Cochise or the Comanche chief, Quanah Parker. In his last years, after imprisonment and alcoholism had taken their toll, the once-invincible Geronimo engaged in beggary and souvenir peddling. Nonetheless, Geronimo's very name will always be associated with grim warfare, relentless opposition to authority, and unflinching defiance against impossible odds.

Overview of Biographical Sources

Much of the early biographical material about Geronimo was written not to present the historical facts but to exploit the reading public's interest in the Wild West or to claim some of the glory that resulted from his capture. Only after more than fifty years did historians attempt to give a balanced account of Geronimo's life and its significance. The biographies of Geronimo by Angie Debo, *Geronimo: The Man, His Time, His Place* (1976), and Odie B. Faulk, *The Geronimo Campaign* (1969), are particularly careful, detailed, and reasonable.

Evaluation of Principal Biographical Sources

Debo, Angie. *Geronimo: The Man, His Time, His Place.* Norman: University of Oklahoma Press, 1976. (A, G, Y) The author is one of the leading historians of Native Americans, and presents Geronimo in a highly favorable light, perhaps as an antidote to earlier commentators who saw him merely as a bloodthirsty savage. Since many of the facts of Geronimo's life are in doubt, Debo has the advantage of reviewing the earlier accounts with the objective of setting the record straight or at least noting where there are questions. For example, she disputes the birthdate that Geronimo himself gave, presenting evidence that he may have been born as early as 1823.

Faulk, Odie B. *The Geronimo Campaign.* New York: Oxford University Press, 1969. (A, G, Y) Faulk places Geronimo's life story in the context of the larger military effort to subdue the Native Americans. This is a complete account of the life of the warrior, well researched and written in a clear, readable style.

Syme, Ronald. *Geronimo: The Fighting Apache.* New York: William Morrow, 1975. (Y) This children's biography presents Geronimo as a hero and is unique in placing most of the blame for the Apache problem on the U.S. Army's Apache scouts. Syme gets a number of facts wrong, such as placing Geronimo's surrender to Crook in January 1886, when it actually occurred in March.

Wyatt, Edgar. *Geronimo: The Last Apache War Chief.* New York: Mc-Graw-Hill, 1952. (Y) A highly favorable biography of Geronimo for young teenagers which makes use of fictional techniques (e.g., imagined dialogue between the Native Americans). Young readers can get the basic events in Geronimo's life from this book, but it is only a starting point.

Overview and Evaluation of Primary Sources

Geronimo's autobiography as narrated to S. M. Barrett is *Geronimo's Story of His Life* (New York: Duffield, 1906; A, G, Y). Barrett was a Lawton teacher to whom Geronimo spoke through an Apache interpreter, Asa Daklugie. With such a procedure, one might expect errors to creep in, and occasionally Barrett disassociates himself from Geronimo's opinions, but his own disclaimers show that he is trying to be fair to Geronimo rather than suppress the war chief's viewpoint. It is best to use the modern edition of this book, *Geronimo: His Own Story* (New York: Dutton, 1970; A, G, Y), which contains an introduction and notes based on recent scholarship by Frederick W. Turner III. This later edition corrects errors or raises questions about statements made by Geronimo, Daklugie, or Barrett.

There are two other Native American accounts of Apache resistance, both by warriors who were young men when Geronimo fought. These men survived into the middle of the twentieth century and related their life histories to editors. Jason Betzinez told his story with W. S. Nye in *I Fought With Geronimo* (Harrisburg, PA: Stackpole, 1959; A, G, Y), which is copiously illustrated. James Kaywaykla's life is presented in Eve Ball's *In The Days of Victorio: Recollections of a Warm Springs Apache* (Tucson: University of Arizona Press, 1970; A, G, Y). Both books are detailed and fascinating, and correct many errors presented in conventional histories written from the invading American point of view.

Other contemporary accounts of the Apache uprising were written to support one side or the other of the army debate over who should be credited for Geronimo's last surrender. General Crook presented his case in *General George Crook: His Autobiography,* edited by Martin F. Schmitt (Norman: University of Oklahoma Press, 1946; A, G). Other Crook advocates include John G. Bourke, who in *An Apache Campaign in the Sierra Madre* (New York: Scribner's, 1958; A, G, Y), gives his version of the 1883 expedition into Mexico and in *On the Border With Crook* (New York: Scribner's, 1891; A, G, Y) carries the story up to Geronimo's 1883 surrender to Crook. Britton Davis, *The Truth About Geronimo* (New Haven: Yale University Press, 1929;

A, G, Y), attempted to understand the Native Americans on their own terms, and his book is particularly helpful.

General Miles's viewpoint appears in his two autobiographies, *Personal Recollections and Observations* (Chicago: Werner, 1896; **A, G, Y**) and *Serving the Republic* (New York: Harper, 1911; **A, G, Y**). Some of the Geronimo material is fabricated. Ironically, the self-effacing lieutenant who was largely responsible for Geronimo's final surrender, Charles Gatewood, is represented in the Miles-Crook debate by only one article, "The Surrender of Geronimo," in *Arizona Historical Review* IV (April 1931). This article is an abridged version of his "An Account of the Surrender of Geronimo," a manuscript in the Gatewood Collection of the Arizona Pioneers' Historical Society in Tucson.

Fiction and Adaptations

Geronimo's story is a natural subject for films, and three movies have featured him as a central character. He was played by Chief Thundercloud in *Geronimo* (1938), Jay Silverheels (the Lone Ranger's television companion Tonto) in *The Battle at Apache Pass* (1952), and Chuck Connors in *Geronimo* (1962). None of these films attempts to be historically accurate. Secondary characters based on Geronimo have also appeared in several other western films.

Paul Horgan's novel *A Distant Trumpet* (1960) is a fictional account of the Crook campaign against Geronimo.

Museums, Historical Landmarks, Societies

Chiricahua National Monument (near Willcox, AZ). The visitor's center offers exhibits on Geronimo and the army's campaign against the Apaches.

Geronimo's Grave (Lawton, OK). Marked with an impressive monument at the Apache Cemetery, Fort Sill. The U.S. Army Artillery and Missile Center Museum, also at Fort Sill, has material on the Apache settlement there.

Other Sources

Bigelow, John, Jr. *On the Bloody Trail of Geronimo*. Los Angeles: Westernlore Press, 1968. The title is precise; the author, part of Miles's command, never saw Geronimo, so the book tells the reader nothing about the Native American but does present background on army life in old Arizona. Original illustrations by Frederic Remington.

Clum, Woodworth. *Apache Agent: The Story of John P. Clum*. Boston: Houghton Mifflin, 1936. This account of the life of the only man who ever captured Geronimo is presented by his son, using John Clum's notes for a projected autobiography. Since Clum was mayor of Tombstone and editor of *The Tombstone Epitaph*, there is much about early Arizona history in this book, including Clum's account of the gunfight at the O.K. corral.

Mazzanovich, Anton. *Trailing Geronimo*. Los Angeles: Gem, 1926. Reprint. 3d. ed. Hollywood, CA: Mazzanovich, 1931. This soldier who later became a movie cowboy spent most of his time in the rear echelon, but his book contains many contemporary photographs which do not appear elsewhere.

Santee, Ross. *Apache Land*. New York: Scribner's, 1947. This objective account of the history and customs of the Apaches by an Arizona cowboy and artist is an excellent introduction to the study of the Apaches. Uncle Jimmie Stevens, an old settler, gives an interesting negative view of Geronimo in Chapter 17.

Thrapp, Dan L. *The Conquest of Apacheria*. Norman: University of Oklahoma Press, 1967. A complete history of the Apaches and their final defeat with special emphasis on Geronimo in the last three chapters.

_____. *General Crook and the Sierra Madre Adventure*. Norman: University of Oklahoma Press, 1972. A history of Crook's 1883 expedition into Mexico to capture Geronimo and other Apaches who had gone on the warpath.

Weems, John Edward. *Death Song*. Garden City: Doubleday, 1976. This general history of the suppression of Native Americans in the last half of the nineteenth century covers Geronimo and the Apaches.

Wood, Leonard. *Chasing Geronimo: The Journal of Leonard Wood: May-September, 1886*. Edited by Jack C. Lane. Albuquerque: University of New Mexico Press, 1970. The Geronimo campaign was the first step in the brilliant career of Leonard Wood, who rose to become not only a general officer but chief of staff. He received the Medal of Honor for his work in the Miles expedition, more for his amazing stamina than for his impact on the surrender. Nonetheless, his journal provides important background material and Jack Lane's introduction and notes help to place Wood's role in the historical context.

Jim Baird
University of North Texas

ROSE GREENHOW
c. 1817-1864

Chronology

Born Rose O'Neale (later changed to O'Neal) about 1817, probably at Port Tobacco, Maryland, to John O'Neale, an affluent planter; *1817* John O'Neale murdered by his black servant; family moves north to Poolesville in Montgomery County, Maryland; *c.1830* moves to Washington, D.C., with her sister Ellen to live with their aunt, Mrs. H. V. Hill, who runs a fashionable boarding house in the Old Capitol Building; *1835* Ellen marries James Madison Cutts and joins the social orbit of her husband's aunt, Dolly Madison; Rose marries Robert Greenhow, whom she meets through her Cutts connections; *March 31, 1850* serves John C. Calhoun as nurse in his dying hours; *June 1850* embarks for Mexico City, where Robert studies archives for the validation of land claims in California; becomes, with her husband, an unwitting accessory in illegal land operations; *October 1850* proceeds to San Francisco and is impressed with the vigor of the fledgling metropolis; *1853* returns to Washington, D.C., for the birth of her fourth child; *March 27, 1854* Robert Greenhow dies at 54, after falling down an embankment in San Francisco; *August 1854* makes another trip to California, this time to enter suit against the city of San Francisco for damages, and is awarded $10,000; *1856* her beloved niece and namesake Rose Adele Cutts marries Stephen A. Douglas; travels once more to California to campaign for James Buchanan in his presidential bid; *1856-1860* enjoys peak of her political influence during presidency of her friend Buchanan; *1861* given a cipher code by a member of Confederate General Beauregard's staff; informs him of Union plans for the First Bull Run Campaign; *August 23, 1861* arrested by order of the War Department after being watched by Allan Pinkerton, head of the Federal secret service; is charged with being a spy, and placed under house arrest; *January 18, 1862* removed to Old Capitol Prison because security leaks continue; *June 1862* released and sent to Richmond; given a hero's welcome and paid a fee of $2,500 from Confederate secret service funds; *August 5, 1863* leaves Wilmington, North Carolina, on the blockade runner *Phantom,* carrying with her the manuscript of her book, *My Imprisonment and the First Year of Abolition Rule at Washington,* which is published in London by early November; *late 1863* presented to Queen Victoria; crosses over to France and puts daughter Rose in a convent school; *January 1864* received by Napoleon III at Tuileries; *August 1864* leaves Scotland on the blockade runner *Condor* in order to convey dispatches and a trunkful of medicines to the hospitals in Richmond; *October 1, 1864* demands to be lowered into a small boat while the *Condor* is running the blockade in waters off Wilmington, North Carolina, a mere two hundred yards from the Confederate guns at Fort Fisher; drowns when boat overturns; her body is washed ashore; *October 2, 1864* buried in a Catholic ceremony in Oakdale Cemetery, Wilmington, North Carolina.

Activities of Historical Significance

As a major spy for the Confederacy who died in service to her government, Greenhow was decried as a traitor in the North and revered as a patriot in the South. A greatly respected hostess in the social life of antebellum Washington, D.C., she was acquainted personally with nine presidents, including James Buchanan, in whose 1856 campaign she was actively involved, and with whom she was on the most intimate of terms. It also appears she was loved by Henry Wilson of Massachusetts, who was later to serve as vice president under President Grant.

Although Greenhow was in unhampered active service to the Confederacy for a total of only five months, she claimed that all of her years as a socialite had been in preparation for this service in the "War for Southern Liberation." Instead of joining the Southern exodus from Washington at the onset of war, she stayed, feigning friendship with Republican politicians and Union officers in order to provide military intelligence to her Southern friends. She converted her home on 16th Street into a clearing-house for military information, which she disseminated through a network of fifty spies, some of them stationed as far away as Texas.

The evening after her arrival in Richmond, Jefferson Davis called on her and acknowledged that without her, the Federal rout at Bull Run would not have happened. This tribute from Davis was, according to her, the proudest moment of her whole life.

Greenhow continued to be loyal to President Davis and was a frequent caller at his home. When she realized that the Richmond *Examiner* was in the hands of an anti-Davis faction and printed news that she felt was hurting the cause of the South "by exaggerating our internal differences and exposing our difficulties," she campaigned vigorously against the paper. To his credit, Davis refused to interfere with the Confederacy's freedom of the press.

Greenhow sailed to Europe in 1863 on a mission to inspire enthusiasm for the Confederate cause in England and France through personal appeals and the publication of her book of anti-Union propaganda. Despite a rumored proposal of marriage from an English nobleman, Greenhow returned to America the following year on another mission. When she died attempting to run a naval blockade, she was carrying needed medicine and $2,000 in gold for the Confederacy.

Overview of Biographical Sources

Most biographical material on Greenhow is found in general books devoted to Civil War spies. The only full-length biography of Greenhow, *Rebel Rose: Life of Rose O'Neal Greenhow, Confederate Spy* (1954) by Ishbel Ross, makes the most of the meager facts known about Greenhow's life, and incorporates peripheral background information. A pioneering journal article by Louis A. Sigaud, "Mrs. Greenhow and the Rebel Spy Ring," appeared in the *Maryland Historical Magazine* (September 1946) and is remarkably thorough and minutely documented.

Evaluation of Principal Biographical Sources

Grant, Dorothy Fremont. *Rose Greenhow, Confederate Secret Agent.* New York: P. J. Kenedy and Sons, 1961. (Y) This sympathetic treatment of Greenhow is designed for readers between ten and fourteen, and emphasizes her rather nominal ties to the Catholic faith.

Ross, Ishbel. *Rebel Rose: Life of Rose O'Neal Greenhow, Confederate Spy.* New York: Harper & Brothers, 1954. (G) The only full-length biography, it contains a four-page bibliography but no footnotes.

Sigaud, Louis A. "Mrs. Greenhow and the Rebel Spy Ring." *Maryland Historical Magazine* 41 (September 1946): 173-198. (A) Explores the intricacies of Greenhow's spy network and gives a complete enumeration of her pro-Union Cutts family in-laws. Sigaud suggests that the status of her in-laws is the reason for the genteel treatment she received while under house arrest.

Overview and Evaluation of Primary Sources

Greenhow's memoir, *My Imprisonment and the First Year of Abolition Rule at Washington* (London: Richard Bentley, 1863; G) was dedicated "to the brave soldiers who have fought and bled in this our glorious struggle for freedom" and became an immediate best seller. However, the book's propagandistic purpose gives it little enduring historical value. By the time of its publication Greenhow's hatred of Yankees was so fierce—rising almost to the pitch of madness—that her English friend Lady Georgiana Fullerton feared for her Christian salvation. Revealing little about the particulars of her espionage or the Washington society over which she reigned supreme, the memoir is principally a harangue against the Union lasting for three hundred rather tiresome pages. The accuracy of her account of her own activities is confirmed by other sources such as the wartime memoir of Allan Pinkerton, *Spy of the Rebellion* (New York: G. W. Carleton, 1883; **A, G**); the unpublished memoir of Pinkerton agent Pryce Lewis (which was in the estate of Harriet H. Shoen of New York City, who obtained it from Lewis's daughter); and Greenhow's own correspondence at the National Archives (Captured Confederate Correspondence, Departments of State and War). Although generally discreet about naming names in her prison memoir, Greenhow names former friends she felt had failed her in her hour of need: Secretary of State W. H. Seward, former attorney general Jeremiah Black, and Senators R. J. Walker and Henry Wilson.

Ironically, some in Richmond felt Greenhow arrived in the South as a spy for the North, an observation recorded by diarist Phoebe Yates Pember on November 29, 1862 (*A Southern Woman's Story*, New York: G. W. Carleton, 1879; **G**). Mary Boykin Chesnut felt obliged to comment on this view on June 6, 1862, in *A Diary From Dixie* (Edited by Ben Ames Williams. Boston: Houghton Mifflin, 1949; **G**): "One half of these ungrateful Confederates say Seward sent her. Mr. Chesnut says the Confederates owe her a debt they never can pay."

Northern impressions of Greenhow are recorded in Erasmus Darwin Keyes, *Fifty Years' Observation of Men and Events* (New York: Charles Scribner's Sons, 1885; **G**), and in W. E. Doster, *Lincoln and Episodes of the Civil War* (New York: G. P. Putnam's Sons, 1915; **G**). The man who found her body on the beach at Wilmington, North Carolina, Thomas E. Taylor, wrote about it in *Running the Blockade* (New York: Charles Scribner's Sons, 1896; **G**). Additional correspondence by Greenhow is included in the Jefferson Davis Papers, Manuscript Room, Duke University Library.

Fiction and Adaptations

A movie made for Armstrong Cable Television starring Madolyn Smith Osborne as Greenhow and Christopher Reeve as Allan Pinkerton was called *The Rose and the Jackal* and aired on April 16, 1990, on TNT. Designed as a docudrama, the romantic element prevailed, as can be seen from the advertisement: "Because of her, 1,100 Union soldiers lost their lives. He lost his heart." In addition, Greenhow is a background character in Shirley Seifert's historical novel *The Senator's Lady* (1967), which is narrated by Greenhow's niece, Adele Cutts, the second wife of Stephen A. Douglas. Since the novel ends with the death of Douglas on June 3, 1861, the author does not explore what must have been a welter of conflicting emotions that the pro-Union Mrs. Douglas had for her secessionist aunt.

Just after Greenhow's death, Lady Georgiana Fullerton wrote "Mrs Greenhow," a thirty-eight-verse poem about her American friend. It appeared in the November 1870 issue of *Temple Bar: A London Magazine For Town and Country Readers*. After noting that "She loathed the Northern foe; / With that intensity of hate, / Impassioned women know,'' Lady Fullerton goes on to record her impression that Greenhow mellowed somewhat in the months before her death.

Museums, Historical Landmarks, Societies
New Hanover Museum of the Lower Cape Fear (Wilmington, NC). Contains memorabilia connected with Greenhow's last days, such as the address book she used during her stay in London. There is also a diorama of her drowning.

Oakdale Cemetery (Wilmington, NC). Greenhow's grave is marked by a marble cross bearing the inscription: "Mrs. Rose O'N. Greenhow, a bearer of dispatches to the Confederate Government. Erected by the Ladies Memorial Association."

Other Sources
Bakeless, John. *Spies of the Confederacy*. Philadelphia: Lippincott, 1970. Devotes the first four chapters to the story of Rose Greenhow.

Horan, James. *Desperate Women*. New York: G. P. Putnam's Sons, 1952. The long first chapter gives a substantial account of Greenhow's life.

————. *The Pinkertons: The Detective Dynasty That Made History*. New York: Bonanza Books, 1967. Includes a chapter on Greenhow's espionage.

Jones, Katherine M., ed. *Heroines of Dixie*. Westport, CT: Greenwood Press, 1973. Includes examples of Greenhow's correspondence.

Kane, Harnett T. *Spies for the Blue and Gray*. New York: Doubleday, 1954. A chapter chronicles the clash between Greenhow and Allan Pinkerton.

Schafer, Joseph. "Greenhow, Robert." In *The Dictionary of American Biography*. New York: Scribner's, 1931. Offers as substantial a portrait of Robert Greenhow as exists anywhere, stressing his scholarly pursuits and his importance as a pioneer historian.

Stern, Philip Van Doren. *Secret Missions of the Civil War*. New York: Bonanza Books, 1959. Contains excerpts from Pinkerton's *Spy of the Rebellion* as well as excellent commentary on other aspects of Greenhow's life.

Jack Shreve
Allegany Community College

SARAH JOSEPHA HALE
1788-1889

Chronology

Born Sarah Jospeha Buell on October 24, 1788 near Newport, New Hampshire, the third child of American Revolution veteran Gordon Buell and model of Republican Motherhood Martha Whittlesey Buell; *1788-1810* grows up on her parent's farm; taught to read by her mother and greatly influenced by the Bible, *Pilgrim's Progress,* and Mrs. Radcliffe's *The Mysteries of Udolpho;* tutored by her older brother Horatio during his vacations from Dartmouth College; *1806-1813* teaches children in local private school; *1811-1813* moves to Newport with her parents and younger sister Martha when her father establishes The Rising Sun Tavern in 1811; takes care of her father after the deaths of both her mother and younger sister Martha in late 1811 and the subsequent closing of the inn; *1813-1822* marries self-educated lawyer David Hale on October 23, 1813; bears four children between 1815 and 1822; her husband replaces Horatio as her mentor; the couple pursues a disciplined course of home study in composition, natural sciences, and French; *1822-1828* delivers the last of her five children four days after the death of her husband on October 25, 1822; remains in Newport and struggles to establish first a school and then a millinery shop while continuing to write; *1823* financed by her husband's lodge brothers and friends, publishes her tribute to David Hale, a collection of poems entitled *The Genius of Oblivion;* subsequently her award-winning poetry, fiction, and critical reviews appear in New England magazines; *1827* publishes her first novel, *Northwood,* which brings her to the attention of Reverend John Blake of Boston who invites her to move to Boston and edit the *Ladies' Magazine; 1828-1836* edits the *Ladies' Magazine* (renamed *The Ladies' Magazine and Literary Gazette* in 1833 and the *American Ladies' Magazine* in 1835 when she becomes part-owner); *1830* issues the enduringly popular *Poems for Our Children,* which includes her own contribution to children's literature, "Mary Had A Little Lamb"; *1835* publishes *The Ladies' Wreath,* a well-received collection of contemporary women's poetry with biographical sketches; *1837* merged her magazine with *Godey's Lady's Magazine,* an expensive and popular women's periodical distinguished only by its lavish fashion plates; *1837-1877* edits *Godey's,* instituting what became the standard content formula for women's magazines (fiction, poetry, features, and domestic arts instruction); continues to author and edit works promoting the "woman's sphere" and lauding women's achievements in the public sphere; *1840* successfully promotes women's crafts fair to raise funds to complete the Bunker Hill Monument; *1841* moves to Philadelphia; *1853* edits and publishes *Woman's Record: Or, Sketches of All Distinguished Women . . .,* a monumental collection of biographical sketches of historical and contemporary women; publishes *Liberia: or, Mr. Payton's Experiment* which supports the colonization movement as a conservative response to the indictment of slavery in *Uncle Tom's Cabin*; *1863* after a seventeen-year one-woman lobbying campaign, secures President Abraham Lincoln's executive decree to establish the last Thursday in November as Thanksgiving, an annual national holiday; *1865* witnesses fruition of her life-long commitment to women's education with the opening of Vassar College (she successfully lobbies to change its name from Vassar Female College), which offers a liberal arts curriculum comparable to that of contemporary men's colleges, and which is the first college to hire a substantial number of women professors; *1877* retires in December after a fifty-year career as the most renowned woman's magazine editor of the Victorian era; *1879* dies at the age of ninety-one on April 30 in the Philadelphia home of her older daughter and son-in-law.

Activities of Historical Significance

As editor of a prestigious national magazine, Hale sought original works of major writers of the 1840s and 1850s while other American women's magazines were still plagiarizing copy from foreign periodicals. Hale's editorship of *Godey's* brought substance to the superficial and showy periodical and demonstrated the possibilities for influencing public opinion, while ostensibly ignoring all political issues and events. Hale was one of the first authors to use American scenes, and *Northwood*, with its New England setting, is one of the first truly American novels. Her editorial policies established literary standards for women's magazines and promoted the development of a national literature. Hale's own literary career exemplified that of a generation of informally educated "scribbling women" who came to dominate the domestic fiction and instructional market of the Victorian era.

As a successful woman writer and magazine editor, Hale served as a role model and example of the achievements and contributions of conservative white middle class women. Protected from charges of radicalism by the apolitical respectability of the magazines she edited, for fifty years Hale pursued the improvement of women's status through a discreet but determined editorial policy that championed the domestic role of women and supported increased educational and employment opportunities. While the contents of *Godey's* promoted distinctly domestic roles for women, Hale's monthly column, "Editor's Table," promoted women's education and the extension of "women's work" from the private to the public sphere. She spoke out for women's entry into the professions of writing, teaching, and medicine, as well as newly emerging occupations such as office work and industrial design.

Hale's participation in benevolent activities helped create a nineteenth-century pattern of women's involvement in public charities and welfare issues.

In the 1830s she was instrumental in establishing the Seaman's Aid Society in Boston and the ladies' crafts fairs, which raised the funds to complete the Bunker Hill Monument; in the 1850s, she publicized the need to establish Mount Vernon as a national historic site, and supported the efforts of the Mt. Vernon Ladies Association to purchase the property in 1860.

Overview of Biographical Sources

Biographical information on Hale can be found in various biographic directories of American women, histories of nineteenth- and twentieth-century American magazines, and in studies of *Godey's Lady's Book*. Feature articles highlighting Hale's contribution to the establishment of Thanksgiving as a national holiday became a tradition in November issues of twentieth-century popular magazines.

However, Hale has been the subject of few biographies: *The Lady of "Godey's"* (1931) by Ruth E. Finley; *Sarah Josepha Hale: The Life and Times of a Nineteenth-Century Career Woman* (1975) by Norma R. Fryatt; and *Sarah Josepha Hale; A New England Pioneer, 1788-1879* (1985) by Sherbrooke Rogers. Neither Rogers' brief account nor Fryatt's book (written for juveniles) has superseded Finley's pioneering work, which is a reliable, well-researched, and thorough reconstruction of Hale's private and professional life.

Isabelle Webb Entrekin's *Sarah Josepha Hale and "Godey's Lady's Book"* (1946) provides a professional and thorough appraisal of Hale's literary career and life and includes an exhaustive bibliography of her publications. Hale's influence on activities at the time to increase women's education and employment opportunities provides the focus for *"For the Improvement of My Sex": Sarah Josepha Hale's Editorship of "Godey's Lady's Book," 1837-1877* (Ph.D. diss. Ohio State University, 1978) by Angela Howard Zophy.

Hale has been featured in textbooks on American women's history to illustrate historical trends. Gerda Lerner's *The Woman in American History* (1971), Nancy Woloch's *Women and the American Experience* (1984), and Glenda Riley's *Inventing the American Woman: A Perspective on Women's History* (1986, 1987) have accounts of Hale's life and career..

Evaluation of Principal Biographical Sources

Entrikin, Isabelle Webb. *Sarah Josepha Hale and "Godey's Lady's Book."* Philadelphia: Lancaster, 1946. (A) This well-written, thorough study of Hale's life and literary career has not been superseded. Originally a dissertation, it offers exhaustive documentation and a complete listing of Hale's publications.

Finely, Ruth E. *The Lady of "Godey's."* Philadelphia: Lippincott, 1931; Reprint. Arno, 1974. (G) Collects vital information from primary sources. The author's admiration and enthusiasm for her subject compensates for an informal tone and lack of methodology.

Fryatt, Norma R. *Sarah Josepha Hale: The Life of a Nineteenth-Century Career Woman.* New York: Hawthorn Books, 1975. (Y) This short biography lists sources but provides no documentation within its simply constructed text.

Rogers, Sherbrooke. *Sarah Josepha Hale; A New England Pioneer, 1788-1879.* Grantham, NH: Thompson & Rutter, 1985. (G) This brief biography covers the major events in Hale's life and career, with some effort at designation of the sources utilized.

Zophy, Angela Howard. "'For the Improvement of My Sex': Sarah Josepha Hale's Editorship of *Godey's Lady's Book*, 1837-1877." Ph.D. dissertation. Ohio State University, 1978. (A) Focuses on Hale's use *Godey's* to influence public opinion on women's issues and examines the implications of Hale's campaign to increase women's educational and employment opportunities. Its listing of primary and secondary source material facilitates access to the historical context, as well as material on her life and career.

Overview and Evaluation of Primary Sources

Hale's literary style reflects both the pomposity of her era and her own lack of formal education. Over a sixty-year career her published output is large and varied: poetry, fiction, children's books, works on historical topics and figures, household manuals and cookbooks.

Hale's novel *Northwood; A Tale of New England*, 2 vols. (Boston: Bowles & Dearborn, 1827; **A, G**) made her reputation as a minor nineteenth-century American author, and *The Genius of Oblivion; and Other Original Poems, By a Lady of New Hampshire* (Concord: Jacob B. Moore, 1823; **A, G**) contained her earlier poetry, which was typical of the popular women writers of the period. Her *Poems for Our Children* (Boston: Marsh, Capen and Lyon, 1830; **A, Y**), her first juvenile collection, contains her classic "Mary Had A Little Lamb." Hale also produced many instructional works for women, such as *Flora's Interpreter: or, The American Book of Flowers and Sentiments* (Boston: Marsh, Capen, & Lyon, 1832; **A, G**), *Keeping House and Housekeeping* (New York: Harper & Brothers, 1845; **A, G**), *Mrs. Hale's Receipts for the Million* (Philadelphia: T. B. Peterson, 1857; **A, G**), and *Manners; or, Happy Homes and Good Society all the Year Round* (Boston: J. E. Tilton, 1867; **A, G**).

As an editor, Hale's contribution to the form and substance of *The Ladies' Magazine* (Vols. 1-3. Boston: Putnam & Hunt, 1828-1830; Vol. 4, Boston: Marsh, Capen and Lyon, 1831) shows her determination "to amuse and instruct'' her own sex, as well as her support for women's education. Although the magazine changed titles, to *The Ladies' Magazine and Literary Gazette* (Vols. 5-6. Boston: Marsh, Capen and Lyon, 1832-1833) and then to *The American Ladies' Magazine* (Vols. 7-9. Boston: James B. Dow, 1834-1836), Hale's editorial presence permeated every issue.

That editorial presence persisted when she merged her own monthly periodical with that of Louis A. Godey, *Godey's Lady's Book and American Ladies Magazine* (Vols. 14-95, Philadelphia: Louis A. Godey, 1837-1877), and her influence as a spokeswoman for women's issues was more widely felt.

Hale emerged as an editor of collected works early on with *The Ladies' Wreath; A Selection from the Female Poetic Writers of England and America* (Boston: Marsh, Capen and Lyon, 1837; **A, G**), which reflected her efforts to increase the esteem of women writers, as did her monumental *Woman's Record; or Sketches of all Distinguished Women* (New York: Harper & Brothers, 1853; **A, G**). Biographical information on herself that she included in these works and prefatory remarks in other publications have constituted the core of primary sources available to modern biography series such as *Notable American Women* (Cambridge, MA: Belknap Press, 1971; **A, G**).

The most significant collections of Hale's letters are found in the Department of Rare Books and Manuscripts of the Boston Public Library; the Manuscripts Department of the Houghton Library, Harvard University, Cambridge, MA; The Connecticut Historical Society, Hartford, CT; The Historical Society of Pennsylvania, Philadelphia, PA; the Library Company of Philadelphia; Vassar College Library, Poughkeepsie, NY; and the Huntington Library, San Marino, CA.

Other Sources

Boyer, Paul S. "Sarah Josepha Hale." In *Notable American Women*, edited by Edward T. James, et al. Cambridge, MA: Belknap Press, 1971. Concise summary of Hale's life and works.

Zophy, Angela Howard. "Sarah Josepha Hale, Matron of Victorian Womanhood." In *For the General Welfare: Essays in Honor of Robert H. Brenner*, edited by Frank Annunziata and Roy T. Wortman. New York: Peter Lang, 1989. Twenty-eight pages are devoted to Hale.

————. "Sarah Josepha Hale." In *Handbook of American Women's History*. New York: Garland, 1990. Zophy places Hale's career in the context of currents and concepts of nineteenth-century American women's history and supplies accessible sources to further research on Hale.

Angela Howard Zophy
University of Houston, Clear Lake

HANDSOME LAKE
1735-1815

Chronology

Born 1735 in Seneca village of Gano'wages on the Genesee River, near present-day Avon, New York, into the Wolf clan; neither the names of his parents nor his baby name is known; marries and has two or three children; nothing known of wife; Handsome Lake is described as thin and unhealthy looking; fights as common warrior with Seneca on the British side during the American Revolution; *1779* after Seneca villages are raided, moves with family to Tonawanda, New York, near Buffalo; *1780* moves to village of Burnt House on Allegheny River on grant of half-brother Chief Cornplanter; assumes name of Ganioda'yo or Handsome Lake; is dissolute, alcoholic and depressed. *1798* Quakers arrive at Burnt House to teach and help Native Americans; *June 15, 1799* has first vision; *1799* others follow and he forms ministry of Gaii'wiio or Good Message; commences preaching; *1802* visits Washington, D.C., with delegation of Seneca and Onondaga chiefs; Secretary of State Dearborn and President Jefferson send messages of support; *1801* at Buffalo Creek Council, is made supreme leader of Six Nations; gradually loses political support with Seneca, but continues to preach with great success; *1815* visits Native American town of Onondaga Castle; dies and is buried there.

Activities of Historical Significance

After the collapse of the Iroquois Confederacy, the Seneca tribe was restless and in despair. Alcoholism and domestic violence were commonplace. Some reforms had been instituted with help from the Quakers, but more were needed. The religion of Handsome Lake provided a stimulus for change. Its syntheses of traditional Iroquois beliefs with those of the Quakers was perfectly suited to the situation. He preached against alcoholism and stressed the value of a strong home life and the importance of social cooperation. Handsome Lake was especially concerned with the care of children. He held, but later discarded, a belief in witchcraft. The benefits to the Seneca were economic as well as moral, and enabled them to survive as a cultural entity. There are seven thousand members of the Handsome Lake religion today.

Overview of Biographical Sources

Handsome Lake cannot be separated from the religion he founded. Very little is known about him until the time of his first vision, when he was sixty-four, and there are no "pure" biographies of him. For this reason, biographical information is most readily found in accounts of the Handsome Lake religion.

Arthur C. Parker in *Parker on the Iroquois* (1913) has much to offer, and more can be learned from his transcription of the code of the Handsome Lake religion. Since its publication, more information has become available from diaries and interviews, and Anthony F. C. Wallace's *Death and Rebirth of the Seneca* (1969) has made full use of them in his definitive treatment. Aren Akweks's pamphlet shows how Handsome Lake's teachings were used by twentieth-century Seneca. Additional articles offer different perspectives and discuss the effects of his religion.

Evaluation of Principal Biographical Sources

Akweks, Aren. *Sa-Ko-Ri-On-Nie-Ni, Our Great Teacher*. Malone, NY: Ray Fadden, 1947. (A, G) A pamphlet printed for the Akwesasne Counselor Organization for use on the St. Regis Reservation, Hogansburg, New York. Gives the story of Handsome Lake's life and teachings. Drawings in sign language by the author.

Deardorff, Merle H. "The Religion of Handsome Lake: Its Origin and Development." In *Symposium on Local Diversity in Iroquois Culture No. 5, Bureau of American Ethnology Bulletin*, No. 149. Washington DC: Government Printing Office, 1951. (A) Brief but accurate ethnological study. Bibliography lists primary sources.

Morgan, Lewis H. *League of the Ho-de-no-sau-nee or Iroquois*. Edited by Herbert M. Lloyd. New York: Franklin, 1966. (A) This classic anthropological study, first published in 1851, includes information that Morgan learned from contemporaries of Handsome Lake and describes the religion. Morgan terms Handsome Lake's influence salutary and preservative of the Seneca people.

Parker, Arthur C. *Parker on the Iroquois*. Edited by William N. Fenton. Syracuse, NY: Syracuse University Press, 1968. (A) Includes a transcription of the Code of Handsome Lake which was originally published as a bulletin of the New York State Museum in 1913. Parker, of Iroquois and Quaker stock, persuaded Chief Edward Cornplanter, one of Handsome Lake's ministers, to commit to writing his version of the Code. William Bluesky, a Baptist minister, served as interpreter. Parker recounts what was known about Handsome Lake at the time and notes that nothing of any consequence was known about his life until he had his vision. Fenton's edition is illustrated by the delightful drawings of Jesse Cornplanter, son of Chief Cornplanter.

Wallace, Anthony F. C. "Cultural Composition of the Handsome Lake Religion." In *Bureau of American Ethnology Bulletin 180*, No. 14. Washington, DC: Government Printing Office, 1961. (A) An examination of the Handsome Lake religion, which maintains that it reveals the culture, personality, and situational stresses of its founder. Notes new religions begin as revitalization movements in demoralized social groups. Uses Morgan, Parker, and the Quaker journals.

————. *Death and Rebirth of the Seneca: The History and Culture of the Great Iroquois Nation, Their Destruction and Demoralization and Their Cultural Revival at the Hands of the Indian Visionary, Handsome Lake*. New York: Knopf, 1969. (A, G) Wallace, an anthropologist and medical research scientist, has produced a synthesis of Iroquois history and ethnology that uses psychological concepts to explain the Handsome Lake phenomenon. He gives many new details of the prophet's life. Contains forty-four pages of notes and references. While one might disagree with some of Wallace's interpretations, this is the definitive study of the Handsome Lake religion, and includes more biographical information than any other work.

Overview and Evaluation of Primary Sources
The most important primary sources are the Quaker diaries of that time, some of which have been published. Wallace has published Halliday Jackson's journal to the Seneca Indians in *Pennsylvania History* 19 (1952): 117-147. Excerpts from others have been reprinted in his *Death and Rebirth of the Seneca*.
The Chester County Historical Society (Pennsylvania) holds transcripts of Henry Simmons' journals and his letter books, as well as some of the Halliday Jackson journals. The Philadelphia Yearly Meeting Archives, located at the Friends Book Store, Philadelphia, holds a large amount of material from this period. The Swarthmore College Friends Historical Library in Philadelphia holds the journals and letter books of Halliday Jackson and Henry Simmons. The Historical Society of Pennsylvania holds papers of Captain John Logan who was living at Burnt House at the time of Handsome Lake's vision. Some biographical information can be found in the Code of Handsome Lake, mentioned above.

Fiction and Adaptations
The story of Handsome Lake is one of seven told on the audiocassette *More Tales of the Eastern Woodlands* (Greenville, NC: Stove Story, 1987).

Museums, Historical Landmarks, Societies

New York State Library (Albany, NY). State Education Building has an outstanding collection on the Iroquois.

Reed Library (Fredonia, NY). State University of New York at Fredonia has extensive collection on the Iroquois.

Grave of Handsome Lake (Onondaga, NY). Near Onondaga Council House, Onondaga Reservation.

Other Sources

Bowden, Henry Warner, ed. *Dictionary of Religious Biography.* Westport, CT: Greenwood, 1977. A brief, accurate entry.

Eliade, Mircea, ed. *Encyclopedia of Religion.* New York: Macmillan, 1987. Solid two-page entry with annotated bibliography.

Lanternari, Vittorio. *The Religions of the Oppressed; A Study of Modern Messianic Cults.* New York: Knopf. 1962. Contains section on Handsome Lake religion. Describes social and cultural conditions and stresses message of hope.

Tooker, Elizabeth. "On the New Religion of Handsome Lake." *Anthropological Quarterly* 41 (October 1968): 187-200. An analysis of his religion. Tooker argues that Handsome Lake was attempting to introduce values that would be consistent with the new economic and social system. Cooperation was necessary and "impulse control" was codified and preserved in the oral tradition.

Wilson, Bryan R. *Magic and the Millenium; a Sociological Study of Religious Movements of Protest Among Tribal and Third World Peoples.* New York: Harper, 1972. Includes a section on the Handsome Lake religion. Primarily a sociological study, yet contains biographical and background material.

Patricia Brauch
Brooklyn College Library
City University of New York

MATTHEW A. HENSON
1866-1955

Chronology

Born Matthew Alexander Henson on August 8, 1866, on a farm in Charles County, Maryland, the son of Lemuel Henson, a sharecropper, and Caroline Gaines Henson; *1866-1878* details of early life are uncertain; grows up in Charles County and Washington, D.C., where he moves following the death of his mother; *1879-1884* serves on board the merchant ship *Katie Hines*, rising from cabin boy to able-bodied seaman; *1877* meets Lt. Robert E. Peary, a naval civil engineer officer and is hired as Peary's valet; *1887-1888* travels to Nicaragua with Peary, who is surveying a route for a possible inter-ocean canal; *1891-1897* accompanies Peary as his assistant on four expeditions to Greenland; *1898-1902* makes first exploration of polar region with Peary; *1905-1906* Henson and Peary come within 174 miles of North Pole; *1907* marries Lucy Ross; *April 6, 1909* Henson, Peary, and four Eskimos reach North Pole (according to Peary's calculations); *1913-1937* works as messenger boy, later clerk, at the Federal Customs House in New York City; *March 9, 1955* dies of a cerebral hemorrhage and is buried at Woodlawn Cemetery in New York City; *April 6, 1988* reburied next to Peary at Arlington National Cemetery.

Activities of Historical Significance

Matthew A. Henson was the constant and invaluable companion of Robert E. Peary during four expeditions to explore the interior and northern coast of Greenland, and during three Polar expeditions. On April 6, 1909, Henson and four Eskimos accompanied Peary on the final dash toward the North Pole. Although Peary's claim to have reached the Pole continues to generate controversy, there is no question that he and Henson rank among the foremost Arctic explorers.

Henson, unlike Peary, learned to speak the local dialect of the native language. He became a skilled sled driver and an expert hunter. It was Henson who perfected the equipment and led the drive on Peary's expeditions across the Arctic icecap. When Peary neared the Pole, he selected Henson to accompany him on the final dash, explaining "I can't get along without him."

Henson's many contributions to Peary's triumphs at first received little notice. While a grateful nation showered Peary with honors, it ignored Henson. Only later in life, thanks to the efforts of Donald B. MacMillan and other supporters, did Henson receive a measure of recognition. A legendary figure among the Eskimos of the Far North, Henson fared poorly in a society that all too often judged a man by the color of his skin.

Overview of Biographical Sources

Henson has been the subject of two biographies, both admiring and neither a satisfactory account of his life. Bradley Robinson, *Dark Companion* (1947), was written with Henson's assistance. Filled with invented dialogue, the book records Henson's contributions to Arctic exploration but does not probe deeply into his personality or his relationship with Peary. Floyd Miller, *Ahdoolo! The Biography of Matthew A. Henson* (1963) borrows heavily from Robinson and contains few insights; it is best suited for younger, uncritical readers.

Evaluation of Principal Biographical Sources

Herbert, Wally. *The Noose of Laurels: Robert E. Peary and the Race to the North Pole.* New York: Atheneum, 1989. (A, G, Y) Although Herbert concludes that Peary and Henson failed to reach the Pole, he writes with admiration of both men as pioneering Arctic explorers. The book focuses on Peary but includes an extensive treatment of Henson.

Hobbs, William Herbert. *Peary.* New York: Macmillan, 1936. (G, Y) This flattering portrait of Peary, the standard biography of the explorer for many years, depicts Henson as a loyal and faithful "negro servant and assistant."

Logan, Rayford W. "Matthew Alexander Henson." In *Dictionary of American Negro Biography*, edited by Rayford W. Logan and Michael R. Winston. New York: Norton, 1982. (A, G) This brief sketch argues, persuasively, that "there is little question that Henson's race was the predominant factor in denying him due recognition."

Miller, Floyd. *Ahdoolo! The Biography of Matthew A. Henson.* New York: Dutton, 1963. (G, Y) Obviously a labor of love, this biography seems more suitable for a younger audience.

Robinson, Bradley. *Dark Companion.* New York: National Travel Club, 1947. (G, Y) Although a somewhat dated account of Henson's many contributions to Arctic exploration, this remains the best treatment of his life.

Weems, John Edward. "Matthew Alexander Henson." In *Dictionary of American Biography, Supplement 5 (1951-1955)*, edited by John A. Garraty. New York: Scribner's, 1977. (A, G) This is the best brief account of Henson's life.

————. *Peary: The Explorer and the Man.* Boston: Houghton Mifflin, 1967. (A, G, Y) Replacing Hobbs as the standard biography of Peary, this volume devotes a good deal more attention to Henson.

Overview and Evaluation of Primary Sources

The Papers of Robert E. Peary can be found at the Center for Polar Archives, National Archives, Washington, D.C. There is no collection of Henson Papers.

Matthew A. Henson, *A Negro Explorer at the North Pole* (New York: Stokes, 1912; A, G, Y) is a ghost-written account of his life that retains some of the flavor of the man. It has been republished as *A Black Explorer at the North Pole* (Lincoln: University of Nebraska Press, 1989), with an excellent, short introduction by Susan A. Kaplan, director of Bowdoin College's Peary-MacMillan Arctic Museum.

Henson's activities can be seen, indirectly for the most part, in Peary's books: *Northward Over the "Great Ice,"* 2 vols. (New York: Stokes, 1898; A, G, Y), an account of the Greenland expeditions; *Nearest to the Pole* (New York: Doubleday, 1907; A, G, Y), the story of the 1905-1906 attempt to reach the Pole; and *The North Pole* (New York: Stokes, 1910; A, G, Y), which records the final adventure.

Henson also makes brief appearances in the memoirs of other individuals who accompanied Peary on his various expeditions: Robert A. Bartlett, *The Log of "Bob" Bartlett* (New York: Putnam, 1928; A, G, Y); George Borup, *A Tenderfoot with Peary* (New York: Stokes, 1911; A, G, Y); and Donald B. MacMillan (who later led the fight to obtain proper recognition for Henson), *How Peary Reached the North Pole* (Boston: Houghton Mifflin, 1934; A, G, Y).

Museums, Historical Landmarks, Societies

Matthew A. Henson Grammar School (Chicago, IL). School on South Avers Avenue has been named in Henson's honor.

Matthew A. Henson State Park (Aspen Hill, MD). This park near Washington, D.C., was established in 1989.

National Geographic Society (Washington, DC). Contains artifacts from the polar expeditions.

Peary-MacMillan Arctic Museum (Brunswick, ME). This museum at Bowdoin College, Peary's alma mater, has a small but important collection of polar material.

Plaque (Annapolis, MD). Plaque honoring Henson stands in the Maryland State House.

Other Sources
Counter, S. Allen. "The Henson Family." *National Geographic* 174 (September 1988): 422-29. This article brought to public attention Henson's descendants by his Eskimo wife. Counter found that tales of Maripaluk (Matthew the Kind One) have become part of the Polar Eskimo legends and songs.

Green, Fitzhugh. *Peary: The Man Who Refused to Fail.* New York: Putnam's, 1926. This first major biography of Peary barely mentions Henson.

William M. Leary
University of Georgia

ISABELLA BEECHER HOOKER
1822-1907

Chronology

Born Isabella Beecher on February 22, 1822, to Lyman Beecher, a prominent minister, and his second wife, Harriet Porter Beecher, in Litchfield, Connecticut; *1832* moves to Walnut Hills, Ohio, when father is appointed head of the Lane Theological Seminary; *1835-1838* attends Hartford Female Seminary and Western Female Institute, founded by her half sister, Catherine Beecher; *August 5, 1841* marries John Hooker, a lawyer; *1842-1855* gives birth to two sons and two daughters; the eldest son dies in infancy; *1861* reads Harriet Mill's "Enfranchisement of Women"; *1868* meets Susan B. Anthony and Elizabeth Cady Stanton in Providence, Rhode Island; helps found New England Woman Suffrage Association; publishes first article advocating women's suffrage; *1869* presides over the founding of the Connecticut Woman Suffrage Association; *1870* introduces a married woman property bill, drafted by her husband, in the Connecticut legislature; *1871* meets Victoria Claflin Woodhull; *1872* beginning of Beecher/Tilton controversy, as half-brother Henry Ward Beecher defends himself against charges of adultery; *1874-1875* tours Europe to escape controversy surrounding half-brother's trial; *1877* Connecticut legislature passes married woman's property bill; *1901* John Hooker dies; *1907* dies January 5; is buried in Cedar Hill Cemetery in Hartford.

Activities of Historical Significance

A member of one of the most notable American families of the nineteenth century, Isabella Beecher Hooker has been overshadowed by her more flamboyant brother Henry Ward Beecher and her sisters Harriet Beecher Stowe and Catherine Beecher. Only recently has Isabella begun to receive attention for her own merits. After she brought up her children, she became active in the movement to secure the right to vote for women. In 1869, she played a supporting role in the division of the women's movement, siding with the more radical National Woman Suffrage Association. At the same time she began to push for legislation which would protect the property of married women, succeeding when the Connecticut state legislature passed such an act in 1877. She also asserted that the female's inherent maternal nature endowed women with a superior moral sense. Although this in itself was not a new position, she used it to justify her philosophy that women in the public life would act to elevate the ethical character of society and politics.

In her early life Hooker had enjoyed a fairly amiable relationship with her famous siblings. But in affiliating with Victoria Woodhull, deemed infamous by many for her advocacy of "free love," Hooker strained her relations with her half-sisters. The relationship endured even more tension when she questioned the veracity of her half-brother, Henry Ward Beecher, after the minister proclaimed his innocence in response to Woodhull's accusation that he had committed adultery with Elizabeth Tilton, wife of prominent reform editor Theodore Tilton. Despite public tensions relating to Henry that cast doubts on her work, Hooker continued her efforts in support of the movement for woman suffrage throughout the remainder of her life.

Overview of Biographical Sources

There is no full biography of Isabella Beecher Hooker. The best examinations of her life are to be found in Jeanne Boydston, Mary Kelley, and Anne Margolis, *The Limits of Sisterhood* (1988) and in Margolis's introductory essay which accompanies the microfilm guide to Hooker's papers. Milton Rugoff's chapters on Hooker in his study, *The Beechers: An American Family in the Nineteenth Century* (1981), provide a short, readable summary.

Evaluation of Principal Biographical Sources

Boydston, Jeanne, Mary Kelley, and Anne Margolis. *The Limits of Sisterhood: The Beecher Sisters on Women's Rights and Woman's Sphere.* Chapel Hill: University of North Carolina Press, 1988. (A, G) A combination of essays and primary sources that delves into the efforts of Hooker, Catherine Beecher, and Harriet Beecher Stowe to define women's role in society.

Margolis, Anne. "A Tempest Tossed Spirit: Isabella Beecher Hooker and Woman Suffrage," *The Isabella Beecher Hooker Project.* Hartford, CT: Stowe-Day Foundation, 1879. 9-45. (A) Skillfully examines the interaction between Hooker's public and private life.

Rugoff, Milton. *The Beechers: An American Family in the Nineteenth Century.* New York: Harper and Row, 1981. (A, G) Places Hooker in the context of the Beecher family, and devotes two chapters to her life.

Overview and Evaluation of Primary Sources

Hooker composed a brief, yet revealing autobiographical sketch, which appeared in *The Connecticut Magazine* 9 (May 1905). *A Mother's Letters to a Daughter on Woman Suffrage* (Hartford, CT: Case, Lockwood and Brainard, 1870; A, G) contains her early advocacy of a woman's right to vote, while

Womanhood: Its Sanctities and Fidelities (Boston: Lee and Shepard, 1873; **A**), written in the midst of the Beecher-Tilton scandal, asserts the superior moral character of women inherent in their role as mother. Future studies of Hooker will be based upon the microfilm edition of her papers, available as *The Isabella Beecher Hooker Project* (Hartford, CT: The Stowe-Day Foundation, 1979; **A**).

Museums, Historical Landmarks, Societies

Beecher Birthplace (Litchfield, CT). The house has been moved to the Forman School, where it is closed to the public, but a historical marker on State Highway 63 designates the original site.

Memorial Library (Hartford, CT). Contains over 15,000 volumes, 6,000 pamphlets, and 100,000 manuscript items, most concerning the suffrage movement.

Nook Farm (Hartford, CT). Center of Hooker's neighborhood, whose residents included Mark Twain and Charles Dudley Warner, as well as the Beecher sisters.

Stowe-Day Foundation (Hartford, CT). Endowed by Katherine Seymour Day, Hooker's granddaughter, the foundation supports Nook Farm, the Memorial Library, and the Hooker Project.

Stowe House Community Center (Cincinnati, OH). Located in the Walnut Hills section, this was Isabella Beecher's home intermittently between 1832 and 1838. Most of the center is devoted to collections on black history, but one room has been set aside for artifacts of the Beecher family.

Other Sources

Dubois, Ellen Carol. *Feminism and Suffrage: The Emergence of an Independent Women's Movement in America, 1848-1869.* Ithaca, NY: Cornell University Press, 1978. This standard account of the early years of the women's suffrage movement emphasizes the links between it and the later feminist movement through the creation of a distinct female identity and consciousness.

Flexner, Eleanor. *Century of Struggle: The Women's Rights Movement in the United States.* rev. ed. Cambridge: Harvard University Press, 1975. A pioneering work, still essential to understanding the fight for suffrage after 1869.

Gurko, Miriam. *The Ladies of Seneca Falls: The Birth of the Woman's Rights Movement.* 1974. Reprint. New York: Schocken Books, 1976. A lively, but not always accurate or critical account.

Scott, Anne F., and Andrew M. Scott. *One Half the People: The Fight For Woman Suffrage.* New York: Lippincott, 1975. Combining documents and commentary, this short volume provides a useful and insightful introduction to the history of the suffrage movement.

Stanton, Elizabeth Cady, Susan B. Anthony, et al. *History of Woman Suffrage.* 6 vols. 1881. Reprint. New York: Arno Press, 1969. A documentary history of the effort to secure the right to vote for women, this remains a standard and essential source.

Waller, Altina L. *Reverend Beecher and Mrs. Tilton: Sex and Class in Victorian America.* Amherst: University of Massachusetts Press, 1982. The best study of the famous adultery trial, emphasizing the political and social backdrop against which the drama was played out.

Brooks Donohue Simpson
Arizona State University

LANGSTON HUGHES
1902-1967

Chronology

Born James Langston Hughes on February 1, 1902, in Joplin, Missouri, to Carrie Langston Hughes and James Nathaniel Hughes; *1902-1914* lives in Missouri, Kansas, and Mexico for brief periods with his parents, then, after they separate, with his grandmother in Lawrence, Kansas; *1914* moves to Lincoln, Illinois, to join his mother and stepfather; *1916* elected class poet for grammar school graduation at Lincoln; *1920* graduates from Central High School, Cleveland, Ohio; spends a year in Mexico with his father; *1921* publishes poem "The Negro Speaks of Rivers" in *The Crisis*; spends a year at Columbia University; *1923* works as cook's helper on tramp steamer to Africa and Europe; *1924* returns to Washington, D.C., to live with his mother; *1925* wins prizes for poetry and essay in *Opportunity* and *The Crisis* contests; *1926* enters Lincoln University in Pennsylvania; publishes *Weary Blues* and *Fire*; *1927* publishes *Fine Clothes to the Jew*; *1929* graduates from Lincoln University; *1930* publishes *Not Without Laughter*; wins Harmon Award for literature; visits Haiti; *1931* goes on poetry reading tour in the southern and western United States; *1932* travels to Russia; *1933* returns to California via Japan; *1934* publishes *The Ways of White Folks*; *1935* awarded Guggenheim Fellowship; *1937* travels to Spain to report on the civil war; *1940* publishes *The Big Sea*; *1941* awarded Rosenwald Fellowship; *1942* publishes *Shakespeare in Harlem*; *1946* awarded grant from American Academy of Arts and Letters; *1947* publishes *Fields of Wonder*; *1950* publishes *Simple Speaks His Mind*; *1951* publishes *Montage on a Dream Deferred*; *1952* publishes *Laughing to Keep from Crying* and *First Book of Negroes*; *1953* publishes *Simple Takes a Wife*; receives Anisfield-Wolf Award; *1954* publishes *Famous American Negroes*; *1955* publishes *Sweet Flypaper of Life*; *1956* publishes *I Wonder as I Wander*; *1958* publishes *Tambourines to Glory*; *1959* publishes *Selected Poems*; *1960* awarded Spingarn Medal; publishes *African Treasury*; *1961* publishes *Ask Your Mama*; elected to membership in National Institute of Arts and Letters; *1962* publishes *Fight for Freedom*; *1963* publishes *Five Plays*; *1965* publishes *Simple's Uncle Sam*; *1967* dies on May 22 in New York City; *The Panther and the Lash* published posthumously.

Activities of Historical Significance

Langston Hughes may be the best-known African-American writer of the twentieth century. An author of poetry, fiction, and autobiography, he was also an anthologist, librettist, songwriter, columnist, translator, theater founder, and dramatist. His poems, novels, short stories, dramas, translations, and anthologies cover the span of years from the Harlem Renaissance in the 1920s to the black arts movement of the 1960s. A champion of social justice and racial equality, Hughes expressed the idea that all people have inherent dignity. His versatile and experimental writings demonstrate great insight and generous humor.

For over forty years, Hughes sought to develop one theme in almost all of his writings: the sorrows and the joys in the enduring lives of African Americans. His poetry may be grouped by some unifying themes: protest and social commentary; Harlem poems; folk-influenced poetry; and African and negritude themes.

Hughes's fiction, twelve volumes in all, includes two novels, a novella, three collections of short stories, and six books devoted to Jesse B. Semple. Semple (or Simple), probably the best-known character created by Hughes, began his life in a 1943 column in the Chicago *Defender*. Simple is an African American whose wry commentary on American society falls into the tradition of folk humor.

As a playwright, Hughes made outstanding contributions to African-American theater. He not only wrote plays and musicals, but founded three theater groups. In his dramas, as in his poetry and fiction, Hughes made excellent use of folk material.

Overview of Biographical/Critical Sources

In the past fifty years, more than fifteen volumes on Hughes have been published and more than a score of doctoral dissertations have been written. Hughes enjoyed a long and productive career as a professional writer. His reputation outside the United States is perhaps greater than within his native land. A possible reason for this lack of recognition in his own country is that Hughes produced no single work that achieved the status of masterpiece. Despite this void, Hughes's output is so overwhelming—he authored more than forty books, edited or translated fourteen more, and wrote hundreds of reviews and essays—that he rightly deserves to be called the "Dean of Black Letters." Since Hughes's death, his stature has grown as critics gain a new appreciation for his creativity and versatility.

Evaluation of Principal Biographical/Critical Sources

Barksdale, Richard K. *Langston Hughes: The Poet and His Critics*. Chicago: American Library Association, 1977. (A, G) An assessment of major critics' responses to Hughes's poetry.

Berry, Faith. *Langston Hughes Before and Beyond Harlem*. Westport, CT: Lawrence Hill, 1983. (A) Traces Hughes's career up to his permanent move to Harlem in the 1940s. A well-documented history of the early years, the Harlem Renaissance, and the influence of Marxist aesthetics on Hughes's work. Because Berry maintains that Hughes was a homosexual, the book has been the object of controversy.

Dickinson, Donald C. *A Bio-Bibliography of Langston Hughes*. Hamden, CT: Archon, 1967. Rev. Ed. 1972. (A) Based on a doctoral dissertation, this book consists of a biographical essay and a bibliography of works by and about Hughes. Dickinson maintains that his subject's output was uneven but that Hughes produced memorable work that has been ignored by the critics.

Emanuel, James A. *Langston Hughes*. New York: Twayne, 1967. (G, Y) A brief, well-written book intended to offer an overview of Hughes's life and work. Emanuel concludes that Hughes is the dean of African-American writers who illuminate the black condition.

Jemie, Onwuchekwa. *Langston Hughes: An Introduction to the Poetry*. New York: Columbia University Press: 1976. (A, G) The first full-length study of Hughes's verse is an introduction to his collected poems from the perspectives of the African-American oral tradition (jazz and blues) and the tradition of social protest. Contains an excellent chronology and sketch.

Miller, R. Baxter. *Langston Hughes and Gwendolyn Brooks: a Reference Guide*. Boston: G. K. Hall, 1977. (A) A carefully annotated list of secondary literature from 1924 to 1977.

Mullen, Edward J. *Langston Hughes in the Hispanic World and Haiti*. Hamden, CT: Archon, 1977. (A, G) Offers a bibliographic view of Hughes's Latin-American connections.

O'Daniel, Therman B. *Langston Hughes, Black Genius: A Critical Evaluation*. New York: William Morrow, 1971. (A) Fourteen essays as well as an extensive selected classified bibliography that helps to further the image of Hughes as father of black American letters.

Rampersad, Arnold. *The Life of Langston Hughes*. New York: Oxford University Press, 1986, 1988. (A) This scholarly, definitive, two-volume study is readable and reliable. Volume 1, covering 1902-1941, is subtitled "I, Too, Sing America." Volume 2, covering 1941-1967, is called "I Dream a World." Rampersad has constructed a masterful biography from primary sources, interviews, and correspondence.

Evaluation of Biographies for Young People

Davis, Ossie. *Langston*. New York: Delacorte, 1982. In this play, Hughes visits a church basement where a drama group is rehearsing one of his plays, and he uses the actors to recreate scenes from his early life. For secondary school students.

Dunham, Montrew. *Langston Hughes: Young Black Poet*. Indianapolis: Bobbs-Merrill, 1972. This volume in the Childhood of Famous Americans Series concentrates on the early years. An illustrated book for middle school.

Meltzer, Milton. *Langston Hughes: A Biography*. New York: Thomas Y. Crowell, 1968. A National Book Award finalist in 1969, this work draws heavily on Hughes's autobiography. For Meltzer, "the man was his work, the work, the man." For secondary school students.

Myers, Elisabeth P. *Langston Hughes: Poet of His People*. Champaign, IL: Garrard, 1970. Using excerpts from Hughes's autobiographies and poetry, Myers traces his life from unsettled childhood to successful maturity. Illustrated with drawings and photographs. Written for middle school students.

Rollins, Charlemae H. *Black Troubadour: Langston Hughes*. Chicago: Rand McNally, 1970. Offers a sympathetic portrait of Hughes as a spokesman for all blacks. Written for junior high students.

Rummel, Jack. *Langston Hughes*. New York: Chelsea House, 1988. One of the Black Americans Achievement Series of interesting and well-illustrated books for secondary school students.

Walker, Alice. *Langston Hughes, American Poet*. New York: Thomas Y. Crowell, 1974. Walker's first book for children grew out of a desire to write about Hughes after meeting him. She writes, "Hardly a day goes by that I don't think of him or speak of him." Illustrated. For elementary readers.

Overview and Evaluation of Primary Sources

The main depository of Langston Hughes's papers is the James Weldon Johnson Memorial Collection in the Beinecke Rare Book and Manuscript Library at Yale University. Other sources of primary materials may be found in the acknowledgments section of Rampersad's biography. A volume of published letters is Charles H. Nichols's *Arna Bontemps-Langston Hughes Letters, 1925-1967* (New York: Dodd, Mead, 1980; **A, G**), which introduces the reader to the lively intellectual milieu of African-American writers.

Hughes wrote two volumes of autobiography. *The Big Sea* (New York: Knopf, 1940; **A, G, Y**) tells of his life up to 1931 in gently humorous straightforward prose. It gives a particularly vivid picture of the Harlem Renaissance. The second autobiographical volume, *I Wonder as I Wander* (New York: Rinehart, 1956; **A, G, Y**), is a collection of memoirs covering 1931-1937. Here Hughes, the world traveler, tells about his travels in Russia, Japan, China, and Spain.

Museums, Historical Landmarks, Societies
Fisk University (Nashville, TN). The library houses a collection of Hughes memorabilia.

Langston Hughes Society, Brown University (Providence, RI). Founded in 1981, this organization publishes the *Langston Hughes Review*.

Lincoln University (Lincoln University, PA). The library of Hughes's alma mater hold a collection of the author's memorabilia.

Schomburg Collection (New York, NY). Located in the New York Public Library, this collection includes Hughes memorabilia.

Other Sources
Bloom, Harold, ed. *Langston Hughes*. New York: Chelsea House, 1989. A collection of twelve previously published critical essays on Hughes and his work, arranged in chronological order of their original publication.

Miller, R. Baxter. *The Art and Imagination of Langston Hughes*. Lexington: University Press of Kentucky, 1989. This scholarly book reconsiders the complex patterns of meaning in Hughes's literary imagination.

Mullen, Edward J. *Critical Essays on Langston Hughes*. Boston: G. K. Hall, 1986. Includes a fine introduction to reprinted reviews, articles, and essays on Hughes's poetry, prose, and drama.

Tracy, Steven C. *Langston Hughes and the Blues*. Champaign: University of Illinois Press, 1988. Explores Hughes's use of the blues tradition, which he considered folk poetry worthy of comparison with the world's best folk literature.

Jacob L. Susskind
Pennsylvania State University

JESSE JACKSON
b. 1941

Chronology

Born Jesse Louis Jackson in Greenville, South Carolina on October 8, 1941, son of a teenage student, Helen Burns, and a married man who was her neighbor; *1941-1959* grows up in the segregated southern city of Greenville; is subject to the social indignities against African Americans during this time; *1950* mother marries Charles Henry Jackson, who legally adopts Jesse; mother works as a domestic servant; family lives in relative poverty; *1955-1959* attends Sterling High School where he excells academically and athletically; *1959* unable to attend Furman University in Greenville because of its policy of racial exclusion, he obtains an athletic scholarship to the University of Illinois with the help of the Furman basketball coach; although he excels as a quarterback, he is told by an Illinois coach that quarterback is a "white-only" position; *1960* transfers to the predominantly black North Carolina Agricultural and Technical College in Greensboro, where he is star quarterback and student body president; *1962* graduates from North Carolina A&T; moves to Chicago and attends Chicago Theological Seminary; *1964* marries Jacqueline Brown, with whom he has five children; *1965* leaves his studies to work in the civil rights movement with Dr. Martin Luther King, Jr. in Alabama; becomes a top aide in King's Southern Christian Leadership Conference (SCLC); *1966* sent to Chicago by SCLC leadership to establish Operation Breadbasket, a project to win economic concessions from big businesses operating in the black community; *1968* in attendence when King is assassinated in Memphis, Tennessee, on April 4; *1969* named by King's successor, Rev. Ralph David Abernathy, as "mayor" of Resurrection City, an SCLC tent encampment in Washington, D.C., protesting the plight of the poor; leads protests against hunger at the Department of Agriculture; *1971* meets with Abernathy in Chicago over alleged financial irregularities in Operation Breadbasket; *1972* leaves SCLC and founds Operation PUSH (People United to Save Humanity, later altered to People United to Serve Humanity); leads a successful effort to challenge Chicago's democratic delegates to the Democratic National Convention in Miami; *1972-1984* heads Operation PUSH in Chicago; works for economic empowerment of black community and greater access for blacks to city jobs and services; organizes voter registration drive instrumental in electing Chicago's first black mayor, Harold Washington; *1984* runs for the presidential nomination of the Democratic Party; campaigns as leader of the "Rainbow Coalition" on the issues of racial and economic justice; controversy erupts over his support for a Palestinian state in the Middle East; attends the Democratic National Convention in San Francisco with 384 delegates won in two primaries; *1984* obtains the release of prisoners held in Cuban jails; travels to Syria and obtains release of downed U.S. pilot Lt. Robert Goodman; *1988* campaigns for the presidential nomination of the Democratic Party on the platform of racial and economic equality; *1989* campaigns for David Dinkins in his successful bid to become the first black mayor of New York City; *1990* travels to South Africa to greet Nelson Mandela of the African National Congress as he is freed from prison; elected "shadow senator" from Washington, D.C., to lobby for its admission to statehood; travels to the Middle East as a journalist after Iraq's invasion of Kuwait to work for the release of foreign hostages and interview President Saddam Hussein of Iraq; inagurates hour-long, weekly television news show.

Activities of Historical Significance

Jackson's political activism began in the civil rights movement of the 1950s and 1960s. During the early 1960s he played a pivotal role in local Congress of Racial Equality (CORE) demonstrations that led ultimately to the destruction of legally sanctioned racial segregation. Later, while attending Chicago Theological Seminary, he was outraged by news reports of the beating of civil rights demonstrators in the South. When he subsequently left the seminary to join Dr. Martin Luther King, Jr. in Alabama, it was the turning point of his career. Later, working for the SCLC in Chicago, Jackson played a major role in the success of Operation Breadbasket, which eventually was emulated by the NAACP and other civil rights organizations.

Jackson was at the Lorraine Motel in Memphis, Tennessee, when Dr. King was murdered on April 4, 1968. His appearance on national television in a shirt allegedly stained with King's blood remains controversial.

In 1971 Jackson left the SCLC to form his own organization, Operation PUSH, which became well-known for the Saturday morning sessions where overflow crowds gathered to hear Jackson's chants—"I Am Somebody"—and his powerful and persuasive preaching on social and political issues.

Jackson's success in preventing Chicago Mayor Daley and the Cook County Democratic Party regulars from being seated at the Democratic National Convention in Miami won the notice of the national news media and, as a result, he began appearing more frequently on television and in news magazines throughout the 1970s. PUSH was recognized as being effective in forcing major corporations to employ more African Americans and to grant more contracts to minority businesses. As a political organization, PUSH organized a number of well-attended "expositions" that featured black entertainers such as Roberta Flack and Bill Cosby.

Jackson was instrumental in convincing a popular black congressman, Harold Washington, to enter the race for mayor of Chicago. However, before he agreed to run, Washington insisted that Jackson and others spearhead a massive voter registration drive, and the success of this campaign contributed to the election of Chicago's first black mayor. It also served as a model for Jackson's race for the presidency in 1984.

In the campaign for the 1984 Democratic nomination, Jackson's goal was to open the convention process so that minority concerns would be included in the platform, to establish a power base that would ensure that the Democratic nominee would introduce legislation to help minorities, and to boost voter registration.

Jackson's race for the Democratic presidential nomination was not without incident. In an off-the-record conversation with an African-American reporter for the Washington Post, Jackson referred to New York City with an ethnic slur, which complicated his already checkered relations with major Jewish organizations opposed to his controversial position that there should be a Palestinian state. His alliance with anti-Jewish Chicago cleric, Louis Farrakhan, further alientated Jewish groups.

In spite of these obstacles, Jackson's support remained solid, especially in the black community. He received over 3.5 million votes, winning the primaries in Louisiana and Washington, D.C., and carrying forty-one congressional districts and seven major cities.

Jackson's success in the 1984 primaries established him as a leader for the poor and for those opposed to the social policies of the Reagan administration. It also won him respect among leaders of third world nations. President Fidel Castro of Cuba released forty-eight Cuban and Cuban-American prisoners to him. He also met with Syrian president resident Hafez Assad and won the freedom of Lt. Robert Goodman, who had been shot down in a military mission over Syria. He linked the deteriorating situation in American ghettos and barrios with foreign policy and escalating defense spending.

This was the backdrop for his second race for the presidential nomination in 1988. He had the smallest campaign treasury of any Democratic candidate and was questioned closely by the press because of his lack of experience in electoral politics and his Middle East views. But again he surprised political analysts by winning seven million votes, many from non-blacks.

Some argued that Jackson would have been nominated if he were not black; others argued that he was treated seriously and with kid gloves only because he was black. Whatever the case, it was clear that Jackson was widely viewed as a pre-eminent political leader and a progressive voice in national politics.

Overview of Biographical Sources

Although a number of books on Jackson have appeared, it is fair to say that a balanced and comprehensive biography has yet to be written. Because he is such a controversial figure, the literature on him is dominated by the works of passionate critics and supporters. Elizabeth Colton's *The Jackson Phenomenon: The Man, the Power, the Message* (1989) is sharply biased against Jackson. A somewhat more objective treatment is given by Bob Faw and Nancy Skelton in *Thunder in America* (1986), which is a breezy journalistic account focusing on Jackson's 1984 presidential race. Ernest House's *Jesse Jackson and the Politics of Charisma: The Rise and Fall of the PUSH, Excel Program* (1988) is an attempt to expose the mismanagement of Jackson's Chicago organization. Though narrowly focused, *Jesse Jackson's 1984 Presidential Campaign: Challenge and Change in American Politics* (1989), edited by black political scientists Lucius J. Barker and Ronald W. Walters, stands virtually alone in seeking to understand Jackson in a balanced manner. However, the prevailing tone of most writing about Jackson is negative, as exhibited by the attacks of Adolph Reed's *Jesse Jackson Phenomenon: The Crisis of Purpose in Afro-American Politics* (1986) and Barbara A. Reynolds's *Jesse Jackson, the Man, the Movement, the Myth* (1985).

Evaluation of Principal Biographical Sources

Barker, Lucius J., and Ronald W. Walters, eds. *Jesse Jackson's 1984 Presidential Campaign: Challenge and Change in American Politics*. Urbana: University of Illinois Press, 1989. (A, G) This is the best treatment of Jackson's political career, especially the 1984 campaign. Includes a substantial bibliography.

Colton, Elizabeth. *The Jackson Phenomenon: The Man, the Power, the Message*. New York: Doubleday, 1989. (G) This sharply biased account of Jackson, his goals, and his politics focuses on Jackson's 1988 attempt to win the Democratic presidential nomination.

Faw, Bob, and Nancy Skelton. *Thunder in America*. Austin: Texas Monthly Press, 1986. (G) This journalistic account focuses heavily on Jackson's 1984 presidential race, using media reports and exerpts from Jackson's speeches.

Hatch, Roger D. *Beyond Opportunity: Jessie Jackson's Vision for America*. Philadelphia, PA: Fortress Press, 1988. (A, G) Hatch explains Jackson's political, economic, and social views. Includes a twenty-page bibliography.

House, Ernest. *Jesse Jackson and the Politics of Charisma: The Rise and Fall of the PUSH, Excel Program*. (A, G) Boulder, CO: Westview Press, 1988. House examines the allegations of mismanagement that surrounded one of PUSH's educational programs.

Reed, Adolph. *Jesse Jackson Phenomenon: The Crisis of Purpose in Afro-American Politics*. New Haven: Yale University Press, 1986. (A) Although Reed's treatment of Jackson's contribution to black electorial politics is highly critical, this is the most thorough analysis of Jackson's impact on American politics.

Reynolds, Barbara A. *Jesse Jackson, the Man, the Movement, the Myth*. 1975. Reprint. Washington, DC: JFJ Associates, 1985. Another critical view of Jackson's public persona. The reprint contains a new introduction and postscript, but otherwise the text is the same and somewhat outdated. Contains fifteen pages of photographs.

Overview and Evaluation of Primary Sources
Correspondence between Jackson and Martin Luther King, Jr. can be found at the Martin Luther King Center in Atlanta; this archive is the principal source for material on Jackson's years with the Southern Christian Leadership Conference. Ironically, some of the most extensive material on Jackson, consisting primarily of files detailing surveillance, can be found at the library of the Federal Bureau of Investigation (FBI) in Washington, D.C. National Public Radio in Washington, D.C., has audio tapes of numerous Jackson speeches and interviews, as do the National Broadcasting Co. (NBC), the American Broadcasting Co. (ABC), and the Columbia Broadcasting System (CBS)—all located in New York City. Both Purdue University and Vanderbilt University have archives containing television news broadcasts that include much material on Jackson. A collection of Jackson's speeches, *Straight from the Heart* was published in 1987 by Fortress Press. Boston University's archive of material on Martin Luther King, Jr. contains some primary material on Jackson.

Other Sources
Barker, Lucius J. *Our Time Has Come: A Delegate's Diary of Jesse Jackson's 1984 Presidential Campaign*. Urbana: University of Illinois Press, 1988. Barker gives a sense of how and why Jackson has evoked such enormous support among African Americans and such skepticism from many whites.

Broh, C. Anthony. *A Horse of a Different Color: Television's Treatment of Jesse Jackson's 1984 Presidential Campaign*. Washington, DC: Joint Center for Political Studies, 1987. Broh gives a valuable close analysis of the news media's view of Jackson's 1984 campaign.

Cavanagh, Thomas E. *Jesse Jackson's Campaign: The Primaries and Caucuses.* Washington, DC: Joint Center for Political Studies, 1984. This treatment of the 1984 campaign covers much of the same ground as Barker but in a more expansive manner.

Collins, Sheila D. *The Rainbow Challenge: The Jackson Campaign and the Future of U.S. Politics.* New York: Monthly Review Press, 1986. Collins focuses on the social and political forces that have backed Jackson. Includes a comprehensive forty-page bibliography.

Landess, Tom. *Jesse Jackson and the Politics of Race.* Ottawa, IL: Jameson Books, 1985. Landess presents the traditional view of Jackson as a champion of the poor against an uncaring government.

Gerald Horne
University of California, Santa Barbara

JACK JOHNSON
1878-1946

Chronology

Born John Arthur Johnson on March 31, 1878, in Galveston, Texas, the first son of Henry and Tiny Johnson; *1878-1897* grows up in a large household and works at a variety of menial jobs to assist his father, a partially disabled school janitor; *1897-1901* learns the craft of the prizefighter at local athletic clubs; *1901-1907* develops into an accomplished boxer in bouts held throughout the nation; experiences discrimination as white champions decline to fight against him; *December 26, 1908* wins the world heavyweight championship at age 30 by knocking out Tommy Burns in Sydney, Australia; *1909-1910* defends his title against nondescript opponents and antagonizes the American public with his extravagant lifestyle and his disregard for racial conventions; *July 4, 1910* defeats Jim Jeffries, the former champion and celebrated "White Hope" at Reno, Nevada; *January 1911* marries Etta Terry Duryea, a white acquaintance who commits suicide twenty months later; *July 1912* opens a lavish nightclub in Chicago; *October 1912* faces charges for violations at his establishment of the White Slave Traffic Act (Mann Act); *December 1912* marries Lucille Cameron, a white prostitute and once a government witness in his case; *June 1913* upon conviction receives a one-year prison sentence but flees the country while out on bail; *1913-1915* spends an unhappy exile in France and England; *April 5, 1915* surrenders his title to Jess Willard in a controversial fight at Havana, Cuba; *1915-1920* remains in exile in England, Spain, and Mexico; *July 20, 1920* returns to the United States and serves term in Leavenworth penitentiary; *1921-1946* performs boxing exhibitions in theaters and at carnivals; offers lectures on his sport; *1946* dies on June 10 from injuries sustained in an automobile accident near Raleigh, North Carolina.

Activities of Historical Significance

In 1908 Jack Johnson's ascension to the heavyweight boxing title stunned and dismayed white Americans who placed a premium value upon virile accomplishments. His victory jolted their assumptions about black inferiority. His disregard for social customs and traditions soon infuriated them. In a nation nearly obsessed with racial distinctions, the new champion became a symbol and a threat to a way of life.

Ironically, Johnson never sought involvement in a cause. He was interested only in earning professional praise, acquiring material gain, and enjoying the freedom to pursue the hedonistic lifestyle closely associated with prizefighting culture. Yet his battle in 1910 against Jim Jeffries, "The Great White Hope," became a central racial issue. His triumph over the formerly invincible champion provoked confrontations between celebrating blacks and enraged whites in fifty cities. The fight was so vital to Americans that white suprema-cists tried to prevent the screening of the fight films. Editors and politicians predicted that Johnson could destabilize the system of racial segregation.

After his conquest of Jeffries, Johnson discovered that he had become the most despised figure in America. The hatred resulted from his athletic accomplishments and from his preference for relations with white women. His two marriages to white women broke what was then the ultimate American racial taboo. An angry public rejoiced in 1913 when the federal government successfully prosecuted Johnson for violations of the Mann Act, which prohibited transporting women across state lines for "immoral purposes." His detractors experienced a sense of relief when the aging champion lost his title to Jess Willard in 1915 in a bitterly contested match at Havana, Cuba.

Black Americans had strong but ambivalent feelings about Jack Johnson. Many praised his accomplishments and looked upon him as the "Bad Nig-ger," a greatly admired figure from black folklore who will not conform to white expectations. Yet black editors denounced Johnson for immorality and accused him of retarding progress and of inadvertently strengthening Jim Crow institutions. Within the realm of professional sports, Johnson undoubted-ly helped to prolong the policy of segregation that excluded black athletes until the mid-twentieth century. Only a few slipped through that barrier. One who succeeded was the boxer Joe Louis, who won the heavyweight title in 1937. He received that opportunity only because he projected an image exactly opposite to the public's memory of Jack Johnson.

Overview of Biographical Sources

Jack Johnson lacked a biographer for many decades after he had attained the heavyweight boxing championship. Nat Fleischer, a noted authority on the sport and the editor of *Ring* magazine, produced the first meaningful account on the eve of World War II. His *"Fighting Furies": Story of the Golden Era of Jack Johnson, Sam Langford, and Their Contemporaries* (1939) contains a lengthy summary of Johnson's career and an evaluation of his boxing skill. John Lardner's *White Hopes and Other Tigers* (1951) offers similar material. Neither work qualifies as a comprehensive biography.

Interest in Johnson enjoyed a renaissance as the civil rights movement reached its peak during the 1960s. Finis Farr's *Black Champion: The Life and Times of Jack Johnson* (1964) is the best of several popular biographies that appeared during that decade. By the 1970s, scholars started to examine the symbolic importance of Jack Johnson. The best work in this genre, Al-Tony Gilmore's *Bad Nigger! The National Impact of Jack Johnson* (1975), evaluates the threat that he posed to traditional racial values. The resurgence of academic interest in Johnson culminated with the publication of a definitive biography. Randy Roberts's *Papa Jack: Jack Johnson and the Era of White Hopes* (1983) provides a penetrating account of the boxer, the symbol, and the man.

Evaluation of Principal Biographical Sources

Anderson, Jervis. "Black Heavies." *American Scholar* 47 (1978): 387-395. (A, G) This article evaluates the impact of Jack Johnson and compares his experiences with those of subsequent black champions Joe Louis and Muhammad Ali.

Farr, Finis. *Black Champion: The Life and Times of Jack Johnson.* New York: Charles Scribner's Sons, 1964. (G) The first modern biography of Johnson adequately describes his career but provides few insights into his complex personality. The work lacks documentation and relies heavily upon Johnson's memoirs.

Fleischer, Nat. *"Fighting Furies": Story of the Golden Era of Jack Johnson, Sam Langford, and Their Contemporaries.* New York: C. J. O'Brien, 1939. (G) This work provides a thorough analysis of Johnson's boxing skills. The author also attests to the high quality of Johnson's character but avoids comment upon the Mann Act prosecution. Twenty-four photographs and illustrations about Johnson from the files of *Ring* magazine enhance the book.

Gilmore, Al-Tony. *Bad Nigger! The National Impact of Jack Johnson.* Port Washington, NY: Kennikat Press, 1975. (A, G) This book describes the controversial features of Johnson's career, including the riots and disturbances that followed his bout with Jim Jeffries, the movement to suppress the screening of interracial fight films, and the federal government's efforts to remove Johnson through the court system. Gilmore suggests that the nation's press intentionally exacerbated racial tensions by dwelling upon Johnson's personal life and by stressing the necessity for a "white hope" to arise and redeem Caucasian honor.

Jaher, Fredric Cople. "White America Views Jack Johnson, Joe Louis, and Muhammad Ali." In *Sport in America*, edited by Donald Spivey. Westport, CT: Greenwood Press, 1985. (A, G) In this important work, the author maintains that all of these famous boxers were protagonists who forced whites to consider an adjusted social role for blacks. Americans responded to Johnson with violence and repression, but they modified racial attitudes during the careers of Louis and Ali.

Lardner, John. *White Hopes and Other Tigers*. Philadelphia: J. B. Lippincott, 1951. (G) This study offers an intriguing description of the origins of the "white hope" phenomenon. The author also argues that the only legitimate challengers to Johnson after 1910 were other blacks and that the paucity of white contenders who might eliminate him inside the ring compelled the public to demand that he be prosecuted for shortcomings in his personal life.

Roberts, Randy. *Papa Jack: Jack Johnson and the Era of White Hopes*. New York: The Free Press, 1983. (A, G) Based upon solid research, this biography supersedes all previous studies about Jack Johnson. The author concludes that his turbulent life resulted primarily from an enormous ego that could not conform to any social conventions.

Wiggins, William H., Jr. "Boxing's Sambo Twins: Racial Stereotypes in Jack Johnson and Joe Louis Newspaper Cartoons, 1908 to 1938." *Journal of Sport History* 15 (Winter 1988): 242-254. (A, G) This article reproduces and analyzes samples of the vicious cartoons that newspapers routinely employed to depict the black fighters. Racist imagery permeated illustrations about Johnson throughout his career. Yet as Louis became acceptable to white America, cartoonists replaced stereotypical drawings with more realistic portraits.

————. "Jack Johnson as Bad Nigger: The Folklore of His Life." *Black Scholar* 2 (January 1971): 35-46. (A, G) This study suggests that black Americans perceived Johnson as an admirable figure who shared with heroes from folklore such traits as disregard for danger and extravagant living.

Overview and Evaluation of Primary Sources

Reliable primary material about Jack Johnson is limited. Johnson readily furnished details about his personal life in an autobiography that he produced several years after his retirement from serious ring competition. *Jack Johnson Is a Dandy* (1927. Reprint. New York: New American Library, 1969; G) contains factual errors and fabricated tales. Scholars must approach it with great caution.

General newspapers and sporting periodicals devoted an enormous amount of space to heavyweight championship fights during the "Era of White Hopes," but they generated little substantive information about Jack Johnson. Boxing commentators filled their accounts of his fights with derogatory racial remarks. Excellent samples of such descriptions are available in *Jack London Reports*, edited by King Hendricks and Irving Shepard (Garden City, NY: Doubleday, 1970; A, G). The files of the nation's black press offer more valuable accounts about Johnson. The Chicago *Defender* provided especially detailed coverage of his boxing matches and his clash with the federal government.

The government agencies that prosecuted Johnson furnish important material. Record Group 60 of the General Records of the Department of Justice contains field reports from federal agents, pictures, and trial records. A few items that relate to Jack Johnson are available in the Schomburg Black History Collection at the New York Public Library. The richest source of information is a documentary released in 1970. Produced by Jim Jacobs and directed by William Cayton, *Jack Johnson* offers rare footage from Johnson's epic battles against Jeffries and Willard. It also contains footage that depicts his interest in automobiles, expensive clothes, and female companionship.

Fiction and Adaptations

On October 3, 1968, *The Great White Hope*, written by Howard Sackler and starring James Earl Jones, opened at the Alvin Theater in New York City and ran for 556 performances. The play was a thinly disguised dramatization of the rise and fall of Johnson, represented here as a black fighter named Jack Jefferson. The story line was inaccurate, adhering to the interpretations of controversial events that Johnson offered in his memoirs. Nevertheless, the production received popular acclaim and won Pulitzer, New York Drama Critics, and Tony awards for the best play of the year. In 1970 Twentieth Century Fox released a film version of *The Great White Hope*, with Jones again cast in the title role. It suffers from the same shortcomings as the play.

Other Sources

Fredrickson, George M. *The Black Image in the White Mind: The Debate on Afro-American Character and Destiny, 1817-1914.* 1971. Reprint. Middletown, CT: Wesleyan University Press, 1987. This excellent work analyzes white attitudes about blacks from the time of slavery through the Progressive Era. It suggests that the concepts of black inferiority that Johnson challenged were shared by both southern conservatives and northern liberals.

Levine, Lawrence W. *Black Culture and Black Consciousness: Afro-American Folk Thought from Slavery to Freedom.* New York: Oxford University Press, 1977. A comprehensive description of African-American folklore from slavery until World War II. It confirms that Johnson shared with mythical heroes behavior traits that black Americans greatly admired.

Jack Patrick
Youngstown State University

JAMES WELDON JOHNSON
1871-1938

Chronology

Born James William Johnson on June 17, 1871, in Jacksonville, Florida, to freeborn parents James Johnson of Richmond, Virginia, and Helen Dillet of Nassau; *1871-1887* grows up in Jacksonville and attends Stanton School where his mother teaches; *1887* graduates from Stanton and enrolls in preparatory school at Atlanta University; *1894* graduates from Atlanta University; *1894-1902* serves as principal of Stanton School, supervising one thousand students and twenty-five teachers; *1895* founds a newspaper, the *Daily American*, in Jacksonville; *1898* after studying eighteen months with Thomas A. Ledwith, a white Jacksonville attorney, is admitted to the Florida Bar; *1900* writes "Lift Every Voice and Sing" with his brother Rosamond; *1902* leaves Jacksonville for New York; *1902-1906* writes songs and musical comedy with Rosamond and their partner, Bob Cole; *1904* receives honorary M.A. degree from Atlanta University where he first meets author and activist W. E. B. Du Bois; joins the Colored Republican Club in New York; campaigns for Theodore Roosevelt; *1906* leaves musical comedy to head U.S. consulate in Puerto Cabello, Venezuela; *1909* leaves Venezuela to head consulate in Corinto, Nicaragua; *1910* marries Grace Nail, the daughter of John D. Nail, a prosperous real estate investor and tavern owner; *1912* while on leave in New York, publishes *The Autobiography of an Ex-Colored Man* anonymously; *1913* publishes "Fifty Years" commemorating the fiftieth anniversary of the Emancipation Proclamation; *1914* with a change in administration and little hope of receiving a promotion, resigns from foreign service; becomes contributing editor of the *New York Age*, a weekly paper; *1916* works for the National Association for the Advancement of Colored People (NAACP) as field secretary in charge of organizing and reviving branches around the country; *1920-1930* serves as secretary of the NAACP; *1922* edits *The Book of American Negro Poetry*; *1925* edits *The Book of American Negro Spirituals*; *1926* edits *The Second Book of American Negro Spirituals*; *1927* publishes *God's Trombones*; republishes *The Autobiography of an Ex-Coloured Man* (changing the spelling of colored) during height of the Harlem Renaissance; *1929-1930* exhausted and ill, takes leave from duties at NAACP to accept a Rosenwald Fellowship; travels, studies writes, and lectures; *1930* publishes *Black Manhattan* and *St. Peter Relates an Incident*; resigns as secretary of NAACP; *1931* publishes revised edition of *The Book of American Negro Poetry*; changes his name from James William Johnson to James Weldon Johnson because, as he says in a letter to a friend, "Jim Bill will not do for a man who pretends to write poetry or anything else"; *1932* appointed to the

Adam K. Spence Chair of Creative Literature and Writing at Fisk University in Nashville, Tennessee; *1933* publishes his autobiography, *Along This Way*; *1934* writes *Negro Americans, What Now?*; *1935* publishes *St. Peter Relates an Incident: Selected Poems*; *1938* dies when his car is hit by a train near Wiscasset, Maine.

Activities of Historical Significance

Eulogizing James Weldon Johnson in 1938, Mayor Fiorello LaGuardia of New York sounded the dominant theme of Johnson's life, declaring that his "many faceted genius produced a wide variety of fine things." Certainly Johnson was one of the most accomplished men of this century during a time in America's past when black achievement was impeded by segregationist laws and other forms of bigotry. Yet from the time he returned to Jacksonville, Florida, in 1894 to become principal of Stanton School until his death in 1938, Johnson's life was a series of triumphs for himself and, as he saw it, for African Americans. Each of his several careers left its legacy.

Johnson's earliest contributions came from his work as educator, lawyer, and newspaperman committed to changing the second-class status of blacks in Jacksonville. As the young principal of the largest public school in the state, he expanded his students' opportunities, adding two years to an existing eight-year curriculum. He was the first black since Reconstruction to attain the Florida bar by examination; and although his newspaper, the *Daily American*, closed within a year of its founding, it played a role in shaping community opinions on racial issues.

As a songwriter Johnson is most remembered for the lyrics to "Lift Every Voice and Sing," written in Jacksonville with his brother Rosamond to celebrate Lincoln's birthday. The song was subsequently popularized and dubbed the Negro National Anthem. Today it is often sung in churches, colleges, political meetings, and other gatherings, where blacks find inspiration in its message of hope. Later, in New York, Johnson wrote musical comedy. With popular tunes like "Nobody's Lookin but de Owl and de Moon" (1901), "Under the Bamboo Tree" (1902), and "Congo Love Song" (1903), Johnson, to some extent, rejected the genre of "coon songs" of the period and the negative racial stereotypes they promoted.

At age thirty-five Johnson set aside songwriting for a long career of public service and activism, beginning with his appointment as U.S. consul to Puerto Cabello, Venezuela, followed three years later by a promotion to Corinto, Nicaragua, as the first American consul there. Johnson was in Nicaragua during the 1912 revolution against President Adolfo Diaz and was the chief governmental policy officer during the crisis. He proved an effective diplomat but resigned in 1914 with the change in administration. His years in the foreign service taught him that success in Latin America did not necessarily mean rewards at home. The limited number of foreign service posts allowed blacks discouraged his ambitions and forced him to seek other opportunities for service.

Within a year of leaving Nicaragua, Johnson was contributing editor of the influential black weekly, the *New York Age*, and within two years he was a driving force at the NAACP. As the first black secretary of the organization, many believe his work there to be his most significant. Organizing marches, providing legal aid to besieged blacks, lobbying tirelessly for the Dyer Anti-Lynching Bill, and decrying discrimination and racial violence wherever it occurred, Johnson was a brilliant strategist able to articulate issues facing black Americans.

During his many years as a political spokesperson, Johnson was also a man of letters, offering his poetry and fiction as poignant commentary on democracy's failings. Indeed, his novel *The Autobiography of an Ex-Colored Man* marked a new literary treatment of race relations in the U.S. As valuable as were his own writings, his efforts to publish the works of others placed him at the forefront of the Harlem Renaissance, that period in the 1920s when New York became the center for black politics and art. His anthologies of Negro poetry and spirituals symbolized a new consciousness which promoted pride and self-respect among blacks. These works stimulated an outpouring of poems, stories, paintings, sculpture, and drama from many black writers and artists in celebration of their culture.

Johnson, who dedicated himself to achieving excellence, was in many ways the renaissance man—educator, diplomat, musician, poet, novelist, journalist, historian, editor, critic, and university professor. His model of character compelled many to reassess black contributions to the intellectual, artistic, and social life of America.

Overview of Biographical Sources

Johnson was not the subject of serious biography during his lifetime. A few brief sketches appeared as portions of larger projects chronicling contributions by blacks. The best of these is Mary Ovington White's "James Weldon Johnson" in her *Portraits in Color* (New York: Viking Press, 1927). Robert Wohlforth profiles Johnson in "Dark Leader: James Weldon Johnson," *New Yorker* 9 (1933); and Benjamin Brawley offers a short biography in "Protest and Vindication," *The Negro Genius* (New York: Dodd, Mead, 1937).

Johnson's death in 1938 inspired several retrospectives in journals and newspapers of the day. Typical of these is "James Weldon Johnson," *The Journal of Negro History* (July 1938): 405-408. One article during this period, however, does not praise. Kelly Miller in his column "Kelly Miller Writes About: James Weldon Johnson the Negro Poet Laureate," *New York Age* 9 (July): 6, characterizes the author as a "literary dilettante" pandering to white values. The year following Johnson's death, Fisk University's Department of Publicity brought out a thirty-six page biography called *James Weldon Johnson* (Nashville: Fisk University, 1939). Almost a decade later, Mary Ovington White examined Johnson's years at the NAACP in "James Weldon Johnson 1920-1931; We Meet the Nation," *The Walls Came Tumbling Down* (New York: Harcourt, Brace, 1947).

The focus in the late 1960s and early 1970s on black history sparked a renewed interest in Johnson's life and work. Two studies appeared in 1967, a short one on Johnson's role in society, Lynn Adelman, "A Study of James Weldon Johnson," *Journal of Negro History* 52 (April): 128-145, and Ellen Tarry's *Young Jim: The Early Years of James Weldon Johnson* (New York: Dodd, Mead). Two other brief articles of this period are Welhelmina Robinson's "Johnson, James Weldon: Author and Diplomat" in *Historical Negro Biographies* (New York: Publishers, 1969): 213-214; and Gloster Current's "James Weldon Johnson: Freedom Fighter," *Crisis* 78 (June 1971): 116-118+. In 1973 Eugene Levy published the most comprehensive biography to date, *James Weldon Johnson: Black Leader, Black Voice* (Chicago: University of Chicago Press). This has been followed by Robert Fleming's concise treatment, *James Weldon Johnson* (Boston: Twayne, 1987).

Evaluation of Principal Biographical Sources

Bronz, Stephen H. "James Weldon Johnson." In *Roots of Negro Racial Consciousness, the 1920s: Three Harlem Renaissance Authors.* New York: Lebra, 1964. (A, G) Concise, detailed discussion of Johnson's life and writings. Bronz asserts that Johnson was not a literary giant but used his work to advance the cause of blacks. Bronz also examines what many view as Johnson's conservative stand on issues and concludes that despite a "controlled, urbanely phrased protest," Johnson was an important leader.

Fleming, Robert E. *James Weldon Johnson.* Boston: Twayne, 1987. (A, G) This is the latest of several articles and books that Fleming has written on Johnson. Beginning with a twenty-page biography, Fleming examines every phase of Johnson's life. After analyzing the social and literary value of most of the important works, Fleming concludes with an assessment of the author's lasting contributions. With only 111 pages of text, this is a complete yet manageable source.

Levy, Eugene. *James Weldon Johnson: Black Leader, Black Voice.* Chicago: University of Chicago Press, 1973. (A, G) Levy's work is as much the study of an era of black struggle as it is the story of Johnson. Each important event in Johnson's life and career is given a larger setting with histories of individuals and institutions that significantly shaped the literary and political life of the period. Levy's narrative is thoroughly engaging. Includes extensive bibliographies of primary and secondary sources.

Tarry, Ellen. *Young Jim: The Early Years of James Weldon Johnson.* New York: Dodd, Mead, 1967. (Y) Tarry focuses on Johnson's youth from his birth in Jacksonville to his departure for New York. A synopsis of his later life is presented in an epilogue. Illustrations are included. This is a good source for young readers.

Overview and Evaluation of Primary Sources

In the late 1940s Carl Van Vechten, Johnson's literary executor, established the James Weldon Johnson Collection of Negro Arts and Letters. Johnson's papers are part of this collection in Yale University's Beinecke Rare Book and Manuscript Library.

All of Johnson's principal works have been reprinted. Of these, *The Autobiography of an Ex-Coloured Man* is most available. Arna Bontemps writes an introduction for one edition (New York: Hill & Wang, 1960) in which he praises the novel's treatment of its tragic mulatto protagonist; historian John Hope Franklin edits *Three Negro Classics* (New York: Avon Books, 1965), which includes, in addition to Johnson's novel, Booker T. Washington's *Up from Slavery* (1900) and W. E. B. Du Bois's *The Souls of Black Folk* (1903). The latest edition of this work is in paperback (New York: Random House, 1989).

AMS Press has reprinted three works: *St. Peter Relates an Incident* (New York: AMS, 1974); *Negro Americans, What Now?* (New York: AMS, 1981); and *Fifty Years and Other Poems* (New York: AMS, 1988). As part of its American Negro: History and Literature Series, Ayer has reprinted *Black Manhattan* (New York: Ayer, 1968). Two volumes of *God's Trombones* have been republished, a 1961 Viking edition and a 1976 Penguin edition.

As part of its Civil Liberties in American History series, Da Capo has reprinted three works: Johnson's autobiography, *Along this Way* (New York: Da Capo, 1973); *Negro Americans, What Now?* (New York: Da Capo, 1973); and *The Books of American Negro Spirituals* (New York: Da Capo, 1977).

Fiction and Adaptations

Several of Johnson's poems have been recorded on video or audio discs. "James Weldon Johnson" (video) includes an adaptation of "The Creation" read by Raymond St. Jacques (Oxford films, 1972). The author Margaret Walker Alexander reads "Go Down Death," "The Prodigal Son," "Judgement Day," and "Listen Lord" on a sound recording (Folkways, 1975). "God's Trombones," a sound recording, is read by Bryce Bond with music by William Martin. Included are biographical notes by Walter White, and texts of the poems (Folkways Records, 1965).

Museums, Historical Landmarks, Societies

James Weldon Johnson Residence (New York, NY). Johnson lived here at 187 West 135th Street from 1925 to 1938 and on May 11, 1976, the U.S. Department of Interior named it a National Historical site.

Other Sources

Adelman, Lynn. "A Study of James Weldon Johnson." *The Journal of Negro History* 52 (1967): 128-145. Interesting discussion of Johnson's response to the racial climate in which he lived and worked.

Fleming, Robert E. *James Weldon Johnson and Arna Wendell Bontemps.* Boston: G. K. Hall, 1978. A valuable and comprehensive guide to secondary sources. This annotated bibliography cites book-length studies and shorter articles on Johnson, conveniently arranged by the year of their publication. Covers the years 1905-1976. An introductory overview of criticism is included.

Gibbs, William E. "James Weldon Johnson: A Black Perspective on 'Big Stick' Diplomacy." *Diplomatic History* 8 (1984): 329-347. Insightful analysis of Johnson's role as U.S. consul in Venezuela and Nicaragua. Examines Johnson's subsequent criticism of American hypocrisy in South America and the Caribbean.

Jackson, Miles M., Jr. "Letters to a Friend: Correspondence from James Weldon Johnson to George A. Towns." *Phylon* 29 (1968): 182-198. Towns was Johnson's friend and roommate at Atlanta University where Towns also taught for twenty-seven years. These letters, from the Negro Collection, Trevor Arnett Library, Atlanta University, date from 1896 to 1934 and offer insights into Johnson's personality.

Logan, Rayford W. "James Weldon Johnson and Haiti." *Phylon* 32 (1971): 396-402. Fascinating look at Johnson's criticism of U.S. occupation of Haiti. Logan's conclusions are based on four articles Johnson wrote for the *Nation* in 1920.

Jan Furman
University of Michigan, Flint

MOTHER JONES
1830-1930

Chronology

Born Mary Harris on or about May 1, 1830, in County Cork, Ireland, daughter of Richard and Helen Harris; *1835* father emigrates to the United States; *1841* with her mother and siblings joins her father in New York; the family settles in Toronto, Canada, where Richard Harris works as a railroad laborer; *1841-1847* attends school in Toronto and becomes first member of her family to graduate from high school; *1847-1849* works as a dressmaker with her mother; *1849* becomes one of the first women accepted at the recently established "normal school" in Toronto; *1850-1857* leaves Canada for the United States and a series of positions as a governess; *1857* teaches at St. Mary's, a Catholic school in Monroe, Michigan; *1858-1860* moves to Chicago and works as a dressmaker; *1860* moves to Memphis, Tennessee, where she meets and marries George Jones, a staunch member of the Iron Molders Union; *1867* her husband and four young children all succumb to a yellow fever epidemic; *1867-1871* after volunteering as a nurse during the yellow fever outbreak, she returns to Chicago, works as a dressmaker, joins with the Knights of Labor, and commits herself to the cause of the working-man; *1877* travels to Pittsburgh to support striking railroad workers; witnesses the bitter Pittsburgh riots; *1880-1890* travels throughout the country speaking on behalf of the labor movement; *1890s* acts as an organizer for the United Mine Workers; *1900, 1902* participates in the "anthracite strikes"; organizes the mine workers' wives; *1903* disguised as a peddlar, she obtains information on the exploitation of miners in Colorado; conducts a caravan of striking child textile workers to summer home of President Theodore Roosevelt in Oyster Bay, New York; *1903-1905* works in cotton mills in southern states to gain personal knowledge of conditions of child labor; *1912-1913* following West Virginia mine strike is tried by a state militia military court, convicted of conspiracy to commit murder, sentenced to twenty years in prison; freed by new governor of West Virginia; *1914* testifies before House Mines and Mining Committee about machine gun "massacre" of striking mine workers and their families in Ludlow, Colorado; *1915-1916* organizes workers during the New York City streetcar and garment-worker strikes; *1921* attends the Pan American Federation of Labor meeting in Mexico; *1930* in Silver Spring, Maryland, celebrates what was thought to be the one hundredth anniversary of her birth; *1930* dies November 30, in Silver Spring; is reinterred in Union Miners Cemetery, Mount Olive, Illinois.

Activities of Historical Significance

Called "the most dangerous woman in America" by her opponents, Mother Jones was one of the most effective organizers and agitators in the labor movement in the United States. She was influential in the founding of both the Social Democratic Party in 1898 and was the only woman involved in the organization of the International Workers of the World in 1905. She later broke with the "Wobblies" over issues of internal factionalism and its increasingly radical policies. Although she was already middle-aged when she began her most active role as a labor organizer, she tirelessly devoted over fifty years to the movement, making her last major speech when she was probably ninety-four years old.

Her empathy with the workers and her concern for the plight of their families earned her the sobriquet "Mother Jones." Next to her compassion, her most striking characteristic was her effectiveness as a rhetorician. Her impassioned speeches called upon the language of the revivalist preachers of the day to mobilize workers: "The labor movement, my friends, was a command from God Almighty. He commanded the prophet to redeem the Israelites that were in bondage . . . he organized the men into a union . . . led them out of the land of bondage and robbery and plunder and into the land of freedom." She shamed politicians and industrialists with the quickness of her wit, once telling John D. Rockefeller that if he alleviated the conditions in his Colorado mines he would be "one of the greatest of Americans." When he responded that she was too inclined to give compliments, she replied, "Oh, no, I am much more inclined to throw bricks." She also utilized her theatrical abilities to enlighten the public. She took a ten year old textile worker to Princeton, stood him in front of an economics class and announced, "Here's a textbook in economics."

In spite of her involvement with socialist causes, she vehemently opposed woman suffrage, seeing it as primarily a fad to direct the energies of upper-class women away from the workers' struggle. She told working-class women, "You don't need a vote to raise hell." Although she did not live to see the passage of federal laws that would guarantee union rights, her fearless dedication to the cause ultimately paved the way for this legislation. When she celebrated what was believed to be her one hundredth birthday, she received tributes from industrialists and presidents, as well as from the working class people to whom she had devoted her life.

Overview of Biographical Sources

Until relatively recently, Mother Jones's life has been largely ignored by biographers. Despite her prominence as an agitator and field organizer for the American labor movement, she was not instrumental in developing either the philosophy or the structure of the unions. Her effect was primarily on individual workers who responded to her intense concern and compassion for them, as well as to the power of her rhetoric. Researchers are hampered by the paucity of accurate information about her personal life prior to the death of her husband and children in 1867. Although her long and sensational career spawned numerous newspaper and periodical accounts of her activities, much of the material is biased or apocryphal.

Mother Jones herself was vague as to such essential biographical details as the date of her birth and the number of children she had. The fullest, and in some ways least accurate, account of her life appears in *The Autobiography of Mother Jones* (1925), edited and co-written by Mary Field Parton. The two standard critical biographies are Dale Fetherling's *Mother Jones: The Miners' Angel* (1974) and Linda Atkinson's *Mother Jones: The Most Dangerous Woman in America* (1978).

Evaluation of Principal Biographical Sources

Atkinson, Linda. *Mother Jones: The Most Dangerous Woman in America.* New York: Crown Publishers, 1978. (A, G) One of the two standard biographies, this work compensates for the lack of information about Mother Jones's family and early life by its treatment of relevant social background. Highly sympathetic to its subject and her activities, occasionally to the point of idolatry, the book is less than critical in some controversial areas, especially in Mother Jones's hostility towards the woman suffrage movement and her conflicts with other prominent figures in the labor movement.

Fetherling, Dale. *Mother Jones: The Miners' Angel.* Carbondale: Southern Illinois University Press, 1974. (A, G) The standard critical biography, this extremely well-researched work carefully examines Mother Jones's role within the organized labor movement. The author avoids idealizing his subject while at the same time paying tribute to her real dedication to the cause of the workers. He presents a believable portrait of this complex individual.

Long, Priscilla. *We Don't Need a Vote to Raise Hell: Mother Jones, Woman Organizer, and Her Relations with Miners' Wives, Working Women, and the Suffrage Movement.* Cambridge, MA: Red Sun Press, 1974. (A) A brief, informative work which examines Mother Jones as a woman in relation to the labor movement, as well as her relationships with miners' wives, women workers, and the organized suffrage movement. It concludes that because Mother Jones's success with male workers resulted from her exploitation of the traditional female role, she was less than sympathetic to working women and women who demanded a role in the political arena.

Overview and Evaluation of Primary Sources

The main primary source for information about Mother Jones's life is *The Autobiography of Mother Jones*, edited by Mary Field Parton (1925. Chicago: Kerr Publishing; 3d rev. ed. 1980, edited by Fred Thompson; **A**). Although fascinating reading, Mother Jones's autobiography consists of the undocumented recollections of a very old woman and was in part co-written by its original editor. The autobiography contains inaccuracies (the older she grew, the earlier, for example, Mother Jones dated her own birth), contradictions, and omissions (of the Ludlow, Colorado, miners' massacre, for instance). Mother Jones's account of her career is lively and readable; her extraordinary rhetorical gifts are evident throughout. Even in extreme old age, she manages to convey her indignation at the exploitation of the working class, as well as her compassion for the individuals she encountered. The original edition contains a highly laudatory forward by famed attorney Clarence Darrow. Fred Thompson's introduction to the most recent edition contains an excellent bibliography.

Museums, Historical Landmarks, Societies

Mother Jones Monument (Union Miners' Cemetery, Mt. Olive, IL). An eighty-ton monument of pink granite that features a *bas relief* portrait of Mother Jones flanked by statues of two miners. Dedicated on October 11, 1936 in commemoration of the bloody Virden, Illinois, mine riot of 1898.

Other Sources

Dilliard, Irving, and Mary Sue Dilliard Schusky. "Mary Harris Jones." In *Notable American Women 1607-1950*, edited by Edward T. James. Cambridge: Harvard University Press, 1971. A brief but informative account of the major events of Mother Jones's life. The bibliography is outdated.

Mary Anne Hutchinson
Utica College of Syracuse University

SCOTT JOPLIN
1868-1917

Chronology

Born Scott Joplin on November 24, 1868, near what is now Linden, Texas, the second of six children of Jiles Joplin, a former slave musician who spent most of his adult life as a railroad laborer, and Florence Givins Joplin, a free black from Kentucky whose father had moved to Texas to work as an overseer for white farmers; *1873-1888* grows up in Texarkana, on the Texas-Arkansas border, receiving a haphazard education from tutors in the black community and then from a public school for black children; exposed to music by his parents, in the black churches, and from various local teachers; very precocious musically, plays engagements in dance halls by the age of fifteen and the next year forms a group called the Texas Medley Quartette to tour the small towns of East Texas; *1888-1897* leaves Texarkana to take up the life of an itinerant pianist, appearing primarily in saloons and brothels in St. Louis, Chicago, and innumerable smaller cities of the Middle West and Old Southwest; absorbs the popular musical influences of the day, such as minstrelsy, that were to be incorporated into "ragged time" or "ragtime"; *1897-1903* settles in Sedalia, Missouri, where he gains some formal musical training at George R. Smith College, writes "Maple Leaf Rag" (1897), and signs a long-term publishing agreement with John Stark & Son; after languishing for three years, "Maple Leaf Rag" is the first ragtime composition to become a popular hit nationally; Stark & Son establish a new printing plant in St. Louis to meet the demand for sheet music, and Joplin quickly becomes known as "The King of the Ragtime Composers," publishing "The Entertainer" in 1902; *1901-1903* marries Belle Hayden of Sedalia and moves to St. Louis; their only child dies in infancy and they separate after only two years, apparently because Mrs. Joplin has no interest in her husband's music and resents his long hours of working alone; *1903-1907* resumes his earlier itinerant existence, performing his compositions throughout the Middle West and East; organizes a performance company to showcase a ragtime opera called *The Guest of Honor* (1903) in Missouri and Iowa, but the effort quickly fails and the work itself is soon lost; writes "The Chrysanthemum" (1904) and "The Gladiolus Rag" (1907); *1907* marries Lottie Stokes of Washington, D.C. and settles in New York City; *1907-1911* concentrates most of his energy on touring and on writing his folk opera *Treemonisha*, which he completes in 1910 and publishes himself in 1911; *1911-1917* with his own style of classical ragtime being eclipsed by the simpler tunes pouring from the commercial music houses of Tin Pan Alley, he supports himself by giving piano lessons and occasional performances, but has to rely increasingly on his wife's earnings as a domestic, while laboring incessantly but to no avail to get *Treemonisha* performed; *1917* dies on April 1 of syphilis in New York City and is buried with two other paupers in an unmarked grave at St. Michael's Cemetery in Astoria, Queens.

Activities of Historical Significance

Although he did not invent classical ragtime, Joplin became one of the musical form's principal exponents. Classical ragtime was generally written as a piano solo or as a song with piano accompaniment. It combined a regular 2/4 or 4/4 beat and conventional harmony in the left hand with an infectious syncopated melody in the right hand. The form itself thus grew out of European dances, but the melodic and rhythmic elements were distinctly African American. Joplin always insisted that his rags should be played slowly and exactly as written, hence "classical ragtime." He made no allowance for the improvisation that characterized the emerging jazz style of piano playing and thoroughly disliked the sprightlier tempos favored by some ragtime pianists. He likewise resisted the simpler melodies and rhythms favored by the tunesmiths of Tin Pan Alley, who churned out music that was easier to play and who applied the term "ragtime" to anything even vaguely syncopated. (With the phonograph still in an experimental stage of development and radio a generation away, the only form of musical mass commercialization was the sale of sheet music.)

In addition to his enormous contribution to the development of classical ragtime, Joplin aspired to write more "serious" compositions. As early as 1902 the original version of "The Ragtime Dance," conceived as a piece for formal performance, ran fully twenty minutes. Publisher John Stark reluctantly agreed to bring out the sheet music for this work, but correctly predicted that there would be little market interest in it. The next year Joplin tried to produce a road show of his ragtime opera *The Guest of Honor*. Without adequate capital, the effort was doomed to failure. The score was never published and the manuscript subsequently disappeared.

Refusing to be discouraged, Joplin in 1910 completed the manuscript for a folk opera named *Treemonisha* (after its main character). Unable to interest a producer in the work, he published the piano score himself and in 1915 was able to mount a single public rehearsal without benefit of sets, costumes, or orchestra. Not until more than half a century after his premature death would the opera be staged, to generally enthusiastic reviews, by a professional company.

In addition to *Treemonisha*, Joplin gave the world some sixty-five published rags, dances, and songs. These shorter works, too, largely disappeared from public listening, despite the efforts of a small circle of aficionados to keep their memory alive, until a ragtime revival began to gain momentum after

World War II. The culmination of this revival was the use of some of Joplin's best rags as the background score for the Academy Award-winning caper film, *The Sting*, in 1973. At about the same time Gunther Schuller's New England Conservatory Ragtime Ensemble recorded a series of Joplin rags, arranged for wind orchestra, that also became very popular.

Overview of Biographical Sources

Information about Scott Joplin's life and career is sparse and fragmentary. His biographers have had to invest a great deal of effort into reconstructing even the most basic facts, such as his parents' background, his place of birth, and his musical education. The fugitive nature of these details is attributable partly to the fact that he was an African American living in the era of segregation and partly to the itinerant nature of his career. As a consequence, even James Haskins and Kathleen Benson, authors of *Scott Joplin* (1978), the best biography that has yet appeared, have had to fill in extensive gaps in the biographical record with material focusing on the context of Joplin's life— what it was like for a black musician to travel around the turn of the century or the state of ragtime music generally. A number of books have appeared that describe the development of ragtime as a musical form. Joplin figures prominently in all of them, but often more as a composer of specific works than as an identifiable individual.

Evaluation of Principal Biographical Sources

Berlin, Edward A. *Ragtime: A Musical and Cultural History*. Berkeley: University of California Press, 1980. (A) Berlin, Senior Research Fellow at Brooklyn College's Institute for Studies in American Music, began this scholarly analysis as a doctoral dissertation at the City University of New York. He includes ragtime songs in order to provide a historical context for evaluating the more traditional piano solos. His book presumes some technical musical knowledge and is extremely thorough. Joplin is prominent throughout the narrative.

————. *Reflections and Research on Ragtime*. New York: Institute for Studies in American Music, Brooklyn College, 1987. (A, G) This slender volume contains just two chapters, the first a thoughtful and rather technical essay on unanswered research questions about ragtime music, the second a fascinating guided tour of New York in the ragtime era, designed to highlight the city's importance in fostering the musical form. Joplin lived in New York for the last decade of his life.

Blesh, Rudi, and Harriet Janis. *They All Played Ragtime.* 3d ed. New York: Oak Publications, 1966. (A, G) This is the seminal work on the history of ragtime by the man who did the most to recover the story and keep it alive during the decades when the music was all but forgotten. Still indispensable for the study of ragtime. There are several chapters on Joplin.

Gammond, Peter. *Scott Joplin and the Ragtime Era.* London: Angus & Robertson, 1975. (A, G) Gammond is the musical editor of England's *Hi-Fi News* and the author of numerous books on jazz. Although intended for a popular audience, this book is surprisingly uneven. Like other Joplin biographers, Gammond must recreate the context of Joplin's life when there is a lack of biographical information. He also incorporates arrays of indigestible factual data, such as a listing of each year's most popular songs. His commentary on each of Joplin's known works, arranged in the order they were written, is more useful.

Haskins, James, and Kathleen Benson. *Scott Joplin.* Garden City, NY: Doubleday, 1978. (A, G) Offers as complete a biographical treatment as Joplin is likely to receive. Haskins and Benson have verified factual details wherever possible. They have also inferred as much as they can from Joplin's musical publications, the few published references to appearances, and the recollections of people interviewed sixty years later.

Hasse, John Edward, ed. *Ragtime: Its History, Composers, and Music.* New York: Schirmer Books, 1985. (A, G) This scholarly anthology is the best way to sample recent research on ragtime. Except for a few musical analyses, the collection does not presuppose musical training on the part of the reader. Includes essays on the origins of ragtime, ragtime songs, banjo works, ragtime on piano rolls, ragtime's influence on jazz, an excellent essay on Joplin by Addison W. Reed, and even a short piece on ragtime revivalist Rudi Blesh.

Jasen, David A., and Trebor Jay Tichenor. *Rags and Ragtime: A Musical History.* New York: Seabury Press, 1978. (A, G) Jasen and Tichenor are leading collectors of ragtime music and their study begins with a good introductory chapter on the development of ragtime as a musical form. The main portion of the book consists of an annotated listing of the rags written and performed by classicists like Joplin; by the more commercial composers associated with Tin Pan Alley; by the great jazz pianists who developed out of the ragtime tradition (Eubie Blake, Fats Waller, Willie "The Lion" Smith, and Jelly Roll Morton); and by the ragtime revivalists after World War II.

Schafer, William J., and Johannes Riedel. *The Art of Ragtime: Form and Meaning of an Original Black American Art.* Baton Rouge: Louisiana State

University Press, 1973. (A, G) Schafer and Riedel have written the best musical analysis of ragtime. It explores in detail what ragtime is, its impact on both black and white culture, and how it should be performed. Joplin, of course, is a key reference point. Among the lengthy appendixes are a comparison of the ragtime and jazz piano styles and a musical analysis of *Treemonisha*. Most of this volume is readily accessible to the general reader, but some parts do presume the ability to read music.

Waldo, Terry. *This Is Ragtime*. New York: Hawthorne Books, 1976. (A, G) Pianist Waldo has produced an excellent historical account of ragtime that explores musical antecedents, the characteristics of the classical form, and the postwar revival embodied in the film score for *The Sting*. The book includes an excellent short discography.

Overview and Evaluation of Primary Sources

There are no significant published primary sources or manuscript collections relating to the life of Scott Joplin. Indeed, the only documents James J. Fuld was able to locate were the contract for the publication of "Maple Leaf Rag," a few applications to the Library of Congress for copyright protection, and some handwritten notations on a copy of the *Treemonisha* piano-vocal score given to Rudi Blesh by Joplin's widow Lottie. (See Fuld's report in "The Few Known Autographs of Scott Joplin," *American Music* 1 [Spring 1983]: 41-48.) Fortunately, one need not consult original manuscripts to study his music. Vera Brodsky Lawrence, *The Complete Works of Scott Joplin* (2 vols. New York: New York Public Library, 1981; A, G), assembles all of the known piano solos and piano scores for all of the vocal works, including *Treemonisha*. Each volume contains a rollography and discography. An earlier edition appeared in 1971 as *The Collected Works of Scott Joplin*.

Joplin had definite ideas about how his music should be played. His conception of classical ragtime can be documented by consulting reissued recordings of original player piano rolls, available on the Biograph label. Piano rolls cannot capture the subtle variations in dynamics and rhythm that mark a live performance, but they do convey Joplin's thinking about proper tempos. There are also many modern solo performances and instrumental arrangements to choose from. David A. Jasen, *Recorded Ragtime, 1897-1958* (Hamden, CT: Shoe String Press, 1973; A, G) lists all commercial first-issue recordings from throughout the world, but includes only eighteen Joplin rags and omits the reissues and dubs. The triumphant Houston Grand Opera production of *Treemonisha* (1976), orchestrated and conducted by Gunther Schuller, has been preserved on videocassette by Sony Corporation of America and a studio recording with the original cast is available from Deutsche

Grammophone. Consult the current *Phonolog Reports* and *Videolog Reports* to determine which recordings of Joplin music are available at any given time.

Fiction and Adaptations

Scott Joplin: King of Ragtime Composers. A fifteen-minute color, sound film produced by Amelia Anderson for Pyramid Films, Santa Monica, 1977. Nar- rated by singer Eartha Kitt, this short film briefly reviews Joplin's life, from his discovery and initial success following the publication of "Maple Leaf Rag," to his failure to get *Treemonisha* performed, and his subsequent early death. It includes samples of his ragtime music and excerpts from the Houston Grand Opera production of *Treemonisha*.

The Sting. George Roy Hill's 1973 feature film has little to do with Scott Joplin, just as ragtime has little to do with the year 1936 when the film was set. However, Marvin Hamlisch's score, based on Joplin rags, marked the culmination of the postwar ragtime revival. The film won Academy Awards for Best Picture, Best Title Song ("The Entertainer"), and Best Score.

Other Sources

Berlin, Edward A. "Scott Joplin." In *The New Grove Dictionary of American Music*, 4 vols., edited by H. Wiley Hitchcock and Stanley Sadie. London: Macmillan, 1986. Presents brief summaries of Joplin's life and music, followed by a concise listing of his compositions.

Keith Ian Polakoff
California State University, Long Beach

CORETTA SCOTT KING
b. 1927

Chronology

Born Coretta Scott on April 27, 1927 in Marion, Alabama, the second of three children of Obidiah (Obie) Scott, a landowner and storekeeper, and Bernice McMurray Scott; *1927-1945* grows up in Alabama, where she attends the segregated Crossroads School in Heiberger and Lincoln High School, a semi-private institution in Marion run by the American Missionary Association of New York; studies voice and piano privately; *1951* earns a bachelor's degree in elementary education from Antioch College, where she encounters racial discrimination in the student-teacher placement program; *1953* marries Martin Luther King, Jr., with whom she has four children; *1951-1954* earns a music degree from the New England Conservatory of Music, where she studies on a Jessie Smith Noyes Fund fellowship; *1954* begins actively assisting husband's civil rights struggle by undertaking speaking and concert engagements; *1959* tours Europe and Asia and sings before many groups in India; *1960* serves as a delegate to the White House Conference on Children and Youth; *1962* teaches voice in the music department of Morris Brown College in Atlanta; *1964-1968* performs over thirty freedom concerts; engages in protests against the war in Vietnam; *1968* husband assassinated; assumes his speaking engagements; launches Poor People's Campaign March on Washington; *1969-1971* writes memoirs; receives honorary degrees and awards from many institutions and organizations; becomes president of the Martin Luther King, Jr. Memorial Foundation and raises money to establish a memorial that would comprise the neighborhood around the family home in Atlanta; becomes the first woman to preach in London's St. Paul's Cathedral; *1971-present* serves as president of the Martin Luther King, Jr. Center for Nonviolent Social Change; engages in concerts and public appearances; active as director or trustee of numerous civil rights groups; *1985* helps arrange anti-apartheid demonstrations outside South African Embassy in Washington; *1986* meets with anti-apartheid leaders in South Africa.

Activities of Historical Significance

While fulfilling traditional roles as wife and mother, Coretta Scott King was instrumental in supporting her husband's civil rights leadership activities throughout the turbulent years of his demonstrations, frequent arrests, and assassination. Because of her education, public speaking and singing skills, and personality, she was able to assume his duties and speaking engagements when political emergencies called him away. Knowing that she could stand in for him provided Dr. King with the luxury of being able to serve in two places at the same time. Her freedom concerts were, themselves, an important source of funding for the Southern Christian Leadership Conference, and for raising public awareness of its goals. By the time Dr. King was assassinated, Coretta had established herself as a committed and effective activist, not only for civil rights but also for educational and antiwar causes.

Following her husband's assassination, Coretta King's visibility increased dramatically, and she became an important spokesperson for the continuing struggle for racial equality. Her close identification with Dr. King's career improved her effectiveness as a diligent fund-raising and organizational leader to develop the Martin Luther King, Jr. National Historic Site and Preservation District in Atlanta, and to make the Martin Luther King, Jr. Center for Nonviolent Social Change a force for continuing and documenting the civil rights movement. King continues to speak out on a broad range of social issues.

Overview of Biographical Sources

Despite the significance of her life and the remarkable quality of her personality and experiences, most of the biographical materials available on Coretta King are contained in magazine articles, and not all of it is reliable. The best biographical data is found in three biographies for young people, and in various sections of biographies about her husband, especially David L. Lewis, *King: A Critical Biography* (New York: Praeger, 1970; **A, G**); Stephen B. Oates, *Let the Trumpet Sound* (New York: Harper & Row, 1982; **A, G**); and David J. Garrow, *Bearing the Cross: Martin Luther King, Jr., and the Southern Christian Leadership Conference* (New York: Morrow, 1986; **A, G**).

Evaluation of Biographies for Young People

Patterson, Lille. *Coretta Scott King.* Champaign, IL: Garrad, 1977. Illustrated and indexed, this ninety-six-page book traces King's life and explains her role in the civil rights movement. For junior and senior high school readers.

Taylor, Paula. *Coretta King: A Woman of Peace.* Mankato, MN: Creative Education, 1974. Only thirty pages long, this laudatory account focuses on the nonviolent social change that Coretta Scott King promotes.

Vivian, Octavia. *Coretta: The Story of Mrs. Martin Luther King, Jr.* Philadelphia, PA: Fortress Press, 1970. Written by a friend and neighbor whose husband served with Dr. King on the executive committee of the Southern Christian Leadership Conference, this account is warm but dated, and short on substantive information.

Overview and Evaluation of Primary Sources

Mrs. King's book, *My Life with Martin Luther King, Jr.* (New York: Holt, Rinehart & Winston, 1969; **A, G**), written as a tribute to her husband's memory, focuses as much on Dr. King's public life as upon their married life. She is more concerned with portraying the dynamics of his personality than in presenting any portrayal of herself. Nontheless, there are some revealing autobiographical passages, particularly those dealing with her emotional relationship with her husband and her passionate conviction about the importance of his work.

Museums, Historical Landmarks, Societies

Dexter Avenue Baptist Church (Montgomery, AL). The Montgomery bus boycott of 1955 was organized on these premises while Dr. King was pastor.

Martin Luther King, Jr. Center for Nonviolent Social Change (Atlanta, GA). Located on the King National Historic Site and Preservation District, the center's facilities include a 5,000-volume library and reading room. Collections contain materials relating to the Kings, the civil rights movements, and black history. Specifically related to Mrs. King are taped interviews and financial records related to her fund-raising activities. The center, which Mrs. King heads, arranges educational programs for college students.

Martin Luther King, Jr. National Historic Site and Preservation District (Atlanta, GA). Maintained by the National Park Service, this historic site offers walking tours of the neighborhood, the King family house, and the Center for Nonviolent Social Change.

Other Sources

Abernathy, Ralph David. *And the Walls Came Tumbling Down: An Autobiography*. New York: Harper & Row, 1989. Refers frequently to Coretta Scott King's activities until the time of her involvement with the Poor People's Campaign.

Joseph M. McCarthy
Suffolk University

JOHN MERCER LANGSTON
1829-1897

Chronology

Born John Mercer Langston on December 14, 1829, the third son of white planter Ralph Quarles and Lucy Jane Langston, a half-black, half-Native American woman, in Louisa County, Virginia; *1834* after the death of his parents, moves to Ohio, emancipated by his father's will; *1844* enters Oberlin College, where he earns a bachelor's degree, a master's degree, and studies theology; *1849* attends and speaks at first black convention; *1854* marries Caroline Mathilda Wall on October 25 with whom he has five children; passes the bar exam; *1855* elected town-clerk of Brownhelm, Ohio, becoming perhaps the first black elected official in American history; *1859* refuses to join John Brown's ill-fated expedition to Harpers Ferry; *1862-1863* helps recruit black regiments during the Civil War; *1864* elected president of the National Equal Rights League; *1867-1869* works for Freedmen's Bureau, inspecting educational operations; *1869-1875* joins faculty of Howard University as dean of the law school, vice president, and acting president; *1871* appointed by President Ulysses S. Grant to serve on the Board of Health for Washington, D.C.; *1877-1885* serves as minister to Haiti and diplomatic representative to the Dominican Republic; *1885-1887* serves as president of the Virginia Normal and Collegiate Institute in Petersburg; *1888* runs for Congress, is declared defeated, and contests result; *1890* is seated by House Elections Committee on September 23; loses reelection bid; *1897* dies November 15 and is buried in Woodlawn Cemetery, Washington, D.C.

Activities of Historical Significance

John Mercer Langston fought not only for the emancipation of blacks from slavery but also asserted their right to an equal place in American society. He holds the distinction of being the first black elected to office in the United States, having secured the post of town clerk in Brownhelm, Ohio, near Oberlin, in 1855. During the Civil War he helped to recruit black regiments, including the Fifty-fourth Massachusetts of Fort Wagner fame; at war's end he had been recommended for a colonelcy. During Reconstruction he pursued his belief in black advancement and self-improvement through education in the Freedman's Bureau and at Howard University.

His prominence led to appointments to office by Republican presidents, starting in 1871, when Ulysses S. Grant chose him to serve on the Board of Health for the District of Columbia. Presidents Hayes, Garfield, and Arthur employed him as a diplomat in Haiti and the Dominican Republic. Langston's effort to win election as the representative from Virginia's Fourth District, including Petersburg, in 1888, won him national attention as he successfully contested the initial results which asserted that he had lost to Democrat E. C. Venable. During his lifetime he was recognized as one of the most prominent leaders of black America.

Overshadowed for some time by Frederick Douglass and more radical black leaders like Martin Delany, Langston is only now being given the recognition by historians that he was accorded by his fellow Americans during his lifetime.

Overview of Biographical Sources

Curiously enough, until recently Langston has suffered from the neglect of historians. While there are scattered references to him in much of the historical literature about northern blacks, abolition, and the civil rights movement during the Civil War and Reconstruction, he received little sustained study. The work of William Cheek and Aimee Lee Cheek, *John Mercer Langston and the Fight for Black Freedom* (1989) promises to remedy this shortcoming. Their two-volume biography, when complete, will assume its place as the definitive study. The first volume, covering Langston's life through the Civil War, is an impressive piece of research, bringing together material to present a portrait not only of Langston but also of the world in which he and other free northern black leaders operated during the nineteenth century.

Evaluation of Principal Biographical Sources

Cheek, William, and Aimee Lee Cheek. *John Mercer Langston and the Fight for Black Freedom, 1829-1865.* Urbana: The University of Illinois Press, 1989. (A, G) The first of a projected two-volume biography, this work fulfills the need for a modern biography of Langston.

————. "John Mercer Langston: Principle and Politics." *Black Leaders of the Nineteenth Century.* Leon Litwack and August Meier, eds. Urbana: The University of Illinois Press, 1988. (A, G) The best short interpretation of Langston's career and contributions.

————. "John Mercer Langston: Black Protest Leader and Abolitionist." *Civil War History* 16 (June 1970): 101-120. (A, G) A short introduction to many of the themes developed in depth in the 1989 biography by the Cheeks.

————. "A Negro Runs for Congress: John Mercer Langston and the Virginia Campaign for 1888." *Journal of Negro History* 52 (January 1967): 14-34. (A, G) A recounting of Langston's independent race for Congress in

1888, when he challenged both the parties and the leadership of former Confederate general William Mahone.

Overview and Evaluation of Primary Sources

Most of Langston's personal papers have been destroyed or lost; others are at Howard University. His autobiography, *From the Virginia Plantation to the National Capital* (1894. Reprint. New York: Arno Press, 1969; A, G), remains an essential source, in part because Langston uses his own life to illustrate his philosophy of black uplift through education. Many of Langston's speeches through the early 1880s are collected in *Freedom and Citizenship* (1883. Reprint. Miami, FL: Mnemosyne, 1969; A, G).

Other Sources

Bromberg, Alan B. "John Mercer Langston: Black Congressman from the Old Dominion." *Virginia Cavalcade* 30:2 (1980): 60-67. An introductory overview of Langston's life.

Pease, Jane H., and William Pease. *They Who Would be Free: Blacks' Search for Freedom, 1830-1861.* New York: Atheneum, 1974. A study of the endeavors of northern blacks in the decades prior to the Civil War to assert their equal place in American society.

Quarles, Benjamin. *Black Abolitionists.* New York: Oxford University Press, 1969. A comprehensive overview of black abolitionists, including Langston and his brother Charles.

Brooks Donohue Simpson
Arizona State University

MARY TODD LINCOLN
1818-1882

Chronology

Born Mary Ann Todd on December 13, 1818, in Lexington, Kentucky, the fourth child and third daughter of Robert S. Todd, a banker, and a senator in the Kentucky state government, and Eliza Parker Todd, who died on July 5, 1825 after bearing her seventh child; *1826* father marries Betsy Humphreys, mother of nine more Todd children; *1832* enters the school of Madame Mentelle; *1837* visits Springfield, Illinois, home of two married sisters (Elizabeth, Mrs. Ninian W. Edwards, and Frances, Mrs. William Wallace), then returns to school in Lexington; *1839* finishes school, moves to Springfield, and meets Abraham Lincoln; *1840* engages to marry but plans collapse on following "fatal first of Jany.''; *1842* marries Lincoln at Edwards home; moves to Globe Tavern; *1843* Robert Todd Lincoln born; *1844* Lincolns purchase house on Eighth Street; *1846* Edward Baker Lincoln born; *1847* accompanies husband to Washington, D.C., for opening of 30th Congress, to which Lincoln was elected; *1848* resides in Lexington while Lincoln remains in Washington; *1849* father dies; Lincolns reside in Lexington; *1850* Edward Lincoln dies; William Wallace "Willie'' Lincoln born; *1853* Thomas "Tad'' Lincoln born; *1857* adds second story to Springfield house while Lincoln is in Chicago on Rock Island Bridge case; *1858* attends one of the Lincoln-Douglas debates; *1860* accompanies president-elect Lincoln to Chicago for cabinet consultations; *1861* leaves Springfield for Washington; in summer and fall visits Saratoga, New York, Long Branch, New Jersey, and Niagara Falls; *1862* William Lincoln dies; *April 14, 1865* Lincoln assassinated; *May 22, 1865* leaves White House for Chicago; *December 22, 1865* arrives in Springfield for transfer of Lincoln's body to tomb; *1867* proposes to sell her jewelry and clothes, garnering popular disapproval; *1868* sails for Europe with Tad, settles in Frankfurt; *1870* awarded pension by Congress; *1871* returns to Chicago; Tad dies; *1875* judged insane and moved to sanatorium in Batavia, Illinois; *1876* released from custody and sails for France; *1880* returns to U.S., lives with sister in Springfield; *1882* dies July 16 in Springfield.

Activities of Historical Significance

Mary Lincoln entered the White House in 1861 bent on a course of self-assertion that left a legacy of controversy, not yet resolved. A troubled childhood after her mother's death, marriage to a rising lawyer-politician, and social prominence in provincial Springfield—due more to her family connections than her own talents—did little to prepare her for life in the White

House. She transferred the emotional and physical problems that generated tempests in Illinois to a larger stage in Washington. She sometimes blatantly attempted to influence presidential appointments to further her social or financial goals, and she was not averse to publicly stating her strong likes and dislikes, a habit which attracted censure from the press, politicians, and her social peers. Bizarre behavior, beginning after the death of her son Willie in 1862, gradually degenerated into a serious mental disorder. She appears never to have recovered from Willie's loss or her husband's assassination and was committed to an asylum a decade after President Lincoln's death.

Raised in a slave-holding family in the upper South, Mary Lincoln's politics were initially attuned to her husband's Whig affiliations, but diverged when he joined the Republican Party. In 1856 she expressed a preference for the American (Know-Nothing) Party. Ambition, however, eventually reconciled her to her husband's politics. During the Civil War, many in her family supported the Confederacy, and she was herself falsely accused of disloyalty.

Abraham Lincoln's marriage to Mary tied him into the political and social elite of Illinois and Kentucky and tied Mary Lincoln to his own rising career. Her personal relationships inside and outside the home were frequently unpleasant, and Abraham Lincoln's original disinclination toward domestic life increased as discord pushed him into the legal and political arena, a move which gratified his ambitious wife. Since Lincoln never held executive office before his election as president, Mary's capacity as hostess was untested. She entered the White House inexperienced in social diplomacy and was harshly judged as inept by public opinion.

When Lincoln was assassinated, his widow deserved the care and comfort of the nation he had reunited, but in this regard Mary Lincoln was her own worst enemy. She demanded lavish public financial support in excess of her true needs, probably more through emotional imbalance than greed, and quarreled with those closest to her, alienating her supporters. Her unpopularity grew so that her commitment for insanity in 1875 received surprisingly little public attention or sympathy.

Overview of Biographical Sources

Throughout the Springfield years, Mary Lincoln snubbed and traduced her husband's law partner, William H. Herndon, who later produced a major Lincoln biography, *Herndon's Lincoln: The True Story of a Great Life* (1889). Herndon, as a result, was merciless in his treatment of Mary Lincoln. He disclosed Lincoln's youthful romance with Ann Rutledge, spitefully enlarging it as Lincoln's only love, and gathered gossip and reminiscences of the tempestuous marriage. By the end of the nineteenth century, due to Herndon's efforts and embellished by other biographers, Mary Lincoln was generally regarded as an affliction to her husband, an obstacle that he overcame to rise to greatness.

In the twentieth century, the tide turned with a series of sympathetic studies based upon a common assumption that Mary Lincoln suffered from the malice of Herndon and a general lack of understanding of the problems of women. Ruth Painter Randall, wife and collaborator of the most respected Lincoln scholar of the day, J. G. Randall, *Lincoln the President* (1945-1955), turned her considerable talents to *Mary Lincoln: Biography of a Marriage* (1953), the first scholarly biography. This work remained the standard until supplanted by Jean H. Baker, *Mary Todd Lincoln: A Biography* (1987). Randall romanticized Mary Lincoln's life into a touching love story; Baker used the perspectives of social history and feminism to repaint the portrait for modern tastes.

Somehow, however, modern biographers have failed to sway public opinion. A 1982 ranking by history professors of the effectiveness of First Ladies, for example, places Mary Lincoln last. The evidence that Abraham Lincoln truly loved his wife is overwhelming, but a convincing explanation of the dynamics of their relationship presents a lasting challenge.

Evaluation of Principal Biographical Sources

Baker, Jean H. *Mary Todd Lincoln: A Biography*. New York and London: W. W. Norton, 1987. (**A, G**) A skillful and engrossing biography, strongly argumentative, and dedicated to demonstrating that "popular stereotypes of Mary Lincoln are classic instances of a male-ordered history that is no longer acceptable." This book is the subject of an acrimonious symposium in the *Psychohistory Review* 17 (Fall 1988): 3-48.

Barton, William E. *The Women Lincoln Loved*. Indianapolis: Bobbs-Merrill, 1927. (**A, G**) By including Lincoln's grandmother, mother, and sister (among others), Barton creates a catchy title. As for contents, Barton excelled in research rather than interpretation.

Evans, W. A. *Mrs. Abraham Lincoln: A Study of her Personality and her Influence on Lincoln*. New York: Alfred A. Knopf, 1932. (**A, G**) A careful study by a pathologist interested in both physical and emotional health, especially their interrelationship. Thoughtful scholarship distinguishes this neglected classic. Later biographers concerned with a defense of Mary Lincoln have generally ignored the conclusion that she was emotionally impaired in the White House years, not responsible for her behavior afterward.

Helm, Katherine. *The True Story of Mary, Wife of Lincoln*. New York and London: Harper & Brothers, 1928. (**A, G**) An affectionate portrait by her niece, who drew upon her mother's recollections. Valuable as a repository of family sources and lore, less reliable as interpretation.

Herndon, William H., and Jesse William Weik. *Herndon's Lincoln: The True Story of a Great Life*, 3 vols. Chicago: Belford, Clarke, 1889. (A, G) Herndon emerged as Lincoln's Boswell in this classic treatment of Lincoln's life. Mary Lincoln, however, suffers from her portrayal in these pages. There was little love lost between Herndon and Mary Lincoln.

Keckley, Elizabeth. *Behind the Scenes*. New York: G. W. Carleton, 1868. (A, G) An account, probably ghost-written, by Mary Lincoln's White House seamstress, a former slave who became Mary's confidante.

Neely, Mark E., Jr., and R. Gerald McMurtry. *The Insanity File: The Case of Mary Todd Lincoln*. Carbondale and Edwardsville: Southern Illinois University Press, 1986. (A, G) The standard account of Mary Lincoln's commitment for insanity, based upon a careful analysis of Illinois law and the first use of Robert Todd Lincoln's assemblage of important documents, which he labeled the "Insanity File."

Randall, Ruth Painter. *Mary Lincoln: Biography of a Marriage*. Boston: Little, Brown, 1953. (A, G) Impressive scholarship harnessed to a passionate defense of Mary Lincoln. Randall attempts to rehabilitate Mary Lincoln's reputation and in many respects is convincing.

Ross, Ishbel. *The President's Wife: Mary Todd Lincoln, A Biography*. New York: G. P. Putnam's Sons, 1973. (A, G) Written by an accomplished journalist and biographer, this is perhaps the best, balanced study of Mary Lincoln, but lacks verve and insight.

Sandburg, Carl, and Paul M. Angle. *Mary Lincoln: Wife and Widow*. New York: Harcourt, Brace, 1932. (A, G) Two books in one: Sandburg's sympathetic biography combined with Angle's compilation of letters and other documents.

Schreiner, Samuel A., Jr. *The Trials of Mrs. Lincoln: The Harrowing Never-Before-Told Story of Mary Todd Lincoln's Last and Finest Years*. New York: Donald I. Fine, 1987. (G) A shrill defense of Mary Lincoln, especially emphasizing the sanity issue, using the same sources as Neely and McMurtry to reach opposite conclusions. Like several other Mary Lincoln biographers, Schreiner invents dialogue in an undocumented book that straddles the fence between fact and fiction.

Townsend, William H. *Lincoln and the Bluegrass: Slavery and Civil War in Kentucky.* Lexington: University of Kentucky Press, 1955. (A, G) A revision and expansion of Townsend's *Lincoln and His Wife's Home Town* (1929), a study that illuminates Mary Lincoln's early years and continuing Kentucky connections.

Overview and Evaluation of Primary Sources

Mary Lincoln's writings consist of personal letters carefully collected by Justin G. Turner and Linda Levitt Turner, *Mary Todd Lincoln: Her Life and Letters* (New York: Knopf, 1972; A, G). Other letters, squirreled away by her son Robert Todd Lincoln to demonstrate that she had once freely given gifts to the daughter-in-law that she later repudiated, appear in Mark E. Neely, Jr. and R. Gerald McMurtry, *The Insanity File: The Case of Mary Todd Lincoln* (Carbondale and Edwardsville: Southern Illinois University Press, 1986; A, G). Minor letters are collected in Thomas F. Schwartz and Anne V. Shaughnessy, "Unpublished Mary Lincoln Letters," *Journal of the Abraham Lincoln Association* 11 (1990): 36-49.

Fiction and Adaptations

Fictional defenses of Mary Lincoln include Honoré Willsie Morrow, *Mary Todd Lincoln: An Appreciation of the Wife of Abraham Lincoln* (New York: William Morrow, 1928) and Irving Stone, *Love is Eternal: A Novel About Mary Todd and Abraham Lincoln* (Garden City, NY: Doubleday, 1954). Both employ fiction to enhance considerable research.

James Prideaux's play, "The Last of Mrs. Lincoln" (first performed in 1972, published in 1973), starring Julie Harris, had some success on Broadway and has been shown on television. The play shines a sympathetic light on its subject.

Leading motion pictures have contributed to a negative image of Mary Lincoln: D. W. Griffith's *Abraham Lincoln* (1930), John Ford's *Young Mr. Lincoln* (1939), and John Cromwell's *Abe Lincoln in Illinois* (1940).

Museums, Historical Landmarks, Societies

Mary Todd Lincoln House (Lexington, KY). The original girlhood home of Mary Todd, restored with period furnishings.

Lincoln's Home (Springfield, IL). Rebuilt and refurnished, then reopened in 1989 to more accurately reflect Mary Lincoln's taste.

Other Sources
Anthony, Carl Sferrazza. *First Ladies.* New York: Morrow, 1990. Anthony devotes about thirty-five pages to Mary Todd Lincoln, discussing her character and personality, political interests, relationship with Lincoln, and her life after his assassination.

Bradford, Gamaliel. "Mrs. Abraham Lincoln." In *Wives* (New York and London: Harper & Brothers, 1925). A brief, trenchant and sensible essay.

Lewis, Montgomery S. *Legends that Libel Lincoln* (New York and Toronto: Rinehart & Company, 1946). An Indianapolis attorney, determined to uphold a genteel Abraham Lincoln, devotes more than half the book to a defense of his wife.

Ostendorf, Lloyd. "The Photographs of Mary Todd Lincoln." *Journal of the Illinois State Historical Society* 61 (Autumn 1968): 269-332. Reproduction and careful analysis of twenty-six photographs.

John Y. Simon
Southern Illinois University at Carbondale

ANNE MORROW LINDBERGH
b. 1906

Chronology

Born Anne Spencer Morrow on June 22, 1906, in Englewood, New Jersey, the second daughter of Dwight Whitney Morrow, later ambassador to Mexico and senator from New Jersey, and Elizabeth Reeve Cutter, later acting president of Smith College and children's book writer; *1906-1924* grows up in Englewood with two sisters and a brother; *1924-1928* attends Smith College and graduates with two literary prizes; *May 27, 1929* marries Charles A. Lindbergh, world famous aviator who made the first solo nonstop transatlantic flight from New York to Paris; *June 22, 1930* gives birth to Charles Augustus Lindbergh, Jr.; *1931* flies as co-pilot and radio operator with her husband in a survey flight to Orient; *1932* grieves for kidnapped and murdered son, Charles, and gives birth to Jon Morrow Lindbergh; *1933* flies North Atlantic survey flight with husband; *1935* publishes *North to the Orient*; *1936-1939* resides in England and France; gives birth to Land Morrow Lindbergh; completes *Listen! the Wind*; *1940* gives birth to Anne Spencer Morrow Lindbergh; publishes *The Wave of the Future* just prior to her husband's campaign for America First; *1942* gives birth to Scott Morrow Lindbergh; *1944* publishes *The Steep Ascent*; *1945* gives birth to second daughter, Reeve Morrow Lindbergh; *1955* publishes *Gift from the Sea*; *1971-1980* publishes five volumes of diaries and letters; *1974* Charles Lindbergh dies; *1975-present* resides in Scott's Cove, Darien, Connecticut.

Activities of Historical Significance

Anne Lindbergh's fame rests on her autobiographical writings and upon her partnership with her aviator husband. She served as co-pilot, radio operator, and best-selling historian of their flights. She wrote and published her first book about their flight to the Orient soon after the kidnapping-murder of their first son. In subsequent years, this shy and introverted writer came under the intense scrutiny of "Movietone News" publicity associated with the Lindberghs' efforts to promote aviation. After the Lindberghs flew over five continents around the North Atlantic, the National Geographic Society awarded her the Hubbard Gold Medal for distinction in exploration, research, and discovery. She was the first woman to receive the medal and the first woman licensed as a glider-pilot.

Her literary fame and achievement derive from several works: her early trilogy on flight, especially *North to the Orient* (1935); her still-popular, meditative essay on woman's choices, *Gift from the Sea* (1955); and her five published volumes of diaries and letters, detailing her life from 1922-1944. Though consistently best-selling, Lindbergh's writing has sometimes been severely attacked by critics. *The Wave of the Future* (1940), published just before her husband spoke out against American intervention in the war in Europe, brought her into the middle of the intense public debate. A scathing critique of *The Unicorn and Other Poems* (1956) made her writing the focus of a literary furor over the merits of "popular-genteel" versus "serious-disciplined" poetry.

Overview of Biographical Sources

Lindbergh's privacy has been maintained because her papers and correspondence at the Yale University Library are closed and unavailable to anyone but authorized researchers. Permission for research may be granted by Lindbergh or two of her children. Personal family correspondence is restricted throughout her lifetime and for fifty years after her death. Still, several recent accounts offer partial insights based upon Lindbergh's own published writings. David K. Vaughan, *Anne Morrow Lindbergh* (1988), Elsie Mayer, *My Window on the World: The Writings of Anne Morrow Lindbergh* (1988), and Roxane Chadwick, *Anne Morrow Lindbergh: Pilot and Poet* (1987), all offer critical interpretations of her life and writings. Harold Nicolson's biography of her father, *Dwight Morrow* (1932), and her sister Constance Morgan's biography of their mother, *A Distant Moment* (1978), help explain the Morrow family background, fortune, and commitment to education and political life. Charles Lindbergh's *Wartime Journals* (1970) include revealing notations about his wife as his companion-traveler in Europe and his posthumous *Autobiography of Values* (1978) offers further commentary on his views of courtship and marriage.

Sensational books about the kidnapping and murder of Charles Lindbergh, Jr., portray in heart-wrenching detail the grieving but brave mother. One example is P. J. O'Brien, *The Lindberghs* (1935). Most recent biographies of Charles Lindbergh mention his wife and her part in his public life. Brendan Gill in *Lindbergh Alone* (1977) writes the most perceptive comments about Lindbergh.

Evaluation of Principal Biographical Sources

Chadwick, Roxane. *Anne Morrow Lindbergh: Pilot and Poet.* Minneapolis: Lerner, 1987. (**A, G, Y**) An appealing, accurate and concise biography for young people, this brief overview might serve every critical reader in spite of its author's obvious strong admiration for her subject.

Gill, Brendan. *Lindbergh Alone*. New York: Harcourt Brace Jovanovich, 1977. (G) A breezy, admiring portrait of Charles Lindbergh, with perceptive passages on his wife and his marriage. However, it lacks footnotes or bibliography.

Mayer, Elsie F. *My Window on the World: The Writings of Anne Morrow Lindbergh*. New York: Shoestring Press, 1988. (A, G) A careful and sensitive reading of Lindbergh's writing, this work offers summary biographical information taken from the published diaries. Mayer offers a useful chronology of Lindbergh's life and extensive, sometimes insightful literary interpretation of Lindbergh's writing and its critical reception. The historical analysis of the context of Lindbergh's writings is not entirely accurate or complete but Mayer's chief interest is in noting Lindbergh's "romantic" or Wordsworthian concentration on feelings instead of events. Complete with footnotes, bibliography, and index.

Morrow, Elizabeth C. *Mexican Years: Leaves from the Diary of Elizabeth C. Morrow*. Croton Falls, NY: Spiral Press, 1953. (G) Diary entries by Anne's mother reveal aspects of the Lindberghs' courtship, early marriage, and the birth of their first son.

Morgan, Constance Morrow. *A Distant Moment*. Northampton, MA: Smith College, 1978. (A, G, Y) A daughter's balanced, thoughtful account of her mother's childhood, education, years at Smith College, post-graduate tensions, courtship, and marriage. This biography puts into perspective the lasting influence of Anne's mother on her children, especially Anne herself. The book unfortunately lacks footnotes, bibliography, or index.

Nicolson, Harold. *Dwight Morrow*. New York: Harcourt, Brace, 1935. (A, G). Contracted by the Morrow family to write this "official" biography, Nicolson included a chapter written by Anne Lindbergh and succeeded in producing a literate if sometimes patronizing assessment of Morrow. Nicolson's encouragement of her literary ability led Anne to continue her efforts to produce her first book, *North to the Orient*.

Vaughan, David Kirk. *Anne Morrow Lindbergh*. Boston: G. K. Hall, 1988. (A, G) A critical study of Lindbergh's writings by this aviator-professor is straightforward and concise. Vaughan believes Lindbergh's writing is chiefly philosophical, aimed at promoting an individual's development of clear perception and understanding in the spheres of family, nation, and world. Vaughan gives little significance to the historical context of the writings but includes a chronology of Lindbergh's life, several biographical chapters based on published accounts, a selected bibliography, and an index.

Overview and Evaluation of Primary Sources

Anne Morrow Lindbergh's autobiographical publications form the basis of a substantial chronicle of her life. Her descriptions of the Lindberghs' famous flights remain in print. *North to the Orient* (1935) and *Listen! the Wind* (1938) are currently more widely read than *The Steep Ascent* (1944), a fictionalized account of a flight over the Alps. Her still popular *Gift from the Sea* (1955), describing her personal struggle to resolve the many conflicts in a woman's life, and a collection of her poetry, *The Unicorn* (1956), preceded her fictional meditation on marriage, *Dearly Beloved* (1962). Her two *Life* magazine essays on environmental conservation were published as *Earth Shine* (1966, 1969).

Five volumes of published diaries form the matrix of any study of her life. *Bring Me a Unicorn: 1922-1928* (1972) describes her sheltered childhood in a privileged family that was astonished by her choice to marry the aviator, Charles Lindbergh. *Hour of Gold, Hour of Lead: 1929-1932* (1973), details her early marriage, the intense publicity associated with the Lindberghs' work to promote aviation, the kidnapping of Charles, Jr. and the fruitless months of searching for him. *Locked Rooms and Open Doors: 1933-1936* (1974) describes her recovery from the deaths of her father, her son, and her sister; the publication of her first book; and the flight around the Atlantic. *The Flower and the Nettle: 1936-1939* (1976) recounts the Lindberghs' residence in England and France just before the beginning of war. *War Within and Without: 1939-1944* (1980) explains through letters and diary entries the internal conflict of loyalties Lindbergh suffered as she tried to remain neutral while her husband worked to keep America out of the war in Europe. Her introductory essay recalls the historical context of the "Great Debate" of 1940-1941, now largely ignored by many historians of the period.

Beyond her own published writings, the collected material now restricted to authorized researchers in the Yale University Library is the chief repository of material on Lindbergh's life with Charles Lindbergh. The Library of Congress holds public documents and photographs related to their flights and activities during the pre-war debate over American intervention. Other significant items may be found at the Smith College Library, Northampton, Massachusetts, where Anne Lindbergh gave a 1978 lecture, "The Journey Not the Arrival." This brief speech was later published under the same title by Harcourt Brace Jovanovich on whose editorial board Lindbergh has recently served. In it, she pinpoints the major choices and turning points of her life.

In addition, the writings of her husband Charles are valuable in rounding out a portrait of her marriage. Among other meditative topics in *Autobiography of Values* (New York: Harcourt Brace Jovanovich, 1978; **A, G**) the famed aviator recounts his sensible, scientific method of falling in love and choosing a wife. This is the closest that the fiercely private Lindbergh came to revealing his heart to the public, and it was published only after his death. In an attempt to put the record straight about his pre-war political and military work, Lindbergh published *Wartime Journals*, (New York: Harcourt Brace Jovanovich, 1970; **A, G**), which he kept while traveling with Anne in Europe before the war.

Fiction and Adaptations

Lindbergh published two works of fiction. *The Steep Ascent* is (1944) an allegory in which a young woman, flying over the Alps with her husband, overcomes her fear of death and learns to live aware of the value of each moment. *Dearly Beloved* (1962) is a metaphor for the "marriage feast" of life. The stream-of-consciousness technique allows family members, who are gathered for a wedding, to tell their private views on marriage,

Although the made-for-television movie, *The Lindbergh Kidnapping Case* (1976), emphasizes the sensational, it provides a moving portrait of the young mother (portrayed by Sian Barbara Allen).

Lindbergh agreed to her only television interview with historian David McCullough for the series "Smithsonian World" (aired 1983 and 1984). In it she recalls with humor her early marriage and flights with Charles Lindbergh, putting their lives into some personal and historical perspective. Eric Sevareid recorded a "Conversation with Anne Morrow Lindbergh" for Encyclopedia Americana/ CBS News Audio Resource Library (c #05773, May 23, 1977), in the fiftieth anniversary year of Charles Lindbergh's solo flight across the Atlantic. Random House Audiobooks has recorded Claudette Colbert reading *Gift from the Sea.*

Museums, Historical Landmarks, Societies

Lindbergh Museum (Jefferson Memorial, St. Louis, MO). Among the artifacts, medals, and portraits of the famous aviator in this collection is a copy of the bronze head of Anne Morrow Lindbergh by the French sculptor, Despiau. Some of her memorabilia, costumes, and gifts are on display.

Lindbergh House (Little Falls, MN). The interpretive slide show in Lindbergh's childhood home refers to their marriage and his flights with Anne. A panel exhibit on her life includes the McCullough television interview for *Smithsonian World.*

Falaise (Sands Point, NY). Anne and Charles visited this Guggenheim estate many times in the first year of their marriage and after the murder of their child. Their rooms with memorabilia are now preserved for public viewing.

Other Sources
Eisenhower, Julie Nixon. "Anne Morrow Lindbergh." In *Special People.*
New York: Simon and Schuster, 1977. A thoughtful, personal essay based
upon published information, extremely rare interviews with Lindbergh and her
daughter, Reeve, and private letters. Mindful of historical perspective, Eisenhower probes, analyzes, and comments with considerable critical insight.

Mayer, Elsie F. "Anne Morrow Lindbergh." In *American Women Writers,*
edited by Lina Mainiero. New York: Frederick Ungar, 1981. A brief biographical analysis precedes a more detailed if debatable literary interpretation of
Lindbergh's works.

Wurz, Trude. *Anne Morrow Lindbergh: The Literary Reputation: A Primary
and Annotated Secondary Bibliography.* New York: Garland, 1988. Concluding
a fifty-year bibliography in 1978, Wurz omits probably the most controversial
and historically important volume of Lindbergh's published diaries and letters,
War Within and Without (1980). Still, this volume documents the considerable
published writing by and about Anne Morrow Lindbergh.

Gretchen R. Sutherland
Cornell College

LITTLE TURTLE
c. 1752-1812

Chronology

Born about 1752 in a Miami village on the Eel River northwest of modern day Fort Wayne, Indiana; his father was a Miami chief and his mother was probably a Mahican; given the name Me-she-kin-no-quah; *1752-1770* matures among his people at a time of great turmoil and stress among the tribes of the Great Lakes region; *1771-1779* becomes renowned for his fearlessness in combat, his skill as a warrior, and his immense talent as an orator; *1780-1790* watches white settlements in Ohio threaten the Native Americans' way of life in the Northwest Territory and emerges as one of the principal leaders of the growing resistance to the post-Revolutionary War invasion of his homeland by white settlers; *1790-1791* plays an active role in the war against the U.S. and receives much of the credit for the defeats administered to the armies of Josiah Harmar in 1790 and Arthur St. Clair in 1791; *1792-1794* serves as rallying point for the Native American forces determined to resist the advance of the white settlers' frontier; *1794* is involved in the fateful Battle of Fallen Timbers and endures defeat at the hands of General Anthony Wayne; decides to make peace with the U.S. while counseling other Native American leaders to follow a similar policy; *1795-1800* continues his peace policy with the U.S. and signs the Treaty of Greenville (1795), in which he actively espouses a conciliatory attitude toward the U.S.; *1801-1808* visits the U.S. several times and becomes something of a hero to white Americans; meets with the French philosopher Volney in the U.S. and gradually becomes one of the more notable spokesmen for the U.S. among the Great Lakes nations; *1809* participates in the negotiation of the Treaty of Fort Wayne, in which the Miami, Delaware, and Potawatomi nations cede nearly three million acres of land to the U.S. for minor increases in their annuities and $5,200 in trade goods; *1810-1811* continues to advocate friendship with the U.S. and actively opposes the Native American unification movement inaugurated by Tenskwatawa (the Shawnee Prophet) and Tecumseh; *1812* is badly discredited among the younger men of the Miami nation and other tribes because of his pro-U.S. stance; during a visit to Fort Wayne, where he often receives medical treatment, Little Turtle dies on July 14.

Activities of Historical Significance

In an era that brought dramatic changes in the Great Lakes Native Americans' way of life, Little Turtle emerged as one of the U.S.' earliest and most effective foes. He built a coalition among several Native American tribes and played a major role in administering two embarrassing defeats to the fledgling republic in the early 1790s. After his defeat at Fallen Timbers, however, Little Turtle underwent a change in attitude and began to urge his brethren into a policy of peace. He evidently decided that white settlement in the area north of the Ohio River could not be stemmed and chose to try to live side-by-side with his erstwhile foes. He devoted the last eighteen years of his life to seeking peace with the U.S. and to reconciling his people to an accommodation with the white settlers. Little Turtle was one of several chiefs who agreed to the terms of the Treaty of Fort Wayne and thereby began his decline as an influential leader among his nation and neighboring tribes. From the time of the Treaty of Fort Wayne until his death in 1812, Little Turtle suffered failing health and gradually forfeited his role as a leader of consequence in the Northwest Territory's complex political environment. Even though he was eclipsed as a leader in his later years, Little Turtle remains a formidable figure in the military and political history of the American frontier.

Overview of Biographical Sources

Little Turtle lived a life of many achievements, but he has not drawn the attention of biographers. The obvious problem is the paucity of source materials. He lived in a pre-literate society and did not leave a corpus of papers that would permit a study of his perspective on the events that surrounded his life and times. Calvin M. Young attempted a biography in *Little Turtle (Me-She-Kin-No-Quah), The Great Chief of the Miami Indian Nation* (1917). Though useful, Young's work is not a definitive study. Readers may discover that they must examine a great many sources to construct a comprehensive view of the Miami chief's feats. Little Turtle's activities and viewpoints are essential items of discussion in studies relating to Tecumseh, Bluejacket, Tenskwatawa, William Henry Harrison, Arthur St. Clair, and Josiah Harmar. These men had important encounters with Little Turtle and his Miami nation, and any complete biography of their lives must necessarily include aspects of his.

Evaluation of Principal Biographical Sources

Young, Calvin M. *Little Turtle (Me-She-Kin-No-Quah), The Great Chief of the Miami Indian Nation.* Greenville, OH: 1917. (A, G) Readers may gain a satisfactory perspective of Me-She-Kin-No-Quah's life from this study, but it must be supplemented with other materials.

Overview and Evaluation of Primary Sources

Little Turtle left no personal papers. Researchers must consequently depend on the bits and pieces they may find in documents that deal with the lives of those who crossed his path. Observations concerning Little Turtle may be found in such collections as the William Henry Harrison Papers in the Library of Congress, Washington, D.C., and Harrison's letterbooks, housed in the collections of the Department of the Interior, Office of Indian Affairs, Washington, D.C. Other strands of information concerning Little Turtle's activities may be located in the Josiah Harmar Papers in the William L. Clements Library, Ann Arbor, Michigan, and in the Arthur St. Clair Collection in the Ohio State Historical Society, Columbus. The Burton Historical Collection, located in the Detroit Public Library, contains many small collections of papers of men who also encountered Little Turtle, and these documents are useful for developing an overview of the period. The Anthony Wayne Papers in the Historical Society of Pennsylvania, Philadelphia, also deserve attention. An important foreign observer of the American scene, French philosopher Constantin-Francois Chasseboeuf, comte de Volney, produced *A View of the Soil and Climate of the United States of America* (1804. Reprint. New York: Hafner Press, 1968; A), which provides useful insights into the environment in which Little Turtle lived. Another useful item to consult is J. P. Dunn, William Wesley Wollen, and Daniel Wait Howe, eds., *Executive Journal of Indiana Territory, 1800-1816* (Indianapolis: Bowen-Merrill, 1900; A).

Other Sources

Dunn, J. P. *True Indian Stories, with a Glossary of Indiana Indian Names.* Indianapolis: Sentinel Printing, 1908. An interesting volume of local history.

Huber, John Parker. "General Josiah Harmar's Command: Military Policy in the Old Northwest." Ph.D. diss., University of Michigan, 1964. An excellent study of the situation in which Little Turtle temporarily flourished as an adversary of the U.S. Army.

Mansfield, Edward Deering. *Personal Memories, Social, Political, and literary with Sketches of Many Notable People, 1803-1843.* 1879. Reprint. Salem, NH: Ayer, 1970. This volume contains interesting tidbits of information. Mansfield was a prolific writer who addressed a host of subjects.

Prucha, Francis Paul. *The Sword of the Republic: the United States Army on the Frontier, 1783-1845.* London and Ontario: Collier-Macmillan, 1969. An excellent study of the military situation on the frontier during a disastrous time for the Native American.

Sword, Wiley. *President Washington's Indian War: The Struggle for the Old Northwest, 1790-1795*. Norman: University of Oklahoma Press, 1985. The best study of the period during which Little Turtle was at the peak of his fame and influence.

Van Every, Dale. *Ark of Empire: The American Frontier, 1784-1803*. New York: William M. Morrow, 1963. A good account of Little Turtle's times that any reader will enjoy.

Larry G. Bowman
University of North Texas

ALICE ROOSEVELT LONGWORTH
1884-1980

Chronology

Born Alice Lee Roosevelt on February 12, 1884, in New York City to Theodore Roosevelt and Alice (Lee) Roosevelt; mother dies two days later of Bright's disease on the same day that her paternal grandmother dies; *1884-1898* lives as an unwanted child with her father, his second wife, Edith Kermit Carow, and her five children; spoiled with attention and money by maternal grandparents during two extended yearly visits; because of polio, one leg is shorter than the other; wears leg braces until age thirteen but suffers no apparent disability as an adult; educated almost wholly by tutors; resides in Washington, D.C., when her father is a civil service commissioner, in New York City when he serves as police commissioner, and again in Washington when he is appointed assistant secretary of the Navy during the Spanish-American War; *1898-1900* lives in the executive mansion in Albany, New York, when her father is state governor, and in Washington when he becomes vice president; *1901-1909* father serves as president of the U.S.; makes her debut or "coming out" at age seventeen (the first president's daughter to do so while in the White House); becomes an object of "yellow press" criticism for associating with the "fast, frivolous, and fabulously wealthy" at Newport, Rhode Island; because she prefers to dress in a shade of blue gray, she inspires a popular song, "Alice Blue Gown"; accompanies Secretary of War William H. Taft and others, including the wealthy Ohio Republican representative, Nicholas Longworth, on a tour of Hawaii, the Philippines, Japan, Korea, and China; their trip takes place five years after the Boxer Rebellion of 1900; *1906* marries Longworth and begins to devote more time to politics than to social affairs; *1912* torn between supporting her father's presidential bid on the Progressive Republican ticket and her husband's reelection bid to the House of Representatives on a stalwart Republican ticket; both men are defeated but Longworth runs again in 1914 and is reelected; *1917-1919* supports America's entrance into World War I but opposes reduction of naval armaments and participation in the League of Nations and World Court; *1924* husband is elected speaker of the House; *1925* bears a daughter, Paulina, at the age of forty-one; *1925-1930* gains importance as a behind-the-scenes adviser to conservative Republicans, dispensing advice on political matters from her Washington home; *1931* husband dies; *1932* opposes the election of Franklin D. Roosevelt and labels Franklin's Eleanor, her first cousin, "a very dear bore"; *1933* publishes her autobiographical *Crowded Years*; *1933-1941* believing in political isolationism, she entertains such members of the America First Committee as John L. Lewis and Charles A. Lindbergh; serves on

Herbert Hoover's National Committee on Food for five democracies con-
quered by Hitler; *1940, 1948* supports Robert A. Taft's presidential campaigns
but tires of him in 1948; *1949-1980* known as "the other Washington
Monument," she continues to entertain and advise conservative Republican
leaders at her home until her death on February 20, 1980; her body was
cremated and the ashes buried next to her daughter, Paulina, who apparently
committed suicide in 1957 after her husband's death.

Activities of Historical Importance

During various periods of history, social Washington has exerted unusual
influence over national politics because of the presence of a strong socialite.
Alice Roosevelt Longworth, daughter of a president, niece of another president's wife (Eleanor Roosevelt), and wife of the speaker of the House of
Representatives wielded her position and her tongue to intimidate congress-
men, and their wives, to support her political ideas. A ferocious Republican
and defender of American superiority and isolation, she vehemently opposed
the New Deal policies that her "uncle" Franklin D. Roosevelt envisioned
would bring economic stability to middle-class Americans ruined by the
depression. When FDR decided to run for an unprecedented third term, Alice
announced that she would rather vote for Adolf Hitler than for FDR. Typical
of her rude, razor-quick wit, she said that FDR was "a real light weight . . .
ninety percent mush and ten percent Eleanor." When William A. Taft, who
succeeded her father as president and then became chief justice of the
Supreme Court, remarked that he liked his job on the court so much that he
could hardly remember having been president, Alice quipped "neither can the
country."

Her elegant, inattentive husband, Congressman Nicholas Longworth, had
little interest in his acerbic wife, which left Alice free to pursue her own
interests. She wrote her autobiography "for profit, not literature," and from
1935 to 1938 she competed with Eleanor Roosevelt's "My Day" newspaper
column with her own anti-New Deal "Capital Comment." For a brief time,
she applied herself to the lecture circuit but was not well received. An atheist,
Longworth rejected the religious views of her daughter, Paulina, who was a
practicing Catholic.

Longworth remained a center of political attention during the Kennedy and
Nixon White House years until the Watergate affair, when she lost credibility
as a barometer of social opinion in Washington. However, Gerald Ford visited
on her ninety-second birthday because, he said, "if she likes you, you were
less in danger of being poisoned." She was well known to President Jimmy
Carter, the last president she attempted to influence. There are few people in
American history who began their adult lives in the inner circle of the
presidency and remained at the center through every president for eighty

years. The books that document her life are more interesting for understanding the evolution of American politics and societal attitudes than for the biography of an irreverent woman, who requested that her death certificate state her profession as "gadfly."

Overview of Biographical Sources

To date, three substantial biographies of Longworth have appeared: James Brough, *Princess Alice: A Biography of Alice Roosevelt Longworth* (1975); Howard Teichman, *Alice: The Life and Times of Alice Roosevelt Longworth* (1979); and Carol Felsenthal, *Alice Roosevelt Longworth* (1988). Also useful is Michael Teague's, *Mrs. Longworth: Conversations with Alice Roosevelt Longworth* (1981). However, to understand the milieu in which "Princess Alice" and then Mrs. Longworth lived, researchers should peruse the many biographies of famous family members and of the many persons she knew or caricatured, as well as more general histories of her days. For Longworth's obituary, see the *New York Times* (February 22, 1980).

Evaluation of Principal Biographical Sources

Brough, James. *Princess Alice: A Biography of Alice Roosevelt.* Boston: Little, Brown, 1975. (G) Written in popular style and published five years before Alice Longworth's death, this biography relies upon the correspondence of persons who knew her, biographies of the Roosevelt and Longworth families, and Alice Longworth's own *Crowded Hours*. It covers the subject's childhood rejection by a father who for years failed to acknowledge her existence, and the doting of her maternal grandparents. Her escapades as a teenager and the creation of the "Princess Alice" legend are fully documented. The author tells of Alice's strained marriage to Nicholas Longworth, an arrangement in which each partner went his or her own way. Interspersed are examples of her destructive quips about leading political and social personalities of the 1920s and 1930s. The narrative ends with a description of the continuing soirees held by "an old Narcissus" at her home at 2009 Massachusetts Avenue in Washington, D.C.

Felsenthal, Carol. *Alice Roosevelt Longworth.* New York: Putnam, 1988. (G) This full-scale biography is solidly based on historical sources and many personal interviews. Felsenthal cites many of her subject's quips in a portrayal that includes "warts and all." If only one biography is to be read, this is the one.

Teague, Michael. *Conversations with Alice Roosevelt Longworth.* Garden City, NY: Doubleday, 1981. (G) Teague "bumped into Mrs. L." in a minor

Alice Roosevelt Longworth

car accident in Washington in 1961 and soon thereafter was granted a number of taped interviews. In these interviews, Longworth shares memories of her childhood, the White House years, the aftermath of her marriage, and her later years. Although she rarely talks about her marriage or daughter, she gives many examples of her spontaneous wit, even poking fun at herself. For instance, after having her second mastectomy, she described herself as "the only topless octogenarian in Washington." These interviews reveal that Longworth was petrified of public speaking, and that she thought her autobiography, *Crowded Hours*, was incredibly dull. This autobiographical portrait is beautifully illustrated with photographs and cartoons.

Teichman, Howard. *Alice: The Life and Times of Alice Roosevelt Longworth*. Englewood Cliffs, NJ: Prentice Hall, 1979. (G) Relying primarily on newspaper and magazine articles, Teichman tells much the same story as Teague. As a teenager in the early 1900s, Alice brought a sense of glamor and style to the U.S. and was blamed by some for causing a generation gap. Teichman describes her as "eternally courageous, provoking, cynical, logical, impossible, incredible, and rebellious to the point of doing just what she pleases. And no more."

Overview of Primary Sources

Longworth's autobiography, *Crowded Years: The Reminiscences of Alice Roosevelt Longworth* (New York: Scribner's, 1933; G), was highly touted by a number of leading literary critics, but it is difficult reading. Little of her spontaneous personality and wit comes through. She is highly selective about what she tells, leaving out, for example, the death of her young half-brother, Quentin; the deaths of her father (who had not mentioned her in his autobiography) and of her husband; and the very existence of her daughter. On the other hand, although she detested her stepmother, she treats her here with kid gloves. Serious historians will be interested in Longworth's descriptions of many national political conventions and her characterization of numerous political figures.

The syndicated column, "Capital Comment" (G), which appeared in newspapers nationwide through United Press Syndicate, is valuable for the views of an anti-New Dealer and isolationist. The column also ran as "Alice Longworth Says" in the *Toledo Blade*; "Alice in Blunderland" in the *San Francisco Chronicle*; "The National Scene" in the *Washington Star*; and "Chatting with Alice" in the *Reading Eagle*. Good examples of Longworth's magazine articles may be found in *Ladies Home Journal*: "Lion Hunting in the New Deal," 51 (December 1934): 27+; "Some Reminiscences," 49 (November 1932): 4+; and "Why I Would Not Run for the Senate," 51

(August 1934): 23+. She also contributed "What's the Matter with Bob Taft?" to the *Saturday Evening Post* 212 (May 4, 1940): 29+.

The Alice Roosevelt Longworth Collection, Manuscript Division, Library of Congress, contains many letters to Longworth, but few replies, for she was a poor correspondent. Longworth destroyed many of her personal papers, but the Nicholas Longworth Collection, Manuscript Division, Library of Congress, is useful for an overview of political matters.

Other Sources

"Alice Roosevelt Longworth." In *Current Biography*. New York: H. W. Wilson, 1975. A brief biographical entry.

Cassini, Countess Marguerite. *Never a Dull Moment*. New York: Harper & Brothers, 1956. Cassini moved in the same social circle as Longworth.

De Chambrun, Clara Longworth. *The Making of Nicholas Longworth*. New York: Ray Long and Richard R. Smith, 1933. Alice Longworth is a prominent feature in this account of her husband's career.

Hoover, Irwin H. *Forty-two Years in the White House*. Boston: Houghton Mifflin, 1934. Inside views by the chief usher of the White House.

Morris, Edmund. *The Rise of Theodore Roosevelt*. New York: Coward, McCann, and Geohagen, 1979. Very detailed study of the young Roosevelt.

Pringle, Henry F. *Theodore Roosevelt: A Biography*. New York: Harcourt, Brace, 1931. Describes Roosevelt as having the "mind of a six-year old boy."

————. *The Life and Times of William Howard Taft*. 2 vols. New York: Farrar & Rinehart, 1939. Includes a description of Longworth's antics during the 1905 trip to the Far East.

Roosevelt, Eleanor. *The Autobiography of Eleanor Roosevelt*. Boston: G. K. Hall, 1984. No love was lost between Eleanor and Alice Longworth.

Schriftsgeisser, Karl. *The Amazing Roosevelt Family*. New York: Wilfred Funk, 1942. Provides useful details of the family, but told in glowing terms.

Paolo Coletta
U.S. Naval Academy (Ret.)

MARY MANN
1806-1887

Chronology

Born Mary Tyler Peabody on November 16, 1806 in Cambridge, Massachusetts, the second daughter and second of seven children to Nathaniel Peabody, a dentist, and Elizabeth, a schoolteacher; raised with little formal education in Salem, Massachusetts, she is self-educated; *1824* teaches in Hallowell, Maine; *1825* opens a dame school with her sister Elizabeth, who in time becomes a significant figure in the history of American transcendentalism and reform; *1832* meets and becomes close friends with widower Horace Mann; *1833-1835* accompanies her sister Sophia (future wife of Nathaniel Hawthorne) to Cuba for her health; *1835-1843* works at various teaching positions, while helping Mann with his educational reforms; *May 1, 1843* marries Horace Mann and visits Europe on a double honeymoon with Samuel Gridley and his bride Julia Ward Howe; studies European educational and charitable institutions; the Manns will have three sons—Horace, George Combe, and Benjamin Pickman; *1850* supports Mann in his criticism of Daniel Webster and the Compromise of 1850; *1853-1859* Horace Mann accepts the presidency of Antioch College, a new school in Yellow Springs, Ohio; *1859* returns to Concord as a schoolteacher after Horace Mann dies of fever; *1866-1887* active with Elizabeth in the kindergarten movement; publishes material on Friedrich Froebel's theories, a biography of her husband, and a novel; *February 11, 1887* dies of chronic bronchitis in Boston and is buried beside Horace and his first wife in the North Burial Ground in Providence, Rhode Island.

Activities of Historical Significance

Plain and modest Mary Mann is noted by history as the second wife of the famous educator Horace Mann and as the sister of the imminent educator Elizabeth Palmer Peabody. Her achievements, however, transcended these associations. With her sister Elizabeth, Mann was an active proponent of the fledgling kindergarten movement. Together, they wrote *Moral Culture of Infancy and Kindergarten Guide* (1863) and edited the *Kindergarten Messenger* (1873-1875) in which Mary Mann translated many articles from German. She wrote a three-volume biography of her husband, *Life and Works of Horace Mann* (1865-1875), and published *Christianity In the Kitchen: A Physiological Cookbook* (1857), which was a collection of recipes, commonsense health rules, and admonitions against drink. In her later years, she wrote a novel, *Juanita: A Romance of Real Life in Cuba Fifty Years Ago* (1887).

Evaluation of Principal Biographical Sources
Messerli, Jonathan. *Horace Mann, A Biography.* New York: Knopf, 1972.
(A, G) A first-rate biography with a solid bibliography, containing factual
information on Mary. The book explains in words of Mann how he and Mary
worked to advance "the agenda of the Almighty."

————. "Mann, Mary Tyler Peabody." In *Notable American Women, A
Biographical Dictionary,* edited by Edward T. James. Cambridge: Harvard
University Press, 1971. (G) This brief entry is a good starting place for any
research on Mary Mann. It is accurate in detail and a fine guide to the few
sources that exist on her life.

Tharp, Louise H. *Until Victory, Horace Mann and Mary Peabody.* Boston:
Little, Brown, 1953. (G) The citations in this book are few and summary in
nature. The text, however, provides a good narrative of the two remarkable
American reformers.

————. *The Peabody Sisters of Salem.* Boston: Little, Brown, 1950. (G)
Although this book provides insight into Mary's world, the documentation is
inadequate. Tharp uses direct quotes and dialogue without proper citation.

Evaluation of Primary Sources
Surviving letters and other documents of Mary Mann are in the Mann
Papers in the Massachusetts Historical Society, in the Berg Collection in the
New York Public Library, and in the Robert L. Straker Collection at Antioch
College. Because of the large number of letters, journal entries, and similar
materials knitted together by her brief narrative, the researcher should consult
Mary Mann's biography of her husband, *Life of Horace Mann* (Boston:
Willard Small Publisher, 1888; Reprint. Miami, FL: Mnemosyne Publishing,
1969; A, G). Clyde S. King, ed., *Horace Mann, 1796-1859: A Bibliography*
(Debbs, Ferry, NY: Oceana Publications, 1966; A) contains annotated citations
on Mary Mann.

Donald K. Pickens
University of North Texas

LUCY RANDOLPH MASON
1882-1959

Chronology

Born Lucy Randolph Mason on July 26, 1882, near Alexandria, Virginia, to Landon Randolph Mason, an Episcopalian minister, and Lucy Ambler Mason, who is active in prison reform; *1882-1891* lives in West Virginia and then Georgia, where her father takes pastorates, before moving with her family to Richmond, Virginia, her home for the next four decades; *1906-1914* works as stenographer with Braxton and Eggleston, a large law firm in Richmond; *1914-1918* serves as industrial secretary of the Richmond branch of the Young Women's Christian Association (YWCA); *1912-1920* serves as member of the board, then president, of the Richmond branch of the Equal Suffrage League; *1921-1923* serves as president of the Richmond League of Women Voters; *1923-1932* serves as general secretary, Richmond YWCA; *1931* spends two months in the Deep South as executive secretary of the Southern Council on Women and Children in Industry; *1932-1937* serves as general secretary of the National Consumers' League, based in New York City; *1937-1953* based in Atlanta, oversees public affairs, organizational matters, and workers' civil rights for the Congress of Industrial Organizations (CIO); *1952* receives the National Religion and Labor Foundation's annual Social Justice Award; publishes her autobiography, *To Win These Rights*; *1953* retires from CIO work; *1959* dies on May 6 in Atlanta, Georgia, and is buried at the Ivy Hill Cemetery in Alexandria, Virginia.

Activities of Historical Significance

Lucy Randolph Mason participated in the development of progressive southern politics from the Progressive Era through the New Deal and beyond. Throughout the 1910s, she worked to secure the right to vote for women; and, during the first few years after ratification of the Nineteenth Amendment in 1920, she worked with the League of Women Voters to promote the vote's effective use. Volunteer work aside, she worked with the YWCA from 1914 to 1932, first as industrial secretary and then as general secretary. During those years, the YWCA took the lead in promoting labor legislation in the southern states to protect women and children, and Mason consistently steered the Richmond branch in that direction. She continued her quest for labor legislation as general secretary of the National Consumers' League between 1932 and 1937. And she testified before Congress in June 1937 in support of a bill that became the Fair Labor Standards Act (1938), which regulated wages and hours for large numbers of industrial workers who did not belong to labor unions.

Mason's major historical importance derives from her labor activities across the Deep South in the wake of the Wagner Labor Relations Act (1935), which recognized American workers' right to organize labor unions of their own choice and to bargain through those unions over wages, hours, and working conditions. In 1937 she moved to Atlanta to promote the work of the Congress of Industrial Organizations in general, and the Textile Workers Organizing Committee in particular. Her work for the CIO, which lasted from July 1937 to February 1953, focused on public affairs; she sought to explain the CIO to southern preachers, journalists, politicians, and businessmen, and thus create a more favorable organizing environment. She argued that the CIO would not only bring dignity to labor, but also promote higher wages, safer working conditions, and a growth in the regional economy.

In many respects, the work of the CIO marked the beginning of the modern civil rights movement in the South. Mason's job was to promote the "civil rights" of workers seeking to organize and join unions—the right to free speech and peaceable assembly, and the right to join labor unions and to engage in collective bargaining. The CIO unions incorporated all workers in a given industry, regardless of race, sex, or specific job. Earlier unions, if they existed at all, were rigidly segregated by race. Increasingly, workers of all races found themselves on the same side in negotiating with management.

Though Mason focused most of her energies on the CIO, she also worked with other groups seeking to change the status quo in the South on race and labor. Chief among these were the Highlander School—whose statement of purpose called for "broadening the scope of democracy to include everyone"—and the Southern Conference for Human Welfare. Both of these organizations maintained links to the CIO, and Mason served at times on both groups' executive councils.

Mason proved effective in her indefatigable efforts to change the South because she was able to make the case that her causes were inherently southern. In support of the Bill of Rights, she invoked her Revolutionary forebear George Mason, author of the Virginia Declaration of Rights, and worked to apply his ideals to a broader constituency. She also spoke of her kinsman Robert E. Lee to demonstrate that she was no "outside agitator" seeking to transplant alien ideas in southern soil. Her lifelong dedication had an incalculable effect in enhancing both industrial and political democracy throughout the region, regardless of race, class, or gender.

Overview of Biographical Sources

Although she appears as a minor figure in a number of studies of the twentieth-century South, Mason has not been the direct subject of much historical inquiry. In 1969 Margaret Lee Neustadt completed an unpublished master's thesis, "Miss Lucy of the CIO: Lucy Randolph Mason, 1882-1959," at the University of North Carolina. Neustadt emphasizes Mason's CIO tenure, claiming that Mason played her most important role during her early years with the organization. Only in 1988 did a book-length study of Mason's life appear. John A. Salmond's, *Miss Lucy of the CIO: The Life and Times of Lucy Randolph Mason, 1882-1959*, which largely supersedes Neustadt's study, covers Mason's entire life. Salmond explores Mason's motivation, as well as describing her activities as a Southern reformer.

To a degree, both Neustadt and Salmond fail to develop the story of Mason's Richmond years. Some context can be drawn from Michael B. Chesson, *Richmond after the War, 1865-1890* (1981). This book's coverage stops just about the time that Mason took up residence in Richmond, but it evokes the atmosphere of the city in which she lived as a child and for many years thereafter. Christopher Silver, *Twentieth-Century Richmond: Planning, Politics, and Race* (1984), focuses on urban planning and housing. Especially useful for information about Richmond during the 1920s is Raymond Gavins, *The Perils and Prospects of Southern Black Leadership: Gordon Blaine Hancock, 1884-1970* (1977).

Evaluation of Principal Biographical Sources

Salmond, John A. *Miss Lucy of the CIO: The Life and Times of Lucy Randolph Mason, 1882-1959*. Athens: University of Georgia Press, 1988. (A, G) The only book-length study of Mason's life. While not particularly detailed, it does a fine job of placing Mason in her cultural, political, and economic contexts.

White, Nancy Ann. "Lucy Randolph Mason." In *Notable American Women: The Modern Period*, edited by Barbara Sicherman and Carol Hurd Green. Cambridge: Harvard University Press, 1980. (A, G) Contains an excellent biographical summary and guide to the primary and secondary sources.

Overview and Evaluation of Primary Sources

Lucy Randolph Mason told, and told well, much of the story of her life in her autobiographical *To Win These Rights: A Personal Story of the CIO in the South* (1952. Reprint. Westport, CT: Greenwood, 1970; A, G, Y). This work is both a memoir of her fifteen years with the CIO and a report on the history of the organization during that period. Her other publications include several pamphlets: *The Divine Discontent* (Richmond: Equal Suffrage League of Virginia, 1912; A, G); *The Shorter Day and Women Workers* (Richmond:

Virginia League of Women Voters, 1922; **A**); and *Standards for Workers in Southern Industry* (New York: National Consumers' League, 1931; **A**). With the first of these, she sought to generate support for women's right to vote; with the second and third, to promote legislation to protect women and children workers by limiting their hours and raising their wages.

The major manuscript collection on Mason, at Duke University, focuses on her years with the CIO and includes her correspondence with Eleanor Roosevelt. The Library of Congress has the papers of the National Consumers' League and of the League of Women Voters. Salmond's biography of Lucy Mason includes a useful guide to these and other materials. Mason's papers at Duke have been reproduced on microfilm and are available on reels 62-65 of "Operation Dixie: The CIO Organizing Committee Papers, 1946-1953" (Microfilm Corporation of America, 1980). The most complete guide to the Duke papers can be found in Katherine F. Martin's guide to that microfilm edition.

Other sources for Mason's public life include the two major Richmond newspapers, the *News Leader* and the *Times-Dispatch*; a microfiche index to these papers, "The Freeman File," is available from the James Branch Cabell Library at Virginia Commonwealth University. Also at Virginia Commonwealth University is the Adele Clark Collection, which fills well over a hundred boxes and contains important materials related to Mason's work in Virginia. Though that collection has not yet been catalogued, the Virginia Historical Society has a guide to it; when it has been catalogued, it will permit a richer reconstruction of women's reform efforts in Richmond and across Virginia in the years that center on the 1920s.

Museums, Historical Landmarks, Societies
Valentine Museum of the Life and History of Richmond (Richmond, VA). Here can be found a rich collection of photographs of Richmond's history, including the pre-CIO world of Lucy Mason.

Other Sources
Glen, John M. *Highlander: No Ordinary School, 1932-1962*. Lexington: University Press of Kentucky, 1988. Mason worked for a time with the Highlander Folk School, one of the institutions that worked to reshape the South's society and economy.

Griffith, Barbara S. *The Crisis of American Labor: Operation Dixie and the Defeat of the CIO*. Philadelphia: Temple University Press, 1988. This assessment of the CIO's operations in the South during the late 1940s includes information about Mason's participation.

Krueger, Thomas A. *And Promises to Keep: The Southern Conference for Human Welfare.* Nashville: Vanderbilt University Press, 1967. A study of an association with which Mason worked in the late 1930s and the 1940s.

McDowell, John P. *The Social Gospel in the South: The Woman's Home Mission Movement in the Methodist Episcopal Church, South, 1886-1939.* Baton Rouge: Louisiana State University Press, 1982. McDowell supplies a context for understanding Mason's Social Gospel beliefs.

Scott, Anne Firor. *The Southern Lady: From Pedestal to Politics, 1830-1930.* Chicago: University of Chicago Press, 1970. A pioneering work that studied the participation of white women in southern politics and culture in general and in progressive efforts of the 1920s in particular. Mason is one of the women examined.

Tindall, George B. *The Emergence of the New South, 1913-1945.* Baton Rouge: Louisiana State University Press, 1967. A comprehensive history of the South that covers most of the period of Mason's public career. Two chapters place her in the larger context of "Building Unions in the South" and "Southern Politics and the New Deal."

Peter Wallenstein
Virginia Polytechnic Institute and State University

ALEXANDER McGILLIVRAY
1759-1793

Chronology

Born Alexander McGillivray in 1759 on a plantation at Little Tallassee near present Montgomery, Alabama, son of a wealthy Scots trader, Lachlan McGillivray, and Marchand Sehoy, daughter of a French soldier and a Creek woman of the Tribe of the Wind; *1773* studies in Charleston, South Carolina; *1777* returns to Little Tallassee as assistant commissary in the British Indian service; *1777-1783* emerges as a chief of the Creek tribes due to his knowledge of English, his diplomacy, and his alliance with British trader William Panton, which ensures his influence over trade in Creek towns; *1783* resists British conveyance of Creek lands to Spain or the U.S. at end of Revolutionary War; conducts raiding parties, while skillfully bargaining with governments of Spain, America, and state of Georgia; *1784* signs Treaty of Pensacola in which Spain provides assurances of Creek sovereignty and cedes all Creek trading rights to William Panton; *1785* opposes Georgia's effort to establish Bourbon County on the Mississippi; *1786-1787* effectively halts Georgian expansion by driving all settlers from Creek lands; *1789* fearing his growing power and bowing to American political pressure, Spain withdraws support and demands he make peace with U.S.; *1790* signs Treaty of New York with U.S., guaranteeing the integrity of Creek lands but recognizing U.S. territorial authority; *1792* induces Spain to reestablish support and repudiates treaty; negotiates with Spain in New Orleans to support a Native American confederation allied against the U.S.; *1793* dies after a protracted illness on February 17 in Pensacola, Florida.

Activities of Historical Significance

Alexander McGillivray was one of the leaders of the Creek Confederacy, a loose organization of Southeast Native American tribes in the region that is now Georgia and Alabama. Although he was only one-quarter Creek, he identified strongly with his Native American heritage and rose quickly to leadership of the tribes in the post-Revolutionary War years. McGillivray is remembered for his use of European-style statesmanship—a strategy almost unique among Native American leaders. Through his skill at forging compromises, he was able, for a time, to unite the diverse interests of the tribes and sub-tribes of the Creek nation in order to present a united front against encroaching white settlement. As a diplomat, he shrewdly exploited the conflicting claims and expectations of the U.S., Spanish, and the Georgia state governments, to champion the cause of Creek independence. His efforts enabled the Creeks to survive as a sovereign people for a full generation longer than neighboring tribes.

McGillivray's successes brought him notoriety, and contemporary newspaper accounts compared him to European monarchs. A leader who operated through consensus and persuasion rather than by coercion, he implemented reforms that strengthened the traditional Creek governmental system of councils. Although primarily a diplomat, he was not averse to backing up his demands by sending raiding parties to force settlers from Creek hunting grounds. The Creeks referred to him as *"Great Beloved Man."*

McGillivray's efforts were ultimately undone by the Creek War, fought against white settlers in 1813-1814, twenty years after his death. In this war, an army of militiamen led by Andrew Jackson suppressed the outnumbered Creeks at the Battle of Horseshoe Bend, slaughtering over eight hundred warriors. The defeated Creeks were forced to cede twenty-three million acres of their lands by the Treaty of Fort Jackson and were subsequently relocated in the territory of Oklahoma. In 1907, when Oklahoma became a state, tribal lands were opened to settlement and the Creek nation ceased to exist. It is estimated that nearly 20,000 individuals of Creek blood, many of whom have assimilated into white society, still live in Oklahoma.

Overview of Biographical Sources

Two articles by A. P. Whitaker, appearing in the *North Carolina Historical Review* in 1928, mark the first serious attempt to survey McGillivray's life. These works employ rare original sources, quoting generously. Following Whitaker, Randolph Downes published two informative articles in *Georgia Historical Quarterly* (1937) and *Journal of Southern History* (1942). J. W. Caughey's *McGillivray of the Creeks* (1938) is the only full-length biography to date. It is considered the standard work on the subject but is increasingly dated in its approach and conclusions.

Such recent historiographical and sociological works as that of Michael D. Green have challenged R. S. Cotterill's well-documented and written narrative, *The Southern Indians: The Story of the Civilized Tribes Before Removal* (1954). Articles by J. Leitch Wright (1967) and James H. O'Donnell (1965) provide unduplicated coverage of such specific aspects of McGillivray's career as the effects of his diplomacy and his rise to leadership.

Evaluation of Principal Biographical Sources

Caughey, John Walton. *McGillivray of the Creeks.* Norman: University of Oklahoma Press, 1938. **(A, G)** This standard work on McGillivray offers generous reproductions of his correspondence with the Spanish, gleaned from the Archivo General de Indias, Seville, Spain.

Cotterill, R. S. *The Southern Indians: The Story of the Civilized Tribes Before Removal.* Norman: University of Oklahoma Press, 1954. (**A, G**) A chapter on McGillivray appears in this well-researched and well-written narrative of events on both the Native American and white settlers' sides in the years preceding the Creeks' removal from their traditional lands.

Downes, Randolph. "Creek-American Relations, 1782-1790." *Georgia Historical Quarterly* 21 (June 1937): 142-184. (**A, G**) In this, and the following article, Downes examines McGillivray's political savvy and his role in influencing U.S. policy toward the Creeks.

————. "Creek American Relations, 1790-1795." *Journal of Southern History* 8 (August 1942): 350-373. (**A, G**) Continuation of the above article.

Green, Michael D. "Alexander McGillivray". In *American Indian Leaders,* edited by R. David Edmunds. Norman: University of Oklahoma Press, 1980. (**A, G**). Places McGillivray in modern Native American historical and sociological context. Green is one of the first to see McGillivray from a Native American rather than a Spanish, British, or U.S. point of view. Green quotes copiously from McGillivray's letters preserved in Spanish archives.

Holmes, Jack. "Spanish Treaties with West Florida Indians, 1784-1802." *Florida Historical Quarterly* 48 (October 1969): 140-145. (**A**) Brings out McGillivray's place within the larger context of Native American and Spanish intrigues on the American frontier of the mid- to late-eighteenth century.

O'Donnell, James H. "Alexander McGillivray: Training for Leadership, 1777-1783." *Georgia Historical Quarterly* 19 (June 1965): 172-186. (**A**) Traces McGillivray's education and his rise to Creek leadership.

Tanner, Helen. "Pipesmoke and Muskets: Florida Indian Intrigues of the Revolutionary Era." In *Eighteenth-Century Florida and Its Borderlands,* edited by Samuel Proctor. Gainesville: University of Florida Press, 1975. (**A**) Places McGillivray in an informative historical context.

Whitaker, Arthur Preston. "Alexander McGillivray, 1783-1789." In *North Carolina Historical Review* (April 1928): 181-203. (**A**) Whitaker deftly weaves McGillivray into the pattern of postwar politics on the Georgia frontier in one of the most detailed narratives available on his career as Creek leader.

————. "Alexander McGillivray, 1789-1793." *North Carolina Historical Review* (July 1928): 289-309. (**A**) This article continues Whitaker's skillful assessment of McGillivray to the time of his death.

Wright, J. Leitch. "Creek-American Treaty of 1790: Alexander McGillivray and the Diplomacy of the Old Southwest." *Georgia Historical Quarterly* 21 (December 1967): 379-400. (A) Focuses on McGillivray's effect on the balance of power in what would be the states of Georgia, Tennessee, and Alabama. Extensive use of Spanish archival sources.

Overview and Evaluation of Primary Sources

Many collections of official documents contain materials by or about McGillivray. His viewpoints were well documented, due to his ability to excite government attention and his habit of corresponding voluminously with his friends and adversaries alike. Spanish collections, such as the Archivo General de Indias in Seville and Archivo Historico Nacional in Madrid, contain correspondence and the reports of Spanish commissioners whose territory included the lands of the Creeks. Fortunately, many of these largely inaccessible sources have been described, translated, and quoted generously by McGillivray scholars. Caughey's *McGillivray of the Creeks* (see above) is a gold mine of such information.

D. C. Corbitt compiled and edited many of these sources in "Papers Relating to the Georgia-Florida Frontier, 1784-1800," published in the *Georgia Historical Quarterly* 20 (1936): 356-365; 21 (1937): 73-83, 185-188, 274-293, 373-381; 22 (1938): 72-76, 184-191, 286-291, 391-394; 23 (1939): 77-79, 189-202, 300-303, 381-387; 24 (1940): 77-83, 150-157, 252-271, 374-381; 25 (1941): 67-76, 159-171 (A). D. C. Corbitt and Roberta Corbitt compiled "Papers from the Spanish Archives Relating to Tennessee and the Old Southwest, 1783-1800," published in *East Tennessee Historical Society Publications*, vols. 9-20 (1937-1948; A). Not all of these Archivo General materials relate specifically to McGillivray.

The National Archives, *American State Papers: Foreign Relations,* vol. 1 (Washington, DC: Gales & Seaton, 1832; A), contains the Treaty of Pensacola and related correspondence. Walter Clark, ed., *The State Records of North Carolina,* vols. 20-22 (Goldsboro, NC: P. M. Hale, 1902; A), contains considerable correspondence relating to McGillivray's efforts to expel settlers from Creek lands. Charles J. Kappler, ed., *Indian Affairs: Laws and Treaties,* vol. 2 (Washington, DC: Government Printing Office, 1904; A), contains the Treaty of New York.

Frank L. Humphreys, *The Life and Times of David Humphreys* (New York: Putnam's, 1917; G), is the biography of one of the U.S. commissioners sent to deal with McGillivray. William W. Willett, *A Narrative of the Military Action of Colonel Marinus Willett, Taken Chiefly from his Own Manuscript* (New York: G. C. H. Carvil, 1831; A), contains the eyewitness account of another of the commissioners that brought McGillivray to New York. The Lachlan McIntosh Papers, dated 1763-1799, comprise seventy-seven items in the Georgia Historical Society, Savannah, Georgia. A Revolutionary Army officer and Georgia planter, McIntosh's papers contain a few of McGillivray's letters. Most of this collection was published as Willa M. Hawes, ed., "Collections of the Georgia Historical Society and Other Documents: Papers of Lachlan McIntosh," *Georgia Historical Quarterly* 38 (1954): 101-141, 148-169, 253-267, 356-398; 39 (1955): 52-67, 172-186, 253-267, 356-374; 40 (1956): 152-173 (A) and reprinted in one volume as Willa M. Hawes, ed. *Collections of the Georgia Historical Society* XII (1957; A).

The Papers of Andrew Pickens, a Revolutionary Army officer and later U.S. congressman from South Carolina, are in the Charleston Library Society Collections, Charleston, South Carolina. These papers contain several of McGillivray's letters. Joseph Brown was an Army officer and Presbyterian minister from Tennessee captured by Creeks. A transcript volume in the Texas Archives of the University of Texas Library (Austin) contains Brown's contemporary description of McGillivray.

A. J. Pickett, *History of Alabama*, 2 vols. (Charleston, 1851; A, G), is one of the most widely quoted sources on affairs between the Creeks and the settlers, and provides an older account of McGillivray's beginnings.

Museums, Historical Landmarks, Societies
Panton Trading Post (Pensacola, FL). Part of the restored historical district, along with Spanish colonial headquarters and other buildings.

Other Sources
National Cyclopedia of American Biography. New York: James T. White, 1891; Reprint. Ann Arbor, MI: University Microfilms, 1967. Contains short biographical sketches of such figures as James Robertson, the founder of Nashville, who faced McGillivray's war parties during the years of contested incursions on Creek lands.

Kinniard, Lucia Burk. "The Rock Landing Conference of 1789." *North Carolina Historical Review* 9 (October 1932): 349-65. Contains an account of the events surrounding McGillivray's diplomacy with the state of Georgia at the peak of his power.

Steven Agoratus

CLAUDE McKAY
1890-1948

Chronology

Born Festus Claudius McKay on September 15, 1890, in Sunny Ville, Jamaica, the eleventh child of Thomas Francis, a farmer and deacon in the Baptist Church, and his wife Hannah Ann Elizabeth Edwards; *1890-1896* spends formative years under the tutelage of his parents; develops a strong sense of racial pride and an interest in his African roots; *1897-1904* accompanies his brother Uriah Theodore (U'Theo), a schoolteacher and freethinker, to a small village near Montego Bay, where he reads widely and begins to write poetry; *1904-1906* returns to his parents' home and finishes schooling after U'Theo and his wife move to Clarendon Parish; *1907-1909* works as an apprentice to a wheelwright, carriage builder, and cabinetmaker in St. Ann; meets Walter Jekyll, an English linguist and folklorist who befriends him and encourages him to write dialect poetry; *1911* becomes a constable in Kingston; *1912* publishes *Songs of Jamaica* and *Constab Ballads* and receives the Jamaica Institute's Musgrave Silver Medal; leaves Jamaica to study at the Tuskegee Institute (Alabama); *1912-1914* transfers to Kansas State College (Manhattan, Kansas) to study agriculture; *1914* moves to New York City, opens a restaurant, and marries Eulalie Imelda Lewars on July 30, 1914; both the marriage and the restaurant are short-lived; *1915* Ruth Hope McKay is born, a daughter McKay will never see; *1915-1917* works at various odd jobs while developing his poetic craft; *1917* publishes "Invocation" and "The Harlem Dancer" in *Seven Arts* magazine under the pseudonym of Eli Edwards; *1918* meets Frank Harris and has five poems published in *Pearson's Magazine*; *1919* meets Max and Crystal Eastman and publishes "If We Must Die" in the *Liberator;* *1919-1921* resides in England; joins the staff of Sylvia Pankhurst's *Worker's Dreadnought*, which prints some of his poems; has his work published in C. K. Ogden's *Cambridge Magazine*; studies Karl Marx and becomes interested in communism; *1920* publishes *Spring in New Hampshire*; *1921-1922* returns to Harlem; becomes an associate editor of the *Liberator*; *1922* resigns as editor of *Liberator* and publishes *Harlem Shadows*; *1922-1923* travels to Moscow to attend the Fourth Congress of the Third International, where he is warmly welcomed by the Russians despite the objections of American Communist Party delegates; publishes *Negry v Amerika* (*The Negroes in America* translated from the English by P. Okhrimenko); *1923-1933* travels throughout Europe and Africa while beginning to write fiction; works at various jobs to support himself including modeling nude in Paris and working as an extra and reader for filmmaker Rex Ingram; *1927* published in Alain Locke's landmark anthology *Four Negro Poets*; *1928* publishes *Home To Harlem*, a popular though controversial first novel; *1929* receives the Harmon Gold award for literature; publishes *Banjo*, which fails to do well commercially; *1932* publishes *Gingertown*, a collection of short stories, to mostly positive reviews; *1933* publishes *Banana Bottom*, generally regarded as his best work; *1934* returns to New York City but has difficulty making a living; enters Camp Greycourt, a work camp in upstate New York, in October, but leaves before Christmas; *1935* receives a grant from the Rosenwald Fund in Chicago to write a memoir of his years abroad; publishes two articles, "There Goes God! The Story of Father Divine and His Angels" and "Harlem Runs Wild," an account of the March 19, 1935 Harlem street riots, in the *Nation*; *1937-1938* is active in the establishment of the Negro Authors League; publishes *A Long Way From Home*; *1938* begins work on *Harlem: Negro Metropolis*; *1939* loses his position with the federal Works Project Administration; *1940* publishes *Harlem: Negro Metropolis*; becomes U.S. citizen on April 13; *1940-1943* lives and writes in New York City; works on "Harlem Glory," a novel set in post-Depression Harlem and Paris; *1942* becomes seriously ill with influenza, hypertension, and heart disease; recovers with the assistance of his friend, Ellen Tarry, a Catholic children's writer; *1943* suffers a stroke on June 25 while working as a riveter in a Port Newark shipyard; leaves for Chicago to work for Bishop Bernard J. Sheil as an advisor on Russian and Negro affairs; *1944* baptized into the Roman Catholic Church; *1945-1948* publishes articles and poems on his conversion to Catholicism; prepares a volume of his selected poems for publication and writes "My Green Hills of Jamaica," a short memoir of his Jamaican childhood; *1948* dies of congestive heart failure on May 22; memorial services held in Harlem; buried at Calvary Cemetery, Woodside, New York.

Activities of Historical Significance

McKay is a minor writer, more important for the influence he exerted on later authors than for his own literary talent. As a young man in Jamaica, he experimented with dialect poetry, wedding local themes to traditional English metrical forms. In both *Songs of Jamaica* (1912) and *Constab Ballads* (1912), poems based on his brief experience as a constable, McKay expressed a growing social consciousness and a strong sympathy for the poor and the downtrodden. His concern for and identification with the masses would later attract him to communism and provide important themes for his work.

Shortly after these initial volumes of poetry were published, McKay left to study in the U.S., never to see his homeland again. The racial prejudice he experienced in the U.S. shocked him and was responsible for the militant tone of much of his poetry and prose—a tone that alienated many of the black intellectuals of the Harlem Renaissance but attracted activists during the 1960s.

McKay's militancy is directly expressed in his most celebrated poem, "If We Must Die," which first appeared in the *Liberator* in July 1919. Written in sonnet form, the poem is a call to arms beginning: "If we must die, let it not be like hogs/ hunted and penned in some inglorious spot"; it ends with an exhortation to confront the oppressors "Pressed to the wall, dying, but fighting back." This poem, reprinted in *Harlem Shadows* (1922), made McKay's reputation. It has been widely anthologized and is said to have been recited by Winston Churchill during World War II to bolster English resolve. The poem even figured in the 1971 Attica prison riots. *Time* magazine reported in its September 27, 1971, issue that some of the rebellious prisoners ". . . passed around clandestine writings of their own; among them was a poem written by an unknown prisoner, crude but touching in its would-be heroic style." The poem, as Gwendolyn Brooks later pointed out (*Time,* October 18, 1971), was an excerpt from McKay's "If We Must Die."

McKay's social and political views and his friendship with Max Eastman led to his growing interest in communism. In 1919 he left for London, where he studied Karl Marx and wrote for Sylvia Pankhurst's Communist publication, the *Worker's Dreadnought.* In 1921 McKay returned to New York and became an associate editor of the *Liberator.* Among his noteworthy pieces were "How Black Sees Green and Red," a sympathetic essay on the Irish nationalist Sinn Fein movement and "He Who Gets Slapped," an angry editorial written after McKay and *Liberator* artist William Gropper were humiliated by being asked to leave their front-row press seats for the balcony at a performance of Leonid Andreyev's *He, The One Who Gets Slapped.*

In June 1922 McKay resigned from the editorial board of the *Liberator* after quarreling with associate editor Michael Gold, and attended the Fourth Congress of the Third International in Moscow. Upon McKay's arrival, the chairman of the American Communist delegation, because of political rivalries within the group, tried to prevent him from attending. Through the influence of Sen Katayama, an old friend and the leading Japanese dele-gate at the congress, McKay was eventually seated.

McKay's visit was an overwhelming success. He was strongly supported by the Russian people, who found him an exciting personality, and he was influential in bringing the problems of American blacks to the party's attention through speeches, articles, and a full-length book, *Negry v Amerika* (*The Negroes in America,* 1923).

McKay then traveled widely through Europe and North Africa for over ten years before returning to the U.S. During his self-imposed exile, he wrote three novels *Home to Harlem* (1928), *Banjo* (1929), and *Banana Bottom* (1933). All were class-conscious, deeply sympathetic to the masses, and imbued with a strong sense of black pride. These novels were important—especially *Banjo*—for influencing writers such as Léopold Sedar Senghor and Aimé Césaire, the leaders of the Nègritude movement, who stressed the positive values of African culture over the corrupt rationalism of the Western colonizers.

After his return to the U.S. in 1934, McKay became increasingly disillusioned with communism. He criticized the party for failing to adequately address the race problem and for demanding propaganda, rather than art, from its writers. He struggled with party leaders for control of the Negro Authors Guild. At the same time, W. E. B. Dubois and other leaders of the Harlem Renaissance attacked McKay for depicting the seamier side of Harlem life. His continuing quarrels with both the Communists and the black intelligentsia further alienated him from many of his former supporters.

McKay continued as a journalist for the *Amsterdam News,* the *Nation,* and other periodicals. He also completed *Harlem: Negro Metropolis* (1940), a sociological history of Harlem focusing on the operation of illegal businesses such as numbers and bootlegging, the role of spiritualism and occultism, and the leaders of political and religious movements such as Marcus Garvey, Father Divine, and Sufi Abdul Hamid. McKay would return to this material again in his unpublished novel, "Harlem Glory."

McKay believed that blacks had to develop their own social and political agenda in order to obtain power. For McKay, building a sense of black solidarity was more important than pursuing integration—a philosophical difference that separated him from W. E. B. DuBois, Walter White, and the NAACP (National Association for the Advancement of Colored People). His emphasis on black pride and African culture, and his desire to unite blacks of all nations, were concepts far ahead of the times.

Overview of Biographical Sources

McKay's reputation declined in his later years. As a result, interest in his life and work diminished during the 1940s and 1950s. However, with the onset of the Black Power movement in the 1960s and the accompanying surge of black pride, interest in McKay and other neglected black writers grew. This growth was spurred by the creation of black or Afro-American studies departments throughout the nation's universities, and it is no coincidence that much of the early biographical work on McKay was published in doctoral dissertations.

M. James Conroy's *Claude McKay: Negro Poet and Novelist* (1968) was the first overall study of McKay. Conroy's concern with the rural-urban opposition in McKay's work, his celebration of primitivism, and his strong sense of alienation were themes that later biographers would elaborate. Conroy's biography was followed by two complementary studies: Charles Terrance Donohue's *The Making of a Black Poet: A Critical Biography of Claude McKay for the Years 1889-1922,* and Phyllis Martin Lang's *Claude McKay: The Later Years, 1934-1948,* both written in 1972. Tyrone Tillery's

Claude McKay: Man and Symbol of the Harlem Renaissance 1889-1948 (1981) attempts to separate the facts of McKay's life from his legend and to measure his importance as a writer, activist, and social critic.

The most comprehensive biography, Wayne Cooper's *Claude McKay: Rebel Sojourner in the Harlem Renaissance* (1987), is a meticulously researched, highly readable study that treats McKay's life and work in relation to the major social, political, and historical events of his times. James R. Giles's *Claude McKay* (1976), the only other full-length published study, is more critical of McKay's art and emphasizes literary rather than biographical concerns.

In summary, while the focus of each biography varies, all agree on the complexity of McKay's personality. All note his sense of alienation, the importance of his role as a social critic, and his influence on literary and social movements including the Harlem Renaissance, Nègritude and Black Power.

Evaluation of Principal Biographical Sources

Conroy, M. James. "Claude McKay: Negro Poet and Novelist." Ph.D. diss. (Order number 69-4058), University of Notre Dame, 1968. (A) Begins with a biographical sketch and examines three of the major thematic concerns of McKay's work: "the Jamaican peasant, the Harlem Negro, and the international Negro vagabond." Good discussion of McKay's primitivism.

Cooper, Wayne. *Claude McKay: Rebel Sojourner in the Harlem Renaissance*. Baton Rouge: Louisiana State University Press, 1987. (A, G) This is the definitive biography of McKay. Cooper assesses McKay and his work against the historical, political, and social events of his time. His portrait draws on McKay's published works, secondary sources, and a wealth of unpublished material in private hands as well as in public collections. Includes extensive notes and a detailed essay on scholarly sources.

Donohue, Charles Terrance. "The Making of a Black Poet: A Critical Biography of Claude McKay for the Years 1889-1922." Ph.D. diss. (Order number 73-8857), Temple University, 1972. (A) Deals with McKay's development as a poet from his early influences in Jamaica through the publication of *Harlem Shadows* (1922), the book responsible for McKay's reputation as a leader in the Harlem Renaissance. Argues that McKay's radical politics were an emotional rather than a rational response to the racism he suffered in the U.S. and England.

Giles, James R. *Claude McKay*. Boston: Twayne, 1976. (A, G) Typical of the Twayne series, a solid introduction to the man and his work. Giles begins with a biographical survey that treats McKay's Jamaican origins, his attraction to the Communist Party, his role in the Harlem Renaissance, and his conversion to Catholicism. He then devotes separate chapters to McKay's poetry, novels, short stories, and nonfiction. He concludes that McKay's fiction and his development of a black aesthetic were his most important contributions to Afro-American literature. Includes a chronology and a partially annotated bibliography.

Lang, Phyllis Martin. "Claude McKay: The Later Years, 1934-1948." Ph.D. diss. (Order number 73-9977), University of Illinois at Urbana-Champaign, 1972. (A) Covers McKay's work during the last fourteen years of his life including poetry, fiction, and nonfiction. The first section deals with McKay's biographical works and *Harlem: Negro Metropolis*; the second section analyzes "Harlem Glory" and relates it to McKay's earlier Harlem stories in *Gingertown* and to *Home to Harlem*; the last section discusses McKay's later poems including those written after his conversion to Catholicism.

Tillery, Tyrone. "Claude McKay: Man and Symbol of the Harlem Renaissance, 1889-1948." Ph.D diss. (Order number 81-20257), Kent State University, 1981. (A) Emphasizes the complexity of McKay's character and discusses his role as a black Jamaican interacting with various cultural and political groups. Attempts to rescue McKay from the stereotypical image created by critics who too closely identified the author with his fictional characters.

Overview and Evaluation of Primary Sources
McKay began his literary career as a poet with the publication of *Songs of Jamaica* (London: Gardner, 1912; Reprint. Miami: Mnemosyne, 1969; **A, G**) and *Constab Ballads* (London: Watts, 1912; Reprint. New York: Gordon, 1977; **A, G**). These collections were reissued under the title *The Dialect Poetry of Claude McKay* (Freeport, NY: Books for Libraries, 1972; Reprint. Salem, NH: Ayer, 1987; **A, G**). They were followed by *Spring in New Hampshire and Other Poems* (London: Grant Richards, 1920; **A, G**) and by McKay's most famous collection, *Harlem Shadows* (New York: Harcourt, Brace, 1922; Reprint. Charlottesville: Teleprint Publishing, 1985; **A, G**). McKay's *Selected Poems* (New York: Bookman Associates, 1953; Reprint. Harcourt, Brace & World, 1981; **A, G**) was published posthumously with a biographical sketch by Max Eastman.

After the publication of *Harlem Shadows*, McKay began writing fiction. He wrote three novels: *Home to Harlem* (New York: Harper, 1928; Reprint. Boston: Northeastern University Press, 1987; **A, G**); *Banjo: a Story Without a*

Plot (New York: Harper & Brothers; 1929. Reprint. London: Pluto, 1986; **A, G**); and *Banana Bottom* (New York: Harper, 1933. Reprint. New York: Harcourt, Brace, Jovanovich, 1974; **A, G**). He also published a collection of short stories, *Gingertown* (New York: Harper, 1932. Reprint. Freeport, NY: Books for Libraries Press, 1972).

After 1934 McKay devoted himself to journalism and wrote a sociological history of Harlem, *Harlem: Negro Metropolis* (New York: E. P. Dutton, 1940. Reprint. New York: Harcourt, Brace, Jovanovich, 1968; **A, G**). It was the last book to be published in his lifetime. Several additional works, however, were published posthumously, including *The Passion of Claude McKay* (New York: Schocken, 1973; **A, G**), an excellent collection of McKay's poems, letters, and essays edited by Wayne Cooper. *The Negroes in America* (Port Washington, NY: Kennikat, 1977; **A**) and *Trial by Lynching: Stories About Negro Life in North America* (Karnataka, India: Centre for Commonwealth Literature and Research, University of Mysore, 1977; **A**) were both retranslated into English by Robert Winter and issued under the editorial supervision of Alan L. McLeod.

McKay wrote several autobiographical works that biographers and critics have relied on heavily. These include *A Long Way From Home* (New York: Lee Furman, 1937. Reprint. New York: Harcourt, Brace, 1970; **A, G**), and *My Green Hills of Jamaica*, edited by Mervyn Morris (Kingston, Jamaica: Heinemann Educational Books, 1979; **A**). McKay also wrote several important autobiographical articles including "On Becoming a Roman Catholic" *(Epistle* 2 [Spring 1945]: 43-45; **A, G**), "Why I Became a Catholic" (*Ebony* 1 [March 1946]: 32; **A, G**), and "Boyhood in Jamaica" (*Phylon* 14 [1953]: 134-145; **A, G**), a brief essay published after his death.

McKay's papers are scattered in various locations throughout the country. The largest collection of his manuscripts is in Yale's Beinecke Library. Max Eastman's correspondence in the Lilly Library at Indiana University contains a substantial amount of McKay material. Finally, the Schomburg Collection at the New York Public Library contains several typescripts of McKay's as well as correspondence in both the Schomburg Papers and the Schomburg Center Archives. There are two microfilm collections (over 130 feet) of exhibit material and primary sources including manuscripts of two unpublished novels, "Harlem Glory" and "Romance in Marseilles." Those seeking a more detailed discussion of archival collections should consult the "Essay on Sources" in Cooper's biography.

Fiction and Adaptations

Reverberations: The Poet Dreams of Africa (Ames, IA: Media Resources Center, 1977). A thirty-minute videotape exploring themes common to African, Caribbean, and Afro-American poetry through readings of the works of a dozen black poets including McKay. Since McKay's works draw heavily on his experiences, these readings reveal much about his life and opinions.

Other Sources

Ali, Schavi Mali. "Claude McKay." In *Dictionary of Literary Biography*, vol. 51. Detroit: Gale Research, 1987. A good overall portrait of McKay, although the bibliography is dated for so recent a publication.

Collier, Eugenia. "Claude McKay." In *Fifty Caribbean Writers: A Bio-Bibliographical Critical Sourcebook*. Westport, CT: Greenwood Press, 1986. Contains a biographical introduction, a discussion of major works and themes, and a brief evaluation of McKay's critical reception.

Stone, Les. "McKay, Festus Claudius 1889-1948." In *Black Writers: A Selection of Sketches from Contemporary Authors*. Detroit: Gale Research, 1989. A concise, accurate account of McKay's life, work, and reputation. Excellent bibliography. The most current source for a short sketch of McKay's life.

William M. Gargan
Brooklyn College, City University of New York

EDNA ST. VINCENT MILLAY
1892-1950

Chronology

Born Edna St. Vincent Millay on February 22, 1892, in Rockland, Maine, the first of three daughters born to Henry Millay and Cora Buzzelle Millay; *1900* her parents divorce, largely because of the compulsive gambling of her father, a school principal and superintendent; *1905-1909* attends high school in Camden, Maine, and serves as editor-in-chief of the school magazine; *1906* begins publishing poems in *St. Nicholas Magazine*; *1912* acclaimed for "Renascence" when it appears in the anthology *The Lyric Year*; her benefactor, Carolyn B. Dow, arranges for her enrollment at Vassar College; *1913* attends Barnard College as preparation for entering Vassar in the fall; *1917* graduates from Vassar with a bachelor's degree after distinguishing herself with Vassar theater groups; publishes *Renascence and Other Poems*; moves to New York and acts with the Provincetown Players; *1918* has love affairs with Floyd Dell and others while living in Greenwich Village and eking out a meager existence from her acting; *1919* publishes poems and pseudonymous stories (as Nancy Boyd) in popular *Ainslee's* magazine; directs *Aria da Capo* (her own work) with Provincetown Players in December; *1920* publishes *A Few Figs and Thistles* and *Aria da Capo*; wins $100 from *Poetry* for her poem "The Bean-Stalk"; goes to Europe to write for *Vanity Fair*; *1921* publishes *Two Slatterns and a King, The Lamp and the Bell*, and *Second April*; *1922* brings her mother to Europe; *1923* returns to U.S.; receives Pulitzer Prize for poetry; becomes seriously ill; marries Eugen Jan Boissevain on July 18; publishes *The Harp-Weaver and Other Poems*; *1924* begins a series of reading tours; visits Asia with her husband; publishes *Distressing Dialogues* under pseudonym of Nancy Boyd; *1925* continues reading tours; receives honorary doctorate from Tufts College; with her husband, buys Steepletop farm in Austerlitz, New York, where they live until their deaths; *1927 The King's Henchman* premieres at the Metropolitan Opera; joins protests in Boston against the executions of Sacco and Vanzetti; *1928* publishes *The Buck in the Snow* and the ten sonnets of "Epitaphs for the Race of Man"; *1929* publishes *Poems Selected for Young People* and is elected to National Institute for Arts and Letters; *1931* publishes *Fatal Interview* and receives Helen Haire Levinson Prize for her sonnets in *Poetry*; *1932* publishes *The Princess Marries the Page*; on Christmas Day gives the first of eight national radio broadcasts to read her poems; *1933* is honored by the General Federation of Women's Clubs; receives honorary doctorates from the University of Wisconsin and Russell Sage College; *1934* publishes *Wine from These Grapes*; *1935* with George Dillon translates Baudelaire's poetry; *1936* publishes, with Dillon, a translation of Baudelaire's *Flowers of Evil*; loses the manuscript of *Conversations at Midnight* in a hotel fire; suffers back injury; begins rewriting *Conversations at Midnight*; *1937* receives honorary degrees from New York University and Colby College; publishes the rewritten *Conversations at Midnight*; *1939* publishes *Huntsman, What Quarry?*; *1940* writes propaganda; is elected to American Academy of Arts and Letters; publishes *Make Bright the Arrows*; *1941* records her poems for RCA Victor; publishes *Collected Sonnets*; *1942* publishes *The Murder of Lidice*; *1943* receives the Gold Medal of the Poetry Society of America; *1944* suffers nervous breakdown and gives up writing for two years; *1949* returns to live alone at Steepletop after husband dies of a stroke on August 30; *1950* dies there of heart failure on October 19.

Activities of Historical Significance

After Edna St. Vincent Millay's father left the household, she assumed much of the responsibility for herself and her two younger sisters while her mother worked as a district nurse. Her mother was careful to nurture her children's imaginations, however, and Millay grew up well trained as a pianist as well as a poet. Her precocious lyric talent brought her quick attention with "Renascence" in 1912, and from the publication of *Renascence and Other Poems* in 1917 until the late 1930s Millay's reputation was strong. Edmund Wilson, perhaps the most prestigious American literary critic of the first half of the twentieth century, held her poetry in high regard. (He was also in love with Millay, who rejected his proposal of marriage.) There is no strong consensus on what made Millay's poetry so moving, but her work's powerful concern with political, social, and personal injustice; its philosophy of radical humanism; its examination of individual integrity; and its detailed exploration of the evolving self have all been mentioned as important factors in its appeal.

Millay's critics have always cited an excessive emotionalism as a crippling flaw in her work; the very qualities they find embarrassing are often praised by her admirers. Millay's sonnets are clearly her major achievement, praised by Wilson and other admirers above all her works. Although they received perhaps excessive praise when her career was at its peak, they remain masterpieces of bittersweet feeling couched in perfect meter and diction. Although many critics claim, with some validity, that her works lack intellectual substance, the best of her lyrics—such as "What Lips My Lips Have Kissed" and "Euclid Alone Has Looked on Beauty Bare"—will endure in the anthologies.

Two reasons can be cited for the rather abrupt falling off by 1940 of Millay's critical reputation. First, her poetry became propaganda, devoid of any expression or feeling. Also, following the appearance of Brooks and

Warren's *Understanding Poetry* in 1936 there was a general reorientation in academe toward poetry that demanded intense explication. This legacy of the New Criticism discouraged any expansion of Millay's reputation in the classroom. When a more personal note entered into American poetry in the 1950s, it was in the anguished confessions of poets such as Anne Sexton and Sylvia Plath—a note not at all like Millay's, whose cries of regret and sadness are always generalized.

Harper's 1988 revised and expanded edition of the *Collected Sonnets* is a welcome publication, representing as it does the heart of a lyric output strong enough to secure Millay a definite place in the second rank of American poets.

Overview of Biographical Sources

Although there are no major areas of scholarly controversy attached to Millay's life story, the poet still lacks a definitive biographer. The first full-length biography was Elizabeth Atkins, *Edna St. Vincent Millay and Her Times* (1936), a generally reliable account that suffers from the author's inability to maintain an objective tone about a writer she admires very much. Miriam Gurko's *Restless Spirit: The Life of Edna St. Vincent Millay* (1962) is a reliable, smoothly written biography composed on a level best suited for younger readers. James Gray's *Edna St. Vincent Millay* (1967) is a well-written, pamphlet-length study; Jean Gould wrote a detailed, full-length life titled *The Poet and Her Book: A Biography of Edna St. Vincent Millay* (1969), which is informative but short on documentation.

Several special studies are also worth noting. Vincent Sheehan, *The Indigo Bunting: A Memoir of Edna St. Vincent Millay* (1951), focuses on the 1940s and examines Millay from the unusual perspective of her interest in birds, revealing what Sheehan interprets as an uncanny closeness to them. Toby Shafter's *Edna St. Vincent Millay; America's Best-Loved Poet* (1957) was written for youthful readers, but is neither as well-written nor as reliable as Gurko's volume. Anne Cheney's *Millay in Greenwich Village* (1975) treats Millay's bohemian existence in Greenwich Village, exploring the poet's psychology and her relations with men at the time. Even more determinedly psychoanalytical in her approach is Joan Dash in her essay on Millay in *A Life of One's Own: Three Gifted Women and the Men They Married* (1973). These psychological studies should be read with Jane Stanbrough's "Edna St. Vincent Millay and the Language of Vulnerability" in *Shakespeare's Sisters: Feminist Essays on Women Poets* (1978), edited by Sandra M. Gilbert and Susan Gubar.

Several of the men with whom Millay had close relationships have written revealing memoirs of their friendships with her. The earliest of these was Floyd Dell's unsigned "Edna St. Vincent Millay" in *The Literary Spotlight*

(1924). Dell wrote not so much a memoir as an analysis of the poet's sensibilities. Max Eastman, a friend of both Millay and her husband, Eugen Boissevain, wrote "My Friendship with Edna Millay" in *Great Companions: Critical Memoirs of Some Famous Friends* (1959). The most important of the recollections is undoubtedly that of the eminent man of letters, Edmund Wilson, who knew her intimately and regarded her very highly as a poet. His "Epilogue, 1952: Edna St. Vincent Millay" was published in *The Shores of Light: A Literary Chronicle of the Twenties and Thirties* (1952). Elizabeth Breuer's description of life at Steepletop, "Edna St. Vincent Millay," appeared in *Pictorial Review* (1931).

By far the best all-around view of Millay and her poetry is given by Norman A. Brittin in *Edna St. Vincent Millay* (rev. ed., 1982), an appreciative, balanced, and well-informed work.

Evaluation of Principal Biographical Sources

Atkins, Elizabeth. *Edna St. Vincent Millay and Her Times.* Chicago: The University of Chicago Press, 1936. (**G, Y**) Published fourteen years before the poet's death, this study captures the ambiance of the poet's early life. Some of Atkins's criticism is apt, but on the whole the book suffers from too high an evaluation of Millay's work. The literary history will be welcomed by those who know nothing of the period, but the work is too elementary to appeal to scholars and contains no documentation.

Brittin, Norman A. *Edna St. Vincent Millay.* 1967. Rev. ed. Boston: Twayne, 1982. (**A, G**) A well-written and reliable introduction to the poet's life and work, this book's sensible criticism, crisp style, and compact bibliography make it indispensable. Brittin stresses Millay's "unusual combination of heart and head," and finds her a combination of "a teasing boy, an indignant satirist, a schoolmarmish feminist, and a tough-minded agnostic." An excellent study.

Cheney, Anne. *Millay in Greenwich Village.* University: University of Alabama Press, 1975. (**A, G**) This short book begins with a chapter on Millay's Maine childhood, followed by an overview of Greenwich Village in the 1920s. Cheney then devotes separate chapters to the men (including Arthur Davison Ficke, Edmund Wilson, and Floyd Dell) who shared Millay's life there, and concludes with a study of the man she married, Eugen Boissevain.

Dash, Joan. "Edna St. Vincent Millay." In *A Life of One's Own: Three Gifted Women and the Men They Married.* New York: Harper and Row, 1973.

(A, G) A psychoanalytical study focusing on Millay's problems adjusting to life and on her husband's role in her struggle. Good feminist interpretation.

Gould, Jean. *The Poet and Her Book: A Biography of Edna St. Vincent Millay.* New York: Dodd, Mead, 1960. (A, G) Gould's study is the longest and most detailed account of Millay's life and is generally reliable. She includes a selected bibliography but no documentation.

Gray, James. *Edna St. Vincent Millay.* Minneapolis: University of Minnesota Press, 1967. (A, G) Gray's brief sketch assigns to Millay "a permanent place in the history of American poetry."

Gurko, Miriam. *Restless Spirit: The Life of Edna St. Vincent Millay.* New York: Thomas Crowell, 1962. (A, G, Y) Gurko's book is gracefully written, sensible in its tone and judgments. Includes a selected bibliography but no documentation.

Shafter, Toby. *Edna St. Vincent Millay: America's Best-Loved Poet.* New York: Julian Messner, 1957. (G, Y) A good introduction for young readers.

Sheehan, Vincent. *The Indigo Bunting: A Memoir of Edna St. Vincent Millay.* New York: Harper & Brothers, 1951. (A, G) Sheehan knew nothing of birds until he met Millay in 1948, and became fascinated by her feeling for the winged creatures. An engaging memoir on an unusual topic.

Overview and Evaluation of Primary Sources

There is no edition of Millay's collected works. The general reader interested in the poems will need the *Collected Poems,* edited by Norma Millay (New York: Harper & Brothers, 1956; A, G). This volume lacks a preface, notes, or other editorial matter; the sonnets are simply arranged according to the volume they originally appeared in. Scholars will need to consult Karl Yost, *A Bibliography of the Works of Edna St. Vincent Millay* (New York: Harper & Brothers, 1937; A, G). Yost gives full descriptions of all the primary materials published through 1936. The post-1936 writings were all published by Harper & Brothers and are conveniently listed in Brittin's bibliography.

A good collection of the *Letters of Edna St. Vincent Millay,* edited by Allan Ross Macdougall (New York and London: Harper & Brothers, 1952; A, G), divides the correspondence into nine chronological periods and includes a useful index. *Edna St. Vincent Millay's Poems Selected for Young People* (New York and Evanston: Harper & Row, 1951; G, Y) features drawings by J. Paget-Fredericks. Elizabeth Barnett prepared *Collected Sonnets of Edna St.*

Vincent Millay (New York: Harper & Row, 1988; **A, G, Y**). She includes all of the sonnets that Millay herself chose for the 1941 *Collected Sonnets*, plus twenty more that the poet's sister, Norma Millay, added to the posthumous volume *Mine the Harvest* (1954). Barnett also reprints Millay's brief foreword to the 1941 volume, as well as a note by Norma Millay on the poet's sonnet-writing practice. Finally, all students of Millay will want to consult Judith Nierman, *Edna St. Vincent Millay: A Reference Guide* (Boston: G. K. Hall, 1977; **A, G**). Nierman provides an annotated bibliography of secondary writings, making the work indispensable.

Museums, Historical Landmarks, Societies

Memorial Marker (Austerlitz, NY). This memorial was erected in June 1959. Accounts of the dedication ceremony are found in the *New York Times* for June 28 and 29, 1959.

Other Sources

Cook, Harold Lewis. "Edna St. Vincent Millay—an Essay." In Yost's *Bibliography*. This fifty-page analysis and appreciation of the poems is introduced by a foreword by Millay.

Stanbrough, Jane. "Edna St. Vincent Millay and the Language of Vulnerability." In *Shakespeare's Sisters: Feminist Essays on Women Poets*, edited by Sandra M. Gilbert and Susan Gubar. Bloomington and London: Indiana University Press, 1978. This distinctively feminist essay emphasizes Millay's understanding of the victimization of women by men.

Frank Day
Clemson University

MARILYN MONROE
1926-1962

Chronology

Born Norma Jeane Mortensen (also known as Norma Jeane [or Jean] Baker) on June 1, 1926, to Gladys Monroe Baker Mortensen, a film cutter at Consolidated Film Industries, and C. Stanley Gifford, her co-worker; mother, who marries and divorces twice, never marries her father; *1935* enters Los Angeles Orphans Home Society after living in foster homes as a result of her mother's mental illness; *1937* leaves orphanage and returns to a series of foster homes; *1942* marries neighbor James E. Dougherty; *1944* works at Radio Plane Company while her husband serves in the merchant marine; *1945* begins posing for men's magazine photographs; *1946* signs film contract with Twentieth Century-Fox; acquires the name Marilyn Monroe; divorces James Dougherty; *1947* contract dropped by Fox; makes first screen appearance in *Dangerous Years* (*Scudda Hoo! Scudda Hay!*, in which Monroe also appears, was shot before *Dangerous Years*, but not released until 1948); *1948* signs contract with Columbia Pictures but is dropped six months later; *1949* poses nude for calendar photographs by Tom Kelley; *1950* plays first substantial dramatic role in *The Asphalt Jungle;* signs second contract with Twentieth Century-Fox; *1951* meets playwright Arthur Miller; *1952* nude calendar story revealed by press; allegedly marries Robert Slatzer in Mexico, but destroys evidence of marriage three days later; *1953* has first starring role in *Niagara;* appears nude in the first issue of *Playboy* magazine; *January 1954* marries baseball hero, Joe DiMaggio; *February 1954* entertains troops in Korea; *October 1954* divorces DiMaggio; *December 1954* walks out on Fox contract, moves to New York and forms Marilyn Monroe Productions; *1955* begins attending Actors Studio, although never as a member; signs new contract with Twentieth Century-Fox; *February 1956* returns to Hollywood; *June 1956* returns to New York and marries Arthur Miller; *August 1956* release of *Bus Stop*, her most acclaimed dramatic film; *1959* release of *Some Like it Hot*, her most financially successful film; *1960* acts in *The Misfits*, her last film; *1961* divorces Miller; *1962* fired in June by Fox from cast of *Something's Got to Give*; found dead on August 5 of apparent barbiturate overdose.

Activities of Historical Significance

With Greta Garbo, Marilyn Monroe is one of America's most powerful and haunting film actress. Lacking Garbo's acting credentials and classic beauty, Monroe had to overcome the public's perception that her features were gross and her behavior vulgar. She portrayed a series of "dumb blondes" so effectively that audiences believed it was her true personality and scoffed at her ambitions, such as forming her own production company, acting with Laurence Olivier, and studying at the Actors Studio. But it is clear that she was both serious and successful in these efforts. The old studio production system was broken down in part because of the challenges of pioneers like Monroe, who created their own production companies to fight the control the big studios had on their careers, and their monopoly on publicity and distribution.

Monroe possessed not only a beautiful face and a stunning figure, but, as those who photographed her have attested, an extraordinary ability to project herself on film. Joshua Logan, who directed her in *Bus Stop*, called her "one of the greatest talents of all time." An exhibitionist in love with the camera, she felt no shame or guilt about revealing her body (as in the famous skirt-blowing scene from *The Seven Year Itch*, 1955) or appearing nude during an era when the general public did not approve of disrobing. While filming *The Misfits*, Monroe accidentally displayed a bare breast and then asked director John Huston to include the shot in the finished film.

Monroe quickly discovered that her physical appeal and special relationship with the camera attracted attention and opened doors to opportunity. To her beauty and sexual appeal, Monroe added the special trait of vulnerability, which drew audiences to her, made them feel that they knew her, and led them to care about her. That vulnerability, the source of her appeal, was very likely the quality that killed her.

At the time of her death, Monroe was seen as a victim of a confused personal life, manipulation by others, and society's patronizing view of women. Her accomplishments, despite the forces working against her, were extraordinary, and she is historically significant, not only for her films that are considered classics, but for playing an important role in breaking down the sexual mores and repression of the 1950s. Respected by people who knew her privately as an extraordinarily intelligent person, Monroe became a symbol of sexual rebellion. She was a woman who, despite the lavish attention paid her by men, would not succumb to male dominance, and she is regarded today more as a liberator than "sex symbol."

Overview of Biographical Sources

While Marilyn Monroe was alive, she seemed wrapped in mystery. On screen, she perfected the dumb blond role; in private she was admired for her wit and intelligence. She was obviously troubled, raising many questions for her biographers. Was she insecure because of her shattered childhood, spent largely in an orphanage and foster homes? Or because of her inability to maintain a marriage or bear a child? Did she feel guilt over the people she had exploited, such as her agent Johnny Hyde, who fell so in love with her that he left his family and finally died from the strain? Or was it humiliation over having been manipulated by lovers such as John and Robert Kennedy? Was she hurt by the public's scornful reaction to her efforts to improve herself as an actress? Was she dependent on drugs, using them to get up for a performance and to wind down afterwards? Or perhaps most chillingly, was she the victim of the mental illness which had engulfed both her grandmother and mother?

Her biographers' failure to unravel the enigma of Monroe suggests that there is no final answer; that perhaps all these factors played a part in her tragedy. Many books about Monroe are merely exploitative. Others are mainly collections of photographs, such as Michael Conway and Mark Ricci, *The Films of Marilyn Monroe* (Secaucus, NJ: Citadel, 1964); John Kobal, *Marilyn Monroe: A Life on Film* (New York: Hamlyn, 1974); Janice Anderson, *Marilyn Monroe* (New York: Hamlyn, 1983); and Roger Baker, *Marilyn Monroe* (New York: Crown, 1990). Works such as these offer information, but little analysis of the riddle of Marilyn Monroe.

The serious biographies of Monroe include Maurice Zolotow, *Marilyn Monroe* (1960); Fred Lawrence Guiles, *Norma Jean* (1969) and *Legend: The Life and Death of Marilyn Monroe* (1984); Norman Mailer, *Marilyn* (1973); Carl E. Rollyson, Jr., *Marilyn Monroe: A Life of the Actress* (1986); and Anthony Summers, *Goddess: The Secret Lives of Marilyn Monroe* (1986).

Monroe's final mystery is her death. A few months before she died, she had ended an intimate relationship with President John Kennedy and had begun another with Attorney General Robert Kennedy. At the time of her death he was trying to break off the relationship. Her death has been variously described as suicide, accident, or murder. Speculation about her death is prominent in James A. Hudson, *The Mysterious Death of Marilyn Monroe* (1968); Robert Slatzer, *The Life and Curious Death of Marilyn Monroe* (1974); Tony Sciacca, *Who Killed Marilyn?* (1976); and Milo Speriglio, *The Marilyn Conspiracy* (1986).

Evaluation of Biographical Sources

Guiles, Fred. *Legend: The Life and Death of Marilyn Monroe*. New York: Stein and Day, 1984. (**A, G**) This is not a new edition of the author's earlier *Norma Jean* but a complete rewriting based on new research and what Guiles contends is "a clear understanding of the woman." Guiles is explicit about Monroe's relationship with the Kennedys, which was only hinted at in his earlier book. Contains filmography and bibliography.

————. *Norma Jean*. New York: McGraw-Hill, 1969. (**A, G**) As the title suggests, Guiles' thesis is that Marilyn Monroe was a creation of Norma

Jean Mortensen, which remained the actress's basic identity. Guiles also contends that there was no intellectual gap between Monroe and Arthur Miller because he was an instinctive artist like Marilyn, rather than a thinker. Well written and with many surprises. With filmography and bibliography.

Hudson, James A. *The Mysterious Death of Marilyn Monroe*. New York: Volitant, 1968. (A, G) Hudson raises questions about Monroe's death, which have yet to be answered, although subsequent research makes his account dated.

Kahn, Roger. *Joe and Marilyn: A Memory of Love*. New York: William Morrow, 1986. (A, G) An account of Monroe's marriage to the baseball star, which, because Kahn is primarily a sportswriter, focuses as much on DiMaggio as on Monroe. Not to be confused with *Marilyn and Joe DiMaggio* (1977) by Robin Moore and Gene Schoor, a less scholarly work.

Mailer, Norman. *Marilyn*. New York: Warner, 1973. (A, G) Less a biography than an analysis of Monroe's life with particular emphasis on what her screen performances reveal about her personality. Mailer's account is explicitly based on the facts presented in Guiles' *Norma Jean*. As always, Mailer is as fascinated with his own relationship with the subject as he is with the subject itself. Includes filmography. Mailer also discusses Monroe in his *Of Women and Their Elegance* (New York: Simon and Schuster, 1981; G), a book of photographs and commentary.

Rollyson, Carl E., Jr. *Marilyn Monroe: A Life of the Actress*. Ann Arbor, MI: UMI Research, 1986. (A, G) Rollyson attempts to relate Monroe's life to her film roles. This approach is intended to correct the overemphasis on her public persona. Includes extensive bibliography and descriptive filmography.

Scaccia, Tony (Anthony Scaduto). *Who Killed Marilyn?* New York: Manor, 1976. (A, G) Despite the provocative title, Scaccia gives no clear idea of who killed Monroe nor any hard evidence that she was murdered. He offers a list of people who might have been interested in silencing her and speculates that she was killed after threatening to reveal her affairs with John and Robert Kennedy.

Speriglio, Milo. *The Marilyn Conspiracy*. New York: Pocket Books, 1986. (G) This update of the author's earlier *Marilyn Monroe: Murder Cover-Up* (1982) contains little new information and serves only to demonstrate that, with physical evidence missing and many key figures dead, the truth about Monroe's death will probably never be known.

Steinem, Gloria. *Marilyn*. New York: Holt, 1986. (**A, G**) Although not planned as such, Steinem's book is an answer to Mailer's *Marilyn*. Steinem views Monroe from a feminist perspective in an attempt to determine the meaning of the actress's life.

Summers, Anthony. *Goddess: The Secret Lives of Marilyn Monroe*. New York: Macmillan, 1985. (**A, G**) Summers has unearthed new information about Monroe's last years, including details of her relationships with John and Robert Kennedy, but is careful not to draw sensational conclusions about her death. Since others had covered Monroe's early life in detail, Summers devotes more than half of his book to her last four years. Often considered the best book ever written about the actress, the paperback edition (New York: New American Library, 1986) contains further new material about the cancellation of a planned segment on Monroe for the television "news magazine" *20/20*.

Zolotow, Maurice. *Marilyn Monroe*. New York: Harcourt, Brace, 1960. (**A, G**) This carefully researched book was the first truly scholarly biography of Monroe. The fact that it appeared before her death is both its strength and weakness; it avoids the sensational tone of some books that examine Monroe's entire career, but lacks coverage of the eventful last year of her life. Based in part on interviews with Monroe.

Overview and Evaluation of Primary Sources

Monroe wrote a partial autobiography, *My Story* (New York: Stein and Day, 1974; **A, G, Y**), which was most likely ghost written by screenwriter Ben Hecht. It was copyrighted and finally published by her one-time manager and business partner, Milton Greene. *My Story* presents Monroe's life up to her 1954 visit to Korea in its most favorable light. Books based largely on interviews with Monroe include Pete Martin, *Will Acting Spoil Marilyn Monroe?* (New York: Doubleday, 1956; **A, G, Y**); George Carpozi, Jr., *Marilyn Monroe: Her Own Story* (New York: Belmont, 1961; **A, G**); and W. J. Weatherby, *Conversations with Marilyn* (New York: Mason Charter, 1976; **A, G**). Edward Wagenknecht edited *Marilyn Monroe: A Composite View* (Philadelphia, PA: Chilton, 1969; **A, G**), which contains interviews with her, as well as essays by critics and friends. *Marilyn Monroe: In her Own Words* (New York: Putnam, 1983; **G**), edited by Roger G. Taylor, is a collection of her quotations.

There are also a number of accounts of Monroe's life written by friends and associates. Her first husband, James Dougherty, tells the story of their marriage in *The Secret Happiness of Marilyn Monroe* (Chicago: Playboy Press, 1976; **A, G**). Andre de Dienes, a photographer who worked with Monroe early in her career, recounts his experiences in *Marilyn Mon Amour* (Paris: E. P. Filipacchi, 1985; A, G), which includes his account of a rare visit between Monroe and her mother. Robert F. Slatzer offers two interesting revelations in *The Curious Death of Marilyn Monroe* (New York: Pinnacle, 1974; A, G). His claim that he was married to Monroe for a few days in 1952 is corroborated by a witness, although all documentary evidence of the marriage was destroyed. Slatzer was also among the first to raise questions about Monroe's death, contending that she was actually murdered. Photographer Sam Shaw published two collections of photographs with text which offer personal glimpses of Monroe: *Marilyn Monroe as the Girl: The Making of the Seven Year Itch* (New York: Ballantine, 1955; G), later incorporated in his *The Joy of Marilyn in the Camera Eye* (New York: Exeter, 1979; G) and, together with poet Norman Rosten, *Marilyn Among Friends* (New York: Bloomsbury, 1987; A, G). Rosten, who knew Monroe in New York, writes in *Marilyn: An Untold Story* (New York: Signet, 1973; A, G) that she was a wistful girl who wrote poetry and yearned to be a better artist. Arthur Miller gives his view of their marriage in his autobiography, *Timebends* (New York: Grove, 1987; A, G). Photographer Bert Stern, who took nudes of Monroe a few weeks before her death, gives an account of her behavior—an unwitting comment on voyeurism—in *The Last Sitting* (New York: Morrow, 1982; A, G). Eunice Murray, Monroe's housekeeper who might better be described as her live-in psychiatric nurse, was in Monroe's house the night she died and recounts the story of her final days in *Marilyn: The Last Months* (New York; Pyramid, 1975; A, G). The accuracy of Murray's book, however, must be considered suspect in light of the fact that she has changed her account of that period several times.

Fiction and Adaptations

Marilyn Monroe's face, body, personality, and life story have been used as material by other artists more than any other film performer. The most significant plays featuring a character resembling Monroe include George Axelrod's *Will Success Spoil Rock Hudson?* (1955), which was made into a movie with the same title in 1957; Arthur Miller's play *After the Fall* (1964); and Terry Johnson's *Insignificance* (1982), also made into a film with the same title in 1985. Other films which feature a character based on Monroe include Paddy Chayefsky's *The Goddess* (1958), Larry Buchanan's *Goodbye Norma Jean* (1976), and Vernon Zimmerman's *Fade to Black* (1985). Among the hundreds of artistic representations of Monroe are William de Kooning's *Marilyn Monroe* (1954) and Andy Warhol's multiple silk screen images of Monroe's face (1964). Songs about Monroe include Ervin Drake and Jimmy Shirl's "Marilyn" (1952) and Bernie Taupin and Elton John's "Candle in the Wind" (1974).

2046 Marilyn Monroe

Museums, Historical Landmarks, Societies

Two fan clubs continue to keep the memory of Marilyn Monroe alive. They are the Marilyn Forever Fan Club in Northridge, California, and the Marilyn Remembered Fan Club in Los Angeles.

Other Sources

Manvell, Roger, ed. *The International Encyclopedia of Film.* New York: Bonanza, 1972. A brief account of the highlights of Monore's career.

Riese, Randall and Neal Hitchens. *The Unabridged Marilyn: Her Life from A to Z.* New York: Bonanza, 1987. Every bit of information about Marilyn Monroe, every book written about her, every person mentioned in the accounts of her life, and every person who made a film with her are collected, analyzed, and cross referenced in this indispensible research guide. Other topics covered include "Books That Marilyn Read" and "Abraham Lincoln," who was Monroe's hero.

Rosen, Marjorie. *Popcorn Venus.* New York: Avon, 1973. A general analysis of the sex-goddess phenomenon, which includes a great deal of material on Monroe.

Thomson, David. *A Biographical Dictionary of Film.* New York: William Morrow, 1981. Contains a biographical sketch of Monroe.

Jim Baird
University of North Texas

LOTTIE MOON
1840-1912

Chronology

Born Charlotte Digges Moon on December 12, 1840, at Viewmont, a plantation between Charlottesville and Scottsville, Albemarle County, Virginia, to devout Baptists Anna Maria Barclay Moon and Edward Harris Moon, a merchant and planter; *1840-1850* grows up in a comfortable, happy family with six brothers and sisters; *1850* sees uncle, James Barclay, off to Jerusalem for the American Christian Missionary Society; *1853* after father dies, assists mother in running female-dominated household and plantation, where she will live until after the Civil War; sister Orianna Moon graduates from Female Medical College of Pennsylvania; *1854-1856* attends Virginia Female Seminary (later Hollins College), near Roanoke, Virginia, earning a bachelor's degree; *1857* matriculates at Baptist-affiliated school for women, Albemarle Female Institute, in Charlottesville, Virginia, intended by its founders to be the academic equivalent of the University of Virginia; *1858* experiences conversion during a revival in Charlottesville's Baptist Church, whose pastor, John A. Broadus, advocates mission work for young people; *1861* graduates from Albemarle with a master's degree; *1861-1865* spends Civil War years helping to run Viewmont; tutors children at various other plantations; *1866-1870* teaches at Danville Female Academy (later Caldwell Institute) in Danville, Kentucky; becomes acquainted with returned Southern Baptist missionaries to China; *1866-1870* Viewmont is dismantled and family fortune is dissipated as a result of changing economic conditions in the South; *1871* with Danville colleague Anna Cunningham Safford, organizes a new school for girls in Cartersville, Georgia; *1872* sister Edmonia Moon goes to Dengzhou, Shandong Province, China, as a missionary after Foreign Mission Board of the Southern Baptist Convention eliminates prohibition on single women missionaries; *1873* joins Edmonia, and both sisters begin teaching in mission school; *1876* accompanies Edmonia on return to U.S.; *1877* returns to Dengzhou, China; *1878* opens school for girls in Dengzhou; *1879* makes first lengthy evangelization tour of country; *1881* moves into what will become her well-known home, Little Crossroads, in Dengzhou; considers and decides against marriage to Prof. Crawford Howell Toy of Harvard, formerly one of her teachers at the Albemarle Female Institute; *1885-1890* maintains winter residence in city of Pingdu, 115 miles west of Dengzhou, for evangelizing in interior of China; *1887* establishes what is considered her most successful evangelical work in village of Shaling, about ten miles from Pingdu; *1886-1888* publishes "Letters from Pingdu" in Southern Baptist periodicals, crystallizing support for overseas missions and resulting in the creation of

Women's Missionary Union (WMU), Auxiliary to the Southern Baptist Convention, whose fundraising efforts eventually put both the North China mission and the Foreign Mission Board on firm financial footing; *1887* proposes WMU Christmas offering, later to become the Lottie Moon Christmas offering, for the support of overseas missions; *1889* evangelizes Confucian scholar who eventually becomes Pastor Li of North China; establishes, in Shaling, first Christian church in Pingdu area; *1891-1894* takes furlough; *1892* mediates ideological differences between the Foreign Mission Board and Tarleton Perry Crawford of the North China Mission, founder of the Gospel Mission Movement; *1895-1900* returns to Dengzhou, resumes teaching in city and countryside; *1895* remains in Dengzhou during bombardment of city during Russo-Japanese war; *1900-1901* flees Boxer rebellion, teaches English in Japan; *1903-1904* takes furlough; *1905-1911* teaches in Dengzhou; *1911* deprives herself of food to aid famine relief; takes ill and is sent home by mission colleagues; *1912* dies December 24, 1912 aboard ship at Kobe, Japan.

Activities of Historical Significance

Lottie Moon, Southern Baptist missionary to China, is remembered for her influential role in mobilizing the Southern Baptist church for missionary support through the founding of the Women's Missionary Union (WMU). Her persistence and faith have been credited with saving the Southern Baptist North China mission during times of ideological conflict and financial trouble. Moon was the first successful single female Southern Baptist missionary to the North China mission at Dengzhou (her sister Edmonia, who preceded her there, returned to the U.S. after a short stay).

Moon immersed herself in the study of Chinese culture, eventually taking the then-unusual step—for a female missionary—of living alone in the Chinese interior, cut off from all Western contact. Since her death, the invocation of her name for the Lottie Moon Christmas Offering has helped to keep her in the public eye. Present-day interest in Moon within the Southern Baptist denomination is evidenced by several references in current issues of *Southern Baptist Periodical Index*.

Overview of Biographical Sources

For many years the only book-length biography of Moon, Una Roberts Lawrence's *Lottie Moon* (1927), has gone through many printings and is still widely read in the South. The Southern Baptist church has used the book extensively over the years as a fundraising vehicle for overseas missions. It contains some period racial stereotypes in references to Moon's pre-Civil War childhood plantation.

Catherine Allen's *The New Lottie Moon Story* (1980), updates Lawrence's more romantic account. Both books are written from a devotional point of view, but Allen gives a more convincing historical narrative of how Moon's life in a pious, female-dominated household prepared her for her independent life as a missionary. She also examines Moon's schooling in effective missionary techniques. Both Lawrence and Allen offer remarkable, if sometimes biased, descriptions of the Chinese people and culture.

Irwin T. Hyatt, Jr.'s concise, clearly written *Our Ordered Lives Confess: Three Nineteenth-Century American Missionaries in East Shantung* (1976) provides perspective of Moon's influence and place in mission politics. Margie Black has written an affectionate review of Moon's life and work in *Viewpoints* (1974), while the brief, devotional treatments of Helen Albee Monsell (1958) and Jester Summers (1971), both intended for juvenile audiences, illustrate Moon's popular appeal within the Southern Baptist denomination. An impartial, full-length treatment of Moon's life, taking advantage of current scholarship on Christian missions in China, has yet to be written. There are numerous popular treatments in Southern Baptist periodicals written as spiritual inspiration for her followers.

Evaluation of Principal Biographical Sources

Allen, Catherine. *The New Lottie Moon Story.* Nashville: Broadman Press, 1980. (G) An inspirational work intended to update Lawrence. Informative and well-researched, it is particularly valuable on Moon's acclimation to China and the Chinese.

Black, Margie. "Our Own Lottie Moon." *Viewpoints, Georgia Baptist History.* Vol. 4. Atlanta: Georgia Baptist Historical Society, 1974. (G) Focuses on Moon during her years in Cartersville, Georgia.

Hyatt, Irwin T., Jr. *Our Ordered Lives Confess: Three Nineteenth-Century American Missionaries in East Shantung.* Cambridge: Harvard University Press, 1976. (A) The most impartial work to date. Hyatt critically examines Moon's career in the context of contemporary scholarship on China missions. An indispensable work.

Lawrence, Una Roberts. *Lottie Moon.* Nashville: Sunday School Board of the Southern Baptist Convention, 1927. (G) The standard work on Moon for many years, written by the director of mission studies for the WMU and valuable as a source of interviews of Moon's acquaintances. Over the years, the book itself has become part of the Moon legend.

Monsell, Helen Albee. *Her Own Way: The Story of Lottie Moon*. Nashville: Broadman Press, 1958. (Y) An inspirational sketch for readers ages ten to fourteen.

Summers, Jester. *Lottie Moon of China*. Nashville: Broadman Press, 1971. (Y) A sixty-two page sketch for ages eight to twelve.

Overview and Evaluation of Primary Sources

Because foreign mission work required much correspondence and many reports between missionaries, mission stations, and home offices in the U.S., there is a great deal of original source material in the official records of mission organizations.

One of the best sources of Moon's voluminous correspondence is the Southern Baptist Convention Papers, at the Foreign Mission Board (FMB) of the Southern Baptist Convention (SBC) in Richmond, Virginia. There are four volumes of Moon's correspondence, each containing three to four hundred letters. Researchers should consult the copy books of corresponding secretaries and treasurers (1872-1913) for responses to Moon's communication with the Board. Other records at this location include the minutes of the FMB (1845-1914); photo files; minutes of the North China mission; and some of Moon's personal effects. The minutes, reports, and other materials of the Southern Baptist Conventions—published annually since 1845 as *SBC Proceedings: Proceedings of the Southern Baptist Convention*—are valuable for tracing the financial rise and fall of the FMB, the evolution of mission policy, and the rise of the WMU. The Office of Communications and Public Relations, Resource Coordination, has about 4,000 photos of the work of Southern Baptist missionaries in China, dating from 1847 to 1947. Although Moon herself was reticent about appearing in photographs, these photos illustrate conditions faced by missionaries in North China.

The official records at the Women's Missionary Union Archives in Birmingham, Alabama, are important for understanding the WMU's role in saving Moon's North China mission from financial ruin. The records include minutes of annual meetings, records of WMU business, and missionary reports, correspondence, and photographs. A Lottie Moon file contains memorabilia and a few of Moon's letters. The FMB archives also hold research materials, such as transcripts of interviews, compiled by Catherine Allen in writing *The New Lottie Moon Story*.

Una Roberts Lawrence's research material—including letters and papers from Lottie Moon and unique interviews with missionaries and other acquaintances—can be found in the Lottie Moon Room at the Southern Baptist Theological Seminary, Louisville, Kentucky.

Much of Moon's fundraising correspondence remains in private hands. The First Baptist Church in Cartersville, Georgia, where she taught for two years, has twenty letters from Moon, written between 1873 and 1899. These are available by appointment with Margie Black, Georgia Women's Missionary Union, South Atlanta, Georgia. Fifteen letters, dating from 1887 to 1908 are archived at the Virginia Baptist Historical Society, University of Richmond, Boatwright Memorial Library. The SBC Historical Commission Library and Archives in Nashville also has a file of Moon letters and other memorabilia. Three letters from the last year of Moon's life, as well as her undergraduate school records, can be found in the Fishburn Library of Hollins College, her alma mater. In her biography, Allen lists a number of churches and individuals that currently hold Moon correspondence. References to these materials in *The New Lottie Moon Story* may assist the researcher in gauging the importance of various sources.

Articles by and about Moon, her colleagues, and the work in North China appeared in many contemporary Southern Baptist periodicals, such as *Foreign Mission Journal* (Richmond, VA: Foreign Mission Board of the Southern Baptist Convention, 1851-1916; A, G). These articles often contain accounts of Moon's policy and provide a barometer of her success. These and a number of other denominational periodicals are available from the SBC Historical Commission. Among other major China mission periodicals are *Chinese Recorder* (Shanghai: China Editorial Board [and other publishers], 1868-1941; A, G) and *Woman's Work in China* (later known as *Woman's Work in the Far East* (Shanghai: American Presbyterian Mission Press, 1877-1921; A, G), founded by Moon's friend Anna Cunningham Safford. Both are available at the Library of Congress, Washington, D.C., and the Presbyterian Historical Society Archives and Library, Philadelphia. The bibliographies in Allen and Hyatt serve as an excellent guide to these articles.

Fiction and Adaptations

The SBC Archives Center in Richmond holds two inspirational motion pictures, created largely for fundraising purposes: *The Lottie Moon Story* (1960) and *Journey Home: Lottie Moon of China* (1983). Other multimedia materials include filmstrips and slides about the Lottie Moon Christmas offerings. A booklet entitled "Lottie Moon in Pictures" (1961) contains stills from *The Lottie Moon Story*. All of these materials are more important as examples of the continued interest in and influence of Moon than as historical documentation.

"The Life of Miss Lottie Moon" is an inspirational but balanced forty-five-minute tape cassette by E. Luther Copeland (Kansas City, MO: Christian Cassettes-Onesimus, 1972).

There are several inspirational, romanticized playlets emphasizing Moon's faith and Southern origins. Some of those include Lucy Hamilton Howard, "Her Lengthened Shadow: Scenes from the Life of Lottie Moon, 1840-1912," (1964); Miriam Robinson, "Faithful unto Death: Narration of the Life of Lottie Moon," (1964); and Dorothy Lehman Sumerau, "Make His Name Glorious: A Dramatic Service of Worship on the Life and Work of Lottie Moon," (1958). Carole Tomlinson and Doris Standridge collaborated on "It Cannot End at Kobe: How Lottie Moon Lives in Missions in the 1970s" (n.d.). This play, more recent than the others, incorporates the legend of Lottie Moon into an examination of social change occurring in the Southern Baptist church.

Museums, Historical Landmarks, Societies

Grave (Crewe, VA). Both Moon and her brother, Isaac, are buried in a Baptist cemetery in Crewe, a small town about fifty miles west of Richmond. The Crewe Baptist Church has a stained glass window honoring Moon.

Lottie Moon Room (Cartersville, GA). The First Baptist Church at 114 West Cherokee Avenue, where Moon was a much-beloved teacher for two years, has twenty of her letters concerning conditions in China and progress of the missions. The Women's Missionary Society, organized almost immediately upon Moon's departure from Cartersville for China, supported her throughout her career.

Lottie Moon Room (Louisville, KY). Located at the Southern Baptist Theological Seminary.

Marker (between Charlottesville and Scottsville, VA). The Virginia Women's Missionary Union placed a marker on Highway 20 opposite the former location of Viewmont.

Other Sources

Beaver, R. Pierce. "Lottie Digges Moon." In *Notable American Women 1607-1950*, edited by Edward T. James, vol. 2. Cambridge: Belknap Press of Harvard University Press, 1971. A succinct, scholarly analysis and chronology of Moon's life.

DeWeese, Eldonna, ed. *Southern Baptist Periodical Index*. Bolivar, MO: Estep Library of Southwest Baptist University, 1989. Contains a number of references to articles about Moon.

Rhea, Claude, comp. *Lottie Moon Cook Book: Recipes Used by Lottie Moon, 1875-1912* (1969). Based upon a cookbook found among Moon's personal effects.

Roth, E. C. "Lottie (Charlotte) Moon." In *Encyclopedia of Southern Baptists*, vol. 2. Nashville: Broadman Press, 1958. A one-paragraph account of Moon's life.

Steven Agoratus

LUCRETIA MOTT
1793-1880

Chronology

Born Lucretia Coffin on January 3, 1793, on Nantucket Island, Massachusetts, to Quaker parents Anna Folger Coffin and Thomas Coffin, Jr., a sea captain; *1804* family moves to Boston where Thomas Coffin, Jr. becomes a merchant; *1806* attends Nine Partners, a Quaker boarding school in Dutchess County, New York; *c. 1807* meets James Mott, teaching at Nine Partners; *1808-1810* assists girls' teacher at Nine Partners; *1809* Coffin family moves to Philadelphia; *April 10, 1811* marries James Mott and sets up housekeeping in Philadelphia where James Mott engages in cotton and wool trade; *1812-1828* six children are born to Lucretia and James Mott, of whom five survive; *1821* recognized as a minister in Society of Friends in Philadelphia; *1827* along with husband joins followers of Elias Hicks in split of Quaker church; *1830-1835* elected clerk of Philadelphia Women's Yearly Meeting; *1830s* begins speaking out at Hicksite branches of Quaker meeting; *August 1830* meets William Lloyd Garrison; *December 1833* helps organize Philadelphia Female Antislavery Society; *1840* with James Mott travels to Great Britain as a delegate to the World's Anti-Slavery Convention in London; refuses a seat at the convention, but attends its meetings; *1840s* speaks out against slavery and for women's rights at Quaker and various other meetings; *May 9, 1848* delivers first major speech, "Law of Progress," at American Anti-Slavery Society in New York City; *1848* helps organize Seneca Falls Convention and write women's Declaration of Rights and Resolutions; *1849* delivers "Discourse on Woman" in Philadelphia as an answer to Richard Henry Dana, Sr.'s attack on the women's rights movement; *1850s* speaks at various antislavery, women's rights, and temperance meetings; *1857* James and Lucretia Mott move to the farm, "Roadside," near Philadelphia; *1866* chosen first president of Equal Rights Association meeting in New York; *January 26, 1868* James Mott dies; *1870s* delivers numerous addresses to Pennsylvania Peace Society; *1878* in Rochester, New York, delivers last public address, commemorating the thirtieth anniversary of the Seneca Falls Convention; *November 11, 1880* dies at "Roadside."

Activities of Historical Significance

Like other nineteenth-century reformers, Lucretia Mott did not confine her struggles to a single cause. Early in her career she recognized the power of the Quaker tradition enabling her to take public positions on a variety of social problems. When the Quakers split, she favored the liberal Hicksite sect which espoused free interpretation of the Bible and involvement in worldly affairs. Mott's antislavery efforts began well before her advocacy of women's rights, but the two were closely connected. As a Quaker she denounced war, including the Civil War, although she clearly sympathized with the war's emancipation goals. She also spoke for temperance and school reforms. With her husband's constant support, she traveled and spoke across the eastern U.S. Despite frequent periods of ill health, Mott raised five children, read constantly, and participated in a dozen or more local and national causes. An incisive, challenging mind, a clear sense of mission, and a level-headed personality made her a natural leader and, among reformers, a major figure.

Although she played a predominant role in establishing the women's rights movement, Mott's reputation has been eclipsed in the twentieth century by Elizabeth Cady Stanton and Susan B. Anthony. Perhaps because she withdrew from the politics of women's rights organizations in the 1860s, she was regarded chiefly as an elderly figurehead and peacemaker. Mott's contributions have been slighted in the twentieth century.

Overview of Biographical Sources

Considering her major role in reform movements, Mott has received only limited biographical treatment. In 1884, her granddaughter Anna Davis Hallowell published *James and Lucretia Mott: Life and Letters,* chiefly a compilation of letters and anecdotes. From the 1960s onward scholars of women's history have discussed Mott's activities in the nineteenth-century women's rights movement. Margaret Hope Bacon's biography, *Valiant Friend* (1980) reflects a shift in the historical picture of Mott from a woman of "sweetness and calm" to "a very human person with a quick temper, a sharp tongue" as well as "a healthy love of life."

Evaluation of Principal Biographical Sources

Bacon, Margaret Hope. *Valiant Friend: The Life of Lucretia Mott.* New York: Walker, 1980. (A, G) Bacon relieves Mott of the mantle of sainthood and portrays her as a brilliant, tough-minded, and vulnerable woman. The well-written biography draws upon primary sources and contains a useful list of all Mott's principal speeches. Although Bacon's biography contains fourteen pages of notes, the fact that not all quotations are documented could frustrate the scholar wishing to research further.

Cromwell, Otelia. *Lucretia Mott.* Cambridge: Harvard University Press, 1958. (A, G) Cromwell's scholarly biography draws on primary sources and documents its assertions carefully. This readable, informative chronicle contains little analysis of Mott's motives and behavior.

Hare, Lloyd C. *The Greatest American Woman: Lucretia Mott.* New York: American Historical Society, 1937. (G) A narrative of Mott's life, this biography assumes no reader background on the Quaker, reform, and anti-slavery movements. Hare's style at times tends to hyperbole, and there are a few factual errors.

Overview and Evaluation of Primary Sources

Mott's 1830 sermons, delivered at Quaker meetings, were apparently never recorded. Dana Greene has collected and published, with little scholarly apparatus, *Lucretia Mott, Her Complete Speeches and Sermons* (New York: E. Mellen, 1980; A). According to Greene, Mott rarely corrected these addresses, so the reader must rely on stenographic versions. A few other printed "re-marks" and sermons are available, as cited in Bacon's helpful list of "Prin-cipal Sermons and Speeches of Lucretia Mott" in *Valiant Friend.* The three-volume *History of Woman Suffrage* (comp. Susan B. Anthony, Elizabeth Cady Stanton, and Matilda Joslyn Gage, New York: Fowler and Wells, 1881-1922; A) contains several letters to and from Mott, petitions she signed, and some convention remarks not included in Greene's edition. Mott's diary of her trip to England has been published as *Slavery and the "Woman Question," Lucretia Mott's Diary, 1840,* edited by Frederick B. Tolles (Haverford, PA: Friends Historical Association, 1952; A).

No scholarly edition of Mott's articles and letters exists. The largest single collection of Mott papers is at Swarthmore College, Swarthmore, Pennsyl-vania. In *James and Lucretia Mott: Life and Letters* (Boston: Houghton Mifflin, 1884; A). Mott's granddaughter included a few complete letters to and from Lucretia Mott, and excerpts from over eighty letters between Mott and her family and friends. The microfilm edition of the records of the Pennsylvania Abolition Society (published by the Historical Society of Pennsylvania, with a guide by Jeffrey N. Bumbrey; A) contains on Reels 30 and 31 minutes and correspondence of the Philadelphia Female Anti-Slavery Society in which Mott was a leading figure.

Fiction and Adaptations

Mott is a principal character in the play *Seneca Falls, 1848: All Men and Women Are Created Equal* by Elizabeth C. Shultis (Seneca Falls, New York, 1984).

Museums, Historical Landmarks, Societies

Sculpture (Washington, DC). Adelaide Johnson's sculpture of Mott, Stanton, and Anthony is in the crypt of the U.S. Capitol.

Other Sources

Brown, Ira. "Cradle of Feminism: the Philadelphia Female Anti-Slavery Society, 1837-1840." *Pennsylvania Magazine of History and Biography* (April 1978): 143-166. Brown describes Mott's role in the development of this antislavery organization.

DuBois, Ellen. "Women's Rights and Abolition: The Nature of the Connection." In *Antislavery Reconsidered: New Perspectives on the Abolitionists*, edited by Lewis Perry and Michael Fellman. Baton Rouge: Louisiana State University Press, 1979. Using Mott as one of her examples, DuBois argues that women's organizational abilities acquired in the antislavery movement helped them in their women's rights activities.

Gurko, Miriam. *The Ladies of Seneca Falls: The Birth of the Women's Rights Movement*. New York: Schocken Books, 1976. Gurko devotes chapter six to a biography of Mott, and elsewhere analyzes her role in the 1848 Seneca Falls convention.

Lutz, Alma. *Crusade for Freedom: Women of the Antislavery Movement*. Boston: Beacon, 1968. This general study devotes several sections to Mott's role in the women's rights and antislavery movements.

Beverly Wilson Palmer
Pomona College

KATE RICHARDS O'HARE
1876-1948

Chronology

Born Carrie Katherine Richards on March 26, 1876, on a homestead near Minneapolis, Ottawa County, Kansas, the third of five children of Andrew and Lucy Sullivan Richards; *1887* experiences economic hardship as drought forces father into bankruptcy; *1888-1893* lives in slum in Kansas City, Missouri, where father eventually finds work as machinist; active in religious and social-purity causes; completes high school and works as vest-maker; *1892-1895* studies at normal school in Nebraska and teaches briefly; *1895* returns to Kansas City, works as machinist in father's shop, and converts to socialism after hearing Mary Harris "Mother" Jones speak; *1899-1901* joins, in succession, Socialist Labor Party, Social Democratic Party, and Socialist Party of America; *1901* studies to become Socialist organizer at International School of Social Economy in Girard, Kansas; *1902* marries Francis (Frank) Patrick O'Hare of St. Louis; *1902-1917* becomes one of Socialist Party's most effective speakers and writers; *1910* runs for House of Representatives in Second Congressional District of Kansas; *1911* joins editorial staff of *National Rip-Saw* (St. Louis) and helps build it into second largest Socialist newspaper in circulation; *1911-1913* recognized by election to Woman's National Committee and National Executive Committee of Socialist Party and to International Socialist Bureau in Brussels; *1916* runs for U.S. Senate in Missouri; *1917* chairs Committee on War and Militarism at party's Emergency Convention in St. Louis; is arrested, tried, and convicted under Espionage Act for antiwar speech at Bowman, North Dakota; *1919-1920* serves fourteen months of five-year term at Missouri State Penitentiary before sentence is commuted; becomes critic of American penology; *1920* resumes lecturing and publication of paper (renamed *Social Revolution* in 1917); *1922* organizes Children's Crusade as part of campaign for amnesty for wartime "political prisoners"; *1923* joins Llano Co-operative Colony in Leesville, Louisiana, where she continues paper as *American Vanguard* and helps found Commonwealth College; *1924* because of factional disputes, withdraws from Llano Colony and helps relocate Commonwealth College to Mena, Arkansas; *1924-1926* conducts study of contract labor in prisons, thereby contributing to congressional reforms in 1929; *1928* divorces Frank O'Hare, marries Charles C. Cunningham, a California engineer, and moves to West Coast; *1934* supports Upton Sinclair's "End Poverty in California" gubernatorial campaign; *1937-1938* serves on staff of Congressman Thomas R. Amlie of Wisconsin; *1939* as assistant director of Department of Penology, contributes to far-reaching reforms in California's prison system; *1948* dies in January of coronary thrombosis at home in Benicia, California, and remains are cremated.

Activities of Historical Significance

O'Hare's efforts as orator, party organizer, pamphleteer, and writer for numerous periodicals placed her in the front rank of American radicals during the heyday of the Socialist Party in the first two decades of the twentieth century. A tall, thin, motherly individual with a commanding presence, she alone rivaled perennial presidential candidate Eugene V. Debs as the party's most charismatic spokesperson in the nation's heartland. Especially in the Southwest, where weeklong summer "encampments" often drew thousands of dirt farmers, lumberjacks, miners, and railroad workers and their families, she drew upon local traditions of primitive Christianity and democracy and the Populist legacy to fuse an effective anti-capitalist message in native idiom. Her contribution to building the party's membership was great.

A mother of four children, O'Hare yielded some of her preference for "love, home, and babies" and regard for her own health to the demands of building the "Co-operative Commonwealth." She worked for a time in tandem with her first husband, himself a masterful publicist and strategist, but eventually eclipsed him in reputation among rank-and-file Socialists—an unusual accomplishment in a movement in which women, even those in leadership positions, traditionally worked in their husbands' shadows.

O'Hare's contributions as a writer were also prolific. In addition to her role as editor of the *National Rip-Saw,* she wrote for the *Appeal to Reason,* the *International Socialist Review,* and other party organs. In 1902-1903 she authored one of the first regular columns for Socialist women in the *Coming Nation.* Several of her periodical pieces enjoyed longevity as leaflets or pamphlets.

Brought up in a devout Disciples of Christ home, she had hoped to enter the ministry. She eventually rejected the church but not the moral fervor of her evangelical background. Distinguishing between "churchianity" and Christianity, she denounced the former for sham, bourgeois respectability, and disloyalty to the teachings of Christ, whom she continued to admire. This distinction, and the fact that she frequently drew upon biblical language, helped make her message palatable to the native-born Protestants who were her principal audience.

O'Hare gained a reputation as "Red Kate" after her indictment in 1917, and she is sometimes identified with the left wing on the party's ideological spectrum. She was, however, pragmatic and oriented toward the ballot box. A "constructive" Socialist, she endorsed numerous immediate demands, tempered orthodox Marxist opposition to private land ownership to appeal to farmers, and repudiated the direct-actionist Industrial Workers of the World. Believing that class exploitation was the cause of oppression for both blacks and women, O'Hare held that the struggle for socialism took precedence over the causes of racial and sexual equality. This belief, compounded by her own racial prejudice and the quest for white votes in the South, led her to employ race-baiting rhetoric and to propound, in her pamphlet *"Nigger" Equality* (1912), a separate-but-equal policy for a socialized America.

O'Hare campaigned actively for woman suffrage, decried the moral degradation of women under capitalism, and, by the mid-1910s, hesitantly supported the cause of birth control. Yet, remaining traditionalist in her views on women's roles and lagging behind younger socialist women in her commitment to sexual emancipation, she is best seen as a transitional figure in socialist feminism.

Her early and vocal opposition to World War I, highlighted by her role in shaping the party's position in 1917, her antiwar speeches, and her imprisonment, made O'Hare a significant figure in the antiwar and civil-liberties causes of that era. The abiding interest in penology she gained from her prison experience provided a second focus to her life, as the Socialist party's decline and her anti-Communist stance moved her toward the political mainstream.

Overview of Biographical Sources

There is as yet no comprehensive biography of O'Hare, and limited primary sources make the task of writing one formidable. Few sources on her childhood and adolescence have survived. During their marital difficulties in the 1920s, her first husband, Frank O'Hare, burned most of her personal papers. Since her career as a prominent Socialist was over by then, the loss of that material is tragic. Many of her party activities can be pieced together from accounts in numerous Socialist periodicals, and her contributions to those periodicals and other writings provide insight into her investigative forays into industrial conditions, ideological position, rhetorical style, and topical interests. Official party records offer limited information about her work in elective positions. Standard secondary works on the Socialist party usually mention O'Hare in passing, without much analysis. Despite the obstacles, the two closest students of her life, Neil K. Basen and Sally M. Miller, have both undertaken to write book-length biographies.

Evaluation of Principal Biographical Sources

Basen, Neil K. "Kate Richards O'Hare: The 'First Lady' of American Socialism, 1901-1917." *Labor History* 21 (Spring 1980): 165-199. (A, G) This is the most accurate, thoroughly researched, and detailed account available for the years indicated. It corrects factual errors, including the year of O'Hare's birth and circumstances of her early life, found in most previous works. Though the author is sympathetic to O'Hare and the Socialist movement, he offers critical judgments about her positions on racial and gender issues.

Brommel, Bernard J. "Kate Richards O'Hare: A Midwestern Pacifist's Fight for Free Speech." *North Dakota Quarterly* 44 (Winter 1976): 5-19. (A, G) Flawed by several inaccuracies about O'Hare's early life, this article focuses on her speech in Bowman, a local political controversy that her defense contended was behind her prosecution, and her trial. It offers little interpretation other than implicit criticism of the judge's conduct of the trial.

Buhle, Mari Jo. *Women and American Socialism, 1870-1920.* Urbana: University of Illinois Press, 1981. (A) In the chapter entitled "Sexual Emancipation," Buhle offers the most sensitive interpretation in print of O'Hare's feminism: a combination—not successfully reconciled—of the beliefs that the exploitation and moral degradation of women derived entirely from economic causes (i.e., capitalist inequality) and that women were also exploited as a sex. O'Hare's endorsement of birth control receives special emphasis.

Cobb, William H. "Commonwealth College Comes to Arkansas, 1923-1925." *Arkansas Historical Quarterly* 23 (Summer 1964): 99-122. (A, G) In this very detailed account of the internal disputes in the Llano Colony that led to the relocation of Commonwealth College in Arkansas, Cobb discusses briefly the decision of Kate and Frank O'Hare to join the colony, the place of their *American Vanguard* in the controversy, and Kate's instrumental role in starting the college.

Green, James R. *Grass-Roots Socialism: Radical Movements in the Southwest, 1895-1943.* Baton Rouge: Louisiana State University Press, 1978. (A, G) Given his focus on the region where O'Hare spent most of her time as a Socialist agitator, Green covers her more extensively than do most authors of secondary works. The summer encampments; O'Hare's equivocations on race and private farm ownership; her role in building the party in the Southwest, in campaigns for woman's suffrage, and in the antiwar movement; and the impact of the *National Rip-Saw* all receive careful interpretation in the context of southwestern Socialist activity.

Hanley, Marla Martin. "The Children's Crusade of 1922: Kate Richards O'Hare and the Campaign to Free Radical War Dissenters in the Era of America's First Red Scare." *Gateway Heritage* 10 (Summer 1989): 34-43. (A, G) Hanley sympathetically recounts O'Hare's role in organizing a march of children of imprisoned war critics as part of a wider amnesty movement.

Lovin, Hugh. "The Banishment of Kate Richards O'Hare." *Idaho Yester-days* 22 (Spring 1978): 20-25. (**A, G**) In an interesting, though not very significant, slice of local history in the aftermath of the Red Scare, Lovin tells the story of O'Hare's abduction from Twin Falls, Idaho, on July 1, 1921, by men determined to prevent her from speaking there during a western tour, her transportation across the Nevada border, and unsuccessful efforts to have her abductors apprehended by state and local authorities.

Miller, Sally M., ed. *Flawed Liberation: Socialism and Feminism.* Westport, CT: Greenwood Press, 1981. (**A**) References to O'Hare in chapters by Miller and Neil K. Basen relate her to the work of Socialist women and to the attitudes of male Socialists toward them.

Shannon, David A. *The Socialist Party of America: A History.* New York: Macmillan, 1955. (**A, G**) This pioneering history provides occasional references to O'Hare's role among western Socialists. Shannon erroneously has her imprisoned at Leavenworth.

Weinstein, James. *The Decline of Socialism in America, 1912-1925.* New York: Monthly Review Press, 1967. (**A**) Weinstein integrates O'Hare into his history of the Socialist party and includes valuable information about her political orientation in the 1920s.

Overview and Evaluation of Primary Sources
O'Hare's writings reflect the qualities that made her an effective speaker. She employs vivid imagery, drawn from the daily lives of working-class Americans and laced with deprecative humor about the evils of capitalism. She appeals directly to both heart and mind. In the genre of Socialist "conversion" stories, her "How I Became a Socialist Agitator" (*Socialist Woman* 2; October 1908: 4-5; **A, G**) recounts her radicalization. She relates some of her experiences in religious rescue work in Kansas City in the pamphlet *Church and the Social Problem* (St. Louis: National Rip-Saw, 1911; **A, G**). *Law and the White Slaver, "Nigger" Equality,* and *Socialism and the World War* (St. Louis: National Rip-Saw, 1911, 1912, and 1919; **A, G**), and *Wimmin Ain't Got No Kick* (Chicago: Socialist Party, Woman's National Committee, n.d.; **A, G**) were among her other influential pamphlets. Her longest discussion of women's issues—including love, marriage, white slavery, child and female labor, and intemperance—can be found in *The Sorrows of Cupid* (a revised and enlarged version of *Whatever Happened to Dan?* [1904]; St. Louis: National Rip-Saw, 1912; **A, G, Y**) Prior to U.S. intervention in the First World War, she and Frank P. O'Hare wrote *World Peace: A Spectacle*

Drama in Three Acts (St. Louis: National Rip-Saw, 1915; **A, G, Y**), which was widely performed before Socialist and other antiwar audiences.

Besides her regular contributions as an editor of the *National Rip-Saw* (and its successors *Social Revolution* and *American Vanguard*), she wrote numerous articles for other Socialist papers, including the *Appeal to Reason* (Girard, Kansas) and the *International Socialist Review* (Chicago). Her observations about prison conditions, first published privately by Frank P. O'Hare in 1920, were reprinted as *In Prison* (New York: Alfred A. Knopf, 1923; **A, G**).

Little remains of O'Hare's correspondence, and what does is scattered among several archives. The Tamiment Institute Library at New York University has a selection of photographs, pamphlets, and letters (mostly from the immediate postwar years). The inventory to the Socialist Party Collection at the Perkins Library of Duke University lists only one O'Hare item, but there may be other correspondence in this large collection of radical materials. The Kate Richards O'Hare Papers and Frank P. O'Hare Papers at the Missouri Historical Society in St. Louis contain a more substantial, but still fragmentary array of materials. These include "Dear Sweethearts," a volume of 124 letters O'Hare wrote to her family during her imprisonment. The most accessible collection of her writings is Philip S. Foner and Sally M. Miller, eds., *Kate Richards O'Hare: Selected Writings and Speeches* (Baton Rouge: Louisiana State University Press, 1982; **A, G, Y**). Accompanied by a fine interpretive introduction, this volume contains a representative sample of prewar articles, antiwar writings (including the speech for which she was convicted, her courtroom speech prior to her sentencing, and a farewell address before she entered prison), prison letters, excerpts from *In Prison*, and several selections from the 1920s and 1930s.

Fiction and Adaptations

In "She Stirred Up the People," a chapter in *Twelve Daughters of Democracy: True Stories of American Women, 1865-1930* (1941), Eleanor Sickels offers a heroic rendition of O'Hare's idealism, opposition to injustice, wartime conviction, and work for prison reform, but ignores her socialist indictment of industrial capitalism. Though much of the information is correct, made-up dialogue and a heavy admixture of inaccuracies give this account the character of a historical fiction.

Other Sources

Burke, Robert E. *Olson's New Deal for California.* Berkeley: University of California Press, 1953. Burke describes the prison reforms in California to which O'Hare contributed in the late 1930s, but does not delineate her specific role.

Dubofsky, Melvyn. "Kate Richards O'Hare Cunningham." In *Dictionary of American Biography: Supplement 4, 1946-1950*, edited by John A. Garraty and Edward T. James. New York: Scribner's, 1974. This sketch is a useful skeletal introduction to O'Hare's life.

Goldman, Emma. *Living My Life*. 2 vols. New York: Alfred A. Knopf, 1931. A fellow "political prisoner" at the Missouri State Penitentiary, the anarchist Goldman offers personal impressions of O'Hare and credits her with using her outside connections to gain improvements in prison conditions.

Shannon, David A. "Kate Richards O'Hare Cunningham." In *Notable American Women, 1607-1950: A Biographical Dictionary*, edited by Edward T. James. Cambridge: Harvard University Press, 1971. A basic overview.

Shore, Elliott. *Talkin' Socialism: J. A. Wayland and the Role of the Press in American Radicalism, 1890-1912*. Lawrence: University Press of Kansas, 1988. Though it mentions O'Hare only a few times, this is a valuable study of the Socialist movement in the Midwest and Southwest, the regions where her impact was greatest.

Jacob H. Dorn
Wright State University

OSCEOLA
c. 1804-1838

Chronology

Born c. 1804 in Creek country in what is now Georgia or Alabama; there is no record of his birth name; name of his father, who dies early in Osceola's life, is not known; his mother, a Creek, is known as Polly Copinger; after the death of husband, she marries a man known as Powell [or Powel]; Osceola is known as Billy Powell as he is growing up. *1804-1826* family is forced to move frequently because of harassment by whites; eventually, Osceola, with mother and grandmother, settles in north Florida; assumes manhood name of Osceola, (varient spellings: Asseola, Assiola, Oceola, Oseola and others), generally believed to mean "Black Drink Singer" from Asi (black drink) plus Yaholo (singer); assists the medicine man with the ritual black drink given at the Green Corn Festival; begins to think of himself as a Florida Indian or Seminole; assists the army at Fort King as scout or reservation line runner; always talks through an interpreter but seems to understand English. *1826* marries Che-cho-ter or Morning Dew and by most accounts has four children; *1832* opposes Treaty of Payne's Landing signed by fifteen Seminole chiefs, who agree to removal across the Mississippi in three years to join Creeks; *1833* rejects treaty of Fort Gibson where lesser chiefs, led by Charley Emathla, agree to immediate removal; begins to assume leadership of Seminoles, although not born to rank or formally elected; *1835* takes second wife; some reports claim she is part Negro; *April 1835* present at meeting with General Wiley Thompson, the Indian agent, to persuade rest of chiefs to acknowledge Payne's Landing Treaty; allegedly, plunges knife into paper instead of signing; *June 1835* argues with Thompson and is put in irons; feigns change of heart, agrees to sign treaty, and is released; *December 1835* along with other braves, murders Wiley Thompson and Lt. Smith; murders Charley Emathla who is preparing to emigrate; war commences; *December 1835* Battle of Withlacoochie where Native Americans decisively defeat whites; writes letter of defiance to the U.S. Calvary commander, General Clinch; Native Americans withdraw to Everglades with families, wage guerilla warfare, and engage in small battles; *1836* occupies Fort Drane, which has been abandoned; contracts malaria; *1837* accompanied by other chiefs, attends parley with General Thomas S. Jesup under flag of truce; all are seized and imprisoned at St. Augustine; becomes hero with the American public because of courage and manner of capture; *1838* is moved to Fort Moultrie, Charleston, South Carolina, where he dies on January 30 of quinsy complicated by malaria; two wives and two children are in attendance; given full military funeral; after his death his head is removed and exhibited, with assistance of Dr. Weedon, the attending physician

Activities of Historical Significance

As the Seminole leader during the Second Seminole War (1835-1837), Osceola inspired the Seminoles to resist removal from Florida to Mississippi. His military genius cost the Americans over $30 million and about fifteen thousand deaths. He became a hero to both Native Americans and whites, as well as to slaves, whose runaways he protected. It is largely his legacy that, despite a federal policy of removal, there are still Seminoles in Florida today. The U.S. Court of Claims has ruled (1964) that the Seminoles of Florida and Oklahoma are entitled to compensation for the lands taken away from them at the Treaty of Moultrie Creek. His legend remains a source of pride and an example to his people.

Overview of Biographical Sources

Little is known about Osceola before the advent of the Second Seminole War. There has been a single substantial biography, *Osceola, the Unconqured Indian* by William and Ellen Hartley (1973). A short biography is included with those of other Native American chiefs in Alvin M. Josephy's *Patriot Chiefs: A Chronicle of American Indian Leadership* (1961); and there are a number of children's biographies. Histories of the Second Seminole War provide information for that period of Osceola's life. The studies cited below by Coe, Mahon, and Sprague are particularly useful. In 1955 the *Florida Historical Quarterly* produced a special "Osceola Issue."

Evaluation of Principal Biographical Sources

Coe, Charles H. *Red Patriots, the Story of the Seminoles.* Gainesville: University Presses of Florida, 1974. (A) A facsimile of the 1898 edition with an introduction by Charleton W. Tebeau. The author, a printer, became sympathetic to the Seminoles while he lived in Florida, and he continued his research on them after moving to Washington, D.C., Coe argues the right of Native Americans to remain in Florida. He uses most of the contemporary printed sources, as well as documentary sources, that he found in Washington. He tries, without success, to trace Osceola's family.

Florida Historical Quarterly 33, 3/4 (1955). (A) This special issue devoted to Osceola includes articles on his history, appearance, parentage, decendants, and relationship with blacks.

Hartley, William, and Ellen Hartley. *Osceola, the Unconquered Indian.* New York: Hawthorne, 1973. (**A, G**) The only full-length, adult biography available. This synthesis of the literature on Osceola is readable and reasonably accurate. The authors have read widely in the primary and secondary sources, but they perpetuate some myths, and there is some improvisation and contrived dialogue. Includes photographs, footnotes, and index.

Josephy, Alvin M. *Patriot Chiefs: A Chronicle of American Indian Leadership.* New York: Viking, 1961. (**A, G**) Osceola is one of nine chiefs chronicled in this work. In a brief factual account, Josephy pictures him as a freedom fighter and places him in the broad historical context. Contains maps, an index, and bibliography.

Mahon, John K. *History of the Second Seminole War, 1835-1942.* Gainsville: University of Florida Press, 1967. (**A**) Mahon's history gives excellent coverage to Osceola's part in the Seminole War. He claims to have read or examined every known manuscript on Osceola to date. The study sets the war in its historical context and demonstrates its connection with the issue of slavery.

Sprague, John T. *Origin, Progress, and Conclusion of the Florida War.* Gainsville: University of Florida Press, 1964. (**A**) Facsimile of 1848 edition with an introduction by John K. Mahon. Sprague was a major in the U.S. Army. His comprehensive study combines research with his personal experience. He considers Osceola a brave and generous enemy. Half of book consists of documents.

Evaluation of Biographies for Young People

Alderman, Clifford Lindsey. *Osceola and the Seminole Wars.* Englewood Cliffs, NJ: Messner, 1973. Factual, interesting, and well-written, this work treats both sides objectively. Confirms that little is known about Osceola's family. Includes an index, an outstanding annotated bibliography, and reading list.

Blassingame, Wyatt. *Osceola, Seminole War Chief.* Champaign, IL: Garrard, 1967. One of Garrard's American Indian Series, supervised by anthropologist Alice Marriott. A brief popular, workmanlike biography, plentifully illustrated, and with a map to show historical places.

Grant, Matthew G. *Osceola and the Seminole War.* Sacramento, CA: Cougar Books/Creative Editions, 1974. Historically accurate, but Grant admits there is scant biographical information on the subject. Attractive format, illustrations on almost every page, large print and easy vocabulary for younger grades.

McNeer, May Yonge. *War Chief of the Seminoles*. New York, Random House, 1954. A full-length bibliograpy for young people (grades 5-9). The author is a descendant of Dr. Weedon, who attended Osceola in prison. She writes with sympathy for the Seminoles but without sentimentality.

Overview and Evaluation of Primary Sources

Documentation about Osceola commenced with the onset of the Second Seminole War. Letters can be found for this period in the Adjutant General's Office, Old Files Division and Records Division, the National Archives, Washington, D.C. and in the Missionary Letters Collection of the Harvard-Andover Theological Library. Further information can be found in American State Papers: Indian Affairs. Washington, 1832-1834, and the Territorial Papers of the United States, vols. 7-26: Florida Territory, 1856-1862, compiled by Clarence E. Carter, (Bureau of Indian Affairs, Washington, D.C.), which contain unpublished correspondence, reports, and journals of events.

Fiction and Adaptations

In 1976 O. Z. Tyler, a colonel in the U.S. Army, published a blank verse poem, *Osceola, Seminole Chief: An Unremembered Saga* (Ocoee, FL: Anna Publishers, 1976), that is well-researched, and contains footnotes, an index, and a lengthy bibliography. It would probably have been more useful and less tedious if written in prose.

Museums, Historical Landmarks, Societies

Historical Association of Southern Florida (Miami, FL). Collection contains material on the Seminoles, including books, tapes, microforms, contemporary newspapers, maps, pictures, and slides.

Hillsborough County Historical Museum (Tampa, FL). Contains books, periodicals, and other materials relating to the Seminoles.

Smithsonian Institution (Washington, DC). Has death-cast of Osceola.

Fort Marion (St. Augustine, FL). Contains the room where Osceola was held prisoner. Open to the public.

Other Sources
   Dictionary of American Biography. New York, Scribner's, 1928-1936 (vol. 14): 76-77. Concise thumbnail sketch with bibliography.

   Handbook of American Indians North of Mexico. Washington, DC: Smithsonian Institution/Bureau of American Ethnology, 1910 (GPO Bulletin 30): 159. A brief accurate account.

   Foreman, Grant. *Indian Removal, the Emigration of the Five Civilized Tribes of Indians.* Norman: University of Oklahoma Press, 1932. Book five, covering the Second Seminole War, provides an "uncolored day-to-day recital of events" with no interpretation. Author uses primary documents, contemporary newspapers, and government documents.

   Welch, Andrew. *A Narrative of Oceola Nikhanochee with a History of Oceola.* Gainesville: University Presses of Florida, 1977. Facsimile of the 1841 edition. The author, a physician from England, adopted Nikhanochee, whom he believed was a relative of the elder Osceola. This work includes an admiring account of the life of Osceola.

   McCarthy, Joseph E. *Portraits of Osceola and the Artists Who Painted Them.* Jacksonville, FL: Jacksonville Historical Society Papers, vol. 2, 1949.

Patricia Brauch
Brooklyn College, City University of New York

JESSE OWENS
1913-1980

Chronology

Born James Cleveland Owens on September 12, 1913, in Oakville, Alabama, the last of ten surviving children (three others died in childbirth) of Henry Cleveland Owens, a sharecropper and son of slaves, and Mary Emma Fitzgerald; *1913-1922* grows up in rural Alabama in abject poverty, troubled by several bouts with pneumonia and mysterious lumps on his legs and chest; *1922-1933* attends public schools in Cleveland where his family moves in search of employment; *1928* sets world age group records in the high jump and long jump while attending Fairmount Junior High School; *1933* sets a world record of 20.7 seconds in the 220-yard dash and ties the world record of 9.4 seconds in the 100-yard dash while a senior at Cleveland East Technical High School; *1933-1936* attends Ohio State University but does not return after the 1936 Olympics; *May 25, 1935* sets world records in the 220-yard low hurdles, the 220-yard dash, and the long jump and ties the world record in the 100-yard dash, all within one hour; *1935* marries Minnie Ruth Soloman with whom he will have three daughters; *1936* wins gold medals at the Berlin Olympics in the 100- and 200-meter dashes, the long jump, and the 4x100-meter relay; on the day of the final ceremonies in Berlin the Amateur Athletic Union ends Owens amateur career when it suspends him for refusing to compete in an exhibition in Sweden; returns to the U.S. and receives $10,000 to campaign for Alf Landon for President; runs in a series of well-paid exhibitions, including the first of several races against a horse; *1937-1941* continues making personal appearances, including leading a touring band; works as a playground director in Cleveland and starts a dry cleaner business; *1939* declares bankruptcy; *1942* is appointed by the Office of Civil Defense to help train black soldiers; *1943* moves to Detroit to work in public relations for Ford Motor Company; briefly sells sporting goods; continues giving exhibitions, including running several handicapped races against Helen Stephens, the women's 1936 100-meter gold medalist; tours with the Harlem Globe Trotters; *1949* moves to Chicago to work in public relations for several businesses; becomes increasingly popular as an inspirational and motivational speaker, especially during the height of the Cold War; *1950* Associated Press votes him "Athlete of the Half Century"; *1951-1952* serves as Director of the South Side Boys Club; *1953* is appointed Secretary of the Illinois State Athletic Commission; *1955* tours Asia as goodwill ambassador for the U.S. State Department; *1956* is appointed Executive Director of the Illinois Youth Commission; *1963* launches Owens-West and Associates, a sales and promotions agency; *1964* begins a life-long relationship with the Atlantic Richfield

Company, including staging their annual Jesse Owens Games for Boys and Girls; *1965* indicted and convicted in Federal Court for not filing tax returns for 1954-1962; *1968* publicly criticizes John Carlos and Tommy Smith's black-glove salute on the victory stand at the Mexico City Olympics; *1970* publishes *Blackthink*, an uncompromising attack on black militancy; *1971* is sent on a goodwill mission to Africa by President Nixon; *1973* appointed to the Board of Directors of the United States Olympic Committee; *1974* receives the National Collegiate Athletic Association's Theodore Roosevelt Award for distinguished achievement since leaving competitive athletics; is inducted as a charter member into the Track and Field Hall of Fame; *1976* receives the Presidential Medal of Freedom, the nation's highest civilian award; *1979* receives the Living Legends Award from President Carter; *1980* dies of lung cancer on March 31 in Tucson, Arizona.

Activities of Historical Significance

Arguably only Babe Ruth has enjoyed greater recognition among American sports fans than Jesse Owens, the man who was voted the greatest athlete of the first half of the 20th century by the Associated Press in 1950.

Owens began breaking world track and field records in 1928 while still in junior high school and did not stop until the AAU ended his amateur career shortly after his triumph in Berlin in 1936. He won seventy-five of seventy-nine races while a schoolboy, setting a world record of 20.7 seconds in the 220-yard dash in 1933. On May 25, 1935 he enjoyed perhaps the single greatest day in track and field history when in the course of a single hour at the Big Ten Conference Championship in Ann Arbor, Michigan, he broke world records in the 220-yard low hurdles (22.6 seconds), the 220-yard dash (20.3 seconds), and the long jump (26 feet, eight and one-quarter inches) and tied the world record in the 100-yard dash (9.4 seconds). His long jump record remained unsurpassed for twenty-five years.

Owens is best known for winning Olympic gold medals in the 100- and 200-meter dashes, the long jump, and the 4x100-meter relay at Berlin in 1936. Many admirers, and later Owens himself, saw these extraordinary victories as a personal defeat for Hitler and his racial policies.

Throughout his life Owens stood as a national symbol, admired by practically everyone, although often for different reasons. White Americans proudly cited him as an example of how anyone could rise above race or class to achieve individual greatness. Blacks embraced him because he greatly surpassed his competition at a time when racial boundaries permitted little opportunity to do so. Along with his contemporary, Joe Louis, Owens also inspired at least two generations of black youngsters to pursue dreams of athletic greatness.

Politically and socially conservative and noncontroversial, the personable and indefatigable Owens became one of America's most popular public speakers. His inspirational but conciliatory addresses proved appealing to corporations, service organizations, and youth groups, especially after the Civil Rights movement became increasingly divisive in the late 1960s and 1970s. A life-long Republican, he served both the Eisenhower and Nixon administrations as a globe-trotting, goodwill ambassador. Black Americans always took great pride in his athletic accomplishments, but during the late-1960s many found his public pronouncements to be outdated, embarrassing apologies for the country's inability or unwillingness to deal effectively with its racial problems.

Overview of Biographical Sources

William Baker's superb and scholarly *Jesse Owens: An American Life* (1986) is the only full-length biography of Owens. There are several brief biographies, but these tend to target juvenile audiences and chronicle the popular, and often mythical, stories Owens himself told in his speeches and in the four autobiographies he wrote with Paul Neimark. Readers should compare the countless articles about Owens in major periodicals to assess the considerable symbolic importance he had for these audiences. Articles in such magazines as *Reader's Digest, Life, TV Guide, Newsweek,* and *Time,* can be compared with those appearing in publications that target a primarily black audience, such as *Ebony* and *Crisis.* Metropolitan newspapers where Owens once lived such as the *Cleveland Plain Dealer, Detroit Free Press,* and *Chicago Tribune,* as well as the *New York Times,* followed his career closely, as did such black newspapers as the *Cleveland Call and Post, Cleveland Gazette, Michigan Chronicle, Chicago Defender, Pittsburgh Courier, New Amsterdam News,* and *Baltimore Afro American.*

Evaluation of Principal Biographical Sources

Baker, William J. *Jesse Owens: An American Life.* New York: Macmillan, 1986. (A, G) Baker presents the man behind the myths in this scholarly, objective, and meticulously detailed study. Baker portrays Owens as a warm, generous, friendly, patient and unwavering patriot who always tried to do what was expected of him. But he also described him as an insensitive, self-centered, greedy man who willingly went along with those seeking financial gains by exploiting his fame. Owens's human foibles were all too common, but Baker does not allow them to overshadow his athletic and public greatness.

Gentry, Tony. *Jesse Owens*. New York: Chelsea House, 1989. (**Y**) This 122-page biography, containing many superb photographs, is a fine addition to the fifty-volume Black Americans of Achievement Series. While applauding Owens's great athletic talents and his considerable public service, Gentry does not ignore the real problems he faced both in himself and in the often hostile world around him. The result is a realistic and truthful portrayal for young readers.

Sabin, Francene. *Jesse Owens, Olympic Hero*. Mahwah, NJ: Troll, 1985. (**Y**) Part of the Easy Biographies series for elementary school children, this biography takes Owens through his childhood and Olympic victories in forty-eight pages that contain more myths than facts about the man.

Overview and Evaluation of Primary Sources

Jesse Owens collaborated with Paul Neimark on four books about his life. Each contains the familiar stories made popular by his speeches, and each is filled with factual errors and contradictions. Nevertheless, these books present a fascinating chronicle of a black superstar in a white man's world. *The Jesse Owens Story* (New York: Putnam, 1970; **G, Y**) contains all the myths an adoring public had come to associate with Owens's brief but spectacular athletic career. Among other things, he reflects on his humble and sickly beginnings, his working three jobs during high school and college, his inspirational friendship with Luz Long, and the alleged snub by Hitler.

Owens's controversial *Blackthink: My Life as Black Man and White Man* (New York: William Morrow, 1970; **A, G**) is a strident attack on black militancy. Owens warns readers that black militants were driving off liberal whites and destroying any chance for understanding between the races. *Blackthink* abounds with platitudes about opportunity and self-reliance. Owens uses the familiar stories of his own life as examples of how whites have helped blacks, but the cited examples occurred during his athletic career rather than during his often futile search for meaningful employment in his later years. This book was well received by most white reviewers and excerpted in *Reader's Digest*. Black critics were not enthusiastic about the memoir.

Clearly surprised and hurt by his black critics, Owens wrote *I Have Changed* (New York: William Morrow, 1972; **A, G**) as an apologia for many of the views he expressed in *Blackthink*. Owens was genuinely disturbed that so many blacks believed he had sold out to the white establishment. *I Have Changed* is a rather plaintive cry for readers to understand that his too was a noteworthy struggle. *Jesse: The Man Who Outran Hitler* (New York: Random House, 1978; **A, G, Y**) chronicles Owens's search for spiritual salvation. Owens was 64 years old and in poor health when he set out on what he calls a spiritual journey. The result was a return to the same familiar territory that he had written about in his previous memoirs, but this time he sought some higher meaning to his life.

Jesse Owens also wrote a short track and field manual entitled *Track and Field*, edited by Dick O'Connor (New York: Atheneum, 1976; **Y**). This 120-page volume in Atheneum's Instructional Books Series introduces the beginning athlete to the basic techniques of track and field buttressed by Owens's inspirational comments on the value of sports, morality, and life.

There are several recordings of interviews with Owens. Barbara Moro's 1961 interviews with Owens and his wife Ruth are transcribed in the Illinois State Historical Library, Springfield, Illinois. The Atlantic Richfield Company Archives in Los Angeles, California, also has transcribed its interviews with him.

Owens has also appeared in many Olympic documentaries, including *Jesse Owens Returns to Berlin* (New York: Cappy Productions, 1968). Narrated by Owens himself and written, produced, and directed by Olympic filmmaker Bud Greenspan, this documentary provides an excellent showcase for Owens's inspirational and effective speaking talents. The film's most moving moment focuses on Owens's chatting with Karl Long, the son of Luz Long, the German who befriended Owens during their long jump competition in Berlin. The film contains excellent coverage of Owens competing, but, as with most footage featuring him at Berlin, it never credits its source, Leni Riefenstahl, the legendary German filmmaker whose magnificent documentary, *Olympia*, was completed shortly after the Games themselves.

Fiction and Adaptations

The Jesse Owens Story (1984), written by Harold Gast, produced by Harve Bennett Productions in Association with Paramount Television, and directed by Richard Irving, is a three-and-one-half hour, made-for-television movie, starring Dorian Harewood as Jesse Owens. The film contains the stories so central to his autobiographies, but treats them more accurately than Owens did himself. It devotes considerable footage to his public service, his work with disadvantaged youngsters, and his life with his wife, Ruth Soloman Owens. It does a respectable job of portraying Hitler's alleged refusal to shake Owens's hand but highly romanticizes Owens's relationship with Luz Long. One of the film's most interesting scenes involves the controversial decision of the American coaches to remove the two Jewish athletes from their 4x100-meter relay team, a decision that Owens supposedly tried to prevent. The film portrays his unwillingness to make waves, but is most unconvincing when it suggests that Owens's IRS tax problems stemmed from his need to strike back at the system that had so often misused him.

Museums, Historical Landmarks, Societies
Jesse Owens Strasse (Berlin, Germany). Street leading to the Olympic stadium.

Jesse Owens Track and *Jesse Owens Recreational Center* (Columbus, OH). Buildings located at Ohio State University, named in Owens's honor and dedicated October 4, 1980.

Monument (Oakville, AL). Four-foot tall marble monument set near Owens's birthplace.

Other Sources
Ashe, Arthur R., Jr. *A Hard Road to Glory: A History of the African-American Athlete, 1919-1945.* New York: Warner Books, 1988. This superb history contains a brief, objective account of Owens's life, especially as it related to other black athletes of his era.

Carlson, Lewis H. and John J. Fogarty. *Tales of Gold: an Oral History of the Summer Olympic Games Told by America's Gold Medal Winners.* Chicago: Contemporary Books, 1987. This oral history includes the remembrances of many of Owens's 1936 Olympic teammates. It also includes the accounts of several later black Olympians who credited Owens for inspiring their own pursuit of athletic greatness.

William O. Johnson. *All That Glitters Is Not Gold.* New York: Putnam, 1972. Johnson's irreverent history of the Olympic games cuts behind the glitter to describe incidents not usually found in chronicles of the Games. Johnson was also one of the few white reporters to criticize Owens for his platitudinous speeches and his unflagging willingness to please the white establishment.

Lewis H. Carlson
Western Michigan University

CISSY PATTERSON
1881-1948

Chronology

Born Eleanor Josephine Patterson on November 7, 1881, in Chicago, the daughter of Robert Wilson Patterson, Jr., publisher of the *Chicago Tribune,* and Elinor Medill, daughter of Joseph Medill, former publisher of the *Chicago Tribune*; adopts name Eleanor Medill Patterson and nickname "Cissy" in her youth; *1896-1899* attends Miss Hersey's School, Boston; *1899-1901* attends Miss Porter's School, Farmington, Connecticut; *1904* marries Count Joseph Gizycki and moves to Moravia, Russian Poland (divorced 1917); *1908* returns to the U.S.; *1925* marries Elmer Schlesinger, a corporate lawyer (died 1929); *1930* hired by William Randolph Hearst as editor, then publisher of *Washington Herald*; *1939* purchases *Washington Herald* and *Washington Times,* which she combines into one paper; *1948* dies on July 24, in Washington, D.C.

Activities of Historical Significance

Patterson did not achieve eminence until the last ten years of her life. As publisher of the *Washington Times-Herald,* she was one of the nation's leading press magnates. *Collier's* magazine called her "the most powerful woman in America" and *Time* found her "the most hated woman in America." In 1939 she bought the *Times-Herald* when it was fourth in circulation among Washington's five dailies. By 1943 it led the city in circulation and made a profit for the first time in years. She entered the newspaper business a novice, but learned quickly. Ruling with an iron hand, she revamped the entire newspaper. Seeking to attract female readership, she invented the modern woman's page and recruited so many women reporters that *Time* referred to the paper as "Cissy's Henhouse." She created a prototype gossip-and-scandal section called Page 3. She was the first person to cable fashion news out of Paris. Respected for her strong news sense, she possessed an instinct for good prose, ~hotography, and typography.

Politically she was a strong New Dealer, even backing Franklin Roosevelt for a third term. When Roosevelt called for lend-lease, however, she was convinced the president sought all-out war and opposed him bitterly. The president in turn cast aspersion on the patriotism of her whole family, and she, her brother Captain Joseph Medill Patterson, publisher of the *New York Daily News,* and Colonel Robert R. McCormick, publisher of the *Chicago Tribune*, were referred to as "The Three Furies." Yet the family's archnationalism and isolationism were of long standing, far antedating FDR.

Her personality had many facets. Arthur Brisbane, her journalistic father-confessor, called her "The Bird of Paradise." Writer Adela Rogers St. John thought of her as the reincarnation of Queen Elizabeth I. Cissy referred to herself as "just a plain old vindictive shanty Irish bitch." She was famous for her feuds with such people as Alice Roosevelt Longworth, columnist Drew Pearson (who had married and divorced her estranged daughter Felicia), columnist Walter Winchell, and cabinet member Harold Ickes. An erratic, lonely woman, her impulsive cruelties are more remembered than her acts of kindness.

Overview of Biographical Sources

There is still no biography that does justice to Patterson as a woman and as a journalist. For many years, the account most cited was a hostile one, John Tebbel's *An American Dynasty: The Story of the McCormicks, Medills, and Pattersons* (1947). The image changed in such favorable journalistic biographies as Paul F. Healy, *Cissy* (1961), and Alice Albright Hoge, *Cissy Patterson* (1970). Even the more critical Ralph G. Martin, *Cissy* (1979), shows a far more complex woman than is typically revealed.

Evaluation of Principal Biographical Sources

Healy, Paul F. *Cissy: The Biography of Eleanor M. "Cissy" Patterson.* Garden City, NY: Doubleday, 1961. (G) The author, a Washington columnist and White House correspondent for the *New York Daily News,* stresses the journalistic aspects of her career.

Hoge, Alice Albright. *Cissy Patterson.* New York: Random House, 1970. (G) Written by her grandniece, this is a thin account, though helpful on personal and family background.

Martin, Ralph G. *Cissy.* New York: Simon and Schuster, 1979. (G) The first two-thirds of this book offers a serious, if error-filled, exploration of Cissy's life, even if the perspective is more like a tempestuous romance than an orthodox biography. Martin focuses on the unfaithful Polish count with his "cruel nostrils;" Cissy's affairs with German ambassador Count von Ber-storff, diplomat William Bullitt, and a Wyoming cowboy; and her contemplation of Louis XVI chairs and gold taffeta. This, however, brings the reader only to 1938. When Martin finally discusses her role as a journalist, his superficial treatment fails to engage the exhausted reader.

Fiction and Adaptions

Under the name Eleanor Gizycki, Patterson wrote two autobiographical novels. *Glass House* (titled *André en Amérique* in French, 1923; in English, 1926), a witty if cruel satire on Washington society, refers to her rivalry with Alice Roosevelt Longworth over Senator William E. Borah. *Fall Flight* (1928) deals with her childhood, youth, life in pre-revolutionary Russia, and marriage to Count Gizycki. Her preface contains a perceptive self-analysis. Her daughter also wrote two novels both of which attacked Cissy: *The House of Violence* (1932) and *Flower and Smoke* (1939).

Other Sources

Brinkley, David. *Washington Goes to War.* New York: Knopf, 1988. Discusses Patterson's prominent role in the Washington of World War II.

Cheney, Lynne. "The Countess of Flat Creek." *Annals of Wyoming* 55:2 (1983): 28-32. A brief sketch of Patterson's life, with emphasis on the ranch she built at Flat Creek, Wyoming.

Denker, David. "Eleanor Medill Patterson." In *Notable American Women,* edited by Edward T. James. Cambridge, MA: Belknap Press, 1971. Though candid on her personality, Denker stresses her journalistic astuteness.

Ickes, Harold. *The Secret Diary of Harold L. Ickes.* 3 vols. New York: Simon and Schuster, 1953-1954. Franklin Roosevelt's acerbic secretary of the interior first reveals genuine affection for Patterson, then shows why the relation cooled.

Tebbel, John. *An American Dynasty: The Story of the McCormicks, Medills and Pattersons.* Garden City, NY: Doubleday, 1947. Contains a brief if hostile treatment of Patterson.

Waldrop, Frank C. *McCormick of Chicago: An Unconventional Portrait of a Controversial Figure.* Englewood Cliffs, NJ: Prentice-Hall, 1966. In this biography of the powerful publisher of the *Chicago Tribune,* who was Patterson's cousin, the former editor-in-chief of the *Washington Times-Herald* gives an insider's view of Cissy.

Justus D. Doenecke
New College of the
University of South Florida

DANIEL PAYNE
1811-1893

Chronology

Born Daniel Alexander Payne on February 24, 1811, in Charleston, South Carolina, son of London and Martha Payne, two free-born blacks; *1819-1823* both parents die before he reaches his ninth birthday; becomes the ward of his grandaunt, Sarah Bordeaux, who enrolls him in the Minor's Moralist Society school, where he studies for three years under the tutelage of Thomas S. Bonneau, one of the best educated blacks in Charleston; *1824-1825* enters the carpenter trade of his brother-in-law, Charles Holloway; educates himself by studying botany, geography, natural philosophy, chemistry and astronomy; *1826* joins the Cumberland Street Methodist Episcopal Church; experiences a religious conversion after which he receives a "call" to be an educator of black people; *1829* opens his first school for black youths but the school falters because of lack of interest in the black community; *1830* reopens his school; damages his left eye by watching a total eclipse; school expands dramatically, offering courses in arts and sciences; *1835* South Carolina General Assembly, fearing unrest among slaves, outlaws black education, forcing him to close his school; leaves South Carolina for Pennsylvania, where he enrolls at Gettysburg Seminary and studies theology under the famous Lutheran educators, Samuel S. Schmucker and Charles Krauth; *1837-1839* forced to end his studies at Gettysburg Seminary because of severe eye strain; joins the Franckean Synod of the Lutheran Church; receives permission from the Franckean Synod to pastor a Presbyterian Church at East Troy, New York; leaves the church after one year because of an injury to his throat caused by long and arduous preaching; *1839* ordained as Presbyterian minister; delivers an address before the Franckean Synod entitled, "Protestation of American Slavery"; *1840* moves to Philadelphia where he opens a school for black youths; *1841* persuaded by Bishop Morris Brown of the African Methodist Episcopal (A.M.E.) Church to unite with that denomination, despite his belief that African Methodists were hostile towards education; joins the quarterly conference of "Mother Bethel" A.M.E. Church; *1843-1845* publishes "Epistles on the Education of the Ministry," which nearly splits the denomination between anti-intellectual and pro-education factions; ordained an itinerant elder and assigned to pastor Israel A.M.E. Church in Washington, D.C.; leaves Israel Church after one year and pastors a church in Baltimore, Maryland; *1846* represents his denomination at the Evangelical Alliance convention in London, England; *1847* marries Julia A. Faris, who dies one year later while giving birth to a daughter; *1848* appointed historian of the A.M.E. Denomination; *1848-1851* travels throughout the eastern states to research the denomination; *1852* elected the sixth bishop of the A.M.E. Church and assigned to preside over the First Episcopal District, which includes Maryland, Pennsylvania, Ohio, and Canada; serves as bishop for forty-one years; *1854* marries Eliza Clark of Cincinnati, Ohio; *1856* becomes a member of the board of trustees of Wilberforce College, which was owned and operated by the Cincinnati Conference of the white Methodist Episcopal Church; moves his family to Wilberforce, Ohio, which was then called "Tawawa Springs"; *1862* visits President Lincoln at the White House and encourages him to sign the Emancipation Proclamation; *1863* purchases Wilberforce College for ten thousand dollars without first receiving permission from his denomination; *1863-1876* serves as president of Wilberforce, while continuing his duties as bishop; *1865* racist whites burn the school, forcing classes to be held in private homes in the Wilberforce community; *1867* visits England in search of financial support for his school; *1868* returns to Wilberforce and solicits funds from the Society for the Promotion of Collegiate and Theological Education, the American Unitarian Association, the Freedmen's Bureau, the John Pfaff Endowment, and individual donors, including Chief Justice Salmon P. Chase; *1867-1876* divides his attention between the bishopric, Wilberforce College, and his literary efforts; *1876* resigns from the presidency of Wilberforce to complete his history of the A.M.E. Church; *1881* presides over a session of the Methodist Ecumenical Conference, the first black to do so; *1893* represents the A.M.E. Church at the World's Parliament of Religions meeting in Chicago; dies in his sleep on November 21 at home in Wilberforce, Ohio.

Activities of Historical Significance

As an A.M.E. bishop and the first black president of the first black church-owned college in America, Payne was one of the most influential African Americans of the late nineteenth century. His crusades for higher education for black people and for a more rational approach to religion through an educated ministry were significant for the social and spiritual elevation of African Americans during this time.

Payne was born to pious parents and raised by an equally pious grandaunt. At the age of eighteen he experienced a conversion in which he said God had "called" him to help free and improve his race through education. As a result, Payne early dedicated himself to the idea that education and piety were inseparable.

Payne has been rightly called a "theologian of black education" because he was the first black clerical leader to insist that education carry theological as well as social consequences. He was so fervently dedicated to the notion that education was a divine command that he came close to insisting that intellectual development was among the means to achieve grace. He was so committed to enlightening and improving the A.M.E. ministry that he broke with his denomination's tradition of accepting untrained clergy by withholding ordination from those who refused to acquire an education.

Although he insisted that an educated ministry was essential, Payne also believed that higher learning would enable former slaves and free blacks to function in a more productive manner in a society dominated by racism. He actively recruited young black men and women to his college by pointing out how education was vital to their social and economic well-being.

Payne's decision to leave the Lutheran Church and unite with the African Methodist Episcopal Church in 1841 helped elevate the denomination to the forefront of the struggle for racial equality during the post Civil-War decades. When he purchased Wilberforce College in 1863, one of his first tasks was to attract a faculty that could not only train black people in the arts and sciences but also in Christian history, theology, and the critical study of the Bible. The curriculum he emphasized enabled hundreds of blacks, many of whom were former slaves, to acquire an education that, in turn, aided them in carving out a niche in American life and culture.

Overview of Biographical Sources

Although references to Payne appear in numerous monographs and surveys of African-American religious and social history, there have been few comprehensive treatments of his life. Several memoirs appeared in eulogistic articles and brief biographies published after his death. Foremost among these biographies is Charles Spencer Smith, *The Life of Daniel Alexander Payne, D.D., LL.D.* (Nashville, TN: A.M.E. Publishing, 1894), which appeared one year after Payne's death.

William J. Simmon's *Men of Mark: Eminent, Progressive and Rising* (Cleveland, OH: George M. Rewell, 1887) and Hallie Q. Brown's *Pen Pictures of Pioneers of Wilberforce* (Xenia, OH: Aldine, 1937) both contain important biographical information about Payne. Several unpublished dissertations and theses also examine his life and views on education and an educated ministry. Only two book-length studies of Payne exist: a somewhat dated but comprehensive examination of his life and work as a Christian educator by Josephus Coan (1935), and a recent comprehensive analysis of his theological ideas and social views by Paul R. Griffin (1984).

Evaluation of Principal Biographical Sources

Coan, Josephus. *Daniel A. Payne: Christian Educator*. Philadelphia: A.M.E., 1935. (A, G) This is the first major biography of Payne's life and activities as an educator. Coan, a devout A.M.E. educator, makes it clear in his preface that his objective is to reestablish Payne's educational philosophy of an enlightened ministry. Although his research was broad, Coan's work is largely a sympathetic celebration of Payne's activities in forcing education and high ethical standards upon his church.

Griffin, Paul R. *Black Theology As the Foundation of Three Methodist Colleges: The Educational Views and Labors of Daniel Payne, Joseph C. Price and Isaac Lane.* Lanham, MD: University Press of America, 1984. (A, G) This definitive monograph on the role of theology in the founding of black Methodist Colleges draws on Payne's sermons, autobiography, and numerous books, articles, and denominational papers to critically assess Payne's life and educational philosophy. The first chapter analyzes how Payne's early experiences shaped his dedication to black education. Succeeding chapters examine how he fashioned a theology of education to advance the belief that black intellectual development was a divine command. Griffin concludes by discussing how Payne shaped the curriculum of Wilberforce and why his denomination refused to financially support that institution.

Wills, David, and Richard Newman, eds. *Black Apostles at Home and Abroad: Afro-Americans and the Christian Mission from the Revolution to the Reconstruction.* Boston: G. K. Hall, 1982. (A, G) A chapter by Wills on "Womanhood and Domesticity in the A.M.E. Tradition: The Influence of Daniel Alexander Payne" provides basic biographical details and a discussion of Payne's views on education and the ministry. Wills skillfully assesses Payne's refusal to accept women in the ordained ministry of the A.M.E. Church, although the study largely ignores how Payne's theology was responsible for this bias.

Overview and Evaluation of Primary Sources

Payne was one of the most prolific Afro-American writers of the nineteenth century. His writings tend to reflect particular moments in his development as an educator, theologian, bishop, historian, and race leader. His *Recollections of Seventy Years* (1888. Reprint. New York: Arno Press, 1969; A, G), *A Treatise on Domestic Education* (Cincinnati, OH: Cranton and Stove, 1889; A, G) and his unpublished journal of 1835-1851 (A, G) are essential for researchers. The recollections flow chronologically and detail his life and experiences from his birth to shortly before his death in 1893. This work also provides important insight into his often troublesome relationship with the A.M.E. Church, his purchase and shaping of Wilberforce College, and his theology. His *Treatise* details what he believed were divine principles for proper and pious living, especially those related to matters such as childrearing, family life and ethical and moral social conduct.

In addition to these two sources, numerous other books, articles, sermons, and addresses are critical primary sources. The major books include *A History of the African Methodist Episcopal Church, 1816-1958* (Nashville, TN: A.M.E., 1991; **A, G**) and The Semi-Centenary and Retrospect of the African Methodist Episcopal Church (Philadelphia, PA: A.M.E. Sunday School Union, 1888; **A, G**), which focus on his understanding of African Methodism and his own work in that denomination as a pastor, bishop, and educator.

Payne's major speeches include "Protestation of American Slavery" in Douglas C. Stange, Journal of Negro History 52 (1967; **A, G**); Welcome to the Ransomed (Baltimore, MD: Bell and Tuttle, 1862; **A, G**); and, The Moral Significance of the Fifteenth Amendment (Xenia, OH: Xenia Gazette Company, 1870; **A, G**). Each of these speeches reflects his understanding of the plight and condition of his race and the theological and educational response to these needs.

The sermons and addresses include "God" in the Repository of Religion and Literature 2 (January 1859; **A, G**), "The Christian Ministry: Its Moral and Intellectual Character" (1859) in Sermons and Addresses, 1853-1891, edited by Charles Killian (New York: Arno Press, 1972; **A, G**), "An Evil Behind a Right" in the Repository of Religion and Literature 3 (April 1861; **A, G**), "Christian Perfection" in the Repository of Religion and Literature 3 (April 1862; **A, G**) and, "The Church of the Living God, Its Priesthood and Ministry in All Ages" (1888; **A, G**) at the archives at Howard University in Washington, D.C. Each of these writings reveals his continuing efforts to construct an enlightened orthodox theology to replace the popular religious orientation, which his Church had espoused since its founding in 1787.

Consistent with his bookishness and interest in preserving history, Payne left a large body of correspondence, sermons, addresses, and other documents. These sources, however, have become scattered over the years. Some are at Wilberforce University and Payne Theological Seminary, both in Wilberforce, Ohio. Others are at Howard University, in Washington, D.C., the Schomburg Collection at the New York City Public Library, and the Indiana Historical Society Library at Indianapolis. Others have simply disappeared.

Fiction and Adaptations

Even though Payne has not been the subject of any works of fiction, he wrote poetry and hymns. His most famous poem was "The Mournful Lute, Or The Preceptor's Farewell," which is found in his Recollections and was written on the occasion of the South Carolina General Assembly's legislation banning black education in that state in 1835. The hymns he wrote include "Personal and Home Consecration, No. 1," "Personal and Home Consecration, No. 2," "Reveal Thyself to Me," and "Hymn for the Consecration of Children," all of which are in his Treatise on Domestic Education.

Museums, Historical Landmarks, Societies

Wilberforce University (Wilberforce, OH). This university remains the major landmark in memory of Payne.

Payne Theological Seminary (Wilberforce, OH). A hand painted portrait of Payne is kept in the Archives at Payne Seminary, which is named in his honor.

Laurel Cemetery (Baltimore, MD). Payne's grave is located in this cemetery.

Numerous churches throughout the African Methodist connection are named after him, including one in Hamilton, Ohio.

Other Sources

Cromwell, John W. *The Negro in American History.* Washington, DC: The American Negro Academy, 1914. Draws on some of Payne's writings and locates him within the context of nineteenth-century Afro-American history and its leaders.

McGinnis, Frederick A. *A History and an Interpretation of Wilberforce University.* Blanchester, OH: Brown, 1914. Discusses the relevant sections of Payne's life and provides useful information about his purchase and remolding of Wilberforce College.

Richings, G. F. *Evidence of Progress Among Colored People.* Philadelphia: George S. Ferguson, 1903. Draws on original sources to highlight Payne's efforts to advance his race through education.

Scarborough, William S. "Address." *Negro Quarterly* 5, 2 (June 1943). This speech celebrates Payne's achievements as an educator and sole shaper of Wilberforce College from 1863-1876.

Paul R. Griffin
Wright State University

ELIZABETH PEABODY
1804-1894

Chronology

Born Elizabeth Palmer Peabody on May 16, 1804 in Billerica, Massachusetts, the eldest of seven children, four of them girls, to Nathaniel Peabody, a dentist who later settled in Salem, Massachusetts, and Elizabeth Palmer Peabody, a school teacher, whose education and emotional support of her daughter allowed Elizabeth to master ten languages and several academic disciplines; *1820-1824* school teacher and private tutor in Massachusetts and Maine; *1826-1849* cultivates intellectual relationship with William Ellery Channing and other New England thinkers and develops a life-long interest in romanticism and liberal theology; *1832* writes *First Steps to the Study of History* and several textbooks; *1837* charter member of the Transcendentalist Club; meets Horace Mann who marries her sister Mary; *1834-1836* works at Bronson Alcott's elementary school based on Platonic-Transcendentalist precepts; *1835* publishes *Record of a School,* an account of this experience; *1836-1840* unemployed and living in Salem; friendship with Ralph Waldo Emerson results in several literary events, such as the publication of Jones Very's *Poems and Essays* in 1839; *1840* secures for Nathaniel Hawthorne a position at the Boston Custom House; two years later he marries her sister Sophia; *1840-1850* runs a bookstore out of her Boston home that becomes a major center of transcendentalism and various expressions of radicalism; publishes a wide-range of literary and reform materials including Thoreau's "Civil Disobedience"; her own writings reveal an interesting synthesis of Christian and Transcendentalist notions particularly focused on early childhood education; *1850-1884* after closing her bookstore, writes and lectures on education (ten books and fifty articles); *1859* with her sister Mary Mann, opens an infant school in Concord; *1863* with Mary, authors *Moral Culture of Infancy and Kindergarten Guide,* revealing her philosophy of education; visits European kindergartens based on the ideals of Friedrich Froebel; *1873* establishes and edits the *Kindergarten Messenger*; *1877* organizes and becomes first president of the American Froebel Union; in later years, she becomes a colorful eccentric—poor, overweight, with poor eyesight, indifferent personal appearance, but a strong conversationalist; *January 3, 1894* dies at her home in Jamaica Plain, Boston; buried in Sleepy Hollow Cemetery, Concord; *1896* friends establish the Elizabeth Peabody House, a Boston settlement house in her memory.

Activities of Historical Significance

The two major activities in Elizabeth Peabody's life were her relationship to New England transcendentalism and her interest in educational reform, particularly kindergarten reform based on the principles of Friedrich Froebel. These two activities were not unrelated. As she once observed, "The final cause of human society is the unfolding of the individual man into every form of perfection, without let or hindrance, according to the inward nature of each." (*Dial*, October, 1841, p. 226)

Elizabeth Peabody knew all the leading transcendentalists. As student and friend of William Ellery Channing, she wrote *Reminiscences of Rev. Wm. Ellery Channing* (1880). She also wrote about the educational experiences of Bronson Alcott and introduced him to Ralph Waldo Emerson, another long-time friend. Together Peabody and Emerson championed the career of the mystic Jones Very. In addition she recognized quickly the talent of her friend and brother-in-law Nathaniel Hawthorne. During her bookstore days, she associated with Margaret Fuller, George Ripley, and Theodore Parker. She contributed to the *Dial* and to the establishment of Brook Farm. Her concept of transcendentalism was more Christian in tone and emphasis than the unitarian concept of the literary transcendentalists. As a strong abolitionist she knew the Grimke sisters and later supported the Indian Rights movement. Although a strong intellectual in her own right, her major contribution was her ability to recognize and encourage New England sages, novelists, and poets. Her *Last Evening With Allson* (1886) analyzed her friendship with the American artist Washington Allson. Her collected essays, published in 1886, is long out of print and difficult to locate.

From her earliest days, Elizabeth Peabody was a teacher and philosopher of education. In 1860 she established in Boston the first organized kindergarten in the country, based on the ideas of Friedrich Froebel, whose ideas she tirelessly promoted. She helped Bronson Alcott with his infant school and taught at his Concord School of Philosophy in the 1880s.

Elizabeth Palmer Peabody's life and thought embody important elements in the history of American reform and education. Her historical reputation, unfortunately, has not matched her impressive achievement.

Evaluation of Principal Biographical Sources

Baylor, Ruth M. *Elizabeth Palmer Peabody, Kindergarten Pioneer.* Philadelphia: University of Pennsylvania Press, 1965. (A, G) In the absence of a major scholarly biography, this work provides the best overall coverage of Peabody's life, with emphasis on her work in the kindergarten movement. It traces fully the influence of Friedrich Froebel's ideas on her educational program. A fine bibliography includes her publications. Appendixes include a list the books from her library and book shop located in the Concord Free

Public Library, Baylor's collection of holograph material, and a chronology of the kindergarten movement in America from 1836 to 1992.

Brooks, Gladys. *Three Wise Virgins*. New York: E. P. Dutton, 1957. (A, G) Despite an unattractive title, no documentation, and a breezy style, Brooks's book has merit. It illustrates clearly the influence of William Ellery Channing on Dorothea Lynde Dix, Elizabeth Palmer Peabody, and Catherine Maria Sedgwick. "Described in modern psychological parlance the heroines of this book were three virgins who succeeded so far in sublimating their sexual drives that they escaped severe neuroses." Be that as it may, Brooks investigates the cultural transformation of Calvinism into transcendentalism and unitarianism in which sin was rejected but duty retained in the lives of these three remarkable women.

Brown, Arthur W. *Always Young for Liberty, A Biography of William Ellery Channing*. Syracuse: Syracuse University Press, 1956. (A) Because of the massive intellectual effect Channing had on Peabody, studies of Channing are important for understanding Peabody, and most have information about her. Brown also wrote *William Ellery Channing* (New York: Twayne, 1961; A, G), a popular and briefer version of this work.

Foster, Charles H. "Peabody, Elizabeth Palmer." In *Notable American Women, a Biographical Dictionary*, edited by Edward T. James. Cambridge: Harvard University Press, 1971. (A, G) This brief entry is the best scholarly account of Elizabeth's activities. Its bibliography is a good guide to nineteenth-century journalism dealing with Elizabeth. It also cites several unpublished doctoral dissertations on Elizabeth and her sisters.

Tharp, Louise Hale. *The Peabody Sisters of Salem*. Boston: Little, Brown, 1950. (G) Using direct quotation and dialogue without proper citation, this book reveals how publishers treated the history of women nearly half a century ago. Nevertheless, the illustrations are good and the text, while informal, does give the reader a sense of Peabody's life experiences. Also provides a good introduction to Elizabeth's interesting sisters, Mary and Sophia.

Evaluation of Primary Sources

Letters of Elizabeth Palmer Peabody (Bruce A. Ronda, ed. Middletown, CT: Wesleyan University Press, 1984; A) is the best available primary source for her life. Ronda provides excellent footnotes and a revealing introduction that places Peabody in the historical context of republicanism, feminism, and Scottish Common Sense philosophy. Organized in chronological order and according to her developing interests, the result is tantamount to an "autob ography," revealing a woman who was selfless and, despite her eccentricitie a proper lady of nineteenth-century New England.

Another important primary source is Peabody's *Record of a Schoo Exemplifying the General Principles of Spiritual Culture* (Boston: Russel Shattuck, 1836. Reprint. Arno Press and the *New York Times,* 1969), he account of Bronson Alcott's "Temple School." She carefully records Alcott' ideas and methodology and explains her educational views.

Glimpses of Peabody can be found in the papers of leading transcender talists and in such collections as the Horace Mann Papers at the Massachu setts Historical Society, the Berg Collection in the New York Public Librar and the Robert L. Straker Collection at Antioch College.

Fiction and Adaptations

In the *Century Magazine* for February 1885, Henry James published hi first installment of his novel "The Bostonians" and introduced Miss Birdsey a reformer who, with humorous good-intent, tries to set the world arigh Although James denied that Elizabeth Palmer Peabody was his model, ev dence gathered by Bruce A. Ronda is conclusive. James's fictional portrait c Peabody was an attempt to reject her reforming ideas as being out of date i post-Civil War America. The truth is, however, that to the end of her lon life Elizabeth Peabody had insightful notions about her time, her place, an her America.

Other Sources

Delbanco, Andrew. *William Ellery Channing, An Essay on the Liberal Spirt of America.* Cambridge: Harvard University Press, 1981. (**A, G**) Delbanc examines the intellectual factors that made Channing such a force in th liberal and reform circles of his day.

Edgell, David P. *William Ellery Channing, An Intellectual Portrait.* Boston Beacon Press, 1955. (**A, G**) A good study but less insightful than the Delban co volume.

Rice, Madeleine Hooks. *Federal Street Pastor, The Life of William Eller Channing,* New York: Bookman Associates, 1961. (**A, G**) This book is a ordinary treatment of Peabody's mentor.

Donald K. Picken.
University of North Texa.

JOSEPH CHARLES PRICE
1854-1893

Chronology

Born Joseph Charles Dozier on February 10, 1854 at Elizabeth City, North Carolina to a free mother, Emily and a slave father, Charles Dozier who was separated from his family shortly after Joseph's birth; *1862* removed by his mother to New Bern, North Carolina, which recently had become free territory; takes the last name of his stepfather, David Price; parents enroll him in the Freedmen's Lowell Normal School where he completes eight years of study; *1871* becomes principal of a black elementary school at Wilson, North Carolina, even though he only has eight years of formal education; *1873* leaves principalship and enrolls at Shaw College at Raleigh, North Carolina; converts during a campus revival; *1874* becomes a member of the African Methodist Episcopal Zion Church of New Bern; *1875* chooses the ministry as his vocation and is immediately ordained an elder; enrolls in the College Department of Lincoln University at Lincoln, Pennsylvania where he graduates valedictorian four years later; *1879* enters the Theological Department of Lincoln University and graduates two years later with a degree in theology; *1880* elected a delegate to the General Conference of his denomination; *1881* represents his denomination at the Ecumenical Methodist Conference which was held in London, England; convinces his denomination to close its fledgling Zion Wesley Institute School and build Livingstone College at Salisbury, North Carolina; serves as the president of Livingstone College until his death; *1882* marries Jennie Smallwood—his childhood sweetheart—and five children were born to that union; *1890* elected president of the newly founded Afro-American League; *October 25, 1893* dies from nephritis at Salisbury.

Activities of Historical Significance

Price's death at the early age of thirty-nine cut short a promising career as a race leader. Still, he was one of the most influential Afro-American clerical and educational figures of the Reconstruction and post-Reconstruction decades. Though he never pastored a church, his academic study of Christian theology enabled him to articulate a theology for his largely untrained clerical colleagues that was grounded in the notion that if Afro-Americans were to be truly free, they must begin by replacing the heart-felt, otherworldly religion which slaveholders had taught them during slavery. To that end, he argued for a Christian theology that was both rational and consistent with black struggles for socio-political liberation in this country as well as throughout the world. His insistence upon a gospel that resonated with the Afro-American struggles for socio-political liberation made him a precursor of theologians of black liberation such as James Cone, Gayraud Wilmore, and others who emerged during the 1960s.

Convinced that slavery's denial of education to slaves and even free blacks had left the majority of post-Civil War era Afro-Americans ill-prepared for their newly acquired freedom, Price's greatest work was the founding of Livingstone College in 1881. He believed that higher education was indispensable if Afro-Americans were to overcome the ignorance, superstition, immorality, and indolence that slavery had fastened upon them. Moreover, he viewed education as invaluable in his race's struggles to assert their common humanity and Constitutional rights to freedom and equality. In molding his college to aid the full liberation of his people, Price insisted upon a curriculum that would prepare Afro-Americans to function in every aspect of this society. Thus, although he favored education in the arts and sciences, he also instituted manual arts education as a part of his school's curriculum. In his view, education—whether in the arts and sciences or in the manual arts—was no mere luxury for a race that was fighting to pull itself out of the smoldering ashes of slavery and the fires of American racism.

In addition to his work as an educator, Price was active as a black political leader during the decades following the Civil War. Anticipating that the Compromise of 1877 would lead to disenfranchisement and legal segregation of Afro-Americans in the South, he traveled and lectured throughout the U.S. on the subject of how Afro-Americans must use their ballots wisely and judiciously. For him, such usage meant that Afro-Americans should not be tied to the Republican Party simply because it had helped effect their legal emancipation. On the contrary, he believed that Afro-Americans should cast votes for local, state, and federal representatives who were sympathetic to their condition, regardless of whether they were Republicans or Democrats.

Overview of Biographical Sources

References to Price appear in only a few monographs and studies of Afro-American religious history, despite the existence of a large body of available sources. Immediately after his death, a number of eulogistic articles appeared, particularly in religious publications of his African Methodist Episcopal Zion Denomination. Three of the best are tributes to Price by George E. Biddle, John C. Dancy, and James W. Hood which appeared in *The A.M.E. Zion Quarterly Review, 4:2 (January 1894)*. One of the best non-denominational eulogistic publications is William B. DuBois, "An Estimate of Joseph Charles Price," *The Crisis Magazine*, March 1922.

Only two book-length studies of Price exist: a comprehensive biography by William Jacob Walls (1943) and a study of his life and ideas by Paul R. Griffin (1984).

Evaluation of Principal Biographical Sources
Battle, Thomas C. *Memorial Address on Life of J. C. Price*. North Carolina: Richardson and Son Printers, n.d. **(A, G)** Battle was Price's Sunday School teacher, counselor, and best friend when Price joined the A.M.E. Zion Church at New Bern, North Carolina in 1874. Thus, he does not move beyond celebrating Price's life and achievements as an educator and race leader in a filio-pietistic encomium.

Griffin, Paul R. *Black Theology As The Foundation Of Three Methodist Colleges: The Educational Views and Labors Of Daniel Payne, Joseph Price, and Isaac Lane*. Lanham, MD: University Press of America, 1984. **(A, G)** Growing out of the author's doctoral dissertation, this definitive study utilizes Price's sermons, addresses, and denominational publications to examine his life and ideas. The first chapter is devoted to examining his biography and comparing it with those of two of his peers—Daniel Alexander Payne and Isaac Lane. Succeeding chapters proceed topically, critically examining his theological and educational philosophies and comparing them with those of Payne and Lane. The final chapter examines Price's labors as founder and president of Livingstone College.

Walls, William Jacob. *Joseph Charles Price: Educator And Race Leader*. Boston: Christopher Publishing, 1943. **(A, G)** A bishop of the A.M.E. Zion Church, Walls draws on a wealth of sources and presents a thorough examination of Price's life and work as an educator and race leader. The study, however, occasionally fails to move beyond an uncritical presentation of the facts.

Overview and Evaluation of Primary Sources
Possibly because of his premature death, Price never wrote an autobiography. His short life notwithstanding, he was a prolific writer and produced a significant number of articles and pamphlets which form an important primary source. His most significant writings include "The Negro in America—His Special Work" in the *Christian Educators in Council* (New York: Philips and Hunt, 1888; **A, G**), "Education and the Race Problem" in the *Proceedings of the National Education Association* (St. Paul: July 1890; **A, G**), "The Times Demand Elevation of the Educational Standards of the Christian Ministry" (*A.M.E. Zion Quarterly Review*, October 1892; **A, G**), "The Race Question in the South" (*A.M.E. Zion Church Quarterly*, April 1893; **A, G**), "Temperance Mission Work Among the Colored People of the South" (*A.M.E. Zion Church Quarterly*, April 1894, **A, G**), "The Negro and the Ballot" (*Alumni Magazine*,

1891, A, G) and *The Race Problem in America* (New York: n.p., 1888, A, G).

The Archives at Livingstone College and Hood Theological Seminary at Salisbury, North Carolina, contain additional unpublished writings, college records, and church documents pertaining to Price's work and thoughts.

Museums, Historical Landmarks, Societies

Livingstone College (Salisbury, NC). The two landmarks to Price are his tomb in front of Huntington Hall and the Price Memorial Building.

Other Sources

Cromwell, John. *The Negro In American History: Men And Women Eminent In The Evolution Of The American Of African Descent.* Washington, DC: American Negro Academy, 1914. In a short but lively chapter, Cromwell—one of the pioneers in the study of Afro-American history—presents a very useful discussion of Price's achievements as an educator and race leader.

Meier, August. *Negro Thought In America, 1880-1915.* Ann Arbor: University of Michigan Press, 1973. Devotes several important pages to Price's educational and political views.

Simmons, William J. *Men of Mark: Eminent, Progressive And Rising.* Cleveland, OH: George Rewell, 1887. Although dated, provides excellent biographical information about Price.

Paul R. Griffin
Wright State University

RED CLOUD
1822-1909

Chronology

Born in the winter of 1822 (although Red Cloud stated to Charles W. Allen that his birth occurred in May of 1821) near the forks of the Platte River, probably near where Blue Water Creek empties into the river, near present day North Platte, Nebraska, son of Lone Man (may have also been named Red Cloud), a Brule chief, and of Walks-as-She-Thinks (a Saone and a sister of Old Smoke), named Makhpiya-luta; *1838* takes first scalp in raid on the Pawnees; *1841* kills Bull Bear, leader of Koyas; leads his first war party against the Pawnees and suffers a near-fatal wound; *1840s* marries Pretty Owl and has five children (either one son and four daughters or two sons and three daughters); *1860s* contact with whites increases as more settlers and prospectors move through the Powder River and Platte River areas; *1865* participates in Platte Bridge fight on July 25-26; *1866* U.S. government recognizes Red Cloud and Spotted Tail as "rulers of the Sioux"; *1866* walks out of council at Fort Laramie, and Bozeman Road War begins in June; leads the fighting at the Fetterman massacre in which more than eighty U.S. troopers are killed in December; *1867* participates in the Wagon Box fight on August 2; *1868* signs treaty on November 6 with the U.S. effectively abandoning the Bozeman Road and closing the forts erected to protect the trail; thereafter, becomes a peace advocate; *1870-1900* visits Washington and the East Coast on numerous occasions to lobby for better treatment of his people and their rights under the various treaties signed during this period; often included in major treaty negotiations with the Plains Indians; *1876* although suspected of aiding Sitting Bull and Crazy Horse, advocates peace; his son, Jack Red Cloud, fights at the Little Big Horn; *1877* helps persuade Crazy Horse to surrender; *1881* Valentine McGillycuddy, an Indian agent, attempts to depose Red Cloud as chief of the Oglala Sioux; *1889* the Ghost Dance movement comes to the reservations; *1890* massacre of Native Americans at Pine Ridge on December 29; *1897* makes final trip to Washington; *1903* on July 4 makes formal renouncement of his position as chief; *1909* dies on December 10 at his home on the Pine Ridge Reservation.

Activities of Historical Significance

For many nineteenth-century Americans, Red Cloud represented the menace and fierce opposition of the Plains Indians to the advancement of the white civilization across North America. Red Cloud had one claim to distinction that virtually no other Native American could make: he won a war against the forces of the U.S. Government. In the Bozeman Road War in the late 1860s, Sioux warriors led by Red Cloud and other war leaders were able to temporarily arrest the advancement of whites into their beloved Powder River country.

Following the signing of the Peace Treaty of 1868, Red Cloud became a staunch advocate of peace. He traveled to Washington on numerous occasions to speak with presidents, Indian Bureau officials, and other government officials to seek better conditions and support for his people. On many of these trips, Red Cloud would make speeches in eastern cities attempting to explain the position and way of life of the Plains Indians.

Red Cloud's role in the continuing conflicts on the Great Plains has been greatly debated. After the signing of the Treaty of 1868, Red Cloud was always suspected of directly encouraging and aiding the resistance to further incursions into Native American lands. He most likely looked the other way when warriors left the reservation, but probably did not directly participate in any armed conflicts after the Treaty of 1868.

Red Cloud became blind and feeble towards the end of his life, but was held in high esteem by his contemporaries for his role in defending the rights of his people.

Overview of Biographical Sources

As one of the principal leaders of the Sioux nation, Red Cloud has been mentioned in many of the histories of the Indian Wars and of the period. Like many other Native American leaders he has had only a few biographers. His life and activities also are examined in the biographies of his principal military adversaries.

There are very few sources available for study from the Native American viewpoint. Many of the primary sources are the documents and correspondence of the military and Indian Bureau officials who dealt with the Native Americans in warfare or on the reservations. Interviews with Native American participants were often done long after the wars had taken place. One of the best biographies on Red Cloud is James Olson's *Red Cloud and the Sioux Problem* (1965).

Evaluation of Principal Biographical Sources

Garst, Shannon. *The Picture Story and Biography of Red Cloud.* Chicago: Follett, 1965. (Y) This volume is part of the Library of American Heroes Series and is illustrated by Art Seiden.

McGaa, Ed. *Red Cloud: the Story of an American Indian.* Minneapolis: Dillon, 1971. (Y) This biography is intended for younger readers and is by a member of the Sioux tribe. He discusses the values, aspirations, and motives of his people.

Olson, James C. *Red Cloud and the Sioux Problem*. Lincoln: University of Nebraska Press, 1965. (A, G) This is probably the most scholarly treatment of Red Cloud's life and the role he played in the lives of the Oglala Sioux.

Voight, Virgina F. *Red Cloud; Sioux War Chief*. Champaign, IL: Garrad, 1975. (Y) A biography written for grades 3-5.

Overview and Evaluation of Primary Sources

Few collections have extensive research material written by Native Americans. Researchers are forced to rely on the papers of the contemporary white combatants and government officials. Probably the most important depository of information concerning Red Cloud is located in the Nebraska State Historical Society Collection, Lincoln. Included in this archive are the papers and records of the interviews conducted by Judge Eli Seavey Ricker. The Ricker interviews were conducted with both white and Native American participants in the conflicts on the Great Plains. Also in the archive are the papers of Charles Philander Jordan, an Indian agent in the Dakota Territory, and Luther Hedden North, a scout from Platte County, Nebraska, who participated in the capture of Red Cloud in 1876.

The Yale University Library contains the papers of Othniel Charles Marsh, a paleontologist at Yale, who carried on an extensive correspondence with Red Cloud.

For information on the various engagements with Red Cloud's warriors, one should consult any of the collections containing materials from the various military leaders who fought in the Plains Indian wars. One also should consult the records pertaining to the Red Cloud and Pine Ridge agencies.

Fiction and Adaptations

The resistance of Native Americans to the coming of the white man has served as the plot device for numerous works of fiction and the cinema. Many motion pictures have depicted Red Cloud, the earliest being the 1925 Vital release entitled *Warrior Gap*. This silent film was based on Charles King's novel *Warrior Gap, A Story of the Sioux Outbreak of '68*. Red Cloud was played by Len Haynes. Three years later MGM released *Spoilers of the West*. Red Cloud was portrayed by Chief Big Tree. Tim McCoy starred as an army officer who was aided by Red Cloud in preventing bloodshed between the Indians and the settlers.

Columbia Pictures was the next studio to make a movie with Red Cloud as a central character. *End of the Trail* (1932), starring Tim McCoy and Chief White Eagle as Red Cloud, was based on a Zane Grey story.

The 1950s saw a series of pictures in which Red Cloud and the events in his life would serve as a centerpiece. Universal released *Tomahawk* (1951), based on a story by Daniel Jarrett and directed by George Shuman. The movie starred Van Heflin as Jim Bridger, Yvonne DeCarlo as Julie Madden, Preston Foster as Col. Carrington, Rock Hudson as Burt Hanna, and John War Eagle as Red Cloud. The events surrounding the Fetterman massacre are depicted as part of the story-line. Two years later Universal produced a second picture on Red Cloud. *The Great Sioux Uprising* (1953) starred Jeff Chandler as Jonathan Westgate and John War Eagle as Red Cloud. Set at the time of the Civil War, one of the Indians was a confederate officer. *The Gun That Won the West* (1955) from Columbia starred Dennis Morgan as Jim Bridger and Robert Bice as Red Cloud. The building of the railroad in the west was blended with the fighting on the Bozeman Road. Red Cloud was depicted as a "good Indian." The character of Red Cloud was also included in the 1955 picture from Universal entitled *Chief Crazy Horse*. Victor Mature starred as Crazy Horse and Morris Ankrum played Red Cloud. Kirk Douglas starred as Johnny Hawks in the Bryan/UA picture *The Indian Fighter* (1955). Eduard Franz played Red Cloud in a minor role. *The Last Frontier* (1955) starred Victor Mature as Jed and Manuel Donde as Red Cloud. Although the picture had many stars (Guy Madison, Robert Preston, James Whitmore, and Anne Bancroft) and was directed by Anthony Mann, it depicted a typical Indian attack on a frontier army post. In *Run of the Arrow* (1957), Rod Steiger played a Confederate army officer who moves west after the Civil War and lives with the Sioux so he can continue to fight Yankees. Frank de Kova played Red Cloud. Continuing the Civil War theme, *Revolt at Fort Laramie* (1957) depicts the personnel of a frontier fort divided by their loyalties at the start of the war but uniting later to fight the Indians. Eddie Little played the role of Red Cloud.

In 1977 Ed Friendly Productions made *Peter Lundy and the Medicine Hat Stallion* for NBC-TV. The two-hour movie centered on a boy who became a Pony Express rider in the Nebraska Territory prior to the Civil War. Ed Romero played Red Cloud.

A very early fictional biography of Red Cloud was written by Lt.-Colonel C. B. Butler. The work was entitled *Red Cloud the Solitary Sioux. A Story of the Great Prairie* (London: Sampson Law, Marston, Searle, and Rivington, 1882). The story was centered on the early life of Red Cloud and his association with an explorer/adventurer from England.

Richard S. Wheeler has written one of the latest novels using Red Cloud as a central character. *Dodging Red Cloud* (Boston: G. K. Hall, 1987) is an account of three adventurers trying to pass the Bozeman Road in 1868.

Museums, Historical Landmarks, Societies

Fort C. F. Smith Historical District (East of Fort Smith, Big Horn County, MT). The fort was burned by Red Cloud during the Bozeman Road War.

Fort Fetterman (Orpha, WY vicinity); *Fort Phil Kearny* (Story, WY vicinity) and *Fort Reno* (Sussex, WY vicinity) are all forts associated with the Bozeman Road fights.

Other Sources

Brininstool, E. A. *Fighting Indian Warriors: True Tales of the Wild Frontiers.* Harrisburg, PA: AMS Press, 1953. Originally titled *Fighting Red Cloud's Warriors.* The first two chapters deal with the fighting at Fort Phil Kearny and the Wagon Box Fight.

DeLand, Charles Edmund. "The Sioux Wars Minnesota Outbreak; Red Cloud and Other Wars of 1867; Little Big Horn; Wounded Knee." In *South Dakota Historical Collections,* Vol. 15. Pierre, SD: Hipple, 1930. Places Red Cloud in the context of the Sioux struggle against the encroachment by whites into their territory. The majority of the volume deals with the battle at the Little Big Horn.

Dockstader, Frederick J. "Red Cloud." In *Great North American Indians: Profiles in Life and Leadership.* New York: Van Nostrand Reinhold, 1977. Contains a short biographical sketch with questionable dates.

Faulk, Odie B. "Red Cloud." In *The McGraw-Hill Encyclopedia of World Biography.* New York: McGraw-Hill, 1973. Along with a short biography is a list and evaluation of other sources.

Ghent, W. J. "Red Cloud." In *Dictionary of American Biography,* edited by Dumas Malone. New York: Charles Scribner's Sons, 1935. The accurate biography also includes a list of authoritative, but dated sources.

Hebard, Grace Raymond, and E. A. Brininstool. *The Bozeman Trail. Historical Accounts of the Blazing of the Overland Routes into the Northwest, and the Fights with Red Cloud's Warriors,* 2 vols. Cleveland: Arthur H. Clark, 1922. Provides good coverage of the Bozeman Road fights.

Hoover, Herbert T. "Red Cloud." In *Dictionary of American Military Biography,* edited by Roger J. Spiller. Westport, CT: Greenwood, 1984. Contains a short biographical sketch from a military point of view.

Hyde, George E. *Red Cloud's Folk; a History of the Oglala Sioux Indians.* Norman, Ok.: University of Oklahoma Press, 1937.

————. *A Sioux Chronicle.* Norman: University of Oklahoma Press, 1956. In these two works, the author attempts to provide a history for the Oglala Sioux from before their contact with whites until the incident at Wounded Knee. Both works are part of The Civilization of the American Indian Series.

Metcalf, P. Richard. "Red Cloud." In *The Reader's Encyclopedia of the American West,* edited by Howard R. Lamar. New York: Thomas Y. Crowell, 1977. A one-page biographical sketch that notes the main events of Red Cloud's life.

Maurice G. Fortin
University of North Texas

PAUL ROBESON
1898-1976

Chronology

Born Paul Leroy Bustill Robeson on April 9, 1898, in Princeton, New Jersey, the son of William Drew Robeson, a clergyman, and Maria Louisa Bustill, an educator; *1898-1918* grows up in Princeton and Somerville, New Jersey; *1919* receives bachelor's degree from Rutgers College; *1921* marries Eslanda Cardozo Goode; performs in *Simon the Cyrenian*; *1922-1943* acts in plays *All God's Chillun Got Wings, Othello,* and *Toussaint L'Ouverture,* in films *Body and Soul, Taboo, The Hairy Ape, The Emperor Jones, Sanders of the River,* and *Show Boat;* performs in concerts and makes recordings including *Show Boat; 1923* receives law degree from Columbia University; admitted to the Bar of New York, employed in law firm; *1934* travels to Germany and the Soviet Union; *1947* announces that he will take a two-year sabbatical from performing to work to eliminate racism in the U.S.; *1948* speaks to the World Peace Congress in Paris; performs in the Peekskill concerts; *1952* receives Stalin Peace Prize from the Soviet Union; *1958* publishes autobiography, *Here I Stand; 1963* returns to the United States; *1970* receives Civil Liberties Award from the American Civil Liberties Union; *1976* dies on January 23 in Philadelphia after suffering a stroke.

Activities of Historical Significance

While Paul Robeson demonstrated that he was a premier performer from the 1920s through 1950, he is remembered equally for his political activism and his sympathy for the Soviet Union. Among the numerous memorable moments in Robeson's performing career were his performances with the Provincetown Players during the 1920s in the production of two plays by Eugene O'Neill, *All God's Chillun Got Wings,* and *The Emperor Jones.* Robeson's fame was enhanced in the 1930s with his performances in *Othello* and *Show Boat.*

By 1930 Robeson was involved with a variety of leftist causes, and his interest in political activities was extended during the 1930s and 1940s. While on a tour in Germany in 1934, Robeson was discriminated against by Nazi officials because of his race; in the Soviet Union he was received as a great artist. These receptions influenced Robeson greatly, and he would emerge as an anti-fascist during the Spanish Civil War. Robeson met the aspiring African nationalists Kwame Nkrumah and Jomo Kenyatta; later, Robeson assisted in the establishment of the Council on African Affairs with the goal of ending the European colonial empires. Robeson performed in benefit concerts and plays to assist the republicans during the Spanish Civil War, to raise funds to assist Jewish refugees who were fleeing the Nazis, and to assist American blacks in their efforts to achieve equality. Despite the political controversy surrounding his career, Robeson maintained his general popularity to the end of World War II.

As conflict between the U.S. and the Soviet Union deepened into the Cold War and with the growth of civil rights activism in the U.S., Robeson's prestige declined. His unflagging support of the Soviet Union, his endorsement of Henry Wallace and the Progressive Party platform in 1948, his pro-Soviet speech to the World Peace Congress in Paris in 1949, and his performances in the violence-marred Peekskill (New York) concerts in 1949 all combined to ruin Robeson's performing career. During the McCarthy era, Robeson refused to take a loyalty oath to the U.S. and was denied a passport to travel abroad. His career never recovered from the public reaction to his political activism and his expressed sympathy for Moscow. In 1958 Robeson published his autobiography, *Here I Stand*, designed to awaken ordinary American blacks to the need to be assertive to acquire equality. While Robeson's reputation began to be restored during the late 1960s and early 1970s, he became an insular personality and refrained from public appearances.

Overview of Biographical Sources

Robeson's controversial life has attracted the interests of several biographers. Marie Seaton, *Paul Robeson* (1958), Edwin Hoyt, *Paul Robeson: The American Othello* (1967), and Dorothy Butler Gilliam, *Paul Robeson, All-American* (1976) are important contributions to our understanding of Robeson.

The most comprehensive and scholarly biography is Martin Bauml Duberman, *Paul Robeson* (1988). Duberman's study has been critically acclaimed because of its scholarship and thoroughness. Robeson emerges as an intensely energetic and intelligent man who nevertheless lacked the necessary skills for political confrontation. Robeson gradually became submerged in depression; his art and artistic values were in many ways corrupted by his politics.

Evaluation of Principal Biographical Sources

Cripps, Thomas. "Paul Robeson and Black Identity in American Movies." *Massachusetts Review* 11, 3 (1970): 468-485. (A, G) A sympathetic review of Robeson's impact on the image of American blacks in films.

Cruse, Harold. *The Crisis of the Negro Intellectual*. New York: Morrow, 1967. (A, G) This work fills in a significant chapter of Robeson's life in which he is criticized for his romantic approach to Stalinism.

Duberman, Martin Bauml. *Paul Robeson*. New York, Alfred A. Knopf, 1988. (A, G) This is the most comprehensive and balanced biography of Robeson. The author, who had access to correspondence and private papers, portrays Robeson as a fundamentally depressed artist; Robeson's art suffered because of his political involvement.

Ellison, W. James, "Paul Robeson and the State Department." *Crisis* 84 (May 1977): 184-189. (A, G) This is an important article that interprets Robeson as the victim of the Red Scare hysteria that gripped America during the late 1940s and 1950s.

Gilliam, Dorothy Butler. *Paul Robeson, All-American*. Washington: New Republic, 1976. (A, G, Y) A very sympathetic and uncritical biography of Robeson.

Graham, Shirley. *Paul Robeson, Citizen of the World*. New York: Messner, 1946. (A, G) A defensive biography of Robeson by the wife of W. E. B. DuBois.

Hoyt, Edwin P. *Paul Robeson: The American Othello*. Cleveland: World, 1967. (A, G) A solid critical biography in which Hoyt argues that Robeson was politically naive and that he was manipulated by the Communists; however, Hoyt acknowledges that Robeson reflected the changing political and social aspirations of American blacks.

Seaton, Marie. *Paul Robeson*. London: Dennis Dobson, 1958. (G) Seaton's biography provides an adequate profile of Robeson that focuses on the period since 1945.

Smith, Ronald A. "The Paul Robeson-Jackie Robinson Saga and a Political Collision." *Journal of Sport History* 6, 2 (Summer 1979): 5-27. An interesting article that compares the values of two prominent American blacks during the Cold War.

Stuckey, Sterling. "'I Want To Be African': Paul Robeson and the Ends of Nationalist Theory and Practice, 1914-1945." *Massachusetts Review* 17, 1 (1976): 81-38. (A, G) A sympathetic account of Robeson's early expressions of his black identity.

Williams, Roger M. "A Rough Sunday at Peekskill." *American Heritage* 27, 3 (1976): 72-79. (A, G, Y) An accurate account of Robeson's concerts and the subsequent riots that occurred in Peekskill, New York.

Wright, Charles H. "Paul Robeson at Peekskill." *Freedomways* 15, 2 (1975): 101-111. (**A, G**) Wright presents a uncritical account of the Peekskill riot and Robeson's connection with it.

Yeakey, Lamont T. "A Student Without Peer: The Undergraduate College Years of Paul Robeson." *Journal of Negro Education* 42, 4 (1973): 489-503. (**A, G**) A sympathetic portrait of Robeson at Rutgers that provides valuable information about his student years.

Overview and Evaluation of Primary Sources
The most significant primary source is Robeson's autobiography, *Here I Stand* (Boston: Beacon Press, 1958; **A, G, Y**). This work has been criticized for its lack of sophistication. While it provides a general portrait of Robeson's career, it is organized and written in a very elementary manner. Robeson intended this work to be read by the general public—especially American blacks and others who were not advanced in their education. One should also consult Robeson's numerous writings in the following journals and periodicals: *People's Voice, African Observer, Afro-American, American Dialog, American Scholar, Daily Worker, Freedomways, Jewish Life, Masses and Mainstream, Messenger, National Guardian, New Statesman and Nation, New World Review, New York Age, Opportunity, Spectator,* and *Worker.*

Many of Robeson's articles, speeches, and interviews have been collected in Philip S. Foner, ed., *Paul Robeson Speaks: Writings, Speeches, Interviews, 1918-1974* (New York: Brunner/Mazel, 1978; **A, G**). This is an outstanding and readily available collection. Two other collections of Robeson's writings and speeches are *Paul Robeson: Tributes, Selected Writings* (New York: The Archives, 1976; **A, G**), compiled by Roberta Yanct Dent, Marilyn Robeson, and Paul Robeson, Jr., and *Paul Robeson: The Great Forerunner* (New York: Dodd, 1985; **A, G**).

Although Robeson was a major political figure during a turbulent period in American history, few noteworthy memoirs have been attempted by his friends or associates. Perhaps the stigma of his political activities deterred would-be chroniclers. One early primary source is Eslanda Good Robeson, *Paul Robeson, Negro* (London: Victor Gollancz, 1930: **A, G**), which interprets Robeson as the most outstanding American black performing artist.

Fiction and Adaptations
Phillips Hayes Dean's play "Paul Robeson" was produced in 1979 and was subsequently denounced by prominent black leaders, such as Coretta Scott

King and Paul Robeson, Jr., for its failure to recognize the substance of Robeson's political agenda. The play has, however, continued to be performed to acclaim, most recently at the Kennedy Center in Washington, D.C. in 1989.

Other Sources

Davis, Lenwood G. *Paul Robeson Research Guide: A Selected, Annotated Bibliography*. Westport, CT: Greenwood Press, 1982. Provides useful sources through 1982 for researching Robeson's career and political views.

Hoggard, Bishop J. Clinton. "Paul Robeson: A Remembrance." *Crisis* 83 (March, 1976): 81-83. Hoggard presented this eulogy at Robeson's funeral at Mother A.M.E. Zion Church in New York on January 27, 1976.

William T. Walker
Philadelphia College of Pharmacy and Science

EDITH KERMIT CAROW ROOSEVELT
1861-1948

Chronology

Born Edith Kermit Carow on August 6, 1861, in Norwich, Connecticut, the first of two daughters of Charles Carow, member of a prosperous New York shipping family, and Gertrude Elizabeth Tyler Carow, whose ancestors helped settle New England; *1861-1886* grows up in New York City, living near Union Square with her family in her early years and near the family of Theodore Roosevelt, with whom she develops a strong friendship; her father's death (1883) leaves the family in "reduced circumstances"; studies privately and attends Miss Comstock's School on West 40th Street; *1886* in March moves to London with her mother and younger sister; on December 2 marries Theodore Roosevelt, whose first wife died nearly three years earlier; the couple will have five children; *1887* returns to New York with her husband and goes to live at Sagamore Hill, Oyster Bay, Long Island; *1889-1895* except for summer months, transfers her family to Washington, D.C., where Theodore serves as civil service commissioner; *1895-1897* returns to New York during Theodore's tenure as police commissioner; *1897-1898* uproots her family once more to follow Theodore (now assistant secretary of the navy) to Washington, D.C.; *1899-1901* presides over the Governor's Mansion in Albany following Theodore's election as governor of New York; *1901-1909* serves as first lady after Theodore's elevation to the presidency upon McKinley's assassination; *1909-1948* makes Sagamore Hill her home but travels widely after Theodore's death in 1919; *1927* purchases Mortlake Manor in Brooklyn, Connecticut, a house in which her ancestors had once lived and which she uses as a summer home for the rest of her life; *1948* dies on September 30 at Sagamore Hill of myocardial insufficiency and congestive failure.

Activities of Historical Significance

Edith Roosevelt is most often remembered as the patient, supportive wife of an extremely active, ebullient president, but she deserves recognition in her own right for reshaping the job of presidential spouse. In 1901 she became the first in that role to employ her own social secretary, relying on this assistant to help shape the news that the public received about the Roosevelt family. She also worked with Theodore to enlarge the White House and to separate public areas from those sections where the family lived. Theodore repeatedly commented on her excellent literary taste and on her good political instincts, but she refrained from taking public positions on any substantive issues and never ran for office herself. After Theodore's death, she traveled widely, spoke publicly in favor of Herbert Hoover's 1932 presidential campaign (in which he was defeated by Franklin D. Roosevelt), and contributed a section to a history of her mother's family—writing that comes as close to an autobiography as this reserved, elegant nineteenth-century lady was likely to compose.

Overview of Biographical Sources

Although several books about her husband and her stepdaughter, Alice Roosevelt Longworth, treat Edith Roosevelt as an important figure, she is the subject of only one full-length biography: Sylvia Jukes Morris's carefully researched and gracefully written *Edith Carow Roosevelt* (1979). The insistence with which Edith Roosevelt guarded her privacy may help explain the paucity of biographical materials. She reportedly concurred in the view—current in her time and among her friends—that a lady's name appeared in print only twice, at her marriage and at her death. Even in the conspicuous position of first lady, she clung to that view. Many magazines published photographs of her and her children while she lived in the White House, but very little text accompanied the pictures.

As stepmother to flamboyant, attention-hungry Alice, Edith is usually portrayed as caring but stern, and she is always described as differing from the younger woman in personality and style. Alice Longworth's autobiography, *Crowded Hours* (1933), treats Edith kindly. Theodore Roosevelt's biographers have not agreed on Edith's personality or her influence. Carleton Putnam, *Theodore Roosevelt: The Formative Years* (1958), describes her as ruthless and the subject of considerable fear among Roosevelt associates, but Edmund Morris, *The Rise of Theodore Roosevelt* (1979), takes the more common position that Edith was a supportive and intelligent companion, careful household manager, and stabilizing influence on Theodore.

Evaluation of Principal Biographical Sources

Hagedorn, Hermann. *The Roosevelt Family of Sagamore Hill.* New York: Macmillan, 1954. (G) Although centered on life at the Long Island residence, this very readable book also examines Edith Roosevelt's White House role and concludes that, avoiding the casualness and the provincial ways of some of her predecessors, she brought a dignity to the presidential mansion not seen since the Federal period.

Morris, Edmund. *The Rise of Theodore Roosevelt.* New York: Coward, McCann, Geohegan, 1979. (A, G) In its coverage of Theodore up to the time he assumed the presidency, this award-winning first volume of a projected multi-volume biography notes Edith's considerable influence on her husband. She opposed, for instance, his running for the mayoralty of New York in 1894.

Morris, Sylvia Jukes. *Edith Carow Roosevelt: Portrait of a First Lady*. New York: Coward, McCann, Geohegan, 1979. (A, G) For this, the most complete and thoroughly documented record of Edith's life, the author interviewed several family members and gained access to privately held collections of relevant materials. Although generally admiring of her subject, Morris captures a special sternness when she reports that Edith Roosevelt once said, "If I could not have both, I should choose my children's respect rather than their love."

Robinson, Corinne Roosevelt. *My Brother Theodore*. New York: Scribner's, 1921. (G) This very admiring biography by Theodore's younger sister is most useful for its description of the president's childhood and the first meetings between "Teedie" Roosevelt and "Edie" Carow (who was Corinne's good friend).

Overview and Evaluation of Primary Sources

Rather than writing a complete autobiography, Edith teamed up with son Kermit to document her mother's illustrious ancestors in *American Backlogs: The Story of Gertrude Tyler and Her Family, 1660-1860* (New York: Scribner's, 1928; G). The book consists mostly of letters, covering the Tylers from the time they arrived in America to the time when Edith's mother, Gertrude Elizabeth Tyler, married Charles Carow.

Edith's other attempt at published self-examination came in a chapter entitled "The Odyssey of a Grandmother" that she contributed to the book *Cleared for Strange Ports* (New York: Scribner's, 1927; G). Although failing to divulge a great deal, she describes her world travels after Theodore's death, and she prefaces her account with a revealing comment: "Women who marry pass their best and happiest years in giving life and fostering it . . . and those born with the wanderfoot are sometimes a bit irked by the weight of the always beloved shackles."

Because so few primary sources are available for Edith Roosevelt, Mrs. Theodore Roosevelt, Jr.'s *Day Before Yesterday: Reminiscences of Mrs. Theodore Roosevelt, Jr.* (Garden City, NY: Doubleday, 1959; G) is useful. Although much of this book is devoted to the author's own world travels, it also includes family stories about Edith, who was the author's mother-in-law. The younger Mrs. Roosevelt, whose name was actually Eleanor Butler (Alexander) and who was sometimes dubbed "the second Eleanor," is generally admiring in her treatment of Edith but also implies that she could be critical and sarcastic.

Unpublished letters and papers of Edith Carow Roosevelt are located in the Theodore Roosevelt Collection, Widener and Houghton Libraries, Harvard University, Cambridge, Massachusetts, and in the Kermit Roosevelt Papers and the Theodore Roosevelt Papers at the Library of Congress, Washington, D.C. The Harvard collection was enriched in the 1980s by the addition of her diaries, which had been privately held. Edith's multi-volume scrapbook, "White House Record of Social Events, 1901-1909," is in the National Archives, Washington, D.C. Additional memorabilia are at the Sagamore Hill estate, Oyster Bay, New York, and at the Theodore Roosevelt Birthplace in Manhattan.

Fiction and Adaptations

The Roosevelt family, with special emphasis on young Quentin Roosevelt, are the subject of *The White House Gang*, Earle Looker's 1929 account of the antics of these rambunctious inhabitants of the presidential mansion.

A 93-minute documentary, "The Indomitable Teddy Roosevelt," made for ABC-TV in 1986, follows the president from birth to death and includes footage of his birthplace, ranch, and Sagamore Hill. In reviewing the film for the *Journal of American History* (December 1986), John Milton Cooper, Jr., regretted that "fictionalized reminiscences" were used rather than surviving recordings of the Roosevelt family. The part of Edith Roosevelt is played by Philippa Roosevelt. This film is available on videocassette.

Museums, Historical Landmarks, Societies

Sagamore Hill (Oyster Bay, NY). Although Theodore began this house for his first wife, Alice, he and Edith completed it, and she made it her primary residence from her marriage until her death. Much of the house reflects her husband's interest in big game hunting, but the parlor bears her strong imprint. Maintained by the National Park Service and open to the public, it houses furniture, books, and other family memorabilia.

Theodore Roosevelt Birthplace (New York, NY). This brownstone, constructed on the site where the Roosevelt mansion once stood at 28 East 20th Street, is furnished as it would have been in Theodore's youth. Although the emphasis is on his early years, some of the memorabilia relate to his later years and to Edith and the children. Maintained by the National Park Service, the house is open to the public.

Theodore Roosevelt Association (Oyster Bay, NY). This organization, formed after the president's death, now publishes the *T.R.A. Journal* and sponsors conferences and other activities focusing on the Roosevelt family. Mailing address: Box 720, Oyster Bay, NY 11771.

Other Sources

Caroli, Betty Boyd. *First Ladies.* New York: Oxford University Press, 1987. Places Edith in the context of White House history and credits her with institutionalizing the role of first lady.

Morison, Elting E. "Edith Kermit Carow Roosevelt." In *Notable American Women*, vol. 3, edited by Edward T. James et al. Cambridge: Harvard University Press, 1971. Short interpretive biographical sketch with bibliography for further study.

Betty Boyd Caroli
Kingsborough Community College,
City University of New York

JOHN ROSS
1790-1866

Chronology

Born John Ross (native name Caaweescoowe) on October 3, 1790, near Lookout Mountain, Tennessee (some sources cite Coosa River at Tahnoovay-ah, Georgia; Center, Alabama; or Rossville, Georgia), the third child of Daniel Ross, a Scottish trader among the Cherokees and Mary McDonald Ross, a woman of Cherokee descent; *1796-1806* educated at home by private tutors; attends an academy in Kingston, Tennessee; *1809* sent by a federal Indian agent on a mission to the Western Cherokees of Arkansas; *1812-1814* serves as an adjutant of the Cherokee Regiment in the army of Andrew Jackson; *March 13, 1813* fights in the Battle of Horseshoe Bend against the Creeks; *1813* marries Quatie (Elizabeth Brown Henley); they have five children; *1817* becomes a member of the National Council of the Cherokee Nation; *1819-1826* elected president of the council; leads or serves on numerous delegations to Washington to clarify treaties and represents Cherokee demands to the authorities; *1827* serves as president of Cherokee Constitutional Convention and helps to draft the Cherokee Constitution; elected assistant chief; *1828* elected and serves as principal chief of the Eastern Cherokees until 1839; *1828-1839* makes numerous trips to Washington to represent the needs of his people to the authorities; *1830s* leads Cherokee party opposed to removal of tribes to the West; *March 3, 1832* Supreme Court rules on *Worcester* v. *Georgia;* *1838-1839* Eastern Cherokees are removed to the western Indian Territory, a journey that came to be called the "Trail of Tears"; wife dies during journey; *1839* helps draft the constitution that unites Eastern and Western Cherokees into one nation; *1839-1866* serves as chief of the United Cherokee Nation; *September 2, 1844* marries Mary Bryan Stapler of Wilmington, Delaware; they have three children; *May 17, 1861* declares Cherokee neutrality in the Civil War; *October 1861* Cherokee Council signs a treaty of alliance with the Confederacy over his objections; *1862-1863* leaves Indian Territory, moves to Philadelphia, and repudiates alliance with the Confederacy; *1865* second wife dies; *August 1, 1866* dies in Washington, D.C., and is later buried in Park Hill, Oklahoma.

Activities of Historical Significance

Chief John Ross provides an early example of the frustration and pain experienced by Native Americans in attempting to deal with the federal government. After initial violent encounters with white settlers, the Cherokees voluntarily adopted many of the ways of the whites, forming a constitutional government with elected officers and establishing a separate nation within the borders of the U.S. In spite of these concessions and earnest efforts to seek solutions to property conflicts within the law, the Cherokees, along with the other "civilized" tribes of the eastern United States, were forceably removed to the Indian Territory in 1838.

For over fifty years, Chief John Ross served the Cherokee tribes in a variety of roles. Although he was only one-eighth Cherokee, he became the tribe's principal chief from the 1830s until his death in 1866. Ross worked vigorously to allow the Cherokees to remain in their traditional homeland, appealing to local, state, and federal governments. He petitioned Congress and filed law suits, one of which was appealed to the Supreme Court. But, in the end, he was forced to lead his people into exile on the infamous Trail of Tears. It is estimated that nearly four thousand Cherokees lost their lives during their removal to the western reservations.

Once in the Indian Territory, Ross was instrumental in reconciling the Eastern and Western Cherokees into a single nation. Unfortunately, this unity was not easily maintained due to constant infighting among the various factions within the tribe. With the advent of the Civil War, the rift became irreconcilable, and the Cherokee Nation split along sectional lines, with opposed groups supporting the North and the South. Although Ross was a slaveholder, he eventually sided with the North and lived in exile for most of the war. At the end of the conflict, Ross worked until his death in 1866 for a policy of reconstruction that would again unify the Cherokees into a single nation.

Overview of Biographical Sources

Ross has attracted the attention of several biographers over the years, some of whom wrote for younger readers. One of the most important of the works for adults is Rachel Caroline Eaton, *John Ross and the Cherokee Indians* (1914). For evaluations of Ross's political career, one should see Morris Wardell, *A Political History of the Cherokee Nation, 1838-1907* (1938), and Grace Steele Woodward, *The Cherokees* (1963). Gary Moulton, *John Ross Cherokee Chief* (1978), is the most current biography.

Evaluation of Principal Biographical Sources

Clark, Electa. *Cherokee Chief: The Life of John Ross.* London: Crowell-Collier Press, 1970. (Y) This biography is written for young readers and was illustrated by John Wagner.

Eaton, Rachel Caroline. *John Ross and the Cherokee Indians.* Menasha, WI: George Banta, 1914. (A, G) Based on the author's dissertation, this work is recognized as one of the best studies on Ross and his leadership of the Cherokees.

Harrell, Sara Gordon. *John Ross.* Minneapolis: Dillon Press, 1979. (Y) Written for grades 4-8, this work is part of the Story of an American Indian Series.

Moulton, Gary E. *John Ross Cherokee Chief.* Athens: University of Georgia Press, 1978. (A, G) The author presents a well-documented history and analysis of Ross's life and accomplishments. It is the most current scholarly biography available.

Overview and Evaluation of Primary Sources

Researchers into the life of John Ross are fortunate in that the Cherokees developed a written language, based on an alphabet devised by Sequoyah in 1821. The Cherokee Nation had its own constitution, as well as a national newspaper. Ross also left extensive correspondence and other papers. In addition, there is a wealth of official documents concerning the treaties and court cases involving the Cherokee Nation.

The most important primary sources are the personal papers of John Ross, which have been collected and edited by Ross biographer Gary E. Moulton. These papers were published in two volumes as *The Papers of Chief John Ross* (Norman: University of Oklahoma Press, 1985; A).

Ross's original manuscripts are housed in several locations. The largest collection is available for study at the Thomas Gilcrease Institute of American History and Art Library in Tulsa, Oklahoma. Some of the items included in this collection are correspondence, proclamations, accounts, and petitions to Congress. The University of Oklahoma Library also includes correspondence, speeches, reports, and proclamations from John Ross. An additional archive for Ross papers can be located in the Cherokee National Historical Society and Museum in Tahlequah, Oklahoma.

The "Cherokee Collection" in the Tennessee State Library and Archives in Nashville include material on the Cherokee Nation and John Ross.

Fiction and Adaptations

Jan Jordan, *Give Me the Wind: A Biographical Novel of John Ross, Chief of the Cherokees* (1973) is a biographical novel that treats John Ross's life and his role in the Cherokee Nation. The line between fact and fiction is not well defined in this work.

Museums, Historical Landmarks, Societies
Cherokee Nation Site (Tahlequal, OK). Along with other buildings are the Cherokee Supreme Court and the First Cherokee Female Seminary.

John Ross House (Rossville, GA). Located at Lake Avenue and Spring Street, the home was built in the 1830s. It is not currently open to the public.

Ross's Landing (Chattanooga, TN). Located at 101 Market St., this is the landing site for the first example of a pendulum ferry in North America, originated by John Ross in 1813. Not currently open to the public.

Other Sources
Dale, Edward E. "John Ross." In *Dictionary of American Biography,* vol. 16, edited by Dumas Malone. New York: Scribner's, 1935. Provides a list of older sources for further reading on Ross's career.

Dockstader, Federick J. "John Ross." In *Great North American Indians: Profiles in Life and Leadership.* New York: Van Nostrand Reinhold, 1977. Gives principal facts on Ross's life, but many are not collaborated elsewhere.

Faulk, Odie B. "John Ross." In *The McGraw-Hill Encyclopedia of World Biography,* vol. 9. New York: McGraw-Hill, 1973. Provides a short article on the life of John Ross and an analysis of additional works.

Gabriel, Ralph H. "John Ross." In *The Reader's Encyclopedia of the American West.* New York: Thomas Y. Crowell, 1977. Places Ross as the most important Cherokee leader in the first half of the nineteenth century.

Malone, Henry Thompson. *Cherokees of the Old South; a People in Transition.* Athens: University of Georgia Press, 1956. A history of the Cherokees until their removal to the Indian Territory.

Wardell, Morris L. *A Political History of the Cherokee Nation, 1838-1907.* Norman: University of Oklahoma Press, 1938. A study of the political history of the Cherokees from the time of their removal to the disbandment of the Cherokee Nation in 1907. Concentrates less on Ross's role than Woodward's.

Woodward, Grace Steele. *The Cherokees.* Norman: University of Oklahoma Press, 1963. A history of the Cherokee Nation to 1866.

Maurice G. Fortin
University of North Texas

SUSANNA ROWSON
1762-1824

Chronology

Born Susanna Haswell on February 10 in Portsmouth, England, the only child of William Haswell, Royal Navy lieutenant, and his first wife, Susanna Musgrave, who died ten days after giving birth; *1767* joins her father in Nantasket, Massachusetts, journeying to America in a voyage that ends in shipwreck on Lovell's Island, off the New England coast; *1768-1775* enjoys the privileges of a private education in the classics and the advantages of aristocratic life in the colonies; *1775* after a failed attempt to flee revolutionary fervor, she and her family are interned as loyalists, under guard, in Hingham, Massachusetts and their property is confiscated; *1777* the family is imprisoned in Abington, Massachusetts, where Rowson's father and step-mother suffer health problems; *1778* the family is allowed to leave for London as part of a prisoner exchange, where they live in poverty without a government pension; *1778-1786* Rowson works as a governess for the children of the Duchess of Devonshire; to support her family, writes songs for Vaux-hall amusement park; claims to have travelled across the continent as a governess to observe aristocratic values and foibles, providing source material for her first novel, *Victoria* (1786), dedicated to the Duchess; *1787* resigns as governess to marry William Rowson, a London hardware merchant and trum-peter in the Royal Horse Guards; *1788* anonymously publishes *Poems on Various Subjects,* the poem "A Trip to Parnassus; or a Critique of Authors and Performers," and a collection of tales in novel form, *The Inquisitor, or the Invisible Rambler*; *1789* anonymously publishes *Mary, The Test of Honour,* written solely for money and never acknowledged by her; *1791* publishes *Mentoria, or the Young Ladies' Friend,* another collection of tales in novel form, as well as her most famous and successful novel, *Charlotte Temple: A Tale of Truth,* an extravagantly sentimental novel about the seduction of a pampered English schoolgirl, who is lured into a sexual alliance and then abandoned by a British army officer; *1792* publishes the autobiographical novel *Rebecca; or the Fille de Chambre*; *1793-1797* after the bankruptcy of her husband's hardware business, the Rowsons take to the stage and perform in Edinburgh, Philadelphia, Annapolis, Baltimore, and Boston, in a total of 129 different parts in 126 different productions, many written by Susanna herself; *1794* appears in the most successful of her operettas, *Slaves in Algiers, or a Struggle for Freedom,* about a group of American women who escape from North African pirates; the play's "feminism" and democratic values cause her to become the subject of a pamphlet controversy between William Cobbett and John Swanwick; *1795* publishes the four-volume, largely autobiographical *Trials of the Human Heart, The Volunteers,* a farce for the stage, and her most popular song, "America, Commerce and Freedom"; *1796* moves to Boston to perform and write for the Federal Street Theater; *1797* performs in *Americans in England,* her last stage appearance; *1798* publishes *Reuben and Rachel,* a fictionalized account of the heirs of Christopher Columbus; *1797-1822* founds and administers the Young Ladies Academy in Boston; writes textbooks on geography, history, spelling, and the Bible for secondary-level students; *1802* becomes an American citizen when her husband is naturalized; *1802-1813* contributes weekly columns to the *Boston Weekly Magazine,* the *Monthly Anthology,* and the *New England Galaxy*; *1804* publishes *Miscellaneous Poems,* including several of her best-known songs; *1813* publishes *Sarah, the Exemplary Wife,* a series of moral tracts taken from her journalistic writings (originally published as *Sincerity*); *1822* retires and entrusts her Academy to her niece and adopted daughter; *1824* dies on March 2 and is buried in St. Matthew's Church, South Boston; *1828* her sequel to *Charlotte Temple, Charlotte's Daughter; or, The Tree Orphans,* is published posthumously; *1866* St. Matthew's Church is demolished and her remains are removed to Mount Hope Cemetery in Dorchester.

Activities of Historical Significance

Rowson's fame in literary history rests on her authorship of *Charlotte Temple* (1791), generally considered to be the first American bestseller. Although the novel lacks the literary values we prize today—ambiguity, subtlety, irony—it does have historical value as the first work of fiction to use the American Revolution as a setting. The novel also functioned as a powerful enforcer of female sexual morality—the sexual double standard—and served as an object lesson in the "separate sphere" concept, which maintained that women should attend to domestic affairs, while men handled public affairs. Contemporary feminist critics claim that Rowson's novels, while ostensibly about the evils and dangers of illicit sexuality, also subvert and criticize those social and economic conventions that encourage dependence in women.

As the founder of the Young Ladies Academy, Rowson was one of the first women to provide formal education for American women at the secondary level. The textbooks she wrote for the female students in her Academy had the unusual characteristic of including material relevant to women. Rowson's school was also one of the first to offer instruction in music and public speaking for women.

Although she was raised as a loyalist, Rowson eventually became a fierce American patriot, using the musical theatre as a forum to expose citizens to democratic ideals and such topical subjects as the Whisky Rebellion and the evils of slavery.

Overview of Biographical Sources

Rowson's reputation as a figure of some prominence in early American culture has been rescued only in the past decade, largely through the efforts of feminist critics determined to restore to the canon forgotten women of letters. Early biographical sources (Knapp, Buckingham, Nason, Halsey) stressed Rowson's role as an educator and author of the hugely successful *Charlotte Temple.* Modern attempts to place Rowson more clearly within the early American political and social scene began with the recent feminist biographies written by Dorothy Weil, *In Defense of Women: Susanna Rowson* (1976), Patricia L. Parker, *Susanna Rowson* (1986), and Cathy N. Davidson, *Introduction to "Charlotte Temple."* (1986).

The earliest source for biographical information is the obituary in Boston's *Evening Gazette,* March 6, 1824. Samuel L. Knapp's "Memoir," which served as the preface to *Charlotte's Daughter* (1828), is the earliest extended biographical and critical source. Other early sources include Joseph T. Buckingham, *Personal Memoirs and Recollections of Editorial Life* (1852), I, 83-85; and Francis W. Halsey's editorial introduction to *Charlotte Temple* (1905 ed.).

Evaluation of Principal Biographical Sources

Davidson, Cathy N. Introduction to *Charlotte Temple,* by Susanna Rowson. New York: Oxford, 1986. (**A, G**) An extended biographical introduction prefaces this modern edition of the novel. Davidson explains the huge popularity of the novel by seeing it as an allegory of the changing political and social conditions in early America.

Nason, Elias. *A Memoir of Mrs. Susanna Rowson, with Elegant and Illustrative Extracts from Her Writings in Prose and Poetry.* Albany: Munsell, 1870. (**A**) Generally considered to be a highly laudatory early source for her life, this biography depends for "facts" on letters from Rowson's former students.

Parker, Patricia L. *Susanna Rowson.* Boston: Twayne, 1986. (**A**) Generally considered to be the best modern biography of Rowson. The study includes extended discussions of Rowson's novels, her writings for the stage, her textbooks, essays, and poems. Parker concludes that "like the new nation, Rowson showed herself to be eager, energetic, didactic, experimental, uncertain, opportunistic, and flexible." Also contains the best and most extensive bibliography on Rowson.

Weil, Dorothy. *In Defense of Women: Susanna Rowson.* University Park: Pennsylvania State University Press, 1976. (**A**) Weil provides an extensive overview of all of Rowson's writings. She attempts to prove that Rowson was "a robust teacher who stresses the Christian religion, democratic ideals, reality over fantasy, and sense over sensibility, [one] who tries to tie these teachings to a realistic and practical view of life.''

Overview and Evaluation of Primary Sources

Rowson's own novels (particularly *Rebecca, Victoria,* and *Trials of the Human Heart*) are generally considered largely autobiographical, although much of the material cannot be substantiated and may be part of the legend Rowson tried to construct about herself.

Charlotte Temple is Rowson's only novel to consistently remain in print since its publication in 1791. Her other novels—*Charlotte's Daughter* (1828), *Rebecca, or the Fille de Chambre* (1792), *The Inquisitor; or Invisible Rambler* (1788), *Mentoria; or the Young Lady's Friend* (1791), *Reuben and Rachel; or, The Tales of Old Times* (1798), *Sarah, or the Exemplary Wife* (1813), *Trials of the Human Heart* (1795), and *Victoria, A Novel* (1786)—are little more than variations on a few sentimental morality tales, seduction novels, or historical fiction.

Her dramatic works stand as historical curiosities, several of them never published, with no copy known for others. Those for which copies exist include *Slaves in Algiers; or, A Struggle for Freedom* (1794) and *The Volunteers* (1795).

Her educational writings, which have a certain importance as documents in the history of women's education, include *Universal Geography, Together with Sketches of History* (1805); *Biblical Dialogues Between a Father and His Family* (1822); *Exercises in History* (1822); *A Present for Young Ladies* (1811); *A Spelling Dictionary* (1807); and *Youth's First Steps in Geography* (1818).

Her poetical writings were anthologized in *Miscellaneous Poems* (1804) and the anonymously published *Poems on Various Subjects* (1788), although no copy of the latter is known to exist.

Fiction and Adaptations

In 1875 Caroline Dall published *The Romance of the Association; or, One Last Glimpse of Charlotte Temple and Eliza Wharton* (Cambridge: Wilson), an unreliable and imaginative version of the supposed historical events upon which *Charlotte Temple* was based.

Museums, Historical Landmarks, Societies

Charlotte Temple Tombstone (New York, NY). The most famous historical landmark connected with Rowson is a tombstone erected to "Charlotte Temple" in Trinity Churchyard. Thousands of people during the nineteenth and early twentieth century flocked to this tomb to leave love letters, bouquets of flowers, and personal mementoes on the tombstone. No one knows exactly who is buried under the stone or when the burial occurred.

Other Sources

Charvat, William. *Literary Publishing in America: 1790-1850*. Philadelphia: University of Pennsylvania Press, 1959.

Davidson, Cathy N. *Revolution and the Word: The Rise of the Novel in America*. New York: Oxford University Press, 1986.

Fiedler, Leslie. *Love and Death in the American Novel*, Rev. ed. New York: Stein and Day, 1966.

Hogan, Charles B. *The London Stage, 1778-1800: A Critical Introduction*. Carbondale: Southern Illinois University Press, 1968.

McNamara, Brooks. *The American Playhouse in the Eighteenth Century*. Cambridge: Harvard University Press, 1969.

Martin, Wendy. "Seduced and Abandoned in the New World: The Fallen Woman in American Fiction." In *American Sister-hood: Writings of the Feminist Movement from Colonial Times to the Present*, edited by Wendy Martin. New York: Harper & Row, 1972.

Meserve, Walter J. *An Emerging Entertainment: The Drama of the American People to 1828*. Bloomington: Indiana University Press, 1977.

Norton, Mary Beth. *The British-Americans: The Loyalist Exiles in England, 1774-1789*. London: Constable, 1974.

Seilhamer, George O. *History of the American Theatre from 1774 to 1797*. Philadelphia: Globe, 1891.

Vail, Robert W. G. *Susanna Haswell Rowson, the Author of Charlotte Temple: A Bibliographical Study*. Worcester: American Antiquarian Society, 1933. Lists all the editions of Rowson's works.

Diane Long Hoeveler
Marquette University

ANNE ROYALL
1769-1854

Chronology

Born Anne Newport on June 11, 1769, in Baltimore, Maryland to William Newport, possibly an illegitimate member of the Calvert family, and Mary Newport; father has ties to the Royalist cause and is considered a Tory; *1772* family leaves Maryland for the Pennsylvania frontier, where her mother becomes a physician skilled in herbal medicines; taught to read by her father, who mysteriously disappears and is presumed dead; *1782* flees to Virginia with her mother after Hanastown, Pennsylvania, where the family had settled, is completely destroyed by Native Americans; *1797* marries William Royall, scholar, farmer, Revolutionary veteran, and Freemason, in whose household she had been living as a servant; *1803* William Royall dies and leaves her the bulk of his estate; *1813* Royall's other heirs break his will, leaving Anne Royall nearly penniless; moves to Washington, D.C., to petition Congress for a Revolutionary War veteran widow's pension; *1824* begins to travel through the U.S. to earn a living by writing travel accounts; *1826* publishes *Sketches of History, Life and Manners in the United States by a Traveller*; *1827* publishes a novel, *The Tennessean*; *1828-1829* publishes the three volumes of *The Black Book, or Continuation of Travels in the United States*; *1829* publishes the two volumes of *Mrs. Royall's Pennsylvania*; *1829* is the first and only American to be tried and convicted on the charge of being a common scold; *1830* publishes *Letters from Alabama*; *1830-1831* publishes two volumes of *Mrs. Royall's Southern Tour*; *1831* begins editing and publishing a newspaper, *Paul Pry*, in Washington in December; *1836* starts a new paper, *The Huntress*, in December; *1848* finally receives her widow's pension, but most of it goes to her husband's other heirs; *1854* dies at her home on B Street in southeast Washington on October 1; buried in the Congressional Cemetery.

Activities of Historical Significance

One of Anne Royall's biographers commented in 1907 that she was "not a figure of historical national importance. Neither do her writings possess sufficient intrinsic merit to rank as literature." Nonetheless, she was a pioneering female figure in journalism and an acute, if biased and acerbic, observer of the social and political scene in Washington and throughout the young nation. Her strong defense of the Freemasons, of which her husband had been a loyal member, and her attacks on the harsh Calvinistic tenets of the Presbyterian church earned her many enemies during the 1820s. After

Presbyterian clergymen in Washington brought complaints against her in the District court, she was tried and convicted of being a common scold, an offense designed to protect others from being harangued by zealots. She evaded penalty when the justices decided that ducking was an old-fashioned and unsuitable punishment.

After her conviction, she turned to journalism and remained in Washington. Her newspapers earned the reputation of publishing thorough investigative stories about corruption among members of the Washington journalistic and political establishment. She never recouped the fortune she lost when her husband's will was broken in 1813, and she died a virtual pauper. While today she would be hailed as an example of women's entrepreneurial spirit, most of her contemporaries thought of her as a crank. This view has dogged her reputation over the years, and those few voices who lauded her generosity to the poor, the sick, and the down trodden, as well as her integrity and commitment to journalism, have seldom been heard.

Overview of Biographical Sources

There are three biographies about Royall, and none is of the highest quality. Porter's *The Life and Times and Anne Royall* (1909) is the best work but may be difficult to find in local libraries. Alice S. Maxwell's *Virago!* (1985) should be the best since it is the most recent and should benefit from new feminist scholarship about the period. George S. Jackson's *Uncommon Scold* (1937) presents an old-fashioned account of the events leading to Royall's trial. The most convenient and reliable account is the sketch of her life and times in *Dictionary of American Biography* (New York: Scribner's, 1928-1936)

Evaluation of Principal Biographical Sources

Jackson, George Stuyvesant. *Uncommon Scold*. Boston: B. Humphries, 1937. (G) A slim and pedestrian monograph.

Maxwell, Alice S. *Virago!* Jefferson, NC: McFarland, 1985. (G) The most recent and longest of the three biographies, Maxwell's account of Royall's life and times is only adequate.

Porter, Sara Harvey. *The Life and Times of Anne Royall*. Cedar Rapids, IA: Torch Press Book Shop, 1909. (G) Porter's study, the first full-length treatment of Royall, presents an even and objective tone. It is the primary source of much of what is known about her.

Overview and Evaluation of Primary Sources

Royall is best known today for her lively and engaging travel writings which contain her witty and acerbic observations on nineteenth-century American society and morals. Various reprint editions of them are currently available. Her often unkind and exaggerated comments generated hard feelings against her. Like other nineteenth-century travelers, she found America rough-hewn, crude, and lacking the "civilizing virtues." She did not try to understand the hardships faced by those in the many frontiers and backwaters she visited, which is surprising considering her early life in western Pennsylvania.

Her only foray into fiction, *The Tennessean*, has not stood the test of time. She also wrote plays, probably of similar quality, which have not survived in any form. Her newspapers, on the other hand, were very good, especially by the standards of the day, and examined the motives of politicians and statesmen more closely than more circumspect publications. Her stories and columns reflected a different view of Washington and the federal government than were found in the established newspapers. Full collections of her newspapers and her personal papers are in the Manuscripts Division of the Library of Congress. Filling twenty-two boxes, these documents provide a rich source of information about Royall and early nineteenth-century Washington.

Other Sources

Porter, Sarah Harvey. "The Life and Times of Anne Royall, 1769-1854." *Records of the Columbia Historical Society* 10 (1907): 1-37. This preliminary article by Royall's first biographer is a useful introduction to the woman and her work.

Jean V. Berlin
Correspondence of William T. Sherman

ROSEMARY RADFORD RUETHER
b. 1936

Chronology

Born Rosemary Radford Armstrong on November 2, 1936, in St. Paul, Minnesota, to Robert Armstrong, an Anglican Republican from Virginia, and Rebecca Cresap Ord Radford, born in Monterey, Mexico, of English and Austrian Catholic descent; mother's family traces its roots to colonial America, and boasts a line of West Point officers, as well as pioneers in California and Mexico; grows up in the Radford house in Georgetown, Washington, D.C. *1941-1945* has little contact with father who is away at war; *1948* father dies in Greece; *1952* moves with family to her mother's childhood home in La Jolla, California; *1957* marries Herman J. Ruether, with whom she has three children; *1958* receives bachelor's degree from Scripps College in Claremont, California; *1960* receives master's degree in classics and Roman history from Claremont Graduate School; associates with a creative community based at the Benedictine priory of St. Andrews in Valyermo, California; awarded a Danforth Grant; *1962* awarded a Kent Fellowship; becomes deeply involved in the civil rights movement; *1965* receives Ph.D. in classics and patristics from Claremont Graduate School; works as a Delta Ministry volunteer in Mississippi; teaches at Immaculate Heart College, Los Angeles; *1966* returns to Washington, D.C., with her family; *late 1960s* corresponds with and befriends Thomas Merton and Gregory Baum; becomes involved with the Harrisburg Defense Group to defeat the FBI's conspiracy charges against activists Philip Berrigan and Elizabeth McAlister; develops close ties with the Washington-based Community for Creative Non-Violence, which provides social services for the poor; *1966-1976* serves as associate professor of historical theology in the School of Religion, Howard University, with term lectureships in theology and women's studies at George Washington University, Princeton Theological Seminary, Harvard Divinity School, Yale Divinity School, and Sir George Williams University, Montreal, Canada; *1975-1976* serves as preceptor in theology for Inter-Faith Metropolitan Theological Education in Washington, D.C.; *1977-present* serves as Georgia Harkness Professor of Applied Theology at Garrett-Evangelical Theological Seminary, Northwestern University; *1984* attends the universities of Lund and Uppsala, Sweden, as a Fulbright Scholar.

Activities of Historical Significance

Ruether, along with Elizabeth Schussler-Fiorenza and Mary Hunt, was influential in shaping the Women-Church movement in the early 1980s. In this role, she served as a bold spokesperson for Catholic and Protestan women experiencing sexism and oppression by male-dominated church struc‐ tures. Between 1965 and 1983 she delivered nearly six hundred speeches a major universities and church conventions.

Between 1963 and 1990, Ruether published nearly four hundred article: and reviews, edited four books, co-edited two books, co-authored three books, and authored fourteen books. She has contributed over sixty articles anc chapters to books and reference works on a variety of subjects, analyzing sexism inherent in the male-dominated practices and structures of every modern institution. Classically and theologically trained, but unorthodox in hei conclusions, Ruether is one of the first women scholars to use the academic forum to call for sweeping social change in commerce, politics, religion education, the economy, and the environment.

Ruether's profound effect on women's networks and feminist groups come: from her ability to meld theology with the findings of other disciplines, sucl as anthropology, sociology, psychology, history, political science, and wo‐ men's studies. Although ill-regarded by some mainstream Catholic theologian: who criticize her for mixing Christianity with socialism, Ruether's principlec stance and her passionate appeals have won the respect of thousands who are committed to fighting social injustice. Many regard her words as prophetic.

Overview of Biographical/Critical Sources

There are no convenient sources for biographical information about Rueth‐ er, and researchers must piece together scattered accounts of her life. She addresses her childhood in context of its influence on her religious views in *Disputed Questions: On Being a Christian* (1982), and Mary Hembrow Snyder, in *The Christology of Rosemary Radford Ruether, A Critical Introduc‐ tion* (1988), addresses the influences that led Ruether to study the relationship between Christianity and feminism. Because Ruether has published so exten‐ sively, and because some of her publications touch on deeply personal beliefs, skillful biographers can deduce many psychological influences, but to date Ruether's work has stood without the benefit of biographical data. On the other hand, her treatises have been widely read and analyzed. Ruether's vision for a just world has been captured by William M. Ramsay's "Rosemary Radford Ruether and Feminist Theology" (1986). In addition, several scholars have written dissertations on aspects of Ruether's theology, including Evans (1980), Vaughan (1982), and Weir (1982).

Evaluation of Selected Biographical/Critical Sources

Evans, Ruth. "Women as Other: A Study of Alienation in Rosemary Ruether, Mary Daly, and Sheila Collins." Master's thesis. St. Michael's

College, Toronto, 1980. (A) This work analyzes the philosophical stances of three noted social critics.

Ramsay, William M. "Rosemary Radford Ruether and Feminist Theology." In *Four Modern Prophets: Walter Rauschenbusch, Martin Luther King, Jr., Gustavo Gutierrez, and Rosemary Radford Ruether.* Westminster, England: John Knox, 1986. (A) A brief, dispassionate examination of Ruether's vision of justice for the world.

Snyder, Mary Hembrow. *The Christology of Rosemary Radford Ruether: A Critical Introduction.* Mystic, CT: Twenty-Third Press, 1988. (A) A luminous and careful exposition of Ruether's radical reevaluation of Christology.

Vaughan, Judy. *Sociality, Ethics and Social Change.* Lanham, MD: University Press of America, 1983. (A) Adapted from Vaughan's 1982 dissertation, this book provides a critical appraisal of Reinhold Niebuhr's ethics in the light of Ruether's works.

Weir, Mary Kathryn. "The Concept of Freedom in the Work of Rosemary Ruether." Ph.D. dissertation. Faculty of Divinity, St. Mary's College, University of St. Andrews, Scotland, 1982. (A) An insightful analysis of a basic theme of Ruether's philosophy and writings.

Overview and Evaluation of Primary Sources
Ruether's few autobiographical writings in print are worth pursuing for a critical understanding of her ideas. In "Professing Theology: Essays in Praise of Teachers; Robert Palmer: First the God, Then the Dance" (*The Christian Century* 107 [February 7, 1990]: 125; A), Ruether credits a historian at Scripps College with inspiring the development of her feminist theology, which is based on three principles: a recognition that there is more than one true religion; an acknowledgement that social arrangements other than those dominated by a patriarchy have existed; and a belief that the "text is dead" if it doesn't lead back to liturgy and theophany.

A fuller exposition of her theological tenets appears in "The Development of My Theology" (*Religious Studies Review* 15 [January 1989]: 1-4; A). Two other worthwhile critical commentaries follow in this journal: Kathryn Allen Rabuzzi, "The Socialist Feminist Vision of Rosemary Radford Ruether: A Challenge to Liberal Feminism," and Rebecca S. Chopp, "Seeing and Naming the Word Anew: The Works of Rosemary Radford Ruether."

In *Disputed Questions: On Being a Christian* (Maryknoll, NY: Orbis Books, 1982; A, G) Ruether succinctly describes the intellectual and personal influences of her childhood and young adulthood, and her questioning of

Christian theology in its institutional forms including the politics of patriarchy, sexism, racism, and Jewish-Christian relations.

From 1967 to 1990, Ruether wrote fourteen books, many of which are considered ground-breaking theological studies. *The Radical Kingdom: The Western Experience of Messianic Hope* (San Francisco: Harper & Row: 1970; **A, G**), offers a sophisticated and somewhat evangelistic analysis of theological motifs in radical social change movements. In *Liberation Theology: Human Hope Confronts Christian History and American Power* (New York: Paulist/ Newman, 1972; **A, G**), Ruether espouses a positive vision of an active, witnessing role for Christianity. *Faith and Fratricide: The Theological Roots of Anti-Semitism* (New York: Seabury, 1974; **A, G**) is considered the most brilliant and penetrating critique of traditional Christianity's anti-Semitism to date. *New Woman/New Earth: Sexist Ideologies and Human Liberation* (New York: Seabury, 1978; **A, G**) provides a valuable assessment of parallel, inbred racist and sexist structures of prejudice. Ruether expounds on a range of contemporary issues in *To Change the World: Christology as Cultural Criticism* (New York: Crossroads, 1981; **A, G**), offering her insights into possible solutions. *Sexism and God-Talk: Toward a Feminist Theology* (Boston: Beacon, 1983; **A**) offers a systematic Christian theological framework that encompasses the feminist viewpoint. Intended to shake loose stereotypical thinking on Western Christianity, Ruether's *Womanguides: Readings Toward a Feminist Theology* (Boston: Beacon, 1985; **A, G**) provides a provocative selection of texts along with her own commentary and reflections. *Women-Church: Theology and Practice of Feminist Liturgical Communities* (San Francisco: Harper & Row, 1985; **A, G**) presents a synthesis and vision of feminist theology and liturgies that indicate a direction for future work.

Other authored works include: *The Church Against Itself* (New York: Herder and Herder, 1967; **A, G**); *Communion Is Life Together* (New York: Herder and Herder, 1968; **A, G**); *Gregory Nazianzus, Rhetor and Philosopher* (New York: Oxford University Press, 1969; **A**); *Mary: The Feminine Face of the Church* (Philadelphia: Westminster, 1977; **G**); and *Contemporary Roman Catholicism: Crisis and Challenges* (New York: Sheed and Ward, 1987; **A, G**).

Correspondence between Ruether and Thomas Merton (August 12, 1966-February 18, 1968), housed in the Thomas Merton Center, Bellarmine College, Louisville, Kentucky, provides informal, candid glimpses of a dialogue on monasticism versus life in the world. In February 1967 Ruether wrote to Merton, "I distrust all academic theology. Only theology bred in the crucible of experience is any good." Representative of Ruether's ongoing critique of church hierarchy is "Dear U.S. Bishops, You Insult Our Intelligence" (*National Catholic Reporter* [May 18, 1990]: 6; **A, G**).

Ruether's co-authored books are: *From Machismo to Mutuality: Essays on Sexism and Woman-Man Liberation* (with Eugene Bianchi; New York: Paulist

Press, 1975; **A, G**) and *The Liberating Bond* (with Wolfgang Roth; New York: Friendship Press, 1978; **A, G**), and *The Wrath of Jonah: The Crisis of Religious Nationalism in the Israeli-Palestinian Conflict* (with Herman Ruether; San Francisco: Harper and Row, 1989; **A, G**). She edited *Religion and Sexism: The Image of Women in the Judaeo-Christian Tradition* (New York: Simon and Schuster, 1978; **A, G**) and co-edited both the three-volume *Women and Religion in America* (with Rosemary Keller; San Francisco: Harper and Row, 1981, 1983, 1986; **A, G**) and *Beyond Occupation: American Jewish, Christian, and Palestinian Voices For Peace* (with Marc H. Ellis; Boston: Beacon, 1990; **A, G**).

Other Sources

Wei-hsun Fu, Charles, and Gerland E. Spiegler, eds. *Religious Issues and Interreligious Dialogue: An Analysis and Sourcebook of Developments since 1945*. New York: Greenwood Press, 1989. "The Feminist Critique in Religious Studies" provides a good overview of contemporary religious issues that concern Ruether.

Evelyn E. Hunt
Cleveland State University

SACAGAWEA
c. 1787-1812?

Chronology

Born about 1787, a member of the northern Lemhi band of Shoshoni (Snake) Indians, probably in the central part of present-day Idaho; *c. 1800* captured and enslaved by the Hidatsa (Minnetari) tribe and taken to present-day North Dakota; *1804* made the property, and the wife, of Toussaint Charbonneau, a French fur trader from Canada living with the Hidatsa; *1805* bears their son, Jean-Baptiste Charbonneau, on February 11; family joins Meriwether Lewis, William Clark, and their men when they leave their winter quarters in April; *1805-1806* contributes variously as interpreter, guide, finder of food, and good-will emissary as the Lewis and Clark Expedition travels from North Dakota to the mouth of the Columbia River and back; *1806-1812* lives in Dakota and St. Louis with her husband and/or son; *1812* bears a daughter, Lisette, sometime before dying on December 20, at Fort Manuel, South Dakota; *1884* according to other reports dies April 9 [near Lander, Wyoming, on the Shoshonis' Wind River Reservation].

Activities of Historical Significance

Sacagawea is a legitimate heroine in American history because of her role in the Lewis and Clark Expedition in 1805 and 1806. Though her importance is often exaggerated, or at least misunderstood, she did not merely "tag along" on the trip, as an occasional detractor has insisted. She was less important as a guide, however, than as an interpreter (she spoke Minnetari and Shoshoni) and a good-will emissary. Of particular importance was her role in the expedition's acquisition of horses and guides from the Shoshonis, which were essential for the successful crossing of the Rocky Mountains. She also found food to supplement the men's diet and rescued important materials after a boating accident. When the party divided during the return trip, she accompanied Clark to the Yellowstone River and served as guide through Lemhi tribal land. She contributed to the security of the expedition since her presence, and that of her baby, gave unspoken proof that the group was not a war party. Without doubt her resourcefulness and cheerfulness promoted the group's resilience.

To the extent that her contributions made a difference in the success of the expedition, its consequences, too, must be credited to her account. Lewis and Clark made their way through the entire Louisiana Territory and across the Rocky Mountains to the Pacific Ocean. Their reports spurred migration into both the upper Louisiana Territory and the Pacific Northwest. Mapping this vast region, they promoted the expansion of the American fur trade and, perhaps of greatest consequence, enhanced American claims to the Pacific Northwest. They also served as naturalists (studying the plant and animal life of the region) and ethnographers (studying the tribes of resident Native Americans).

Sacagawea is also important in light of the mythology that has developed around her. She is an icon of American culture, similar to Pocahontas, the only other Native American woman most Americans can name. Speaking of the "canonization of the legendary Sacajawea," the historian Bernard DeVoto (in *The Course of Empire,* 1952), expressed his admiration not only for her personal traits but for the hold she had gained on the American imagination. Her image has been tapped for purposes ranging from woman suffrage (in the early twentieth century) to state tourism.

If, in fact, she is the same woman as "the Sacajawea of the Shoshonis" who died in Wyoming in 1884, she has a further claim on the history of the American West, for that woman played a number of important roles in the development of Native American culture and the course of Indian-white relations in the Northwest.

Overview of Biographical Sources

Sacagawea received little historical notice until a century after the Lewis and Clark Expedition. Then came a historical novel published in 1902, on the eve of the centennial celebrations (between 1903 and 1906) of the Louisiana Purchase and the Lewis and Clark Expedition. Belated recognition was characterized by overreaction, as writers typically gave her too much credit. This was so much the case that DeVoto, while admiring the young Indian woman, wryly deprecated the apparent widespread belief that Lewis and Clark "were privileged to assist in the Sacajawea Expedition." There followed a quest for the historical Sacagawea, which led at first to another overreaction, one that insisted that she had made no significant contributions to the expedition. At present a consensus has gathered around a middle ground, though the debate continues.

Comparable to the debate over her role in the expedition is the debate over the date of her death. Library catalogers indicate that she was born in 1786 and died in 1884, but most scholars now place her death in 1812 (and she was more likely born in 1787 or even 1788). Readers are encouraged to assess the evidence and come to their own conclusion. The debate is related to the sources relied on—oral tradition among some western American Indians or written sources from the years during and soon after the expedition. Her name, too, has been the subject of extended debate as to spelling (Sacajawea and Sakakawea as well as Sacagawea), pronunciation, origins, and meaning.

Popular works on Sacagawea almost inevitably include fictional ingredients, particularly for the years before and after the expedition. Some of those works announce themselves as novels, but they may be as factual as those that do not. One novelist, Donald Culross Peattie, declared his book to reflect the historical record fleshed out by reading "between the lines." Another writer, Anna Lee Waldo, stated, "I do not know if Sacajawea died in 1812 or 1884, but as a novelist I prefer the long-life story." Whatever an author's intent, the ready availability of the Lewis and Clark journals has long made it possible for historians and novelists alike to know the outlines of what Lewis and Clark knew about her in 1805 and 1806.

Journal articles provide an excellent introduction to the continuing debates over Sacagawea's identity and importance. In particular, Irving W. Anderson has reviewed the evidence and the arguments: "Probing the Riddle of the Bird Woman," *Montana: The Magazine of Western History* 23 (October 1973): 2-17; "A Charbonneau Family Portrait" (with essays on Sacagawea, Toussaint Charbonneau, and Jean-Baptiste Charbonneau), *The American West: The Magazine of Western History* 17 (March-April 1980): 4-13, 58-64; and "Sacajawea, Sacagawea, Sakaawea?" *South Dakota History* 8 (Fall 1978): 303-311. In addition, E. G. Chuinard offers a balanced assessment in "The Actual Role of the Bird Woman: Purposeful Member of the Corps or Casual 'Tag Along'?" *Montana: The Magazine of Western History* 26 (July 1976): 18-29. These journal articles supply, among them, not only guides to the literature and documentation but also valuable illustrations that include painters' and sculptors' depictions of Sacagawea.

As for books written for young audiences, Sacagawea has been a favorite subject since the time that Katherine Chandler's book for beginning readers, *The Bird-Woman of the Lewis and Clark Expedition,* appeared (1905) during the centennial celebrations. The past half-century has brought a large number of new entries beginning with two on her childhood and capture: Flora Warren Seymour's *Sacajawea: Bird Girl* (1945), soon followed by Evelyn C. Nevin's version, *The Lost Children of the Shoshones* (1946). Seymour's book is clearly less fictional than Nevin's, but both are catalogued as fiction. Similarly, Jerry Seibert's *Sacajawea: Guide to Lewis and Clark* (1960), though he describes the expedition as a "true story as exciting as any adventure story ever written" (and takes the story of Sacagawea only to 1806), is listed in the National Union Catalogue as "juvenile fiction" rather than "juvenile literature." In the late 1980s, new books appeared nearly every year, including Marion Marsh Brown, *Sacagawea: Indian Interpreter to Lewis and Clark* (1988), and Martha F. Bryant, *Sacajawea: A Native American Heroine* (1989). Shorter versions of her life can be found by means of Karen Breen's *Index to Collective Biographies for Young Readers* (4th ed., 1988).

Evaluation of Principal Biographical Sources

Clark, Ella E., and Margot Edmonds. *Sacagawea of the Lewis and Clark Expedition.* Berkeley: University of California Press, 1979. (A, G) Although the authors accept the notion that Sacagawea lived until 1884, they offer a thoughtful argument and are critical of other treatments that share their position on her date of death. The study includes a history of the literature on Sacagawea, a striking "Indian Children's Story," and an appendix on "Sacagawea Memorials." An important book by folklorists.

Hebard, Grace Raymond. *Sacajawea: A Guide and Interpreter of the Lewis and Clark Expedition.* Glendale, CA: Arthur H. Clark, 1933; Reprint. 1967. (A, G) An influential early work that remains important, even though it engaged in myth-making about Sacagawea's role on the expedition and traced her life for seven decades past the time she likely died. In an earlier article (1907), Hebard first published the thesis that the Sacagawea of Lewis and Clark was the same woman as the "Sacajawea of the Shoshonis," who died in 1884, documented only as "Bazil's mother. In her book, she developed the idea partially on the basis of the research of Dr. Charles Eastman, a physician, who in 1925 interviewed various western Native Americans who had known the woman who died in 1884.

Howard, Harold P. *Sacajawea.* Norman: University of Oklahoma Press, 1971. (A, G) The most reliable book-length biography. It includes a thoughtful assessment of the controversy over her "later life" (coming to the conclusion that she did, in fact, die in 1812) and an appendix on "Memorials to Sacajawea."

Evaluation of Biographies for Young People

Blassingame, Wyatt. *Sacajawea, Indian Guide.* Champaign, IL: Garrard, 1965. A brief illustrated biography that highlights the more dramatic events from her capture in 1800 to her return with the expedition in 1806. For grades 2 to 6.

Burt, Olive. *Sacagawea.* New York: Franklin Watts, 1978. A creditable effort to convey to young readers—and older ones, too—the texture of the sources and the nature of the debates over her life.

Farnsworth, Frances Joyce. *Winged Moccasins: The Story of Sacajawea.* New York: Julian Messner, 1954. An engaging recreation of her life, with half the book focusing on her participation in the expedition, the other half reaching back to her birth and forward to her alleged death in 1884. For young adult and general readers.

Frazier, Neta Lohnes. *Sacajawea: The Girl Nobody Knows.* New York: David McKay, 1967. An effort to convey the saga of Sacagawea to young adult and general readers. Frazier's book may be suspect in that she adopts material from Schultz (see below) for the early years, but she offers a thoughtful rendition of the expedition, and is suitably skeptical in her treatment of the allegedly lengthy later years.

Gleiter, Jan, and Kathleen Thompson. *Sacagawea.* Milwaukee: Raintree, 1987. An engaging, illustrated rendition for grades 2 to 4.

Jassem, Kate. *Sacajawea, Wilderness Guide.* Mahwah, NJ: Troll Associates, 1979. A brief, illustrated version for grades 2 to 6.

Johnson, Ann Donegan. *The Value of Adventure: The Story of Sacagawea.* La Jolla, CA: Value Comunications, 1980. A creative use of the story of Sacagawea to convey "the value of adventure" to readers in grades 2 to 6.

Rowland, Della. *The Story of Sacajawea, Guide to Lewis and Clark.* New York: Dell, 1989. Despite its traditional title, spelling of Sacagawea's name, characterization of her as "guide," this is a creditable recent account, generally faithful to the known facts, on the period from her capture to her return from the expedition. For grades 4 to 8.

Seymour, Flora Warren. *Bird Girl: Sacagawea.* Indianapolis: Bobbs-Merrill, 1945. Reissued in 1959 as *Sacagawea: Bird Girl.* A sensitive and plausible rendition of Sacagawea's childhood, together with a chapter on the expedition and a retrospective on her importance. For middle-school and up.

Skold, Betty Westrom. *Sacagawea: The Story of an American Indian.* Minneapolis: Dillon, 1977. A deftly realized and culturally sophisticated narrative of Sacagawea's childhood and journey. For middle-school as well as older readers.

Overview and Evaluation of Primary Sources
    The major documentation of Sacagawea's life focuses on her travels from Dakota to the Pacific and back, between the time Lewis and Clark left the Mandan village for the west on April 7, 1805, and their departure from the village for St. Louis on August 17, 1806. That documentation consists of the journals kept by various members of the Corps of Discovery, as it called

itself, or the Lewis and Clark Expedition, as it is now known. These are available in a number of editions. In particular, see Reuben Gold Thwaites, *Original Journals of the Lewis and Clark Expedition, 1804-1806* (8 vols. New York: Dodd, Mead, 1904-1905; Reprint. New York: Arno, 1959, and New York: Antiquarian Press, 1959; **A, G**). A new edition of the journals is nearing completion, edited by Gary E. Moulton and published (1983-) by the University of Nebraska Press. Paul Russell Cutright, *A History of the Lewis and Clark Journals* (Norman: University of Oklahoma Press, 1976; **A, G**), provides an excellent guide to these journals (as well as a critique of secondary accounts). Another essential source is Donald [Dean] Jackson, *Letters of the Lewis and Clark Expedition, with Related Documents, 1783-1854,* 2d ed. 2 vols. (Urbana: University of Illinois Press, 1978; **A, G**).

Fiction and Adaptations

Sacagawea has been the subject of film, painting, sculpture, and historical fiction. As part of a series called "You Are There," designed for grades 4-9, BFA Educational Media produced for the Columbia Broadcasting System a 21-minute color movie, "Lewis and Clark at the Great Divide" (1971), which dramatizes the critical encounter with the Shoshonis when Sacagawea proved instrumental in securing the horses needed by the expedition; Walter Cronkite narrates the story as if giving the evening news, and other members of the CBS news team report in as "White House correspondent" or "with" Captain Lewis or Captain Clark, while Trudy Tenaya Torres plays Sacagawea.

MGM Family Network TV produced a 24-minute, 16 mm. motion picture, "Sacagawea" (1975), which dramatizes the expedition and seeks to tell the story from Sacagawea's perspective. Eye Gate House produced a 35 mm. color filmstrip on "Sacajawea, Guide to Lewis and Clark" (1953), for its series on "Famous American Women." More recent is Southerby Productions' "Sacajawea" (1984), a 24-minute color video, suitable for all ages, that dramatizes her experiences on the expedition.

Sacagawea is the subject of a 108-minute movie, *The Far Horizons: The Story of the Lewis and Clark Expedition,* produced in 1955 by Paramount Pictures and developed from the novel, *Sacajawea of the Shoshones* (1943), by Della Gould Emmons. Centered on a fictional love affair between Captain Clark and Sacagawea (one which goes well beyond that presented in the novel), the movie features Charlton Heston as Clark and Donna Reed as the Indian woman he comes to love. The movie tells a good story, but, for a viewer acquainted with the facts, much of its entertainment value lies in the liberties taken to tell that story. For example, in the movie Sacagawea has no son Jean-Baptiste, and she accompanies Clark back to Washington, D.C., where she meets President Thomas Jefferson.

Sacagawea continues to be the subject of works of historical fiction. The first to appear was Eva Emery Dye's *The Conquest: The True Story of Lewis and Clark* (1902). More recently, Anna Lee Waldo's sprawling *Sacajawea* (1979) was a best-seller. Others are Ethel Hueston, *Star of the West: The Romance of the Lewis and Clark Expedition* (1935); Claire Warner Churchill, *South of the Sunset: An Interpretation of Sacajawea, the Indian Girl That Accompanied Lewis and Clark* (1936); Donald Culross Peattie, *Forward the Nation* (1942); Della Gould Emmons, *Sacajawea of the Shoshones* (1943); Winfred Blevins, *Charbonneau: Man of Two Dreams* (1975), on Sacagawea's son Jean-Baptiste; James Alexander Thom, *From Sea to Shining Sea* (1984), based on the Clark family; and Scott O'Dell, *Streams to the River, River to the Sea: A Novel of Sacagawea* (1986), intended for a young adult audience.

Museums, Historical Landmarks, Societies

Markers to honor Sacagawea have been placed to the west of Lemhi Pass (near Tendoy, Idaho); to commemorate her reunion with her brother Cameah-wait in 1805 (Armstead, Montana; 1914); at the grave of "Sacajawea of the Shoshonis," who died in 1884 (at the Wind River Indian Reservation, near Lander, Wyoming; 1909); and elsewhere, including the site designated a Registered National Historic Place, in Corson County, South Dakota, where she is thought to have died in 1812.

Sacagawea has any number of mountains, rivers, and lakes named after her (using one or another among the three spellings of her name): Lakes in Washington and North Dakota; one mountain peak each in the Bridger Range (Montana), the Wind River Range (Wyoming), the Wallowa Range (Oregon), and the Lost River Range (Idaho); and a creek named for her by Lewis and Clark (Montana). Even a crater on the planet Venus carries her name.

Among the major sculptures is one on the Capitol grounds in Bismarck, North Dakota, by Leonard Crunelle (1910). Others are by Alice Cooper (with Sacagawea stereotypically pointing the way westward), in Washington Park, Portland, Oregon (1905); by Charles M. Russell, at the National Cowboy Hall of Fame, in Oklahoma City, Oklahoma; by Robert M. Scriver, at Fort Benton, Montana (1976); and by Harry Jackson, at the Plains Indian Museum of the Buffalo Bill Historical Center (see Harry Jackson et al., *Sacagawea: A Monument in Bronze* [Cody, WY: Buffalo Bill Historical Center, 1980]).

Among the paintings of Sacagawea are one by Henry Altman of her on an Indian pony (1905); a painting by Edward Samuel Paxson (Library, State University of Montana; 1906) and mural by him, "Lewis and Clark at Three Forks" (Capitol, Helena, Montana; 1912); and a mural by Charles M. Russell (Capitol, Helena, Montana; 1912). For an introduction to the painters, see the final chapter, "They Illustrated Lewis and Clark," in Paul Russell Cutright, *A History of the Lewis and Clark Journals* (1976).

Lewis and Clark Trail Heritage Foundation (Portland, OR). The foundation publishes *We Proceeded On*, a quarterly magazine that focuses on the expedition, including Sacagawea's participation.

Sacajawea Interpretive Center (Sacajawea State Park, near Pasco, WA). The center maintains exhibits relating to Sacagawea, the expedition, and its brief stay in that area in October 1805.

Other Sources

Hawke, David Freeman. *Those Tremendous Mountains: The Story of the Lewis and Clark Expedition*. New York: Norton, 1985. This excellent recent treatment of the subject somewhat underemphasizes her role.

Kingston, C. S. "Sacajawea as Guide: The Evaluation of a Legend." *Pacific Northwest Quarterly* 15 (January 1944): 3-18. The pioneer debunking essay, it heralded a major downgrading of her role in the expedition. Kingston notes that Lewis and Clark served as guides along the Missouri and Columbia rivers, that they relied on local Indian guides across the Rockies, and that Sacagawea had little importance even as a guide to the Yellowstone River.

Madsen, Brigham D. *The Lemhi: Sacajawea's People*. Caldwell, ID: Caxton, 1979. Though it makes only occasional reference to Sacagawea, it traces the story of her people into the twentieth century.

Ronda, James P. *Lewis and Clark among the Indians*. Lincoln: University of Nebraska Press, 1984. Contains, as a brief appendix, a valuable recent reassessment of the historical Sacagawea, and guide to some of the literature.

Schultz, James Willard. *Bird Woman (Sacajawea), the Guide of Lewis and Clark*. Boston: Houghton Mifflin, 1918. Schultz styled himself a white New Yorker who had married a Native American and lived in the West among her people for many years. He stated that he was now telling, for the first time, the true story of Sacagawea's long life. Well-written, engaging.

Taber, Ronald W. "Sacagawea and the Suffragettes." *Pacific Northwest Quarterly* 58 (January 1967): 7-13. An important review of Sacagawea's historical place as a symbol for the woman suffrage movement in the West.

Wells, Merle W. "Sacajawea." In *Notable American Women, 1607-1950: A Biographical Dictionary*. Cambridge: Harvard University Press, 1971. A tendentious but scholarly review of her life and the literature on her.

Peter Wallenstein
Virginia Polytechnic Institute and State University

DRED SCOTT
c. 1797-1858

Chronology

Facts about early life uncertain; Dred Scott possibly born as Sam Blow, in 1797, a slave to the Blow family of Southampton, Virginia; *1827* settles with the Blow family in St. Louis after a short period in Alabama; *1833* sold to Dr. John Emerson about the time of Peter Blow's death; *1834-1836* accompanies his owner when the U.S. Army transfers Emerson to Rock Island, Illinois (a free state); *1836-1838* accompanies Emerson when the doctor is transferred to Fort Snelling in the Wisconsin Territory (free territory under the terms of the Missouri Compromise); *1836* meets and marries Harriet, a slave sold to Emerson by Major Lawrence Taliaferro, a St. Peter's Indian Agency agent (this appears to have been Scott's second and Harriet's only marriage); they later have two children; *1838* briefly left behind with one of Emerson's friends when Emerson is transferred again; sails with Harriet to Jefferson Barracks, Missouri; spends time hired out; works on a steamboat; *1843* the Scotts' title transferred to Mrs. Emerson after her husband dies, and she hires them out to the Blows (relatives of Scott's original owners); *1846* Scott files unsuccessful suit in Missouri Circuit Court seeking his family's freedom based on their time living in free territories (*Dred Scott v. Irene Emerson*); *1850* wins a second suit for his freedom filed in Missouri Circuit Court for the County of St. Louis; *1852* circuit court decision reversed by the Missouri Supreme Court; Mrs. Emerson transfers Scott's title to her brother John Sanford; *1853* files a federal lawsuit seeking his family's freedom, *Dred Scott v. John F. A. Sandford* (the misspelling of the defendant's name was the result of a clerical error in the official documents); the jury finds for Sanford; *December 1855* the case is argued before the U.S. Supreme Court, but no decision is reached; *December 1856* the case is re-argued; *March 1857* the Court finds against Scott, ruling that he is not a citizen and thus has no standing to sue in federal court; *May 1857* the Scotts' title is transferred to Taylor Blow, who emancipates them; *1858* Scott dies on September 17 of tuberculosis in St. Louis, Missouri, fifteen months after his emancipation.

Activities of Historical Significance

The case of *Dred Scott v. John F. A. Sandford* (1857) was among the most important and influential cases ever to come before the U.S. Supreme Court. The Missouri Compromise of 1820 had outlawed slavery in the Louisiana Purchase territory north of the 36° 30'N parallel but excepted Missouri from this restriction. In 1854 passage of the Kansas-Nebraska Act undermined this system for determining where slavery was legal. Drawing upon the concept of popular sovereignty, the Kansas-Nebraska Act allowed each territory to decide for itself whether to be free or slave. Kansas had become a battleground for the opposing forces as both advocates and opponents of slavery struggled to control the territorial government that would write the state constitution. The *Dred Scott* case became a focus for the concerns of both sides in the pre-Civil War fight over slavery.

The Court first had to decide whether Scott had the right to sue in federal courts, a right reserved for citizens. Chief Justice Roger B. Taney, writing for the majority, found that because blacks were brought to America as slaves, they were "beings of an inferior order;" thus Scott could not be a citizen of the United States or Missouri, and had no standing to sue in the federal courts.

Once the Court determined that Scott was not a citizen, the case required no further rulings, but the Court also ruled that the Missouri Compromise violated the Fifth Amendment to the U.S. Constitution by depriving people of their property without due process. According to the chief justice, even if Emerson had intended to stay in a free territory, he should have been allowed to keep his property, as the Constitution affirmed slavery, and no body of the government had the legal power to encroach on that property right.

The Court's decision caused an immediate problem. The decision both overturned the Missouri Compromise, which had been the basis for peace between free and slave states, and brought into question the constitutionality of popular sovereignty. The decision increased hostilities as anti-slavery forces portrayed the case as a pro-slavery scheme to overturn the Missouri Compromise. The question of popular sovereignty remained a source of tension between the opposing forces until the outbreak of the Civil War. The legal ambiguities that the decision generated were not resolved until the passage of the Thirteenth Amendment (1865), which outlawed slavery, and Fourteenth Amendment (1868), which affirmed the citizenship of all persons born or naturalized in the United States.

It has been suggested that the Court's decision to have the case re-argued was based on the desire of some justices to see Democrat James Buchanan elected to the presidency in 1856. By waiting until after the election to hand down a decision, the Court dampened public debate about the slavery issue, a development that possibly contributed to Buchanan's victory over the Republican candidate, John C. Frémont.

Overview of Biographical Sources

Much about Dred Scott's life remains a mystery. While most texts that discuss the U.S. Supreme Court decision provide some coverage of his life, no biographies are available.

The short biographical sketches of Scott are too numerous to mention. All but a few are of substantial interest for their efforts. Almost every work about American constitutional law has a section on the *Dred Scott* decision with some lead-in about Scott's life. There are also numerous works on the case itself. Among the works with biographical sections on Scott's life are Walter Ehrlich's *They Have No Rights: Dred Scott's Struggle for Freedom* (1979), Don Fehrenbacher's *The Dred Scott Case: Its Significance in American Law and Politics* (1978), and Joel Joseph's *Black Mondays: Worst Decisions of the Supreme Court* (1987). All of these works use the life of Scott as background to the filing of the case.

Scott's reasons for filing the suit are still open to debate. Ehrlich and Fehrenbacher both argue that the original suit was filed simply to obtain the freedom of Scott and his family. Other authors believe that the case was designed to advance the interests of either pro-slavery forces or abolitionists.

Evaluation of Principal Biographical Sources

Barclay, Thomas S. "Dred Scott." In *Dictionary of American Biography*, edited by Dumas Malone. New York: Charles Scribner's Sons, 1963. (G) This work gives a good short biographical account of Scott's life. It is well-documented but was written before the works of Ehrlich and Fehrenbacher brought important new information to light.

Ehrlich, Walter. *They Have No Rights: Dred Scott's Struggle for Freedom.* Westport, CT: Greenwood Press, 1979. (A, G) The background sections focus on the whites involved in the case, but the author does an excellent job in presenting the unresolved questions about Scott's life and providing possible answers. Ehrlich's major strength is his use of source material, including copies of original transcripts of the case that had been believed lost or destroyed.

Fehrenbacher, Don E. *The Dred Scott Case: Its Significance in American Law and Politics.* New York: Oxford University Press, 1978. (A) The majority of the text covers the period of the court cases. Fehrenbacher notes a possible early attempt by Scott to win his freedom in court; this event is referred to by Emerson, but there is no court record of any such attempt. The author's comparison of the justices' opinions is particularly valuable.

_____. *Slavery, Law and Politics: The Dred Scott Case in Historical Perspective.* New York: Oxford University Press, 1981. (A, G) Here Fehrenbacher shortens chapters from *The Dred Scott Case* to make the material more accessible to a general audience.

Joseph, Joel. *Black Mondays: Worst Decisions of the Supreme Court.* Bethesda, MD: National Press, 1987. (**G**) The short section on Scott is useful but weak on documentation. It is most valuable as an overview, rather than as an in depth analysis of either Scott's life or the case. The author's bias is evident from the title of the work.

Overview and Evaluation of Primary Sources

The number of primary sources is extremely limited, as Scott never wrote about his experiences. The primary sources fall into two categories: newspapers and court records. The numerous newspaper articles include an interview with Dred Scott for *Frank Leslie's Illustrated Newspaper* 4 (June 27, 1857; **A**, **G**). There are no reprints of this article available, but it is on microfilm in the New York Public Library, the Library of Congress, in Washington, D.C., the San Francisco Public Library, and the St. Louis Public Library. This interview should be read carefully, because some statements are contradicted by other reliable sources. The State Historical Society of Missouri in Columbia has many local newspapers that contain references to both Dred Scott and the case.

The court records at both the state and federal level are another important source. The original trial court records for *Dred Scott v. Irene Emerson* are available at the St. Louis County Circuit Court archives. Transcripts for the two trial court cases are published in *American State Trials*, vol. 13 (St. Louis: Thomas Law Book Company, 1921; **A**), The original records of the Missouri Supreme Court are located in the court library in Jefferson City. The state supreme court decision is published in the *Reports of Cases Argued and Decided in the Supreme Court of the State of Missouri*, vol. 15 (Jefferson City: James Lusk Public Printer, 1852; **A**). The state court records provide information about Scott's background and the motives behind filing the suit.

The federal trial court records are available through the U.S. government repository in Kansas City, Missouri. These records have been reproduced in *American State Trials*, vol. 13. The U.S. Supreme Court's decision is found under *Dred Scott v. John F. A. Sandford* in *Reports of Cases Argued and Adjudged in the Supreme Court of the United States*, vol. 19 (Washington, DC: William Morrison, 1857; **A**). The court records offer a good short biography of Scott and his family; these are reliable in that both the plaintiff and defendant accepted the statements as facts.

The Missouri Historical Society Library in St. Louis has a Dred Scott collection that is a central source for primary materials on Scott and the case. The collection contains typeset and photostatic copies of the Missouri court records, as well as letters from acquaintances of the participants, and newspaper and scholarly articles about the case and its history.

Museums, Historical Landmarks, Societies

The Gateway Arch and Old County Courthouse National Historical Landmark (St. Louis, MO). The courthouse has restored a courtroom to resemble the one where the *Dred Scott* cases were heard. The courthouse also has microfilm copies of the court records.

Other Sources

Basler, Roy, ed. *The Collected Works of Abraham Lincoln.* 7 vols. New Brunswick, NJ: Rutgers University Press, 1953. This collection shows the importance of the *Dred Scott* decision to Lincoln and presents the case in the context of the Republican party's philosophy.

Blaustein, Albert, and Robert Zangrando, eds. *Civil Rights and the Negro American: A Documentary History.* New York: Trident Press, 1968. The book excerpts court documents from the state and federal trials, and explores the case's influence on black history.

"The Case of Dred Scott in the United States Supreme Court. The Full Opinions of Chief Justice Taney and Justice Curtis, and Abstracts of the Opinions of other Judges; with an analysis of the Points Ruled and some concluding observations." New York: The Tribune Association, 1860. This is a reprint of the chief justice's majority opinion and Justice Curtis's dissenting opinion.

Cox, Archibald. *The Court and the Constitution.* Boston: Houghton Mifflin, 1987. Cox discusses the *Dred Scott* case and its effect on constitutional law and the stature of the Supreme Court.

Ehrlich, Walter. "The Origins of the *Dred Scott* Case." *Journal of Negro History* 59 (April 1974): 132-142. This work is the product of the research that was later expanded into Ehrlich's book *They Have No Rights.* It is an excellent examination of the case and the motives of those involved. This is the author's first use of copies of transcripts he found in the Missouri Supreme Court archives.

Elliott, E. N., ed. *Cotton is King and Pro-Slavery Arguments; comprising the writing of Hammond, Harper, Christy, Stringfellow, Hodge, Bledsoe and Cartwright on this subject with an Essay in the Light of International Law by the Editor.* 1860. Reprint. New York: Negro Universities Press, 1969. This collection of essays that attempt to justify slavery includes a section on the U.S. Supreme Court decision on the *Dred Scott* case.

Fehrenbacher, Don. "*Dred Scott v. Sandford*." *Encyclopedia of the American Constitution*, edited by Leonard Levy, Kenneth Karst, and Dennis Mahoney. New York: Macmillan, 1986. A concise sketch of the case and its impact on constitutional law prior to the Civil War.

Hopkins, Vincent. *Dred Scott's Case*. New York: Fordham University Press, 1951. This provides an excellent overview of the case, but it has been superseded by later works.

Howard, Benjamin, ed. *Report of the Decision of the Supreme Court of the United States, and the Opinions of the Judges thereof in the Case of Dred Scott v. John F. A. Sandford. December Term 1856*. 1857. Reprint. New York: DaCapo Press, 1970. This is a printing of the opinions handed down by the Supreme Court.

Kleber, Louis. "The *Dred Scott* Decision." *History Today* 22 (December 1972): 873-878. This good, short overview puts the decision in historical context by discussing the origins of slavery and the tensions in 1850s America.

Kutler, Stanley, ed. *"Dred Scott" Decision: Law or Politics*. Boston: Houghton Mifflin, 1967. The editor has compiled the opinions of politicians, Supreme Court justices, and newspaper editors of the period, as well as the opinions of historians.

Romero, Patricia, ed. "*Dred Scott* Case." *I Too Am America: Documents from 1619 to Present*. New York: Publishers Company, 1968. The editor excerpts the opinions of Chief Justice Taney and Justice Curtis for the general reader.

Donald E. Heidenreich, Jr.
Kemper College

SEQUOYAH
c. 1770-1843

Chronology

Born c. 1770 in the Cherokee village of Tuskeegee, Tennessee, the son of a Cherokee woman, Wut-teh, of the Red Paint Clan and her white husband, probably Nathaniel Gist, who left her before or soon after Sequoyah's birth; given English name of George Gist but called Sequoyah (The Lame One) by villagers; *1770-1789* grows up in Tuskeegee, where he learns the arts of woodworking and silversmithing (uses trademark of "George Guess"); *1791* moves near Willstown, Alabama, after his mother dies; *1791-1812* works as a blacksmith; marries Utiya and begins a family; contemplates writing down symbols to represent the syllables of the Cherokee language; *1813* enlists in U.S. Army under name of George Guess; *1814* fights in Battle of Horseshoe Bend under Andrew Jackson; returns from war and devotes himself to work on his syllabary of the Cherokee language; acquires divorce from Utiya; *1815* marries Sally and continues work on syllabary; *1816* agrees to treaty that gives large part of Cherokee land to the United States; *1818* moves to Arkansas in Cherokee Nation West and continues work on his syllabary; *1821* takes completed syllabary back to Cherokee Nation East and teaches his people the written word; *1822* returns to Arkansas and teaches Cherokee the written language; *1828* his syllabary is used in *Cherokee Phoenix* newspaper; travels to Washington, D.C., and signs treaty exchanging Cherokee land for land in Oklahoma; *1829* moves family to Oklahoma territory, where he runs a saltworks and farms; *1832* awarded silver medal from Cherokee Nation for his invention of the Cherokee syllabic characters; *1839* plays major role in reuniting the Western Cherokees with the Eastern Cherokees, who were removed to Oklahoma Territory on the "Trail of Tears"; *1842* departs Cherokee Nation for Mexico in search of original Cherokee tribe; *1843* dies in August near San Fernando, Mexico.

Activities of Historical Significance

That an apparently illiterate man could invent a syllabary, called Agayuh, to represent the sounds (made partly through the nose and partly with the throat) of the Cherokee language is little short of miraculous. In slightly more than a decade, Sequoyah invented his eighty-six characters and opened up the world of the written word to his people. His genius transformed the Cherokees into a literate society virtually overnight. Cherokees could learn the Agayuh in three days, and comfortably read and write it within a week. With the written word came a new sense of power and a stimulus to self-expression.

Seven years after Sequoyah completed his syllabary the *Cherokee Phoenix* newspaper was printed half in English, half in Cherokee, providing communication between the Eastern and Western Cherokees. Portions of the Bible were soon translated into the Cherokee language and helped the spread of Christianity.

Overview of Biographical Sources

Little is known of Sequoyah's early years, and his parentage is uncertain, but biographers have made educated guesses. Grant Foreman's book *Sequoyah* (1938), which sums up what is known about the Cherokee, passes over much of Sequoyah's unknown childhood, but declares that Nathaniel Gist, a British explorer, hunter, and soldier, was his father. Foreman qualifies George Gist, a vagabond German trader, as a ruffian who could not have fathered such a philosopher as Sequoyah. Biographer C. W. Campbell disagrees. In *Sequoyah* (1973), he explains that Native American women many times named their children after the father, and because Sequoyah's white name was George Gist, Campbell supports the theory that the German was indeed Sequoyah's father. Mystery still surrounds the issue, but current research leans toward Nathaniel Gist. Disagreement also arises over the number of wives Sequoyah had. Numbers from two to five are debated without a definitive answer. The circumstances of Sequoyah's death remain mysterious as well. His final resting place is unknown, and the stories surrounding his trip to Mexico are akin to legends.

Biographers do agree that Sequoyah was a genius. At the time he completed his syllabary, he did not speak or read English. Whether he learned this skill and merely refused to speak any tongue but his own is one of the mysteries still surrounding his life.

Evaluation of Principal Biographical Sources

Foreman, Grant. *Sequoyah*. Norman: University of Oklahoma Press, 1938. (A, G) This thin volume concentrates on Sequoyah's astonishing accomplishment and its effect on the Cherokees. It includes accounts of Sequoyah's life given by his contemporaries.

Foster, George E. *Se-Quo-Yah, the American Cadmus and Modern Moses*. 1885. Reprint. New York: AMS Press, 1979. (A, G) The subtitle, "A complete biography of the greatest of redmen, around whose wonderful life has been woven the manners, customs and beliefs of the early Cherokees, together with a recital of their wrongs and wonderful progress toward civilization," aptly states the author's wide focus and indicates his cultural biases. This volume was originally published by the Office of the Indian Rights Association.

Kilpatrick, Jack Frederick. *Sequoyah of Earth and Intellect.* Austin, TX: Encino Press, 1965. (A, G) The author, who understands the intricacies of Sequoyah's syllabary, presents a short biography.

West, C. W. Dub. *The Mysteries of Sequoyah.* Muskogee, OK: Muskogee Publishing, 1975. (G) West's volume is a very general biography of Sequoyah.

Evaluation of Biographies for Young People

Browin, Frances Williams. *Captured Words: The Story of a Great Indian.* New York: Aladdin Books, 1954. This fictionalized biography, written on the fourth through sixth grade level, highlights the relationship between Sequoyah and his daughter Ah-yoka.

Campbell, C. W. *Sequoyah.* Minneapolis: Dillon Press, 1973. Campbell's biography presents a clear and concise picture of Sequoyah for fourth through sixth-grade readers.

Coblentz, Catherine. *Sequoya.* New York: Longmans, Green, 1946. This biography, illustrated by Ralph Ray, Jr., provides a valuable reference for junior high school readers.

Cwiklik, Robert. *Sequoyah.* Morristown, NJ: Silver Burdett Press, 1989. This volume is part of Alvin Josephy's History of the Native American Series for grades five through seven.

Kohn, Bernice. *Talking Leaves: The Story of Sequoyah.* New York: Prentice-Hall, 1969. This volume, illustrated by Valli, is for fourth through sixth grade readers.

Marriott, Alice Lee. *Sequoyah: Leader of the Cherokees.* New York: Random House, 1956. Illustrated by Bob Riger, this is a fictionalized account of Sequoyah's life for fifth through seventh grade readers.

Oppenheim, Joanne. *Sequoyah, Cherokee Hero.* Mahwah, NJ: Troll, 1979. Illustrated by Bert Dodson, this is written for fourth to sixth grade readers.

Patterson, Lillie. *Sequoyah, the Cherokee Who Captured Words.* Champaign, IL: Garrard, 1975. For third to fifth grade readers, this volume is illustrated by Herman B. Vestal.

Radford, Ruby Lorraine. *Sequoyah.* New York: G. P. Putnam's Sons, 1969. Illustrated by Unada, this easy-to-read book is for second and third grade readers.

Roper, William L. *Sequoyah and His Miracle.* Billings: Montana Council for Indian Education, 1972. This volume, part of the Indian Culture Series, is written for high school students.

Snow, Dorothea J. *Sequoyah: Young Cherokee Guide.* New York: Bobbs-Merrill, 1960. This fictionalized biography for fourth through sixth grades is illustrated by Frank Giacoia.

Overview and Evaluation of Primary Sources
The story of the great Cherokee Sequoyah emerges in papers and diaries of contemporaries, and interviews with Sequoyah that found their way into newspapers of the time. Papers of Cherokee Chief John Ross mention his friendship with Sequoyah. General Ethan Allen Hitchcock, an army officer who toured the Oklahoma Indian country, wrote in his diary of meeting with Sequoyah. John Howard Payne, while collecting material to write a history of the Cherokees, wrote a long account of his conversations with Sequoyah. The manuscript is housed at the Library of Congress. For information about Sequoyah's trip into Mexico in search of other Cherokees, historians rely on a companion's account. The Worm, a Cherokee who accompanied Sequoyah, related his experiences to the editor of the *Cherokee Advocate,* who published the story. The *Cherokee Advocate* can be found on microfilm at Northeastern State University at Tahlequah, Oklahoma, where the newspaper was printed; a few other copies can be found in museums that house Indian collections.

Government records place dates on some of Sequoyah's movements. Military records are housed in the United States War Department and the Pension Office in Washington, D.C.; reports to the commissioner of Indian Affairs are at the U.S. Office of Indian Affairs in Washington D.C.; and treaties Sequoyah signed, and official papers of the Cherokee Nation are found at the Cherokee Nation Complex in Tahlequah, Oklahoma.

Debates continue over the credibility of Traveller Bird's *Tell Them They Lie: The Sequoyah Myth* (Los Angeles: Westernlore Publishers, 1971; G). Traveller Bird and sixteen other heirs of Sequoyah planned the book about their forefather, using documents supposedly written by Sequoyah and his children.

Fiction and Adaptations

Weyman Jones based his 1968 novel, *Edge of Two Worlds,* on incidents in Sequoyah's life. In this book for sixth and seventh grade readers, a young Missouri boy and Sequoyah journey together across the plains, first as adversaries, then as friends.

Museums, Historical Landmarks, Societies

Cherokee National Museum, Cherokee Heritage Center (Tahlequah, OK). This museum contains a showcase of Sequoyah miscellany, including a recorded oral history of the philosopher and pronunciation of the Cherokee syllabary.

Museum of the Cherokee Indian (Cherokee, NC). A 3,000-volume rare document reference library is housed here, along with artifacts and relics. One of the key research fields is language.

New Echota (Calhoun, GA). A replica of the Cherokee Phoenix print shop stands in the 1825 capital of the Cherokee Nation. A monument to Sequoyah stands two miles north of Calhoun.

Sequoia National Park (California). The giant redwood trees (*Sequoiadendron giantea*) that grow on the western slope of the Sierra Nevada Mountains were named after the Native American genius.

Sequoyah Home Site (Sallisaw, OK). Sequoyah's one-room log cabin, designated as a National Historic Landmark in 1966, is preserved inside a stone building. Displays about Cherokee history and Sequoyah's Agayuh are housed in a separate information building on the ten-acre homesite.

Statuary Hall in the National Capitol (Washington, DC). In 1911 the young state of Oklahoma commissioned sculptor George Julian Zolnay to make the statue of Sequoyah for the U.S. Capitol building.

Other Sources

Holmes, Ruth Bradley, and Betty Sharp Smith. *Beginning Cherokee.* Norman: University of Oklahoma Press, 1924. The authors present twenty-seven lessons for learning the Cherokee syllabary and arithmetic symbols.

Kilpatrick, Jack Frederick, and Anna Gritts Kilpatrick. *The Shadow of Sequoyah—Social Documents of the Cherokees, 1862-1964.* Norman: University of Oklahoma Press, 1965. This volume illustrates the wide variety of applications found for the syllabary.

McKenney, Thomas L., and James Hall. *The Indian Tribes of North America: With Biographical Sketches and Anecdotes of the Principal Chiefs.* 3 vols. Edinburgh: John Grant, 1933-1934. A capsule biography of Sequoyah is presented.

McLoughlin, William G. *Cherokee Renascence in the New Republic.* Princeton, NJ: Princeton University Press, 1986. Chapter 17, "Sequoyah and the Christians, 1819-1827," discusses the religious changes brought by Sequoyah's invention.

Malone, Henry Thompson. *Cherokees in the Old South, A People in Transition.* Athens: University of Georgia Press, 1956. Chapter 12, "The Sequoyah Miracle: Talking Leaves and Printed Pages," details Sequoyah's syllabary.

Mooney, James. *Myths of the Cherokee.* 1900. Reprint. New York: Johnson Reprint Corporation, 1970. A history of the Cherokees originally published by the Government Printing Office.

Veda Jones

SITTING BULL
c. 1831-1890

Chronology

Born Hunk-es-ni about 1831 near the Grand River, in present-day South Dakota, son of Jumping Bull (also called Returns-Again) and Her Holy Door of the Hunkpapa tribe of the Teton Sioux Nation; *c. 1831-1852* earns name of Tatanka Yotanka, Sitting Bull; counts first coup (striking enemy with a stick) as a Sioux warrior at an early age; successfully dances the tortuous Sun Dance and has first Vision Quest; becomes member of Strong Heart Warrior Society; *1848* accompanies father on the warpath against the Crow and distinguishes himself as a warrior; *c. 1862* becomes a chief of the Hunkpapas, a leader in the Strong Heart Warrior Society, and a participant in the Silent Eaters, a select group concerned with tribal warfare; *1864* declares war on whites as a result of the Sand Creek Massacre in Colorado; *1865* refuses to sign Harney-Sanborn Treaty which allowed safe passage for whites on the Bozeman Trail; *1868* mandates many demands for Treaty of 1868, which promised all the Black Hills and Powder River country to Native Americans, but which he never signed; *1869-1874* enjoys temporary peace with whites until miners pour into Black Hills searching for gold; *1876* as head of the war council, organizes Sioux Nation against General George Custer at Little Big Horn in Montana; *1877* flees with his tribe to Canada; *1881* surrenders at Fort Buford, Montana, and arrested; *1833* joins own people near Standing Rock Indian Agency; *1885* travels with Buffalo Bill's Wild West Show; *1889* reveals that he does not believe in the new Ghost Dance religion but defends other Native American's rights to believe; *1890* killed on December 15 by Native American police sent to arrest him because of Ghost Dance fervor; leaderless Hunkpapas shot in indiscriminate killing on December 28 at Massacre of Wounded Knee, bringing an end to Indian hostilities.

Activities of Historical Significance

Sitting Bull, the most famous Native American chief, epitomizes the courage and stalwartness of the Plains Indians. This intelligent man, staunch defender of the customs and traditions of his people, was honored not only as a warrior and chief, but also as a mystic medicine man whose trance-evoked visions were viewed as prophecies. Capable of inciting fervor with his rare but eloquent speeches, Sitting Bull galvanized not only the Hunkpapas, but also the many tribes of the Sioux Nation, uniting them against their common foe.

As the foremost opponent of white settlement of the plains, Sitting Bull organized a resistance force of Native Americans that used the white's own method of fighting. Having learned from the soldiers that the only way to win a battle was to have overwhelming forces, in 1876 Sitting Bull called the Sioux together and welcomed Cheyenne warriors into their fold. Two thousand warriors, led by Oglala Chief Crazy Horse and other tribal war chiefs, were waiting when General George Armstrong Custer attacked with some 220 soldiers on June 25, 1876. Sitting Bull watched the battle from a distance and planned strategy. He later said of the Battle of Little Big Horn, "We did not go out of our country to kill them. They came to kill us and got killed themselves."

Sitting Bull, who exemplified the spirit of the warrior society, fought to stave off the destruction of the Native American way of life. Only when the buffalo food supply was eliminated did he and his followers, the last of the Native American holdouts, bow to the white strength and retire to the reservation.

Overview of Biographical Sources

Many accounts of Sitting Bull's life have been written for children, but few have been written for adults. Perhaps this is because Stanley Vestal's *Sitting Bull, Champion of the Sioux* (1932; rev. ed., 1957) has been pronounced the definitive biography and few have challenged that opinion. Vestal's book, which is based on interviews with those who fought with and against Sitting Bull, provides a clear picture of the warrior-leader of the Sioux. Alexander Adams's *Sitting Bull: An Epic of the Plains* (1973) provides context for both the U.S. government's military actions against the Native Americans and the wars the tribes fought among themselves. Adam's complete account moves from the military action in the West to politics in the East and the advance of settlers with the plow.

Evaluation of Principal Biographical Sources

Adams, Alexander B. *Sitting Bull, an Epic of the Plains*. New York: G. P. Putnam's Sons, 1973. (**A, G**) Adams chronicles the conflict between Native Americans and whites, focusing occasionally on Sitting Bull. Includes notes and a bibliography.

Capps, Benjamin. *The Great Chiefs*. Alexandria, VA: Time-Life Books, 1975. (**G**) Excellent pictures supplement the text in the chapter entitled, "The Threatened World of Sitting Bull." A bibliography and index are included.

Fielder, Mildred. *Sioux Indian Leaders.* New York: Bonanza, 1975. (G) A chapter, "Sitting Bull, Hunkpapa Medicine Man," contains a brief biography of the chief. Quoted references are noted.

Freedman, Russell. *Indian Chiefs.* New York: Holiday House, 1987. (G) A chapter on Sitting Bull includes many pictures.

Vestal, Stanley. *Sitting Bull, Champion of the Sioux: A Biography.* 1957. Reprint. Norman: University of Oklahoma Press, 1980. (A, G) The definitive biography of the Sioux chief was revised from the 1932 edition. In the revision, Vestal added personal records of Native Americans who would not be quoted while they were alive.

Evaluation of Biographies for Young People
Anderson, LaVere. *Sitting Bull, Great Sioux Chief.* Champaign, IL: Garrard, 1970. This fictionalized biography was written for grades 2 and 3.

Black, Sheila. *Sitting Bull.* Morristown, NJ: Silver Burdett, 1989. This volume is part of Alvin Josephy's History of the Native American Series for grades 5 to 7.

Fleischer, Jane. *Sitting Bull, Warrior of the Sioux.* Mahwah, NJ: Troll, 1979. This volume was written for readers in grades 4 to 6.

Garst, Shannon. *Sitting Bull, Champion of his People.* New York: Julian Messner, 1946. This fictionalized biography, illustrated by Elton C. Fax, was written for readers in grades 6 to 9.

Knoop, Faith Y. *Sitting Bull.* Minneapolis, MN: Dillon Press, 1974. This work is part of the Story of an American Indian Series for readers in grades 5 to 7.

O'Connor, Richard. *Sitting Bull, War Chief of the Sioux.* New York: McGraw-Hill, 1968. O'Connor presents the many sides of Sitting Bull in this biography for readers in grades 5 to 7. Drawings are by Eric von Schmidt.

Smith, Kathie B. *Sitting Bull.* Englewood Cliffs, NJ: Julian Messner, 1987. This volume is part of the Great Americans Series for grades 4 to 6.

Stevenson, Augusta. *Sitting Bull: Dakota Boy.* New York: Bobbs-Merrill, 1956. This volume is part of the Childhood of Famous Americans Series for grades 3 to 5.

Overview and Evaluation of Primary Sources

Sitting Bull is one of the few Native Americans to write something resembling an autobiography. He drew pictures of his exploits in a blank infantry roll-book. He had drawn only forty pictures when the book was stolen by a Yankton Sioux and sold to an army officer. The original is now housed at the Bureau of American Ethnology in Washington, D.C.

Other accounts of his life were made by his contemporaries, who often were recalling events several years after the fact. Sitting Bull's adopted brother, Frank Grouard, told his story to newspaperman Joe DeBarthe in *Life and Adventures of Frank Grouard* (1894. Reprint. Norman: University of Oklahoma Press, 1958; **G**). How much of DeBarthe's book is in Grouard's own words will never be known. South Dakota Historical Collections and North Dakota Historical Collections house many of the papers and interviews of Sitting Bull's contemporaries.

The U.S. Army Military History Institute in Carlisle Barracks, Pennsylvania, houses a collection of first-hand accounts from Crow scouts and Sioux warriors of the Battle of the Little Big Horn, as well as the U.S. Army's casualty reports and the papers of military figures during the Western campaign.

Fiction and Adaptations

War with Native Americans has provided the background for numerous novels, short stories, and movies. As the best known chief, Sitting Bull appears in many of these accounts. Some works, such as Douglas C. Jones's novel *Arrest Sitting Bull* (1977), closely follow documented facts; others distort known truths.

Many movies feature the great chief. Among them are: *Sitting Bull, the Hostile Sioux Chief* (1914), *Hands Up!* (1926), *Flaming Frontier* (1926), *Sitting Bull at the Spirit Lake Massacre* (1927), *Custer's Last Stand* (1936), *Annie Get Your Gun* (1950), *Sitting Bull* (1954), *Cheyenne Autumn* (1964), *The Great Sioux Massacre* (1965), *Buffalo Bill and the Indians* (1976), and *Annie Oakley* (1985). Television movies include *Cheyenne* (1947) and *Branded* (1950).

Museums, Historical Landmarks, Societies

American Indian Culture Research Center (Marvin, SD). The center houses a 2,600-volume library and over 30,000 photos of Dakotas.

Custer Battlefield National Monument (Big Horn Country, MT). A museum is located at the site of the Battle of the Little Big Horn.

Sioux Indian Museum and Crafts Center (Rapid City, SD). The museum contains many Native American artifacts and examples of their handiwork.

Other Sources

Andrist, Ralph K. *The Long Death; the Last Days of the Plains Indian.* New York: Macmillan, 1964. This meticulous history covers the period from 1862 to the white settlement of Oklahoma. Excellent maps supplement the text.

Dockstader, Frederick J. *Great North American Indians: Profiles in Life and Leadership.* New York: Van Nostrand Reinhold, 1977. Contains a biographical sketch of Sitting Bull with a bibliography.

Brown, Dee. *Bury My Heart at Wounded Knee.* New York: Holt, Rinehart and Winston, 1970. A comprehensive and readable history of Native Americans in the West. Contains a complete bibliography, notes, and an index.

Finerty, John F. *War-Path and Bivouac or the Conquest of the Sioux.* 1890. Reprint. Norman: University of Oklahoma Press, 1961. Finerty, a war correspondent for the *Chicago Times,* recalls his experiences during the "Indian Wars."

Foreman, Grant. *Last Trek of the Indians.* Chicago: University of Chicago Press, 1946. This carefully documented history includes a bibliography and an index.

Johnston, Charles H. L. *Famous Indian Chiefs.* 1909. Reprint. Freeport, NY: Books for Libraries Press, 1971. Johnston's volume analyzes the Battle of the Little Big Horn.

Josephy, Alvin M., Jr. *The Patriot Chiefs: A Chronicle of American Indian Leadership.* New York; Viking Press, 1961. Contains objective and vivid biographical sketches of prominent Native Americans.

Whitaker, Jane. *Patriots of the Plains: Sitting Bull, Crazy Horse, Chief Joseph.* New York: Scholastic Book Services, 1973. Accounts of Native American chiefs for high school students.

Veda Jones

BESSIE SMITH
1894-1937

Chronology

Born Bessie Smith on April 15, 1894 in Chattanooga, Tennessee, one of seven children of William Smith, a part-time minister, and Laura Smith; both parents die before she is a teenager; *1903* begins singing on street corners; meets Ma Rainey and joins her touring review; *1903-1918* tours South and East with various musical shows; *1918* appears in her own *Liberty Belles* review in Atlanta; *1918-1937* performs in numerous shows and reviews, sometimes producing her own shows at clubs and theaters as far west as Chicago and Detroit; *c. 1920* marries Earl Love, who dies shortly thereafter; *1923-1933* records for Columbia Records; *1923* marries Jack Gee; *1926* adopts Jack Gee, Jr.; *1929* appears in short film, *St. Louis Blues*, only film record of her work; leaves Jack Gee; *1937* dies September 26 in Clarksdale, Mississippi, of injuries received in a car accident; buried in an unmarked grave in Sharon Hill, Pennsylvania; *1970* grave marked with stone purchased by blues singer Janis Joplin, music producer John Hammond, and others.

Activities of Historical Significance

Blues is the cornerstone of American popular music, and, in many ways, Bessie Smith is the cornerstone of the blues. Blues, which appeared about 1890, greatly influenced later forms, including jazz, rock-and-roll, and mainstream popular music. Unlike spirituals, the other great mainstream of black music whose themes address redemption and the hope of future rewards, the blues were steeped in the disturbing conditions of everyday life for black Americans—poverty, trouble in love, frustration, grief, and inevitable death. The aim of the blues musician, however, was not to wallow in misery but to confront these troubles squarely.

Blues migrated from the fields, roadhouses, and dance halls of the South in the 1890s to reach the big cities by the First World War. The first recorded blues singer was Mamie Smith (no relation to Bessie) whose "Crazy Blues" became a hit in 1920, initiating the era of the "classic" blues singers. These entertainers, primarily women, performed blues numbers in shows, backed by a piano or a small band, and were recorded in the 1920s and early 1930s. Chief among them was Bessie Smith.

Musical critics, historians, and fans have reached rare consensus in their judgment of Bessie Smith. She is considered not only the greatest of the classic blues singers, but the greatest blues singer of all time. She was born with a voice of tremendous range, power, and authority. Performing before the introduction of electronic amplification, she could fill a large hall with her voice alone, holding an audience spellbound. Beyond her natural ability, Bessie Smith projected an unparalleled range and depth of emotion, derived from the experiences of a difficult life. Her live performances were reportedly overwhelming, and in spite of the primitive recording techniques of the time, the recordings still in print on Columbia Records are stunning today.

One of the finest is her own composition, "Backwater Blues," in which she describes being wiped out by floods and having nothing to fall back on; another is "Empty Bed Blues," written on a familiar blues theme—rejection by a lover. In addition to her powerful performances, these recordings feature a panoply of jazz and blues artists who played in her bands, including James P. Johnson, Louis Armstrong, Chu Berry, Jack Teagarden, Fletcher Henderson, and Benny Goodman. During her lifetime Bessie Smith had a huge impact on other performers, and since her death her recordings have continued to influence musicians and musical forms. Most blues and jazz performers today readily acknowledge their debt to Smith.

As more details of her life emerged, Smith came to be seen as a heroine because of her life as well as her music. Black and female—a double handicap in a segregated America—saddled with bad marriages, and frequently finding refuge in a bottle of gin, she nonetheless refused to knuckle under to anyone. She is an inspiring example of a strong, independent woman who led a proud life and stayed with the music she knew best through the most difficult of times.

For a time, the circumstances of Smith's death were considered as significant as any feature in her life. In 1937 she was critically injured in a car wreck outside Clarksdale, Mississippi. A false rumor spread that she had bled to death because she was denied admittance to a white hospital. The rumor was started by famed producer and critic John Hammond and perpetuated in Edward Albee's play *The Death of Bessie Smith*, which treated the irony of the South's greatest artist supposedly dying as a result of racial segregation. Years later, researcher Chris Albertson discovered the truth of the incident. Smith was actually treated by a white doctor who happened upon the accident, then taken to a black hospital where she died from the shock of her extensive injuries.

Overview of Biographical Sources

Recognition of the importance of blues music and blues performers began in the 1950s, but these early attempts were not very scholarly, often relying on hearsay, rumor, and the information on the backs of record albums. In the 1960s British musicologists, who recognized the value of the blues before most Americans, began interviewing performers, record producers, and others associated with the blues. The first and, for a decade, the definitive, biography, *Bessie Smith* (1961), was by the British blues scholar Paul Oliver. This was superseded by Chris Albertson, *Bessie* (1972). Two short biographies, Carman Moore's *Somebody's Angel Child: The Story of Bessie Smith* (1969), and Elaine Feinstein's *Bessie Smith* (1985), are of special interest. Much biographical material is scattered about in histories of the blues and jazz.

Evaluation of Principal Biographical Sources

Albertson, Chris. *Bessie*. New York: Stein and Day, 1972. (A, G) This is the definitive biography of Bessie Smith. Albertson was annoyed at the paucity of biographical material on the singer and performed an invaluable service by tracking down the records of her recording sessions and interviewing her contemporaries, many shortly before their deaths. Another major contribution is Albertson's clarification of the myths surrounding Smith's death. Contains a bibliography and discography for Smith, as well as for Ma Rainey, Ida Cox, and Ethel Waters. An indispensable reference.

Blesh, Rudi. *Shining Trumpets*. New York: DaCapo, 1958. (G) A basic history of jazz with extensive coverage of the life and performances of Bessie Smith.

Feinstein, Elaine. *Bessie Smith*. New York: Viking, 1985. (A, G) Written for the Lives of Modern Women Series, this work emphasizes the singer's struggles as a independent woman in a world not designed to reward such efforts. Less a biography than an analysis of Smith's career. Contains a bibliography and discography of Smith, Ma Rainey, and Ethel Waters.

Hoefer, George. "Bessie Smith." In *The Jazz Makers*, edited by Nat Hentoff and Nat Shapiro. New York: Rinehart, 1957. (G) A good introductory work on Bessie Smith, although somewhat superceded by recent scholarship.

Hughes, Langston. "Bessie Smith." In *Famous Negro Music Makers*. New York: Dodd, Mead, 1955. (Y) A youth biography, but written by a man who was one of America's leading black artists and an influential promoter of the careers of other black artists.

Moore, Carman. *Somebody's Angel Child: The Story of Bessie Smith*. New York: Dell, 1969. (G, Y) This work by a black composer and critic is part of the Women of America Series for young people. Moore dramatizes some scenes from Smith's life, making up dialogue and action. The author says that his primary source of information was Jack Gee, Smith's ex-husband. As a result, some elements of Smith's career (such as her first marriage) are ignored, and because of the intended audience, some troubling aspects of her personality, such as her drinking, are minimized.

Oakley, Giles. *The Devil's Music.* New York: Harcourt Brace, 1976. (G) This well-written and copiously illustrated history of the blues contains a section on Bessie Smith.

Oliver, Paul. *Bessie Smith.* New York: A. S. Barnes, 1961. (A, G) The author is the leading British historian and critic of the blues, but this book, written for a series of short biographies called "Kings of Jazz," focuses primarily on the period of Bessie Smith's life when she was recording, giving Oliver the opportunity to analyze her performances.

Stewart-Baxter, Derrick. *Ma Rainey and the Classic Blues Singers.* New York: Stein and Day, 1970. (A, G) Ma Rainey was one of the first classic blues singers, the originator of the traveling blues review format, and the discoverer of Bessie Smith. There is more information about Bessie Smith in this book than in any other source except the Albertson, Oliver, and Moore biographies.

Overview and Evaluation of Primary Sources

Bessie Smith wrote no autobiography, and at the time she sang, musicians were not considered worthy of detailed interviews, but many people who knew her discuss her in Nat Shapiro and Nat Hentoff's excellent oral history of jazz and blues, *Hear Me Talkin' To Ya* (New York: Rinehart, 1955; A, G), which is a good starting point for those needing an introduction to the music. John Hammond, who assisted Bessie Smith during her career, discusses his relationship with her in *John Hammond on Record* (New York: Ridge Press, 1977; A, G). Ethel Waters, a performer who was often linked with Bessie Smith during the 1920s, describes the blues singer in her autobiography, *His Eye Is On the Sparrow* (Garden City, New York: Doubleday, 1951; G, Y). Mezz Mezzrow (with Bernard Wolfe) also gives a first hand account of Bessie's singing in *Really the Blues* (New York: Random House, 1946; A, G).

Fiction and Adaptations

Edward Albee's play *The Death of Bessie Smith* (1960) is well written, but perpetuates the unfortunate myth about her death.

Museums, Historical Landmarks, Societies
Delta Blues Museum (Clarksdale, MS). The Public Library, 114 Delta Avenue, of the town where Bessie Smith died, has an exhibit of her recordings.

Other Sources
Albertson, Chris. *Bessie Smith: Empress of the Blues.* New York: Kane, 1975. A selection of Bessie Smith's songs by her main biographer.

Brooks, Edward. *The Bessie Smith Companion.* New York: DaCapo, 1982. Not a biography but a detailed musical analysis of Bessie Smith's recordings with chapters for each of her recording sessions. Although the introduction claims that this book can be used by anyone, it is helpful to have a knowledge of music terminology and theory. An essential work for the study of Bessie Smith's contributions to the development of popular music.

Dixon, Robert, and John Godrich. *Recording the Blues.* New York: Stein and Day, 1970. Few observations of Bessie Smith's life and musical career put emphasis on how her records and those of other black performers were produced and marketed.

Harris, Sheldon. *Blues Who's Who.* New Rochelle, NY: Arlington House, 1979. A huge compendium of information about blues and jazz performers. The article on Bessie Smith is particularly good on her road and performance itinerary.

Jones, Leroi (Imamu Baraka). *Black Music.* New York; William Morrow, 1968. Black popular music seen from the perspective of one of America's most important black writers.

―――――. *Blues People: Negro Music in White America.* New York: Apollo, 1965. Similar to *Black Music*, but as the title indicates, it focuses on the impact of black music on the dominant culture.

Murray, Albert. *Stomping the Blues.* New York: McGraw-Hill, 1976. A history of blues and jazz which makes its point that jazz is a direct descendant of the blues by never using the word "jazz" and regarding jazz as an up-tempo version of the blues. Contains much material on Bessie Smith's life and her performances.

Oliver, Paul. *Blues Off the Record.* New York: DaCapo, 1984. A collection of thirty years of album liner notes with many references to Bessie Smith.

————. *Screening the Blues: Aspects of the Blues Tradition.* London: Cassell, 1968. This analysis of blues lyrics and performances makes frequent reference to Bessie Smith's work.

Shaw, Arnold. *Black Popular Music in America.* New York: Schirmer, 1986. This history by a leading blues commentator includes recent scholarship and covers Bessie Smith's career extensively.

Jim Baird
University of North Texas

JULIA EVELINA SMITH
1792-1886

Chronology

Born Juliette Abelinda Smith (later changed to Julia Evelina), on May 27, 1792 in "Eastbury," Connecticut, later known as "Buckingham," to Zephaniah Hollister Smith, a native of Glastonbury, graduate of Yale, scholar, linguist and mechanical genius, and Hannah Hadassah Hickok Smith, a linguist, mathematician, astronomer and poet; father was a former Congregational/Sandemanian pastor-turned-lawyer; reared in Glastonbury, Connecticut; educated at home; in her teens attends school in the home of a French couple in New Haven and, possibly, with Sarah Pierce, in Litchfield, Connecticut; *1823* joins her sister, Laurilla Aleroyla, as a French instructor at the Troy Female Seminary in Troy, New York; *1842* reads the doomsday prophesies of William Miller for the year 1843 with more than passing interest; *1847-1855* organizes weekly Bible study and translation group with her sisters, a friend, Emily Moseley, and her mother, in the course of which she not only teaches herself Hebrew (to add to her knowledge of Greek and Latin), but completes five translations of the Bible (from Greek, Hebrew, and Latin); *1873-1886* along with her youngest sister, Abby Hadassah, becomes politically active regarding the issue of taxation without representation and related suffragist concerns; *1876* together with her sister, obtains an agreement with the American Publishing Company of Hartford, Connecticut, to publish 1000 copies of a literalist, edited, version of her Bible translations; *1877* publishes "Report of the Law Case Decided Contrary to Law"; *1879* becomes the third wife of prominent attorney, retired judge, published poet and author Amos A. Parker, from Fitzwilliam, New Hampshire; *1881* publishes a collection of fifty of her Mother's poems; *1886* dies on March 6 in Parkville, Connecticut; at her request she is buried with her sisters, and her maiden name is etched upon the headstone.

Activities of Historical Significance

In her own words, Julia Evelina Smith undertook publishing her translation of the entire Bible as a woman who, "with no motive but the love of doing it . . . has gone further, alone, in translating [now dead] languages, than any man has ever gone, and without any of his help, *and no law of the land gives her any protection.*" Her upbringing, her training, and her own accomplishments, had confirmed for her that "knowledge rules the world," and she and her sister fought to remedy the injustices they thought were being perpetrated against them and other women.

In 1874 Julia Smith and her sister Abby became embroiled in a controversy over the denial of the vote to women. The sisters refused to pay local taxes on the ground that, lacking the vote, this was a case of taxation without representation. The city of Glastonbury responded on January 8, 1874, by seizing the sisters' seven pet Alderney cows and putting them up for auction. The sisters then bought back the cows. In February of the same year the tax collector, George C. Andrews, again attempted unsuccessfully to retrieve the Smith's taxes. On June 20, 1874, he put their house and fifteen acres of land up for public auction. The Smith's intended to purchase their property again, but Andrews changed the auction location, and their estate was sold to a covetous neighbor for $78.35 (the real value was $2,000.00). The Smiths brought suit against Andrews, on the grounds that he violated a law stating that all movable property must first be sold for unpaid taxes, before real estate can be seized. Judge Hollister of Glastonbury ruled in the Smiths' favor, and fined Andrews ten dollars. Andrews appealed the case. The second trial lasted three days in Hartford Court of Common Pleas. The ruling was reversed in favor of Andrews. The Smiths made a second appeal before the Court of Equity. The case continued for two years and achieved notoriety in the U.S. and abroad. Twice more in 1876 the cows were taken to auction and repurchased by the Smiths. In November of 1876 the final verdict was rendered in the Smiths' favor.

Smith is notable as an early advocate for woman suffrage, which did not arrive until forty-four years after her death. Her spiritual concerns and intellectual accomplishments are representative of the activities and interests of accomplished women of the nineteenth century.

The edited version of her Bible translation was eventually published in 1876 by the American Publishing Company of Hartford, Connecticut, which charged the Smith sisters $4,000 for printing 1,000 copies. For the average reader of the time the language was far too wooden and literal to sustain any interest. New concepts are to be found, however, in Smith's translation of the names for God, the naming of Eve as "Life," the use of "love" for "charity" and "immerse" for "baptize."

Beyond the purely scholastic competency evidenced in producing a work of such scope and magnitude, that such a task could be accomplished by a woman went far to motivate women like Elizabeth Cady Stanton, and forty of her associates, to formulate *The Woman's Bible* (1895; 1898), a work which ignited serious feminist-religious controversy in religious circles and in society at large.

Overview of Biographical Sources

Those historians, journalists, scholars, and friends who have taken notice of Smith, have tended to emphasize her contributions as a suffragist. While it is true that the Bible translation was published primarily as a weapon against the belief that women were incapable of serious intellectual accomplishment, the primary focus of interest on Smith's life has been in the political and social arena. A body of miscellaneous literature is available on the life and times of the Smith family, most especially, Julia and Abby. These include one independent research paper and several articles from periodicals such as *Hartford Daily Courant, Woman's Journal, American Heritage, New England Quarterly,* and *Quarterly Journal of the Library of Congress.* Other sources include encyclopedic entries, reference texts, manuscripts, letters, and diaries from archives and historical associations.

Evaluation of Principal Biographical Sources

Burr, Frances Ellen. "Appendix." In *The Woman's Bible,* edited by Elizabeth Cady Stanton. New York: European Publishing, 1895-1896. (A, G) The appendix is a biographical essay on Julia Smith. While it is one of the more comprehensive, it is not totally accurate. Burr also wrote an extensive "Obituary" for the *Hartford Times* on March 8, 1886.

Cartledge, Pamela. "Seven Cows on the Auction Block: Abby and Julia Smith's Fight for Enfranchisement of Women." *The Connecticut Historical Society Bulletin* 52 (Winter 1987): 16-17. (A, G) This article concentrates upon the political activities of the Smith family, and it is an accurate and dependable source of information.

Hale, Addie Stancliffe. "Those Five Amazing Smith Sisters." *Hartford Daily Courant,* Sunday, May 15, 1932. (G, Y) A necessary article to read about the Smith family even if it is conjectural and anecdotal.

Housley, Kathleen. "'The Letter Kills but the Spirit Gives Life': Julia Smith's Translation of the Bible." *New England Quarterly* 61 (December 1988): 555-568. (A, G) Probably today's most knowledgeable scholar on the Smith family, Housley is the first scholar to treat in detail Smith's translation and the events that led up to it.

Speare, Elizabeth G. "Abby, Julia, and the Cows." *American Heritage* 8 (June 1957): 54-57, 96. (G, Y) This article is important for its interpretation of the historical account, but is inaccurate in some factual data and does not cite outside sources or references.

————. "Abby Hadassah Smith and Julia Evelina." In *Notable American Women,* edited by E. T. James, et al. Cambridge: Harvard University Press, 1971. A brief but useful biographical sketch.

Stern, Madeleine B. "The First Feminist Bible; The 'Alderney' Edition 1876." *Quarterly Journal of the Library of Congress* 34 (June 1977): 23-31. (A, G) This is a comprehensive and captivating retelling of the story of Smith's Bible translation and the events surrounding its publication.

Overview and Evaluation of Primary Sources

The total corpus of Smith's writings is not large, primarily because she devoted more than twenty years of her life to translating the Bible. She translated the Old Testament twice, the New Testament twice, and the Latin Vulgate once. There are twelve extant copies of her Bible translation available in university libraries, historical societies and in private collections. The Wesleyan University Archives (Middletown, CT) contains a copy of the translation, as well as an annotated copy of Julia's personal King James Bible, an 1838 edition, in which she uses different inks to represent the three different classical languages in which she worked.

The Connecticut Historical Society in Hartford is a primary resource center for original documents, ancillary articles, archival and reference materials pertinent to study of the Smith family. The handwritten manuscript leaves (believed to number some ten thousand) are archived here, although the primary repository for material and artifacts dealing with the Smith family is the Historical Society of Glastonbury, Connecticut. The society has a wide, though uncatalogued, collection of articles, newspaper clippings, and memorabilia, including Smith's letters and diaries (fifteen volumes in French and four in English).

Smith's only other publications are two pamphlets. One is a collection of newspaper clippings, articles, correspondences and information about the legal case surrounding her controversy with the city of Glastonbury, *Abby Smith and Her Cows, With a Report of the Law Case Decided Contrary to Law* (1877); the other is a collection of fifty of her mother's poems, *Selections from the Poems of Mrs. Hannah H. Smith, by her Daughter, Julia E. Smith, The Only Survivor of the Family* (1881). Both of these pamphlets are available in the Historical Societies and State Libraries of Connecticut.

Fiction and Adaptations

On January 7, 1958, ABC Television aired a Telephone Time Production entitled, "Abby, Julia, and the Seven Pet Cows," starring Judith Anderson and Dorothy Stickney. No tape or film of this production is known to exist. Occasionally, local Glastonbury schoolchildren reenact the events surrounding the Smith battle over taxation without representation.

Museums, Historical Landmarks, Societies
Historical Society of Glastonbury (Glastonbury, CT). This is the main repository for Smith Family materials.

Smith House (Glastonbury, CT). The original house remains standing on Main Street, as does the cemetery in which the family is buried. Open to the public through the Historical Society of Glastonbury.

The Stowe-Day Foundation (Hartford, CT). This Memorial Library and Historical Foundation has much to offer on the period and some few specific items related directly to Julia and her family.

Other Sources
Grode, Robert. "A Suffrage Saga." *Connecticut* (April 1989): 174-179. A nice retelling of the story but lacking in bibliographical information.

Kidder, Mary Helen, "The Sisters Smith of Glastonbury: Intellectuals, Rebels, and Cranks." Paper presented to the Connecticut Historical Society (March 3, 1936). This is an interesting presentation derived from translations of portions of Julia's French diaries and other anecdotal and legendary stories.

Prudden, Lillian E. "A Paper Written and Read by Lillian E. Prudden at the Fortnightly Club in New Haven, CT." (November 16, 1949). Another "recollection" about the Smith family and the contributions they have made. Available at the Historical Society of Glastonbury (CT).

Susan Shaw

LUCY STONE
1818-1893

Chronology

Born Lucy Stone on August 13, 1818, on a farm at Coy's Hill near West Brookfield, Massachusetts, the eighth of nine children and the third of four daughters born to Francis and Hannah Matthews Stone; *1818-1839* grows up resenting traditional gender roles that require women to be docile, meek, and subservient to men; resolves to go to college; *1839-1843* teaches and attends various local female seminaries; *1843-1847* attends Oberlin College and is first woman from Massachusetts to receive a college degree; *1847-1858* lectures publicly for the Massachusetts Anti-Slavery Society; becomes a leading orator of the women's rights movement after the 1848 Seneca Falls Convention; *1850s* instrumental in organizing women's rights conventions; *1855* marries Henry Browne Blackwell after both sign a prenuptial agreement that allows her to retain her name; *1856* presides over the Seventh National Woman's Rights Convention; *1857* gives birth to Alice Stone Blackwell, her only child to survive infancy; *1867* campaigns with her husband in Kansas on behalf of amendments to the state constitution for extending suffrage to women and Afro-Americans; *1869* helps found the American Woman Suffrage Association, an organization that looks to state legislation as a means of establishing woman suffrage; *1870-1893* reduces her lecture schedule and begins publishing *Woman's Journal,* a high-quality weekly newspaper known for its progressive stances on women's rights; continues lecturing and writing, delivering her last lecture at the World's Columbian Exposition at Chicago in 1893; *1893* dies in Dorchester, Massachusetts, on October 18; her funeral is attended by thousands of mourners.

Activities of Historical Significance

As a newspaper editor, columnist, and leading orator on behalf of abolition, woman suffrage, and prohibition, Stone stands shoulder-to-shoulder with Susan B. Anthony and Elizabeth Cady Stanton in the fight to change nineteenth-century women's lives. Throughout her life she championed the cause of equality—a tradition reaching back to the eighteenth-century work of women's equality advocates such as Mary Wollstonecraft and Abigail Adams.

From an early age, Stone resented the relegation of women to inferior roles; she was especially sensitive to her mother's long working hours and her father's preferential treatment of her older brother. Stone was angered to learn that she had no voting rights as a member of the Congregational Church of

West Brookfield simply because she was female, and her suspicion of inaccuracies in Bible translations made her determined to attend college to study the Greek and Hebrew texts.

By selling nuts and berries, Stone earned enough money to hire a tutor and to buy books denied her by her father. For seven years she "boarded around," teaching in various district schools; she saved her wages and studied for brief periods at Quadoag Seminary in Warren, Massachusetts, the Wesleyan Academy in Wilbraham, Massachusetts, and at Mount Holyoke Female Seminary. Finally in 1843 she entered Oberlin College, one of the few institutions to admit females and African Americans.

In order to meet expenses, Stone taught and did housework in the ladies' boarding hall, and accepted loans from her sister and brother. In her third year, Francis Stone agreed to provide his daughter the financial support he had supplied his sons.

A stop on the Underground Railroad, the town of Oberlin, Ohio, was strongly abolitionist and promoted a progressive agenda. Stone, however, was considered too radical because of her uncompromising advocacy of women's rights. While at Oberlin, Stone met Elizabeth Brown Blackwell, the first female to be ordained a Protestant minister in the U.S.; they became lifelong friends and eventually sisters-in-law. Selected to compose an oration for her college commencement, Stone refused upon discovering that, since females were restricted from public speaking, a male would actually deliver her speech. Thirty-six years later Stone was an honored speaker at the Oberlin College semicentennial jubilee.

After graduation Stone gave her first public address, speaking from her brother's Gardner, Massachusetts, pulpit. She lectured on behalf of the American Anti-Slavery Society, sponsored by William Lloyd Garrison, and soon blended her advocacy of women's rights into her abolition lectures. This tactic caused conflict with abolitionists, many of whom would have preferred their message to reach audiences undiluted. "I was a woman before I was an abolitionist. I must speak for the women," Stone affirmed, agreeing to lecture for women's rights on her own behalf during the week and against slavery for the Society on weekends.

At first Stone charged no fees for her speaking engagements, passing a hat to help meet expenses. She arranged her own lectures, posted her own handbills, and served as gatekeeper and collection-taker, as well as speaker. In spite of hostile, even violent audiences, she attracted large crowds and impressed many with her eloquence. Following the 1848 Seneca Falls Convention, Stone emerged as a national figure. Her speech at the First National Woman's Rights Convention, held in Worcester, Massachusetts, in 1850, is said to have convinced Susan B. Anthony to join the movement.

For the next decade Stone traveled extensively, lecturing on woman suffrage in the South, in Missouri, and in Canada. In 1853 she lectured three times at Louisville, Kentucky, marking the beginning of the suffrage movement in that state. She also sought an alliance between the women's movement and temperance organizations.

After years of shunning marriage because she believed it forced women to give up their rights, she married Henry Brown Blackwell following a lengthy courtship. They signed and published a marital agreement that protested the legal status of women—in particular, women's lack of property or custodial rights—and outlined their vision of equality in marriage. Stone was one of the first women not to adopt her husband's last name, and as the women's movement grew, those who followed her example became known as "Lucy Stoners."

Blackwell came from a distinguished and progressive family: two of his sisters were pioneer physicians, one was a newspaper correspondent, and another was a biographer. Stone and Blackwell respected each other's need to be independent. Their letters reveal a personal intimacy and a shared commitment to women's rights and abolition. After the birth of her daughter Alice in 1857, Stone briefly retired from the lecture circuit. In 1859 a son, born prematurely, died soon after birth.

Upon moving from Cincinnati to Orange, New Jersey, in 1858, to call attention to the plight of women who paid taxes but received no representation, Stone refused to pay her taxes and allowed some of her household goods to be sold at public auction. She also founded, organized, and supported numerous women's rights organizations, including the Women's Loyal National League, and the New Jersey Woman Suffrage Association.

After the Civil War, Stone worked on behalf of the American Equal Rights Association to secure African-American and woman suffrage. When the Republican leaders of Congress passed the Fourteenth and Fifteenth Amendments that advanced the rights of African American males while introducing sex distinctions into the Constitution, Stone resumed a full lecture schedule, actively but unsuccessfully campaigning with her husband for state woman suffrage in Kansas and New York.

In 1869 they moved to Boston and helped organize the New England Woman Suffrage Association. The historic schism that developed in the national movement resulted in Stone, Blackwell, and Julia Ward Howe, among others, aligned against Susan B. Anthony and Elizabeth Cady Stanton. The reasons for the division are manifold, but arose partly from honest differences over policy and tactics, and partly from a scandal made public by the sisters Victoria Woodhull and Tennessee Claflin, supporters of free love.

Advocating numerous social and cultural reforms, Anthony and Stanton led the National Women's Suffrage Association; meanwhile, from 1870 to 1890, Stone chaired the executive committee of the American Woman Suffrage Association (AWSA) and directed its efforts to concentrate exclusively on the issue of suffrage.

As founder and editor of *Woman's Journal* in 1870, Stone concentrated on increasing her readers' awareness of women's issues. The audience of well-educated club women, professionals, and writers consumed editorials by Stone, analyses of legal proceedings by Blackwell, articles featuring women's activities and accomplishments, and reprints of articles from other magazines and newspapers. Neither subscription nor advertising revenue could finance all production costs, so Stone and Blackwell devoted much of their time to meeting cost, while continuing to lecture on behalf of woman suffrage. The magazine, which survived until 1917, was edited by Alice Stone Blackwell after her mother's death.

In 1890 the AWSA and the NASA merged after three years of negotiations led by Alice Stone Blackwell. Stone headed the executive committee, with Stanton elected president, and Anthony vice president. Stone continued her efforts on behalf of women's rights, lecturing at the 1893 Columbian Exhibition at Chicago three months before her death on October 18.

Overview of Biographical Sources

The two full-length biographies of Stone that exist are adequate, but limited. However, because of Stone's central position in the reform movements of her time—abolition, suffrage, women's rights, prohibition—important biographical material appears in texts focused on these topics; analyses of the Blackwell family also cover Stone. Articles and women's studies reference sources offer additional assessments of Stone's considerable accomplishments.

Evaluation of Principal Biographical Sources

Blackwell, Alice Stone. *Lucy Stone: Pioneer of Woman's Rights*. 1930. Reprint. Millwood, NY: Kraus Reprint, 1971. (A, G) Written by Stone's daughter, not as an exposé but as a historic document, this text provides excellent detail and insightful commentary. Blackwell introduces a cast of characters that includes the major figures of the abolition, women's rights, prohibition, and suffrage movements. She draws on her own knowledge of events and on various family documents, but does not provide attribution.

Hays, Elinor Rice. *Morning Star: A Biography of Lucy Stone, 1818-1893*. New York: Harcourt Brace & World, 1961. (A, G) Building on Blackwell, Hays draws significantly on family letters. She significantly broadens the discussion of Stone's influence, particularly the role of *Woman's Journal*. Includes a bibliography and index, but lacks citations. Hays's occasionally dated judgments distract from the text.

Overview and Evaluation of Primary Sources

Two recent editions of Stone's correspondence have shed further light on her personal motivations and public actions. *Friends and Sisters: Letters between Lucy Stone and Antoinette Brown Blackwell, 1846-93,* edited by Carol Lasser and Marlene Deahl Merrill (Urbana: University of Illinois Press, 1987; A, G), documents the intimate friendship and mutual dependence of reformer Stone and her college classmate and sister-in-law, Antoinette Brown. These letters span the period from 1846 to 1893, with a gap from 1861 through February 1869. With informative introductions to each group of letters, notes to each letter, illustrations, index, and the brief bibliography, this book is a major resource.

Loving Warriors—Selected Letters of Lucy Stone and Henry B. Blackwell, 1853 to 1893, edited and introduced by Leslie Wheeler (New York: Dial Press, 1981; A, G), is the result of extensive research in the Blackwell Family Papers in the Library of Congress. Written before and during their long marriage, this correspondence reveals the doubts, passions, philosophical insights, political arguments, financial difficulties, personal trauma, family developments, and physical travail that filled the lives of these two nineteenth-century figures. Valuable for a range of letters that reveal the personalities of the correspondents, the book also features an introduction, editorial notes, and an index.

Issues of *Woman's Journal* dating from 1870 to 1893 are available on microfilm; this publication is an excellent source for articles by Stone, some of which were reprinted as tracts and pamphlets.

Other Sources

Curtis, Mary. "Amelia Bloomer's Curious Costumes." *American History Illustrated* 13, 3 (1978): 11-15. A good discussion of nineteenth-century dress reform. Especially useful for the story of Turkish trousers, the mode of dress that Stone and other women's rights advocates promoted during the 1850s. Well-illustrated.

"Lucy Stone." In *American Reformers,* edited by Alden Whitman. New York: H. W. Wilson, 1985. This entry summarizes the important details of Stone's career, providing an adequate explanation of the historical context and listing other sources of information.

"Lucy Stone." In *Dictionary of Literary Biography,* Vol. 79. Detroit: Gale Research, 1989. This entry is concise and lists certain *Woman's Journal* articles by Stone that represent her beliefs on various topics.

"Lucy Stone." In *Notable American Women: A Biographical Dictionary, 1607-1950,* Vol. 3. Edited by Edward T. James, Janet Wilson James, and Paul S. Boyer. Cambridge: Belknap Press of Harvard University Press, 1971. This noteworthy sketch is self-referenced and lists other sources.

Masel-Walters, Lynne. "A Burning Could by Day: The History and and Content of the *Woman's Journal.*" *Journalism History* 3 (Winter 1976-1977): 102-110. An important assessment of the longest running, most widely circulated suffrage newspaper that highlights the efforts of Stone and her husband, Blackwell.

Wheeler, Leslie. "Lucy Stone: Wife of Henry Blackwell." *American History Illustrated* 16 (1981): 38-45. This well-illustrated article provides insight into Stone's marriage to an equally important nineteenth-century reform advocate.

Sharon M. Rambo
Michigan State University

IDA TARBELL
1857-1944

Chronology

Born Ida Minerva Tarbell on November 5, 1857, on a farm near Watts-
burg, Erie County, Pennsylvania, the eldest of three surviving children of
Franklin Sumner Tarbell, a carpenter, and his wife Esther Ann McCullough
Tarbell, a schoolteacher before her marriage; *1857-1880* moves with family to
Rouseville and then to Titusville, Pennsylvania; abandons formal religious
practice; attracted to women's rights movement; attends local public schools
and then Allegheny College, Meadville, Pennsylvania; receives her bachelor's
degree; *1880-1891* teaches in Ohio at the Poland Union Seminary for two
years; returns to Meadville to join the staff of the *Chautauquan* magazine, a
teaching supplement for the home study program of the Chautauqua movement; travels to Paris to study the role of women in the French Revolution
and attends classes at the Sorbonne and the College de France; contributes
occasional articles to American periodicals and newspapers; *1892-1894* hired
by magazine publisher S. S. McClure to write feature articles on prominent
Frenchmen for *McClure's* magazine; returns to New York to join magazine's
staff; *1895* writes highly successful serialized biography of Napoleon, which is
published as *A Short Life of Napoleon Bonaparte* and sells one hundred
thousand copies; *1896* publishes her *Life of Madame Roland*; *1900* writes
series of articles on Abraham Lincoln that are collected as *The Life of
Abraham Lincoln*; *1900-1903* writes a series of articles on the development of
the Standard Oil trust; *1904* reworks the resulting nineteen articles and
publishes the two-volume *History of the Standard Oil Company*; hailed as the
founder of the journalistic movement that becomes known as "muckraking";
1906 leaves *McClure's* and joins with group of former *McClure's* staffers and
other journalists to purchase *American Magazine*; writes series of articles
attacking the high protective tariff as promoting monopoly; *1911* tariff articles
published as *The Tariff in Our Times*; *1915-1932* lectures on the Chautauqua
circuit for the Coit-Alber Lecture Bureau after the sale of the *American
Magazine*; remains prolific free-lance writer for magazines; writes favorabl
about Frederick W. Taylor's "scientific management" techniques; *1916*
publishes *New Ideals in Business*, which extols experiments underway in
welfare capitalism; *1916-1921* refuses offer by President Woodrow Wilson of
appointment to Federal Tariff Commission; serves as a member of the
Woman's Committee of the U.S. Council of National Defense in World
War I; appointed delegate to Wilson's Industrial Conference; serves as
correspondent at Paris Peace Conference; *1921-1932* attends President Warren
G. Harding's Conference on Unemployment; reports on Washington Naval

Disarmament Conference; goes to Italy to report on Mussolini's fascist regime; writes gushingly admiring biographies of business leaders Elbert H. Gary of United States Steel and Owen D. Young of General Electric; *1932-1938* lives in semi-retirement on her Connecticut farm; expresses ambivalence toward New Deal; writes *The Nationalizing of Business 1878-1898* for the A History of American Life Series; gives course on methods of biography at several colleges; *1939* publishes her autobiography, *All in the Day's Work*; *1944* dies on January 6 in a Bridgeport, Connecticut, hospital of pneumonia.

Activities of Historical Significance

Ida Tarbell was a facile-penned professional journalist whose most persistent lifelong interest was Abraham Lincoln. In connection with her work on Lincoln, she was instrumental in inducing Carl Schurz to write his memoirs, *The Reminiscences of Carl Schurz* (1907-1908) and collaborated with Charles A. Dana in preparing his *Recollections of the Civil War: With the Leaders at Washington and in the Field in the Sixties* (1898). She herself published eight books on Lincoln, including several for children. Although she was unduly modest about these works in her autobiography, she not only discovered important new material about Lincoln but also conscientiously worked to sift fact from legend. The leading student of Lincoln historiography has praised her as "the pioneer scientific investigator whose work foretold the revelation of Lincoln as he really was."

Tarbell's reputation during her lifetime and since rests primarily upon the two-volume *The History of the Standard Oil Company,* (1904). Without question, Tarbell did more thorough research on John D. Rockefeller and the building of his oil empire than any previous writer—more even than Henry Demarest Lloyd for his *Wealth Against Commonwealth* (1894), which strongly influenced her. Her volumes still warrant the attention of historians, most importantly for the information she acquired from personal interviews with early oil industry leaders and Rockefeller associates such as Henry H. Rogers. But the work is marred by the strong personal animus displayed toward Rockefeller and Standard Oil. Tarbell appears to have absorbed this hostility during her childhood from the independent oil men of Titusville. Her father blamed Standard Oil for the failure of his business (he manufactured wooden oil storage tanks) and for the suicide of his partner.

Tarbell gained a reputation from her *History of the Standard Oil Company* as a "muckraker," that is, a reform-minded writer bent on exposing business wrongdoing. But despite her hostility toward Rockefeller, Tarbell was an admirer of business and businessmen, at least those exhibiting proper ethical standards. She became a strong champion of Frederick W. Taylor's "scientific management" techniques to increase worker productivity, extolled Henry Ford's mass-production methods and paternalism toward his workers, and applauded ongoing experiments in welfare capitalism as the "Golden Rule in Industry." Her biographies of United States Steel's Elbert H. Gary (1925) and General Electric's Owen D. Young (1932) were regarded even at the time of their publication as uncritically adulatory. *The Nationalizing of Business 1878-1898* (1936), in the A History of American Life Series edited by Arthur M. Schlesinger, Sr., and Dixon Ryan Fox, reflected a similar pro-business bias, was thinly researched, and lacked analysis.

Tarbell was an ambivalent feminist. As a young woman, she fell under the influence of the women's rights movement. After hearing women's rights activists who visited her parents describe marriage as a "prison," she vowed not to marry and never did. But she remained opposed to woman suffrage, and she appears to have regretted not marrying and having children, declaring in *The Business of Being a Woman* (1912) that "women had a business assigned by nature and society which was of more importance than public life."

Tarbell's significance for modern researchers lies in how her life illuminates the impact of the social, economic, and intellectual changes that took place in the U.S. between the Civil War and the Great Depression.

Overview of Biographical Sources

Despite her secondary importance as a historical figure, Tarbell has attracted a surprising amount of interest. She is the subject of excellent brief biographical sketches by David M. Chalmers (1971) and Geoffrey Blodgett (1973). Virginia Van der Veer Hamilton (1970) favorably reappraises her *History of the Standard Oil Company* and its social impact. Mary E. Tompkins (1970) reviews the full body of her writings. There is even a biography for young people by Alice Fleming (1970), extolling her as "the first and best of the muckrakers." Kathleen Brady's *Ida Tarbell: Portrait of a Muckraker* (1984) is a thoroughly researched and documented full-scale biography.

Evaluation of Principal Biographical Sources

Blodgett, Geoffrey. "Tarbell, Ida Minerva." In *Dictionary of American Biography: Supplement Three 1941-1945*, edited by Edward T. James. New York: Scribner's, 1973. (A, G) An excellent succinct biographical sketch with analysis.

Brady, Kathleen. *Ida Tarbell: Portrait of a Muckraker*. New York: Seaview/Putnam, 1984. (A, G) Brady has assiduously tracked down Tarbell's surviving correspondence and other papers. Approximately eighty percent of the text is devoted to the years up to the sale of the *American Magazine*. While rarely going beyond the surface details of Tarbell's life, the work will probably remain the standard biography for the foreseeable future. Brady chides Tarbell for not being sufficiently feminist; but otherwise she is admiring, even eulogistic. "Hers is a story," Brady writes, "of how one person handled the human dilemma of daring great things, despite galling limitations, and succeeded admirably."

Chalmers, David M. "Tarbell, Ida Minerva." In *Notable American Women 1607-1950: A Biographical Directory*, vol. 3, edited by Edward T. James, et al. Cambridge: Belknap Press of Harvard University Press, 1971. (A, G) Another excellent brief account, more detailed but less analytical than Blodgett's.

Fleming, Alice. *Ida Tarbell: First of the Muckrakers*. New York: Thomas Y. Crowell, 1971. (Y) A gushing, hero-worshipping account apparently intended to provide inspiration for teen-age girls.

Hamilton, Virginia Van der Veer. "The Gentlewoman and the Robber Baron." *American Heritage* 21 (April 1970): 78-86. (G) A piece written for the general reader rather than the scholarly audience that favorably reappraises Tarbell's *History of the Standard Oil Company* and explores its impact.

Tompkins, Mary F. *Ida M. Tarbell*. New York: Twayne, 1974. (A, G) A useful, if pedestrian, survey of the full body of Tarbell's writings.

Overview and Evaluation of Primary Sources
The bulk of Ida Tarbell's surviving papers are in the Pelletier Library, Allegheny College, Meadville, Pennsylvania. Additional significant Tarbell materials are in the following repositories: the Little Chapel of All Nations, Tucson, Arizona (principally youthful correspondence with her family); the Drake Well Museum, Titusville, Pennsylvania (principally letters and memoranda from her history of the oil industry along with scrapbooks of newspaper clippings and reviews); the Sophia Smith Library, Smith College, Northampton, Massachusetts (approximately 1,000 letters); the Petroleum History and Research Center, University of Wyoming, Laramie (Tarbell-John McAlpine Siddall correspondence); and Henry Demarest Lloyd Papers, State Historical Society of Wisconsin, Madison.

Tarbell's autobiography, *All in the Day's Work: An Autobiography* (New York: Macmillan Co., 1939; A, G) lacks the overblown egoism typical of the genre; she is remarkably soft-spoken, at times even unduly modest about her accomplishments. The work is indispensable for its account of her upbringing and young womanhood. Another interesting work is *The Business of Being a Woman* (New York: Macmillan, 1912; G), which reveals some of Tarbell's ideas about feminism.

Information about Tarbell during her *McClure's/American Magazine* years appears in the following autobiographies of her associates: Samuel S. McClure, *My Autobiography* (New York: Frederick A. Stokes, 1914; A, G); Lincoln Steffens, *The Autobiography of Lincoln Steffens*, 2 vols. (New York: Harcourt, Brace, 1931; A, G); Ray Stannard Baker, *American Chronicle: The Autobiography of Ray Stannard Baker* (New York: Scribner's, 1945; A, G); and William Allen White, *The Autobiography of William Allen White* (New York: Macmillan, 1946; A, G).

Other Sources

Case, Victoria, and Robert O. Case. *We Called Its Culture: The Story of Chautauqua.* Garden City, NY: Doubleday, 1948. Includes information on the early days of Chautauqua and the *Chautauquan.*

Chalmers, David. *The Social and Political Ideas of the Muckrakers.* New York: Citadel Press, 1964. Brief sketches of the views of leading muckrakers, including Tarbell.

Ellis, Elmer. *Mr. Dooley's America: A Life of Peter Finley Dunne.* New York: Alfred A. Knopf, 1941. An entertaining and illuminating biography of one of Tarbell's associates on the *American Magazine.*

Filler, Louis. *Crusaders for American Liberalism.* New York: Harcourt, Brace, 1939. Although outdated by more recent scholarship, this work and Regier's *Era of the Muckrakers* remain the only attempts at a comprehensive treatment of the rise and fall of muckraking.

Kaplan, Justin. *Lincoln Steffens: A Biography.* New York: Simon and Schuster, 1974. The best of the treatments of Steffens, one of Tarbell's associates at *McClure's* and *American Magazine.*

Lyon, Peter. *Success Story: The Life and Times of S. S. McClure.* New York: Scribner's, 1963. A readable, though not penetrating, biography of Tarbell's mentor.

Mott, Frank Luther. *A History of American Magazines*, 5 vols. Cambridge: Harvard University Press, 1938-1968. The standard history of magazines in the United States. Material on Tarbell is found in volumes three and four.

Nevins, Allan. *Study in Power: John D. Rockefeller, Industrialist and Philanthropist*, 2 vols. New York: Scribner's, 1953. A far more positive portrait of Rockefeller and Standard Oil than Tarbell's.

Regier, Cornelius C. *The Era of the Muckrakers*. Chapel Hill: University of North Carolina Press, 1932. Outdated by more recent scholarship, but is one of two attempts (see Filler) at an overall account of the period.

Semonche, John E. *Ray Stannard Baker: A Quest for Democracy in Modern America, 1870-1918*. Chapel Hill: University of North Carolina Press, 1969. An excellent study of Baker during his years as a journalist, magazine writer/editor, and muckraker, when he was closely associated with Tarbell.

Thomas, Benjamin P. *Portrait for Posterity: Lincoln and His Biographers*. New Brunswick, NJ: Rutgers University Press, 1947. A survey and evaluation of the writings on Lincoln that praises Tarbell's contribution to Lincoln scholarship.

Wilson, Harold S. *McClure's Magazine and the Muckrakers*. Princeton, NJ: Princeton University Press, 1970. A thoroughly researched and insightful account of McClure, his magazine, its staff, and its influence.

John Braeman
University of Nebraska, Lincoln

TENSKWATAWA
1775-1836?

Chronology

Born Lalawethika in 1775 at Old Piqua, a Shawnee village in western Ohio on the Mad River; he is the son of Puckeshinwa, a Shawnee, killed at the Battle of Point Pleasant before his birth, and Methoataske, a woman of Creek descent; one of his triplet brothers dies in infancy and the other, Kumskaukau, survives; *1775-1779* cared for by his mother until she immigrates westward to join Shawnees living in modern-day Missouri; *1779-1788* reared by his eldest brother, Chiksika, and his sister, Tecumpease; *1788* Chiksika is killed while raiding in Kentucky, and Lalawethika becomes a member of Tecumpease's family; *1788-1791* matures as the Shawnees battle invading whites and loses another brother, Sauwauseekau, killed in the Battle of Fallen Timbers in 1791; *1791-1798* lives in villages in western Ohio and then moves with Tecumseh to the Whitewater River in modern-day Indiana; *1798-1805* lives in Indiana, marries, sires several children, and apprentices himself to a shaman, Penagashea; *1804-1805* upon Penagashea's death succeeds him as shaman but fails to protect his people from an epidemic; *1805-1807* has a vision in which the Master of Life instructs him to lead his people back to the older and better ways of life, and from this point forward Lalawethika is known as Tenskwatawa, "the open door"; preaches the Master of Life's words to the Indiana and Ohio tribes, rapidly establishing a devoted following, and builds a new village on the site of Greenville, Ohio; *1808-1809* moves his people from Greenville to the Tippecanoe River in Indiana and creates a new seat for his movement called Prophetstown; *1809-1811* outraged by the Treaty of Fort Wayne, in which Miamis, Delawares, and Potawatomis cede three million acres of land to the U.S.; with his brother Tecumseh, intensifies efforts to unite the western tribes to stem the white invasion of their homeland; *1811-1813* defeated by William Henry Harrison at the Battle of Tippecanoe and halfheartedly takes part in the War of 1812 until Tecumseh is killed at the Battle of the Thames in 1813; Tenskwatawa's influence wanes, and he remains in exile in Canada; *1813-1824* quarrels with his British benefactors in Canada and returns to Wapakoneta, Ohio, at the invitation of Lewis Cass, the governor of Michigan Territory; *1824-1828* involved in Cass's efforts to relocate the Shawnees and finally leads a small band to the Kansas River Valley; *1828-1832* founds several Shawnee villages on the south bank of the Kansas River near Kansas City; *1832-1836* lives out his final years in the Kansas River area; establishes another village named Prophetstown; poses for a portrait by the famous artist George Catlin; *1836* dies and is buried somewhere in the vicinity of Kansas City, Kansas.

Activities of Historical Significance

Tenskwatawa, the Shawnee Prophet, profoundly affected the lives of the inhabitants of the old Northwest Territory during his lifetime. As a child and as a young man, Tenskwatawa, then known as Lalawethika, was ungainly and ineffectual. His own brother Chiksika apparently despised him, his contemporaries scorned him, and he was completely inept at the favorite pursuits of his peers. He was corpulent, abrasive in personality and unable to establish a rapport with anyone other than his brother Tecumseh. He accidentally blinded himself in one eye with an arrow, and by the time he reached adulthood, he was something of a laughingstock among his nation. He was not a warrior, was a poor hunter and provider for his family, and was addicted to alcohol. Mildly stated, the young Tenskwatawa was an absolute failure at everything he attempted to do.

His life was dramatically transformed on a chilly night in April 1805. While lighting his pipe, Lalawethika fell down as though dead. His family, shocked by his apparent death, began to make funeral preparations. At that point, Lalawethika, roused and informed his astonished family that he had had a vision from the Master of Life. His account of his visit with the Master of Life and his version of the Master's message to his Native American children electrified his listeners. The Master directed his children to change their lives, to throw off the white man's yokes of alcohol, cheap trade goods, and corrupting influences, and to return to their traditional culture and values. He adopted the name Tenskwatawa, and soon came to be known as the "Prophet" among whites. He gathered disciples and his vision altered the balance of religious and political realities among the Native Americans of the western Great Lakes region.

As his following grew, and after his brother Tecumseh joined his movement, the nature of Tenskwatawa's teachings underwent an important metamorphosis. He and Tecumseh were alarmed by the Treaty of Fort Wayne, which they believed proved that Native Americans would never be able to live peacefully with white men. Tenskwatawa and Tecumseh argued that the tribes must set aside their ancient enmities and work together to halt the invasion of their homeland.

By 1809 Tenskwatawa's movement, endorsed by his widely admired brother Tecumseh, became more secular in its concerns. Tenskwatawa built a village, named Prophetstown, at the confluence of the Tippecanoe and Wabash rivers. Scores of Native Americans from throughout the region came to Prophetstown to hear his message. As war with Great Britain threatened the U.S. and as the influence of the Prophet burgeoned, a clash between Native Americans and whites was inevitable. By 1811 neither Tenskwatawa nor Tecumseh quailed at the thought of another open war with the whites. Their only concern was the proper timing for the conflict, which depended solely upon the commencement of hostilities between the U.S and Great Britain.

Hostilities with the whites erupted before Tenskwatawa and Tecumseh were fully prepared to cope with the crisis, however. Ill-timing, combined with English defeats in the War of 1812 and Tecumseh's death, collapsed Tenskwatawa's hopes for an alliance that would halt white expansion. Even though his movement faltered, Tenskwatawa was an extraordinary figure. As a youngster he was ridiculed, as a young adult he was scorned, and then for a brief time he was revered for his message. In his later years, he was a pitiful figure who constantly intrigued to advance his interests in the vain hope he might restore some of his former importance.

Overview of Biographical Sources

The best source for biographical information on Tenskwatawa the Prophet is R. David Edmunds, *The Shawnee Prophet* (1983). Other valuable books that shed light on the Prophet and his calamitous times are R. David Edmunds, *Tecumseh* (1984); Benjamin Drake, *Life of Tecumseh* (1969); Alvin M. Josephy, Jr., "Tecumseh, The Greatest Indian," in *The Patriot Chiefs: A Chronicle of American Indian Leadership* (1961); John Oskison, *Tecumseh and His Times* (1938); and Glenn Tucker, *Tecumseh: Vision of Glory* (1973).

Evaluation of Principal Biographical Sources

Edmunds, R. David. *The Shawnee Prophet*. Lincoln: University of Nebraska Press, 1983. (A, G) The only work devoted solely to the career of Tenskwatawa, this useful biography is a complete account of the Prophet's life from birth to death. Edmunds is a sympathetic biographer who critically examines the Prophet's foibles, as well as his greatness. In addition, this biography describes the roles of Tecumseh and other major Native American leaders in the era of Tenskwatawa's prominence. *The Shawnee Prophet* is well-written, solidly researched, and features an excellent bibliography.

————. *Tecumseh and the Quest for Indian Leadership*. Boston: Little, Brown, 1984. (A, G) A useful companion to *The Shawnee Prophet*, this study focuses on the Prophet's more famous brother. Tecumseh was an extraordinary figure in his own right and has enjoyed an enduring fame. This biography adopts the streamlined format of the Library of American Biography series, but nevertheless provides a handy account of the events and people in the lives of two of the most famous Native American brothers in American history.

Josephy, Alvin M., Jr. *The Patriot Chiefs: A Chronicle of American Indian Leadership*. New York: Viking Press, 1961. (A, G) A first-rate source of information on Native American leaders who tried to unite their peoples against the onslaught of white settlers. The chapter entitled "Tecumseh, the Greatest Indian" deals with Tecumseh's efforts to build a Native American confederacy. Of necessity, Josephy discusses the Prophet's role in these events and consequentially provides readers with a thumbnail sketch of Tenskwatawa. He reiterates a few minor misconceptions about the Prophet.

Overview and Evaluation of Primary Sources

The Prophet left no personal papers, but many whites who dealt with him recorded their concerns and impressions of Tenskwatawa's movement in their papers and correspondence. One useful place to begin studying the Prophet is Logan Esarey, ed., *Messages and Letters of William Henry Harrison*, 2 vols. (Indianapolis: Indiana Historical Commission, 1922; A, G). This valuable source illuminates how Governor Harrison viewed the Prophet. Another useful source is Gayle Thornbrough, ed., *Letter Book of the Indian Agency at Fort Wayne, 1809-1815* (Indianapolis: Indiana Historical Society, 1961; A, G). The Cincinnati Historical Society holds several series of manuscripts—including the William Henry Harrison Papers, the John Johnston Papers, and the Frank J. Jones Collection—that shed light on Tecumseh and the Prophet in those fateful years. The William L. Clements Library at the University of Michigan in Ann Arbor is the repository for papers pertaining to Lewis Cass and to the War of 1812. The Burton Historical Collections of the Detroit Public Library contain several manuscript collections relevant to the activities of Lewis Cass, George Ironside, William Henry Harrison, and the historian Benson J. Lossing; these papers contribute to an understanding of the Prophet's era.

The archives of the Fort Malden National Historical Park at Amherstburg, Ontario, contain useful information regarding Native American activities during the War of 1812. The Draper Manuscripts in the State Historical Society of Wisconsin, Madison, feature thirteen volumes of Tecumseh papers. Other documents that shed light on Tenskwatawa may be found in the Ohio Historical Society in Columbus, the Indiana Historical Society in Indianapolis, and the Battleground Historical Association, in Battleground, Indiana. Information relating to the Prophet's later years is available in the National Archives, in Record Group 75 of the Records of the Bureau of Indian Affairs, and at the Kansas Historical Society, Topeka.

Museums, Historical Landmarks, Societies

Battleground Historical Association (Battleground, IN). A special organization created to maintain files and information concerning the Battle of Tippecanoe and the subsequent burning of Prophetstown in 1811.

Tecumseh Memorial Association (Thamesville, Ontario). In 1924 this organization dedicated a monument to Tecumseh, a fitting memorial to his role in the events of the early nineteenth century. The Prophet also enjoys a certain amount of notoriety as a result of this group's actions.

Other Sources

Clark, Jerry E. *The Shawnee*. Lexington: University of Kentucky Press, 1977. An excellent introduction to the culture and practices of the Shawnee nation.

Klinck, Carl, ed. *Tecumseh: Fact and Fiction in Early Records*. Englewood Cliffs, NJ: Prentice-Hall, 1961. A piecemeal collection of accounts of Tecumseh's life and times, plus poems and fiction commemorating his life. The collection's celebration of Native American nationalism provides insights into the Prophet's place in the movement.

Meek, Basil. "Tarhe—The Crane". *Ohio Archaeological and Historical Publications* 20 (January 1911): 64-73. A short useful account of Tarhe, an influential Wyandot rival of the Prophet.

Prucha, Francis Paul. *The Sword of the Republic: The United States Army on the Frontier, 1783-1845*. London and Ontario: Collier-Macmillan, 1969. An excellent study of the military situation on the frontier during a confusing and bloody time for the Native American. Prucha is the premier historian of this era.

Wallis, Wilson D. *Messiahs: Their Role in Civilizations*. Washington, DC: American Council on Public Affairs, 1943. Readers may find this little-known study fascinating to examine.

Larry G. Bowman
University of North Texas

MARY CHURCH TERRELL
1863-1954

Chronology

Born Mary Church on September 23, 1863, to newly-emancipated slaves Robert Reed and Louise Ayers Church, in Memphis, Tennessee; *1868* her parents divorce and Mary and her brother Thomas live with their mother; *1868-1879* to avoid the segregated schools of Memphis, attends the "model school" run by Antioch College, a forerunner of the kindergarten program, and the all-white elementary and secondary schools in Yellow Springs, Ohio; *1884* receives a degree in classics from Oberlin College; *1885-1887* teaches French and English at Wilberforce University; *1887* meets her future husband Robert while they both teach Latin at the Preparatory School of Colored Youth in Washington, D.C.; *1888-1890* travels throughout Europe with her mother, studying languages; returns to Washington to teach; *1891* marries Robert Terrell, a Harvard graduate, lawyer, and later judge of the Municipal Court of the District of Columbia; *1893* serves as first woman president of the Bethel Literary and Historical Association; *1892-1898* elected president of the National Association of Colored Women; has four children, but only one, Phyllis, survives; *1895-1911* appointed to and serves on the Board of Education in Washington, D.C., the first black woman to hold such a position; *1898-1905* addresses the convention of the National American Woman Suffrage Association on the specific problems of colored women and on "The Justice of Woman Suffrage"; in Berlin, addresses the International Council of Women in English, German, and French; adopts her niece, Mary Church; *1905-1917* intercedes with Secretary of War William Taft for an investigation of the conditions that led to the riot of black soldiers in Brownsville, Texas; lectures and writes on black life and history; is one of the founders of the National Association for the Advancement of Colored People (NAACP); pickets the White House with other suffragists; *1911* publishes *Harriet Beecher Stowe: An Appreciation*; *1919-1924* serves as a delegate to the International Congress of Women at Zurich and is recognized for her work at the Quinquennial International Peace Congress; *1920* during the presidential election, appointed by the Republican National Committee as director of work among black women in the East; *1925* husband Robert dies; *1929* recognized by Oberlin College as one of its hundred most influential graduates; *1932* publishes the pamphlet *Colored Women and World Peace*; *1940* publishes her autobiography, *A Colored Woman in a White World*; *1946* receives an honorary doctorate from Wilberforce; *1948* receives honorary doctorates from Oberlin and Howard University; *1946-1949* fights and finally wins membership in the Washington chapter of the American Association of University

Women (AAUW), bringing an end to discrimination against membership for blacks; *1949* leads the Coordinating Committee for the Enforcement of the District of Columbia Anti-Discrimination Laws, an effort to require restaurants to serve blacks in accordance with the "Lost Laws of 1872-73"; organizes pickets in front of the Thompson Restaurant and department stores that refused to serve blacks in an effort to integrate restaurants; becomes involved in an attempt to free a family of Georgia sharecroppers accused of murder—the Ingram case; appeals on their behalf to the governor of Georgia and to the United Nations, winning them a ten-year sentence rather than a death sentence; *1954* dies at the age of ninety in Anne Arundel General Hospital, Annapolis, Maryland, on July 24, and is buried at Lincoln Memorial Cemetery, Suitland, Maryland.

Activities of Historical Significance

Terrell was one of the first five black women in the U.S. to receive a college degree. As a Wilberforce University lecturer, she was also one of the first black women in the country to teach at the college level. Terrell lectured throughout the country at Chautauqua meetings, American Missionary Association gatherings, women's rights rallies, and for pacifist causes. Her role as a proponent for justice and equal rights for all led to the prominent place she held in a variety of reform-minded organizations.

Terrell's role in black organizations is more problematic. She was the daughter of the South's first black millionaire (her father was also half white), and she was raised with all the privileges her father's money could provide. Such a background produced a woman who was continually torn between separatist and assimilationist tendencies. This split is best reflected in her stormy associations with W. E. B. DuBois and Booker T. Washington, both of whom she supported and opposed at various times. Her involvement in founding the NAACP particularly drew criticism from Washington, while on other occasions she helped Washington block DuBois's reform efforts.

Terrell's most radical activities—enforcing anti-discrimination laws, picketing restaurants, lobbying for the Brownsville soldiers and the Ingram family, and fighting to gain membership in the AAUW—need to be placed alongside her very active work for the Republican Party. Terrell wanted to be accepted fully as a woman in both black and white worlds.

Overview of Biographical Sources

Sterling's brief sketch of Terrell's life, *Black Foremothers: Three Lives* (1988), is clearly simply a summarizing of Terrell's autobiography, *A Colored Woman in a White World*. Because Terrell's autobiography was published in 1940, and she lived another fourteen years, there are two short articles that complete the picture of her last decade: Constance Daniel's "Together—Across New Frontiers" (1949) and Janet McKelvey Swift's "Oberlin's Share" (1949).

Evaluation of Principal Biographical Sources

Daniel, Constance. "Together—Across New Frontiers." *Women United* (October, 1949; A, G) Discusses Terrell's efforts to integrate the AAUW.

Shepperd, Gladys Byram. *Mary Church Terrell—Respectable Person.* Baltimore: 1959. (A) Describes Terrell's later success in desegregating the restaurants of Washington, D.C., a topic not discussed in her autobiography.

Sterling, Dorothy. *Black Foremothers: Three Lives.* 2d ed. New York: Feminist Press, 1988. (A, G) A thirty-page biography of Terrell, bound with biographies of other black female reformers, Ellen Craft and Ida B. Wells. Contains a valuable bibliography.

Swift, Janet McKelvey. "Oberlin's Share." *Oberlin Alumni Magazine* (September 1949; A, G) Describes Terrell's successful fight to gain membership in the AAUW.

Overview and Evaluation of Primary Sources

Terrell's major work is her autobiography, *A Colored Woman in a White World* (Washington, DC: Ransdell, 1940; Reprint. New York: Arno, 1980; A, G). As the major source for information on Terrell's life, her autobiography presents her memories of her work in education and reform. It had less impact than she had hoped it would because of its meek, self-effacing tone. This volume does reprint some of her best known speeches.

Terrell also published a series of articles on such subjects as "Lynching from a Negro's Point of View" (*North American Review,* June 1904; A, G), "Peonage in the United States" (*Nineteenth Century,* August 1907; A, G), "Taft and the Negro Soldiers" (*Independent,* July 1908; A, G), "Woman Suffrage and the Fifteenth Amendment" (*The Crisis,* August, 1915; A, G), "The History of the High School for Negroes in Washington" (*Journal of Negro History,* July 1917; A, G). Along the same lines she also published a short biography, *Harriet Beecher Stowe: An Appreciation* (1911) and the pamphlet *Colored Women and World Peace* (1932).

Terrell's papers, including diaries and letters, are housed in the Library of Congress, Washington, D.C. Sylvia Lyons Render, "Afro-American Women: The Outstanding and the Obscure" in *Quarterly Journal of the Library of Congress* (October 1975: 310-15, 319-21), presents useful summaries of the

Terrell collection held by the Library of Congress. A second collection of Mary Church Terrell papers is held by the Moorland-Spingarn Research Center, Howard University, in Washington, D.C.

Other Sources

Church, Annette E., and Robert Church. *The Robert Churches of Memphis: A Father and Son Who Achieved in Spite of Race.* Ann Arbor, MI: Burke's Book Store, 1974. A family history that details the struggles and successes of family members, particularly Robert Church.

Flexner, Eleanor. *Century of Struggle: The Women's Rights Movement in the United States.* New York: Atheneum, 1971. A classic work on the contributions of black women to the women's rights movement.

Kellogg, Charles Flint. *NAACP.* Baltimore: The Johns Hopkins University Press, 1967. A history of the organization Terrell helped found.

Meier, August. *Negro Thought in America 1880-1915.* Ann Arbor, MI: University of Michigan Press, 1963. Terrell's ideas and activities are discussed in context of other black reformers of the time.

Papachristou, Judith. *Women Together: A History in Documents of the Women's Movement in the United States.* New York: Knopf, 1976. This selection of important documents includes material relevant to Terrell's contributions to the women's movement.

Ploski, Harry A., and James Williams, eds. *The Negro Almanac: A Reference Work on the Afro-American.* 4th ed. New York: Wiley, 1983. Terrell's role is described in context of twentieth-century efforts to achieve equity.

Sterling, Dorothy. *Speak Out in Thunder Tones: Letters and Other Writings by Black Northerners.* New York: Doubleday, 1973. This classic treatment of the black struggle for equality should be consulted to understand Terrell's political ideals.

Woodward, C. Vann. *The Strange Career of Jim Crow.* New York: Oxford University Press, 1974. Traces the efforts of blacks to overthrow those laws that institutionalized prejudice and socio-economic limitation.

Diane Long Hoeveler
Marquette University

SOJOURNER TRUTH
c. 1797-1883

Chronology

Born Isabella Baumfree about 1797 in Hurley, Ulster County, New York, the next to youngest of the several children of James and Elizabeth, slaves belonging to the wealthy Dutch patroon Charles Hardenbergh; not much is known about her early life except that she served as a slave in several different households, and her native language was low Dutch; *1810-1827* serves as a slave in the house of John H. Dumont, New Paltz, New York, where she has five children with a fellow slave, Thomás (although there has always been a suspicion that some of the children may have been fathered by Dumont); four of the children survive infancy, two of the girls are sold away, and she has to use legal means to regain custody of her son; *1827* flees to the house of Isaac and Maria Van Wagener, and takes their last name; *1829* arrives in New York City with her two youngest children and works as a maid; becomes involved with a variety of chiliastic cults; as a self-styled mystic who claimed to hear voices, preaches on street corners, especially to prostitutes, with Elijah and Sarah Pierson, wealthy religious fanatics; *1832* joins with the Piersons in giving their money and allegiance to Robert Matthews, who calls himself Matthias and founds a religious commune in Sing Sing, New York, called "Zion Hill"; commune collapses after two years because of the mysterious death of Elijah Pierson; Matthews tried and acquitted of the murder; involved in the scandal and rumors of sexual irregularities, she brings a successful libel suit to clear her name; *1835-1843* continues to hear mystical voices and becomes involved with the African Zion Church; lives quietly with her children and works as a maid; *1843* is commanded by a voice to take the name "Sojourner Truth" and travel throughout Long Island and Connecticut preaching that God is kind, good, and that all people should love and accept one another; *1843-1846* becomes actively involved with the abolitionist movement under the auspices of the Northhampton Association of Education and Industry, founded by George W. Benson; *1850* Olive Gilbert writes the *Narrative of Sojourner Truth*, a told-to autobiography, which provides financial support during the next few years; *1850-1855* travels throughout the Midwest speaking with other abolitionists and women's rights advocates, often jeered by hecklers, clubbed by Southern sympathizers, defamed by the *St. Louis Dispatch* as a "man" (Truth once exposed her breasts to disprove the allegation); *mid-1850s* moves to Battle Creek, Michigan, to live with her three daughters and their families; *1861-1864* raises food and clothing for Negro volunteers throughout Michigan; *1864* is received at the White House by President Lincoln; forces compliance with the legal desegregation of streetcars in Washington, D.C.; appointed "counselor to the freed people" by the National Freedmen's Association at Freedmen's Village, Arlington Heights, Virginia; *1865-1870* champions the idea of a "Negro State"—settling Negroes on public land in the West—and circulates a petition on the subject, which she presents to President Grant; *1870-1875* preaches to black audiences to "Be clean!"; exhorts white audiences to support temperance and Negro and women's rights, preaching a befuddled religious mysticism; final appearances often ridiculed for attempts to peddle books and photographs; *1875* retires to Battle Creek and receives hundreds of visitors every year; *1883*, dies on November 26, and is buried in Oak Hill Cemetery, Battle Creek.

Activities of Historical Significance

Although her role in the reform movements of the period was relatively small, Sojourner Truth captured the imagination of the country with her dramatic personality and powerful oratorical skills.

She was the first African American to believe that the American legal system could work to the advantage of black citizens. She was the first black to go to a court of law to successfully regain custody of her son, illegally sold into slavery. She was also the first black to win a slander suit against prominent white citizens. She advised the inhabitants of the freedmen's camps after the Civil War that "the law is behind you, get with it!" and she led the fight of the "freedom riders" to force compliance with the legal desegregation of streetcars in Washington, D.C.

Although she could not read or write, Truth left one of the earliest slave narratives, a told-to autobiography, which is a valuable historical record of what life was like for slaves and early freed blacks in New York during the early nineteenth century.

Overview of Biographical Sources

Olive Gilbert's *The Narrative of Sojourner Truth* (1850) stands as the basis for all biographical work on Truth. This told-to autobiography is suspect on at least grammatical grounds, with Gilbert standardizing Truth's own dialectal speech. Truth's relationship with Dumont is also presented in an internally contradictory manner that has always raised questions about the paternity of Truth's children. The first modern retelling of Truth's life was Arthur H. Fauset, *Sojourner Truth: God's Faithful Pilgrim* (1938), which presents a highly romanticized, speculative biography. The first work to apply modern historical methods was Hertha Pauli, *Her Name Was Sojourner Truth* (1962). The most recent biography is the one by Jacqueline Bernard, *Journey Toward Freedom: The Story of Sojourner Truth* (1967).

Evaluation of Principal Biographical Sources
Bernard, Jacqueline. *Journey Toward Freedom: The Story of Sojourner Truth.* 1967. Reprint. New York: Feminist Press, 1990. (A, G) The most recent biography, based on extensive research in primary sources.

Fauset, Arthur H. *Sojourner Truth: God's Faithful Pilgrim.* 1938. Reprint. New York: Russell and Russell, 1971. (A, G) Fauset divides his biography into three sections: "Isabella," "Matthias," and "Sojourner." He also takes liberties with inventing what God's voice must have said to Sojourner at crucial moments in her life. Contains a bibliography.

Gilbert, Olive. *Narrative of Sojourner Truth.* 1850. Reprint. New York: Arno Press, 1968. (A) The standard biographical source. This edition also reprints all contemporary newspaper accounts of her speeches and all of the correspondence she received.

Pauli, Hertha. *Her Name Was Sojourner Truth.* New York: Avon, 1962. (A, G) Written in a dramatic style, this study is the first to try to reassess some of the legends about Truth through historical research. Contains a bibliography.

Sojourner Truth: Narrative and Book of Life. Chicago: Johnson Publishing, 1970. (A, G) A reprint of the Gilbert volume. Contains biographies, essays, and brief commentary on the life of Truth.

Vale, Gilbert. *Narrative of Isabella, or Fanaticism, Its Source and Influence: Illustrated by the Simple Narrative of Isabella.* New York: 1835. (A) Considered the indispensable source for information about the Matthias delusion.

Overview and Evaluation of Primary Sources
Truth was illiterate and left no writings. In addition to her speeches, which are interspersed throughout the various biographies, she left only her *Narrative* as recorded by Gilbert (see above).

Fiction and Adaptations
The record album, *The Negro Woman* (Folkways Records. FH5523), includes speeches by Truth.

Museums, Historical Landmarks, Societies
Sojourner Truth Grave (Battle Creek, MI). Truth is buried at the Oak Hill Cemetery; the grave is marked by the Libyan Sibyl monument sculpted by William Wetmore Story.

Other Sources

Brawley, Benjamin. *Negro Builders and Heroes.* Chapel Hill: University of North Carolina Press, 1937.

Davis, Lenwood G. *The Black Woman in American Society: A Selected Annotated Bibliography.* Boston: G. K. Hall, 1975.

Dictionary of American Negro Biography, ed. Rayford W. Logan and Michael Winston. New York: McGraw-Hill, 1982.

The Encyclopedia of Black America, ed. W. Augustus Low and Virgil A. Clift. New York: McGraw-Hill, 1981.

Flexner, Eleanor. *Century of Struggle: The Women's Rights Movement in the United States.* New York: Atheneum, 1971. A classic work on the contributions of black women to the women's rights movement.

Foster, Frances. "Adding Color and Contour to Early American Self-Portraitures: Autobiographical Writings of Afro-Americans." In *Conjuring: Black Women, Fiction, and Literary Tradition,* edited by Marjorie Pryse and Hortense Spiller. Bloomington: Indiana University Press, 1985.

Giddings, Paula. *When and Where I Enter: The Impact of Black Women on Race and Sex in America.* New York: Morrow, 1984.

Harley, Sharon, and Roslyn Terborg-Penn, eds. *The Afro-American Woman: Struggles and Images.* Port Washington, NY: National University, 1978.

Hooks, Bell. *Ain't I a Woman: Black Women and Feminism.* Boston: South End Press, 1981. An analysis of the interrelation between color and sexism.

Lerner, Gerda, ed. *Black Women in White America: A Documentary History.* New York: Vintage, 1973.

Loewenberg, Bert B. J., and Bogin, Ruth, eds. *Black Women in Nineteenth Century American Life: Their Words, Their Thoughts, Their Feelings.* University Park: Penn State University Press, 1979.

Montgomery, Janey Weinhold. *A Comparative Analysis of the Rhetoric of vo Negro Women Orators: Sojourner Truth and Frances E. Watkins Harper.* rt Hays, KS: Fort Hays State University Press, 1968.

Peterson, Helen Stone. *Sojourner Truth, Fearless Crusader.* Champaign: arrard, 1972. An illustrated biography for children.

Sterling, Dorothy. *Turning the World Upside Down: The Anti-Slavery onvention of American Women Held in New York City, May 9-12, 1837.* New ork: Feminist Press, 1988.

————. *We Are Your Sisters: Black Women in the Nineteenth Century.* ew York: Norton, 1985.

Diane Long Hoeveler
Marquette University

JULIA TUTWILER
1841-1916

Chronology

Born Julia Strudwick Tutwiler on August 15, 1841, in Tuscaloosa, Alabama, third child of Henry Tutwiler, an educator, and Julia Ashe Tutwiler; *1847-c. 1859* grows up near Havana, Alabama, in the plantation district; attends Greene Springs School (founded by her father in 1847); *c. 1859-1861* attends a French school in Philadelphia; *1861-1865* teaches at Greene Springs School; *1865* returns to school in Philadelphia; *1866* attends Vassar College; *1866-1869* teaches at Greensboro Female Academy, Greensboro, Alabama, and serves as principal from 1867 to 1869; *1869-1872* teaches at Greene Springs School; *1872-1873* receives private instruction by faculty members at Washington and Lee University, Lexington, Virginia; *1873* tours England and Europe; *1873-1874* attends a "normal school" and works at the Diakonessen Anstalt (Institute of Deaconesses), in Kaiserswerth, Germany; *1874-1876* studies languages in Berlin, Bonn, and Gottingen; passes Prussian teachers' examinations; *1874-1875* teaches at Steglitz, Germany; *1875-1876* publishes poem "Alabama" in the Tuscaloosa *Times*, as well as pieces in *St. Nicholas* and *Appleton's Journal*; *1876-1881* teaches at Tuscaloosa Female College; *1878* visits Paris Exposition as representative of the *National Journal of Education*; observes French women's trade schools; *1879-1880* founds Tuscaloosa Benevolent Association, which lobbies successfully for statewide health standards for county jails; *1880* advocates public aid to women's vocational education before Alabama Educational Association; *1881* appointed co-principal of Livingston Female Academy, Livingston, Alabama; begins anti-liquor campaign in Livingston and the surrounding area; *c. 1882-1915* involved in attempts to abolish or reform the "convict lease" system (a system by which the state and counties leased the labor of convicts to private businesses); serves for many years as "prison superintendent" of the Alabama Women's Christian Temperance Union; frequently visits and inspects convict camps; lobbies for creation of boys reformatories, a separate women's prison, and improved treatment and facilities for county convicts; *1883-1884* launches Alabama Normal College for Girls, a state subsidized department of the Livingston Female Academy; *1884-1886* serves as "counsellor" to National Education Association; *1889-1896* works successfully with Alabama Educational Association for creation of a state supported vocational school for young women; *1890* appointed "president and sole principal" at Livingston; *1891* advocates coeducation before the Alabama Educational Association; *1891-1893* pushes for coeducation at the University of Alabama, Tuscaloosa; is instrumental in decision of trustees and faculty to begin admitting women students in fall 1893; *1892* serves as president of the Department of Elementary Education of the National Educational Association; *1893* attends Columbian World's Fair, Chicago, and addresses the International Historical Congress of Charities and Corrections on recent trends in Alabama; also speaks before International Congress of Education, and World's Congress of Representative Women; *1898* negotiates for first women's housing on University of Alabama campus; *1899-1907* deals with challenges arising from state reform of teacher certification; continues active in reform organizations and personal charities; *1907-1910* works with state officials to reorganize Alabama Normal College, eliminating private control; *1907* receives honorary doctorate from University of Alabama; *1910* retired by Alabama Normal College trustees; appointed President Emeritus; *1910-1916* suffers from poor health; continues to work for prison reform; *1916* dies March 24, 1916.

Activities of Historical Significance

Champion of women's educational rights, prison reformer, educational pioneer, and prohibitionist, Tutwiler was courageous, persistent, and intelligent. All but forgotten today, she was a power among white Alabamians at a time when the state's politicians ignored women and crushed activists. How could such a woman live, move, have her being, and enjoy success? Several factors must be considered. Among them are her family and early education, an antebellum reform tradition of which she was to an extent representative, and the place she created for herself within the civic and political worlds of her native state.

Tutwiler was raised with ten brothers and sisters in the atmosphere of the Greene Springs School. Her father, Henry Tutwiler, a Virginian and early graduate of the University of Virginia, was one of the most remarkable educators produced in the region. Determined to be free of boards of trustees and politicians, he assembled a faculty which compared favorably with that of the University of Alabama. For nearly forty years (1847-1884) he taught science by experiment, languages by practice, and government through discussions of current ideas. He was famous for treating his students as individuals and for inflicting no corporal punishments. In the classroom and in school devotional meetings, he urged his scholars to work for the betterment of mankind.

A number of the boys who boarded at Greene Springs grew up to be influential men, but not all of the pupils were male. The Tutwiler daughters were educated there, as were other young women. Henry Tutwiler believed that girls and boys should sit in the same classrooms, have the same assignments, and recite together. When young Julia decided that she would devote herself to serving humanity—even when she took the celibate warrior Joan of

Arc as her model—no one discouraged her. As a child, she worked to teach the slave children of Greene Springs to read. This activity was illegal under Alabama law. But Henry Tutwiler was a believer in the equal worth of every human soul, and in his youth had been a sincere, if somewhat hesitant, antislavery man.

Although the Tutwilers were far more liberal than most Alabamians, there was a distinct reformist element in the state. Henry Tutwiler was a Whig; and Whigs tended to view government as a tool for the improvement of human life. A vocal minority in state politics, Whigs hoped to elevate the masses through programs of education and moral suasion. In common with reformist Democrats, they supported the creation of a state penitentiary and a number of humane changes in criminal law. Some of them went so far as to work for the limitation (even the abolition) of capital punishment.

In their attitudes toward slavery and sectionalism, Henry Tutwiler and other Alabama Whigs were more moderate than their Democratic counterparts. Given the political climate of the South and their personal involvement as slave owners, these Whigs were likely to view slavery as an unfortunate, but not necessarily evil, institution. Many of them, including the Tutwilers, opposed secession but afterwards loyally supported the Confederacy. Paternalistic in their attitudes toward blacks, women, lower class whites, and criminals, they did not transcend the prejudices of the time; yet they were pious, optimistic, and open to change.

No doubt the ideal of reform from above influenced Julia Tutwiler. Willing to give lip service to contemporary ideas about the place of women, she was bold enough to pursue her studies in the North as well as abroad. There is no doubt that she was imbued with a sense of mission. Upper class white men might be the leaders of society; but they should give every reasonable opportunity to their present and their former dependents. In addition, she was influenced by the Civil War and its aftermath. For most white Southerners, the experiences of defeat and occupation were intensely painful. For white women, however, the times were to an extent liberating, as manpower shortages forced women to take new roles and responsibilities. The losses and displacement of white men would affect the South for years, as Tutwiler well understood.

Tutwiler spent the final heated years of Reconstruction out of the state. When she returned, Alabama was firmly in the grasp of a coalition of Democratic planters, merchants, and industrialists known as the "Bourbons." The Bourbons advocated rigid governmental economy and white supremacy. Often they were friendly to the booming railroad, coal, and iron interests of North Alabama. Though often challenged, the Bourbons kept power by identifying themselves with the "Lost Cause," by appealing to regional and racial prejudices, and (if pressed) by "counting out" opponents with fraudulent votes.

The atmosphere to which Tutwiler returned was one in which Whiggery seemed dead. Nonetheless, she soon began lobbying for enhanced educational opportunities for women, for better living conditions for prisoners, for separation of convicts by age and gender, and for state sanctioned schooling and religious instruction in camps and jails. Given her educational experiences, she was intimidated by neither the pretensions nor the sarcasms of legislators. her behavior was consistently true to her upbringing—gentle and well-bred in manner, yet compelling of respect. The fact that the Tutwilers were well-connected made her less vulnerable; Julia found many Greene Springs "boys" and former faculty among legislators, school officials, and industrialists.

As a lobbyist, she developed a genius for treading the line between ladylike propriety and (by contemporary standards) disgraceful forwardness. Refusing to be sheltered from ugliness and misery, she visited the most squalid prison camps. On the other hand, she consented to have two important papers read to the Alabama Educational Association by male readers; after all, ladies were not supposed to address "mixed" audiences. An experienced lecturer, she gave several speeches before national educational and reform bodies. Her out-of-state boldness did not seem to hurt her image at home.

Though Tutwiler was in many respects a Progressive reformer, her ability depended as much on her tact as on her sense of moral outrage. She was accepted by Alabama officialdom because her criticisms, however sharp, did not threaten the reigning political order. Unlike the Farmers' Alliancemen and Populists who denounced the Alabama Democratic Party in the 1880s and 1890s, she was seldom overtly political. She condemned the convict lease system as a mechanism by which human beings were subjected to conditions worse than slavery. But she was sometimes content to work for amelioration of the system. Even her victories for women's education depended in part on convincing male audiences that women would be even more womanly if properly educated.

Overall, Tutwiler created her own semiofficial position in Alabama. She was the woman to whom legislators would listen; she represented whole classes of voteless citizens. In this respect she was like Booker T. Washington. To be sure, she could afford to be more assertive than Washington because of her color and her connection. In 1891 she urged *him* to work for creation of a black boys' reform school, apparently long before he was willing to act. Still, both Tutwiler and Washington were vocational educators whose friends included local oligarchs as well as Northern reformers; both accomplished remarkable things in a hostile world.

It would be easy to overstate Tutwiler's achievements. As she freely admitted, she was not a lone crusader for reform. In Alabama, labor leaders, several politicians, and a host of club women opposed the existing prison system or worked for its reform. During the mid-1880s, their efforts secured better physical conditions for convicts and strict state supervision of convict camps. In the 1890s, under pressure from reformers, the state might have abolished the lease system altogether had funds for an alternative approach been available. As for women's educational rights, it is true that Tutwiler was the state's most important promoter of girls' vocational education as well as coeducation. Yet, these subjects were much discussed in Alabama; and several prominent men supported changes in the status quo. Radicalism was not Tutwiler's forte; neither was originality.

Her strength did lie, however, in calm courage, backed by the conviction that things as they were could be made better. Her career goes far to prove, to a twentieth century reluctant to believe it, that Old South and New South possessed a social conscience.

Overview of Biographical Sources

Tutwiler has not lacked for biographers, though no fully satisfactory work about her has been written. Most biographical studies were written by admirers. As such, they contain many useful anecdotes about her teaching methods, her personal eccentricities, and the golden atmosphere of the Alabama Normal College during her tenure. After her unwilling retirement in 1910, Tutwiler's supporters quarreled bitterly with her successor, George W. Brock; traces of that quarrel may be found in most treatments of her life. In general, Tutwiler's biographers lack a sense of historical distance. Too often they give her credit foɪ all the educational and penal reforms of the era. Recently, Tutwiler has been the subject of two books, by Bynum and Cooper, designed for young readers.

Evaluation of Selected Biographical Sources

Farmer, Hallie. "Tutwiler, Julia Strudwick." In *Dictionary of American Biography*. New York: Scribner's, 1981. (G) A summary of her life and work, containing some incorrect dates. Farmer also wrote the entry on Henry Tutwiler.

Hargrove, Henry Lee. "Julia S. Tutwiler of Alabama." n.p.: n.d. (A, G) This pamphlet makes Tutwiler out to be a more radical reformer than she was.

Kunkel, Robert Raymond. "A Rhetorical Analysis of Julia Strudwick Tutwiler's Reform Speeches, 1880-1900." Ph.D. diss. Louisiana State University, 1978. (A, G) Not a conventional biography, Kunkel's dissertation gives a sense of the historical context for Tutwiler's speeches. The closest examination of her writings thus far.

Lyon, Ralph M. "Julia Tutwiler." Livingston, AL: Alabama-Tombigbee Rivers Regional Planning and Development Commission, 1976. (A, G) A well-written pamphlet by a former Livingston president.

Moore, Eoline Wallace. "Julia Tutwiler Teacher." *Birmingham Southern College Bulletin* 27 (January 1934). (A, G) This short essay is useful for its anecdotes and its citations to Tutwiler's writings and speeches.

Pannell, Anne Gary, and Dorothea E. Wyatt. *Julia Tutwiler and Social Progress in Alabama.* University: University of Alabama Press, 1961. (A, G) This is the standard work on Tutwiler. It is well-written, if somewhat elementary, with fine citations and bibliographical references. However, the authors do not provide an adequate historical context for Tutwiler's career as a prison reformer.

Pitts, Clara L. "Julia Strudwick Tutwiler." Ed.D. diss. George Washington University, 1942. (A, G) This work concentrates on Tutwiler's educational work and speeches, but contains information on her upbringing and prison reform work. The citations to newspaper and other original sources are useful. Pitts places Tutwiler firmly in historical context, and avoids giving her the sole credit for reforms.

Evaluation of Biographies for Young People
Bynum, Rusty. *Julia Tutwiler: The Pathfinder.* Huntsville, AL: Writers' Consortium Books, 1989. Written in an inspirational vein, this is a fine work for junior high school readers.

Cooper, Richard. *Julia Tutwiler: Teacher, Leader.* Raleigh, NC: Creative Productions, 1987. This brief book is well written and suitable for elementary school children.

Overview of Primary Sources
The Special Collections Department of Gorgas Library at the University of Alabama has an important body of Tutwiler's papers, together with printed and manuscript writings. The Alabama Department of Archives and History in Montgomery has a collection of miscellaneous Tutwiler materials, as well as a card file of information compiled by one of Tutwiler's former students. The Archives Department of the Birmingham Public Library holds a small collection of Tutwiler family materials. The Carmichael Library of the University of Montevallo has a small collection of Julia Tutwiler letters. Published correspondence between Tutwiler and Booker T. Washington can be found in

Louis Harlan, editor, *The Booker T. Washington Papers,* Vol. 3 (Urbana: University of Illinois Press, 1974). Manuscript materials on Henry Tutwiler can be found at the Alabama Department of Archives and History and in the University of Virginia Library. For Henry Tutwiler's correspondence with an abolitionist, see Dwight L. Dumond, *Letters of James Gillespie Birney, 1831-1857,* Volume I (New York: D. Appleton-Century, 1938).

For samples of Tutwiler's early writings, see "Christinchen's Answer" in *St. Nicholas* II (1875); "St. Nicholas' Day in Germany" in *St. Nicholas* III (1876); and "On the Baltic" in *Appleton's Journal* I (New Series, 1876). Tutwiler wrote several occasional poems. Though she did not think herself a great poet, her work was admired; her "Alabama" became the state song. For the text of "Alabama" see Pannell and Wyatt, *Julia S. Tutwiler and Social Progress,* cited above. A number of Tutwiler's speeches, public writings, and reports survive. The following is a chronological listing and evaluation of selected works that are often cited, easily accessible, or otherwise typical.

Evaluation of Primary Sources

"The Technical Education of Women." *Education: An International Magazine* 3 (1883). (A, G) A plea for women's education rights, and a discussion of the schools that Tutwiler had observed in Paris.

"Our Brother in Stripes, in the School-Room." In *National Educational Association. Journal of Proceedings and Addresses: Session of the Year 1890.* Topeka, KS: The Association, 1890. (A, G) One of Tutwiler's best essays, a revealing account of her lobbying, educational and missionary work for convicts.

"A Year in a German Model School." In *National Educational Association. Journal of Proceedings and Addresses: Session of the Year 1891.* New York: The Association, 1891. (A, G) The story of Tutwiler's year at Kaiserswerth.

"Coeducation and Character." In *Alabama Educational Association: Proceedings and Papers of the Tenth Annual Session . . .* Birmingham, AL: Silver Book and Stationary Printers, 1891. (A, G) An argument for coeducation, skillfully adapted to community mores.

"Individualization by Grouping." In *National Education Association: Journal of Proceedings and Addresses; Session of the Year 1892.* New York: The Association, 1893. (A) Tutwiler's speech as president of the NEA Department of Elementary instruction.

Richmond Pearson Hobson: The Preparation for His Life Work. Livingston, AL: Hobson Campaign Club, c. 1904-1906. (A) A campaign biography of a Spanish-American War hero and prohibitionist. An exception to Tutwiler's usually apolitical stance.

"Woman Commends Work of Three Prison Officials: Julia Tutwiler Also Recommends More Comforts for Alabama's Convicts." Montgomery, AL, *Advertiser,* December 10, 1911. (A) Copied in Clara L. Pitts, "Julia Strudwick Tutwiler." Ed.D. diss. George Washington University, 1942, p. 218-221. Typical of Tutwiler's later reform work.

Museums, Historical Landmarks, Societies

The University of Alabama, Livingston University, and the University of Montevallo have buildings named for Julia Tutwiler. Portraits of Tutwiler have been presented to various schools and agencies, including the University of Alabama and the State Department of Archives and History. The Julia Tutwiler state penitentiary for women is located north of Wetempka, Alabama. A bridge across the Tombigbee River at Gainesville, Alabama, is named for Tutwiler. Sharp-eyed tourists can read a roadside monument to Henry and Julia Tutwiler at Havana, south of Moundville in Hale County, Alabama.

Other Sources

Cable, George Washington. *The Silent South, Together With the Freedman's Case in Equity, The Convict Lease System, The Appendix to the 1889 Edition and Eight Uncollected Essays on Prison and Asylum Reform.* Montclair, NJ: Patterson Smith, 1960. Essays that provide an understanding of the convict lease system.

Felton, Rebecca L. "The Convict System of Georgia." In *The Forum* 2 (1886): 484-490. An example of the work of a contemporary woman prison reformer.

Going, Allen Johnston. *Bourbon Democracy in Alabama, 1874-1890.* University: University of Alabama Press, 1951. The standard account of public life in Alabama during the late nineteenth century. An excellent, comprehensive history.

McCorvey, Thomas Chalmers. "Henry Tutwiler and the Influence of the University of Virginia on Education in Alabama." In *Transactions of the Alabama Historical Society* 5 (1904): 82-106. Contains information on Henry Tutwiler's educational philosophy.

Sellers, James B. *History of the University of Alabama.* Vol. 1. University: University of Alabama Press, 1953. Contains a good treatment of Tutwiler's work in bringing coeducation to the university.

Thornton, J. Mills. *Politics and Power in a Slave Society: Alabama, 1800-1860.* Baton Rouge: Louisiana State University Press, 1978. This complex but useful work provides background necessary to understand the political culture of antebellum Alabama.

Ward, Robert David, and William Warren Rogers. *Convicts, Coal, and the Banner Mine Tragedy.* Tuscaloosa: University of Alabama Press, 1987. The best account of the convict lease system in Alabama, focused on one particularly tragic incident.

Paul M. Pruitt, Jr.
University of Alabama
School of Law Library

DENMARK VESEY
c. 1767-1822

Chronology

Born about 1767 in Africa or the Caribbean; named Telemaque; *1781* brought from the Virgin Islands to Saint-Dominque on a slave ship commanded by Captain Joseph Vesey, a Bermuda slave trader; *1781-1782* reacquired by Captain Vesey; *1783* settles with Captain Vesey in Charleston, South Carolina, where he learns the carpentry trade; *1800* after winning $1,500 in the East Bay lottery, buys freedom for $600; settles down as a carpenter; *1817* joins Second Presbyterian Church; *1821* begins to recruit co-conspirators for a slave rebellion, planned for July 14, 1822; *1822* details of plot leak to Charleston whites at the end of May; arrested on June 22; tried and convicted of inciting insurrection, and executed on July 2.

Activities of Historical Significance

Denmark Vesey's efforts to engineer a slave rebellion in Charleston, South Carolina, constitute his claim to historical notice. Brought to Charleston in 1783 as the slave of Captain Joseph Vesey, Denmark learned the carpentry trade, and after he won $1,500 in a lottery in 1800, he bought his freedom. In the wake of the debate over the expansion of slavery, which culminated in the Missouri Compromise, Vesey began to consider the possibility that slavery, far from being a "temporary evil," was now defended by white southerners as a "positive good" that ought to be sustained. He read accounts of the debates, finding common ground with the anti-slavery remarks of New York's Rufus King. He began to contemplate a slave uprising to resist the perpetuation of black enslavement.

Although Vesey was a free black, he sought his co-conspirators among the slave community in Charleston and the surrounding plantations, including two slaves belonging to Governor Thomas Bennett. He used both Christian and African appeals to persuade slaves to join his movement. Originally he planned for an uprising on July 14 (Bastille Day), a Sunday when most whites would be out of town and the darkest night of the month. But at the end of May news of the conspiracy reached Charleston's whites, who commenced searching for the conspirators. Vesey immediately advanced the date of the uprising to June 16, but Charleston authorities discovered more details of the plot just two days before the uprising was to take place. Vesey fled for his life, but was captured on June 22. The following day he was tried for inciting insurrection. Found guilty, he was executed on July 2. Eventually thirty-five blacks were hanged, thirty-four exiled, and sixty-one acquitted.

Although Vesey's conspiracy ended in failure, its exposure alerted white southerners once more to the possibility of slave rebellion, and increased their distrust of free blacks as agents of insurrection. For decades to come the free black community of Charleston struggled to overcome white suspicions.

Vesey's death may have had a bigger impact on the abolitionist cause than any of the events of his life. Whites, petrified by the specter of slave rebellion, cracked down on slave autonomy and education. Blacks pointed to Vesey as a symbol of resistance to oppression. "Remember Denmark Vesey!" cried Frederick Douglass in speaking to black recruits for the Union army during the Civil War.

Overview of Biographical Sources

Scattered and fragmentary sources have made it very difficult to piece together a satisfactory biography of Vesey. Instead, scholars have looked at Vesey's life only in terms of the extent and the seriousness of the conspiracy. Richard Wade's "The Vesey Plot: A Reconsideration" (1964) questions whether a conspiracy did in fact exist. Other scholars, including William Freehling, *Prelude to Civil War: The Nullification Controversy in South Carolina, 1816-1838* (1966) and the leading expert on the conspiracy, John Lofton, *Denmark Vesey's Revolt* (1983), accept it as real. Other work on Vesey celebrates his act of resistance, holding him up as a martyr to freedom and an exemplar to Afro-Americans.

Evaluation of Principal Biographical Sources

Edwards, Lillie Johnson. *Denmark Vesey.* New York: Chelsea House, 1990. (Y) A biography suitable for children in fourth through seventh grade.

Grimke, Archibald H. "Right on the Scaffold, or the Martyrs of 1822." *The American Negro Academy Occasional Papers 1-22*, edited by Ernest Kaiser. 1901. Reprint. no. 7. New York: Arno Press, 1969. (A) A celebration of Vesey's exploits and the example he set.

Kleinman, Max L. "The Denmark Vesey Conspiracy: An Historiographical Essay." *Negro History Bulletin* 37 (February-March 1974): 225-228. (A) A discussion of Richard Wade's interpretation of the planned insurrection. Kleinman argues that the conspiracy was real and should be taken seriously as historical fact.

Lofton, John M. *Denmark Vesey's Revolt.* Kent, OH: Kent State University Press, 1983. (A, G) Originally published in 1964 under the title *Insurrection in South Carolina: The Turbulent World of Denmark Vesey*, this remains the standard study.

Spencer, Philip. *Three Against Slavery: Denmark Vesey, William Lloyd Garrison, Frederick Douglass*. New York: Scholastic, 1969. (Y) A children's biography, suitable for grades four through six.

Starobin, Robin S. *Denmark Vesey: The Slave Conspiracy of 1822*. Englewood Cliffs, NJ: Prentice Hall, 1970. (A, G) A combination of primary sources and discussions of Vesey's conspiracy. Starobin takes issue with Richard Wade's assertion that the conspiracy was more figment than fact.

Stuckey, Sterling. "Remembering Denmark Vesey." *Negro Digest* 15 (February 1966): 28-41. (A, G) A reply to Richard Wade's article, maintaining that a conspiracy existed and that it posed a serious threat.

Wade, Richard C., "The Vesey Plot: A Reconsideration." *Journal of Southern History* 30 (May 1964): 143-161. (A) Questions whether the reaction to Vesey's plot was more of a product of white hysteria than the actual dimensions of the conspiracy. His conclusion that no conspiracy actually existed has been subject to severe criticism.

Overview and Evaluation of Primary Sources

Starobin's volume, cited above, includes primary documents and excerpts of trial transcripts and letters. *The Trial Record of Denmark Vesey*, edited by John Oliver Killens (Boston: Beacon Press, 1970; A) includes Vesey's, "An Account of the Late Intended Insurrection Among a Portion of the Blacks of this City," as well as two related pamphlets.

Fiction and Adaptations

In 1982 "Denmark Vesey's Rebellion," a television program reciting a version of the Vesey conspiracy, aired on PBS. Robert Brent Toplin, "The Making of 'Denmark Vesey's Rebellion,' " *Film and History* 11 (September 1982): 49-56, described the making of the movie from the point of view of a historical consultant. William W. Freehling criticized the presentation for filtering out unsavory facts about Vesey's life in "History and Television," *Southern Studies* 22 (Spring 1983): 76-81.

John O. Killens's *Great Gittin' Up Mornin'* (Garden City, NY: Doubleday, 1972) is a fictionalized biography of Vesey based upon the trial transcript and historical research.

Other Sources

Aptheker, Herbert. *American Negro Slave Revolts.* 1943. Reprint. New York: International Publishers, 1974. In a highly controversial study, Aptheker explores various slave rebellions and insurrections, placing Vesey's efforts in the context of black resistance. Critics claim that Aptheker exaggerates evidence of slave unrest in his efforts to demonstrate that blacks did not willingly accept enslavement.

Berlin, Ira. *Slaves Without Masters: The Free Negro in the Antebellum South.* New York: Pantheon, 1974. An examination of the status of free blacks in American slave society, including white reaction in the wake of Vesey's execution.

Freehling, William W. *Prelude to Civil War: The Nullification Controversy in South Carolina, 1816-1836.* New York: Harper and Row, 1966. Shows how the Vesey controversy fueled the fears of white southerners about the dangers of slavery, contributing to their tenacious defense of the "peculiar institution."

Genovese, Eugene D. *From Rebellion to Revolution: Afro-American Slave Revolts in the Making of the New World.* Baton Rouge: Louisiana State University Press, 1979. A brief but informative examination of black revolts, including the Vesey conspiracy, in comparative context.

Wade, Richard C. *Slavery in the Cities: The South 1820-1860.* New York: Oxford University Press, 1964. Still the best study of urban slavery, illustrating the problems confronting white slaveowners seeking to control the activities of their slaves.

Brooks Donohue Simpson
Arizona State University

VICTORIO
c. 1825-1880

Chronology

Born about 1825 in Apache region of southwestern United States territories, a member of Mimbres (Warm Springs) tribe; a legend that he was captured as a boy from a Mexican family is probably untrue; acquires name Victorio (the conqueror) and is sometimes called Victoria; may also have been known as Lucero; *1853* as a leader of his tribe, signs peace treaty with American government; *1863-1865* raids and plunders through eastern part of American Southwest following the treacherous death of Apache chief, Mangas Coloradas, at the hands of U.S. soldiers; *1872* agrees to live on Tularosa Reservation, but finds it too high and cold for Apache life; *1873* raids into Mexico; *1874* allowed, along with other Apaches, to leave the Tularosa Reservation and return to his home grounds, Ojo Caliente; *summer 1877* moved, along with tribe, to arid San Carlos agency; *September 1877* breaks from San Carlos agency to go raiding; *October 1877* returns to Ojo Caliente; *November 1878* Mimbres Apaches removed to San Carlos by U.S. government; *February 1879* surrenders at Ojo Caliente; *April 1879* leaves Ojo Caliente for raiding again; *June 1879* returns to Ojo Caliente; *September 1879* wanted for murder, leaves reservation for good and lives as raider for the rest of his life; *October 15, 1880* ambushed and killed at Tres Castillos, Chihauhua, Mexico, by superior Mexican force.

Activities of Historical Significance

Victorio was one of the greatest Apache warriors, revered among his people even more than the famous Geronimo. Not only a fierce fighter, he was a superb strategist, usually moving only through familiar terrain, choosing high ground from which to launch attacks, preparing escape routes, and surprising his enemy. American officers who had fought in the Civil War declared him the best guerrilla leader they had ever seen. Victorio and his followers maintained that they had been forced into a renegade life by an American government which failed to understand them, removed them from their beloved Warm Springs homeland, and treated them with contempt.

When settlers of European descent moved into the homeland of the nomadic Native American tribes of the American Southwest, conflict often resulted. The Native Americans were accustomed to roaming freely over the land, hunting, gathering, and taking what they needed. After a period of attempting to negotiate peace with the Native Americans through treaties, the U.S. government next tried to force the Apaches onto reservations (usually land that no

2201

one else wanted) and into an exclusively agricultural life. Many Apaches would not tolerate such a life and rallied to the war cry of Victorio and other Apache leaders.

Very little is known about Victorio because, distrusting whites, he kept silent whenever he was around them. The usual historical sources—military orders, journals, letters of citizens and Indian agents—contain few accounts of his personality. Accounts of him by Native American contemporaries contain gaps and contradictions because they were related as many as eighty years after Victorio's death.

One of the reasons he was held in high regard was that he refused to cooperate with whites, unlike his friend and fellow leader, Loco (who, some say, was given that name, "crazy" because he tried to trust and make peace with whites). In the only known photograph of Victorio, the warrior appears without the usual headband because he refused to have his picture taken and had to be subdued by two men.

After Victorio left the San Carlos reservation in 1877, he and sub-chiefs Loco and Nana raided continuously and terrorized southern New Mexico and the northern Mexican state of Chihuahua until ambushed by a Mexican force under Colonel Joaquin Terrazas and Juan Mata Ortiz in the Chihuahuan desert at Tres Castillos. Tres Castillos are three rocky hills with ponds at their bases in the middle of a barren region. Victorio, who was unfamiliar with the area, was making for the waterholes when he was surprized by a superior force entrenched on high ground. There was no possibility of retreat into the flat surroundings. For once Victorio had abandoned his strategic principles, and he paid for this mistake with his life and those of most of his braves.

The manner of Victorio's death is disputed. Contemporary Mexican accounts say that he was found among the dead after the battle, so that it is not clear from them how he died. James Kaywaykla (see below) says that he stabbed himself in the heart rather than be killed by his enemies, a fitting end for one of the fiercest of Apache warriors.

Overview of Biographical Sources

The only book which purports to be a biography of Victorio is Dan L. Thrapp's *Victorio and the Mimbres Apaches* (1974), but even that contains little solid information about the war chief. Other accounts of Victorio appear as chapters or sections of longer works about Apaches or other Indians.

Evaluation of Biographical Sources

Brown, Dee. *Bury My Heart at Wounded Knee.* New York: Holt, Rinehart, and Winston, 1970. (**A, G, Y**) The account of Victorio's life and final days is quite brief and has been superseded by Dan Thrapp's more extensive research.

Thrapp, Dan L. *The Conquest of Apacheria*. Norman: University of Oklahoma Press, 1967. (**A, G**) In the second of four books about the Apaches and their struggles against the American and Mexican governments, Victorio's story is presented as part of the general campaign. Nonetheless, for the beginning researcher, this book is the place to start. It provides an overall view of the Apaches and is easier to follow than the highly detailed *Victorio and the Mimbres Apaches*.

Thrapp, Dan L. *Victorio and the Mimbres Apaches*. Norman: University of Oklahoma Press, 1974. (**A, G**) Thrapp is the leading historian of the Apaches and the U.S. military campaign to subdue them, and he is a thorough and exacting scholar and writer. By the time Thrapp wrote this book, all of the eyewitnesses to the events of Victorio's life were long dead. Documentary evidence about Victorio is largely limited to the records and letters of U.S. Indian agents and military personnel. As a result, the reader sees the Apaches from the Anglo and Mexican perspective. Most of the evidence presented concerns the general treatment of the Mimbres Apaches; the focus shifts to the activities of Victorio only in the last third of the book. Nonetheless, Thrapp has done an excellent job of marshalling what evidence there is, and his extensive bibliography leads the researcher to most of the available material on Victorio.

Overview and Evaluation of Primary Sources

Victorio wrote no autobiography and conducted no interviews, but there is a remarkable first-hand account of his last breakout in Eve Ball's *In The Days of Victorio* (Tucson: University of Arizona Press, 1970; **A, G, Y**). This book consists primarily of the recollections of James Kaywaykla, who was a member of Victorio's party as a small child and who survived the Tres Castillos massacre. Although some of Kaywaykla's memories are questionable because of his youth at the time of Victorio's last campaign, Ball carefully fills in the gaps through interviews with other Apaches or references to other historical sources. As a result, the book is both fascinating and as accurate as possible.

Geronimo, in *Geronimo: His Own Story* (edited by S.M. Barrett, New York: Dutton, 1970; **A, G, Y**) makes some comments about Victorio. Charles B. Gatewood, the Army officer who was instrumental in the final surrender of Geronimo, gives his impressions of the chase after Victorio in "Campaigning Against Victorio in 1879," *The Great Divide*, April, 1894. John Clum, the Indian agent famous for the capture of Geronimo, provides little new information in his article, "Victorio", *New Mexico Historical Review* 4, 4 (October, 1929).

Museums, Historical Landmarks, Societies

Victorio's final resting place is not known, but even those associated with him are honored. James Kaywaykla's tombstone in the Apache Cemetery, Fort Sill, Oklahoma, bears the inscription, "last survivor of Chief Victorio's band."

Other Sources

Tarin, Don Jesus, as told to Jose Aceves. "Who Was Victorio?" *Frontier Times* 37, 5 (August-September, 1963). An account of the Mexican legend, usually considered false, that Victorio was captured as a child from a Mexican family.

Jim Baird
University of North Texas

MERCY OTIS WARREN
1728-1814

Chronology

Born Mercy Otis on September 25, 1728, the eldest daughter of Colonel James Otis, farmer, merchant, court justice, and politician, and Mary Allyne, of wealthy fourth-generation Puritan gentry, in Barnstable, Massachusetts; educated by family tutor, Reverend Jonathan Russell, and later by her older brother James; *1754* marries James Warren, moves to husband's farm in Plymouth; *1757* occupies Winslow House; son James born; *1759* son Winslow born; *1762* son Charles born; brother James elected to Massachusetts House of Representatives; *1764* son Henry born; *1765* husband elected to House of Representatives; *1766* son George born; *1769* brother James attacked in a Boston tavern by pro-Crown roughs and disabled; *1772* anonymously publishes excerpts of *The Adulateur: A Tragedy; As It Is Now Acted in Upper Servia*; *1773* anonymously publishes excerpts of *The Defeat, A Play*; *1775* anonymously publishes scenes from *The Group, a Farce*; *1775-1776* suffers hardship at home while husband serves with George Washington; begins writing *History*; *1776* may have anonymously published *The Blockheads: or The Affrighted Officers, a Farce*; *1779* may have anonymously published *The Motley Assembly, a Farce*; *1781* husband purchases Thomas Hutchinson's estate, Milton Hall, near Boston; son James wounded in naval combat; *1783* brother James Otis dies; *1784* writes *The Ladies of Castile*; meets Thomas Jefferson in Boston; *1785* writes *The Sack of Rome*; son Charles dies of tuberculosis in Spain; *1786* supports Shay's rebellion; *1788* returns to Plymouth, publishes *Observations on the New Constitution, and on the Federal Conventions*; *1789* beginning of break with John Adams; *1790* publishes under her own name *Poems, Dramatic and Miscellaneous*; *1791* finishes main body of her *History of the Rise, Progress, and Termination of the American Revolution*; after imprisonment for debt, son Winslow joins army and is killed in an ambush by Native Americans; she withdraws from politics and writing of history for a decade; *1800* resumes writing history; youngest son George dies; *1805* publishes *History of the Rise, Progress and Termination of the American Revolution, interspersed with Biographical and Moral Observations*; *1807* estranged from John Adams; *1808* husband James Warren dies; *1811* reconciliation with John Adams; *1814* dies October 19 at Plymouth, Massachusetts.

Activities of Historical Significance

In the diverse roles of sister, wife, mother, writer, polemicist, and historian, Warren was a passionate participant and acute observer of the American

Revolution and the early national period. For forty years Warren lived a domestic life, typical of a well-to-do middle-class Puritan daughter and wife. But in the political crisis of the 1770s, she joined with her brilliant and tragic brother, James Otis, Jr., her husband James Warren, and her friends John and Abigail Adams, to become an active proponent of the patriotic cause.

Highly educated by the standards of her time, Warren wrote religious and nature-inspired poetry in her youth that exhibited strong literary tastes and talents. In the 1770s, she turned to writing deadly satiric political plays aimed at exposing the corruption and vice of Massachusetts Royal Governor Thomas Hutchinson and his loyalist supporters, while praising the virtue of the patriots. Her political plays mark her as one of the founders of American dramatic art.

In the 1780s, she and her husband emerged as leaders of the dissident farmers of western Massachusetts. They soon became identified with the anti-federalist cause and voiced their fear and distrust of centralized political institutions. Their identification with Shay's Rebellion and their vocal opposition to the new constitution all but ended her husband's political career in Massachusetts.

Their disaffection from the new political currents, however, only sharpened Mercy Warren's understanding of her role as a political woman and writer. She emerged as a proponent of what historians have called "republican motherhood," the view that the proper political role for women in post-revolutionary America was the preservation and transmission of true republican values and principles through proper childrearing.

With this role in mind, she authored the only major anti-federalist history of the American Revolution and Constitutional period, her three-volume *History of the Rise, Progress and Termination of the American Revolution, interspersed with Biographical and Moral Observations*, a work that has been returned to by generations of historians seeking insights into republicanism, anti-federalism, and federalism. Perhaps more than any other woman of her time, she found a way to integrate domesticity with important intellectual accomplishments.

Overview of Biographical Sources

Mercy Otis Warren has attracted a small but noteworthy biographical corpus. Several book-length popular biographies written as early as the mid-nineteenth century generally express a laudatory point of view. Although Warren was designated the "first lady" of the American Revolution, the evaluation of her political and social ideas was largely superficial. Her admirers were prone to stress her achievements as a writer without appreciating the tensions or dilemmas with which she grappled. Nor did they well appreciate the historical significance of her actions.

Beginning in the 1950s, Warren's activities as a pamphleteer received serious attention. In the next decade, her history was the subject of a rigorous scholarly analysis. But this interest was mainly confined to demonstrating the polemical quality of her scholarship and debating the revolutionary character of her history.

Since the 1970s, interest in Warren's private life has increased, spurred by the discovery of the depth and resonance of republican ideology in early American political thought and by the study of women's history. Scholars are now probing Warren's letters and writings for evidence of her understanding of republicanism, and to determine the relationship betwen her ethical and ideological positions and her historical and dramatic works. Feminist scholars view her as one of the founders of the case for women as nurturing mothers of republican institutions, considered an important step in the growth of women's political consciousness.

As a personality, Warren was difficult and demanding. She has been characterized as nervous, worrisome, fretful, excessively dominant, moralistic, and puritanical. Considerable debate surrounds the question of whether she was adjusted to a domestic role or fundamentally unhappy. There is no doubt, however, that present-day biographers have a greater appreciation for the complex evolution of her consciousness and feelings.

A controversy persists over the attribution of several bawdy political farces. Some, such as Moses Coit Tyler, Paul Leicester Ford, and Montrose Moses, have thought her the author, while others, including Maud Hutcheson, Alice Brown, and Jean Fritz, have cast doubt on her authorship of these farces.

Evaluation of Principal Biographical Sources

Anthony, Katharine. *First Lady of the Revolution: The Life of Mercy Otis Warren.* New York: Kennikat Press, 1958. (A, G, Y) A heroic biography, heavily anecdotal, full of sensitive insights and sometimes exaggerated pronouncements, such as crediting her with the invention of the Committees of Correspondence. Anthony has an eye for the domestic as well as the political life of Warren, but is prone to substitute imaginative reconstruction for reliable narrative.

Brown, Alice. *Mercy Warren.* New York: Charles Scribner's Sons, 1896. (A, G, Y) Perhaps the most hostile treatment of her life, this work has the distinction of being the first extensive, although hardly exhaustive, biography of Mercy Warren. As a personality, Brown found Warren lacking in essential interest. As a patriot, Brown judged her too partisan to be admired.

Cohen, Lester H. "Explaining the Revolution: Ideology and Ethics in Mercy Otis Warren's Historical Theory." *William and Mary Quarterly* 37

(1980): 200-218. (**A, G**) A subtle reading of Warren's "hortatory" and exemplary theory of history in which the author argues Warren stressed the priority of ethics (virtue) over ideology (republicanism) in a passionate "jeremiad" to educate Americans on the causes of the revolution and the prerequisites of maintaining freedom.

————. "Mercy Otis Warren: The Politics of Language and the Aesthetic Self." *American Quarterly* 35 (1983): 481-498. (**A, G**) Focusing on Warren's private correspondence in the 1770s and 1780s, the author advances the doubtful claim that a subtle evolution occurred in her consciousness as she changed from a naive republican to a politically self-conscious feminist. Republicanism frustrated Warren as much as it expressed her views because it still denied women an equal voice in politics. Hence, Warren's view that woman's proper role as mother-shepherd of republican principles was a retreat from her alleged true beliefs.

————. *The Revolutionary Histories: Contemporary Narratives of the American Revolution.* Ithaca, NY: Cornell University Press, 1980. (**A, G**) A comparative study of Warren's history and those of Noah Webster and David Ramsey. It presents their works as studies in political ethics, and finds in her ideas a foreshadowing of the neoclassical interpretations of our time.

Crovitz, Elaine, and Elizabeth Buford. *Courage Knows No Sex.* Chris, MA: Christopher Publishing, 1978. (**A, G, Y**) Devotes one chapter to a synoptic and slanted view of Warren's life as exemplifying feminine courage.

Friedman, Lawrence J., and Arthur H. Schaffer. "Mercy Otis Warren and the Politics of Historical Nationalism." *New England Quarterly* 48 (June 1975): 194-215. (**A, G**) An ambitious interpretation of Warren's *History* that stresses the limits of her radicalism based on her presumed embrace of nationalist ideology, which the authors claim she shared with federalist historians. Although not entirely persuasive, the authors were the first to explore the relationship of Warren's political ideology to her position on the subordinate role of women in society.

Fritz, Jean. *Cast for a Revolution: Some American Friends and Enemies 1728-1814.* Boston: Houghton Mifflin, 1972. (**A, G, Y**) A "collective biography" of the Warren-Otis-Adams-Hutchinson circle. Mercy Warren is the star of the story, but not the only subject. It is a work of fine detail and satisfying balance, treating Warren's foibles as well as her strengths. In some respects, this work elaborates themes first presented by Alice Brown. Warren emerges as a fretful victim of real and imagined troubles, and the Warrens' nemeses— first Thomas Hutchinson and then the federalists—are given a fair hearing.

Fritz casts persuasive doubt on Warren's authorship of the vulgar political plays sometimes attributed to her.

Geiger, Marianne B. "Mercy Otis Warren and Catherine Sawbridge Macaulay: Historians in the Transatlantic Republican Tradition." Ph.D. diss. New York: New York University, 1986. (A, G) This study in comparative political philosophy and family history interprets these two friends' correspondence in the context of their families' lives and their individual political commitments. The author argues that neither woman was particularly satisfied with the social roles available to her.

Hutcheson, Maud Macdonald. "Mercy Warren 1728-1814." *William and Mary Quarterly* 3 (July 1953): 378-402. (A, G) This first scholarly assessment of Warren's life and principal works avoids extravagant claims and stresses Warren's contributions as a revolutionary pamphleteer. Hutcheson does not attribute the bawdy plays to Warren.

Smith, William Raymond. *History As Argument: Three Patriot Historians of the American Revolution.* Paris: Mouton, 1966. (A, G) An exercise in intellectual history and historiography, this work skillfully examines how political and philosophical assumptions varied between Mercy Warren and two other patriotic historians—the moderate federalist David Ramsay and tough-minded nationalist John Marshall—producing dramatically different interpretations of the American Revolution, even though all three shared similar styles of thought and language.

————. "Mercy Otis Warren's Radical View of the American Revolution." In *The Colonial Legacy: Some Eighteenth Century Commentators*, edited by Lawrence H. Leder. New York: Harper & Row, 1971. (A, G) Short exposition and analysis of the principal themes in Warren's three-volume history. The author stresses the uniqueness of her place in the history of the revolution based on her association with advocates of radical popular sovereignty.

Warren, Charles. "Elbridge Gerry, James Warren, Mercy Warren and the Ratification of the Federal Constitution in Massachusetts." *Proceedings, Massachusetts Historical Society* 64 (March 1931): 143-64. (A, G) Presents a convincing argument, based mainly on stylistic grounds, that Warren authored the *Observations on the New Constitution* rather than Elbridge Gerry.

Overview and Evaluation of Primary Sources

Mercy Otis Warren's distinct reputation rests primarily upon her three-volume history of the American Revolution, her personal letters to the inner

Adams circle, and a number of political farces written in the midst of the revolution.

Her three-volume history, *History of the Rise, Progress and Termination of the American Revolution, interspersed with Biographical and Moral Observations* (1805. Reprint. New York: AMS Press, 1970; Orem, UT: Liberty Press, 1989; **A, G**), was written in the spirit of the revolutionary pamphleteers. Like her plays, Warren's history saw conspiratorial designs at the heart of the causes of the American Revolution. Her history is a work of a participant, or near participant: heroic, highly personified and highly moral, in which the conspiratorial arguments propounded during the Revolution are the essential stuff of explanation. Older editions of this work are set in Old English type, which makes heavy going for the modern reader. The Liberty Press edition, superbly edited and annotated by Lester H. Cohen, a leading authority on the historical literature of eighteenth-century America, is a modern version in two volumes.

One finds in Warren's letters to family and friends a personal and elegiac view of well-born New England society. Her principal correspondents included her long-standing friend Hannah Winthrop, John and Abigail Adams, James Warren, James Otis, her sons, and Catharine Macaulay, the English author who inspired her to write a history of the American Revolution. Warren's letters are particularly valuable for an understanding of the hardship imposed on domestic society by the Revolution and the doubts this patriotic family suffered during the long struggle. In her letters we see her many domestic struggles: as the dutiful wife of a committed revolutionist; as the mother of a son who lost a leg in naval combat, another killed in an ambush, and a third who died of tuberculosis; and as the commiserating friend of other women in the revolution.

Many of these letters have found their way into publication, but their principal source remains the Mercy Warren Papers and the Mercy Warren Letterbook, both at the Massachusetts Historical Society in Boston. One can also find here invaluable biographical manuscripts and unpublished verse. Warren's correspondence alone runs over a thousand manuscript pages. The Warren Family Letters and Papers, 1763-1814, compiled and arranged by Charles Warren, also reside at the Massachusetts Historical Society.

Warren's published correspondence includes: *Warren-Adams Letters: Being Chiefly Correspondence among John Adams, Samuel Adams and James Warren*, Massachusetts Historical Society Collection vol. 72: 1743-1777 (1917); Vol. 73: 1778-1814 (1925. Reprint, New York: AMS Press, 1972; **A**), containing many letters to and from Mercy Warren; *Correspondence between John Adams and Mercy Warren relating to her History of the American Revolution*, Massachusetts Historical Society Collections, 5th series, vol. 4 (1878; **A**), which includes ten letters by Adams and six by Warren documenting their increasing alienation following the publication of the history in 1807;

and Charles Warren, ed., "Elbridge Gerry, James Warren, and Mercy Warren and the Ratification of the Constitution," *Massachusetts Historical Society Proceedings* 64 (1932; **A**), which reprints the contributions of the three prominent anti-federalists to a critique of the constitution as it emerged from the Philadelphia convention.

Warren's plays and dramas were much influenced by the realism of Raleigh, Molière, and Shakespeare. Because of their satiric content, and because anonymity was often adopted by pamphleteers of the times, her authorship of several of these works has remained in dispute. Benjamin V. Franklin, ed. *The Plays and Poems of Mercy Otis Warren* (New York: Scholars' Facsimiles and Reprints, 1980; **A, G, Y**) collects facsimile reproductions of all her published plays and poems with a superb introduction by Franklin commenting on her literary techniques and the evidence for her authorship of *The Blockheads* and *The Motley Assembly*.

The Adulateur: A Tragedy; As It Is Now Acted in Upper Servia was first excerpted in *The Massachusetts Spy* in 1772 and published as a pamphlet in 1773. Originally a three-act play exposing the "unscrupulous" Royal Governor, Thomas Hutchinson, it was subsequently plagiarized into a five-act play with the Boston Massacre as its focal point. *The Defeat, a Play* was excerpted in the *Boston Gazette* in 1773 and never completed. This play's fragmentary nature—it is her shortest play—has lead critics to judge it her least satisfactory dramatic work, but it is the first play written entirely by Warren. *The Group, a Farce* first appeared in the *Boston Gazette* and was published in full as a pamphlet in 1775. It was once described as a "gallery of unrelieved villainy" and is considered her best play. It appeared on the eve of the fighting at Concord and Lexington. *The Blockheads: or The Affrighted Officers, a Farce* was published in Boston (1776) in response to an unflattering play about the patriots by British General John Burgoyne during his residence in Boston. Because it is written in prose style, and contains sexual and scatological language, doubts of Warren's authorship have persisted. Claims to her authorship rest on internal evidence drawn from the play's structure, themes, and characters. *The Motley Assembly, a Farce: Published for the Entertainment of the Curious* was first published at Boston in 1779. It is a drawing room comedy also written in prose style that records one dimension of the disillusionment of the Adamses circle at the course of the Revolution.

The Franklin volumes also contain materials first published as *Poems, Dramatic and Miscellaneous* (1790), the first of Warren's works to be published under her own name. The original volume contains eighteen poems of modest quality, which are considered by her admirers as "praiseworthy imitations" of Pope and Dryden. Because these poems express Warren's views on politics, nature, friendship, philosophy, reason, and religion, they serve as valuable guides to several of her intellectual concerns.

Observations on the New Constitution and on the Federal and State Conventions, By a Columbian Patriot. Sic Transit Gloria Americana, (Boston, 1788. Reprint. in Paul Leicester Ford, ed., *Pamphlets on the Constitution of the United States,* New York: Franklin, 1968; A), was thought for years to have been written by Elbridge Gerry (Ford made this attribution). It is now recognized as the work of Mercy Warren, but is also considered her least successful political pamphlet in the cause of anti-federalism.

Other Sources

Bailyn, Bernard. *The Ideological Origins of the American Revolution.* Cambridge: Harvard University Press, 1967. Places Warren's literary and historical works within the framework of trans-Atlantic republican ideology.

Kerber, Linda K. *Women of the Republic: Intellect and Ideology in Revolutionary America.* Chapel Hill: University of North Carolina Press, 1980. Perhaps the most important exploration of the changing role of women in the revolutionary war and resulting political system. Mercy Warren figures prominently for her development of a rationale for women's role as republican mother, inculcating civic virtue into husbands and sons. This work is especially useful for assessing the exceptional and conventional in Warren's thought and behavior.

Main, Jackson Turner. *The Anti-Federalists: Critics of the Constitution 1781-1788.* New York: Norton, 1974. Sets Warren's anti-federalism within the context of the larger movement and attributes authorship of the *Observations* to Warren over Gerry.

Waters, John J., Jr. *The Otis Family in Provincial and Revolutionary Massachusetts.* Chapel Hill: University of North Carolina Press, 1968. The story of five generations of the Otis family in colonial and revolutionary America, this work offers a detailed account of the family into which Warren was born and how it conceived political and social relations to its community.

————, and John A. Schutz. "Patterns of Massachusetts Colonial Politics: The Writs of Assistance and the Rivalry between the Otis and Hutchinson Families." *William and Mary Quarterly* 24 (October 1967): 543-567. Important background on the rivalry between the Otis-Warren faction and the principal loyalist.

Julian J. DelGaudio
USAF Space Systems Division History Office
Los Angeles Air Force Base

MARTHA WASHINGTON
1731-1802

Chronology

Born Martha Dandridge on June 21, 1731 in New Kent, Virginia (near Williamsburg) to Colonel John Dandridge, a planter and country clerk, and his wife Frances, whose family were clerics and scholars; oldest of several brothers and sisters; *1746* prominent belle in Williamsburg; received in the governor's palace by Governor Gooch; *1749* marries Daniel Parke Custis, scion of the wealthy and notorious Virginia family; *1754* gives birth to her first surviving son, John Parke Custis; *1757* Daniel Parke Custis dies of fever on July 8, leaving her one of the wealthiest widows in the colonies; *1758* meets George Washington for perhaps the first time in March, and he proposes to her later the same month; *1759* marries George Washington on January 6; *1768* Martha "Patsy" Parke Custis, her daughter, is diagnosed an epileptic on June 14; *1773* Patsy dies after an epileptic fit on June 19; *1774* John "Jacky" Parke Custis marries Eleanor "Nelly" Calvert on February 3; *1775* accompanied by her nephew George Lewis and Jacky and Nelly Custis, joins Washington at his army camp at Cambridge, Massachusetts; *1776* follows Washington and his troops to New York in March; celebrates the birth of her first grandchild, Elizabeth Parke Custis, in August; *1777* travels to Washington's headquarters at Morristown, New Jersey, to nurse him in March; welcomes the birth of her second granddaughter, Martha Parke Custis; *1778* joins Washington at his winter encampment at Valley Forge; *1779* joins Washington at his winter encampment at Somerville, New Jersey; receives word of the birth of her third granddaughter, Eleanor Parke Custis; *1780* spends winter encampment with Washington at New Windsor on the Hudson; *1781* celebrates birth of George Washington Parke Custis, her first and only grandson; Jacky Custis dies of camp fever on November 2 while accompanying Washington to Yorktown; *1781-1782* joins her husband in Newburgh, New York; *1783* returns to Mount Vernon with Washington, where they are shortly joined by her two youngest grandchildren, Eleanor Parke and George Washington Parke Custis; *1789* leaves for New York City as the wife of the first president of the United States; *1797* returns to Mount Vernon with Washington for what they hope will be a peaceful and lengthy retirement; *1799* she and her husband take great pleasure in the marriage of Eleanor Parke Custis to one of Washington's favorite nephews, Lawrence Lewis; *1799* Washington dies on December 14 of a cold contracted while supervising farm activities at Mount Vernon; *1802* dies peacefully at Mount Vernon on May 22 after a long illness and is buried there with her husband.

Activities of Historical Significance

Martha Washington married a man who became perhaps the most famous man in North America, but she herself accomplished nothing of particular note in historical terms. Although her significance may well rest in her domestic role—she was the quintessential wife in the eyes of generations of Americans—she also managed the sizeable Custis estate, perhaps the largest in the colonies, until her remarriage, with only occasional assistance from lawyers.

A good housekeeper and an affectionate, if indulgent, parent and grandparent, Martha Washington presumably supported her husband in all of his endeavors, as would most "properly" trained women of her class and era. Cynics claim that her fortune was her major attraction for the ambitious young Washington. On the other hand, he brought considerable renown to the match, as well as a handsome estate on the Potomac.

Whatever the motivations behind the union, there can be no denying that theirs was a successful marriage. Washington was always solicitous of his wife's health and needs. He ordered her gifts from London and shared his private and public correspondence with her. She spent as much time with him as she could during the Revolutionary War, usually in dirty, cold, and unsanitary winter camps. This devotion to her husband and her cause won her the affection and admiration of the troops.

Martha and George Washington had no children together, but he always treated her children and grandchildren as his own and was, if anything, too indulgent of their misbehavior and too prone to spoil them. The couple's happiest times together were at Mount Vernon, where she worked on the house and garden and he worked on the estate. Perhaps Martha Washington's greatest role in history was to provide a stable and comfortable home from which her husband could sally forth to lead the nation in war and in peace.

Overview of Biographical Sources

As is often the case with wives of famous men who are not famous in their own right, there is no really satisfactory biographical treatment of Martha Washington. Most of the material that does exist was written before the flowering of the women's movement in the 1960s, when lives such as Martha Washington's came to exemplify what most women were rebelling against, not what they aspired to be. Any historian who could write an intelligent, lively, and scholarly biography of the "Mother of Her Country" would quickly be appreciated for understanding and recording her historical context.

Evaluation of Principal Biographical Sources
Conkling, Margaret C. *Memoirs of the Mother and Wife of Washington.*
Auburn, Derby, Miller and Co., 1851. (G) This was the first of the biographies to treat both Martha Washington and her somewhat unpleasant mother-in-law, Mary Washington.

Desmond, Alice Curtis. *Martha Washington, Our First Lady.* New York:
Dodd, Mead & Company, 1942. (G) An adequate, albeit dated, account.

Lossing, Benson John. *Martha Washington.* New York: J. C. Buttre, 1861.
(G) Long out-of-date and out-of-print, this is the first biography to focus only on Martha Washington.

Thane, Elswyth. *Washington's Lady.* New York: Dodd, Mead, 1960. (G)
One of the most recent works whose title suggests its focus.

Vance, Marguerite. *Martha, Daughter of Virginia.* New York: E. P. Dutton,
1947. (G) An uninspired retelling of Martha Washington's life.

Wagoner, Jean Brown. *Martha Washington, Girl of Old Virginia.* Indianapolis: Bobbs-Merrill Company, 1947. (Y) An adequate juvenile biography.

Walter, James. *Memorial of Washington, and of Mary, His Mother, and
Martha, His Wife.* New York: Scribner's, 1887. (G) This dated account nonetheless has much information.

Wharton, Anne Hollingsworth. *Martha Washington.* New York: Scribner's,
1897. (G) Another lengthy, anecdotal account of questionable accuracy.

Overview and Evaluation of Primary Sources
Unfortunately, Martha Washington burned all of the correspondence between herself and her husband shortly before her death; only two letters, which she overlooked, escaped the flames. Some of her letters to other correspondents can be found in various collections of the Virginia Historical Society, which also holds the valuable Custis Family Papers. A collection of manuscripts pertaining to Mount Vernon and the Washingtons' married life is kept at the estate by the Mount Vernon Ladies Association. A few of Martha Washington's letters will be included in the ambitious Papers of George Washington project, published by the University Press of Virginia. The paucity of extant material, compounded by the fact that Martha Washington focused her energies on home and marriage rather than public activities, have

made it difficult for both contemporary and modern observers to get a sense of the woman; even William Maclay, the acerbic diarist of and commentator on the First Federal Congress, had no comments on her personality.

Fiction and Adaptations

Two miniseries based on James Thomas Flexner's biographies of George Washington have appeared on television. *George Washington* concentrated on Washington's youth and Revolutionary War career and aired in March-April 1984, with Patty Duke as Martha Custis Washington, Barry Bostwick as George, and Jaclyn Smith as Sally Fairfax. In September 1986, *George Washington: The Forging of a Nation* depicted Washington as president. Duke and Bostwick "reprised" their roles, while the rest of the cast included Jeffrey Jones as Jefferson, Richard Bekins as Hamilton, and Lise Hillboldt as Maria Reynolds. In both series, Martha appears as a wise and discreet woman, deeply in love with her husband.

The most recent work on Martha Washington is *Lady Washington* (1984), a novel by Dorothy Clarke Wilson. While not a stellar example of fiction, it is as good and accurate a biography as any of the earlier works that purported to be nonfiction.

Museums, Historical Landmarks, Societies

Custis House (Williamsburg, VA). This house, part of the large Custis estate, was used by Martha during her trips to Virginia's capital. It is in the process of being restored by the Colonial Williamsburg Foundation.

Mount Vernon (Alexandria, VA). This was George and Martha's home for many years. Built by George's half-brother Lawrence, the house went through three major periods of restoration during the eighteenth century. The Mount Vernon Ladies Association of the Union was formed in the 1850s to buy and preserve the estate and open it to the public. The Association has recently embarked on an ambitious plan of restoration to bring Mount Vernon back to its 1799 appearance. The house and grounds are both impressive and beautiful.

Other Sources

Minnigerode, Meade. *Some American Ladies.* New York: Putnam's, 1926. The first chapter of this romantic and melodramatic book is devoted to Martha Washington.

Jean V. Berlin
Correspondence of William T. Sherman

PHILLIS WHEATLEY
c. 1753-1784

Chronology

Born c. 1753, most likely in Senegal, Africa, probably a member of the Moslem Fula tribe; *c. 1761* kidnapped from her village; *1761* purchased by Susannah Wheatley directly off a slave ship anchored in Boston harbor; is probably about eight years old when she lands in America, although this hypothesis is based only on the condition of her teeth at the time; *1762-1769* instructed in English by Mary Wheatley, one of the two older Wheatley twins; demonstrates remarkable progress in a short period; within sixteen months is reading the Bible, and by age twelve is learning Latin and reading British literary classics; lives as a daughter rather than as a slave in the household, eating with the family, having her own room, and beginning to write poetry at thirteen; *1767* publishes her first poem, "On Messrs. Hussey and Coffin," in the Newport (Rhode Island) *Mercury* of December 21; *late 1760s-early 1770s* displayed as a sort of curiosity, an educated and educable Negro, and a prop in the arguments of antislavery supporters; writes poetry largely in response to specific requests; *1770* publishes "An Elegiac Poem, on the Death of the Celebrated Divine . . . George Whitefield," a work that attracts a good deal of attention and reveals the influence of Alexander Pope and the neoclassic poets on her style; *1773* in declining health, sent by her family to England, where she spends a brief five weeks in triumph; enjoys a short social whirl as the guest of the methodist Countess of Huntingdon, who functions as her literary patron; her only book of verse, *Poems on Various Subjects, Religious and Moral,* is published in England and dedicated to the Countess; becomes a freedwoman; *1774* her anti-slavery letter to Samuel Occom is reprinted in a dozen New England newspapers; left to support herself as a poet and seamstress following the death of Susannah Wheatley and the dispersal of the Wheatley family; *1776* publishes a poem for General George Washington (in the March issue of the *Virginia Gazette* and the April issue of *Pennsylvania Magazine*), and receives an invitation to visit his headquarters in Cambridge; *1778-1784* marries a free black man named John Peters and moves to Wilmington, Massachusetts; bears three children, only one of whom survives; her husband is jailed for debt; supports herself and her child by working in a lodging house for blacks; suffers from steadily declining health; *1784* dies in Boston on December 5, along with her only child, and is buried in an unmarked grave; *1786* the first American edition of her volume of verse is published posthumously.

Activities of Historical Significance

Hailed as the "Mother of Black American Literature," Wheatley's literary reputation is based on her identity as America's first black woman poet. Her poetry has always been criticized as trivial by white critics, and has also received a fair amount of criticism from black critics (primarily male) for its lack of overt anger or racial consciousness. More recent critical opinion claims that a few poems contain a fair amount of racial and social criticism buried beneath their facile surfaces. Black female literary critics have generally been more appreciative of Wheatley's work, seeing her as the originator of a black women's literary tradition, a tradition distinctly different from the black male's.

Wheatley's poetry reflects the neoclassical heritage so prevalent in British poetry of the period—heavy use of biblical and classical allusions, heroic couplets, Christian piety, and impersonal subjects. That a black slave would immerse herself in such an alien culture serves only to reveal how thoroughly Wheatley was accepted by and assimilated into this culture.

Overview of Biographical Sources

Margaretta M. Odell, a distant relative of the Wheatleys, published her "Memoir" of Phillis Wheatley as a preface to a new edition of her poems (1834), thereby reviving the poet's dwindling reputation. This "Memoir" contains a number of self-serving errors and has been corrected by recent historical scholarship. Other early attempts to write Wheatley's life can be found in Charles F. Heartman (1915), which relies on Odell for facts. The best modern biographies are William H. Robinson, *Phillis Wheatley and Her Writings* (1984), and Merle A. Richmond, *Bid the Vassal Soar* (1974).

Evaluation of Principal Biographical/Critical Sources

Heartman, Charles E. *Phillis Wheatley (Phillis Peters): A Critical Attempt and a Bibliography of her Writings.* 1915. Reprint. Miami: Mnemosyne, 1969. (A) An early biography and attempt to list all of the editions of Wheatley's poems published to date. Also contains Arthur A. Schomburg's "Appreciation" of Wheatley, which states that "there was no great American poetry in the 18th century, and Phillis Wheatley's poetry was as good as the best American poetry of her age."

Odell, Margaretta Matilda. *Memoir and Poems of Phillis Wheatley.* Boston: Light, 1834. (A) The thirty-six-page memoir that prefaces this collection of poems was written by Odell, a great-grandniece of Susannah Wheatley. Odell presents John Peters in less than a fair light, and absolves her own family for not attending Wheatley in her last days or at her funeral. Despite its flaws, it is considered the most accurate of the early biographies, and is the one on which all others are based.

Richmond, Merle A. *Bid the Vassal Soar: Interpretative Essays on the Life and Poetry of Phillis Wheatley and George Moses Horton.* Washington, DC: Howard University Press, 1974. (A) A vivid and lively retelling of the life of Wheatley, using the standard Odell source. The most helpful chapter is "The Critics," which reviews the major attacks on and supporters of Wheatley's poetry.

Robinson, William H. *Critical Essays on Phillis Wheatley.* Boston: G. K. Hall, 1982. (A) A valuable collection of essays edited by the major contemporary critic on Wheatley. The first section contains eyewitness accounts by her contemporaries, as well as early critical assessments of her poetry. The second and third sections reprint the major critics on her work. The preface recounts the various historical controversies involved in dating major events in her life. By far the most valuable critical resource currently available on Wheatley.

—————. *Phillis Wheatley and Her Writings.* New York: Garland, 1984. (A) The major biographical source on Wheatley. Reprints the Odell "Memoir" as an appendix. Includes all of Wheatley's poetry and letters, as well as all of the known portraits of her and the Boston of her day. A briefer, more accessible version has been published as *Phillis Wheatley: A Bio-Bibliography* (Boston: G. K. Hall, 1981; A).

Thatcher, B. B. *Memoir of Phillis Wheatley, A Native African and a Slave.* Boston: Light, 1834. (A) Another early biography, based fully on Odell.

Overview and Evaluation of Primary Sources

All of Wheatley's writings are printed in the Robinson volume cited above (1984). In addition, *The Collected Works of Phillis Wheatley*, edited by John C. Shields (New York: Oxford, 1988; A, G) and drawn from Harlem's Schomburg Library collection on nineteenth-century black women writers, also includes much of Wheatley's correspondence. An early volume of Wheatley's correspondence is the *Letters of Phillis Wheatley, the Negro-Slave Poet of Boston*, edited by Charles Deane (Boston: privately printed, 1864; A, G). Julian D. Mason, Jr., edited *The Poems of Phillis Wheatley* (Chapel Hill: University of North Carolina Press, 1966; A, G).

Fiction and Adaptations

Naomi Long Madgett's poem "Phillis," printed in *Critical Essays on Phillis Wheatley*, edited by William H. Robinson (1982), is a tribute to the poet's subversive skill. Madgett writes, "Lurking behind the docile Christian lamb/ Unconquered lioness asserts: 'I am!'"

Other Sources

Brawley, Benjamin. *The Negro Genius: A New Appraisal of the Achievement of the American Negro in Literature and the Fine Arts.* 1937. Reprint. New York: Biblo & Tannen, 1966. Brawley is also the author of *Early Negro American Writers* (Chapel Hill: University of North Carolina Press, 1935) and *Negro Builders and Heroes* (Chapel Hill: University of North Carolina Press, 1937). All of his books are concerned with celebrating the "talented tenth" among African Americans. He says of Wheatley, "Her ambition knew no bounds, her thirst for knowledge was insatiable, and she triumphed over the most adverse circumstances."

Gates, Henry Louis, Jr. *The Idea of Blackness in Western Discourse.* New York: Oxford University Press, 1982. Sets Wheatley's poetry into the larger social and political context of colonial America.

Greene, Lorenzo Johnston. *The Negro in Colonial New England, 1620-1776.* 1942. Reprint. Port Washington, NY: Kennikat, 1966. Contains valuable historical information about the living conditions of blacks during Wheatley's lifetime.

Johnson, James Weldon, ed. *The Book of American Negro Poetry.* New York: Harcourt, Brace, 1922. Contains a discussion of various critiques of Wheatley's poetry, and compares Wheatley to Anne Bradstreet.

Kunio, Robert C. "Some Unpublished Poems by Phillis Wheatley." *New England Quarterly* 43 (June 1970): 2287-2297. Contains some of the more obscure Wheatley poems.

Loggins, Vernon. *The Negro Author: His Development in America to 1900.* 1931. Reprint. Port Washington, NY: Kennikat, 1964. A pioneering work that criticizes Wheatley for failing to condemn the racism of her period.

Mazyck, Walter H. *George Washington and the Negro.* Washington, DC: Associated Publishers, 1932. Contains information about Wheatley's thirty-minute private audience with Washington.

Redding, J. Saunders. *To Make a Poet Black*. Chapel Hill: University of North Carolina Press, 1939. Attacks Wheatley's poetry for failing to protest against the conditions of black slaves in early America.

Robinson, William H. *Phillis Wheatley in the Black American Beginnings*. Detroit: Broadside, 1975. Contains chapters on Wheatley's life and poetry, and a fairly extensive bibliographical listing of primary and secondary sources.

Watts, Emily. *The Poetry of American Women from 1632 to 1945*. Austin: University of Texas Press, 1977. Examines Wheatley's work in the context of American women's poetry.

Wright, Richard. *White Man, Listen*. New York: Doubleday, 1964. Contains a sympathetic, five-page appraisal of Wheatley's poetry, praising it for its assimilative quality and its ability to sing of "universal" values.

Diane Long Hoeveler
Marquette University

ELLEN GOULD WHITE
1827-1915

Chronology

Born Ellen Gould Harmon on November 26, 1827, on a farm near Gorham, Maine; with her twin sister the youngest child of William and Eunice Gould Harmon; raised in Portland where her father works as a hatmaker; *1837* severely injured by a falling rock which leaves her unconscious for three weeks, permanently disfigured, and subject to dizzy spells for the rest of her life; *1840* schooling abandoned because of her weakened physical condition and repeated illnesses; *1842* undergoes a conversion experience, is baptized by immersion, and joins the Methodist Episcopal Church; *1843* hears William Miller speak, becomes a believer in the imminent Second Coming of Christ; *June 1843* with the rest of her family is "disfellowshipped" by the Methodists as a result of their espousal of adventist beliefs; *October 22, 1844* lives through the Great Disappointment, the failure of Christ to return as predicted by William Miller; *December 1844* has the first of many visions concerning the ultimate Second Coming of Christ; *1846* marries James White, an adventist preacher, with whom she eventually has four sons; shortly after their marriage, they begin keeping the seventh-day sabbath, the correctness of their decision affirmed by another vision; *1847-1855* the Whites continue their role as itinerant preachers, eventually establishing two journals *The Present Truth* and *The Review and Herald*, and seeing groups of adherents emerge as small organized churches; *1851* publishes her first pamphlet *A Sketch of the Christian Experience and Views of Ellen G. White*; *1855* moves to Battle Creek, Michigan, where she experiences the vision which leads to her most famous book *The Great Controversy between Christ and His Angels and Satan and His Angels*; *1860* the Whites' followers are formally organized under the name The Seventh Day Adventist Church; as a result of her continued visions, the Adventists became active in the anti-slavery movement; *1863* as a result of another vision, begins to espouse diet and health reform as part of Adventist regime; Dr. John Harvey Kellogg, one of her followers, transforms the church's water cure health spa in Battle Creek into a renowned sanitorium, and, in response to her dictates on a vegetarian diet, invents corn flakes; *1881* husband James dies after a long illness; she spends the rest of her life writing and speaking on behalf of her beliefs, travelling throughout the U.S., Europe, and Australia to advance her views; *1903* moves to St. Helena, California, where she continues to work on behalf of the Adventist church until her death in 1915.

Activities of Historical Significance

The Seventh Day Adventist Church, founded by Ellen and James White, has a membership of over a half million in the United States and continues to grow at the rate of thirty-five percent each decade. Next to the Church of the Latter Day Saints, it ranks as one of the more long-lived and successful religious organizations to have emerged from the religious reawakening of the early and middle decades of the nineteenth century. It succeeded in making the transition from cult to established church. It has an especially strong medical and religious mission to developing countries. Ellen White's advocacy of a vegetarian diet, abstinence from alcohol and tobacco, emphasis on holistic healing, all developed not only out of her personal struggle with ill-health and the reformist tendencies of the nineteenth century but looked forward to the medical advances of the next. With only three years of formal schooling herself, she was an early proponent of child-centered education, and her influence was largely responsible for the Seventh Day Adventists' strong system of elementary and secondary schools as well as their many church-sponsored colleges and universities. Like many other evangelical reformers, White was active in the anti-slavery movement and the Underground Railroad. She was also an influential figure in such causes as the temperance movement, and in movements advocating sensible clothes for women and the recognition of conscientious objectors during wartime. Finally, her association with Dr. John Kellogg helped spark the development of the commercial breakfast cereal market.

Overview of Biographical Sources

Although numerous biographies of Ellen G. White have been published under the sponsorship of the Seventh Day Adventist Church, no standard unbiased assessment of her career exists. Her life has been of little interest to secular biographers, and her career has been treated primarily in relation to the history of the Great Awakening of evangelical religious thought in the mid-nineteenth century. Biographies written for religious adherents and potential converts naturally tend to be less than critical. Her enormous collection of papers, letters, and writings is located at the General Headquarters of the Seventh Day Adventist Church in Takoma Park, Maryland. Access to primary sources has been generally limited to sympathetic writers who also happen to be practicing Seventh Day Adventists. The best of these biographies is Arthur Spalding's short *There Shines a Light* (1953). Arthur L. White, one of her descendants, has written a more recent book, *Ellen G. White: Messenger to the Remnant* (1969), which deals specifically with her visions and prophecies from the official Adventist view. Hostile anti-Adventist accounts of her teachings appear in Dudley Canright's *Life of Mrs. E. G. White, Seventh-Day Adventist Prophet; Her False Claims Refuted* (1919) and Guy Winslow's "Ellen Gould White and Seventh Day Adventism" (Ph.D. diss., 1933). Francis D. Nichol's *Ellen G. White and Her Critics* (1951) provides the official refutation of charges of charlatanism levelled by these two critics.

Evaluation of Principal Biographical Sources

Ferrell, Vance. *Prophet of the End.* Altamont, TN: Pilgrims' Books, 1984. (G) More proselytizer than biographer, the author interlaces an overly dramatic account of White's life with long passages from her writings and ominous foreshadowings of the coming end of the world.

Spalding, Arthur W. *There Shines a Light.* Nashville, TN: Southern Publishing Association, 1953. (G) Although largely adulatory, this short biography represents the best and most accessible treatment currently available of White's career. The author idealizes his subject but still manages to present the basic outline of her life and an assessment of her accomplishments for the general reader.

Overview and Evaluation of Primary Sources

At her death in 1915, White left all her writings to the White Estate which is located at the General Conference headquarters of the Seventh Day Adventist Church in Takoma Park, Maryland. Her will provided that all royalties from any of her works be paid directly to the church. Over fifty of her books have been published; her works have been reprinted in over eighty languages. These publications are detailed in the *Comprehensive Index to the Writings of Ellen G. White* (3 vols. 1962-63). There are an additional 30,000 manuscript pages of letters, diaries, and other writings to which White Publications continues to control access; new books are continually being prepared for press as these documents are edited.

For the faithful, White's writings represent an authoritative source of spiritual direction, second only to the Bible. The most influential is *The Great Controversy between Christ and Satan,* originally written in 1855 after one of her visions revealed to her a battle between the forces of good and evil. Her general instructions for the church are chronicled in the nine volumes of *Testimonies for the Church,* begun as a sixteen-page pamphlet in 1855. Other important doctrinal material is contained in *Patriarchs and Prophets* (1890). Useful autobiographical information can be found in any of the many editions of *Spiritual Gifts: My Christian Experience, Views and Labors,* first published in 1860; *Life Sketches: Ancestry, Early Life, Christian Experience, and Extensive Labors, of Elder James White, and His Wife, Mrs. Ellen G. White,* originally published in 1880; and *Life Sketches of Ellen G. White* (1915).

Other Sources

Barkun, Michael. *Crucible of the Millenium: The Burned Over District of New York in the 1840s.* Syracuse, NY: Syracuse University Press, 1986. This text places the Whites and the adventist movement in the context of the religious Great Awakening of the nineteenth century.

Cross, Whitney R. *The Burned Over District.* Ithaca, NY: Cornell University Press, 1950. An older though still valuable treatment of the general cultural background of the Millerite and adventist movements.

Culver, Elsie Thomas. *Women in the World of Religion.* New York: Doubleday, 1967. Written for a general audience and readily available, this account discusses White's career in the context of female religious experience.

"Ellen Gould Harmon White." In *Biographical Dictionary of American Cult and Sect Leaders,* edited by J. Gardner Melton. New York: Garland, 1986. A concise account which provides useful bibliographical information.

Goen, C. C. "Ellen G. White." In *Notable American Women 1607-1950: A Biographical Dictionary,* edited by Edward T. James. Cambridge, MA: Belknap Press, 1971. Given the lack of critical biographical material, this brief informative sketch is invaluable.

Mary Anne Hutchinson
Utica College of Syracuse University

EDITH BOLLING GALT WILSON
1872-1961

Chronology

Born Edith Bolling on October 15, 1872, in Wytheville, Virginia, the seventh child and fourth daughter of circuit judge William Holcombe Bolling and Sallie White Bolling; *1872-1896* grows up in a warm, devoutly religious household and is educated by members of her extended family; takes only two years of formal education—one at a finishing school and the other at Powell's School in Richmond; *1896* marries Norman Galt, a Washington jeweler who is in partnership with her brother-in-law; *1908* Galt dies; *1908-1915* relies on employees for help in running the jewelry business so she can enjoy the capital's social life and travel in Europe; *1915-1921* marries widower President Woodrow Wilson in December 1915; presides over White House social life and, after the President's stroke in 1919, takes responsibility for supervising his care and recovery; *1921-1924* resides on S Street in Washington with her husband; *1924-1961* widowed for a second time in 1924; continues to live in Washington, publishes her autobiography in 1938, and participates in social affairs related to capital politics; *1961* dies in her Washington home on December 28 of heart failure.

Activities of Historical Significance

Although she took almost no interest in politics before meeting Woodrow Wilson in 1915, Edith Bolling Galt helped enlarge the idea of a woman's role in politics. One of the first women to drive her own car around Washington, D.C., she had always raised eyebrows, and after her marriage to the president, she increased her reputation as a confident, strong-willed woman.

Edith Wilson enlivened a previously gloomy White House and used her sharp native intelligence to assist the president in examining official papers. Although she had very limited education, she impressed Woodrow Wilson, and he treated her—according to his biographers—as a trusted advisor and confidante. When he attended the Peace Conference in France in 1918-1919, she accompanied him, thus becoming the first president's wife to participate in an international tour. His disabling stroke in the fall of 1919 pushed her into special prominence, and she was often credited with "taking over the presidency." Although she downplayed her role and insisted that she never made a single decision on any important matter, historians have concluded that her role was more complex.

It is generally agreed that during the president's final months in office—and especially between October 1919 and April 1920—Edith Wilson kept important advisers from him and refused to share communications she had been asked to forward to him. Disagreement centers on her motivation. Some historians see her as ruthless towards people whom she disliked or considered disloyal to the president or to herself. Other students of the Wilson presidency have accepted her explanation of her role as mere wifely support in helping a sick husband recuperate. Whatever her motivation, it is generally accepted that she contributed to the president's difficulties with close associates—especially Secretary of State Robert Lansing and the president's personal secretary, Joseph Tumulty. She is also credited with strengthening the president's determination not to compromise on the League of Nations.

Edith Wilson showed little interest in politics after her husband's death, but her record, exposing the Constitution's lack of provision for dealing with a disabled chief executive, was cited in discussions leading to the 25th Amendment (on presidential succession) in the 1960s. Although she was First Lady at the time the Constitution was amended in 1920 to guarantee the vote to women, she gave no help to that change and in fact spoke critically of members of the suffrage movement.

Overview of Biographical Sources

Although she has been the subject of considerable debate, Edith Wilson still lacks the careful, scholarly biography given Woodrow's first wife by Frances Saunders in *Ellen Axson Wilson: First Lady Between Two Worlds* (1985). The dearth of writings may be attributed in part to the fact that Edith Wilson survived the President by several decades and jealously guarded her place in history. Those scholars who did try to set the record straight had to reconcile her own varying accounts of the same event. While Wilson's outspokenness made her somewhat suspect among those who preferred that women keep to traditional roles, she rarely found friends in the feminist camp because she had little use for that movement.

Writings about Edith Wilson have moved beyond the first stage when too much credence was placed in her autobiography, but interpretations of her role still vary. Revelations of new documents, the impact of expanded work in women's history, and considerable scholarship on President Wilson's medical condition have not resulted in complete agreement on Edith Wilson's role.

Edith James, in her article "Edith Bolling Wilson, A Documentary View" in Mabel Deutrich and Virginia C. Purdy, *Clio Was a Woman* (Washington, D.C.: Howard University Press, 1980; A, G) concludes that many "popular" accounts "overstate" Edith Wilson's role. Accused of "running the country," she actually did little more than delay action and keep people from seeing the president.

Judith Weaver, in a well-researched article in *Presidential Studies Quarterly* (Winter 1985), comes to a different conclusion—that the president's wife permitted the Cabinet to handle political questions in which she had no interest but that she interfered when she had a strong opinion.

Evaluation of Principal Biographical Sources

Hatch, Alden. *Edith Bolling Wilson: First Lady Extraordinary.* New York: Dodd, Mead, 1961. (G) This authorized biography, for which the subject made her papers available, is understandably very sympathetic to her. It follows her own interpretation of her role.

Ross, Ishbel. *Power with Grace: The Life Story of Mrs. Woodrow Wilson.* New York: Putnam's, 1975. (G) Anecdotal and heavily dependent on Edith Wilson's own account of her life, this book concludes that she became "by chance . . . one of the most powerful women in White House history in reputation and in legend, if not in fact."

Schachtman, Tom. *Edith and Woodrow: A Presidential Romance.* New York: Putnam's, 1981. (G) Focusing on the relationship between Woodrow and Edith Wilson, this book finds her a powerful influence on him. From the time of their marriage, she shielded him from people and acted the part of a "presidential assistant."

Weaver, Judith. "Edith Bolling Wilson as First Lady: A Study in the Power of Personality." *Presidential Studies Quarterly* 15 (Winter 1985): 51-76. (A) Examines new documents and concludes that Edith Wilson was "not a power-hungry woman, intent upon controlling the reins of the U.S. government." Instead, she used her power to encourage the president to ignore matters she deemed unimportant (such as the question of whether or not to recognize Costa Rica) and to punish enemies.

Overview and Evaluation of Primary Sources

Edith Wilson waited for more than a decade after her husband's death and nearly seventeen years after leaving the White House to write her own account of her years there. Although unreliable, *My Memoir* (New York: Bobbs Merrill, 1938; G) is useful for Wilson's own perspective on her time in the limelight.

Many of her letters are included in the published volumes of her husband's papers, Arthur S. Link, et al., eds. *The Papers of Woodrow Wilson* (Princeton, NJ: Princeton University Press, 1966-; A, G) The letters, describing specific events such as her first meeting with Woodrow Wilson, do not always agree with her autobiography. Her letters to Woodrow before their marriage reveal an animated, amorous woman intent on pleasing him. These courtship letters are published in Edwin Tribble, ed., *A President in Love; The Courtship Letters of Woodrow Wilson and Edith Bolling Galt* (Boston: Little Brown, 1981; G).

The unpublished papers of Edith Wilson, including several thousand items spanning the years 1893-1961, are located in the Library of Congress in Washington, D.C. In addition to family letters, diaries, and financial papers, she left a manuscript for an autobiography which goes beyond 1924, the year she chose to end the published version.

The papers of Edith Bentham, secretary to Edith Wilson in the White House, are also in the Library of Congress. One memo from that collection, as reported by Joyce Williams in "The Resignation of Secretary of State Robert Lansing" (*Diplomatic History* [Summer 1979]: 337-343; A), implicates the First Lady in the resignation of Secretary of State Lansing.

Fiction and Adaptations

Wilson, a full-length film about Woodrow Wilson's life, was made in 1944 by Twentieth Century-Fox. Characters include both Ellen Wilson (played by Ruth Nelson) and Edith Wilson (played by Geraldine Fitzgerald). In reviewing the film favorably in the *New York Times* on August 2, 1944, Bosley Crowther noted that "the second Mrs. Wilson" was depicted as a "remarkably understanding woman."

Museums, Historical Landmarks, Societies

Woodrow Wilson House (Washington, DC). Located at 2340 S Street NW, the residence of the ex-president and his wife after leaving the White House is now a museum maintained by the National Trust for Historic Preservation. Open to the public and furnished as it was during the President's final years, it contains many mementoes of Edith Wilson.

Other Sources

Link, Arthur S. "Edith Bolling Galt Wilson." In *Notable American Women: The Modern Period.* Cambridge: Harvard University Press, 1980. Short biographical sketch, including a bibliography.

Caroli, Betty Boyd. *First Ladies.* New York: Oxford University Press, 1987. Places Edith Wilson in the context of two hundred years of White House history.

Betty Boyd Caroli
Kingsborough Community College, CUNY

WALLIS WARFIELD WINDSOR
1896-1986

Chronology

Born Bessiewallis Warfield, on June 19, 1896, in Blue Ridge Summit, Pennsylvania, the only child of Teackle Wallis Warfield, a clerk, and Alice Montague Warfield; *1896* father dies; *1896-1912* lives in Baltimore, Maryland, with her widowed mother and attends Arundel School; *1912-1914* attends Oldfields School for Girls near Baltimore; *1914* selected as a Baltimore debutante; *1916* marries Lt. Earl Winfield Spencer, Jr., a graduate of the U.S. Naval Academy; *1916-1921* lives with Spencer, a naval pilot stationed at Pensacola, Boston, San Diego, and then Washington, D.C.; *1921-1927* separated from Spencer, lives in Washington, Paris, Shanghai, and Peking; *November 1927* divorces Spencer in Warrenton, Virginia; *1928* marries Earnest A. Simpson, Harvard-educated British shipping broker; *1928-1936* lives in London as Simpson's wife, and after 1931, as the "special friend" of the Prince of Wales; *October 1936* divorces Simpson in Ipswich, England, and is publicly acknowledged as the woman the former prince, King Edward VIII, intends to marry following his abdication; *1937* becomes the Duchess of Windsor by her marriage in France to Prince Edward, now the Duke of Windsor; 1937-1940 lives in France with Edward; *1940-1945* lives in the Bahamas Islands with the Duke, who serves as governor-general of the British colony; *1945-1972* the Duke and Duchess of Windsor live primarily in France, and visit extensively in New York, Palm Beach, and elsewhere outside the British Commonwealth; *1972-1986* after the Duke of Windsor's death, lives in Paris in declining health; *April 1986* dies and is buried beside the Duke of Frogmore, in Windsor, Great Park, England.

Activities of Historical Significance

By her romantic involvement with England's Prince of Wales, who became King Edward VIII (1936), Wallis Warfield Simpson set the stage for her impact on British history. His decision to abdicate from the throne rather than renounce the twice-divorced American established her historical significance as "the woman he loved." Except for her relationship with, and marriage to the former king, who became the Duke of Windsor, the activities of Wallis Warfield Windsor were of little significance, historically. As his wife of thirty-five years, she was prominent in the world of fashion, perennially listed as one of the ten best-dressed women.

Overview of Biographical Sources

A well-researched, unbiased, and scholarly biography of Wallis Warfield Windsor has yet to be written. Those currently available have been written in a popular journalistic style and tend to be either highly sympathetic or harshly critical. Apparently there exists continuing interest in the Windsors. A number of dual biographies of the duke and duchess, or biographies of the duke focusing much attention on the duchess, are more numerous than separate biographies. Within the last decade a number of volumes have appeared. Several were written under the auspices of Maître Suzanne Blum, the French attorney and executor of Wallis Warfield Windsor's estate. In her role as apologist she has exerted great effort to present her late client in the best possible light. Her associate, Michael Bloch, has edited or authored several volumes in this category. Apparently Maître Blum controls the Windsor's private archives. Until these archives are opened to scholars a definitive biography is not possible.

Evaluation of Principal Biographical Sources

Birmingham, Stephen. *Duchess: The Story of Wallis Warfield Windsor*. Boston: Little, Brown, 1981. (G) Superficial popular biography, readable and gossipy. Based on interviews with friends and associates of the Duke and Duchess of Windsor. The historical context is quite shallow in this journalistic, romantic biography.

Bloch, Michael. *The Duke of Windsor's War*. New York: Coward-McCann, 1982. (G) Written on behalf of the Duchess of Windsor, this book was written to discount tales of her husband's incompetence as wartime governor general of the Bahamas. Also focuses on her contributions to his career.

————. *Operation Willi: The Nazi Plot to Kidnap the Duke of Windsor*. New York: Weidenfeld and Nicolson, 1984. (G) Written to discredit accounts published in 1957 suggesting that the Duke and Duchess of Windsor were willing conspirators in a Nazi plot to kidnap them during World War II.

Bocca, Geoffrey. *The Woman Who Would be Queen*. New York: Rinehart, 1954. (G) First full-length biography of Wallis Warfield Windsor. Highly romanticized, stressing her positive qualities. Insists that she seriously attempted to renounce the king's love, and ward off his abdication. Concludes that she would have made a good queen of England.

Bryan, J., III, and Charles J. V. Murphy. *The Windsor Story*. London: Granada, 1979. (G) Murphy who served as ghost writer for *A King's Story* and *The Heart Has its Reasons,* brings great insight to this thoughtful analysis of the Windsor story. Though balanced and provocative, Murphy does reveal his frustrations as a Windsor collaborator. He also details the self-centered inconsiderate behavior of the Windsors.

Hood, Dina Wells. *Working for the Windsors.* London: Wingate, 1957. (G) Written by Wallis Windsor's secretary during the early years of her marriage to the Duke of Windsor, this is an anecdotal insider's account of their relationship. Provides a convincing picture of their commitment and affection.

Martin, Ralph G. *The Woman He Loved.* New York: Simon and Schuster, 1974. (G) Hailed as the "first full story of the romance of the century," Martin's work is a well-balanced dual biography of the Duke and Duchess of Windsor. Without any apparent bias he addresses the difficulties of the Windsor's marriage, their much criticized visit to Hitler's Germany, their wartime sojourn in the Bahamas, their intimacy and problems with Woolworth heir, Jimmy Donahue, and their long self-centered existence in exile.

Parker, John. *King of Fools.* New York: St. Martin's Press, 1988. (G) Advertised as "the dark truth behind the romantic legend of Edward and Wallis," this is a critical, even hostile, treatment of the Windsors. Focusing on Wallis Windsor's checkered past, Parker insists she had intimate connections to fascist and Nazi agents in Europe and China, where he alleges she spent time in a Peking brothel. Parker also portrays the Windsor's visit to Nazi Germany, and later their stay in Portugal, as part of a sinister plan to recapture the throne under Nazi auspices. He even perceives ties to organized crime while the Windsors were in the Bahamas. Parker attributes to the Windsors far greater sophistication in international politics than the traditional view of them as a pair of blundering self-centered dilettantes in a world at war.

Thornton, Michael. *Royal Feud: The Dark Side of the Love Story of the Century.* New York: Simon and Schuster, 1985. (G) British author and journalist focuses on the feud between Queen Elizabeth, wife of George VI, and her sister-in-law, Wallis Windsor. Thornton insists that the Windsor's permanent exclusion from the Royal family was based primarily on Queen Elizabeth's unwavering hostility toward the Duchess, whom she blamed for Edward's abdication. Well-written, in-depth analysis of two strong-willed women.

Windsor, Duke of. *A King's Story.* New York: Putnam's, 1947. (G) Romantic fact-filled account of the Duke of Windsor's childhood, youth and action-packed years as Prince of Wales. Attempts to explain and justify his decision to abdicate from the throne of England rather than renounce Wallis

Warfield Simpson. Unique as the memoirs of an English king, heavily focused on an American woman. Ghost written by Charles J. V. Murphy.

Windsor, Duchess of. *The Heart Has its Reasons*. New York: McKay, 1956. (G) Autobiography designed to improve public image of Wallis Windsor. Candid in many respects, although it ignores the topic of former romances, is vague on the relationship between Simpson and the Prince, and is fuzzy concerning their decision to marry. It also omits any reference to Jimmy Donahue, a close associate with the Windsors during the 1950s. Ghost written by Charles J. V. Murphy.

Overview and Evaluation of Primary Sources
The only available primary source material, except for Wallis Windsor's autobiography, *The Heart Has its Reasons*, is contained in the volume of letters edited by Michael Bloch, *Wallis and Edward: Letters 1931-1937* (New York: Summit Books, 1986; G). Consisting of the intimate correspondence of the Duke and Duchess of Windsor, this volume was authorized by Maître Suzanne Blum, executor of the Duchess of Windsor's estate. These letters were selected ostensibly to reveal the depth and sincerity of the Windsor's relationship. From a researcher's perspective, these letters also present a critical view of the Royal Family, and their hostile relations with the duke and duchess. They provide insight into the middle-class world of the Simpsons of Bryanston Court, their money problems, and servant troubles, as well as her transition to the Prince of Wales's social set. These letters reveal the banality of the lovers' correspondence prior to their marriage. His letters are remarkably immature, suggesting a boy's letters to his revered mother; her's contain affectionate advice and admonitions, as though to a much-loved child.

There is, of course, no way to determine the content of the letters the editor chose not to include in this volume.

Fiction and Adaptations
The Windsors' story is the stuff of romance and human interest. A number of television mini-series have been produced, over the years. The best and most authentic is *Edward and Mrs. Simpson*, produced in England by Andred Brown, for Thames Television in 1978. The seven-part series has been presented several times on American television.

Other Sources
Menker, Suzy. *The Windsor Style*. Topsfield, MA: Salem House, 1988. A beautifully illustrated "coffee table" volume which goes far to substantiate

the author's claim that their magnificent jewels, furniture, fashion, and porcelain collection expressed the Windsor's intense and intimate relationship, in terms of passion, humor, and sensual expression. For those interested in the dispersal of these objects, the author has included a detailed epilogue.

Mary Jo Bratton
East Carolina University

CARTER G. WOODSON
1875-1950

Chronology

Born Carter Godwin Woodson on December 19, 1875, in Buckingham County, Virginia, one of nine children of James Henry Woodson, a former slave who saw action with Union troops during the Civil War, and Anne Eliza Riddle Woodson, also a former slave; works on family farm as youth until he and one brother move to West Virginia to work on the railroad and in the coal mines; *1896* graduates from Frederick Douglass High School in Huntington, West Virginia; *1897* enrolls at Berea College (Kentucky) and graduates in 1903; *1901-1903* teaches and becomes principal of Frederick Douglass High School; *1903-1907* accepted by War Department as instructor of English in the Philippine Islands; *1903-1907* enrolls in correspondence courses from University of Chicago studying Spanish and other subjects to facilitate his teaching in the Philippines; *1907* travels to Europe and studies one semester at University of Paris; *1908* completes coursework for both bachelor's and master's degrees in history and romance languages from the University of Chicago; *1908* enrolls at Harvard and receives Ph.D. in history in 1912; *1909-1919* teaches at Dunbar High School, Washington, D.C.; *1915* publishes *The Education of the Negro Prior to 1861*, first of nineteen books as author, co-author, or editor; *1915* founds the Association for the Study of Negro Life and History (ASNLH, now called the Association for the Study of Afro-American Life and History); *1916* commences publishing the *Journal of Negro History*; *1919-1920* Dean of College of Liberal Arts, Howard University; *1920-1922* Dean of College at West Virginia Collegiate Institute (West Virginia State University); *1921* founds Associated Publishers; *1926* initiates Negro History Week (Black History Month); *1928* begins offering correspondence course in Afro-American history through the ASNLH; *1929* receives Social Science Research Council Grant to collect sources on African-Americans; *1937* begins publishing *Negro History Bulletin;* never marries; *1950* dies on April 5 in Washington, D.C.

Activities of Historical Significance

Woodson adopted a two-fold mission—to promote scholarly research on African-American history, and to make the findings from that research available to the general public. To this end, he established the Association for the Study of Negro Life and History, with headquarters in Washington, D.C. The Association remained the focal point for Woodson's endeavors throughout his life. One of the most influential outgrowths of the Association was the highly regarded *Journal of Negro History*. Edited by Woodson, the *Journal* was published quarterly and included scholarly articles, a "Documents" section, and pertinent "Notes" for those interested in the history discipline. The "Documents" section presented obscure primary sources on African Americans and proved to be invaluable to historians. As well, the *Journal* provided young scholars such as Charles Wesley, Rayford Logan, and John Hope Franklin with an opportunity to publish pioneering articles in black history.

Woodson encouraged scholarship in black history by organizing the Associated Publishers in Washington, D.C., to publish full-length studies of his own and other African-American historians. This, in addition to the Association and the *Journal*, provided a forum and an impetus for serious study of the African-American experience. Woodson himself wrote many scholarly books and articles, but he was still concerned with reaching a more general audience and believed that African-American history should be an integral part of public education. Therefore, he published several standard textbooks on the subject, among them, *The Negro in Our History* (1922), and *The Story of the Negro Retold* (1935). Additionally, Woodson and the Association published the *Negro History Bulletin*, directed at primary and secondary level students. To increase the general public's awareness of the contributions made by African Americans and their significant role in the nation's history, Woodson organized a commemoration called Negro History Week to be held each February, and first celebrated in 1926; participants included ministers, teachers, social workers, businesspeople, state departments of education, principals of schools, presidents of colleges, and noted African-Americans. Celebrating African-American history each February has not only continued but has now been lengthened to embrace the entire month.

Overview of Biographical Sources

There is no published full-length biography on Woodson. A number of scholars, nevertheless, have attempted to reconstruct Woodson's life in published articles and unpublished works. Among the published accounts, a good place to begin is W. E. B. DuBois's assessment, "A Portrait of Carter G. Woodson" (*Masses and Mainstream* 3, 6 (1950): 19-25). Charles H. Wesley, a close associate (although not always in his good graces), left a solid summary, "Carter G. Woodson as a Scholar" (*Journal of Negro History* 36, 1 (1951): 12-24). A longer and worthy treatment of Woodson is presented by Meier and Rudwick, "Carter G. Woodson as Entrepreneur: Laying the Foundation of A Historical Specialty" (*Black History and the Historical Profession, 1915-1980*, 1986).

Another close associate, Rayford W. Logan, provided several notable sketches, including "Phylon Profile, VI: Carter G. Woodson" (*Phylon* 6, 4 (1945): 315-321) and "Carter G. Woodson: Mirror and Molder of His Time"

(*Journal of Negro History*, 58, 1 (1973): 1-17). With Woodson's death in 1950, the *Negro History Bulletin* dedicated its May issue to Woodson's career. Of particular interest in this issue is John Hope Franklin's contribution, "The Place of Carter G. Woodson in American Historiography" (*Negro History Bulletin* 13, 8 (1950): 174-176). Lorenzo J. Greene worked for Woodson at the Association and kept a diary during a two-year period, *Working with Carter G. Woodson, the Father of Black History, A Diary, 1928-1930* (1989).

Among unpublished sources, Patricia W. Romero's Ph.D. dissertation is indispensable ("Carter G. Woodson: A Biography," Ohio State University, 1971). Romero's is the only full length treatment of Woodson's life to date. Another admirable contribution is Jacqueline A. Goggin's Ph.D. dissertation, "Carter G. Woodson and the Movement to Promote Black History" (University of Rochester, 1983). Alfred Young looks at the educational philosophy of Woodson in his Ph.D. dissertation, "The Educational Philosophies of Booker T. Washington and Carter G. Woodson: A Liberating Praxis" (Syracuse University, 1977).

Evaluation of Selected Biographical Sources

Association for the Study of Negro Life and History. *Negro History Bulletin* 12, 8 (1950). (A, G, Y) A memorial issue dedicated to Woodson. Various authors, such as John Hope Franklin, Langston Hughes, and Arthur M. Schlesinger, among others, comment on aspects of Woodson's life, contributions, and achievements.

Greene, Lorenzo J. *Working with Carter G. Woodson, the Father of Black History, A Diary, 1928-1930*. Baton Rouge: Louisiana State University Press, 1989. (A, G) A penetrating portrait by a colleague who travelled and worked closely with Woodson for two years.

Logan, Rayford W. "Phylon Profile, VI: Carter G. Woodson." *Phylon* 6, 4 (1945): 315-321. (A, G, Y) Logan was an associate and has contributed several profiles on Woodson. This article is short, straightforward, but informative. Discusses both strengths and weaknesses of Woodson.

Meier, August, and Elliott Rudwick. "Carter G. Woodson as Entrepreneur: Laying the Foundation of a Historical Specialty." In *Black History and the Historical Profession, 1915-1980*. Urbana: University of Illinois Press, 1986. (A, G) In a lengthy treatment the authors place Woodson in perspective with regard to the "professionalization of historical scholarship." Woodson "laid the foundations" for the development of African-American history as a respectable discipline. The authors also concentrate on the dilemmas faced by Woodson in procuring funds for the *Journal of Negro History*.

Overview and Evaluation of Primary Sources

The most valuable single source of primary materials is the Carter G. Woodson Collection at the Library of Congress, which contains correspondence and personal papers of and relating to Woodson. The Moorland-Spingarn Research Center at Howard University holds a small collection of materials relating to Woodson. It is also fruitful to consult the Rockefeller Archives Center (North Tarrytown, NY), particularly the General Education Board Records and Rockefeller Foundation Records.

An important source are the annual reports included in the *Journal of Negro History*, which provide an ongoing account of the Association's and the *Journal's* progress. The "Notes" section in each issue also provides useful bits of information. Additional material can be found in the *Negro History Bulletin*, where editorial remarks often provide insight into Woodson's beliefs.

Woodson was a prolific writer. He authored numerous articles for the *Journal of Negro History* and the *Negro History Bulletin* on a wide range of African-American themes. Some of the themes included African Americans in business, African-American veterans, and miscegenation. He also published articles in other journals such as the *Southern Workman* and Garvey's *Negro World*. Writing for the *Journal of Negro History*, Woodson sometimes wrote nearly every review in the issue.

The numerous books authored, co-authored, or edited by Woodson complete the works he contributed to the discipline of history. Many historians, including John Hope Franklin, consider *The Education of the Negro Prior to 1861* (New York: Putnam's Sons, 1915; A, G) to be Woodson's most important work based on original scholarship. *The Negro in Our History* (Washington, DC: Associated Publishers, 1922; A, G) was the pioneering text on African-American history. One of Woodson's most popular and frequently quoted works is *The Miseducation of the Negro* (Washington, DC: Associated Publishers, 1933; A, G), revealing his views regarding the erroneous education the African-American elite had received. Woodson's concern for retrieving the African past is exhibited in *The African Background Outlined* (Washington, DC: Associated Publishers, 1936; A, G), which presents an overview of African history including the great empires and a discussion of African societies. He uniquely includes in the book an outline on the history of black people in Africa and America with annotated bibliography. Other important works are: *Free Negro Heads of Families in the United States in 1830* (Washington, DC: Association for the Study of Negro Life and History, 1925; A, G), *Free Negro Owners of Slaves in the United States in 1830* (Washington, DC: Association for the Study of Negro Life and History, 1926; A, G), *The Negro Church* (Washington, DC: Associated Publishers, 1921; A, G), *A Century of Negro Migration* (Washington, DC: Associated Publishers, 1918; A, G), and with Lorenzo J. Greene, *The Negro Wage Earner* (Washington, DC: Associated Publishers, 1930; A, G).

Museums, Historical Landmarks, Societies
Association for the Study of Afro-American Life and History (Washington, DC). Headquarters and administrative offices of Woodson's organization, records closed to public use. The Association continues to publish the *Journal of Negro History* out of Morehouse College in Atlanta, Georgia.

Other Sources
Logan, Rayford W. "Carter G. Woodson." In the *Dictionary of American Negro Biography*, edited by Rayford W. Logan and Michael R. Winston. New York: W.W. Norton, 1982. Biographical sketch by one of Woodson's former students and colleagues.

Scally, Anthony, ed. *Carter G. Woodson, A Bio-Bibliography*. Westport, CT: Greenwood Press, 1985. An invaluable bibliography containing over 800 entries compiled by a librarian who worked at the Association.

Lester S. Brooks
Illinois State University

FRANCES WRIGHT
1795-1852

Chronology

Born Frances Wright on September 6, 1795, in Dundee, Scotland, the second of three children of James Wright, a tradesman, merchant, political activist, and promoter of Thomas Paine's *Rights of Man*, and Camilla Campbell; *1798* orphaned at age two-and-a-half; removed from the liberal atmosphere of the Wright household and made a ward of her Tory maternal grandfather, Major General Duncan Campbell, and his daughter Frances in London; *1798-1813* grows up in rebellion against the environment of her upper-class British army family; educated by tutors; *1810* pronounces a solemn oath to dedicate herself to the cause of the poor and disadvantaged; reads a history of the American Revolution and is excited about a country "consecrated to freedom"; *1813-1816* leaves the Campbell home with her younger sister, Camilla; lives in Glasgow with her uncle, James Mylne, a professor of moral philosophy at the University of Glasgow; studies the U.S.; writes a blank verse tragedy, *Altorf*, and a treatise on Epicurean philosophy, *A Few Days in Athens*; *1816-1818* returns to London and becomes disillusioned with the possibility of social change in England; *1818-1820* resides in New York with her sister; *1819 Altorf* is staged (with anonymous authorship) in New York; published by Matthew Carey under her name; begins life-long friendships with Fanny, Harriet, and Julia Garnett; meets President James Monroe; expresses disappointment about "the sight of slavery"; travels throughout New England, but spends most of her time in the Middle Atlantic states; writes a number of long enthusiastic epistles describing the U.S.; *1820-1824* returns to England with Camilla; edits her American letters and publishes them as *Views of Society and Manners in America*; receives the attention of such reformists as Jeremy Bentham in England and Marquis de Lafayette in France; spends most of her time for the next two and a half years in Bentham's and Lafayette's circles; *1824* returns with Camilla to the U.S.; accompanied by Lafayette, who had arrived in U.S. a month earlier; makes acquaintance of John Quincy Adams, Thomas Jefferson, James Madison, Sam Houston, and Andrew Jackson; *1824-1825* becomes increasingly concerned with the "horrible ulcer" of slavery; impressed by the success of Robert Owen's communal society at New Harmony, Indiana, and George Flower's Birbeck community in Albion, Illinois; selects features of each as part of her Nashoba plan; purchases 320 acres outside Memphis, Tennessee, on the Wolf River and later increases her holding to two thousand acres; names her first property in America "Nashoba," the Chickasaw word meaning "wolf"; *1826* accepts for the emancipation project eight adult slaves and three children; falls dangerously ill with Dengue fever; recovers as a guest of the Owens in New Harmony; *1827* travels with Robert Dale Owen on a fund-raising venture in Europe; *1828* returns from Europe to learn she is being criticized for advocating free love and racial mixing; leaves Nashoba and joins Owen as co-editor of the *New Harmony Gazette*; *1828-1830* writes and lectures on rationalism and freedom; travels widely throughout U.S. as a public lecturer; *1829* relocates the office of the *New Harmony Gazette,* renamed the *Free Enquirer,* to New York City; begins a series of six lectures at Masonic Hall; establishes the Hall of Science as a secular alternative to churches; advocates the cause of the New York Workingmen's Movement and promotes a national system of education; travels to Haiti with former New Harmony teacher Phiquepal D'Arusmont and other Nashoba participants; *1830* returns from Haiti in March, supposedly pregnant by D'Arusmont; leaves for England in July; settles in Paris with Camilla; allegedly gives birth to a daughter in either December 1830 or January 1831 (much confusion surrounds Wright's Parisian years, 1830-1835, especially as related to her marriage and pregnancies); *1831* marries D'Arusmont; *1832* gives birth to her second daughter, who dies within three months; *1835-1839* returns to U.S. to lecture on growing inequities in American society; *1839* returns to Paris; *1843* buys a home in Cincinnati, Ohio; *1844* writes her autobiography; *1846* separates from D'Arusmont; *1848* publishes her final work, *England the Civilizer; 1851* finalizes her unpleasant divorce suit against D'Arusmont; *1852* dies December 13 in Cincinnati of complications related to a broken hip; buried in Spring Grove Cemetery in Cincinnati.

Activities of Historical Significance

Wright was the first woman in America to use public speaking engagements to challenge nineteenth-century assumptions that women should be pious, pure, submissive, and domestic. A reformer during a time when women could not vote and had no accepted role in public life, Wright devoted her efforts to improving the plight of women and slaves. In establishing her commune, Nashoba, Wright discredited the economic and moral base of slavery; in her July 4, 1828, address in New Harmony, Indiana—perhaps the first occasion in which a woman was permitted to address a large, mixed-gender audience—Wright attacked the social barriers facing women. Her Hall of Science, was the first center for radical free thought, and her social, political, and economic activities during the 1820s preceded the Grimke sisters' work by ten years, and that of Elizabeth Cady Stanton, Susan B. Anthony, and the women at the 1848 Seneca Falls Convention by twenty years. She became a leader in the New York Workingmen's Movement of 1829, and while it would be overstating the case to argue that Wright was the originator of a national, tax-supported education system, she actively espoused the idea years before such noted proponents as Horace Mann, and was a key agent in bringing the idea to public consciousness. Wright also challenged the assumption that the most effective leaders were found among the ranks of major political figures, a bias that excluded the disenfranchised, especially women, from attaining power and historical recognition.

Overview of Biographical Sources

In 1844 Wright attempted to shape public perception by writing an account of her life up to her first lecture in New York. Calling the sketch a biography and composing it in the third person, she set forth her social beliefs, especially those related to the divisive power of organized religion and the unequal treatment of women, the working class, and African Americans.

Three years after Wright's death, Amos Gilbert, a Quaker and an associate printer, wrote the first biography, *Memoirs of Frances Wright* (1855), in which he reverentially portrays his friend. Each of the twentieth-century biographers—William Randall Waterman, *Frances Wright* (1924); Alice Jane Gray Perkins and Theresa Wolfson, *Frances Wright: Free Enquirer* (1930); and Celia Morris Eckhardt, *Fanny Wright: Rebel in America* (1984)—attempts, to some extent, to carve out a "definite niche" for Wright in the social history of the U.S.

The first two biographies are limited by the difficulties the authors encountered during research. According to Frances Wright's grandson, Dr. William Guthrie, Wright's papers had been "misplaced"; Guthrie referred Waterman to Alice Jane Gray Perkins, who had made extensive transcripts of the Wright documents in 1909. However, because Perkins was interested in Wright's relationship with Lafayette, and her idea of American democracy, her notes focus on these two topics. Waterman's work, and the work of other historians, was constrained by Perkins's practice of snipping only limited portions of Wright's letters and diaries.

In the mid-1930s, upon the recommendation of Waterman, Theresa Wolfson, an economist from the Brookings Institution who was interested in Wright's work with the New York Workingman's Party, contacted Perkins. This collaboration was not entirely successful because Perkins's interest in writing a sensational biography conflicted with Wolfson's interest in studying, describing, and evaluating Wright's activities in the labor movement.

Unlike previous biographers, Eckhardt had access to Wright's correspondence published in 1975. Writing after the social movements of the 1960s and 1970s that focused on the civil and social rights of African Americans and women, Eckhardt portrays Wright as instrumental in the history of women's rights. It is curious that, in light of her disdain for religion, Wright's first biographer, Gilbert, and the latest biographer, Eckhardt, compared Wright to earlier religious champions of human liberty, including Jesus of Nazareth.

To date, no biographer has taken the position that Wright's rhetoric and inspiration directly contributed to helping individuals, particularly workingmen, blacks, and women, realize and respond to their oppression. These biographers view Wright's career as "meteoric." Their focus on the ire she ignited, and their emphasis on how she was limited by her sex tend to de-emphasize the ways in which Wright inspired people to initiate change.

Evaluation of Principal Biographical Sources

Bradlaugh, Charles, ed. *Biographies of Ancient and Modern Thinkers,* vol. 13. Boston: Mendum, 1871. (A, G) Short biographical sketch that examines Wright's ideas on religion, free thought, and America. The entry describes her as a poetess, politician, and writer on ethics. Not documented, but of interest to historians and researchers for its nineteenth-century perspective.

Eckhardt, Celia Morris. *Fanny Wright: Rebel in America.* Cambridge: Harvard University Press, 1984. (A, G) By far the most complete and scholarly biography of Wright. Includes extensive footnotes, and comments on primary source materials. Eckhardt's work presents Wright as a figure of heroic proportions engaged in a series of adventures important to the history of a nation, of a race, of a sex. Eckhardt portrays Wright as a misunderstood messianic hero who was unable to offer leadership in her time. Somewhat problematic for researchers is Eckhardt's failure to include locations of collections used and the lack of a bibliography.

Perkins, A. J. G., and Theresa Wolfson. *Frances Wright, Free Enquirer: The Study of a Temperament.* New York: Harper & Brothers, 1939. (A, G) This useful account is valuable for its numerous citations of letters and speeches. However, it is not footnoted, contains noticeable errors in direct quotations, and suffers from the uneasy collaboration between Perkins and Wolfson. Perkins's main intent was to engender controversy and excitement, while Wolfson sought a more dispassionate investigation. The authors portray Wright as the pioneering leader in social service, and regard the Hall of Science as a precursor to Jane Addams's Hull House and Lillian Wald's Henry Street settlement.

Stiller, Richard. *Commune on the Frontier: The Story of Frances Wright.* New York: Thomas Y. Crowell, 1972. (G, Y) A valuable volume in the Women of America Series. Although intended for the non-historian, Stiller's book is an accurate and interesting biography. Written especially for the young reader, Stiller pictures Wright as a driving force within the reform movements of the Jacksonian Era.

Waterman, William Randall. *Frances Wright.* New York: Columbia University Press, 1924; Reprint. New York: AMS Press, 1967. (**A, G**) Well-documented and significant as the first twentieth-century biography of Wright. Waterman, a political scientist, was interested in Wright's views of American political institutions. By attempting to praise her "masculine" qualities, Waterman grounded Wright in a "famous man" approach to historiography.

Overview and Evaluation of Primary Sources

Wright's biography, notes, and political letters have been published in the collections, *Biography, Notes, and Political Letters of Frances Wright D'Arusmont No. 1 Containing Biography and Notes* (New York: John Windt, 1844; **A, G**); *Biography, Notes, and Political Letters of Frances Wright D'Arusmont No. 2 Containing Political Letters* (New York: John Windt, 1844; **A, G**); and *Biography and Notes of Frances Wright D'Arusmont from the Dundee Northern Star* (Boston: J. P. Mendum, 1848; **A, G**). *Life, Letters and Lectures* (New York: Arno Press, 1972; **A, G**) is a modern edition containing some of Wright's biography, letters, and lectures. All are important as sources of chronology and as presentation of Wright's ideas.

Wright prolifically set forth her ideas in her literary works, *Altorf, A Tragedy* (Philadelphia, PA: M. Carey, 1819; **A, G**); *A Few Days in Athens* (Reprint. New York: Arno Press, 1972; **A, G**); *Views of Society and Manners in America in a Series of Letters from that Country to a Friend in England During the Years 1818, 1819, and 1820,* edited by Paul R. Baker (Cambridge, MA: Belknap Press, 1963; **A, G**); *England the Civilizer: Her History Developed in Its Principles* (London: Simpkins, Marshall, 1848; **A, G**). Also important is her work as editor and writer for the *New Harmony Gazette* (1827-1828), the *New Harmony and Nashoba Gazette* (1828-1829), and the *Free Enquirer* (1829-1832). Most of her orations were printed in the *Gazette* and the *Free Enquirer* and reprinted in penny press publications. Researchers can find Wright material in the Library of Congress and in the archives under the name of Frances Wright D'Arusmont or Frances Wright Darausmont.

Mrs. Frances Trollope, *Domestic Manners of the Americans* (1832. Reprint. Gloucester, MA: Peter Smith, 1974; **A, G**), and Thomas Adolphus Trollope, *What I Remember* (New York: Harper & Row, 1888; **A, G**), describe Wright's oratorical style. The Trollopes' work plus Robert Dale Owen's *Threading My Way* (1874. Reprint. New York: A. M. Kelley, 1967; **A, G**) are significant accounts of how contemporaries viewed Wright. Researchers, however, must be wary of Owen's description of Wright since evidence shows that the two had a falling out over financial matters in the late 1830s.

Perceptions on Wright by two literary contemporaries, William Cullen Bryant and Walt Whitman, can be found respectively in "Ode to Miss Frances Wright," (*New York Evening Post,* January 12, 1829; **A, G**) and *With*

Walt Whitman in Camden (1905. Reprint. New York: Rowman and Littlefield, 1961; **A, G**). Where Bryant's ode was sarcastic and biting, Whitman remembered her as "one of the sweetest of sweet memories."

The biographical works of Amos Gilbert and Joel Brown are particularly useful since both knew Wright after 1830. Gilbert's, *Memoirs of Frances Wright: The Pioneer Woman in the Cause of Human Rights* (Cincinnati, OH: Amos Gilbert, 1855; **A, G**) is valuable as a primary source and biographical interpretation by a friend. Written to memorialize Wright, it lacks footnotes and avoids criticism. Joel Brown's handwritten, "Frances Wright," (unpublished ms., Cincinnati and Hamilton County Library, Cincinnati, OH; **A, G**) gives Wright's version of her own life colored by her public experiences.

Of special interest is *The Garnett Letters,* a collection of letters written among the Wright sisters, the Garnett sisters, and other women, such as Frances Trollope. Privately printed by Dr. Cecillia Payne Gapochkin, the great-granddaughter of Julia Garnett (1979; **A, G**), the letters reveal the friendships that existed between these nineteenth-century women.

An extensive collection of Wright documents and correspondence is housed at the Workingmen's Institute, New Harmony, Indiana. The Cincinnati Historical Society contains the Gholson Collection; the Public Library of Cincinnati and Hamilton County contains the unpublished Brown memoir; and the Ohio Historical Society houses Amos Gilbert's memoir. The Theresa Wolfson Papers, Martin B. Catherwood Library, Cornell University (Ithaca, New York) contains the Perkins's snippets, parts of Wright's letters, and the correspondence that surrounded the Perkins/Wolfson collaborative biography. Libraries with smaller collections include the British Museum, The Arthur and Elizabeth Schlesinger Library at Radcliffe College, the Houghton Library at Harvard University, the Historical Society of Pennsylvania, the Memphis Public Library, the Library of Congress, the University of Chicago Library, the New York Public Library, the New York Historical Society, and Teachers College at Columbia University.

Fiction and Adaptations

Edd Winfield Parks has written *Nashoba* (New York: Twayne, 1963), a fictional account of Wright's planned community. Coleman McAlister's *Pioneers of Freedom* (New York: Vanguard, 1929) is a collection of short stories, especially for young people, about such pioneers as Thomas Paine, Thomas Jefferson, Wendell Phillips, and Eugene Debs. Wright is the only woman included, and is presented as a role model of courage and utopian vision.

Museums, Historical Landmarks, Societies

Historic marker (Memphis, TN). Only a misplaced road marker for Nashoba outside of Memphis stands as monument to Wright's life and her work.

Historic marker (Cincinnati, OH). Memorial marker on Wright's grave in Spring Grove Cemetary.

Other Sources

Berg, Barbara. *The Remembered Gate: Origins of American Feminism.* New York: Oxford University Press, 1978. Important analysis of the nineteenth-century notion of "true womanhood."

Bestor, Arthur Eugene, Jr. *Backwoods Utopias.* Philadelphia: University of Pennsylvania Press, 1950. Valuable as a description of communitarian efforts, such as Owen's New Harmony and Wright's Nashoba.

Cott, Nancy. *The Bond of Womanhood.* New Haven, CT: Yale University Press, 1977. Important analysis of the emergence of feminism in the U.S. and a description of nineteenth-century assumptions related to "true womanhood."

Engle, Jean, and Glorianne M. Leck. "Frances Wright and Margaret Fuller: Sanctions and Oversights in the Histories of Early American Feminist Philosophy." In *Women in History in the Arts: A Festschrift for Hildegard Schnuttgen in Honor of her Thirty Years of Outstanding Service at Youngstown State University,* edited by Lorrayne Y. Baird-Lange and Thomas A. Copeland. Youngstown, OH: Youngstown State University, 1989. This article compares Wright's and Fuller's approaches to human rights politics and feminist philosophies.

Gutek, Gerald. *Education in the United States.* Englewood Cliffs, NJ: Prentice Hall, 1986. An especially important, but brief analysis of Wright's contribution to education in the U.S.

Heinemen, Helen. *Restless Angels: Friendship of Six Victorian Women.* Athens: Ohio University Press, 1983. Valuable account of the friendship between and among the Garnett sisters, Frances Trollope, and the Wright sisters.

Schlesinger, Arthur M., Jr. *The Age of Jackson.* Boston: Little, Brown, 1950. Traces the historical, cultural, economic, and political life of the U.S. as it burgeoned from Thomas Jefferson to Andrew Jackson. Shows Wright as a social reformer, critic of the Second National Bank, and a campaigner in Van Buren's presidential race.

Taylor, Barbara. *Eve and the New Jerusalem: Socialism and Feminism in the Nineteenth Century.* New York: Pantheon, 1983. Taylor offers a bold new look at the socialist tradition, and Wright, through the lens of feminism.

Wilentz, Sean. *Chants Democratic: New York City & the Rise of the American Working Class, 1788-1850.* New York: Oxford University Press, 1984. Offers a rich contextual interpretation of Wright's importance to the New York Workingmen's movement.

Joan E. Organ
Case Western Reserve University

ANDREW J. YOUNG, JR.
b. 1932

Chronology

Born Andrew Jackson Young, Jr., on March 12, 1932, the son of Andrew Jackson Young, a dentist, and Daisy Fuller Young, a teacher; *1932-1947* grows up in a middle-class environment; attends a segregated black school and graduates from Gilbert Academy, a private high school; *1947-1951* enrolls at Dillard University in New Orleans but transfers after a year to Howard University in Washington, D.C., where he earns a bachelor's degree; *1951-1955* studies Ghandi's nonviolence philosophy at Hartford Theological Seminary and receives divinity degree; ordained a minister in the predominantly white United Church of Christ; *1955-1957* following a failed attempt to become a missionary to Angola, serves as pastor in Thomasville and Beachton, Georgia; leads a voter registration drive; *1957* heads athletic and media programs as associate director of the Department of Youth Work of the National Council of Churches; administers a voter education and registration project for the United Church of Christ; *1961* joins the Southern Christian Leadership Conference (SCLC) as administrator of a citizen education program; *1964* named executive director of SCLC; helps draft the Civil Rights Act of 1964; directs desegregation efforts in Birmingham, Alabama, and marches at Selma, Alabama; *1965* helps draft the Voting Rights Act of 1965; *1968* named executive vice president of the SCLC; helps direct the Poor People's Campaign March on Washington; *1970* runs unsuccessfully for U.S. Representative from Georgia's Fifth Congressional District; chairs Atlanta's Community Relations Commission; *1972* runs for Congress and is elected, then reelected in 1974 and 1976; *1977* appointed by President Carter as U.S. ambassador to the United Nations with cabinet rank; *1979* resigns under pressure after conducting unauthorized talks with the Palestine Liberation Organization; *1981* elected mayor of Atlanta and serves two terms; *1990* runs unsuccessfully for the Democratic nomination for governor of Georgia; is instrumental in winning for Atlanta the site of the 1996 Olympic Games.

Activities of Historical Significance

Andrew Young's commitment to nonviolence during the struggle for civil rights and his experience in voter registration drives made him a valuable and effective member of the Southern Christian Leadership Conference (SCLC), although he was regarded with suspicion by some of its members. Less radical than the leadership, he was the first to sense that the momentum for civil rights was losing ground to broader social issues spearheaded by the anti-Vietnam War movement, and he became instrumental in steering the SCLC along a mainstream path.

As a congressman, Young used his position on the House Banking and Currency Committee to direct appropriations to civil rights causes, including poverty and health care programs. His belief in nonviolence caused him to vote against military expenditures and identified him as one of the congressional voices opposed to the war. When fellow Georgian Jimmy Carter decided to run for president, Young was tapped to head a national voter registration drive, which proved highly successful. Over three million new voters, mostly Democrats, became the key to Carter's narrow victory over President Gerald Ford. As an influential, third-term congressman and a victorious political lieutenant in the Carter campaign, Young seemed to be on the rise in national politics. He received a cabinet-level appointment from President Carter as ambassador to the United Nations and was very successful during his first year. His intelligence, calm demeanor, and charismatic personality made him an effective spokesperson for the U.S. and a role model for Afro-American leaders. Clearly, he was responsible for improving the U.S. relations with third world countries, especially in Africa. This success, however, was interpreted by some interest groups in the U.S. as undermining the U.S. commitment to Israel, and when Young held secret talks with members of the Palestine Liberation Organization, who were not recognized members of the U.N., and in violation of U.S. policy, the Carter administration decided it must force Young to resign.

Back home in Georgia, Young was regarded as having achieved the impossible for an African American—an early civil rights activist had risen to the highest ranks of government. The fact that he talked with the PLO to work toward peaceful negotiations was regarded in Georgia simply as an extension of his social nonviolence background. He was attempting to apply on a larger scale the successful approach he had used on behalf of southern blacks. Having earned the respect of both black and white leaders in Georgia, Young was easily elected mayor and proceeded to bridge racial gaps. His reputation as a national leader and political moderate helped attract industry to Atlanta. The city's economic boom as well as its successful bid to host the 1996 summer Olympic Games, is inextricably linked to Young's leadership. When Young announced his candidacy for governor, he seemed unbeatable. He was facing a white opponent in a predominantly black state in which many white voters ardently appreciated his outstanding record. However, he badly misjudged his constituency. Believing that his civil rights record ensured the African-American vote, he campaigned predominantly among working-class whites outside Atlanta, a group whom blacks have always perceived as hostile to civil rights. Two years earlier he had alienated many black voters by opposing Jesse Jackson's 1988 bid for the presidency. In wooing the opposition camp, Young won few votes from working-class whites and lost the support of his constituency. He lost his primary bid by almost a two to one margin. Most political analysts view this as a technical defeat, not a referendum against Young, and he is expected to continue in important leadership positions.

Overview of Biographical Sources

Three biographies for adults and five for young people cover Young's life through his ambassadorship to the United Nations. None is complete enough, objective enough, or current enough to be considered definitive or even adequate for a person of Young's stature. The best material can be mined from the more scholarly books about Martin Luther King, Jr. and the civil rights movement.

Evaluation of Principal Biographical Sources

Eizenstadt, Stuart E., and William A. Barutio. *Andrew Young: The Path to History*. Atlanta: Voter Education Project, 1973. (G) Written in campaign biography style, this laudatory account concentrates on Young's civil rights work, especially in voter registration.

Gardner, Carl. *Andrew Young: A Biography*. New York: Drake, 1978. (G) The lengthiest account of Young's life, this seems hastily written to meet the demand for information created by Young's U.N. ambassadorship. It is now badly dated.

Stone, Eddie. *Andrew Young: Biography of a Realist*. Los Angeles: Holloway House, 1980. (A, G) Much of this biography is a defense of Young against those who accuse him of a lack of zeal in fighting for civil rights.

Evaluation of Biographies for Young People

Bryant, Ira B. *Andrew Jackson Young: Mr. Ambassador*. Houston, TX: Armstrong, 1979. This is a very short account of Young, the statesman, written prior to his forced resignation from the United Nations. Its inspirational tone makes it most appropriate for middle-school students.

Haskins, James. *Andrew Young: Man with a Mission*. New York: Lothrop, Lee & Shepard, 1979. The most substantial of the biographies for young people, this work emphasizes Young's social consciousness. Haskins carefully explains the controversies of Young's U.N. job, but is too uncritically favorable.

Roberts, Naurice. *Andrew Young: Freedom Fighter*. Chicago: Childrens Press, 1983. Only thirty-one pages long, this book is stronger for its illustrations than for information.

Simpson, Jan. *Andrew Young: A Matter of Choice*. St. Paul, MN: EMC, 1978. Part of a series, Headlines I, this is a very brief and dated account of Young's civil rights and congressional careers.

Westman, Paul. *Andrew Young: Champion of the Poor*. Minneapolis, MN: Dillon, 1983. A short, appreciative biography of Young's work for the poor. It is part of the Taking Part Series, designed to show young people how individuals can make an important social difference.

Overview of Primary Sources
Among the papers and oral-history interviews archived in the Martin Luther King, Jr. Center for Nonviolent Social Change and in the Southern Christian Leadership Conference records, there are materials related to Young's role in the civil rights movement. Federal and City of Atlanta archives should be consulted for primary sources on Young's government activities, as should the Jimmy Carter Library in Plains, Georgia.

Other Sources
Abernathy, Ralph David. *And the Walls Came Tumbling Down: An Autobiography*. New York: Harper & Row, 1989. Frequent references are made to Young, especially to his work on the Poor People's Campaign after Abernathy became president of the Southern Christian Leadership Conference.

Garrow, David J. *Bearing the Cross: Martin Luther King, Jr. and the Southern Christian Leadership Conference*. New York: Morrow, 1986. The most complete study of King's leadership activities, this contains numerous references to Young.

Joseph M. McCarthy
Suffolk University

WHITNEY MOORE YOUNG, JR.
1921-1971

Chronology

Born Whitney Moore Young, Jr., July 31, 1921, in Lincoln Ridge, Kentucky, the only son of Whitney Moore Young, president of Lincoln Institute, a boarding high school for black students, and Laura Ray Young, a postmistress; *1921-1936* grows up in Lincoln Ridge and graduates from Lincoln Institute at fourteen; *1941* graduates from Kentucky State College, an all-black school, where he is president of the senior class; *1941-1946* after a year of teaching and coaching at Rosenwald High School in Madisonville, Kentucky, enlists in the U.S. Army; studies engineering at M.I.T. from 1942-1943; marries Margaret Bruckner, a teacher, on January 2, 1944; goes to Europe with a black anti-aircraft company assigned to road-building; is promoted first sergeant and fights in the Battle of the Bulge; *1946-1947* completes a master's degree in social work at the University of Minnesota with a thesis on the St. Paul Urban League; *1947-1950* joins the St. Paul Urban League as director of industrial relations and vocational guidance; supervises field work of students from University of Minnesota and Atlanta University; teaches at the College of St. Catherine; *1950-1954* as executive secretary of the Omaha Urban League, teaches community organization at the University of Nebraska School of Social Work; teaches at Creighton University from 1951 to 1954; *1954-1961* serves as dean of the School of Social Work at Atlanta University; receives the 1959 Florina Lasker Award, the highest honor in social work; is a member of the 1960 White House Conference on Children and Youth; receives a Rockefeller Foundation grant to study at Harvard University; *1961-1971* is executive director of the Urban League; advises President Johnson on antipoverty legislation; concentrates Urban League efforts on lawsuits and legislation affecting civil rights and voter registration; *1971* drowns March 11 in Lagos, Nigeria, while attending a conference to promote Afro-American understanding.

Activities of Historical Significance

Whitney Young's border state upbringing, army service, and work experience in the Midwest gave him a viewpoint different from that of other civil rights leaders. He had no personal experience of life in the Deep South until his commitment to social change brought him to Atlanta in 1954. There, his academic and practical background in social work led him to view the problem of civil rights as one to be solved by unlocking the white power structure rather than by confrontational tactics. His background also equipped him with excellent skills as a mediator.

As executive director of the National Urban League, Young developed plans for a full-scale national effort to outlaw segregation and eliminate the educational and economic disparities between the races. This "Domestic Marshall Plan" was incorporated in large measure into the Johnson administration's anti-poverty legislation and remains Young's most significant contribution to the civil rights struggle. He increased the effectiveness of the legislation by calling upon blacks to take a forceful role in planning and executing anti-poverty strategies through the development of community action agencies.

Young was a strong voice for moderation in the civil rights movement, and he refused to dilute his influence on the political establishment by joining Martin Luther King, Jr., in opposing the Vietnam War. His professional and social contacts with establishment figures led to accusations that he was an "Uncle Tom," but at the same time brought enormous political and financial support to the Urban League and enlisted many moderates in the civil rights cause. During his tenure, the League's budget increased nearly twenty-fold.

Overview of Biographical Sources

There is only one full adult biography of Young. *Whitney Moore Young, Jr. and the Struggle for Civil Rights* (1989) by Nancy Weiss is the product of ten years of research by a scholar who has written on the early years of the Urban League. In addition, two biographies are available for young adults, Richard Bruner's *Whitney Moore Young, Jr.: The Story of a Pragmatic Humanist* (1972), and Peggy Mann's *Whitney Moore Young, Jr.: Crusader for Equality* (1972).

Evaluation of Principal Biographical Sources

Bruner, Richard. *Whitney Moore Young, Jr.: The Story of a Pragmatic Humanist.* New York: McKay, 1972. (Y) This seventy-three page book explains and justifies Young's views to students of junior high school age.

Mann, Peggy. *Whitney Moore Young, Jr.: Crusader for Equality.* Champaign, IL: Garrard, 1972. (Y) Illustrated and indexed, this is a very useful introduction to Young for junior and senior high school students.

Weiss, Nancy J. *Whitney Moore Young, Jr. and the Struggle for Civil Rights.* Princeton, NJ: Princeton University Press, 1989. (A, G) Carefully researched from primary sources, this biography includes interviews with a broad variety of Young's friends and co-workers. Scholarly and even-handed, although partial to Young's views, this will long remain the standard biography.

Overview and Evaluation of Primary Sources

Young's writings focus on social analysis rather than on autobiography. His books, *To Be Equal* (New York: McGraw-Hill, 1964; **A, G, Y**) and *Beyond Reason* (New York: McGraw-Hill, 1969; **A, G, Y**), grew out of newspaper columns he wrote regularly for the New York *Amsterdam News* and the *World-Telegram and Sun*. They provide an excellent chronicle of his reactions to events in the evolving civil rights struggle. His papers can be found in the Rare Book and Manuscript Library at Columbia University. Also valuable are the National Urban League Papers, Part II in the Manuscript Division, Library of Congress, Washington, D.C.

Other Sources

Hayward, O. H. "Bibliography of Literature by and about Whitney Moore Young, Jr., 1921-1971: An Annotated Checklist." *Bulletin of Bibliography* 31 (July 1974): 122-125. Although dated, this is still a valuable source.

Parris, Guichard and Lester Brooks. *Blacks in the City.* Boston: Little, Brown, 1971. This history of the National Urban League provides detailed coverage of Moore's career as executive director.

Joseph M. McCarthy
Suffolk University

APPENDIX I
HISTORICAL FIGURES GROUPED BY ERA

AGE OF EXPLORATION/COLONIAL (pre-1776)

Crispus Attucks
Susanna Rowson

Mercy Otis Warren
Phillis Wheatley

REVOLUTIONARY/EARLY NATIONAL (1776-1827)

Richard Allen
Crispus Attucks
Captain Paul Cuffe
Handsome Lake
Little Turtle
Alexander McGillivray
Osceola
Susanna Rowson

Anne Royall
Sacagawea
Sequoyah
Tenskwatawa
Denmark Vesey
Mercy Otis Warren
Martha Washington
Phillis Wheatley

JACKSONIAN/ANTEBELLUM (1828-1860)

Richard Allen
Catharine E. Beecher
Black Hawk
William Wells Brown
Mary Boykin Chesnut
Varina Howell Davis
Martin Delany
Jessie Benton Frémont
Rose Greenhow
Henry Highland Garnet
Sarah Josepha Hale
John Mercer Langston
Mary Mann

Lucretia Mott
Daniel Payne
Elizabeth Peabody
John Ross
Anne Royall
Dred Scott
Sequoyah
Lucy Stone
Sojourner Truth
Julia Strudwick Tutwiler
Victorio
Ellen Gould White
Francis Wright

CIVIL WAR AND RECONSTRUCTION (1861-1877)

Catharine E. Beecher
William Wells Brown
Mary Boykin Chesnut
Varina Howell Davis
Martin Delany

Jessie Benton Frémont
Henry Highland Garnet
Rose Greenhow
Isabella Beecher Hooker
John Mercer Langston

Mary Todd Lincoln
Mary Mann
Daniel Payne
Elizabeth Peabody
Joseph Charles Price
Red Cloud
John Ross
Sitting Bull

Julia Evalina Smith
Lucy Stone
Mary Church Terrell
Sojourner Truth
Julia Strudwick Tutwiler
Victorio
Ellen Gould White

LATE NINETEENTH CENTURY (1878-1899)

Ethel Barrymore
Mary Cassatt
Varina Howell Davis
Isabella Stewart Gardner
Henry Highland Garnet
Geronimo
Matthew A. Henson
Isabella Beecher Hooker
Mother Jones
John Mercer Langston
Mary Mann
Lottie Moon

Daniel Payne
Elizabeth Peabody
Joseph Charles Price
Red Cloud
Sitting Bull
Julia Evelina Smith
Lucy Stone
Ida Tarbell
Mary Church Terrell
Julia Strudwick Tutwiler
Victorio
Ellen Gould White

PROGRESSIVE ERA (1900-1916)

Josephine Baker
Ethel Barrymore
Carrie Chapman Catt
John Collier
Isadora Duncan
Isabella Stewart Gardner
Matthew A. Henson
Jack Johnson
James Weldon Johnson

Mother Jones
Scott Joplin
Alice Roosevelt Longworth
Claude McKay
Kate Richards O'Hare
Edith Kermit Carow Roosevelt
Ida Tarbell
Mary Church Terrell
Julia Strudwick Tutwiler

WORLD WAR I THROUGH WORLD WAR II (1917-1945)

Marian Anderson
Louis Armstrong
Josephine Baker
Emily Greene Balch
Ethel Barrymore

Ruth Benedict
Carrie Chapman Catt
John Collier
Agnes DeMille
Charles Richard Drew

Isadora Duncan
Duke Ellington
Zelda Fitzgerald
Isabella Stewart Gardner
Langston Hughes
James Weldon Johnson
Anne Morrow Lindbergh
Alice Roosevelt Longworth
Lucy Randolph Mason
Claude McKay

Edna St. Vincent Millay
Jesse OwensCissy Patterson
Kate Richards O'Hare
Paul Robeson
Bessie Smith
Ida Tarbell
Mary Church Terrell
Edith Bolling Galt Wilson
Wallis Warfield Windsor
Carter G. Woodson

POST-WORLD WAR II (1946-present)

Marian Anderson
Josephine Baker
Ruth Benedict
John Coltrane
Agnes DeMille
Charles Richard Drew
Duke Ellington
Zelda Fitzgerald
Dian Fossey
Langston Hughes
Jesse Jackson
Coretta Scott King

Anne Morrow Lindbergh
Alice Roosevelt Longworth
Marilyn Monroe
Jesse Owens
Cissy Patterson
Paul Robeson
Rosemary Radford Ruether
Mary Church Terrell
Wallis Warfield Windsor
Andrew Young, Jr.
Whitney Moore Young, Jr.

APPENDIX II
SELECTED MUSEUMS AND HISTORICAL LANDMARKS

ALABAMA
Birmingham
Arts Hall of Fame (Marian Anderson)

Montgomery
Dexter Avenue Baptist Church (Coretta Scott King)
First White House of the Confederacy (Varina Howell Davis)
State Department of Archives and History (Julia Tutwiler)

Oakville
Jesse Owens Monument

University
University of Alabama (Julia Tutwiler)

ARIZONA
Prescott
Frémont House

Wilcox
Chiricahua National Monument (Geronimo)

CALIFORNIA
Los Angeles
Charles R. Drew Postgraduate Medical School
Marilyn Monroe Remembered Fan Club
Southwest Museum (Jessie Benton Frémont)

Northridge
Marilyn Monroe Forever Fan Club

Sequoyah National Park

CONNECTICUT
Glastonbury
Historical Society of Glastonbury (Julia Evelina Smith)
Smith House

Hartford
Memorial Library (Isabella Beecher Hooker)
Nook Farm (Isabella Beecher Hooker)
Stowe-Day Foundation (Catharine E. Beecher, Isabella Beecher Hooker, Julia Evelina Smith)

Litchfield
Beecher House

DISTRICT OF COLUMBIA
Washington
Marian Anderson Mural
Association for the Study of Afro-American Life and History (Carter G. Woodson)
Charles R. Drew Blood Center
Duke Ellington Home
Duke Ellington Memorial Bridge
National Geographic Society (Matthew A. Henson)
Statuary Hall, U.S. Capitol Building (Sequoyah)
Smithsonian Institution (Varina Howell Davis, Osceola)
Woodrow Wilson House (Edith Bolling Galt Wilson)

INDIANA
Battleground
Battleground Historical Association (Tenskwatawa)

FLORIDA
Miami
Historical Association of Southern Florida (Osceola)

Pensacola
Panton Trading Post (Alexander McGillivray)

Tampa
Hillsborough County Historical Museum (Osceola)

St. Augustine
Fort Marion (Osceola)

GEORGIA
Atlanta
Martin Luther King, Jr. Center for Nonviolent Social Change (Coretta Scott King)
Martin Luther King, Jr. National Historic Site and Preservation District (Coretta Scott King)

Calhoun
New Echota (Sequoyah)

Cartersville
First Baptist Church (Lottie Moon)

Rossville
John Ross House

ILLINOIS
Black Hawk Trail

Chicago
Mathew A. Henson Grammar School

Mt. Olive
Mother Jones Monument

Oregon
Black Hawk Statue

Rock Island
Black Hawk State Park

Springfield
Lincoln Home

IOWA
Black Hawk Trail

Lakeview
Black Hawk Statue

KENTUCKY
Lexington
Mary Todd Lincoln House

Louisville
Southern Baptist Theological Seminary (Lottie Moon)

LOUISIANA
New Orleans
Confederate Memorial Hall (Varina Howell Davis)
Tulane University Archives (Louis Armstrong)

MAINE
Brunswick
Peary-MacMillan Arctic Museum (Matthew A. Henson)

MARYLAND
Annapolis
Matthew A. Henson Plaque

Aspen Hill
Matthew A. Henson State Park

Baltimore
Laurel Cemetery (Daniel Payne)

MASSACHUSETTS
Boston
Crispus Attucks Monument
Isabella Stewart Gardner Museum

Westport
Captain Paul Cuffe Monument

MICHIGAN
Battle Creek
Sojourner Truth Grave

MINNESOTA
Little Falls
Lindbergh House

MISSISSIPPI
Biloxi
Beauvoir (Varina Howell Davis)

Clarksdale
Delta Blues Museum (Bessie Smith)

Natchez
The Briars (Varina Howell Davis)

Vicksburg
Old Court House Museum (Varina Howell Davis)

MISSOURI
St. Louis
The Gateway Arch and Old County Courthouse
National Historical Landmark (Dred Scott)
Lindbergh Museum

MONTANA
Big Horn Country
Custer Battlefield National Monument (Sitting Bull)

Fort Benton
Sacagawea Sculpture

Fort Smith
Fort C. F. Smith Historical District (Red Cloud)

NEW YORK
Albany
New York State Library (Handsome Lake)

Austerlitz
Edna St. Vincent Millay Memorial

Flushing
Queens College (Louis Armstrong)

Fredonia
Reed Library (Handsome Lake)

New York City
Ethel Barrymore Theater
CBS Records Archives (Louis Armstrong)
James Weldon Johnson Residence
New York Public Library (Langston Hughes)
Theodore Roosevelt Birthplace (Edith Kermit Carow Roosevelt)
Charlotte Temple Tombstone (Susanna Rowson)

Onondaga
Handsome Lake Grave

Oyster Bay
Sagamore Hill (Edith Kermit Carow Roosevelt)
Theodore Roosevelt Association (Edith Kermit Carow Roosevelt)

Piermont-on-the-Hudson
Frémont Tomb

Sands Point
Falaise (Anne Morrow Lindbergh)

Seneca Falls
Women's Hall of Fame (Marian Anderson)

NORTH CAROLINA
Cherokee
Museum of the Cherokee Indian (Sequoyah)

Haw River
Charles R. Drew Monument

Salisbury
Livingstone College (Joseph Charles Price)

Wilmington
New Hanover Museum of the Lower Cape Fear (Rose Greenhow)
Oakdale Cemetery (Rose Greenhow)

Winston-Salem
Agnes DeMille Theatre

NORTH DAKOTA
Bismarck
Sacagawea Sculpture

OHIO
Cincinnati
Frances Wright Grave
Stowe House Community Center (Isabella Beecher Hooker)

Columbus
Jesse Owens Track and Recreational Center

Wilberforce
Payne Theological Center
Wilberforce University (Daniel Payne)

OKLAHOMA
Lawton
Geronimo Grave

Oklahoma City
National Cowboy Hall of Fame (Sacagawea)

Sallisaw
Sequoyah Home Site

Tahlequal
Cherokee Heritage Center (Sequoyah)
Cherokee National Museum (Sequoyah)
Cherokee Nation Site (John Ross)

OREGON
Portland
Sacagawea Sculpture

PENNSYLVANIA
Lincoln University
Lincoln University (Langston Hughes)

Philadelphia
Marian Anderson Scholarship Foundation
Mother Bethel African Methodist Episcopal Church (Richard Allen)

Swarthmore
Swarthmore College Peace Collection (Emily Greene Balch)

RHODE ISLAND
Providence
Langston Hughes Society

SOUTH DAKOTA
Marvin
American Indian Cultural Research Center (Sitting Bull)

Rapid City
Sioux Indian Museum and Crafts Center (Sitting Bull)

TENNESSEE
Chattanooga
Ross's Landing

Nashville
Fisk University (Langston Hughes)

VIRGINIA
Alexandria
Mount Vernon (Martha Washington)

Arlington
Charles R. Drew's Boyhood Home

Crewe
Lottie Moon Grave

Richmond
Hollywood Cemetery (Varina Howell Davis)
Museum of the Confederacy (Varina Howell Davis)
Valentine Museum of the Life and History of Richmond (Lucy Randolph Mason)

Williamsburg
Custis House (Martha Washington)

WISCONSIN
Black Hawk Trail

WYOMING
Cody
Plains Indian Museum of the Buffalo Bill Historical Society (Sacagawea)

Orpha
Fort Fetterman (Red Cloud)

Story
Fort Phil Kearny (Red Cloud)

Sussex
Fort Reno (Red Cloud)

Wind River Indian Reservation
Sacagawea Grave

CUMULATIVE INDEX FOR VOLUMES I-IV
OF FIGURES AND SOURCES REVIEWED

W. E. B. Du Bois: Negro Leader in a Time of Crisis (Broderick)
W. E. B. Du Bois Speaks (Foner, ed.)
Writings (Huggins, ed.)

DULLES, JOHN FOSTER, 424-430

American Foreign Policy
John Foster Dulles (Gerson)
John Foster Dulles, 1888-1959 (Beal)
John Foster Dulles: A Reappraisal (Goold-Adams)
John Foster Dulles: A Statesman and His Times (Guhin)
John Foster Dulles: The Last Year (E. L. Dulles)
John Foster Dulles: The Road to Power (Pruessen)
Memoirs by Harry S Truman
Ordeal of Power (Hughes)
Papers of Senator Vandenberg (Vandenberg, Jr., ed.)
Papers Relating to the Foreign Relations of the United States
War or Peace (Dulles)
War, Peace, and Change (Dulles)
White House Years (Eisenhower)

DUNCAN, ISADORA, 1892-1896

Fifteen Years of A Dancer's Life (Fuller)
Isadora and Esenin (McVay)
Isadora Duncan (Kozoday)
Isadora Duncan (Magriel)
Isadora Duncan, An Intimate Portrait (Stokes)
Isadora Duncan in Her Dances (Walkowitz)
Isadora Duncan: Her Life, Her Art, Her Legacy (Terry)
Isadora Duncan: Pioneer in the Art of the Dance (Duncan-Rogers)
Isadora Duncan: The Russian Years (Schneider)
Isadora Duncan's Russian Days and Her Last Years in France (Duncan and Ross)
Isadora: A Revolutionary in Art and Love (Macdougall)
Isadora: Portrait of the Artist As A Woman (Blair)
My Life (Duncan)
My Life in Art (Stanislawsky)
The Real Isadora (Seroff)
Untold Story: The Life of Isadora Duncan (Desti)
Your Isadora: The Love Story of Isadora Duncan and Gordon Craig (Steegmuller)

DYER, MARY, 431-436

Antinomian Controversy (Hall, ed.)
Apprenticeship of Washington and other Sketches (Hodges)
Boston Common (Howe)
General History of the Quakers

Great Women of the Christian Faith (Deen)
History of New England (Winthrop)
Mary Dyer of Rhode Island (Rogers)
New England Judged (Bishop)
Procession of Friends (Newman)
Quaker Reader (West, ed.)
Quiet Rebels (Bacon)
Short Story of the Rise, Reign and Ruine of... (Winthrop)

EARHART, AMELIA, 437-442

20 Hrs. 40 Min. (Earhart)
Amelia Earhart Lives (Klaas and Gervais)
Amelia Earhart: The Final Story (Loomis and Ethell)
Amelia, My Courageous Sister (Morrissey)
Courage Is the Price (Morrissey)
Daughter of the Sky (Briand)
Fun of It (Earhart)
Last Flight (Earhart)
Letters from Amelia, 1901-1937 (Backus)
Search for Amelia Earhart (Goerner)
Soaring Wings (Putnam)
Stand By To Die (Myers)
Winged Legend (Burke)
World Flight (Pellegreno)

EDDY, MARY BAKER, 443-446

Life of Mary Baker Eddy (Wilbur)
Life of Mary Baker Eddy and the History of Christian Science (Milmine)
Manual of the Mother Church (Eddy)
Mary Baker Eddy (Beasley)
Mary Baker Eddy: An Interpretive Biography (Silberger)
Mary Baker Eddy: The Truth and the Tradition (Bates and Dittemore)
Mary Baker Eddy: The Years of Authority (Peel)
Mary Baker Eddy: The Years of Trial, 1876-1891 (Peel)
Mrs. Eddy: The Biography of a Virginal Mind (Dakin)
Prose Works Other than Science and Health (Eddy)
Retrospection and Introspection (Eddy)
Science and Health with the Key to the Scriptures (Eddy)
Years of Discovery (Peel)

EDISON, THOMAS, 447-452

Diary and Sundry Observations of Thomas Alva Edison (Runes, ed.)
Edison: A Biography (Josephson)
Edison As I Know Him (Ford)
Edison: His Life and Inventions (Dyer and Martin)
Edison: His Life, His Work, His Genius (Simonds)